COLLECTED PAPERS ON LATIN POETRY

Oliver Lyne at his house in Italy, summer 2004.

Collected Papers on Latin Poetry

R. O. A. M. LYNE

OXFORD
UNIVERSITY PRESS

Great Clarendon Street, Oxford OX2 6DP

Oxford University Press is a department of the University of Oxford.
It furthers the University's objective of excellence in research, scholarship,
and education by publishing worldwide in

Oxford New York

Auckland Cape Town Dar es Salaam Hong Kong Karachi
Kuala Lumpur Madrid Melbourne Mexico City Nairobi
New Delhi Shanghai Taipei Toronto

With offices in

Argentina Austria Brazil Chile Czech Republic France Greece
Guatemala Hungary Italy Japan Poland Portugal Singapore
South Korea Switzerland Thailand Turkey Ukraine Vietnam

Oxford is a registered trade mark of Oxford University Press
in the UK and in certain other countries

Published in the United States
by Oxford University Press Inc., New York

© L. A. Lyne 2007

The moral rights of the author have been asserted
Database right Oxford University Press (maker)

First published 2007

All rights reserved. No part of this publication may be reproduced,
stored in a retrieval system, or transmitted, in any form or by any means,
without the prior permission in writing of Oxford University Press,
or as expressly permitted by law, or under terms agreed with the appropriate
reprographics rights organization. Enquiries concerning reproduction
outside the scope of the above should be sent to the Rights Department,
Oxford University Press, at the address above

You must not circulate this book in any other binding or cover
and you must impose the same condition on any acquirer

British Library Cataloguing in Publication Data

Data available

Library of Congress Cataloging-in-Publication Data

Data available

Typeset by SPI Publisher Services, Pondicherry, India
Printed in Great Britain
on acid-free paper by
Biddles Ltd., King's Lynn, Norfolk

ISBN 978–0–19–920396–3

1 3 5 7 9 10 8 6 4 2

Preface

This book collects the articles of Oliver Lyne and was conceived by a group of his former pupils and colleagues as a memorial to Oliver, and as a work valuable to scholars and students. To make it the more accessible, effective, and compact, it was eventually decided to omit articles which were particularly short or technical, or which had been superseded through Oliver's later work or changes of view. The principal loss here is the early articles on the *Ciris*. Two items not strictly articles proved too interesting to omit: Oliver's introduction to C. Day Lewis's translation of the *Eclogues* and *Georgics*, and an unpublished presentation on Sulpicia.

The realization of this book has been a team effort. Gregory Hutchinson and Stephen Harrison have co-ordinated the project; Claudia Strobel has laboured on the bibliography and on unearthing computer files; Rebecca Armstrong has done significant work on the editing; Bruno Currie and Matthew Leigh have produced the indexes. At OUP Hilary O'Shea, a former pupil of Oliver's at Cambridge, took up our proposal with enthusiasm, and arranged for the re-keying of the papers, funded by a generous grant from the Jowett Copyright Trustees, to whom warm thanks are due; Daniel Johnson's professional help with the volume's re-keying and bibliography was much appreciated. Comments from two readers for the Press were useful and encouraging. Linda Lyne has given us every assistance. She will know that, although most of the work in this book is Oliver's, its appearance marks in a small way our lasting gratitude to him—and our unpayable debt.

Contents

List of Acknowledgements and Original Places of Publication	vii
Introduction (Gregory Hutchinson)	ix
1. Propertius and Cynthia: *Elegy* 1. 3 (1970)	1
2. Propertius 3. 10 (1973)	24
3. Propertius 1. 5 (1974)	32
4. *Scilicet et tempus ueniet...*: Vergil, *Georgics* 1. 463–514 (1974)	38
5. The Neoteric Poets (1978)	60
6. *Seruitium Amoris* (1979)	85
7. Introduction to C. Day Lewis's Translation of Vergil's *Eclogues* and *Georgics* (1983)	101
8. Vergil and the Politics of War (1983)	115
9. Lavinia's Blush: Vergil, *Aeneid* 12. 64–70 (1983)	136
10. Ovid's *Metamorphoses*, Callimachus, and *l'art pour l'art* (1984)	146
11. Vergil's *Aeneid*: Subversion by Intertextuality. Catullus 66. 39–40 and Other Examples (1994)	167
12. Introductory Poems in Propertius: 1. 1 and 2. 12 (1998)	184
13. Love and Death: Laodamia and Protesilaus in Catullus, Propertius, and Others (1998)	211
14. Propertius 2. 10 and 11 and the Structure of Books '2a' and '2b' (1998)	227
15. Propertius and Tibullus: Early Exchanges (1998)	251
16. Notes on Catullus (2002)	283
17. Horace *Odes* Book 1 and the Alexandrian Edition of Alcaeus (2005)	293
18. Structure and Allusion in Horace's Book of *Epodes* (2005)	314
19. [Tibullus] Book 3 and Sulpicia (2004–5)	341
Bibliography of Oliver Lyne	368
References	370
Index Locorum	383
General Index	405

List of Acknowledgements and Original Places of Publication

1. 'Propertius and Cynthia: *Elegy* 1. 3', *Proceedings of the Cambridge Philological Society* 16 (1970), 60–78.
2. 'Critical Appreciations I: Propertius iii. 10', *Greece and Rome* 20 (1973), 38–48.
3. 'Propertius I. 5', *Mnemosyne* ser. IV, 27 (1974), 262–9.
4. '*Scilicet et tempus veniet*...: Virgil, *Georgics* 1. 463–514', in T. Woodman and D. West (eds.), *Quality and Pleasure in Latin Poetry* (Cambridge, 1974), 47–66.
5. 'The Neoteric Poets', *Classical Quarterly* NS 28 (1978), 167–87.
6. '*Servitium amoris*', *Classical Quarterly* NS 29 (1979), 117–30.
7. *Virgil: The Eclogues, the Georgics*, translated by C. Day Lewis (Oxford, 1983), Introduction, i–xx.
8. 'Vergil and the Politics of War', *Classical Quarterly* NS 33 (1983), 188–203.
9. 'Lavinia's Blush: Vergil, *Aeneid* 12.64–70', *Greece and Rome* 30 (1983), 55–64.
10. 'Ovid's *Metamorphoses*, Callimachus, and *l'art pour l'art*', *Materiali e Discussioni* 12 (1984), 9–34.
11. 'Vergil's *Aeneid*: Subversion by Intertextuality. Catullus 66.39–40 and Other Examples', *Greece and Rome* 41 (1994), 187–204.
12. 'Introductory Poems in Propertius: 1.1 and 2.12', *Proceedings of the Cambridge Philological Society* 44 (1998), 158–81.
13. 'Love and Death: Laodamia and Protesilaus in Catullus, Propertius, and others', *Classical Quarterly* NS 48 (1998), 200–12.
14. 'Propertius 2.10 and 11 and the Structure of Books "2a" and "2b"', *Journal of Roman Studies* 88 (1998), 21–36.
15. 'Propertius and Tibullus: Early Exchanges', *Classical Quarterly* NS 48 (1998), 519–44.
16. 'Notes on Catullus', *Classical Quarterly* NS 52 (2002), 600–8.
17. 'Horace *Odes* Book 1 and the Alexandrian Edition of Alcaeus', *Classical Quarterly* NS 55 (2005), 542–58.
18. 'Structure and Allusion in Horace's Book of *Epodes*', *Journal of Roman Studies* 95 (2005), 1–19.

Introduction

Gregory Hutchinson

This volume brings together Oliver Lyne's most substantial articles on Latin poetry. It thus offers a collection of primary importance for the contemporary study of Latin literature. It also enables the reader to see more easily the relation of these pieces to each other and to the total body of Lyne's work; this in turn gives fresh point to the individual pieces. The present introduction aims at helping the reader to appreciate the corpus of his writings, not at drawing the character of an extraordinarily generous, colourful, and lovable man; this form was favoured by the editing team. I may say that the detachment which a scholarly discussion imposes (including the appellation 'Lyne') goes much against the grain: Oliver was a dear friend of mine. Something of his personality is none the less bound to come through, especially in the numerous quotations: an account of this unusual writer must engage with the detail of his expression. The discussion follows a chronological sequence, like the book itself: this seems to suit a scholar whose œuvre is marked by growth and evolution. The account is not meant to be authoritative: it should begin rather than end consideration of Lyne's work as a whole.

R. O. A. M. Lyne was born in 1944. He went to Highgate School, and became a Scholar of St John's College, Cambridge, where Guy Lee was his main supervisor. F. R. D. Goodyear supervised his doctoral dissertation on the pseudo-Vergilian *Ciris*, submitted in 1970. Lyne was made a Research Fellow at Fitzwilliam College, Cambridge, and a Fellow at Churchill College, Cambridge. He became a Fellow and Tutor at Balliol College, Oxford in 1971. His distinction was marked by a Professorship in 1999. He died suddenly in March 2005. He was a much admired lecturer, and a much loved tutor (the best at Balliol: so the students voted). He was devoted to his wife, his children, and his grandchildren. His emails were full of fun, and his hats were famous.

To get some understanding of the shape of his output, the work may be grouped into three periods: the first (A) from the beginning to the publication of *The Latin Love Poets* (Lyne 1980); the second (B) from the Introduction to Day Lewis's translation of the *Eclogues* and *Georgics* (No. 7 in this book) to the publication of *Horace: Behind the Public Poetry* (Lyne 1995); the third (C) the articles that followed. The periods are a convenient simplification, and suit the particular account here. The book on Horace could have been put into period C on grounds of subject-matter; but in other ways it would not belong there, and it was followed by a generic shift: a decision to focus on articles.

Two general points about the *œuvre* may be made at the start. The papers and books present a striking concentration, after the *Ciris* which Lyne then thought to be late, on the most well-known period of Latin poetry, from *c.*60 BC to *c.* AD 20. Yet this concentration was at any rate not inevitable: thus at one time Lyne had planned to write a book which partly concerned Greek tragedy (considerable material survives). The concentration does not represent a limitation of interest. Homer, for example, was one of Lyne's favourite poets; the books on Vergil treat Homer not as a foil but as a poet no less deserving than Vergil of close and sophisticated reading. But the depth of Lyne's involvement with late Republican and Augustan poetry is apparent. Returns to the same material from different perspectives are a characteristic feature of his work on every level. Fertility and restlessness are both involved.

The second point is the relation of personal and public poetry. Period A, the *Ciris* apart, is chiefly preoccupied with personal poetry, which is conceived as reflecting actual personality and opinions. Period B deals with poetry which seems to present a public and Augustan stance. This stance, however, is undermined; undermining indeed (with its more devious congeners) forms perhaps the central concern in Lyne's analysis of poetry. The return to avowedly or professedly personal poetry in period C now gives more emphasis to its literariness: to forms and structures, and to intertextuality. Authors are still fundamental, but more as authors: even in 'Love and Death' (No. 13) an intertextual rivalry with Catullus is the focus of attention. In period C poets undermine and deconstruct each other's works. Intertextuality has helped to modify the approach to personal poetry; but it is a very Lynean take on intertextuality, based on authors' personalities and on subversion.

Discussion begins from No. 1 (only some of the articles will be discussed). It is earlier than the published commentary on the *Ciris* (Lyne 1978*b*), although the work behind the *Ciris* goes further back. The article, a superb account of Propertius 1. 3, is in many ways more fully characteristic than the *Ciris* of Lyne's later productions. It still has much in common with the commentary in form, as does No. 4 (on Verg. *G.* 1. 463–514): the close vision of the commentator would remain central to Lyne's work, even when the form became more distant. The article reads 1. 3 as a dramatization of disillusionment; the subversion of the character's vision of the sleeping beloved is here made into the author's presentation of a basic experience. But the character and author are identified, the basic experience is seen as the author's experience in love: so 'The irony in Propertius' loving description of the very event that will bring about the shattering of his own dreams is masterly' (p. 19 below). The polysemous 'loving' here furthers the entanglements of the irony. The reading could indeed be extended into another subversion (as Lyne (1996), p. vii might encourage): Cynthia's suspicions may be no more or less valid than her lover's. But Lyne does not here proceed thus far, or explore the place of the poem in the book it helps to raise questions about. The engaged reading of the entire poem, where every line is scrutinized and made part of an argument, makes this article a fine embodiment of a critical and scholarly approach.

Earlier too than the published *Ciris* is a small book *Selections from Catullus: Handbook* (Lyne 1975): this comments on the O-Level selection of the time from Catullus, for teachers and fifth-formers. It presents a magnificent series of close readings. So Cat. 64. 50–75 (the depiction of Ariadne) had mysteriously been set as the only portion of poem 64; Lyne's reading, while it still lacks the full notion of embedded focalization, does rich justice to the simultaneous emotionalism and sensuousness of the passage, and to its momentous narrative implications, backwards and forwards. Seeing hints of violence to come, he writes, 'we wait for the resolution (outside our extract!)' (47); in his phrasing here he characteristically plays with first person plurals and with the arbitrariness of the selection. His constant interest in general ideas on practical criticism is apparent in this work. Thus he makes a point in relation to poems which he would emphasize later in relation to books, and makes it with memorable persuasiveness and clarity: '...yet another legitimate way of considering the shape of the poem; incidentally I hope my pointing out alternative structures will not worry: the structure of a poem is not like that of a house; a poem is not rigid, and one seen structure does not exclude others' (40).

Lyne's doctoral dissertation was a commentary on *Ciris* 1–190; this grew into a long commentary on the whole poem, considerably pruned when it was at last published (Lyne 1978*b*). The subject of the dissertation was suggested by F. R. D. Goodyear, and resembles the subject of Goodyear's own dissertation on the *Aetna*. But whereas the early Goodyear had concentrated austerely on textual criticism, and did not really want to get involved even on date and authorship, Lyne's commentary is richly informative. It is particularly so on diction, where the intensity and rigour of his work is remarkable. The book shows his alert and perceptive reading of poetry, though that reading is aimed at a controversial target: strange features of expression are used to find an origin for lines in lost neoteric poetry. Thus, while dating the poem very late, Lyne brings it back into centrality as a source for late Republican poetry. Such reconstruction evokes the methods of German scholarship in the nineteenth and early twentieth centuries; but the deconstruction links with Lyne's exploration elsewhere of subversion *within* specific texts. Lyne came to doubt both the excavation of intact neoteric poetry and the dating (indeed, metrical and other features recommend an Augustan date). The book remains both impressive and highly likeable.

One example will illustrate the moves in this book, and the links with Lyne's characteristic reading. At 166 *ictaue barbarico Cybeles antistita buxo* he well notes the unexpected use of the *gallus* in describing a sexual emotion; his inference is a borrowing. (But *uirgo* in 167 might suggest the poet's own self-consciousness on sex and gender.) Characteristic Lynean reading is then seen in his analysis of *icta . . . buxo*, and especially in his masterly discussion of *antistita* for *antistes*: 'an archaic, solemn and explicitly feminine word for "priest*ess*" has been applied (with a touch of perverseness, even humour?) to Cybele's *galla*.'

The humour, geniality, and candour of the writing make reading the book a pleasure. So on the next page a note on *styrace* (*Cir.* 168), after telling us it was 'an odorous resin used for unguent', adds: 'Interested visitors to Constantza (Tomis) can see pots of the stuff (solidified) salvaged from the sea in the archaeological museum.' The joyfully unacademic 'pots of the stuff' and the ironic 'interested' bring a sense of game into the writing and reading of the commentary Lyne has laboured so hard on. The whole book establishes both the erudition of the scholar and his uncommon skill and grace of exposition.

Two articles, Nos. 5 and 6, point forward and back. The classic article on the neoteric poets draws on Lyne's deep study of this group for the *Ciris*. Characteristic are its firm and clearly argued theses, and in particular the dramatic contention that Catullus is separated even from his colleagues by Lesbia (Ticida is not discussed). What he might later have thought of as more a point about series of poems here becomes primarily an eloquent point about people: 'Of course (for example) Meleager had tied successions of epigrams to Heliodora and Myiscus. But Catullus explores and displays the nature of his love for Lesbia profoundly, obsessively... he shows the interplay of their personalities... All this in related and mutually dependent, mutually deepening poems' (p. 71). Typical of his style and analysis are the two adverbs separated only by a comma ('profoundly, obsessively'), the second *returning* to the same point with a different line of thought. The anaphora and alliteration at 'mutually dependent, mutually deepening' show a more elaborate version of the same figure, with the brilliant 'mutually deepening' reached as a climax.

The piece on *seruitium amoris* (No. 6) ventures a bold literary-historical thesis: that Propertius invents the *seruitium amoris*. The publication of the

Gallus papyrus soon required this thesis to be modified. But the contrast of Tibullus and Propertius (not yet seen as intertextual sparring) again looks forward. The idea of *seruitium amoris* is explored intensely in its historical, linguistic, and communicative resonances; discussion of it is taken, the reader feels, on to a different level.

The Latin Love Poets (Lyne 1980) established itself immediately as a central and indispensable book on its subject. It immerses the reader in the poems, of which it offers many-sided readings. It is intently interested in forms and techniques, but still more so perhaps in ideas on love. The lines of argument are clear; the poets are vividly separated. The book is much influenced by the historical contextualization of love-poetry which Lyne's colleague Griffin had powerfully presented (Griffin 1976). The book insinuates that the poems exhibit the authors' real personalities and exploit their real experiences; but in the details of its readings it offers a more complex account. (A full account of, say, earlier Propertius would have to integrate the representation of passion with generic games.) The book ultimately dwells on subversion. Even in Propertius, the Catullan visions and the mythological transfigurations are subjected to recurring disbelief and humour; at any rate, shifting approaches seem to leave the validity of the 'romanticism' precarious and in tension. In Catullus himself the romanticism is incompatible with reality. Tibullus enjoys the deflation of his own unreal ideals and undignified poses; romanticism is diversely undone by Horace and Ovid. The core of 'romantic' poetry is thus relatively small and fragile: all the more so as Gallus receives little discussion, and Catullus' love-poetry is found to be a series of often unsuccessful experiments. And yet the book is informed by an obvious belief in the value of love.

All independence in the book seems to be relished and appreciated for its provocative individualism, whether it is Horatian independence from elegiac love or Propertian independence from Augustan militarism. Both are valued subversions. Thus Horace's cynicism in *Odes* 3. 20 is enjoyed; the account is enlivened by Lyne's awareness of both the pursued Nearchus and the lectured Pyrrhus as people. 'And the important action is inaction; Nearchus is ineffably indifferent to the whole business. Bored.' (A comically mimetic monosyllable after the choice 'ineffably indifferent'.) 'The studied casualness with which Horace objectively reports on Nearchus, reflecting Nearchus' own lack of interest..., is cruelly pointed in an address to Pyrrhus' (233). Lyne writes more intensely, however, on pacifism in Prop. 2. 14. 21–4 (... *haec spolia, haec reges, haec mihi currus erunt*), 'That implies a triumphant rejection of war...'; of 2. 7. 13–18 he writes, 'These brave lines'... 'splendid and brave insolence' (77–8). 'Brave' and 'triumphant', which alludes of course to 'triumph' (cf. 'triumphal' in the translation), show the individual appropriating military values in a superior act of courage. This will lead into the full confrontation of public poetry and martial epic in period B. The statues on the covers of *The Latin Love Poets* (Eros and Psyche embracing; Rome, Cap. 408) and of *Further Voices in Vergil's* Aeneid (dying Gaul; Rome, Cap. 747) occupy the same room of the Musei Capitolini.

Period B shows a conspicuous evolution, above all through the impact of literary theory. Two close friends are crucial figures here: Gian Biagio Conte and Don Fowler. (No. 16 illustrates Lyne and Fowler working together, on the text and interpretation of Catullus.) Lyne still maintains an independent and wary stance; his explorations draw too on his own long-standing interest in thinking and generalizing about poetic language and procedures.

An article on war in the *Aeneid* (No. 8), which precedes the books on Vergil, offers another classic piece, as some library copies in Oxford indicate only too clearly. The strategy here connects with *The Latin Love Poets*: Roman theory is used to show a gap between Aeneas' ideals and practice; here the author is presenting truths about imperialism and war. The clarity and strength of the exposition are again outstanding, even if it could be argued that Aeneas' values are more coherent—and none the less subjected to scrutiny for that (in books 2, 10, 12 *pietas* is not really the opposite of *furor*; cf. for 12 Hardie (1998), 100).

This treatment leads the way into Lyne's great book *Further Voices in Vergil's* Aeneid (Lyne 1987). The book was seen by some as a reversion to old-fashioned pessimism. First, though, pessimism at present appears not an old-fashioned mistake but part of an undying conflict in debate on the *Aeneid*; and, second, the title announces an advance on Parry's two voices in the *Aeneid* (Parry 1963). Lyne is not, at least in principle, establishing the non-epic voices as uniquely authorial or authoritative (even Parry's two voices had been equipollent); the epic voice is accorded a notional priority. But the non-epic voices have for Lyne the merit of modifying and 'occasionally' subverting the epic voice (2); they do not here defy boldly but question discreetly—this insidiousness and refinement is now valued by Lyne. It is thus rhetorically effective that he does not elaborate greatly on what these voices *are*: that would detract from the impression of their restraint.

And yet—part of the fascination of the book is the passion and emphasis that its argumentation often displays. 'As not infrequently happens when I talk about Dido, I get carried away' (198): the sentence formally refers to digression, but also conveys the writer's self-conscious engagement. In his treatment of Aeneas' leaving of Dido, the rhetoric is that of proving a factual case, one that matters. 'But is this sort of view correct? Is this *all*? Let us grant that Aeneas' response is correctly Stoical, eminently self-possessed, rational, and practical. Does Vergil in fact present it as laudable, or as explained by the special circumstances?... Does this fact not bear on our conclusion?' (166–7). 'Now if Vergil's invention shows unnecessary as well as lamentable consequences ensuing on Aeneas' typical character and elected policy, must we not be meant, at these times, to lament that type of character and policy? Is there not a voice here which we should hearken to?' (177). 'Lament' seems to follow logically from 'lamentable', but brings in more emotional connotations. The final rhetorical question goes beyond the voice itself in *demanding* our attention to that voice.

The book impresses by the vigour of its argument and by its confident tracing of large patterns; at the same time there is much close reading. 56–60 even present a kind of commentary, drawing on an earlier article (Lyne 1984). *Words and the Poet*, which appeared only two years later, comes back to Vergil: a prime example of Lyne's returning. This book concentrates on close reading, partly to exhibit general features of Vergil's writing, but also to continue the exploration of Vergilian questioning and subversion. The book ends, 'Vergil cashes in acquired value to dark effect at the conclusion of our Augustan poem'; 'our' in Lyne's writing often marks irony and a disruption of surfaces. Vergil's disruptions of language to insinuate meaning are seen as partly 'extreme', partly 'discreet' and 'guileful' (17–18); the critical terms (like 'extortion' (extreme), 'incitement' (discreet)) consciously reflect this antithesis, which will continue to be important in Lyne's work. The two sides mingle in sentences like 'Incitement and trespass extort troubling sense from "caduci"' (168: the heroic dead are reduced to insubstantiality). The title *Words and the Poet* neatly conveys both the different focus of this return and the poet's ability within his epic of action to do things with words.

The book is astonishingly fertile and full of material. Taking up the *Ciris*, it amasses information on diction, and exploits it; Axelson is a primary inspiration here. It also takes up the fruitful No. 9 ('Lavinia's blush'), as well as *Further Voices*, to explore the relation of narrative and imagery: here it illuminates far beyond Vergil. While the book returns as a whole, it also keeps returning within itself to an aspect, a passage, a character, enriching and darkening. It is a still more sombre book than *Further Voices*. War and Dido are prime, and connected, concerns. Killing, wounds, death dominate the book more completely than the *Aeneid*. One of the last words considered is *laetus*; it is forcefully argued often to signal disaster. The first entry of Dido forms the climax of that section.

Lyne's final contact with Vergil focuses again on Dido's death (No. 10, 'Subversion by intertextuality'): Dido as a ghost begins, Dido's death closes, in partial subversion of the ghost. In between the Roman mission is subverted. But the tool, and the object of primary attention, is intertextuality. With notable good humour and conscious self-irony, Lyne proclaims a shift to accepting the language of intertextuality rather than of allusion. The theoretical argument is robust, and includes an important argument on readers. The shift to more explicit theory in this article is significant for Lyne, and even for Latin scholarship more widely (cf. Hinds (1998), 47 n. 57); but Lyne deploys a wry humour in various directions. An incongruous 'slightly' enhances the consciously fastidious misgivings over jargon in 'And we pick up the term *intertextuality*, along with its slightly repellent associate *intertext*' (p. 170). 'Faintly' adds to the self-mockery of the reprise in '"This is a problem that the theoreticians seem to me to evade..." Another evasion. For my part, I fell back on Anglo-Saxon empiricism, faintly anti-climactically' (p. 182; cf. Fowler (2000), 83 n. 61).

After this piece, *Horace: Behind the Public Poetry* (Lyne 1995) is strikingly author-centred. The author is especially manifested in the subversion of public stances, in particular of support for the Augustan régime. The language of 'further voices', already called into question in Lyne (1992), is now explicitly replaced by 'sapping'—in fact a more intentionalist and authorial term. But it renders the idea of subversion more vivid; and it partakes in an opposition familiar from *Words and the Poet* between the discreet and the violent (the late 'definition' at 207 n. 1 emphasizes extremity of result, though 'sapping' had sounded insidious). The book often stresses restraint: so 'discreetly subversive insinuation' (168). Somewhat less so: 'if we probe the *uenator* image, it has an irritant value, it mischievously introduces most unwelcome connotations and memories, it is benignly subversive' (183). Against the common view of Horace as infinitely tactful, Lyne often moves to suggest the vigour and impudence of Horace's self-assertion and abandonment of public roles, especially to Maecenas: 'The trick could be played with subtlety... or with cheek. Here it is only mildly exaggerative to say that he plays it with cheek' (78); 'discreetly, indeed not so discreetly, it is a self-assertive poem' (116). Lyne is playing in both places on his own discretion of language. Separate and conflicting sentences mark his lack of restraint on Horace's awkwardness at a later period: 'To try to be more objective.... To declare my hand more candidly' (194). Then with poised understatement he writes, 'He is doing it very well [*sc.* walking a tightrope]; but walking tightropes is not pleasant to the unaccustomed funambulist, and can induce anxiety in the spectator.' In the book the scholar like the poet hovers, but without the poet's risks.

The book is as ever full of valuable close reading, and throws new light on many poems; it engages more fully than before with Roman history (Syme is a vital influence). The negative approach to the most public poems of *Odes* 4—an important if perhaps unsatisfying take—rests in part on Lyne's conception of poetry and prose: directness and poetry do not go well together, in political odes as in amatory epigrams (Lyne (1980), 41–2). The clarity of his own prose heightens this opposition; but the relation between poet and scholar is more complex, as we have seen.

The book makes yet another major contribution to the study of Augustan poetry. However, some adverse elements in the reception of the book had a disproportionate effect on Lyne, and turned him instead to a concentration on articles. These were conceived and written during vacations at his house in Italy. A dazzling series of four (Nos. 12–15), all published in 1998, recurs to the writers of *The Latin Love Poets*, and like that book dwells chiefly on Propertius books 1 and 2 (three books, as Lyne perhaps rightly thinks). Among the differences is a focus on the books as structures. 'Dialogue' between texts—now the favoured term—becomes in the seminal article on Propertius and Tibullus (No. 15) a dialogue between books: books are the salvos in the 'exchanges' of fire. This concern with books is still more visible in the masterly pair on Horace (Nos. 17–18), both published posthumously in 2005. Earlier Lyne had treated Horace's love-poetry, and political poetry; discussion of the latter had been divided by books, though *Odes* 1–3 had been taken more as a unit. Now he explores two books as books.

The article 'Love and death' (No. 13), though its title must allude light-heartedly to Woody Allen, takes a completely positive view of extreme love, as seen in Catullus' Laodamia. In this it follows *The Latin Love Poets*. But its view of Propertius fascinatingly combines the polemical author, 'taking issue' with another text (p. 222), and the tortured author, whose subversion of his own vision subverts his attempt to confute Catullus. No. 15 presents Tibullus and Propertius in more straightforward antagonism, Tibullus parodying Propertius, Propertius mocking and outdoing Tibullus. This rewarding idea would work even if the chronology were changed (cf. Knox 2005). None the less, Propertius also mocks himself and his own reply to Tibullus (p. 270). The piece on introductory poems in Propertius includes polemical dialogue between Propertius and Greek poetry (cf. Lyne 1996). Simultaneously it includes polemical dialogue with public and political values; this is now seen in the context of the book, and the role of 1. 1 as an introduction. (The poem could be seen still further as liminal, at the stage of madness when madness can be recognized.) The fusion in these pieces of textual criticism, close reading, Roman history, and Greek literature shows the particularly impressive range that Lyne's scholarship has attained in these final years.

The two Horatian pieces progress to explore the relation between Latin books and Greek books, not only Callimachus' *Iambi* in the case of the *Epodes*, but Alcaeus' book 1 in the case of *Odes* 1. The latter is a highly original approach, based on a striking observation. The relation between the Greek and the Roman authors is not explored in depth, although Horace's relation to Alcaeus involves a kind of pretend self-subversion. The reader's experience of the author's virtuosity and surprises is vividly and closely evoked; this strong sense of sequence could be thought part of the commentator's outlook. 'When and how will this metrical gymnast settle down?' (p. 297; contrast the funambulist) amusingly conveys the tension in the sequential reader's admiration. The piece on the *Epodes* includes a particularly rich and sympathetic reading of *Epode* 13. The breadth of approach and of scholarship in these pieces increases the frustration of Lyne's own readers as they wonder what might have followed.

A diverse project had been in hand for some years. Lyne had been contemplating work on Sulpicia, i.e. a non-canonical Latin love-elegist; he certainly spoke of a commentary. No. 19, a remarkable draft article (a presentation for a seminar), indicates the depth of his research and reflection on the author. In what it offers, the emphasis is rather more on poetic books than on gender, though clearly gender interests Lyne too (cf. Lyne 1996). His intense concern with female characters, especially Dido, makes the move to a female author of personal poetry both natural and interesting. The return to a commentary format is more unexpected. He never made a decisive resolution to proceed; he said once that giving a text was the obstacle. He may well have envisaged other forms for his material too.

In his last year a very different (but related) project had begun to occupy him: a book on daughters in classical literature. This he had spoken of as a definite plan, and some files indicate his preliminary reading of and pondering on texts. These are predominantly Greek. There are suggestions in his discussions that Latin writers often play down the depiction of daughters (his comments on e.g. Cic. *Ver.* 1. 112 would have been interesting). Euripides on the other hand is here a 'lead player'. The notes show particular interest in the relationship of daughters and fathers: daughters' love for their fathers, and ability to manipulate them. This relationship is set against that of brothers and sisters (Sophocles' Electra is more of a sister). But interaction is not just seen across the sexes: Euripides' Polyxena raises her mother into nobility. Lyne's writing is as alive in these notes as in his books, and still less inhibited by decorum: it is hard to resist the description of Alcinous as 'a bit of a silly old sod'.

The corpus of Lyne's work, though painfully incomplete, radiates achievement. The sheer scale is imposing, all the more when one considers his doubts and diffidence, and the amount of time he had to spend on teaching and administration (the teaching he delighted in). Both the continuities and the development of his work are striking. The books on Vergil, especially the second, could not be imagined in period A, nor the late articles in periods A or B. But returning to enrich is a general feature of the *œuvre*. The concern with subversion predominates throughout; however, the shading of the subversion becomes much more important in period B. Authors, while always fundamental, undergo many changes and modifications. Books and gender grow in significance, especially in period C. Lyne's very individual rapprochement with literary theory displays his development and his humility, but also his capacity to turn common property into something Lynean. Accumulation of expertise and approaches meant that his work was always growing in range; individual articles display this range on a small and concentrated scale. His movement across scholarly genres—commentary, book, article—shows his range as a writer and a creator of structures; one cannot easily say which medium came most naturally to him. It is above all his style which gives cohesion and complexity to his work. The mixture of rhetorical energy and inventive wit, of clarity and subtlety, of engagement and self-mockery, produces scholarly writing of rare distinction and complete individuality. There is so much life in his words. His voice continues to speak clearly and engagingly; it creates or renews an affection both for the vanished speaker and for the poetry to which he devoted himself so ardently.

1

Propertius and Cynthia: *Elegy* 1. 3[1] (1970)

In this article, I shall refer to the standard commentaries on Propertius by the name of the editor alone. I include under this heading Shackleton Bailey's *Propertiana* (Shackleton Bailey 1954), whose comments on 1. 3 are on pp. 11–14. Another work I mention now, *honoris causa*, which will be referred to by name of author alone, is M. W. Edwards, 'Intensification of Meaning in Propertius and Others' (Edwards 1961). Edwards well illustrates and develops the growing awareness of the extent to which Propertius exploits the possibilities of ambiguity, shifting nuance, and linguistic innovation in the creation of his poetry.

At dead of night, Propertius comes to Cynthia's bedside, apparently after leaving a fairly drunken party. He is first tempted by her beauty to take advantage of her there and then, but decides against such a hasty act, and contents himself with presenting her in her sleep with gifts which he has brought back from the party. The straying beams of the moon interrupt this tender scene and, filtering through the window, they wake Cynthia up. She then delivers an harangue to him, among other things accusing him of unfaithfulness. And so the poem closes. This is one of Propertius' best known poems, but one which, in my opinion, still lacks adequate exposition both in the details of its art and in its general purpose and effect.

The poet is describing an incident, presenting it apparently as an actual event; and it has all the vividness and life suitable for a recollection of a personal experience. But if we look more closely, we find that probably the whole, and certainly parts, of the main theme are based upon literary material.[2] We are here faced with one of the fundamental surprises of Latin

---

[1] My thanks are due to Mr E. J. Kenney and Mr A. G. Lee for kindly reading and commenting on a first draft of this paper, and I have since benefited from the advice and criticisms of several other scholars in Cambridge.

[2] The theme of the poem as a whole is closely paralleled by *Anth. Pal.* 5. 275 written by Paulus Silentiarius in the age of Justinian I. Scholars have disagreed as to whether Paulus is there imitating Propertius or whether both have a common source now lost in Hellenistic poetry, but general opinion seems to favour the second of these alternatives, and I am sure this is right: the differences between Paulus' and Propertius' poems seem to me most easily explained if we realise that Paulus is fairly accurately reproducing the Hellenistic motif whilst Propertius has

Elegy. Now A. W. Allen, in a valuable essay,[3] has clearly shown as a basic principle how misconceived and dangerous the 'biographical' approach to Latin Elegy is: the Romans would neither have expected a poem necessarily to mirror details of the author's life, nor dreamt of trying to separate the 'real' from the 'literary'. A poem creates its own reality. The appearance of authenticity and actuality to us is the mark of a good poem, not a 'truthful' or 'sincere' poet. But Propertius clearly cannot just be interested in the vivid description of a borrowed, imaginary scene; this is, of course, a problem that concerns the whole of his work, not just 1. 3. It is, rather, exactly *experience* that he is concerned to portray and examine, his own and other people's, but he does so via scenes and situations that are often basically conventional, manipulating them to serve his own purpose. Whether in fact the material is literary or drawn from 'life' does not matter; it is its potentiality for exemplifying the experience that he wants to convey that interests Propertius. In the narrative of a specific scene, then, he is often making quite a general statement, but one which needs the evocation of a particular instance to become alive and forceful. And this is what is happening in poem 1. 3. He is illustrating a habit of mind he himself was prey to, a habit of mind in fact he would share with many lovers. Let us now look more closely at the general purpose and effect of the poem.

In mood it is quite light and witty, in a wry and rueful sort of way. It is chiefly about, or at least it exemplifies, Propertius' attitudes to his loved one, and it expresses with humour and urbanity his awareness of his own powers of self-deception. It is about Cynthia the woman of wonder, the idealised creation of Propertius' own mind, and Cynthia the woman of reality who inevitably reveals herself, and breaks in upon the eggshell world of dreams.

When Propertius comes upon Cynthia, the sleeping girl seems to him as rare and beautiful as a heroine of the mythical past. She has thus immediately taken on an idealised status in his mind and through various ensuing scenes he allows her to keep it. In this way he is typifying his (and most lovers') illogical romanticism. He resists the temptation to make immediate love to her, and just stares at her in detached awe and amazement, or makes humbly loving offerings to her. Propertius' reactions to Cynthia thus change from descriptive, wondering admiration (1–8) to momentary rash attraction (11–16), thence to suppression and awe (17–20), and finally to humble tenderness (21–30). But all the time Cynthia herself must remain mute and

---

introduced changes to suit his far more subtle purpose. 1. 3 bears thematic similarity also to two other Propertian poems (2. 29A and 2. 29B) and the likelihood that the basic motif is Hellenistic must be very great. Lines 31–3 of the present poem afford a self-contained and interesting illustration of how Propertius uses, but transforms, a borrowed idea.

[3] Allen (1962).

unresponding: the Cynthia of life is asleep, while the ideal Cynthia who takes over in this part of the poem is but a creature of dreams without substantiality. But when the sleeping form wakes up, the ensuing harangue shatters this idealised picture, the loving illusions created by Propertius. With her withering scornful sarcasm and whining *unjustified* reproaches, the real Cynthia introduces a dose of reality into the poet's pathetic dreams, and *herself* shatters the image he has created of her. In this poem, then, Propertius is illustrating a congenital weakness of his (and most lovers): the poem typifies an undignified idealisation of an all too human girl, and the inevitable rude awakening that follows.[4]

I have called Cynthia's reproaches at the end of the poem unjustified; this is I am sure how we are supposed to take them, and it is important for a proper comprehension of the poem to understand this.[5] Cynthia immediately assumes that Propertius' lateness indicates he has been playing around with another girl—nay, he has actually spent most of the night in sexual activity.[6] Now there is not much indication in the poem itself as to what exactly Propertius was doing before he came to Cynthia's, but there is certainly no indication that he has been unfaithful. All we gather is that he is rather tipsy, and presumably he has been at a jolly party. The whole context of Book 1 is here instructive. We never hear of Propertius even *considering* the charms of another—far from it,[7] whilst promiscuity is an accusation often and convincingly levelled at Cynthia.[8] It is not till we get to 2. 22A that Propertius' habits suddenly seem to have changed, if only temporarily. Thus Cynthia's remarks are supposed, I think, to strike us as unjustified, an example of her over-hasty, suspicious, irrational, *real* nature. The very next poem is an indignant rejection by Propertius of a friend's encouragement to him to notice other girls' charms. He is making his position very clear; the fourth elegy is intended, I think, as a belated and indirect refutation of Cynthia's charges at the end of 1. 3, since (the implication is) Cynthia gave little chance for a direct answer when her blood was up, and was not likely to pay heed to it anyway.

There is one other general point to be made that helps towards a fuller understanding of the poem, particularly its humour. When Propertius is seen by Cynthia's side, the impression conveyed, I think, is that he has come *home*. Nothing really explicit suggests this, but, other things being equal, I am sure

---

[4] An obvious parallel suggests itself here: the moon wakes Cynthia from sleep, while Cynthia wakes Propertius from his dream. It may have been intended.
[5] If A. W. Allen, for example, had properly grasped this, he would not have gained his impression that at the end of the poem Cynthia 'returns in the reader's consciousness to a realm of timeless being and permanent reality, which she shares with the heroines' (Allen (1962), 133).
[6] See below p. 20.   [7] Cf. statements of fidelity like 1. 19.
[8] Cf. 1. 8A, 1. 11, 1. 12, 1. 15.

this is the deduction we would most naturally make from the text. Certainly there is absolutely nothing to suggest, as there is in 2. 29B, that Cynthia inhabits a separate house from Propertius. He is portrayed here, I maintain, in terms that suggest for all the world a guilty returning husband (note especially 9 ff.). Similarly, Cynthia's tirade from 35 on seems to assume wifely rights;[9] and line 41, particularly, Cynthia's self-pitying picture of her own lonely spinning, can scarcely fail to evoke a picture of a trusty ancient wife. Nay more, we are probably here meant to be reminded of Penelope, archtimekiller and spouse *par excellence*. Now it was a convention for lovers to describe the ideal of a liaison in terms of 'marriage',[10] but here the convention is being exploited by Cynthia and the romantic vision turns sour. Claiming the rights of the 'wife' that Propertius in his loving moments wants to see in her, she acts up like any irrational, hasty spouse who suspiciously accuses her husband; and of course the posture as a faithful wife, as well as the accusations of promiscuity, is highly droll coming from her—this is the point. The poet has prepared for this perversion of the marriage convention by Cynthia, by depicting himself in its terms at the beginning of the poem, or at least in terms that could be interpreted in this way. We may compare with all this the Cupids' attitude in the kindred 2. 29A (line 22 'i nunc et noctes disce manere domi'), while contrasting the situation in the also related 2. 29B (1–2 'mane erat et uolui si sola quiesceret illa | uisere'). This colouring to the whole poem adds an element of sophisticated humour, and indicates by a manipulation of convention Propertius' rueful awareness that Cynthia rules the roost.

I shall shortly be looking in more detail at how Propertius conveys the above effects, but first it is convenient to comment on a few points of interpretation that admit of separate discussion.

At line 10 there is a possible subsidiary allusion that the commentators seem to have missed. The main picture is of course that of the slaves waving the torches in the air to keep them alight as they accompany the tardy Propertius home. But do not these *pueri* also suggest the Ἔρωτες, the Cupids, who are armed with (clearly symbolic) torches or arrows?—cf. 2. 29. 5 'pueri...quorum alii faculas, alii retinere sagittas'. The waving of the torches would presumably symbolise their fanning the flames of love. And precisely this metaphorical sense is attributed to the action at Prop. 4. 3. 50, only with Venus as the torchwaver: 'omnis amor magnus, sed aperto in coniuge maior | hanc Venus ut uiuat uentilat ipsa facem'; cf. too Ov. *Am.* 1. 2. 11. Thus as

---

[9] Cf. below p. 20.
[10] Cf. 2. 6. 42 'semper amica mihi, semper et uxor eris' (and all 2. 6), 2. 16. 22, etc. The convention seems typically Propertian, but cf. too Tib. 1. 3. 83 ff. and K. F. Smith's note ad loc.

Propertius totters drunkenly home, the fires of love are, it is hinted, already kindled in him. The temptation to rape that follows is in this way subtly prepared for.

The much-discussed lines 15, 16, describing, clearly, this temptation are I think, as many editors have maintained, textually sound: 'Although Bacchus on this side, Love on that, ... urged me, passing my arm beneath her, to make trial of her gently as she lay there, and, caressing her, to take my fill of kisses and take up arms in the lists of love...' The boldness of the syllepsis of 'sumere oscula, sumere arma' is paralleled for example in Rothstein's commentary ad loc. as well as in Shackleton Bailey's discussion, and the context is surely plain enough hereabouts to show that *sumere arma* is being used metaphorically, following the common *militia amoris* image.[11] The phrase contains the climax to these two lines, clearly referring to the commencement of the act of love. There is thus an artistic progression from the rather vague *temptare*,[12] through the preliminaries of *oscula sumere*, to the majestic metaphorical finale. The military metaphor of *arma sumere*, moreover, has been prepared for by *temptare*. This word certainly has sexual connotations but it is also of course used in military contexts meaning 'assail'. Likewise *admota manu* blends in to some extent with the metaphor. The force of this rather elliptic phrase has in fact been generally missed, but the parallels exist which explain it. It refers to the manual caress that is a prelude to the act of love. Camps's adduction of Plaut. *Bacch.* 480 'nisi ... | manus ferat ad papillas' (the text is suspect, but probably mainly right) shows, I think, what is precisely envisaged (though it might be yet more intimate). The phrase itself I suspect may have been a colloquial idiom, which would account for its allusiveness; cf. Ov. *Am.* 3. 7. 74 (of a woman to a man) 'hanc (sc. *partem pessimam nostri*) non est ... dedignata. ... admota sollicitare manu', and Petron. 131; and at Ov. *Met.* 10. 254 the amatory sense is probably at least partially intended. One could think of similarly allusive idioms in English. But as well as being used in erotic situations, the phrase *admouere manum* can have a violent if not military force: cf. Cic. *Agr.* 1. 11, Liv. 5. 11. 16 etc., and thus it happily precedes *sumere arma*.

leuiter (15) has caused difficulty. There is a humorous point being made: Propertius himself originally only tries to approach Cynthia, pressing the

---

[11] It is possible, but unlikely, that *arma* is supposed actually to indicate the offensive weapon of amatory war. The method of expression in these lines seems to me to be too oblique for such an allusion to be in place. On this see Edwards (1961), 138.

[12] Shackleton Bailey is certainly right to object to Enk's equation of *tempto* here with *subigito*. At the stage of the context in line 15 there is nothing to suggest such an explicit interpretation of the verb. Indeed the generality and vagueness of it seem particularly chosen to provide the progression and climax outlined above.

couch *molliter*, just to be near her, without waking her up. Love and Wine on the other hand guilefully suggest that he has a shot at making love to her with similar stealth and gentleness, *leuiter* matching his *molliter*. Perhaps this might seem a reasonable suggestion to a tipsy, love-inflamed mind, but of course in reality it is rather implausibly optimistic to hope that *that* would not wake the girl: therein lies the humour.

Lines 24–6: we are in the middle of the scene where Propertius is making offerings to the sleeping Cynthia. It seems to me incredible that it can still be believed that *cauis... manibus* is ablative and refers to Propertius' hands. The main reason for this is of course that line 8 apparently tells us that Cynthia's head is resting on her hands; so, how can Propertius put apples in them? The problem is of course there; but either we must assume that Propertius is not concerned to maintain strict consistency between the parts of his poem (a not unparalleled ancient habit!),[13] or we must suppose Cynthia has moved meantime (after all she is credited with *raro motu* (27) which could have involved her arm position), or perhaps Propertius did not so much imagine Cynthia as lying exactly on her hands, as on her arms:[14] for one thing is certain—*cauis manibus* makes beautiful sense if it is taken as the dative, i.e. of the sleeping Cynthia's hands, while the epithet is utterly pointless applied to the giver, and could not have been intended by Propertius.

The main force of the phrase *cauae manus* which Propertius is exploiting seemed to me obvious enough, but I have only found it actually pointed out by Shackleton Bailey.[15] The phrase is used of beggars and others who hold out their hands *asking* for something: cf. Tib. 2. 4. 14 (of a girl) 'illa caua pretium flagitat usque manu' and Smith ad loc. Cynthia's hands are cupped in the typical position of a sleeper, but Propertius with a stroke of pathetic whimsy purports to believe she is thus asking for something—all this would of course be clearer to the Roman reader for whom the idiom of 'hollowed hands' was natural. He therefore obliges, giving her the lover's offering.[16] But of course she is not asking, and does not respond. He wastes his gifts on someone who is asleep and thus ungrateful for what is given. *cauis* is clearly picked up by *ingrato* (which is of course significantly juxtaposed with *omnia*): he gave his gifts to someone who was apparently asking, but no, she, or rather sleep, was ungrateful. The pathetic disappointment inherent in *ingrato* is only brought out by a correct understanding of *cauis*.

[13] We would thus be seeing the poem through 'Tychoist' eyes. This is a more convincing method of approach than supposing, as Shackleton Bailey suggests, that Propertius could have 'forgotten' what he wrote in line 8 by the time he got to line 24.

[14] This last alternative is I think, far from impossible. Parallels could be adduced for vague uses of *manus*, and the sort of position I am envisaging is something like the Vatican Ariadne's. Cf. Paulus Silentiarius *Anth. Pal.* 5. 275. 2 περὶ κροτάφους πῆχυν ἑλιξαμένη.

[15] Shackleton Bailey (1949), 23.   [16] See further below, pp. 15–16.

In line 26 I think an interpretation has become general which is wrong. Almost all commentators, remembering their Catullus 65, have taken *sinu* to refer to Cynthia's bosom whence apples deposited by Propertius roll forth owing to her inclined position. Now especially if we accept what I regard as the unavoidable interpretation of 24, this becomes very hard to fit in. *sinu* I think refers quite naturally to the pocket across *Propertius*' breast;[17] the *sinus* was commonly used for carrying things. In 24–6, thus, the datives *manibus* and *somno* give the goal of the gifts, *de sinu* the original source, and taking 21–6 as a whole we see that *de sinu* parallels the *nostra de fronte* of line 21: there was thus no need to repeat the possessive adjective. For the lines have in fact a chiastic structure, an understanding of which makes the sense plain. Propertius first took garlands *from* his forehead (21), and then placed them *on* Cynthia's temples; next follows the central pivotal action (23); then he put apples *into* her hands, which he took *from* his bosom. Only there is a slight variation. Three lines form the concluding action instead of the initial two (a new idea is added in line 25), and Propertius does not say he *took* the apples out, for as he leant over Cynthia, they rolled out of their own accord in profusion, presumably on to the bed, whence he placed them in her hands. In this way he neatly illustrates the abundance and generosity of the lover's gifts he brought back with him, all in vain. The *munera* of 25 and 26 of course still refer to the *poma*; and in view of the interpretation given above, I think *uoluta* is meant to have a preterite force in relation to *dabam* and *largibar*.[18] *prono* clearly makes much easier and better sense if the *sinus* belongs to Propertius himself. There is something to be said I think for the conjecture *omnia quae* in line 25,[19] though the simple paratactic construction of the preceding lines favours the paradosis; I would prefer, though, because of the structure of the lines, to punctuate with just a comma at the end of 24.

To support the above interpretation I think it is relevant to mention Prop. 2. 16. 12; there the poet, in a more cynical mood, is telling us that it is the *sinus* (*qua* the receptacle for the purse) alone which Cynthia cares for in her lovers: *semper amatorum ponderat una sinus*. There, it is the hard cash contents of the *sinus* that please the real Cynthia; here Propertius hopes that a pocketful of romantic sentimentalities will find their way to the heart of his idealised girl.

Finally, of these preliminary points, line 45: 'until sleep touched me with his pleasant wings, while I was already slipping (and thus pushed me over)'. Shackleton Bailey's note ad loc. is one of the most useful to date, and cites

---

[17] Only Butler in the Loeb translation, so far as I have seen, has taken it in this way.

[18] This goes against the general opinion of the commentators.

[19] Shackleton Bailey for one favours the emendation. Catull. 76. 9 *omnia quae ingratae perierunt credita menti* is always quoted by its supporters; the opening unit *omniaque ingrato* does however occur at Prop. 1. 17. 4.

important illustrative passages. That *iucundis... alis* is an instrumental ablative with *impulit* is I think shown by the direct or indirect source Call. *h. Del.* 234...οὐδ' ὅτε οἱ ληθαῖον ἐπὶ πτερὸν ὕπνος ἐρείσει.[20] Propertius has compressed a lot into this line, and has involved himself in the process in an illogicality. The image is clearly that of being pushed over a brink. Sleep comes up and brushes Cynthia with its wings, as she totters on the brink of—most naturally, sleep (and thus pushes her over). The confusion however is easily glossed over in the beguiling smoothness of the words.

I shall now follow in detail the progress of the poem, examining the effects that are being aimed at, and how they are realised.

1–10 THE IDEALISED CYNTHIA (1): THE WORLD OF MYTH

Propertius opens his poem in a strange, unreal world: a parade of heroines[21] occupies the main part of the first section (1–10). The forward-connecting repeated *qualis* shows of course that these heroines are illustrative, but by the time we reach the illustrated Cynthia in lines 7, 8 the world of mythology has really taken over. This is one of the main purposes of the extended mythological illustrations: to establish dramatically and immediately the complete idealism of Propertius' present attitude to Cynthia. It is so complete that he is putting her on a par with mythical heroines. But not only that, these pictures are also the device by which Propertius imparts the subtlety to his conception of the girl at this stage of the poem; and we must remember that it is precisely his idealised conception we are dealing with, which will prove to be far from the actuality. Incidentally, we have here a very good example of Propertius' dynamic, integral use of mythology.[22]

First, of course, the overwhelming beauty of Cynthia, as it seemed to him, is stressed by the comparison to at least two great belles of myth. Cynthia's beauty is truly wonderful, even *mythical*. But there is another point here. It is commonly suggested by the commentators that Propertius has in mind, in the references to the heroines, actual pieces of plastic art; what matters is whether the poet intended his readers (even unconsciously) to be reminded of such figures. Now surviving examples indicate that an actual model, which could

---

[20] This is the first time in surviving literature that sleep appears winged: see Cahen ad loc.

[21] I like L. C. Curran's suggestion (Curran (1966), 193) that the list of the first six lines might recall the Hesiodic *Catalogue of Women*.

[22] There is a good discussion of Propertius' use of mythology in Allen (1962), 130 ff.; we may contrast the practice of Tibullus. Cf. too Ovid's decorative, simple use of a comparison to three mythological heroines, which he *explains*, at *Am.* 1. 7. 13 ff.; note also Lee (1962), 154–5.

well be recalled by a reader, is quite likely for the first and third scenes.[23] And with just the text in front of us, the impression conveyed by the three couplets is surely of a beauty that is precisely *statuesque* in its stillness. The evidence suggests that this feeling would have been stronger for a contemporary reader because of actual associations. Propertius is emphatically transporting the beauty of his girl out of the realm of flesh and blood. High-flown language reinforces the feeling of remoteness and elevation in these lines: we mark the exotic-sounding Greek names,[24] the supra-elegiac diction, and the ornate phraseology.[25]

We notice next the dominant adjective of each clause, *languida* (2), *libera* (4), *fessa* (6): Cynthia seems to Propertius as faint and frail as Ariadne on the shore of Naxos; like Andromeda, she seems to have been freed from great care; and like the Bacchante she appears utterly physically exhausted. Freed from her care, Cynthia requires no action from Propertius: she can remain safely remote in her ideal world. But weary and frail, she can still arouse feelings of romanticising pathos. The Ariadne comparison contributes further to the pathos of Cynthia's figure. The loneliness of the former is carefully marked: *desertis*, though strictly qualifying *litoribus*, clearly emotionally colours Ariadne,[26] and thus adds to the pathos of Cynthia. But these feelings are never allowed to get too strong: the pathos depicted is, as it were, *comfortable*, an extravagance of a romantic mind. The peaceful calm of Andromeda unbound counteracts any excessive involvement with Ariadne's pain.

It is in place at this point to remark upon a misinterpretation of *languida* and *accubuit* that seems to be increasing in popularity. Numerous scholars have imagined that *languida* here is meant to have its overtones of sexual exhaustion. It is of course true that *languidus* does very often have this sense, and it will be subsequently very forcefully exploited. But *here* it is ruinous to the picture the poet is carefully building up, and clearly cannot be intended. Likewise the common habit of understanding *accubuit* (3) in its sexual sense, as though Andromeda is here being pictured as sleeping her first night with Perseus, is completely wrong. For a start she presumably did not spend her first night, after being released from the rocks, with Perseus,[27] and she needs

---

[23] See e.g. Rothstein on lines 1, 3, and 5.

[24] It is possible that Propertius was the first Latin writer to use the forms *Theseus, Cepheius,* and *Edonis*.

[25] See Curran (1966), 192, 193 and also below p. 11.

[26] Cf. Edwards (1961), 140, 141. On p. 141, Edwards also acutely talks of 'the suggestion of exile that lies behind the conventional metonymy *Cnosia*'; it seems brought out by the position of the metonymy in between *desertis* and *litoribus*.

[27] Cf. for example Curran (1966), 197: 'by using this word here [*accubuit*] he boldly fuses the moment of Perseus' discovery of Andromeda with the consummation of their marriage, ignoring the time Perseus had to spend in dealing with Andromeda's suitors and kinsmen'.

to be alone to provide a suitable comparison for the single Cynthia. But no sexual innuendo of any kind has any place in these opening pictures: they are carefully drawn to suggest an untouchable ideal nature for Cynthia, tinged with pathos. Propertius is concerned with the sleeping heroines as single figures, and the impressions they might convey to a watcher who intruded upon the scene. They are frozen like the statues they are into this one situation, and the men who play a part in their lives are outside Propertius' consideration, just as he does not relate himself at all to the present situation of Cynthia—which is of course ominous, as we shall remark below. *accumbo* of course does commonly have sexual connotations,[28] but by far its most frequent use is in contexts of reclining at table. I think the poet is imagining his heroine lying in a position like that of one reclining; she is perhaps stretched out on a couch with a raised end.[29]

A further look at the third comparison is profitable; its qualitative difference to the preceding two and its concluding position suggest, I think, a special role. Cynthia, like the Bacchante, has fallen asleep in the midst of things. There is an obvious and dire warning suggested in this that the idealistic Propertius misses.[30] Though the picture of the Bacchante in 5–6 is softly and pleasantly drawn, almost idyllic,[31] we all know, if we stop to think, that the servants of Dionysus have a harsher reality. The slumbering Bacchante who has fallen asleep from exhaustion will wake, and waking may show herself in her true maddened colours. Cynthia is being compared to just such a one. Propertius lets us see that in the midst of his romanticism, while his conscious self could see only the beauty and attraction, his unconscious was aware of the truth. We soon find that this warning is apt. Of course, when we think about it, there were ominous omissions in the previous two idealised pictures. If Cynthia *was* pathetically deserted and lonely, it was due to *him*; if she seemed to him an Ariadne, he was laying himself open to being called a Theseus.[32] Likewise, if she had worries from which, like Andromeda, she was released, these worries were his fault: he was far from being her Perseus.[33]

---

[28] As commentators point out, this force seems to be at least suggested in the other Propertian uses of the word (though I am not really convinced for 4. 4. 67); but of course since this is the first occurrence of the word in Propertius, we do not have to allow for the active associations of the other instances.

[29] We might compare the position of the Vatican Ariadne.   [30] See Luck (1969), 122.

[31] Propertius places his Bacchante in an unusual locale: see Rothstein on line 5. The almost pastoral-sounding scene seems to me to have been specially chosen for its gentle, attractive sound.

[32] We can see how Propertius' conscious mind hedged this implication by blurring the role of Theseus: it was just the *Thesea carina* that left.

[33] Thus the discrepancies between Cynthia's and Andromeda's situation, which have worried some commentators, are intentional and significant on a subtle level.

Propertius (as, largely, do we) forgets this side of the matter in his rosy romanticism; he sees (and carries us along with him) Cynthia in an isolated statuesque scene, just like the three mythical figures, without past or future, and no thoughts of responsibility occur to him. But the real Cynthia will have other ideas.

It takes a long time for us to express in words the main impressions conveyed by the mythological illustrations of 1–6, and we probably have not yet pinned it all down;[34] but in fact, as I said, their most important function is to indicate that it is precisely into a world of mythology and unnatural, ideal calm that the poet has transported his girl. This is I think again stressed by the bold phrase *mollem spirare quietem*: Cynthia is not just said to breathe *molliter* or *quiete*, but she seems actually to breathe forth *quies*—*quies* is the essence of her breathing. As a result she seems in a way to embody soft rest and peace; we may compare how Horace's Lyce used to 'breathe forth' *love*, embody it (*Carm.* 4. 13. 19), though of course the 'breathing' notion in Propertius is playing a literal role as well. He has compounded for his purpose a phrase that is the obverse of, for example, Lucretius' *spirantes... bellum* (5. 392); cf. too, for example, Cic. *Att.* 15. 11. 1 *Martem spirare*, Aesch. *Ag.* 374 ff. Ἄρη πνεόντων, and all such phrases go back originally to the Homeric μένεα πνείοντες.

The position represented by line 8 *non certis nixa caput manibus* reminds us immediately of that of the Vatican Ariadne, and this is probably roughly what Propertius has in mind, as we saw above. It also fits very well the situation of one who, like the Bacchante, has dropped asleep from exhaustion, and not had time to compose herself. There is thus no ostensible diminution in Propertius' mythicising of Cynthia.[35] But since the line does ultimately refer to a human woman and not to a statue, it surely does suggest the prospect of the subject's moving, and thus waking, with all that that entailed for Propertius' dream. These words then, like the Bacchante image and the other comparisons, will seem perhaps in retrospect to have been uttered with ironical blindness, but in his present romanticism Propertius misses their significance. In reality, the existence of his ideal Cynthia could be destroyed, if the head of the girl who lay before him slipped from its precarious rest.

---

[34] One aspect of Cynthia that the poet is not trying to stress, I think, is the *depth* of her sleep—though this has been the notion of several commentators. Perhaps the three figures of 1–6 were deep asleep, but Propertius does not stress this, as he does other features. In fact, as we learn from 31 ff., Cynthia herself is not presumably very fast asleep. Contrast too *mollem... quietem* (7), which, though not referring itself to light sleep, certainly does not seem designed to suggest great depth.

[35] The emphasis of what I say about line 8 may be contrasted with Curran (1966), 195.

We will note the bold language of line 8: the use of *non certis* to indicate the insecurity of Cynthia's head's support is much more striking, and more subtly suitable in the context, than it appears at first sight. Her hands, *qua* cushion, are 'untrustworthy' much as a friend can be *incertus*; *certus* or *incertus* is not regularly used of physical instability. Likewise the *acc. graec.* of *caput* adds individuality, a certain poetical flavour, to the expression.[36] The line is strikingly written, and the appreciation of a subsequent echo is made the easier.

Upon the romanticised scene of 1–8, Propertius pictures himself as bumbling in, his senses dulled by wine, and thus a ready prey to the kind of idealisation we have seen in process: 'ebria[37] cum multo traherem uestigia Baccho, | et quaterent sera nocte facem pueri' (9 f.). The language describing his entry is vivid and colourful, and the intrusion is thus emphasised. The mode of expression of 9 f. would probably have seemed much more bold and fresh to a contemporary reader, than the literal translation suggests to us. *ebrius* survives[38] a few times in hypallage before Propertius, in colloquial authors: cf. Plaut. *Cas.* 746 'facite cenam mihi ut ebria sit', Varr. *Men.* 144 'saturis auribus scholica dape atque ebriis sophistice aperantologia', Catull. 45. 11 'dulcis pueri ebrios ocellos'; but with the possible exception of the last passage, there is nothing closely similar to the Propertian usage, in which a part which exhibits symptoms of the drunkenness of a whole is actually said to be drunk. After Propertius, such uses of *ebrius* become more common: cf. Ov. *Fast.* 6. 408 'ebria verba', Sen. *Med.* 69 'huc incede gradu marcidus ebrio', etc. And at Claud. *Rapt. Pros.* 1. 19 and Drac. *Romul.* 10. 275 (*ebria... uestigia*) the debt to Propertius is clear. The vividness of Propertius' *ebria...uestigia* is obviously heightened by the combination with *traho*.[39] The incidental detail of line 10, like the fact of the *ebrietas*, emphasises the reality of the world from which Propertius is appearing and thus, by contrast, the mythical nature of what has preceded. The line also, as we have seen, foreshadows by covert allusion the motif of the next section: Propertius is aware of his feelings, but the attitude of respect and awe that rules him only allows him to convey them in an unconscious suggestion.

---

[36] Cf. Prop. 2. 29. 40.

[37] With *ebria*, there is a theoretical possibility of 'transient ambiguity'—we might take *ebria* momentarily as referring to Cynthia; and some scholars have done so: see Edwards (1962), 132. But I cannot see what possible point the poet could intend by this; indeed it seems to me ruinous to the tenor of the poem so far established. It is of course a fallacy that a poet will *always* exploit syntactical ambiguity.

[38] The state of preservation of pre-Propertian literature makes what immediately follows subject to the obvious provisos.

[39] Cf. Ov. *Rem.* 378 '...iambus | seu celer, extremum seu trahat ille pedem' (the image of course being of someone limping).

11–20 THE IDEALISED CYNTHIA (2): A REAL TEMPTATION

Before wine completely drowned his wits,[40] says Propertius, he approached the sleeping Cynthia. At this stage, we gather, he only wanted to sit by her without waking her, for he approaches *softly* (*molliter*), though he finds this, in his inebriated state, a bit difficult (*conor*). In his actions thus he is carefully and tactfully trying to match the gentleness of Cynthia's breathing (*mollem*, 7). This is the first of many significant verbal echoes in the poem. We contrast the harshness (*durus*, 14) of the two Gods who urge him to a very unidealistic rape,[41] and we note their disingenuous suggestion that he do *this* with a tact comparable to the gentleness of his original approach (*leuiter*).[42] The violent metaphors they employ, though, reveal the true state of their minds.

It is the Gods, *Amor* and *Liber*, then, who are made to bear responsibility for the idea of the rape. Propertius himself, who was initially just gently 'approaching' (11–12), rejects it (17–18). The force of the pluperfect *ausus eram* is to push the rejection back in time, to present it as an accomplished fact at the time of the narrative, thus emphasising Propertius' respect for Cynthia's idealised status, by so stressing the instantaneousness of his repression.[43] He also, of course, underlines the fact that such a suggestion was a non-starter by introducing it initially in a *quamuis* clause. After the temptation Propertius is seen respecting Cynthia's *quies*, just as before it he tactfully matched her '*mollita*': the second occasion, like the first, picks up verbally the striking description of the girl's idyllic sleep, *mollem spirare quietem* (7), and a pleasing symmetry is achieved. By the device of blaming third parties for awkward thoughts, Propertius is able to maintain the idealism of mind that befits the ideal creature he has formed.

A word should strike us in line 17, and that is *dominae*. This is of course a conventional term of the elegiac amatory situation, but it stands out in the quasi-mythical picture that we have become used to. It prepares for an unexpected insight in line 18. Propertius rejected the base idea of rape not only out of respect for (the ideal) Cynthia's *quies*, which echoes part of the

---

[40] The expression of this is noteworthy, including the archaic *nondum etiam* (see Tränkle (1960), 46), and again a 'poetic' *acc. graec.* construction. Contrast the more simply expressed Lucr. 3. 527, which is possibly in his mind here.

[41] On the interpretation of lines 15–16, see above p. 5.   [42] Cf. above pp. 5–6.

[43] The force of the pluperfect has been missed: cf. e.g. Camps ad loc.: 'Propertius often makes the pluperfect do duty for preterite or imperfect.' The tense has I think here another function as well as that outlined above. For Propertius to say 'I *had* not disturbed her' seems to imply that something subsequently did. And of course we learn that that was the case (31 ff.). The pluperfect is thus implicitly anticipatory, and adds a structural cohesion to the whole.

previous mythicising description, but also in fear of the *saeuitia* of the real woman. *iurgia saeuitiae* is very strong and highly unmythical, but not incompatible with more normal elegiac situations. We have had hints before of the reality behind the statuesque ideal, but this is the first explicit one, the first one that the Propertius of the poem *consciously* admits to himself.

Lines 19–20, which conclude this section, quickly re-establish the mythical remoteness of Cynthia. The point is made by a striking παρὰ προσδοκίαν—a device popular with Propertius. Line 19 surely sounds as if a conventional amatory situation, suggested by the previous line, is being maintained, with the lover unmoving from the side of the beloved: cf. Tib. 1. 5. 62 'pauper... in tenero fixus erit latere', Ov. *Am.* 3. 11. 17 'quando ego non fixus lateri patienter adhaesi?' This is reinforced by a lexical ambiguity:[44] *figo* is also a common word in various constructions to describe Cupid transfixing his victims: cf. e.g. Tib. 2. 1. 71 'fixisse puellas | gestit', Ov. *Ars* 1. 23 'me fixit Amor', *Pont.* 3. 3. 80 'Phasias est telis fixa puella meis'. It seems to me that the sense of 'transfixed' (by Cupid's darts) is inevitably suggested here. Thus by all accounts line 19 sounds *amatory*. The *intentis... ocellis*, we would suppose, are the eyes of a lover, and of course *ocellus* is redolent of love poetry. I might suggest, too, in passing, that the juxtaposition of *fixus* with *ocellis* leads to further 'intensification of meaning':[45] *figo* is used in contexts of 'fixed gazes'—cf. Verg. *Aen.* 1. 482 'diua solo fixos oculos aversa tenebat', 11. 507 'Turnus ... oculos horrenda in uirgine fixus' and, in an amatory situation, Ov. *Met.* 7. 87 'in uultu... | lumina fixa tenet'; it seems to me that some echo of this is inevitably struck in the reader's mind.

Line 20, though, with calculated surprise, reveals that this is not the simple scene of lover and beloved it appeared to be. Argus,[46] to whom Propertius compares himself, was not activated by love,[47] but *guarded* Io and watched and watched, indefatigably, with his hundred eyes. Propertius surely has in mind the convention whereby the transformed Io is represented as an ordinary girl, but equipped with horns,[48] and thus the sight that met Argus' eyes was distinctly surprising. This is the force of *ignotis*—'strange', 'out of one's

[44] For other examples of lexical ambiguity in Propertius, see Edwards (1962), 133 ff.
[45] For similar effects see Edwards (1962), 139 ff.
[46] It is worth mentioning that the topicality and vividness of this story was probably greater for a contemporary reader, since he would presumably have been familiar with Calvus' *Io*. Very possibly, if we possessed Calvus' depiction of Argus, the point of Propertius' comparison, which seems generally to have been at the most only vaguely grasped, would be clearer.
[47] Rothstein's suggestion ad loc. that Argus has an erotic interest in Io is without foundation in any evidence, and misses the poetic point of the comparison.
[48] See Roscher (1884–1937), ii. 270 ff. The wording of line 20 suggests I think this interpretation, and it is clearly more suitable, since some connection between Io and Cynthia must be being envisaged. Propertius however is not consistent in his depiction of the transformed Io: see Curran (1966), 201 n. 17.

experience'.⁴⁹ Thus Argus in the present version has two reasons for pinning his hundred eyes on Io: the objective one of pure duty (*qua* guardian), and also sheer amazement at the fantastic sight. Propertius deftly adds to the wonder of the line by the exotic form *Inachidos*.⁵⁰ The poet thus, via this sudden and surprising comparison, pictures himself no longer as an interested lover, but as the awed guardian of an incredibly strange heroine, who causes him *wonder* (he is all eyes), but who is not for him to love. Cynthia too, of course, is thus firmly re-established in her former distant, mythical position. It will not be forgotten, also, that Argus came to a sticky end: there is an ominous note in the comparison for our present *custos uirginis*.

21–30 THE IDEALISED CYNTHIA (3): 'TENDRESSE' AND PATHOS

While Propertius' reactions progressed from awed admiration, through base temptation and repression back to wonder, Cynthia remained for him, with just the occasional glimpse of reality, an idealised, distant figure. In this third section Propertius' reactions take the form of humble, one-sided amatory gestures, sentimentally loving.⁵¹ He still idealises her, but she is now no longer so distant; she is coming closer to a figure of real life than to one of myth. We note immediately the address of 22 *tuis, Cynthia, temporibus*. Propertius behaves towards her as though theirs was a happy and sentimental love (which was scarcely the truth). But he now seems more consciously aware of his idealisation, and all but ready to admit that it is a charade he is playing. For the kind of advances he makes (see below) would achieve in a happy situation some reciprocation, and it is heavily ironic that the time he is able to behave in this tender way is when Cynthia is asleep. The rather hopeless tenderness of this final section of idealisation is a perfect foil to the last scene.

In lines 21 f. and 24 ff.,⁵² Propertius is not just giving presents to Cynthia, which he has brought back from the party, but is performing two conventional gestures of love, though this has been curiously unstressed by the

---

⁴⁹ Cf. Camps's note on line 20. Other interpretations of *ignotis* (cf. e.g. Enk ad loc.) miss the point Propertius is trying to make in this comparison. Efforts to emend *ignotis* betray even more lack of comprehension of the force of the poetry.

⁵⁰ The form *Inachis* occurs here for the first time in surviving Latin, and appears in Greek for the first time only at Moschus, *Europa* 44; see Bühler's note ad loc. We note that Propertius maintains the Greek genitive.

⁵¹ All Propertius' reactions in the poem fit in well with the dramatic setting in which he is supposed to have drunk too much: he is now getting maudlin.

⁵² For discussion on the interpretation of these lines, see above p. 6.

commentators. The full pathos of the passage is missed unless this is properly appreciated. For garlands being offered to a loved one, cf. e.g. Theocr. 3. 21; commonly the situation is that the offering, for one reason or another, cannot actually be given to the loved one, and it is then fixed to the door in lieu: cf. Catull. 63. 66, Prop. 1. 16. 7, etc. For apples as the lover's typical and probably symbolic gift, we remember immediately Catull. 65. 19–24 (Propertius may well have this poem in mind here) and the motif has a long history in literature.[53] *furtiua* has a subtlety missed by the commentators. It is commonly just assumed to be put by hypallage for *furtim*; i.e. Propertius gives his presents to Cynthia stealthily to avoid waking her. But offerings to the beloved were conventionally 'furtive' in ordinary situations, for obvious reasons.[54] Thus by what amounts to a play on words, Propertius underlines the true significance of the gift he is making.

There is other subtlety in the phraseology of these lines which seems to have been missed. The construction of *ingrato… somno* is commonly compared to that of *lacrimis… meis* in line 46, and taken thus to be the equivalent of *tibi ingratae dormienti*. But an appreciation of the poem's mood at this point shows that the method of expression serves a specific purpose. Propertius seems by now able and willing to admit some of his idealisation of Cynthia. He realises that all these fond gifts are being wasted. And yet at the last moment he blames, not Cynthia herself, but *sleep* for the unresponsiveness of his loved one. The charge of ingratitude has to be diverted to a convenient third party.

Acting the beloved's coiffeur (line 23) does not appear to be a conventional literary motif of amatory interplay, but it is clearly an intimate and fond gesture. I think too that here, since the ordering of a Roman woman's hair was the duty of a slave, if a high-class one,[55] there is a specific hint towards the *seruitium amoris*; but by all accounts the action, being basically a servile one, is all the more loving. And while on this line let us notice a small example of Propertius' careful choice of language. After the calculated simplicity of the preceding lines, it is easy for us to miss the colour of *formare*. This is no usual word to describe the arranging of hair.[56] It seems to be chosen as a conscious variant of *fingere*, to suggest more vividly the *forming*, *shaping* of ringlets in Cynthia's hair.

With line 27, Cynthia is at last said to move. Inherent in this is clearly the possibility of her waking, and, after the hints that have been given, the

---

[53] See Enk's commentary on line 24.
[54] Cf. Catull. 65. 19 'missum sponsi furtiuo munere malum', 68. 145 'furtiua munuscula'.
[55] Cf. Ovid's Nape in *Am.* 1. 11. 1 f. 'colligere incertos et in ordine ponere crines | docta'.
[56] The closest parallel I can find is Tac. *Agr.* 39 'quorum habitus et crines in captiuorum speciem formarentur', which is rather different.

prospect of the shattering of the idealistic dream. The extreme verbal economy of the line is notable.[57] The full force of 27–30 has largely, I think, been missed: 'As often as you sighed with rare motion, *obstupui*, I stood *dumbstruck, amazed...*' This is the literal sense; but commentators, apparently unanimously, take the latter verb to refer just to the effect of fear. Certainly by the time *ne* is reached in 29, the sense of fearing must be present, but as regards *obstipesco* itself, in its tropaic sense, the primary significance is always strong 'astonishment', 'amazement'. We cannot just ignore this. Until 29 is reached, thus, Propertius appears to say that when Cynthia occasionally moved or breathed perceptibly, he was dumbstruck with amazement.

The point I think lies in the choice of the word *auspicium* 'portent', 'omen'. If Cynthia happens to move in her sleep, it must be, as it were, of religiously important significance. And the common response to a sudden divine portent is amazement: cf. Verg. *Aen.* 5. 90 'lubricus anguis [etc.]...obstipuit uisu Aeneas'. By this choice of vocabulary, Propertius is attributing to Cynthia and her actions an obviously absurdly inflated importance, and the element of self-mocking humour is clearly very near the surface.

So, on seeing Cynthia sigh, Propertius was amazed as though at some divine sign. *auspicio* is of course directly dependent on *credulus*, and we naturally want to know what the *auspicium* portended which Propertius believed—we have already been told that it was not fulfilled (*uano*). But the sentence does not progress obviously. With line 29 ('ne qua tibi insolitos...') we have to realise that inevitably suggested by the discussion of the portent in 28 is *fear* at its significance: hence *ne*. The syntax thus develops along an unexpected route, and the information we awaited is unexpectedly conveyed. And a further surprise follows. When, while acting out furtive fantasies over Cynthia's body, Propertius sees her move in her sleep, the obvious thing for him to fear, surely, would be that she might wake up. Line 29, by a slightly involved route, could still be leading to this end. Line 30 contains the surprise: he is afraid lest she is being disturbed by the unwelcome attentions of phantom lovers in her dreams. We are reminded of the Argus-like watcher of the end of the previous section; here, however, Propertius does indeed have a personal involved interest in the guarded object, but a tender, solicitous,

[57] The compression in fact is such that I am not sure that the full sense of *duxti suspiria* is entirely clear. It is normally, and probably correctly, taken to mean 'give forth sighs'—i.e. on the exhaled breath: cf. Ov. *Met.* 1. 656 'alto tantum suspiria ducis | pectore', 10. 402 'suspiria duxit ab imo | pectore' (Ovid seems to have Propertius' phrase in mind), Verg. *Aen.* 2. 288 'gemitus imo de pectore ducens', etc., but we will note the force of *duco* in these phrases is brought out by the indication of the 'source whence'. And in view of the phrase *aera* sim. *ducere* (e.g. Cic. *Nat. D.* 2. 6) meaning 'breathe (in)', I wonder if Propertius is not rather thinking of the drawing *in* of a deep audible breath; cf. Rothstein's paraphrase '...wird der ruhige Schlaf doch durch einen besonders tiefen und schnellen Atemzug unterbrochen'.

virtuous one. There has been a shift from awed dissociation to an absurdly devoted concern. By the παρὰ προσδοκίαν the poet stresses this sudden burst of almost smug solicitude, bringing out its tender tone by the simple language;[58] and of course virtuous protectiveness presupposes some tender flower that needs protecting, so we see that the idealism is still very much present. We have, also, only to contrast Propertius' concern about the unwelcome importunities of phantom lovers with *his* momentary real thoughts in 13–16 (we can forget now his specious avoidance of responsibility there), to see how much his attitude, even to himself in connection with Cynthia, is imbued with fictional romanticism. These lines thus pick up two motifs in the earlier part of the poem to make their point. We come to the end of the 'Idealised Cynthia' sections with Cynthia imagined as the affrighted lady in distress, and Propertius adopting the role of the gallant guardian. Though we have moved a long way from the mythical remoteness of the earlier part of the poem, the situation is idealistically romanticised and the world quite literally a dream one, and the tender solicitous tone will provide an eloquent contrast to the final section.

LINES 31–33

A moonbeam steals in the window and plays across Cynthia's eyes, so waking her. The motif recalls, as has been pointed out, the opening of *Anth. Pal.* 5. 123 (Philodemus), but it has been transformed by Propertius' application and development of it. It is of course heavily ironic that it needs just the gentle[59] ray of light from the moon (*leuibus radiis* 33) to wake Cynthia and thus to break Propertius' dream. We remember now, too, how *Amor* and *Liber* told Propertius *leuiter temptare* Cynthia: how unreasonable and disingenuous a suggestion that was is now even more clearly understood when we see what mere *leues radii* can do.

Propertius adds to the contrast that is to come in the final section by maintaining in this transition passage the romantic attitude of the previous lines, though the calculated simplicity of the language is replaced by a tone of almost beatific elevation. Line 31 is smoothly and calmly written with no hint of a coming change; unusual language, though, creates I think an elevated

---

[58] Note e.g. the more colloquial verb for 'bear' *portare*: cf. Tränkle (1960), 6 f.; see, also, his remarks on this present line at 10 f., though I am not sure he is making a valid point.

[59] Enk wonders whether the sense of *leuibus* is 'tenuibus et minimas etiam rimas penetrantibus' or 'blandis', 'mitibus'. Clearly, I think, in view of what is said above, the second is the important notion.

impression.⁶⁰ Line 32 then lovingly describes how the moon's rays would have lingered on Cynthia (*moraturis... luminibus*)⁶¹, had not the moon herself been pressing to continue. *sedula*, most obviously referring to the diligence of the moon in sticking to her timetable, also suggests 'officious': the moon is unfair to hurry on her lovelorn rays. Propertius handles this somewhat artificial dichotomy with great charm. *luminibus* of course could suggest also 'eyes' rather than 'rays'—in which case the busy moon is having to hurry on in spite of her own wishes. Propertius again exploits ambiguity for density and richness of meaning. In line 33 *compositos* and *patefecit* maintain the calm and lofty tone. Neither verb is an obvious one to choose for what it describes: *compono* has many uses in contexts of peace, rest and conciliation; *patefecit*⁶² would have seemed, I think, strange and dignified in the context.⁶³ The last word, the diminutive *ocellos*, stresses the continuingly doting attitude, ending the section on a note of elegiac sentimentality. Our attentions are turned not forward, but back, to the idealistic moment of line 19, when Propertius had referred to his own eyes thus. The irony in Propertius' loving description of the very event that will bring about the shattering of his own dreams is masterly.

34–46 THE FINAL SCENE

Line 34 comes with arresting sharpness. The lack of connection, emphasised indeed by the bald, forward-connecting *sic* (especially as this comes after the retrospective *ocellos* of 33), draws attention to the break in the poem; and the positioning of the break in the middle of a couplet heightens its sharpness. The line itself, at least the second half, would, I think, have sounded ugly and violent to the Roman ear. We note first the harsh consonantal sounds (*fixa toro cubitum*); and the use of *figo* in such a context is hard to parallel: it seems specially chosen to sound hard and purposeful.⁶⁴ The real Cynthia thus wakes

---

⁶⁰ The use of *praecurro* is apparently original: see the commentators. For the interpretation of *diuersas*, the difficulty of which seems to have been caused by Propertius' desire for an out-of-the-ordinary word, see conveniently Camps ad loc.

⁶¹ See Shackleton Bailey ad loc. For *lumina* of 'rays', cf. Lucr. 2. 162.

⁶² Propertius uses the phrase *patefecit ocellos* again at 2. 15. 7.

⁶³ There is perhaps an echo with *radiis patefecit* of Enn. *Ann.* 558 'inde patefecit radiis rota candida caelum' (cf. too Ov. *Met.* 9. 795 'postera lux radiis latum patefecerat orbem'). If such an echo were struck in the mind of the reader, it would enhance the tone of elevation I think these lines have.

⁶⁴ The nearest parallel that I can find for the use of *figo* is Apul. *Met.* 10. 17 'et primum me quidem mensam accumbere suffixo cubito... perdocuit', where the context seems to explain the

and drives away the dreams with an outburst of speech that has, and needs, no further comment from Propertius. She condemns herself by her own mouth.[65]

She opens by employing withering sarcasm, which seems to have been largely missed by the commentators. They find *iniuria* an embarrassment, usually interpreting it just 'harshness'. But the word always elsewhere seems to maintain its connection with the notion 'unjust'. Line 35, it seems to me, is calculatedly paradoxical: why should Cynthia say *injustice* is bringing him back? We soon learn she is sarcastically calling the action of the putative other girl in expelling Propertius 'unjust', unjust to 'poor' Propertius. In 35, also, the *nostro*, which could of course be a purely 'poetic' plural (cf. *nostra de fronte* above) is probably meant to be a suggested foretaste of Cynthia's version of the marriage convention, and *nostro lecto* thus equals the 'marriage bed'. The compression in expression of line 36 should cause no difficulty in interpretation (it is perhaps meant to be symptomatic of Cynthia's rage). It has, though, often been misunderstood that Cynthia clearly assumes, as is shown by the language of this and line 38 (*expulit, languidus*; for the latter see below), that Propertius has not only been admitted to a girl's house for some time before being thrown out, but has made good use of his time there. The situation alluded to is *not* thus the conventional one of the *exclusus amator*.

namque magnificently reveals Cynthia's tenuous feminine logic. The thought process is: 'you must have been sleeping with another girl, for where *else* could you have been...'. The splendid proprietary assumption of *meae*—a flat claim to own Propertius' nights[66]—is missed by many a commentator's gloss.[67] The claim, anticipated by *referens*[68] and *nostro... lecto*, is of course part of Cynthia's version of the marriage convention,[69] and the perversion of the elegiac conception is now plain. *nostro lecto* could have turned out all right, but *meae noctis*, given the tone of the speech, is the expression of a domineering wife of terrible reality, not the dream spouse of poetry. The familiar form *consumpsti* takes on an air almost of contempt. The onslaught continues with the bitter *languidus*, clearly implying that Propertius is in an advanced state of sexual exhaustion.[70] And in 39–40 we note the

---

rather mechanical verb. We may contrast more natural phrases like Verg. Aen. 4. 690 *cubitoque adnixa*.

[65] I have mentioned at the beginning how we are meant to appreciate the lack of substance behind her accusations.

[66] *nox* here has the association of a night of love, as often in the amatory poets.

[67] Cf. Enk 'mihi debitae', Camps 'the night that should have been spent with me'.

[68] Cf. Rothstein ad loc.   [69] Cf. above p. 4.

[70] Instances of this force of *languidus* are cited by Rothstein ad loc.

open reproach of *improbe* and the contemptuously careless exaggerations of *semper* and *iubes*. *me miseram*, however, has a note of self-pity that prepares for the switch in tone that follows.

At line 41, Cynthia in a change of tactics sinks to a tone of whining reproach full of self-pity. The allusion in 41 has been mentioned above—a rather incongruous assumption by Cynthia of a role of traditional and pathetic virtue. Likewise 42 maintains the picture of her own pathos, as she depicts herself, still keeping awake though weary,[71] whiling away the time on a lyre in hope of her love's return. *Orpheae* is not just an *epitheton ornans* as the commentators seem to assume.[72] Cynthia, by this implicit reference, mutely contrasts, to gain pathetic point, her own helplessness with the power of the great lonely lover of olden days. The calculated self-pitying pathos of the succeeding lines—all part of the real Cynthia's guile—needs no rehearsing. We may notice, though, how the arbitrary exaggeration, suitable to the tone of the first half of the tirade, is now muted: *semper* becomes *saepe*.[73]

The full contrast between this final section and the earlier portion of the poem is brought out by a series of linguistic echoes, some very obvious, some perhaps just impinging unconsciously on our ears. Cynthia's dream-shattering speech that concludes the poem is made to reuse elements of the wording of the elaborately idealistic opening section. The ironical effect of this is clear: Cynthia, crushingly and conclusively, flings back in Propertius' face his own idealisation of her.

In 38, Cynthia is made to exploit the crude sexual associations of *languidus* to provide an ironic echo of the epithet so sentimentally and guilelessly applied by Propertius to the frailty of her idealised self.[74] Likewise the emotive *desertis* of line 2[75] is turned to the service of self-pitying reproach in the real Cynthia's mouth (line 43). And the *fessa* of line 5 is similarly reused at 42. Indeed the whole stately *qualis...talis...* construction of these opening mythicising comparisons is thrown back at Propertius in the bitter wish of 39–40. In the light of these obvious echoes, I think it is no accident that *lapsam* in the penultimate line of Cynthia's speech (and the poem) picks up one of the charming motifs of the third 'Idealised Cynthia' scene, *lapsos formare capillos* (23); while the affectionately familiar form of *duxti* (27) is perverted in *consumpsti* into an instrument of Cynthia's scornfully patronising tongue.[76]

[71] Thus, simply, *fessa*; many commentators see it as meaning 'when weary with spinning'.
[72] It is seen as a variant for the conventional *Threicius*: see Enk ad loc.
[73] *saepe* should be taken syntactically with *moras*: see e.g. Rothstein and Shackleton Bailey ad loc.
[74] Cf. above p. 9.   [75] Cf. above p. 9.
[76] We might compare the varying effects that can be obtained by judicious use of the familiar 'you' form in modern European languages.

There are more echoes in this speech to be noticed. Cynthia's wild exaggeration *iubes* in line 40 picks up the *iuberent* of line 13, the harsh command of the gods *Amor* and *Liber* which Propertius in his respect and idealism refused. And similarly the self-pitying account of her softly uttered[77] moans in line 43 echoes the guileful *leuiter* of the same gods' suggestion in 15.[78] Cynthia is thus taking up the vocabulary of the rude forces which Propertius, in his idealistic regard for her idealised self, rejected. It is a hard blow for him.

Given this technique of ironic effect by verbal echo, we might look back at the harshly sudden introduction to the final speech 'sic ait in molli fixa toro cubitum' (34). One reason it does sound so harsh is, I think, that it echoes, while jumbling up, sounds and ideas from the idealistic first portion of the poem. As a whole, it is clearly reminiscent in construction and sound of line 8 'Cynthia non certis nixa caput manibus', the description of the idealised Cynthia's statuesque position. That line, we remember, contained as it were a prospect of motion,[79] and it is now realised in this harsh echo. Cynthia rises to a waking position as she prepares to shatter Propertius' dream. The progression from the neutral *nixa* to the more ugly and purposeful *fixa*[80] is masterly,[81] and *fixa* at the same time ironically picks up the idealising faithfulness of line 19 'haerebam fixus ocellis'. Likewise, *mollis* was an epithet which was used by Propertius about the ideal Cynthia ('mollem spirare quietem', 7), and to which consequently he himself respectfully adapted his own movements (line 12); but it is now no more than an epithet of the inanimate *torus*.[82] It has been blatantly transferred away from the girl, to whom in the immediately following scene it will not be suitable:[83] it is an ominous moment.

It remains to say a word about the last line. The interpretation of *cura* as *curatio* has already been established as quite impossible here: see conveniently Shackleton Bailey's note ad loc. But what has not been sufficiently stressed is

---

[77] *leuiter* has caused trouble with those (including some later MSS) who apparently do not understand Cynthia's abrupt change of tone and approach in 41, when she switches from bitter robust sarcasm to wheedling self-pity.

[78] When we remember that this *leuiter* itself was adapted to the *mollitia* attributed previously by Propertius to the idealised Cynthia (cf. above pp. 5–6) and how Cynthia was woken, ironically, by mere *leuibus radiis* (cf. p. 18), it seems clear that the use of *mollis*, *levis*, etc. throughout the poem is a planned idea, the notion being exploited at different times for different effects. See also below.

[79] See above p. 11.   [80] See above p. 19 for a discussion of the force of *figo* here.

[81] And yet the suggestion to read *nixa* in 34 still receives attention.

[82] We are of course reminded of the Homeric εὐνῇ ἐνὶ μαλακῇ; but this is a neat example of how we should beware of assuming Propertius ever uses an epithet *purely* decoratively.

[83] We notice how *mollis* and *torus* are juxtaposed in both lines 12 and 34, but in different syntactical relationships. In this way the transference that has been made is underlined. (In the ideal portion of the poem it is the people who have *mollis* applied to them; in 34 this is dramatically no longer the case.)

that the obvious sense of *cura*, 'anxious thought', 'worry', provides a very pointed and satisfactory conclusion to the poem. It is meant to be infuriatingly typical of the real Cynthia that she should thus hug to herself an unjustified grievance (*cura* refers back to line 44) as her last waking thought; infuriatingly typical, too, that she should be able to inject her words with such haunting pathos, that it is all we can do not to think of her as a wronged innocent. Propertius need add no comment.

2

Propertius 3. 10[1] (1973)

I

As the first in what is hoped to be a continuing series, the editors of *Greece & Rome* have invited two contributors to attempt a critical appreciation of Propertius 3. 10. The contributors were asked to present their opinions independently and no 'rules' were laid down by the editors. It is our intention to publish from time to time further exercises of this type.

      Mirabar, quidnam uisissent mane Camenae,
         ante meum stantes sole rubente torum.
      natalis nostrae signum misere puellae
         et manibus faustos ter crepuere sonos.
5   transeat hic sine nube dies, stent aere uenti,
         ponat et in sicco molliter unda minas.
      aspiciam nullos hodierna luce dolentis;
         et Niobae lacrimas supprimat ipse lapis;
      alcyonum positis requiescant ora querelis;
10   increpet absumptum nec sua mater Itym.
      tuque, o cara mihi, felicibus edita pennis,
         surge et poscentis iusta precare deos.
      ac primum pura somnum tibi discute lympha,
         et nitidas presso pollice finge comas:
15   dein qua primum oculos cepisti ueste Properti
         indue, nec uacuum flore relinque caput;
      et pete, qua polles, ut sit tibi forma perennis,
         inque meum semper stent tua regna caput.
      inde coronatas ubi ture piaueris aras,
20   luxerit et tota flamma secunda domo,
      sit mensae ratio, noxque inter pocula currat,
         et crocino naris murreus ungat onyx.
      tibia nocturnis succumbat rauca choreis,
         et sint nequitiae libera uerba tuae,

[1] [The original publication was headed 'Critical appreciations I: Propertius iii. 10'; Lyne's discussion of the poem was followed by James Morwood's.]

> dulciaque ingratos adimant conuiuia somnos; 25
> publica uicinae perstrepet aura uiae:
> sit sors et nobis talorum interprete iactu,
> quem grauius pennis uerberet ille puer.
> cum fuerit multis exacta trientibus hora,
> noctis et instituet sacra ministra Venus, 30
> annua soluamus thalamo sollemnia nostro,
> natalisque tui sic peragamus iter.

    6 minax   13 at   28 grauibus

II

To interpret a poem in any depth involves discussion of the 'unsaid' areas beyond the printed words—which make the poem a poem. Explicit exposition of the implicit does not sound promising. The risks of destroying the poem—killing it with kindness—or distorting it are high; but worth taking, on the whole, in an effort to prevent the unsaid being unheard. There are innumerable levels of consciousness involved in composition; and just as many in reading. The interpreter is faced with articulating all his responses, and on one plane. The result may appear at times heavy-footed, but this is inevitable. By these remarks I hope to anticipate some criticism of what follows. I stress that if I seem to neglect light to point out shadows it is because light is self-evident.

    The idea of 'birthday' is not simple. Predominantly happy, it has conflicting suggestions and associations. In its very name it evokes the time of birth which, custom decrees, is a happy event. The annual celebration then can be taken as a reminder and symbol of hope. Equally, each birthday records the passing of time, it is a milestone nearer death—a thought which, as candles crowd out the cake, becomes more conspicuous. A birthday is, in short, a highly ambiguous event in one's life. And as a poetic motif it has rich potentialities—symbolizing beginning, renewal, hope, and yet stalked by mortality; stimulating an emotional commingling of past, present, and future. A reservoir of symbolisms that only needs to be channelled.[2]

    Reading through Propertius 3. 10 a couple of times one tends to be most caught by the couplet 15 f.:

---

[2] It is interesting to contrast a rich use of the motif in Hor. *Odes* 4. 11 with the lack of exploitation of it (in the main) in [Tib.] 3. 11 and 12.

> dein qua primum oculos cepisti ueste Properti
> indue, nec uacuum flore relinque caput.

The mention of the lover-poet's own name (and perhaps the aural echoes of the first line of the *monobiblos*) hold one while *oculos cepisti* expands in meaning via the ambiguity of *capio* and the especial significance of 'eyes'[3] from 'caught my eye' to 'won my heart'. And here, by moving out beyond the limits of the immediate situation to the 'birth' of their love-affair, by directly connecting the two occasions, the poet underlines the way he is exploiting the poetic potentiality of 'birthday'. Mortality I maintain indeed shadows this celebration; but it is the love-affair's 'birthday' which the ambiguity concerns. Emotions over *its* inception, present, and future are what lie behind the poem, governing its mood.

1–4: The Birthday Poem starts promisingly. Propertius 'wonders'; the sun prettily 'blushes'—this touch warms the picture and analysis risks destroying it.[4] The girl—and she is a *puella* and not a *domina*—is satisfactorily *nostra*. The Spirits of poetry (Propertius uses for the first [and last] time the Italian, more 'homely' *Camenae*) announce her birthday and give propitious signs. Noticeably it is they and not, say, the *Cupidines*[5] who have come. His loved-one's happiest day, and Song available with which to celebrate it! All is well, then, for the poet-lover. *Nostrae* we note is capable of expanding to include *Camenae* and thus complete the sense of harmony.

5 ff.: May the day be a fine one, he wishes, which is natural enough on the morning of a birthday (5–6):

> transeat hic sine nube dies, stent aere uenti,
> ponat et in sicco molliter unda minas.

But then, seemingly in response to the propitious (*faustos*) introduction (7–10):

> aspiciam nullos hodierna luce dolentis;
> et Niobae lacrimas supprimat ipse lapis;
> alcyonum positis requiescant ora querelis;
> increpet absumptum nec sua mater Itym.

Again something of the sort may seem conventional enough. But I think the nature of these prayers, the obsession with ritual observance that follows, indicate that the lover is a prey to *anxiety* at odds with his apparent cheerfulness.

---

[3] Cf. e.g. Eur. *Hipp.* 525–6 with Barrett's note; Hor. *Odes* 1. 36. 17 with Nisbet and Hubbard (1970), n. Cf. also the phrases cited by Brandt on Ovid, *Am.* 2. 19. 19.

[4] *Because* the phrase is 'unusual' (Shackleton Bailey (1956), 301), I would maintain a personification is suggested. Only *after* this is appreciated does a gloss like Camps's (Camps (1966), ad loc.) become useful. Cf. below, p. 28 n. 14.

[5] Cf. 2. 29A.

Propertius 3. 10

The detail of line 7 attracts attention: *dolor* and its related words are highly pregnant in a context of love elegy.[6] Propertius, who has often been *dolens*, indicates a general area of anxiety. Then, while the very impossibility of 8–10 seems to bespeak exuberance (whatever version of the halcyons' story Propertius has in mind their *querelae* are presumably in 'reality' as unstoppable as the tears of Niobe and the lament of the nightingale),[7] impossibility is two-edged. The echoes of the halcyons' and the nightingale's tragedy do *not* ever end; and cannot, *once mentioned*, entirely be banished from this poem by the fancy of an infatuated lover. To wish their silence is to admit to consciousness of their voices;[8] and for the lover to do this, to recall on this day of days the metamorphosed remnants of tragically, even horrifically, disastrous love stories, must somewhat sabotage his own cheerful front. *Increpet* (10) mars the sounds of *crepuere* (4).

Now let us look back to 5 f. in the light of the emerging complexities. Familiar with the traditional image of the 'storms of love',[9] one finds that these lines too tend to move outwards towards a more substantial anxiety than bad weather on a birthday. Why, we might ask, is Propertius so concerned about the behaviour of the *waves* unless it is that he is thinking of and wants to suggest the normal setting of the *metaphor*? Particularly interesting to compare is 1. 17 where the poet plays between the reality and symbolism of stormy weather; where the winds seem to embody the anger of Cynthia against her lover (5 f., 9):[10]

> quin etiam absenti prosunt tibi, Cynthia, uenti:
> aspice, quam saeuas increpat aura minas...
> tu tamen in melius saeuas conuerte querelas...

But our words themselves are suggestive enough. *Nubes* has obvious metaphorical significations; while *minas* repeats a favourite term of Propertian erotic parlance[11] whose associations must urge the wider reading. (The

---

[6] See Pichon (1902), 132 f.—or simply Phillimore (1905), s.v.

[7] Cf. e.g. Cat. 65. 12 ff., 'semper maesta tua carmina morte canam | qualia...concinit...| Daulias, absumpti fata gemens Ityli'; Ovid, *Met.* 6. 310 ff., [Niobe] 'flet tamen et...| in patriam rapta est; ubi fixa cacumine montis | liquitur, et lacrimas etiam nunc marmora manant'. Contrast Call. 2. 17 ff.; but this *Hymn* is for a *divine* epiphany, and the 'divinity' of Cynthia is at best precarious.

[8] *Lacrimae* and *querelae* have a *particularly* jarring resonance for the same reason that *dolentis* stood out (cf. Pichon (1902), 181 f. and 248 f.; or again Phillimore (1905), s.vv.).

[9] Cf. e.g. *Anth. Pal.* 12. 157 (Meleager). Further references can be found in F. Solmsen's article mentioned below.

[10] My allusions to this complex poem are necessarily rather bare. There are some good remarks in Solmsen (1962), 73–88.

[11] He uses the word to typify what the lover has to bear from his mistress: cf. 1. 7. 12, 1. 10. 26, 2. 25. 18 etc., and Pichon (1902), 202.

pointedness of the resultant text convinces me of the correctness of *minas* against *minax*—which does not occur elsewhere in Propertius—though I am aware that I am in danger of a circular argument.[12]) And *molliter*: this word conjures up everything that is not inimical (*durus*) to love and lovers.[13]

11 ff.: The pattern of sunniness matched by caution is repeated. 'Tuque o cara mihi felicibus edita pennis | surge'—tender and heady words[14] to a Cynthia of propitious birth (*felicibus* picks up *faustos*). But her first thoughts must be of her duties: 'surge et poscentis iusta precare deos'. Prayers are normal on birthdays,[15] but the *timing* of the instruction, the voice of insistence that Propertius seems to hear (*poscentis*), the scrupulousness which here and subsequently he enjoins upon Cynthia, and the sheer space he allots to such topics, all suggest some anxiety—for which graver causes than those alluded to in 5–7 will transpire.

And Propertius has been too precipitous in his urging of prayer. He forgot something (12–15):

> surge et poscentis iusta precare deos—
> at primum pura somnum tibi discute lympha;
> et nitidas presso pollice finge comas;
> dein qua...

I have adopted the reading *at* (a conjunction which Propertius is fond of) and punctuated slightly differently to the editions to bring out the sense. Night pollutes and washing is necessary *before* prayer,[16] as Propertius now hastily reminds Cynthia. *At primum* makes this clear, and the *et* of 14 connects it rather with 12 than 13, which is virtually parenthetic. Haste—anxiety—has displaced the action of 13 from its rightful place between *surge* and *precare*.

It must also be realized that this (rather spartan-sounding) washing is also intended as part of Cynthia's 'toilette'. And veritably it is a plain *munditiae* that Propertius urges upon her. A wash, arrange her own hair—completely against the established habits of Roman ladies[17]—and that too with just a

---

[12] *Minax* is read by Camps and the majority of editors. There is further support for *minas* in Shackleton Bailey.

[13] Fully documented (if documentation is needed) in Pichon (1902), 204–6.

[14] *Felicibus edita pennis* is in the same danger as *sole rubente*. A note on it like Camps's is true enough and valuable; so long as the reader has also responded *before* he analyses—to the delight of what the poet *actually* says.

[15] See Shackleton Bailey on 3. 10. 17; he also explains the syntax of *poscentis iusta precare*.

[16] See Butler and Barber (1933), and Shackleton Bailey, ad loc., who compare Verg. Aen. 8. 68 ff. Cf. too Ausonius' words to his slave on getting up and wishing to pray (2. 2, Loeb ii. 14): 'da, quidquid est, amictui | quod iam parasti, ut prodeam. | da rore fontano abluam | manus et os et lumina. | pateatque, fac, sacrarium...'

[17] Carcopino (1941), 167 f.; Balsdon (1962), 255 ff.

touch;[18] finally that same *uestis* and a flower in her hair. The absence of, indeed the implicit opposition to, normal *cultus* is unmistakable.[19] Comparisons with some other accounts of women are interesting: Ovid, *Ars Amatoria* 3 for instance. And in an account in Ps.-Lucian, *Erotes* (39–40), there are details that underline the tone of Propertius' picture: 'let anyone see women when they get up first thing in the morning, he'll find the sight uglier than ...; they don't just wash away the torpor of sleep in pure water (ὕδατος ἀκράτῳ νάματι) and straightway apply themselves to some useful task ... [they employ masses of make-up and bevies of maids to tart themselves up] ... But their hair-do (ἡ πλοκὴ τῶν τριχῶν) is the greatest expense.' This may be a jaundiced view. But Propertius' attitude smacks of a rather rosy romanticism—which we have seen before.[20] With hair that is *nitidi*, who needs elaborate coiffure? he might say. I suspect Cynthia's (the 'real' Cynthia's) retort would have been short and sharp. Given discrepancy between reality and the lover's idea of reality, we have one reason for his troubles.

But Propertius' anxiety has other and deeper roots. Let us pick up the poem at *o cara mihi* (11) and look ahead. At 17 f. Propertius tells Cynthia to turn again to the gods and ask that *her* power over *him*—in effect her ability to make him say *o cara mihi*—may last for always; and that her beauty (but *forma* since Catullus of course implies more than 'beauty') in which she is 'mighty' may be eternal. An unexpected turn. Other things besides quarrels bring love-affairs to an end, of which perhaps the saddest is the passing of time and the fading of charms that once captivated; the placing of 17 and 18 must imply that the loss of *forma* will see the fall of Cynthia's *regna*. Palpable shadows, then, in the gaiety. The passing of time is inexorable and nothing reminds one more of it than birthdays.

Let us briefly review 11–18, showing incidentally how the manuscript order of lines is right.[21] Line 15 was the first of all to catch our attention (above, pp. 25–6); its pentameter concludes (beautifully, if I may hazard the word) Cynthia's 'adornments': 'nec uacuum flore relinque caput'. Predisposed to concentrate on the line, we find what must be one of the most 'loaded' words in poetry. The 'flower' has vast accretions of association and suggestion;[22] an

---

[18] Something of the sort I take to be implied in *presso pollice* (14). To say that *pollice* 'evidently stands by a metonymy (and as a collective singular) for "fingers"' misrepresents, I think, the effect.

[19] To re-read 1. 2 is illuminating.

[20] In 1. 2 for instance; in another form in 1. 3—as I read the poem at any rate (Lyne (1970) [= Ch. 1, this volume]).

[21] Barber (in his OCT apparatus) suggests putting 17–18 after 12. Others have even wished to expel the couplet (it is accidentally omitted in N): see Shackleton Bailey, ad loc.

[22] A good start is to look up *imagery*, subheading *flower*, in the index to Bowra (1964).

enormous symbolic potential that only needs activating and channelling. Propertius has just mentioned the birth of the love-affair itself. The flower here can hardly but suggest an emblem or token—better words at this stage than symbol—of love.[23] Fittingly thus it caps Cynthia's adornments on this day of days—Propertius' idea of them anyway.

But once the imagistic content of *flore* is freed, other implications must follow: complementing but subverting; beauty and fragility of course, but *transient* beauty. Propertius draws such a lesson from flowers elsewhere (it is of course a commonplace): 'uidi ego odorati uictura rosaria Paesti | sub matutino cocta iacere Noto', the *lena* says (4. 5. 61 f.) with rather surprising superbness. Such symbolism is in fact helped to the surface by 17 f. But the process is one of interaction. Precisely *because* in a context of the birth of their love he concludes a section with this tender but two-edged symbol, the lover is moved to the command of 17 f. Ruinous to move *forma perennis* from its poignant juxtaposition with *flore*.

19 ff.: The anxiety continues. Insistence upon scrupulous religious observance[24] (19 f.) precedes orders for the evening's gaiety; and the idea of propitiousness is less confidently stated: *secunda* (picking up *felicibus* and *faustos*) is attached to the conditions, not assumed—even temporarily. There seems to me, also, some ambiguity in the *purpose* of the anticipated merrymaking; a feverish note to it, an unnecessary lavishness that comes through in the language (note line 22). Demonstrating and celebrating the happiness of the day, it seems also to be chasing away ghosts. This, we may say, no more than corresponds to the natural ambiguity of a birthday. But we must remember what this one signifies, and what therefore mortality is shadowing. And why so eager to defy decorousness and neighbours (24 and 26)? Restraint here might moderate the party but would be irrelevant to the *real* happiness of the day.[25] If Propertius thinks such excess necessary for the day to be convincingly gay, we know who needs convincing. As in 11–16, but in a very different way, he is ducking reality. But his anxiety comes through.

We can observe the ambiguity more closely. Why is drink to speed[26] the night away (21, 'noxque inter pocula currat')? One *protracts*, surely, a time of joy—as 23 is nearer saying, if rather feverishly, with the pipe 'hoarse', and 'yielding' to, i.e. before, the dancers; and as 25 almost unequivocally states ('dulciaque ingratos adimant conuiuia somnos'). 21 and 25, saying more or less the same thing but from completely different standpoints, exemplify the

---

[23] Cf. Cat. 11. 23.
[24] Rothstein (1920), ad loc., gives some parallels for such ritual on birthdays.
[25] Contrast the situation in Cat. 5.
[26] The striking nature of the language (cf. Tränkle (1960), 116) militates against the phrase's being passed over as a mere 'façon de parler'.

lover's ambivalence. And let us think further on 21. In a love poem we expect *nox* to have its familiar associations of a night of love—as it begins to have, with *noctis*, in 30. That such a time should be hastened on its way! The point is that for this lover, prey to anxiety, *nox* intrudes other associations it possesses, darkness and death, the very mortality he is trying to chase away in the licence of this party.[27]

Passing to 29 f. we find that again the passing of the evening is referred to, but this time the portion allotted to drinking is *distinguished* from the *nox*—which begins to open out into its appropriate meaning; and neither *hora* nor *exacta* have perforce any unwelcome tone. Since 27, in fact, the rather frenzied note and its concomitant ambiguities have faded. If the poem has by implication raised and reacted to problems, conflicts, and sadnesses, these now recede. I am inclined to accept the emendation *grauius* in 28: it is neat with *nobis*, which most naturally refers to Cynthia and Propertius; and the result better brings out the point to be made.[28] For the game of 27–8 demolishes all love's *intensity*: suddenly we are in an atmosphere more reminiscent of Greek Epigram than the Propertian *seruitium*.[29] This levity seems to reflect a conscious decision. The lover, harassed by troubles and fears, simply shuts his eyes—and plays. In this way, all the problems besetting the life of the love, including the insuperable obstacle of the mortality of beauty and love itself, are shelved by him; now guying the religiosity that obsessed the more earnest part of the poem,[30] he and Cynthia can go to bed. The questions raised by the poem get no answer. Or perhaps, after all, they do.

---

[27] Catullus catches, and fuses, these two areas of association in *nox* in his 'nox est perpetua una dormienda'.

[28] See further Shackleton Bailey, ad loc. But *grauibus* is far from impossible. There are after all other people present (*choreis*), so *nobis* could—though it would be clumsy—refer to a larger group than Propertius and Cynthia alone, which at first sight seems necessary to give much sense to *grauibus*; however, see also Rothstein, ad loc. But either way, while the dicing would still take the intensity out of love, it would not be explicitly from *their* love, which is most to the point.

[29] No *exact* parallel for such dicing is known: see Shackleton Bailey, Rothstein, ad loc. But the *atmosphere* is reminiscent of, say, Call. *Ep.* 43—or Hor. *Odes* 1. 27. 10 ff. (see further Nisbet and Hubbard (1970), 309 ff.).

[30] See Rothstein's admirable note on 30 and 31; on *iter* see Camps (1966), ad loc.

3

Propertius 1. 5[1] (1974)

The most tangible results of this paper will be to have suggested a reading in line 19 different from that of the vulgate and to have offered clarification of the sense and point of 25–6. In the process however I hope by commenting on some details to help towards a fuller appreciation of the poem; and to give a clearer picture of its structure than seems at the moment to be available.

> non tibi iam somnos, non illa relinquet ocellos:
>   illa feros animis alligat una uiros.
> a, mea contemptus quotiens ad limina curres,
>   cum tibi singultu fortia uerba cadent,
> 15 et tremulus maestis orietur fletibus horror,
>   et timor informem ducet in ore notam,
> et quaecumque uoles fugient tibi uerba querenti,
>   nec poteris, qui sis aut ubi, nosse miser!
> tum graue seruitium nostrae cogere puellae
> 20   discere et exclusum quid sit abire domum;
> nec iam pallorem totiens mirabere nostrum,
>   aut cur sim toto corpore nullus ego.

Thus, Barber's text, in the OCT *Propertius* (2nd edn. 1960), of 1. 5. 11–22. In a few evocative strokes the poet tries to communicate to a rival (who turns out to be named Gallus) what it is like to be in love with Cynthia. The language is highly pregnant; I touch on some points. (They subserve a particular purpose which will become apparent, as well as—I hope—being worthwhile in themselves.)

iam (11) is striking; the situation is thrust before our (and the rival's) eyes: and because it is striking, a repetition will easily be picked up. *non tibi iam somnos... relinquet* suggests not merely insomnia (cf. e.g. Ov. *Am.* 1. 2. 1 ff.) but also—within the tradition of erotic poetry[2]—the vigil of the *exclusus amator*.

Line 12: Cynthia alone 'binds wild men'. *feros* in fact provokes expectation of 'tame' rather than 'bind'. A stock theme, one of the powers of Love, seems

---

[1] Messrs. A. G. Lee and E. J. Kenney kindly read and most helpfully criticised an early draft of this paper.

[2] Copley (1956) makes it clear that the Augustan Elegists both could and did assume great familiarity with the motif on the part of their readers. See especially pp. 70 ff.

Propertius 1. 5 33

to be in mind: cf. Ov. *Fast.* 4. 91 ff. 'illa (sc. Venus) quidem totum dignissima temperat orbem...deposita sequitur taurus feritate iuuencam' (103), '...prima feros habitus homini detraxit' (107); [Tib.] 3. 6. 15 ff., etc. That Cynthia should be credited by implication with the power of the *deity* of love is characteristic;[3] and *una* should thus unequivocally be allowed a full sense 'alone'—cf. the traditional μόνος in prayers and hymns to gods and goddesses (e.g. Eur. *Hipp.* 1281 with, very usefully, Barrett ad loc.). But ideas have been merged in the line. 'Binds' replaces a simple word for 'tame'. Now *alligo* can be loosely and generally metaphorical. But Propertius' favourite image for love, the *seruitium*,[4] has already been in evidence (e.g. 1. 4. 1–4), and the verb must suggest here I think the particular idea of *slave*-binding (for *alligo* literally thus see Columella 1. 8. 16, 1. 9. 4): cf. 3. 11. 4 '...quod nequeam fracto rumpere uincla iugo',[5] 3. 15. 10. (The actual detail of slave-bonds seems more often, or at least more explicitly, utilised in the Tibullan *seruitium*. But it is evident in all three elegists.[6]) Incidentally the bond here in question is Cynthia's *animi*. Propertius often stresses the significance of this side of her, her *will*, her forceful even arrogant spirit (but it is difficult adequately to convey the sense): e.g. 2. 20. 26 'quidquid eram, hoc animi gratia magna tui', 2. 5. 18 'parce tuis animis, uita, nocere tibi'; and see usefully Rothstein's note on 2. 1. 23 (cf. also for example Ov. *Am.* 1. 9. 42). Propertius is making a striking statement about the nature of Cynthia's domination, and I have little sympathy with commentators who take *animis* with *feros*.[7]

Line 13: Gallus will be forced to run to the man he has supplanted. To appreciate the line the reader must be familiar with the traditional situation of the *exclusus amator* (cf. above on 11): the poet plays against the background of the motif. The rival's sorrow will be no ordinary sorrow—for this is no ordinary girl—his plight no ordinary plight. The key word of course is *limina*.[8] Disdained and barred from passing the beloved's threshold he will

---

[3] A development obviously of the *diuina puella* tradition. In particular we may compare how in the concluding couplet (and in 8–9) Cynthia is described in language suiting a goddess: cf. Moritz (1967), 107.

[4] Cf. Copley (1947), 285–300: 'Of all the elegists, Propertius is the one to whom the idea of slavery seems most readily to occur when he thinks of love.'

[5] On Prop. 3. 11. 4 see Lilja (1965), 85.

[6] Cf. Copley (1947), 296; Lilja (1965), 80, 85 f. And cf. Pichon (1902), 295; but it must be remembered that several metaphors and associations can be stimulated by *uincio* etc., and not always singly. Cf. e.g. Nisbet and Hubbard (1970) on Hor. *Carm.* 1. 13. 18.

[7] Thus Rothstein and Enk. Postgate makes no comment at all. Camps at least mentions *animis alligat* as a possibility.

[8] Cf. Prop. 1. 16. 22, 3. 25. 9, etc. Cf. the implications of *heu nullo limine carus eris* at 1. 4. 22: see Rothstein ad loc. (Enk however disagrees). In general see Copley (1956), especially 35–6: the prominence of the *door* (thus the significance of *fores, ianua, limen*) seems a Roman emphasis added to the Greek motif. (In Greek πρόθυρα recurs; cf. Asclepiades 13 and 42 Gow and Page, and Callimachus *Ep.* 63 Gow and Page.) We may note how *limen* already features in Lucretius'

not stay there, at her *limina*, like the conventional 'excluded' lover lamenting and finally sleeping the night. He will come dashing with his sorrows to *Propertius'* threshold of all places, where he *will* gain admission—and provide we may presume some passing *Schadenfreude* for the original lover. This rather mortifying come-down will be forced upon him because only *another* lover of Cynthia understands the pain she inflicts; hence can afford hope of solace. An improbable but, in the circumstances, inevitable bond will have been forged between the two (cf. 29 ff.). (Tibullus does something similar to this—though his point is more obvious and lacks the irony—at 1. 4. 77 f. 'me qui spernentur amantes | consultent: cunctis ianua nostra patet'; *ianua* serves to evoke the motif—as *limina* in our line.)

14–15: brave words (of reproach, anger and the like) that ought to be provoked will 'fall' (*cadent*)—fitting that the brave should be said as it were to be slain[9]—accompanied by an ignominious sob; in their place will rise (*orietur*) *tremulus horror* and tears. These last sound like conventional symptoms of weak-kneed and adolescent love;[10] but they *could* be signs of fear.[11] And real fear is in the air (*timor* 16, and cf. 14). A confusion of responses, 'twists' to the conventions—but there is no-one like the fearsome Cynthia. And our man has not just become a mouse. Who cannot speak his mind is not truly *free*. Cf. e.g. 1. 1. 27 f.:

> fortiter et ferrum saeuos patiemur et ignis,
> sit modo libertas quae uelit ira loqui

—see Rothstein and Enk on 1. 1. 28.[12] Again the *seruitium amoris*, Propertius' conception of it, is indicated: in substance if not in name. For him the impossibility of speaking freely is one of the salient features of the servility of love.[13]

---

reference to the *exclusus amator* (4. 1177 ff.): 'at lacrimans exclusus amator limina saepe | floribus et sertis operit postisque superbos...' etc. See too Pichon (1902), 189; also Nisbet and Hubbard (1970), 290 f. and their note on *Carm.* 1. 25. 4.

[9] *cado* is a natural enough verb to choose for such an expression (see Enk ad loc.), but the juxtaposition with *fortia* intensifies the meaning.

[10] Enk: 'cf. Ter. Eun. 84, ubi Phaedria, Thaidis amator, dicit: *totus, Parmeno,* | *tremo horreoque, postquam aspexi hanc*'.

[11] *horror* thus needs no illustration. For tears as a sign of fear, see Nisbet and Hubbard (1970) on Hor. *Carm.* 1. 3. 18.

[12] *libertas* and its cognates are of course highly emotive with the currency of the *seruitium* image.

[13] See Lilja (1965), 83: 'The most difficult thing about the slavery of love, for Propertius, is the impossibility of speaking like a free man. His wish *sit modo libertas, quae uelit ira, loqui* (1. 1. 28) is only fulfilled when, alone in a forest, he is able to give vent to his grief—*hic licet occultos proferre impune dolores* (1. 18.3).' And Lilja goes on to draw attention to 1. 9. 1 ff. and 2. 21. 5 f. Interesting to compare too is Ov. *Met.* 1. 757 f. (with Bömer ad loc.).

Propertius 1. 5

Line 16: the actual physical symptom caused by *timor* is probably the *pallor* mentioned below[14]—perhaps, though, lines etched into the care-worn face.[15] Neither of these—simply—seem to justify the very emphatic[16] *informem* (a nice paradox incidentally that the *formosa puella* has this effect). The ignominy of a man's being afraid of a woman is partly what provokes it—and in return *informem* strengthens, puts reality into, *timor*. But we should mark well the word *notam*. In what it *suggests* rather than its superficial reference lies its strength. It is a highly coloured word; in this context we associate not so much the *nota censoria*, and the general metaphorical sense 'mark of ignominy' arising therefrom, as its explicit use for the brand-mark of a slave.[17] (Propertius exploits this sense of the word with relation to the *seruitium amoris* more obviously at 1. 18. 8 'nunc in amore tuo cogor habere notam', on which see Camps and, very usefully, Enk. Cf. too Prop. 3. 11. 40 'una Philippeo sanguine adusta nota'. Again, though, it is in the Tibullan *seruitium* that branding is more prominent.[18]) Once more, then, an adumbration of the servility of Cynthia's lover. Of course this implication is not a logical component of the surface sense of the line: there *timor* is the agent, nor has any actual offence on Gallus' part been mentioned—yet. But a reader of Propertius becomes used to disentangling levels of sense and conflated ideas.[19]

Line 18: echoes here of conventional descriptions of madness (including madness caused by love).[20] But the highly 'loaded' toings and froings of the preceding lines, and the doubts thrown not only upon the lover's masculinity but even on his status as a free man revivify both these motifs—and the whole cliché of lover's insanity.

21–2 are retrospective, drawing a conclusion based on 11–18. If and when Gallus has experience of being Cynthia's lover he will no longer wonder at Propertius' pallor and thinness (cf. further below). *iam* (21) picks up *iam* (11) and a section is framed: a future scene has been presented before Gallus' eyes and the same evocative word that introduced it now dramatises the conclusion that is drawn from it. And the couplet 19–20 must be the beginning of this summation. For the *seruitium* has already been adumbrated—allusively but eloquently; likewise the rival's role as an *exclusus amator*. This was the

---

[14] Cf. Shackleton Bailey (1956), 19.   [15] Cf. Postgate ad loc.
[16] Propertius' one other use of *informis* is at 2. 8. 33 'uiderat informem multa Patroclon harena…'
[17] Cf. Suet. *Cal.* 27. 3 'multos honesti ordinis deformatos prius stigmatum notis ad metalla et munitiones uiarum aut ad bestias condemnauit.' We may note that the servile mark of branding was a favourite metaphor of Cicero's: cf. *Sull.* 88 'sed ne qua generi ac nomini suo nota nefariae turpitudinis inuratur', *Phil.* 13. 40 'quem ego inustum uerissimis maledictorum notis tradam hominum memoriae sempiternae', etc.
[18] See Lilja (1965), 77 and 79; cf. Smith (1913) on Tib. 1. 5. 5.
[19] Cf. e.g. Postgate's edn., p. lxxi; or the exemplary remarks of G. Williams (1968), 767–8.
[20] See Enk ad loc.; add (e.g.) Plaut. *Aul.* 713 ff.

drift of my comments above. We were indeed struck by the 'gravity' of that very singular *seruitium*. And the language of 20 recalls the special bitterness which we saw above that 'exclusion' from Cynthia involves; the *domus* is where lover and beloved should reside, or make-believe they reside, together—an imaginative or poetic expression of their unity.[21] Hard and ironic to go *away*, excluded, *domum*. (We may compare the way the intensity of *limina* (13) and *domum* (20) is exploited.)

So while 21–2 epitomises (in conventional symptoms)[22] the physical effects of loving Cynthia which were clearly enough implied in the description of 11–18, 19–20 draw together the 'slavery' and 'exclusion' motifs there involved—which express rather the effect on character and mental state. All seems well: except that I am unhappy about the reading *tum* (19). I find it awkward in the company of *iam* (21)—when *iam* so nicely frames the section. And could it possibly, for the unwary, obscure the fact that 19–20 are indeed retrospective and not *adding* a new point? Rather we should read *tam*,[23] which does exactly what is needed: it stresses the peculiar gravity of *seruitium* to Cynthia, and makes the line manifestly part of the conclusion drawn. (An added little improvement I think would be to replace the conventional semicolon at the end of 20 with a comma.) Incidentally Propertius is fond of *tam* (and its cognates).[24] The line (as emended) is probably echoed at *Ciris* 291 'tam graue seruitium, tam duros passa labores'.

The poem continues (23–6):

> nec tibi nobilitas poterit succurrere amanti:
> nescit Amor priscis cedere imaginibus.
> quod si parua tuae dederis uestigia culpae,
> quam cito de tanto nomine rumor eris.

23–4 present little problem. *amanti* of course means here *amanti Cynthiam*. It is only in the case of a Cynthia that *Amor* is inevitably unyielding to *imagines*; very relevantly for 24 we remember that at the beginning of the *monobiblos*

---

[21] Such a resonance to *domus* arises out of the 'marriage convention': the Roman Elegists (since Catullus) wishing to express permanence or security or involvement in their love—aspired to or attained—sometimes pictured their affairs in terms of marriage. See e.g. Williams (1968), 412–17, Wiseman (1969), 20–5. In this light I think we need to read Prop. 1. 3 (Lyne (1970), 62 [= Ch. 1, p. 4, this volume]). For *domus* itself, cf. its use in Catull. 68 (cf. Wiseman 1969), Prop. 2. 1. 56 'ex hac ducentur funera nostra domo', 2. 16. 22 'atque una fieret cana puella domo', 2. 24. 24 'in primis una discat amare domo', 3. 20. 9 'fortunata domus, modo sit tibi fidus amicus', etc.

[22] Cf. Call. *Ep.* 33 etc.; and for *pallor* cf. (e.g.) Ov. *Ars* 1. 729 'palleat omnis amans'. Both are commonplace.

[23] This emendation was suggested by R. M. Henry but never published by him. See Smyth (1970), ad loc.: it was reported to Smyth by one of Henry's pupils.

[24] Cf. Postgate's edn., p. xxxix.

(1. 1.1–4) Propertius virtually equated Cynthia with *Amor*.[25] Gallus' *nobilitas* will be of no avail in this love. Cynthia is no *uaga puella* to be impressed by rank. On the contrary she is the one who lords it: love of her is by definition slavery and her lover, *nobilis* or not, her *seruus*. The couplet, posing by implication a nice paradox, leads quite naturally from the explicit mention of *seruitium* in 19. But 25–6 have not I think been fully understood. Camps ad loc. lists three ways of understanding 25; none of these brings out the point.

When the predicted suffering of Gallus is described in 11–18, there seems barely any suggestion that he will actively have done anything to merit such treatment.[26] It seems that he is at the mercy of Cynthia's cruel whims. He merely suffers. And part of what he suffers, I think we are supposed to infer, is Cynthia's playing him false—her acts of infidelity, her *culpae*.[27] An obvious reason after all for her excluding Gallus is that she is already occupied. Now in 25 I think Propertius turns to consider what Cynthia's reaction would be (never mind her behaviour) if Gallus should play *her* false, if *he* should be caught out in any *culpa*. The emphasis of the line is on *tuae*, and *parua* is important too: 'but if *you* ever show any tiny trace of infidelity, you will...'. Cynthia can do as she pleases and torture Gallus in the process, but just let *him* try playing loose with her! Just see how quickly *then* he will be reduced to abjectness! (line 26). *rumor* of course refers to the fact that the plight Cynthia will reduce him to will make him a subject of shocked or derisive gossip: 'this man is—or was—a *nobilis*!'[28] The point of the couplet is that the degradation of Gallus at the hands of Cynthia if *he* is unfaithful will happen much more quickly (this is the effect of *quam cito*) than in 11–18. The net result will be much the same: the Gallus of 11–18 was already a *rumor*. But the whole process will be considerably faster.

The articulation of the poem is I think now reasonably clear: setting of the dramatic situation and general admonitions and description (1–8); evocation of the trials awaiting Gallus as a (faithful) lover of Cynthia (9–18); summing-up of this section (19–22); an additional point developing out of this summary (23–4); a brief consideration of what will happen if he lapses in his faithfulness (25–6). As for what follows, *tum* of 27 (uncomplicated now by a *tum* in line 19)[29] refers I think generally and comprehensively to the basic situation imagined in the poem, i.e. Gallus as a lover of Cynthia. In other words it refers to all 9–26. And the transition is naturally effected into the concluding remarks of the poem.

---

[25] By a process of 'transient ambiguity'—see Allen (1950), 266.
[26] Though the connotations of *nota* (see above), and indeed *timor*, may be felt to suggest or to anticipate some offence by Gallus.
[27] The sense of *culpa* I am assuming is of course very common in the elegists. (Full documentation should it be needed in Pichon (1902), 118.)
[28] Cf. Camps ad loc.   [29] Camps's indecision in his note on 27 is instructive.

4

Scilicet et tempus ueniet...: Vergil, *Georgics* 1. 463–514 (1974)

THE WORLD OF THE 'GEORGICS'

Vergil's *Georgics* is scarcely simply a didactic poem to aid the cultivator. To miss any of its sheer descriptive beauty is surely a pity. Yet too much concentration on this can obscure a greater literary worth.[1] It is also a poetical expression of morals and values. It is an emotional response to a datable historical situation, to a time largely dominated by the threat or actuality of civil war; though of course the poem is as timeless as the essence of the historical situation. Only towards the end of the period of composition (36 BC, or possibly earlier—29 BC)[2] was the cycle of civil war, it might be assumed, concluded. The poem argues piety, order, peace, productiveness, *life*—in reaction to chaos, destruction and war. It does so through the metaphor of the Farmer.

'Metaphor' is slightly to overstate; or to oversimplify. The strength of the poetic potential of 'the Farmer' lay in his nearness, or his emotional nearness, to all Roman citizens of Italy. The poem is ultimately about and for man. But it is based as a poem of Italy;[3] and Italy was still largely rural. If, according to the realities of agriculture, the self-sufficient *colonus* of the *Georgics* was increasingly a myth, the myth was not distant[4]—and was highly emotive. It tapped a traditional Roman feeling that the rural and the *moral* life were synonymous. Thus we find a practical man like Varro, in fact a main source for the realities of contemporary agriculture, enthusing over the *dignitas* of the *pastoricia res* and maintaining the essential and moral superiority of the country and its life. More, he even alludes to another tradition which

---

[1] Cf. Wilkinson (1969), 1–15, 49 ff. and chs. 5–7; though I am not sure Mr Wilkinson would agree with my 'greater'; also Otis (1963), 145 ff., R. D. Williams (1967), 14 ff., and especially Klingner (1967), 178–84, and e.g. 194, 220–1.

[2] See Wilkinson (1969), 69; a fuller discussion Klingner (1967), 222–6.

[3] The idea of 'Italy' was increasingly felt and increasingly fostered for various purposes by various people: cf. Klingner (1961), 11–33; Syme (1939), 86 ff., 276–93; Wilkinson (1969), 153–9.

[4] Cf. Syme (1939), 450–2, and 254; Brunt (1971*b*), 129.

contributed to the Farmer's poetic potential, the affinity of rural life to a Golden Age.[5] Here then was an area where, for the Italian consciousness, reality merged with idealizing. Vergil, searching for a poetical obverse to civil war, its causes and concomitants, found a natural and malleable symbol in the *colonus*. Out of his world he created the World of the *Georgics*.

That the *Georgics* upholds and argues in symbolic form the essential values mentioned above becomes obvious in the course of reading Book 1. But I mention some salient points. A basic stance of religious piety is set by the opening invocation to the Gods and maintained throughout: it is Jupiter who has willed and shaped man's present existence (see the famous summary 121 ff.); if a storm is, or images, the anger of Jupiter (328 ff.) we have our answer: *in primis uenerare deos...* (338 ff.). And the Gods *care* for man, it seems: Jupiter is responsible for all those helpful signs, the *prognostica* (352 ff.) whose potential importance we scarcely at first guess.[6] The *Georgics* is a continual and obvious proclamation of 'peace': I single out for mention the military metaphor commonly used of the Farmer's task: see e.g. 145 ff. which lead into the account of the farmer's *arma*.[7] The Farmer's 'war' is with nature. His existence is a perpetual embodiment of the idea of 'swords into ploughshares'. The poem's commitment to *life* is symbolized in the continual personification involved in description of nature;[8] we should note particularly the use of suggestive words like *fetus* (55, etc.), *fecunda* (67, etc.), *grauidus* (111, 319, etc.) whose basic sense of 'pregnant' is never dead in good poets, and the recurrent *laetus* (1, 69, etc.) which contributes its full significance of human joy.[9] These words also adequately indicate the ideal of 'productiveness' that infuses the poem—for which however, in the World of the *Georgics*, hard

---

[5] On Varro see Wilkinson (1969), 50 ff. and 65–8. For Varro's views cf. *Res Rusticae* 2. 1. 6 'de antiquis illustrissimus quisque pastor erat'; or e.g. 2 *Praefatio:* 'uiri magni nostri maiores non sine causa praeponebant rusticos Romanos urbanis...', 3. 1. 4 'diuina natura dedit agros, ars humana aedificauit urbes... necque solum antiquior cultura agri, sed etiam melior. itaque non sine causa maiores nostri ex urbe in agros redigebant suos ciues, quod et in pace a rusticis Romanis alebantur et in bello ab his alleuabantur. nec sine causa terram eandem appellabant matrem et Cererem, et qui eam colerent, piam et utilem agere uitam credebant atque eos solos reliquos esse ex stirpe Saturni regis.' (The allusion to the Golden Age is in the last clause.) Cf. too Cato, *De Agri Cultura* 1. 2 'et uirum bonum quom laudabant, ita laudabant, bonum agricolam bonumque colonum'.

[6] For the religion of the *Georgics* cf. Klingner (1967), 196, 213–14 etc.; also cf. his remarks in connection with *labor*: see n. 10, below.

[7] *arma* was probably first applied to the farmer's tools by Virgil: cf. Wilkinson (1969), 80. Huxley (1963) on line 160 is misleading.

[8] Cf. Wilkinson (1969), 128–9.

[9] The poet brings alive what we know to be a common rustic idiom: see Cicero, *Orator* 81, Conington and Nettleship (1963), on line 1; and quite possibly this idiom was founded on a more concrete sense to *laetus* (cf. *laetamen* 'manure', 'dung')—see Palmer (1954), 69 f., Huxley (1963), 65.

relentless work is essential. But by work we live—and live not only honourably but happily. The necessity of *labor* is stressed in Book 1: see again particularly 121 ff. But in the *Georgics* work *is* productive (as well as perhaps a moral virtue in itself)—this is the point.[10]

Thus the *Georgics*, though it as it were remembers the traditional Golden Age,[11] does not image or try to advocate such a Utopia—where work is unheard of and man is innocent (125–8). It recognizes that man is *not* now innocent. By Jupiter's will he must be inventive to live; *ars*, indeed guile, is required of him. Jupiter, it seems, wants no race of slothful dumbwits: cf. 121–4

>   pater ipse colendi
> haud facilem esse uiam uoluit, primusque per artem
> mouit agros, curis acuens mortalia corda
> nec torpere graui passus sua regna ueterno.

Cf. too e.g. 139 f. 'tum laqueis captare feras et fallere uisco | inuentum', 271 'insidias auibus moliri'. But the sharp wits gained *are* at the expense of innocence. Consequently it is imperative that those artful talents remain in defined pursuits. The *Georgics* realizes this acutely, as soon transpires. The poem recognizes and warns of the dangers attending the ambivalent *durum genus* man, and prescribes for them. We think again of the military metaphor. It in one way is also a warning, ever-present. In such 'war' man should confine his inescapable warlike instincts—the *labor* of the Country must occupy his energies. His violence is only dormant, or channelled. A picture, touched upon, vividly reminds us of the fact. Earth itself, *terra*, the basis of the World of the *Georgics* (see below, p. 48) can become *Terra*, giving birth to the monstrous Titans, symbols of uncivilized violence (278–9 'tum partu Terra nefando | Coeumque Iapetumque creat saeuumque Typhoea';[12] the present tense bears reflecting on).[13] The World of the *Georgics*, because of the nature of man, is only precariously maintained.

Order in fact is supremely necessary—to prevent (for example) the military metaphor spilling over into reality. 'Order' is a theme of the poem. Cf. e.g. 60 f. 'continuo has leges aeternaque foedera certis | imposuit natura locis...';

[10] The remarks of Klingner (1967) on *labor* are particularly perceptive: see e.g. 192–3, 198–201, 208–10 and 212. See too Wilkinson (1969), 54 f. and 59.

[11] Cf. 2. 458 ff.: 'O fortunatos nimium...agricolas!...extrema per illos | Iustitia excedens terris uestigia fecit'; 2. 538 'aureus hanc uitam in terris Saturnus agebat'.

[12] Typhoeus was a monster often associated with the Giants; see e.g. his entry in *OCD*; and Giants and Titans were often confused or identified. See Horace, *Odes* 3. 4 for a famous example of the exploitation of the symbolic import of such monsters, with the discussion of Fraenkel (1957), 273 ff.

[13] Parallels might suggest that the tense is by analogy with Greek practice and not to be pressed: cf. Tränkle (1960), 73. But I think that the full implications should be given a chance; and when they are, that the tense *is* seen to be significant. Cf. my remarks below on *Cyclopum*.

and if, though the earth produced *liberius* before the present Age (128), this still implies a measure of 'freedom' in Nature now, the Roman mind knows that *libertas* is inseparable from *lex*.[14]

Such emotional and philosophical significance to the *Georgics* becomes evident gradually in the course of Book 1. But the peroration at the end, which I examine in detail, makes the whole thing plain; it is a vital part of the book and the poem as a whole—a fact which Macrobius and others have not fully grasped.[15] For it highlights the positive values implicit in the poem by an horrific display of their total negation in the world of actuality.

THE CONCLUSION TO BOOK 1 ANALYSED

```
                solem quis dicere falsum
audeat? ille etiam caecos instare tumultus
saepe monet fraudemque et operta tumescere bella;        465
ille etiam exstincto miseratus Caesare Romam,
cum caput obscura nitidum ferrugine texit
impiaque aeternam timuerunt saecula noctem.
tempore quamquam illo tellus quoque et aequora ponti,
obscenaeque canes importunaeque uolucres                 470
signa dabant. quotiens Cyclopum efferuere in agros
uidimus undantem ruptis fornacibus Aetnam,
flammarumque globos liquefactaque uoluere saxa!
armorum sonitum toto Germania caelo
audiit, insolitis tremuerunt motibus Alpes.              475
uox quoque per lucos uulgo exaudita silentis
ingens, et simulacra modis pallentia miris
uisa sub obscurum noctis, pecudesque locutae
(infandum!); sistunt amnes terraeque dehiscunt,
et maestum inlacrimat templis ebur aeraque sudant.       480
proluit insano contorquens uertice siluas
fluuiorum rex Eridanus camposque per omnis
cum stabulis armenta tulit. nec tempore eodem
tristibus aut extis fibrae apparere minaces
aut puteis manare cruor cessauit, et altae               485
per noctem resonare lupis ululantibus urbes.
non alias caelo ceciderunt plura sereno
fulgura nec diri totiens arsere cometae.
```

[14] Cf. Wirszubski (1950), 7–9; cf. too Klingner (1967), 193–4.
[15] Macrobius, *Saturnalia* 5. 16. 4–5; cf. Richter (1957), on lines 461 ff.

ergo inter sese paribus concurrere telis
490 Romanas acies iterum uidere Philippi;
nec fuit indignum superis bis sanguine nostro
Emathiam et latos Haemi pinguescere campos.
scilicet et tempus ueniet, cum finibus illis
agricola incuruo terram molitus aratro
495 exesa inueniet scabra robigine pila,
aut grauibus rastris galeas pulsabit inanis
grandiaque effossis mirabitur ossa sepulcris.
di patrii Indigetes et Romule Vestaque mater,
quae Tuscum Tiberim et Romana Palatia seruas,
500 hunc saltem euerso iuuenem succurrere saeclo
ne prohibete. satis iam pridem sanguine nostro
Laomedonteae luimus periuria Troiae;
iam pridem nobis caeli te regia, Caesar,
inuidet atque hominum queritur curare triumphos,
505 quippe ubi fas uersum atque nefas: tot bella per orbem,
tam multae scelerum facies, non ullus aratro
dignus honos, squalent abductis arua colonis,
et curuae rigidum falces conflantur in ensem.
hinc mouet Euphrates, illinc Germania bellum;
510 uicinae ruptis inter se legibus urbes
arma ferunt; saeuit toto Mars impius orbe,
ut cum carceribus sese effudere quadrigae,
addunt in spatia, et frustra retinacula tendens
fertur equis auriga neque audit currus habenas.

The sun is the last of the *prognostica*, the weather-signs, that Vergil cites; and just previously the section appeared to be closing (461–3):

denique, quid Vesper serus uehat, unde serenas
uentus agat nubes, quid cogitet umidus Auster,
sol tibi signa dabit.

But it recommences with lines that move through ambiguity and metaphor into a different dimension altogether (463–8). Via transcending examples of the sun's prognostic function the peroration on civil war and the chaos of the present world is introduced. Jupiter's signs show their full potential; the extent of his concern for man is, it seems, revealed.

The pivotal ambiguity is *tumultus* (464)—supported by *instare*. At 311–34 there was a striking set-piece description of a Storm; the sun has in the lines immediately preceding 464 been considered as a prognosticator of bad weather (cf. e.g. 441 ff. or 453–6); and *tumescere* (465) has previously been used in a literal context of weather (357). Thus the literal sense 'storm' for *tumultus* seems momentarily a reasonable assumption.[16] But *caecos* suggests something more sinister. *tumultus* emerges as a metaphor, developing through *tumescere* of 465 into *bella*. The epithets ease the transition; and adumbrate the nature of the *bella*. The 'covered', 'hidden' (*operta*) are naturally 'dark'; and *caecus*, often found meaning unequivocally 'dark', is obviously helped to contribute *its* association of 'hidden'. Both, in the context, obviously suggest sedition.[17] We rightly sensed a warning behind the military metaphor[18]—which in fact was prominent in that Storm of 311–34.

The conception of the sun changes to suit this change in dimension. He now explicitly commands a national attention and shows a transcending and national concern, becoming the anthropomorphic divine Sun, with prognostications to match. First in general he warns of those conflicts regrettably frequent and sinister, manifestly *civil* wars (464–5). And as a climax he gives his response to the assassination of Caesar, covering his head in pity for Rome—but also therein warning of the consequences to follow (466–8). Having moved from metaphor to reality in *tumultus*, we move from general to immediate and crucial particular in *ille etiam... ille etiam*.

This Sun and Caesar are so to speak of the same stature—a feeling which emerges from the balance and phrasing of 466.[19] There, while the Sun displays human emotion (*miseratus*), Caesar's dying (*exstincto*), given the context, manifestly magnifies in significance to suggest the extinction of a cosmic body.[20] The Sun covering his head—the action is one of mourning[21]—pities Rome on the death of an equal or equivalent. But the action *is* also prognostication. If the Sun *covers* his shining head in *darkness* (467 *caput obscura nitidum ferrugine texit*), the portentous significance after the *caecos tumultus* and *operta bella* portended in the past is obvious. All 464–8 turn on the ideas of light and dark, hidden and open. The world, it seems, had in Caesar a 'Sun' capable of preventing the covert darkness of civil war. At his eclipse, the heavenly Sun correspondingly reacts, removing his light: pitying Rome it may be, but warning her *people*, the *impia saecula*, who have abandoned

---

[16] Vergil uses *tumesco* only at *Georgics* 1. 357, 465 and 2. 479; *tumultus* often in the *Aeneid*, but in the *Georgics* only at 1. 464.

[17] *OLD* s.v. *caecus* gives useful documentation on the word.

[18] We find roles reversed in the *Aeneid*: cf. e.g. *Aeneid* 7. 525 f. 'sed ferro ancipiti decernunt atraque late | horrescit strictis seges ensibus...'.

[19] Cf. very interestingly how the historical Caesar, not without precedent, seems to have associated himself with the God *Sol*: Weinstock (1971), 381–4, to which Dr Woodman refers me. (In our present passage the logic or theology of the poetic impression is not of course to be pressed too far.)

[20] Cf. *OLD* s.v. *ex(s)tinguo* 1b. Cf. particularly Cicero, *De Natura Deorum* 2. 14 'Tuditano et Aquilio consulibus... P. Africanus, Sol alter, extinctus est.'

[21] Cf. Plutarch, *Moralia* 267A, Pauly–Wissowa VIA 2231. 4 ff. Compare Lee (1974), 109.

the piety enjoined by the *Georgics*; showing them the 'darkness' they have produced—and the 'darkness' to come. The night feared for all time was real enough. But at the end of these five lines it is also a definitive symbol and portent of civil war.

I have left *fraudem* (465) for special comment. This is a stronger, more wide-ranging word than its English derivative might suggest. It summons from lexicographers glosses like 'harm', 'danger', 'crime' as well as 'dishonest conduct', 'deceit' and 'trickery'. It is something in this latter area that the context (*operta* following immediately) evokes. 'Treachery' to anticipate the 'treachery' of Caesar's killers, for example; or more generally the 'deceit' of insurrection. But the context does not confine the word. There seems to be indicated some basic fault, 'treachery', in the people which keeps surfacing in one form or another—symbolized (in a very different mood) at 502 by the perjury of Laomedon.[22] *fraudem*, and *impia...saecula* (468), are the beginnings of this idea, anticipating *luimus* and *periuria* of 502. While we witness the *Georgics'* military metaphor becoming reality, we appreciate also what dimensions are possible for man's guile (cf. p. 40). The Sun has had repeated occasion to warn of such *fraus*. The crime of Caesar's murder is the ultimate manifestation. There seems no doubt of the people's guilt or the Sun's consciousness of it. It should be stressed that the Sun's pity is for *Roma* as opposed to its people: the *saecula* are *impia* and frightened.

fraudem intensifies in retrospect the Sun's epithet *falsum* in 463 which expands (matching the movement of *sol* from weather sign to 'deity') from 'incorrect' to involve a suggestion of 'deceitful', 'treacherous'. The Sun is the obverse of this benighted generation. So, it would follow, was his equal— Caesar, whom they murdered. Additionally I would suggest that in this context of guilt and crime some moral tone emerges in *ferrugine*, a suggestion of moral corruption which Ovid at any rate seems to have felt the word could imply (see *Metamorphoses* 2. 798). The reaction of the Sun more pointedly mirrors the darkness of the world, and its prognostic significance ramifies. Some scrutiny of *ferrugine* is compelled, for it is not a common word—called 'puzzling' by one scholar.[23] Its basic function is obviously to convey *dark colour*. But the potential overtone suggested above, plus perhaps the simple associations which its root *ferrum* can relevantly contribute in the context, explain its selection.

From the Sun as prognosticator we move to other portents of disaster. The reaction is universal (469–88): the focus of the narrative shifts from the heavens to the broad divisions of the world and vague evocations of its beasts;

---

[22] For the currency of such an idea cf. Wilkinson (1969), 161.
[23] See Fordyce (1961), 304.

from Aetna to the sky in Germany and to the Alps; there follow other portents which involve, more or less immediately, the World of the *Georgics* itself; and these mingled with signs more indefinable and unplaceable broaden back to the opening dimension, to portents in the heavens. Such is the build-up to the actual narrative of calamity.

Several lists of the portents supposedly following Caesar's death survive. Vergil's in fact is the earliest. There is considerable divergence of detail between it and later 'historical' sources, although in essence it may well be based on what was reputed actually to have occurred.[24] But whatever the 'truth', the choice of *which* portents to include, how to treat or embellish them, in what order to arrange and combine them, was Vergil's responsibility. This is Vergil's poetical account of the portentous foreshadowing of civil catastrophe that followed Caesar's assassination; it is Vergil I shall interpret.[25]

Both *obscenae* and *importunae* (470) signify 'boding-ill': cf. e.g. Vergil, *Aeneid* 12. 876 'obscenae uolucres', 12. 864 'quae (sc. *ales*) ... canit importuna per umbras'.[26] But both have other obvious senses; the dogs and birds anticipate in their epithets the horror of the deeds they portend. *obscenus* has general associations of 'hateful', 'disgusting', 'obscene': cf. e.g. *Aeneid* 7. 417 (Allecto) 'frontem obscenam rugis arat'; and Vergil is playing on both areas of sense at *Aeneid* 4. 455 'uidit ... fusaque in obscenum se uertere uina cruorem' (cf. Pease (1935) ad loc.). *importunus* comes close to 'cruel', 'savage': e.g. applied to a tyrant by Livy (29. 17. 20), to Catiline by Cicero (*Catiline* 2. 12). Such significations inevitably emerge in, and affect, this context. Just as, in this context, the signal for battle must be heard behind *signa dabant*[27]— ironically given by creatures of nature. Things have changed since 463, or 439.

Aetna erupts (471–3). The more ominous if one remembers that according to legend beneath Aetna lay trapped one or other of the type figures of violence (there were varying versions): e.g. the Giant Enceladus (Vergil, *Aeneid* 3. 578–82)—or Typhoeus himself, son of Terra, whose buried anger, it was foretold, would violently boil over despite Jupiter's constraint in scenes

---

[24] See e.g. Plutarch, *Caesar* 69; Suetonius, *Caesar* 81; the question is well and concisely discussed by Wilkinson (1969), 204–6. Particularly interesting to compare perhaps is Cicero, *De Diuinatione* 1. 97–8 (published just after Caesar's assassination but not directly referring to it) which has many parallels with Vergil—and interesting differences. But there is a great deal of conventionality in such lists: cf. Dio Cassius 41. 14, Cicero, *Catiline* 3.18 and a quotation from Cicero's poetry in *De Diuinatione* 1. 17 ff. (with Pease (1920) ad loc.), Apollonius Rhodius 4. 1280–7.

[25] I shall not cite parallels for the individual portents unless it illuminates the discussion to do so. The reader has the passages in the previous note to compare, and there is further documentation in the commentaries at the relevant points.

[26] Cf. L & S s.v. *obscenus*; on both see Conington and Nettleship (1963) ad loc. or, more fully, Richter (1957) on line 470.

[27] Cf. L & S s.v. *signum* 11 A 2.

of destruction very (and interestingly) similar to those here described: cf. Aeschylus, *Prometheus* 356–74. I mentioned the picture of Terra and her offspring above; it is perhaps hard not to sense mythical symbolism beneath the present portent.

But first we note the depth to the language. *efferuere* (471) denotes the 'boiling over' in heat and fire of Aetna. However, in the company of words evocative of military violence like *flammae* and *saxa*,[28] it also contains an impression, or suggests the colour, of things to come, the things it portends: cf. Vergil, *Aeneid* 9.692 f. 'hostem | feruere caede noua', or 9.72 (*feruidus*) etc. The significance of *in agros* is intense. Built up by the narrative of Book 1, *agri* are by now in effect symbolic: they are after all the ground of the World of the *Georgics*; and 'living'—living enough to be 'pregnant' (cf. 2. 5 'grauidus... ager'). Hence emotive recipients of violence; and the portent as a whole deepens. *agri* here illustrates—in a simple way—an important technique; we shall see several more examples. A word, by repeated and significant mention in the poem, accumulates implicit but increasing resonance or meaning; and at salient moments (such as in this finale) all such meaning can be realized with explicit and climactic effect.

Cyclopum, now that we have moved into the Roman present, arrests. In such density of writing we should expect it to be more than a method of geographical location.[29] And, if we allow it, it is. Let us accept the full implication. The fields are in the portent the property of these monsters, and not of farmers. According to Hesiod[30] the Cyclopes are, like the Titans and Typhoeus, dreadful offspring of Earth. By other tradition[31] it was actually the Cyclopes who were domiciled in Aetna, forging thunderbolts for Zeus. Conflation has taken place, the Cyclopes (naturally enough) adopting the role of the Titans and Giants as symbols of savagery and by implication being *imprisoned* as such in Aetna. Beneath the surface signification of this portent there is thus an adumbration of another idea as we suspected above. In the boiling over of Aetna is the escape of symbolic monsters of violence—the Cyclopes—taking possession of the fields with the violence foretold for the anger of Typhoeus. *ruptis fornacibus* helps this picture, suggesting the *escape* of the Cyclopes. *fornax*, basically a furnace, is particularly where one smelts metal—precisely these monsters' job—as well as being poetically and more generally applied to volcanoes.[32] The picture is only adumbrated; it will not submit to tight logical analysis and the impression on the reader may be largely subliminal.

---

[28] Our response to the suggestive power of the *words* I think is not affected, not anyway swamped, by the specifications (*globos, liquefacta*) imposed by the literal context of the portent.
[29] Huxley (1963) ad loc. '**Cyclopum... in agros**: i.e. over the region round Etna.'
[30] *Theogony* 139–46 on which see M. L. West (1966), 206.
[31] Cf. Cicero, *De Diuinatione* 2. 43.   [32] See *OLD* s.v. 1c and f.

The sound of battle stirring in 471 is strident in 474. The basic import of the omen is obvious enough. But Germany particularly heard it and for Germany no doubt it was a tuneful sound. The portent has more specific implications than commentators mention: pointing to barbarians exploiting the coming civil strife, the threat of incursions—added repercussions to the murder of Caesar. This is indeed to be the case: *illinc Germania bellum* (509). The Alps tremble, shaken by earthquakes: ominous in itself.[33] But this trembling also indicates *fear*. Both *motus* and *tremo* have emotional potential that interacts.[34] The Alps, long felt as the bulwark and frontier of unified Italy, tremble in fear at the prospect of the barbarian invasion threatened in the previous line.[35] Passages of Livy are instructive to compare for the feeling about the Alps (e.g. 5. 34. 6–7, 21. 30. 6–8, 41. 15); and with the recent completion of Italian unity (cf. note 3), such a feeling must have been enhanced.

The portents become less distinct, ominously juxtaposing opposites (476–8): the *ingens uox* in silent, presumably sacred but also (simply) rural-sounding groves;[36] singularly-hued phantoms in darkness (*obscurum noctis*) pregnant because reminiscent of the Sun's eclipse (cf. 467 f. *obscura... noctem*). We are not told what the voice said, nor who or what these *simulacra* were. Perhaps we can guess; if not we shall soon be in a better position. But then the *pecudes locutae* (478) strike immediately, provoking *infandum* (479). Here is the first of the portents that intimately involve the Country. In each case the essential component is sufficiently typical of the World of the *Georgics* to remind us of it and its normality. But what happens suggests rather a nightmare *Georgics*. We see in these portents pictures not so much of violence inflicted upon the Country which was the basic impression with Aetna, but its internal collapse, distortion, even perversion[37]—something more terrible; and a closer depiction in image of civil war.

However, before considering these in detail, I shall look ahead to the other portents unplaceable and more general like the *ingens uox* and the *simulacra* which are mingled with the specifically 'Country' signs. I take first 483–4 'nec tempore eodem | tristibus aut extis fibrae apparere minaces'. Key here are the framing adjectives *tristibus* and *minaces*. The former is comparable to *obscenus* and *importunus* above, combining a signification virtually equivalent to 'boding-ill' (cf. *Aeneid* 2. 184 'pro numine laeso | effigiem statuere, nefas quae triste piaret', etc. and see Pease (1923), 389) with its more obvious emotional range. *minax* is correspondingly industrious: threatening for the

---

[33] See Pliny, *Naturalis Historia* 2. 194 for the Ancients' belief in earthquakes in the Alps. (And for earthquakes as portents see Cicero, *De Diuinatione* 1. 97.)
[34] For *motus* see L & S s.v. 11 A.   [35] Cf. the use of *tremit* at 330.
[36] Cf. Ovid's imitation at *Metamorphoses* 15. 792 f.; but cf. also e.g. *Eclogues* 8. 86, 10. 58.
[37] Cf. Otis (1963), 162.

future what will be 'threatening' in the present. Both thus, as usual, anticipate as well as forebode.

More dramatic is 480 'et maestum inlacrimat templis ebur aeraque sudant'. The line with its climactic *aeraque sudant* has an extraordinary impact. Yet the portent of 'sweating statues' in isolation might seem no more than a vague if awesome marvel—as e.g. in Cicero, *De Diuinatione* 1. 98. The point is that in our line the emotional potential of *sudant* has been realized. The 'sweating statues' have been coupled with statues that are explicitly 'grieving' and do the overtly emotional thing of 'weeping'.[38] Hence the relevant emotional content or causation of *sudant* surfaces. These statues weep in grief, fittingly, for what the future holds; if they are sweating, it will be for the equally fitting reason of fear.[39]

These portents space the more or less immediately 'Country' ones, which start with the speaking cattle. *pecudes* are part of the *Georgics*. They have been mentioned already in Book 1 (see especially 4; cf. also 263, 444) and will recur as the poem proceeds—particularly (naturally) in Book 3; and each mention increases their emotive 'typicality'. But they do not normally *speak*. (Forced, so it seems, to speak, what had they to say? Again one wonders, again one might guess.) Then *sistunt amnes* (479): pointed in the context since we know the importance of water in the form of natural or artificial streams for the life of the land: cf. especially 106 ff., and 269. In the Golden Age rivers ran with wine (132); the life they contribute to the World of the *Georgics* is more prosaic but still life. Worse follows. The Italian river Po, so to speak in an alien guise (*fluuiorum rex Eridanus* 482), runs riot *destroying* rather than vivifying— linked to the destruction of Aetna by Aetna's image of *undantem* (472). Admittedly rivers do not always run easy but ease was not after all Jupiter's will for man; and this destruction magnifies beyond all reason or expectation the floods of nature (cf. 115 ff., 326 f.).

And *what* is destroyed is emotive. 482 f.: 'camposque per omnis | cum stabulis armenta tulit'. The resonance of *campos* is basic: cf. *agros* in the Aetna portent. And the *armenta* with their *stabula* whom we have already met (355 'quid saepe uidentes | agricolae propius stabulis armenta tenerent') are to become, increasingly, indicative members of this World: thus cf. e.g. 2. 515 (in the praise of the Farmer's life) 'hinc patriam paruosque nepotes | sustinet, hinc armenta boum meritosque iuuencos'; and particularly of course in Book 3.

Perversion of the *Georgics*' norm is the point of or gives strength to *terrae dehiscunt* (479): *terra* is deeply emotionally charged, the very substance of the Country, in our minds from the first line of the poem on. Against that norm,

---

[38] Interestingly, this precise idea, that of 'weeping statues', may be from Virgil's imagination. Tibullus 2. 5. 77 and others are most likely imitations of this passage.

[39] For sweat as a symptom of fear cf. Lucretius 3. 154.

too, the frightfulness of 'nec tempore eodem...aut puteis manare cruor cessauit' (483 ff.: again possibly Virgilian invention in its details, like the 'weeping statues') sharpens. *puteus* though not 'built up' in the *Georgics*, manifestly belongs to ordinary, peaceful life. When *cruor* ('gore') appears in the place of the expected[40] normality, constant *water*, the horror fits into the pattern of perversion and is thereby exacerbated. In fact *puteus* is more or less a symbol—like *armenta* and *amnes* etc.

One does naturally first connect the *puteus* portent with others of the Country. But 'wells' are not of course exclusively rural. As the open evocation of civil war approaches, the signs that at once portend and image it broaden again. In 486 the scene is *urbes*, with which *putei* must, in view of the syntactical inextricability of 485 and 486, also associate; the 'wells', then, start the shift. But the main portent of the cities is that of the wolves— howling in them *per noctem* (again a recall of the Sun's eclipse). In essentials here is a traditional portent. But *lupi* are banes of the *Georgics*: cf. 130 'ille (sc. *Iuppiter*)...praedarique lupos iussit', 3. 407, 537, 4. 435. So the portent takes on a particular significance. A threat to the *Georgics*, wolves are a threat to peace, order and the like. Hence what their presence in the cities portends for those cities is clear. The 'wolves', also, facilitate the return to the scale of the beginning, combining in their portent the Country with the world of cities.

But 487–8 take us right back to the heavens, with signs unparalleled in their profusion. Comets, plainly here the *belli mala signa* (Tibullus 2. 5. 71), the overtones of whose language (*diri* and *arsere*)[41] are a fore-taste of the *bellum*. Thunderbolts falling[42] in a cloudless sky, which admitted various interpretations,[43] but here as often evidence the anger of Jupiter, his response to the *impia saecula* (cf. the remark above, p. 39, on 328 ff.); and more generally portend war: for again the sign images what it portends. Violence (in the shape of *fulgura*) is intruding into peace: the word *serenus* has in Book 1 been associated with peace for the Farmer (cf. 100 'umida solstitia atque hiemes orate serenas', 260, 340 'sacra refer Cereri laetis operatus in herbis |...iam uere sereno. | tum pingues agni et tum mollissima uina...', 393, and 461 'unde serenas | uentus agat nubes...sol tibi signa dabit'). And though there can be *insidiae* in a *serena nox* (426), I suppose *that* is scarcely surprising; and

---

[40] *manare* is a neutral word drawing its colour from its context. Cf. e.g. 3. 310 'laeta magis pressis manabunt flumina mammis', *Aeneid* 3. 175 'tum gelidus toto manabat corpore sudor', *Aeneid* 3. 43 'non...cruor hic de stipite manat'; it therefore contains no clue of the horror to come.

[41] The military-violent potential to *dirus* and *ardeo* is fully exploited by Vergil in the *Aeneid*. It is instructive to look at his use of the words there (via Merguet (1912) or Wetmore (1911)). *dirus* is also a more or less technical term for—'dire'—portents: see *OLD* s.v. 1.

[42] *fulgura* for the more obvious *fulmina*, as *cecidere* shows.

[43] Cf. Nisbet and Hubbard (1970), 376 f. as well as the passages cited in note 24.

anyway the sun is prepared to help (424): on reflection (after 466 ff.) 424–6 is a pregnant little passage.

So a circle has been completed in the portents and on various levels we have been prepared, as the Romans were prepared, for the actuality of civil war (489 ff.). *ergo*: the portents were a consequence of the assassination of Julius Caesar, and so of course is the disaster presaged and imaged in, and now fulfilling, those portents. Now we witness Vergil's most explicit portrayal of the destruction, collapse and perversion of the World of the *Georgics*. There is calculated surprise in 489 but obviously no lack of poetical or logical continuity. The actuality, like salient portents, is phrased in terms of the opposition of the Country and violence.

Lines 489–92 have been much discussed. Which two battles is Virgil referring to? I must propound my own (unfashionable) view summarily, leaving the reader to compare the accounts of other commentators. *iterum* is most naturally taken with *uidere*, though perhaps also by association with *concurrere*. At all events Virgil is indeed talking of two battles at 'Philippi'; and he means the two battles actually at Philippi itself in 42 BC approximately one month apart, the first ending in the suicide of Cassius, the second in that of Brutus.[44] Philippi was in Macedonia on the borders of Thrace: Emathia strictly a district of Macedonia could be extended poetically to signify all of it; Haemus is a mountain range in Thrace. The geography of the passage on this reading, though loosish, is plausible. Virgil is *not* confusing or conflating the sites of Philippi and Pharsalus (which was in Thessaly, approximately 170 kilometres SW): I should not hasten to impute to him such laxity or licence whatever subsequent poets—some possibly through misunderstanding these lines—allowed themselves.[45]

This interpretation most satisfactorily answers the claims of geography and syntax. But does it make poetical sense? Why should Virgil put two parts of what in the light of history is one battle at the heart of his finale when an apparently more powerful conceit might have been engineered with—for example—Pharsalus? Due consideration of the structure of this finale will lead to the solution. Its frame is the two Caesars, the murdered Julius erstwhile Sun of Rome and the new hoped-for redeemer, the young Caesar (466 and 503). The omens, stressed as happening at the time of (i.e. as a result of) Julius Caesar's murder (*tempore... illo* 469, *tempore eodem* 483), portend the *consequences* of it: civil war as here described, adequately epitomized in Philippi—whilst Pharsalus was past history, way outside the frame. But not just 'adequately': there is much more to it. The mood is changing (this I shall

---

[44] See Scullard (1970), 166; Charlesworth (1952), 24 f.
[45] See the passages quoted in Conington and Nettleship (1963) on line 490.

amplify below). The emphasis is shifting from the idea of due if horrible punishment coming upon the *impia saecula* for their wickedness, to bewilderment at a seemingly unending tragic process of crime begetting crime; to bafflement at the Gods' allowing such a thing; to an expression of desperate hope that the new Caesar (the balance in the finale to the old) will be able and be allowed by the Gods to call a halt. Therefore evocation of the two onslaughts on this self-same Caesar by his own suffering people becomes acutely pertinent—onslaughts led we remember by the protagonists of the destruction of the first Caesar. The tragedy of the Romans' fate is that the civil war which is their punishment (but we are less and less happy with this word) for the murder of Julius Caesar involves the murderers leading Romans against the new Caesar, who offers the only chance of escaping from precisely this sort of endless cycle of crime and punishment. That Romans should doggedly pursue this insane (cf. 481) attempt at self-destruction twice on the same field—and not learn from the blood already there—completes the tragedy. Philippi (other 'attacks' on the young Caesar before Actium could have been found) selects itself. We must not forget that these were indeed considered, or promulgated, as two substantial and separable battles at the time: such was Augustus' view—cf. *Res Gestae Divi Augusti* 1. 2 'qui parentem meum interfecerunt, eos in exilium expuli...et postea bellum inferentis rei publicae uici bis [NB!] acie'; historical perspective has allowed, for some commentators, the impact of contemporary events (spontaneous or contrived) to become dulled. Nor must we forget that this whole tragedy of self-destruction took place on a site recalling in its name healthily defeated Macedonians.

The shift in emphasis and mood becomes more apparent in *nec fuit indignum*... (491). Why was such horror not *indignum* in the Gods' judgement? True, there seemed a deep sin in the people (cf. *saepe monet fraudem* 465, *impia saecula* 468, and see above, p. 44); witness the ultimate manifestation, the assassination of Caesar, for which Jupiter appeared justly angry (cf. *fulgura* 488, above p. 49). So perhaps the Gods are right to inflict, or allow, such tragic suffering. Yet the emotional strength of the language (which I shall turn next to consider) expressing the suffering defies such unquestioning acceptance. *nec fuit indignum*... easily gathers to it a tone of bitter incomprehension. In short the statement is ambivalent. The state is intrinsically corrupt, it now murders Caesar, the Gods are angry, and according to tragic justice the guilty destroy themselves. But—'satis iam pridem sanguine nostro | Laomedonteae luimus periuria Troiae'. And is it justifiable to talk so generally of guilt? (With the ambivalence of *nec fuit indignum*...we may compare the famous *dis aliter uisum* at *Aeneid* 2. 428 with the note of Austin (1964) on it.)

Philippi watches the Roman conflict: *Romanae* and *Philippi* (490) are pointedly placed at either end of the line—*Schadenfreude* for ghosts or descendants. The language of the clash (*inter sese paribus*) stresses that this is civil war. The portents, and the premonition sensed in the military metaphor of the book, are vindicated. A detail clinches the latter: the language of the battle also recalls that Storm again (cf. above, p. 42):

> omnia uentorum *concurrere* proelia uidi
> quae grauidam...etc.   (318)

318 and 489 are the only occurrences of *concurro* in *Georgics* 1. The worst of wars has triumphed to mock the 'war' of the peaceful *Georgics*.

Understanding the intimate relation of finale and the body of the book is essential to a full appreciation of 491 f. 'bis sanguine nostro | Emathiam et latos Haemi pinguescere campos'—a superlative example of the technique expounded above, p. 48. The core of strength is in *pinguescere*. The basic idea of bodies fattening land is old;[46] but this is a transformation. A repeated theme of the book has been *pinguis* land or growth; what in the peaceful and sane world of the Italian *Georgics* constitutes it, or will produce it (interestingly the epithet in some of its collocations was probably novel enough particularly to catch the attention):[47] see 8 'pingui...arista', 14, 64 'ergo age terrae | pingue solum...inuertant tauri', 80, 87, 105, 341; and the ironic use at 192—which draws its effect from the previous examples. In all these *pinguis* accumulates an association with the fullness of the *Georgics*; and this accumulation is the basis of the horror conveyed by *pinguescere*. Here is an epitome of the obscene perversion of the *Georgics* that civil war conclusively is. Not only are the *campi* (cf. above, p. 48) of Italy neglected (cf. 507). Here is what richness of land now means: our *blood*—and the poet identifies in *nostro* (cf. now my remark above on guilt)—fattening broad fields; far away, in Emathia, in Haemus.

493–7 bring the *agricola* and war into direct confrontation, and at last there seems to be some optimism: a belief in the final victory of *diuini gloria ruris*. The warriors who fought each other will be gone: we are reminded of a Hesiodic Age, past and buried. The replacement it seems will be the Farmer and his Age: the World of the *Georgics*.[48] The Farmer may marvel at their *grandia ossa*, i.e. the remnants of a race of 'epic heroes', but they will be dead and he will be alive—*grandia* can take on a nice touch of irony. Nor are the warriors' *sepulcra*, we might think, exactly heroic; or indeed *sepulcra* at all.

The Farmer, performing his timeless task, will find the weapons of war eaten away with rust. Manifestly and immediately symbolic; but the symbolism is

---

[46] See Conington and Nettleship (1963) on line 492.   [47] Cf. Wilkinson (1969), 200–1.
[48] Cf. the fine note of Richter (1957) on lines 493 ff.; cf. too Huxley (1963) on line 497.

grounded in the poem. In the course of the narrative 'ploughing', and more particularly *aratrum* itself, has gained special significance. Unexpectedly the poem proper *begins* with the action of ploughing (43 ff.),[49] throwing it into prominence. And the plough is the first of the Farmer's *arma* to be enumerated: 160 ff. 'dicendum et quae sint duris agrestibus arma... uomis et inflexi primum graue robur aratri'—*arma* which are summarized in lines of obvious wider potential significance 'omnia quae multo ante memor prouisa repones, | si te digna manet diuini gloria ruris' (167–8). Of these *arma* it alone claims a passage (169–75) describing, impressionistically, its construction. The *aratrum* is fixed in the memory, prepared by the poem to evoke by itself the World of the *Georgics*;[50] and see too 19, 45, 98, 213, 261. It becomes a symbol of peace and productiveness. And already, I think, we sense that the seemingly formulaic (in essence) epithet *incuruo* makes its own contribution to this symbolism. The *aratrum* was *inflexum* at 162, *curuum* at 170; and the beginning of the description of the plough's construction (169–70) indicates the possible reasoning behind such a symbolic association: 'continuo in siluis magna ui flexa domatur | in burim et curui formam accipit ulmus aratri'. The plough—like, more broadly, the general military metaphor—illustrates the channelling of man's *uis* without which the *Georgics* cannot exist. (The curved plough is again used in a synoptic vision at 2. 513.) Appropriate then for it to turn up the mouldering weapons. Appropriate too for the *rastra*, also listed among the Farmer's *arma* (164)—cf. too 94, 155 (in a passage of obvious 'military metaphor')—to knock the war helmets; here the ironic opposition of *grauibus* and *inanis* is obvious: *rastra* unusually but splendidly enjoy the full ramifications of *grauitas* while *galeae*, symbols of war, are not only literally 'empty' but empty in the sense of useless, worthless, vain. Indeed the right *arma* prevail.

These remarks on 493–7 are true enough so far as they go but they need qualification. The time envisaged sounds very remote: so remote it is phrased in terms that suggest a whole New Age. The present remains nightmarish. And in such a present to introduce a vision of optimism with *scilicet*—a word of most unfortunate ambiguity as a glance at Lewis & Short shows—is not calculated to inspire confidence. Nor anyway is the vision itself totally unequivocal, a simple picture of *diuini gloria ruris* triumphing finally over *gloria militaris*. If War and the Farmer are opposites, there is no such easy opposition between Farmer and soldiers. The soldiers whose bones are turned up *were* once farmers—*squalent abductis arua colonis*—an alien race of heroes though they may seem in that distant future.

---

[49] See Klingner (1967), 192–3.   [50] Huxley (1963) on line 175 is instructive.

The disastrous present remains; the poem leads naturally into an emotional prayer to the Gods to save the state (498 ff.). This balances the opening invocation but in very different mood. The Gods addressed are intimately connected with the Roman Commonwealth:[51] the *di patrii* obviously, then the *Indigetes*, i.e. probably heroes who have been granted divine honours for services to the people; then Romulus the deified founder, and Vesta whose cult was at the heart of Rome and whose eternal and symbolic flame had been brought from Troy (*Aeneid* 2. 296 f.)—Vesta's relative clause involving an allusion to the Tuscan origin of the Tiber and a consequent balancing of *Romana* by *Tuscum* sufficiently and suitably adumbrates the Italianness of the Roman *patria*. But the prayer is not put quite in the way we expect. The Gods are asked not to *prevent* the *iuuenis*, the new Caesar, from reviving the *euersum saeclum*. He, it is implied, can possibly restore piety, justice, law, peaceful life—all that the *Georgics* propounds. Why on earth should they obstruct him? But it must be counted a real possibility. *saltem* (500) implies that in the past the Gods disallowed just such a saviour—the old Caesar. And already the *iuuenis* has been twice in tragic danger. What has become of the Gods—whose statues seemed in sympathy with, and fear for, Rome's plight? Of Jupiter who respected *pietas* and cared for man? If Heaven grudges (*inuidet*, 504) the new Caesar's attention to worldly matters at *this* juncture (*quippe ubi fas*...), where is the value of such a pantheon? It cannot simply be a circuitous form of flattery for Octavian. (*hominum*, 504; *mere* men perhaps, but Vergil emphatically cares about them.)

Problems are crystallizing. Where does lie responsibility, how do we apportion blame? For a time this seemed simple; we could say the Romans simply deserved what they were getting. But we have been increasingly appalled by the suffering and perplexed by the place of men and Gods in it. The apostrophe, first to the Gods and then to Caesar himself (deservedly in their company as the invocation at 25 ff. shows) focuses, though barely answers, the perplexity. While *people* could be blamed for a crime, a guilt in the race supposed, and this accepted as a reason for divine anger and punishment (as seemed the case at 464 ff.) the position was clear. But the poem is moving towards a less facile culprit: war rather than warriors, abstract and generalized forces of violence which must somehow be controlled if the World of the *Georgics* is ever to be attained. The attitude to people in the increasingly inexplicable chaos becomes correspondingly more sympathetic; and the Gods' role mysterious: to compare the beginning and the end of the

---

[51] Cf. Huxley (1963) on line 498. I think Romulus and Vesta are to be considered apart, not just as examples of the aforementioned general categories. The exact sense and origin of *Indigetes* is disputed: see Richter (1957) on lines 498 f., Latte (1960), 43–5.

book is illuminating.[52] Vergil does not really know *what* they are doing—except that if they are still punishing the Romans for some primeval sin, enough is enough: 'satis iam pridem sanguine nostro...' Caesar, the new Caesar, is the only hope. He must *impose* the *Georgics*.

euerso... saeclo in 500 illustrates the shift in attitude. *euersum* itself works like *pinguescere*, though less obviously; the verb, simply or in compounds, is joined in Book 1 to the dominant and symbolic theme of ploughing:[53] cf. 1 f. 'quo sidere terram | uertere', 65 'pingue solum... fortes inuertant tauri', 119, 147 'prima Ceres ferro mortalis uertere terram | instituit'; and in another sense at 98 'rursus in obliquum uerso perrumpit aratro'. Thus *euersum* activates, at least subliminally, associations of the World of the *Georgics*. But here it spells destruction. However, crucial to note is the difference in emphasis to *impia saecula* of 468. They we might say deserve what they get. But an *euersum saeclum*, though evoking the perversion of the age, arouses sympathy; passively phrased, it appears a victim. The same dimension of horror as in *euerso saeclo* is involved in 'quippe ubi fas uersum atque nefas' (505). But it is equally impossible to apportion the guilt.

This is the general configuration as the book closes (505 ff.). *tot bella* face the young Caesar, not numerable concrete enemies. More ominously, *tam multae scelerum facies*. The metaphorical picture with *facies* is a nice touch: elusive faces of virtually personified *scelera* instead of *scelerosi* with faces, identifiable and exposed to conventional defeat. Then follow perhaps the most eloquent lines of the piece (506–8): 'non ullus aratro | dignus honos, squalent abductis arua colonis | et curuae rigidum falces conflantur in ensem'. The disastrous state of Rome is captured in three climactic sentences expressed in the basic imagery of the poem. Caesar is shown the scorn, disruption and perversion of the World of the *Georgics*. This is the reality; 494 f. were a dream. The centrally symbolic plough lacks honour. The hard-won fruits of *labor* are lost, for the emotive *arua* ('fields') are now *squalida*, neglected, their *coloni* led away even 'seduced' to become soldiers.[54] And the sickle, which, naturally making a pair with the *aratrum*[55] and specifically belonging in the *Georgics* (it is mentioned in Book 1 at 157 and 348), has a

---

[52] And perhaps if we think back to the famous account of Jupiter's purpose at 121 ff., questions now occur to us—ambiguities or confusions in it not wholly resolved. Indeed some may be apparent from my allusions to the account at p. 40, which aimed truthfully to represent an initial response. 121 ff. should be closely re-examined. Was Jupiter rather *over*-diligent in providing conditions to sharpen men's wits? How do we react now, for example, to 130 'praedarique lupos iussit' (cf. p. 49)?

[53] For *euerto* itself of ploughing cf. *OLD* s.v. 2.

[54] See *OLD* s.v. for the various nuances of *abduco*; on *squalent* cf. R. D. Williams (1967), 18.

[55] Cf. Varro, *Res Rusticae* 2 *Praefatio* 3, describing the despicable migration from the countryside: 'nunc intra murum fere patres familiae correpserunt relictis falce et aratro...'.

comparable symbolism, is forged into a sword, conclusively signalling the victory of the reality of war over the *Georgics*' metaphor. *rigidus* must in the context involve the idea of *straight* rigidity.[56] It is compelled to by its contrast with *curuae*; and this straightening symbolizes in itself, especially when we recall the symbolism implicit in *curuus*, the epithet also of the plough (see above, p. 53), the perversion that is civil war. But this is not the obvious significance of *rigidus* (see note 56). Also contributed, in conjunction with *ensem*, must be its common metaphorical associations: e.g. it is an epithet which Ovid can apply to Mars (*Metamorphoses* 8. 20). Thus it further interacts with *curuae* reinforcing but conflicting with the aura of peace we sense to that word. In the epithets alone as well as in the conceit of the line we can find an epitome of the defeat of peace.

509 expands the reality of war—threats at either end of the empire. Perhaps it was not to be expected that the World of the *Georgics* would ever be understood there. But 510 moves home (*uicinae...urbes*). It pictures the breaking of *leges* in language (*ruptis*) which recalls the violence of Aetna; and again, still, civil war—and at home, anyway, understanding *was* hoped for. *arma ferunt*: but not the *arma* of the *Georgics* which precisely insists upon *leges* (see p. 41). All however is phrased in the generalized terms we have become accustomed to. And finally war moves into the cosmic picture of Mars rampant in 511 ff. Such is the situation that faces the young Caesar: a vast, inexplicable chaos where simple apportionment of blame and responsibility is impossible. The finale opened with the Romans seeming cursed and guilty, to be punished; specifically they had murdered the old Caesar. But the consequences emerge, so to speak in the telling, to be too awful and tragically self-perpetuating for any easy explanation or comprehension. If Rome is expiating guilt when will it stop? If the Gods are just and care for Rome, surely her people have now suffered enough—and should not be grudged a saviour? Will the Gods watch the consequences of Julius Caesar's murder continue into further inexpiable crime? It is with fine-judged rhetoric that, as the apocalyptic vision of disaster gathers momentum, the notion of primeval sin finds its most explicit statement symbolized in the *periuria* of Laomedon (502); but phrased precisely so as to capture the Vergilian perplexity. Laomedon is prehistory but the blood of 501 is horrifically today's: *sanguine nostro* of 501 picks up the *bis sanguine nostro* of 491. Enough surely is enough: 'satis iam pridem sanguine nostro | Laomedonteae luimus periuria Troiae'. Doubt

---

[56] Thus Conington and Nettleship (1963) ad loc.; contrast Huxley (1963). Huxley is wrong but it is as well he makes us look at the word again. The point *is* that the context imposes this sense; indeed in general we could say that the sickle is as *rigidus* as the sword. The fact that Virgil chose to use an unobvious word for the notion of straightness supports my contention that he was after another effect too.

indeed seems implicitly cast upon the whole idea of collective guilt, primeval or particular. The distinction of Rome and Romans implicit at 464 ff. no longer stands up, and it is Mars who is now called *impius* not the people. And yet the people suffer, as has been brought strikingly home to us. In these circumstances only one thing emerges as certain. Hope for the future rests with the new Caesar who must somehow impose the controls that the *Georgics* needs for its existence. Somehow he must restrain *impius Mars*, whose *saeuitia* opens into the concluding picture of the chariot careering out of control. Initially seeming a general adumbration of the wildness of Mars's rampage, the picture particularizes. The chariot begins to seem the state helpless in the grip of war—for there is no effective *auriga*. This there must be and of course it must be Caesar. He must—somehow—control the state, govern its warlike propensities: he must make sure that the *retinacula* are not unheeded.[57] Did not even the vine need them (265)?

Other implications are clearly involved in the simile; it operates on several levels. Generally adumbrating Mars's wildness, its *carceres* (the 'starting-barriers') intrude their other meaning 'prison': however *Mars impius* chooses to manifest himself, that manifestation must, it seems clear, be summarily dealt with. (Cf. the description of the clearly symbolic winds at *Aeneid* 1. 54: 'luctantis uentos tempestatesque sonoras | imperio premit ac uinclis et carcere frenat'.)[58] When the simile particularizes, the chariot—the state—*is* still running out of control. The book sets in stark contrast the World of the *Georgics*, an ideal (poetically expressed) but to be considered as realizable, and the contemporary actuality. The only hope of replacing the one with the other we now know. The Romans must accept and obey the *auriga*. But we can hardly be confident about the future. The simile gives no signs that the people are yet willing to respond, or capable of it; civil war, as 510 f. showed, persists. Nor can the hope residing in the *auriga* be very sure given a universe of inexplicable Gods and the precedent of Julius Caesar's assassination and the battles of Philippi.

So the conclusion of the book points towards a solution but with little optimism. And (a final thought) could Virgil have viewed the solution—the *imposition* of the *Georgics*, the effective *auriga*—without mixed feelings? It seems a solution if not of despair then at least of compromise, and containing its own dangers. War is clearly going to be necessary—even, likely, more civil war (cf. 510 f.): a sad way to establish the *Georgics*. And the *auriga* image involves external or centralized control. That too needs pondering. Naturally,

---

[57] Cf. the description of Latinus at *Aeneid* 7. 600 (with Conington and Nettleship (1963) ad loc.) and of Aeolus at *Aeneid* 1. 53 f. quoted below.
[58] Cf. Otis (1963), 227–35; Pöschl (1962), 13 ff., esp. 19.

a *currus* is unworkable and unthinkable without an *auriga*. But the whole simile is as it were an alien addition, while the *Georgics* seemed to argue a way of life that worked through mutual respect and agreement, virtue and self-control. The *Georgics* was drawn with its own system of law and treaties—and the vintner applied his own *retinacula*. It is perhaps no more than a certain implicit equivocation; but one should not suppose that Vergil's Caesarianism was naive.[59] The tragedy of Philippi was that there Romans doggedly tried to destroy their one hope of salvation. But it was also the tragedy of, simply, a civil war. The degree of tragedy involved in a civil war is in proportion to the degree with which one is unable to exculpate either side. Book 1 ends therefore poised and rhetorical—and with a touch of ambivalence. The whole poem remains fundamentally rhetorical, a vision and a challenge; now arguing with greater enticement the way of the *Georgics*, now elaborating the threats to it from within and without. It sticks to the Caesarian solution; but the reservations or worries which we sense the poet may feel about it, these too persist, detectable in periodic signs of ambivalence and ultimately to be amplified in the last book, which reflects or should reflect the time when a realization of the World of the *Georgics* was at hand.[60]

ENDNOTE

The best all-round introduction to the *Georgics* is Wilkinson (1969). See too R. D. Williams (1967), 14–22. Stimulating are the relevant chapters of Otis (1963) and Klingner (1967); particularly the latter, a most sensitive and sympathetic discussion. The commentaries I have found most useful are those of Conington and Nettleship (1963), Huxley (1963), and Richter (1957). T. E. Page (1898) is also a steady stand-by. I have assumed the reader has at least one of the English commentaries to hand.

A word about what I have and have not done in this essay. There has not been room, and it has not really been my inclination, to comment except in rare instances on Virgil's word-music and word-patterning. My concern has been within the *sense* of words; to show the poet exploiting their semantic resonances, their associations and backgrounds of meaning; to show how these are made to interact and cooperate; for hence comes the real stuff of poetry. As the piece I have chosen (the end of Book 1) is part, indeed a

---

[59] A weakness of Klingner (1967): e.g. p. 220.
[60] Cf. 4. 560 ff. 'Caesar dum magnus ad altum | fulminat Euphraten bello uictorque uolentis | per populos dat iura ...'. Interesting vocabulary.

climactic part, of a longer poem, my analysis has necessarily involved comment, albeit allusive, on the poem, and its meaning, as a whole. The general remarks with which I begin are indispensable for my analysis.

Mr. J. Griffin very kindly criticized a draft of this essay. He will notice but I hope forgive the fact that stubbornness has sometimes prevailed over wise advice. I am also grateful to the editors for their helpful comments.

References to *Georgics* Book 1 are by line number alone and to the rest of the poem by book and line number.

5

The Neoteric Poets[1] (1978)

I

In 50 BC Cicero writes to Atticus as follows (*Att.* 7. 2. 1): 'Brundisium uenimus VII Kalend. December. usi tua felicitate nauigandi; ita belle nobis *flauit ab Epiro lenissimus Onchesmites.* hunc σπονδειάζοντα si cui uoles τῶν νεωτέρων pro tuo uendito.' The antonomasia, the euphonic sibilance, and the mannered rhythm (the five-word line with fourth foot homodyne; the spondaic fifth foot) are all prominent in Cicero's hexameter. The line is a humorously concocted example of affected and Grecizing narrative. But it is also a line which, Atticus is to suppose, οἱ νεώτεροι would value; presumably therefore it is meant to hit off characteristics of their style. Cicero must in fact be *parodying* what he regards as a *typical* 'neoteric' line, and the significance of this simple fact has perhaps been underestimated.

To parody a group presupposes that one has in mind a group with common characteristics; indeed (it seems to me) if anyone thinks he can hit off a group of poets in a single line, he must regard that group as highly mannered and distinct. And Cicero obviously thinks he can do just that. So he at any rate seems to have in mind a clearly cohering group of νεώτεροι; or, not to beat about the bush, a school. It seems likely that they are the same or the same sort of poets as those whom in 45 BC he refers to as 'cantores Euphorionis' (*Tusc.* 3. 45); poets who, he implies, despised the grandiose style of Ennius.[2] The prima-facie plausibility of this will be substantiated as we proceed. And when Cicero refers in 46 BC (*Orat.* 161) to the practice of 'poetae noui' in avoiding elided *s*, he may again have the same group in mind but the expression there is too general to provide positive support for the notion of a cohering school.

---

[1] My thanks are due to P. G. McC. Brown for kindly reading and acutely criticizing a first draft.

[2] On the meaning of 'cantores Euphorionis' see n. 25 below. Of course Cicero means to imply through this reference other peculiarities besides a warped sense of style. But style is clearly his main preoccupation, here as at *Att.* 7. 2. 1. At *Att.* 7. 2. 1. he hits at poets who cultivate an abstruse stylistic preciosity; at *Tusc.* 3. 45 he stresses the corollary, the scorn of affected stylists for classical Ennian grandeur.

The idea of a school of νεώτεροι has been much questioned and debated in recent years.[3] I think the implications of Cicero's remarks (anyway at *Att.* 7. 2. 1) are clear—and if he thought in terms of a school, there probably was a school. It is the purpose of this paper to try to clarify the picture: to try to identify some or all of the school's members and then to define what precisely their shared characteristics or interests were. Further assistance from Cicero will be limited: he names no names and his comments are chiefly or exclusively in reaction to 'neoteric' *style*. We shall have to work our way beyond him to establish who belonged to the 'neoteric' school and what genres or subject matter it liked.

First, a word on the meaning of νεώτεροι.

II

Professor Alan Cameron has contributed some timely comments on the sense of νεώτεροι and 'neoterici'.[4] The term continually occurs in grammarians and commentators, Greek and Roman. If (for example) Aristarchus wants to distinguish between genuine Homeric usage and what was not found till later writers, these later writers are οἱ νεώτεροι; when Vergil has established the classical Latin canon, the Latin grammarians may then use 'neoterici' of what we might call the Silver Poets. The term is therefore essentially general and relative: 'newer writers'—often with depreciatory tone. Possibly[5] Cicero himself—given that a hexameter is in question, and given his and Atticus' familiarity with Aristarchus—meant more specifically 'newer *epic* writers'; but the term is not in itself as restricted as Wiseman maintains. This, the essentially general nature of the term, might weigh heavy with those who do not believe in a school of 'neoteric' poets.

---

[3] Note the cautious or sceptical views of Crowther (1970), and of Bramble (1974), 180 ff. Quinn (1959) is fairly cautious too (44–8) and refers to articles which forthrightly attack the notion of a school. Bardon (1952–6), i. 358–67, sees the neoterics as a rather vague and general movement (*not* a school) and includes poets and types of poetry which must be excluded. Similarly, Schanz and Hosius (1927), 285–6. Wiseman (1974), 44–58, holds a rather different view from mine as to who the neoterics were and what it was they did that was neoteric. Ross (1969), 11 writes: 'There is no question that Catullus was a neoteric poet' and his book seeks among other things to arrive at a definition of what constituted neoteric poetry. But again his conclusions are rather different from mine, although at times our paths interestingly converge. (It should be noted that my views on neotericism have changed since Lyne (1972), 37—my review of Ross.) Some of the most useful remarks to date on the neoterics are in Wheeler (1934), 77–86.

[4] See Cameron (1980).   [5] Cf. Wiseman (1974), 51.

Cicero however writes a line intended to be typical of the 'newer writers' which is highly idiosyncratic. He must therefore be thinking of very idiosyncratic 'newer writers', *particular* 'newer writers'; he must be thinking of a school of 'newer writers', even if he does not say quite as much. And of course he does say 'newer writers' in a rather particular way. He says it in Greek; he writes σπουδειάζοντα in Greek too. Perhaps a notable part of the particularity of these poets had to do with Grecizing.

And perhaps Cicero did feel their particularity predominantly or only in epic. But that would not mean that *other* particular interests could not be shared by such an idiosyncratic group.

In conclusion, therefore, one should well doubt that the poets in question ever called themselves νεώτεροι (it is ironic that 'neoteric' is the term we shall use for them):[6] it seems quite clear that Cicero meant some of the customary depreciatory tone to attach to the particular poets he had in mind. One may in fact agree with Professor Cameron, with some qualification, that Cicero used the term because he thought they were mere *epigoni*. On the other hand there is nothing to change one's conclusion that Cicero had in mind a cohering school—whose programme is yet to be established; and whatever Cicero thought, the poets themselves may well have considered that they were prophets of a 'new poetry'.[7]

III

Cicero's 'flauit ab Epiro lenissimus Onchesmites' is intended to be *typical*, in a parodying vein, of a fashion of writing. Does it resemble, hit off, any surviving literature? One poem obviously suggests itself. The mannered antonomasia, alliteration, and rhythms of Cicero's line are all striking features of the style of Catullus 64: cf. 'Peliaco quondam prognatae uertice pinus' (1), 'tene Thetis tenuit pulcherrima Nereine' (28), 'a misera, assiduis quam luctibus externauit | spinosas Erycina serens in pectore curas' (71–2), 'incola Itoni' (228), 'Emathiae tutamen, Opis carissime nato' (325), etc., etc.: cf. Fordyce (1961),

---

[6] But what else? 'poetae novi' or 'new poets' is unsuitable for the reason implied above. As for 'cantores Euphorionis', we still require confirmation that the term refers to the same group. Anyway it too is uncomplimentary. We will use the term that derives from the most significant and useful of Cicero's references—confident that the poets themselves would appreciate the irony.

[7] Cameron (1980), writes: 'It is in this sense [i.e. the general, relative sense]...that Cicero ...used the term of certain contemporary writers; *not* because they were prophets of a "new poetry", but precisely because (in his opinion) they were *epigoni*.'

274–6, Quinn (1959), 44–6, (1973), ii. 299 f., Wilkinson (1963), 129 f. Cicero's line could in fact be a parody of Catullus' style in poem 64, the 'Peleus and Thetis'. It is, actually, unlikely to be: Catullus is most probably dead in 50 BC[8] and οἱ νεώτεροι whom Cicero has in mind are presumably alive. This makes the resemblance the more dramatic. If Cicero parodies a group *without* having Catullus specifically in mind and yet *still* reminds us strongly of him, not only (we might infer) must Catullus have been a member of the group but the characteristics hit off must have been prominently and regularly displayed by all members. And the fashion of writing must have been in operation for a number of years.

We have now established the likelihood of a neoteric school, and that Catullus had probably been (as it were) a member. It also seems likely that the mannered miniature *epos,* which we conveniently call epyllion, was a (if not the) typical genre of the school. But the question of what forms the neoterics typically wrote in I am leaving for a moment; it ought anyway to be said that Cicero at *Att.* 7. 2. 1 could have had in mind narrative *elegy*—an affinity between his parody and lines of Catullus 68 might easily have been demonstrated. I continue now on the track of other members of the school; and it is an obvious move to look among Catullus' own contemporaries and confrères, for whom we have a little information.

We look in the Catullan corpus to see if there are any poets for whom Catullus expresses particular affection; more especially we look for poets with whom he shares a definite literary sympathy or interest. Given Catullus' apparent membership of the school these too will be likely candidates—though only as yet candidates.

Catullus addresses poem 35 to a Caecilius, 'poetae tenero meo sodali'; he expresses interest, even anxiety,[9] about the progress of a 'learned' ('doctus') poem of Caecilius' which is called or concerns the 'Dindymi domina', the 'magna mater', i.e. Cybele. In poem 50 Catullus writes to Licinius, who is clearly the orator and poet Licinius Calvus (cf. poem 14 mentioned below, also 53 and 96, all to or about Calvus): the poem comprises Catullus' passionate recollection of, and response to, an evening spent with Calvus experimenting in polymetric *uersiculi.*[10] Poem 95 is a celebration of Helvius Cinna's abstruse epyllion *Zmyrna,* which he contrasts with the rubbishy and lengthy 'annales' of Volusius (Caius Cinna is mentioned as Catullus' 'sodalis'

---

[8] For Catullus' dates see conveniently Quinn (1973), pp. xii–xv.

[9] Catullus heavily emphasizes that the poem has been well *begun*: cf. Quinn (1973), 194–5. I think the implication is that too much attention to the *candida puella* is holding up Caecilius' literary progress.

[10] Catullus seems to have been particularly close to Calvus. Certainly later writers closely associated them—like a kind of double act: cf. Hor. *Serm.* 1. 10. 18 f., etc.; Wiseman (1974), 52 n. 43.

at 10. 29 f.; cf. too 113. 1). As well as these places, where Catullus speaks to or about fellow-poets and explicitly mentions their literature, we should note the following places where he shows affection for people who are probably poets, but where literature is not mentioned: poem 38 is addressed to a Cornificius who is probably the poet of an epyllion *Glaucus*; and poem 56 is addressed to a Cato who seems likely to be the famous poet and grammarian Valerius Cato. These then are poets whom we may suspect—some or all of them—to have belonged to the self-conscious school whose existence we have inferred and to which Catullus seemed to belong. For all of them, except Caecilius, fragments and/or allusions survive to provide further valuable information.[11]

Another fact should now be brought into play which strengthens one's impression of a cohesive group of poets around Catullus. This is the phenomenon of a literary polemic. An attitude of Us against Them presupposes a strong bond of interest among Us. Poem 95 referred to above reads as follows:

> Zmyrna mei Cinnae nonam post denique messem
> quam coepta est nonamque edita post hiemem,
> milia cum interea quingenta Hortensius uno
> . . . .
> Zmyrna cauas Satrachi penitus mittetur ad undas,
> Zmyrnam cana diu saecula peruoluent.
> at Volusi annales Paduam morientur ad ipsam
> et laxas scombris saepe dabunt tunicas.

Callimachus' battle of the books has been transplanted; the allusions and stance are unmistakable.[12] Catullus' poem 36 'annales Volusi cacata carta...' involves another blow in the campaign against the wretched Volusius. Note too poem 14, comprising in-jokes with Calvus on how terrible other poets are; it is interesting to read 14 in conjunction with 50. Catullus therefore associates himself, at least with Cinna and Calvus, 'against the rest'; and with Cinna in strident Callimachean fashion on the particular and traditional topic of *epos*. Disagreement about *epos* may be at the root of another Catullan quarrel.[13]

---

[11] The fragments are collected in Morel (1927). On Calvus see conveniently Schanz and Hosius (1927), 289 f., Bardon (1952–6), i. 341–4. Cinna: Schanz and Hosius (1927), 307 f., Bardon (1952–6), i. 344–7 and now Wiseman (1974), 44–58; Wiseman has in fact pertinent things to say about most of these poets. Valerius Cato: Schanz and Hosius (1927), 287 f., Bardon (1952–6), i. 337–41, Robinson (1923), 98–116, Crowther (1971), 108–9. Cornificius: Schanz and Hosius (1927), 309 f., Bardon (1952–6), i. 355–6, Rawson (1978), 188–201.

[12] Cf. Call. *Epigr.* 27 and 28 Pf., *Aetia praef.* (frg. 1 Pf.), Kroll (1960), 266 f., Clausen (1964), 188 f. Catull. 95b ('at populus tumido gaudeat Antimacho') repeats Callimachean polemic: cf. Call. frg. 398 Pf. Λύδη καὶ παχὺ γράμμα καὶ οὐ τορόν.

[13] I think it quite possible (given the situation with Volusius) that the Furius who has attacked Catullus on literary grounds (poem 16) and who is in turn subjected to banter or

The Neoteric Poets

In fact the polemic suggests an identifiably *Callimachean* faction of Catullus, Cinna, and I think Calvus. We should recall now Catullus' own explicit demonstrations of Callimachean indebtedness: poems 65, 66, and 116.[14] We should recall indeed that Catullus is in very real ways a genuinely Callimachean poet: lavishing care and attention on forms and subjects that would not traditionally have been deemed worthy of such care and attention; a poet to be judged (in much of his work at least) solely according to the canons of art and delight.[15] The polemic not only confirms the cohesion of three candidates for the neoteric school; it may be some guide to the nature of its programme.

IV

A group of sympathetic poets seems to be identifiable around Catullus; and Catullus seems likely to have belonged to the school to which Cicero refers slightingly as οἱ νεώτεροι. Our next step is to look closely at what this group of poets wrote. If they share idiosyncratic interests, this will further confirm their identity as a group—and start to fix their programme; if they all share or could share the characteristics of style which Cicero parodies this will confirm that the group is indeed the neoteric group or school. It will be prudent to note interests that they do *not* share.

Epigrams and polymetric versicles of erotic, humorous, insulting, and indeed multifarious occasional nature were a common interest among them.

abuse by Catullus (poems 16, 23, and 26; and the address in poem 11 is surely ironical) is in fact the disastrous epic poet Furius ('Alpinus') parodied by Horace (see *Serm.* 2. 5. 40, with Porph. ad loc., *Serm.* 1. 10. 36 with Wickham ad loc., and Rudd (1966)), and that at least part of the reason for Catullus' enmity towards him is literary. I am inclined to believe too that Furius 'Alpinus' is one and the same as Furius Bibaculus (those ancient sources who specify do in fact identify the epic Furius with Bibaculus). The main arguments in favour of supposing Furius 'Alpinus' and Furius Bibaculus to be two different people are usefully set out by Rudd (1966), 289 f., together with many more useful references to their (or his) work. On Bibaculus see too Schanz and Hosius (1927), 290–2. A main point for Rudd in favour of separating them is that a 'Neoteric' is hardly likely to have written an historical epic. But there is no reason to suppose Furius Bibaculus to have been a 'Neoteric' or even a poet in sympathy with the Catullan coterie (though this is the usual view: cf. Quinn (1959), 44, Bardon (1952–6), i. 347 ff.). The only Furius that Catullus acknowledges is, as we have seen, no great chum; and Furius Bibaculus' poems on Val. Cato (frgs. 1 and 2 M) strike me as far from unequivocally admiring or friendly. All that Furius Bibaculus has in common with Catullus is the not very striking phenomenon of a taste for abusive versicles; cf. Quint. 10. 1. 96, Tac. *Ann.* 4. 34. In short (though there are problems of chronology which can be argued to and fro) I think there is probably only one Furius in play. I certainly feel there is no cause to divorce Bibaculus from 'Alpinus'.

[14] Poem 116 is very usefully explained by Macleod (1973), 304–9.

[15] Cf. Lyne (1975), 1–5. On Callimachus' aesthetics cf. usefully Brink (1946), 11–26, esp. 16–19, Pfeiffer (1968), 137–8, Reitzenstein (1931), 23–69. The fact is perhaps underestimated

Catullus: *passim*. Calvus: Suet. *Jul.* 73 'famosa epigrammata' (against Caesar: cf. Catull. 29 etc.), frgs. 1–3, 17–19 M (18 is on Pompey: cf. Catull. 29), Sen. *Con.* 7. 4. 7, Ov. *Trist.* 2. 431 f. 'par fuit exigui similisque licentia Calui | detexit uariis qui sua furta modis'. Cinna: frgs. 9–14 M, Ov. *Trist.* 2. 435 'Cinna quoque his [sc. "explicitly erotic poets"] comes est, Cinnaque procacior Anser'. Cato and Cornificius: Ov. *Trist.* 2. 436 'Cinna quoque his comes est... et leue Cornifici parque Catonis opus'; for Cornificius cf. too frg. 1 M (hendecasyl-labic)—and Catullus seems to think him capable of some sort of Simonidean threnody: Catull. 38. 6–8.

Such occasional versicles were a common interest among them. But it was an interest by no means confined to them. And, however exquisitely they penned their own efforts (I return to this point), it seems hardly likely that they could be distinguished as a school on this score alone. One thinks back to the precedents: Porcius Licinus, Valerius Aedituus, Lutatius Catulus, Laevius.[16] Or one thinks of Catullus' contemporaries. There is Memmius, governor of Bithynia in 58 BC. For his erotic verses, cf. Ov. *Trist.* 2. 433 'quid referam Ticidae quid Memmi carmen, apud quos | rebus adest nomen nominibusque pudor?' And Pliny (*Ep.* 5. 3. 5) records that he wrote 'uersiculos seueros parum': comparing Catull. 16. 3–4 'qui me ex uersiculis meis putastis | quod sunt molliculi parum pudicum' we might infer that he wrote in lyric metres. He had Greek literary taste too: cf. Cic. *Brut.* 247; cf. further Owen's note on Ov. *Trist.* 2. 433. Now although Memmius numbered Catullus among his cortège in Bithynia, there is not the slightest evidence that Catullus regarded him as a literary brother-in-arms and dramatic evidence for Catullus' enmity on other scores (poems 10 and 28).

Or there is (for example) the orator Q. Hortensius Hortalus addressed by Catullus in poem 65 but criticized for his literature in the polemical poem 95 (see above, p. 64). The 'milia' of line 3 may refer to *uersiculi* or perhaps rather to epic *annales*.[17] But Hortensius certainly wrote erotic poetry: cf. Ov. *Trist.* 2. 441 'nec minus Hortensi nec sunt minus improba Serui | carmina'; he too is one to whom Pliny attributes 'uersiculi seueri parum' at *Ep.* 5. 3. 5;[18] and

---

that Callimachus will, to an extent, be misrepresenting critics in the preface to the *Aetia*—that of course is in the nature of polemic. No one would really maintain that we should judge poetry by its length (αὖθι δὲ τέχνῃ | κρίνετε, μὴ σχοίνῳ Περσίδι τὴν σοφίην). The real alternative to the yardstick of τέχνη is, I suppose, worth or seriousness of content: cf. Aristotle's μίμησις σπουδαίων or πράξεως σπουδαίας (*Poetics* 1449[b]) etc. (Brink (1946), 18). Callimachus is in many respects close to *l'art pour l'art*.

[16] Cf. Quinn (1959), 5–18, Ross (1969), 137 ff.

[17] Cf. Vell. 2. 16. 3 and Münzer (1914), 196–205 (and Quinn (1973), 432); contrast Fordyce (1961), 384.

[18] Pliny in fact invokes as precedent for his filthy verses M. Tullius, C. Calvus, Asinius Pollio, M. Messalla, Q. Hortensius, M. Brutus, L. Sulla, Q. Catulus, and many other worthies ('doc-tissimi, grauissimi, sanctissimi') including four emperors.

Gellius records an interesting opinion of his and other contemporaries' lyric (so it appears) *erotica*, uttered by 'Graeci plusculi... homines amoeni et nostras quoque litteras haut incuriose docti' (19. 9. 7):

saepeque eum [sc. Iulianum rhetorem] percontabantur, quid de Anacreonte ceterisque id genus poetis sentiret et ecquis nostrorum poetarum tam fluentes carminum delicias fecisset, 'nisi Catullus' inquiunt 'forte pauca et Caluus itidem pauca. Nam Laeuius inplicata et Hortensius inuenusta et Cinna inlepida et Memmius dura ac deinceps omnes rudia fecerunt atque absona.'

But an idiosyncratic interest which our poets do share is epyllion, that brief, highly wrought *epos* which more or less ostentatiously dissociated itself from traditional *epos*: concentrating on unheroic incidentals in the sagas of heroes, or on heroines as opposed to heroes, or on otherwise off-beat subject matter; employing a narrative technique that was often wilfully individual and selective; and yet largely maintaining epic language, metre, and style.[19]

For Calvus and Cinna, as well as Catullus, our information is relatively good. Catullus, of course, writes the 'Peleus and Thetis' which seems at first to be an epic of the Argonauts, switches unexpectedly to the love of Peleus and Thetis, switches to Theseus, to Ariadne, and so on. Calvus writes an *Io*, a potentially off-beat story offering possibilities of humour, pathos, divine indignity—as Ovid, who imitated Calvus, shows (*Met*. 1. 568 ff.).[20] Frgs. 9–14 M are from the poem; frg. 9 'a uirgo infelix herbis pasceris amaris' shows us that Calvus not only emotionally apostrophized his heroine but also anticipated his own plot—both features of the wilful Catullan narrative. The *Zmyrna* of Cinna we have already mentioned (above, p. 64). This must have been a work of extraordinary *doctrina*: the contrast with Volusius' *annales* shows that it was an epyllion of brief compass, yet it took nine years to write— and soon required an explanatory commentary.[21] The story, revolving around a heroine who fell in love with her father, would make a splendidly off-beat *epos*—as Ovid (who imitated Cinna too) again shows.[22] Three lines are preserved (frgs. 6 and 7 M), which include an emotional apostrophe: 'te matutinus flentem conspexit Eous...'.

---

[19] On the epyllion see Crump (1931). I am in the process of completing my own monograph on the nature and history of the epyllion. For further comment which bears on epyllion's subject matter see below, pp. 78–9, 80.

[20] Calvus frg. 9 M: *Met*. 1. 632 (Calvus frg. 9 is also echoed by Vergil at *Ecl*. 6. 47—which is where Servius quotes it); frg. 11: *Met*. 1. 713.

[21] Quint 10. 4. 4 and Serv. on Verg. *Ecl*. 9. 35 repeat or corroborate Catullus' evidence on the time taken in composition. Suet. *gramm*. 18 reports that an explanatory commentary was written by L. Crassicius. This commentary was celebrated in a clever little epigram (parodying Catullus) which Suet. quotes.

[22] Cf. Otis (1970), 420 f.

As for Valerius Cato there is no proof that his *Diana* was an epyllion. But a poem which Suetonius (*gramm.* 11) calls *Diana* and Cinna calls *Dictynna* (frg. 14 M: see below) seems likely to have told of the aetiology of Diana's name Dictynna, i.e. the story of Britomartis who was pursued by Minos and leapt off a cliff. And this, a romantic incidental in the legends of Minos, suits the tenor of epyllion. It is interesting too to note how Cinna's praise of Cato's *Dictynna* 'saecula per maneat nostri Dictynna Catonis' resembles Catullus' praise of Cinna's own masterpiece epyllion *Zmyrna*: 95. 6 'Zmyrnam cana diu saecula peruoluent'. I am fairly confident that Cato's poem told of Britomartis and Minos and that it was an epyllion—though a strong possibility remains that in form it was a narrative *hymn* (on which more anon).[23]

Finally Cornificius: Macr. *Sat.* 6. 5. 13 (Vergil's borrowings are being illustrated): ' "tu nubigenas inuicte bimembres" [*Aen.* 8. 293]. Cornificius in Glauco: centauros foedare bimembres.' I think it would be perverse to doubt that the *Glaucus* was an epyllion; and its subject will have been the fanciful tale, popular with Hellenistic writers, of Glaucus the sea-god, half human and half fish in form, who fell in love with the nymph Scylla (told by Ovid at *Met.* 13. 898 ff.).[24] What of 'centauros foedare bimembres'? One is tempted to posit a substantial digression on these comparable hybrids, in the manner of Moschus' digression on Io, in his epyllion on Europa.

It is hard to find sure signs of Latin epyllion apart from these poets, particularly before them. The Roman adaptation of the genre seems their achievement. It is in short an idiosyncrasy of the group, and the community of the group is thereby confirmed. It is, too, precisely the genre that is likely to offer the sort of line Cicero parodies; and this confirms our impression that the group around Catullus is associable with the school referred to as οἱ νεώτεροι by Cicero. It is also worth reflecting at this point that poets of this ilk (perhaps particularly the exceedingly abstruse Cinna himself) might well have offered justification for the slighting tag 'parroters of Euphorion' ('cantores Euphorionis');[25] they might well have been, or seemed to be,

---

[23] Cf. Sudhaus (1907), 485 n. 3, Bardon (1952–6), i. 340. I think in fact that we can learn much more about Cato's *Diana*, and about Calvus' *Io* and Cinna's *Zmyrna*, from a study of the *Ciris* which most probably borrowed from all of them. See my edition of *Ciris* (Lyne 1978*b*).

[24] Cf. Wiseman (1974), 55, with useful bibliography. The Glaucus story was told by Hedyle, Hedylus, Alexander of Aetolus, and, it seems, Callimachus: cf. Webster (1964), 52 and 130, and the Suda, *s.v.* Callimachus.

[25] The meaning of 'cantor' here is often missed or blurred (and some nuances may indeed escape us); cf. of course Hor. *Serm.* 1. 10. 19 'nil praeter Caluum et doctus cantare Catullum'. The basic sense in both cases must simply be 'chant', 'recite'. Devotees are being referred to who can only, or only want to, chant or recite the verses of their favoured poet. But the implication in 'cantores Euphorionis' (at least) is probably that the devotees also chanted verses of their own, in the style of their idol. Cf. Allen (1972), 1–14, especially 13.

The Neoteric Poets 69

addicts of that ἐποποιός whose ἔπη presumably comprised what we call epyllions, who wrote 'learned poetry in difficult language'—'nimis obscurus' Cicero called him at *Div.* 2. 132—and whose hexameters show studied artistry of style ('alliteration, assonance, internal rhyme and the like to a degree which can hardly be fortuitous') and of metre ('a marked preference for certain types of line, particularly lines with spondaic ending and lines composed of a small number of long words');[26] cf. the references to the Catullan hexameter above, p. 62—and we can now add that Catullus affects not only five-word but four-word hexameters (64. 15, 77, 115, and 319). (I resume the question of 'hi cantores Euphorionis', and whom Cicero may particularly have in mind at that time, in §VIII.)

V

Now we shall turn to see whether some or all of these poets share any *other* striking literary interests: interests remarkable enough to assist in distinguishing them collectively from other poets. We should not of course necessarily expect to find all members of a school adopting all its typical forms or topics; and in the case of the neoterics (given the fragmentary state of our knowledge) we could be in ignorance of such consistency even if and when it occurred. What I think we should watch for is when two or more of the poets jointly write the same sort of idiosyncratic thing—idiosyncratic in form or subject; and we should then look to see if the forms or subjects that we discover show any characteristics or motivation in common among themselves—and in common with the already established neoteric genre, epyllion. Here would be confirmation of the school and clarification of its programme. Finally we can see if any striking form or subject treated by *single* members associates itself with the common characteristics or motivation identified. For this, too, would then be assignable to the neoteric programme.

Catullus writes two epithalamia—to use the term very loosely. Poem 62, in hexameters, is totally fictional, a drama staged at a wedding feast, complete with song contest and developing action.[27] Poem 61, in stanzas of glyconics and a pherecratean, seems to have been written with a real Roman wedding in mind; yet it too is a complex imaginative enactment rather than an actual hymenaeal or epithalamion: an enactment of a song to Hymen, of addresses

---

[26] On Euphorion see conveniently Webster (1964), 221–7 with bibliography. The quotations are from pp. 223–5.
[27] The poem is excellently discussed by Fraenkel (1958), 1–8.

and asides to participants in the course of a procession. Poem 62 especially is something surprising. Why should Catullus write it? There was hardly much precedent in Rome for a fictional, dramatized wedding scene with song. It is hardly the most obvious way to occupy one's pen in any circumstances. But one of Catullus' immediate confrères probably did much the same. Calvus writes, to our knowledge, two epithalamia: one apparently in the same lyric stanzas as Catullus and one in hexameters (frgs. 4 and 5 M). We may infer that the hexameter poem at least was comparably dramatic.

What other shared interests strike one? Caecilius' occupation with Cybele is very remarkable, the 'Magna Mater' or the 'Dindymi domina' (above, p. 63): for perhaps Catullus' most striking and unexpected poem also concerns Cybele, namely his 'Attis', poem 63. Whether Caecilius wrote or meditated writing in galliambics, whether he had a version of Attis in particular in mind we cannot know. But presumably he was occupied with a myth or story connected with Cybele—and not just a description of ritual, which would hardly in itself make an interesting poem. And that Caecilius was doing something similar to Catullus is indicated by the similarity between Catullus' reference to his work and a line of his own 'Attis': cf. 35. 14 'Dindymi domina' and 18 'Magna...Mater' with 63. 91 'dea, magna dea, Cybele, dea domina Dindymi'.[28] Now this again is something extraordinary for Latin literature. Lucretius had had reason to explain the religion and rituals of Cybele, and in the process vividly described it (2. 600–60). Varro of Reate too had touched on the topic in the course of his medley of Menippean *saturae*; and (typically for the genre) he switched to the appropriate metre (galliambics) for the occasion.[29] But neither of these—descriptions of current rites known at Rome—is a parallel for choosing an associated myth (or myths) and making a narrative poem out of it, self-sufficient in itself: as Catullus did and as Caecilius, it seems, was in the process of doing.

It begins to look as if some or all of Catullus' 'longer poems' (61–8) are distinctively neoteric. But that is jumping the gun. We still need to discover what, if any, are the common characteristics or motivations shared by the idiosyncratic subjects and forms noticed in this section—besides extraordinariness. However before doing this, it will be useful further to clarify what in Catullus is *not* typically neoteric. Our sights will in fact then be set more firmly and confidently on (some of) the 'longer poems'.

I have already shown that polymetric and elegiac occasional versicles, though common to the neoteric poets, were as a genre far from exclusively

---

[28] Wiseman (1974), 56 conjectures that Caecilius' story was aetiological, something like Hermesianax's account (for which see Paus. 7. 17. 5, frg. 8 Powell).

[29] Quinn (1973), 284 f. gives some information on the very rare galliambic metre and quotes Varro's lines (*Men.* 79, 131, 132, 275). On galliambics see further below, p. 77.

neoteric; and I ought to stress that however exquisite the *style* of the neoterics' own production was, it can hardly have been so different from other people's that one could reckon membership of the school on that score alone.[30] But there is one feature of *Catullus'* polymetrics and epigrams, or rather of some of them, which would indeed have lifted them out of any crowd. It is in fact arguably the most individual, characteristic, and important feature of his poetry; and I mean, in a word, *Lesbia*. No ancient poet, so far as one can tell, had ever before written a series of poems dealing in depth, in all manner of moods, with one relationship with a single enthralling lover. Of course (for example) Meleager had tied successions of epigrams to Heliodora and Myiscus. But Catullus explores and displays the nature of his love for Lesbia profoundly, obsessively—pursuing its ramifications: he shows the interplay of their personalities and the power of his love to shape his vision of the beloved; he shows the effects of disaster. All this in related and mutually dependent, mutually deepening poems. Catullus and Lesbia, Catullus' intense involvement with Lesbia, Catullus' psychological perception of his feelings for Lesbia, all emerge vividly—from a related cycle of what in other hands would be *uersiculi*.

Here then, in *content*, is a respect in which Catullus' *uersiculi* must by past form have been distinctive, extraordinary, even shocking. If Catullus' other poetical confrères wrote similarly—and if no other contemporary did—then here ought to be a characteristic of their school. 'Lesbia' poetry—poetry to and about the commanding, agonizing, wonderful mistress—would have to be considered a highly distinctive part of their programme. (We might however have to reassess whether this school was indeed the school which Cicero had in mind at *Att.* 7. 2. 1.)

But the evidence is that this is simply not so: Cinna and the rest did not, in all probability, write poetry remotely like Catullus' Lesbia poetry. They wrote occasional erotic versicles, polymetrics and epigrams about *furta*. But not 'Lesbia' poetry. This is a fact of considerable importance, too little noticed. The poetry which we probably regard as most typical of Catullus, the poetry indeed which immediately succeeding generations of Latin poets probably

---

[30] Ross (1969) maintains that Catullus displays an artistry, an originality, and sophistication of style in his polymetrics and 'longer poems' that he does not display in his epigrams—and there is truth in this (cf. Lyne 1972). Ross also calls this artistry of style *neoteric* artistry, which may also (with qualifications) be justifiable. But we could not then say (not that Ross in so many words does) that such precious polymetrics would be sufficient on their own to distinguish a neoteric poet. It is hard to imagine that the *uersiculi* of Memmius and Hortensius were so very different from (e.g.) Catullus' (except in one respect which I am coming to). We may note that the 'Graeci plusculi' in Gellius (above, p. 67) thought that Catullus and Calvus did stand out somewhat in the matter of lyric poetry; but they lumped Cinna with Laevius, Hortensius, and Memmius, considering them all, for much the same reasons, pretty hopeless.

regarded as most typical of Catullus, is *untypical* of the school of poets with which he is intimately connected.[31]

The evidence is basically evidence from silence but I think it is conclusive. It boils down to this: no neoteric poet apart from Catullus is connected with any paramount, commanding mistress; and without a Lesbia there can be no 'Lesbia' poetry. But it is not just that no such girl is mentioned: the silence is at times deafening. For the fashion for Catullan 'Lesbia' poetry caught on after Catullus and caught on dramatically (behind this was no doubt the process of life imitating art as well as art imitating art); and a kind of canon of lover-poets and their mistresses developed, to be listed on various occasions and for various motives. Now sometimes there were obvious or understandable reasons for selectivity and allusiveness of reference.[32] On other occasions there were not, and the silences or variations in one or two such lists are clear in their implications. A case in point is Ov. *Trist.* 2. 427 ff. But in order to draw the available conclusions thence one must first deal with tricky textual and interpretative problems; and there is unfortunately no space for this in the present article. I shall consider Prop. 2. 34. 81 ff.

At 2. 25. 4 Propertius seems to claim that his *libelli* have more power to bestow fame on Cynthia than the works of Catullus and Calvus had had in a comparable situation: 'ista meis fiet notissima forma libellis | Calue, tua uenia, pace, Catulle, tua'. This might suggest a girl for Calvus, to correspond to Catullus' Lesbia and Propertius' Cynthia. But if we look at Prop. 2. 34. 81 ff. we see what Propertius must actually have in mind.

> non tamen haec ulli uenient ingrata legenti
> siue in amore rudis siue peritus erit.
> nec minor hic animis, ut sit minor ore, canorus
> anseris indocto carmine cessit olor.

---

[31] Much of the 'Catullan Revolution' was therefore very particularly a *Catullan* revolution. Quinn (1959), 26, when defining the revolution, talks of the poet becoming 'an independent personality who forces his personality into his poetry' and of the unit becoming 'the short poem, intensely personal...'. But is it not particularly Catullus' *Lesbia* poetry that this suits? And yet on p. 24 Quinn talks of 'The revolution that the *poetae novi* represent'.

Wiseman (1974), 52, referring to the 'beginnings of personal poetry' and noting how most scholars attribute these beginnings to the 'neoteric movement', is himself more circumspect: 'For that, the "Catullan revolution"... we can certainly give the credit to Catullus himself and perhaps also to Calvus...'; later in the paragraph he says that 'Cinna himself wrote love poetry'. But 'personal poetry' and 'love poetry' are terms that must be very clearly defined. There is a world of difference between the 'personal poetry' of Catullus and that of say Anacreon, or Sappho, or Meleager; and there was probably a world of difference between Catullus' and Calvus'. Other scholars, like Schanz and Hosius (1927), 285–6, tend simply to assume or imply that Catullus was completely typical of the neoteric school.

[32] e.g. at Ov. *Am.* 1. 15. 27 ff., and Apul. *Apol.* 10.

> haec quoque perfecto ludebat Iasone Varro,
> Varro Leucadiae maxima flamma suae;
> haec quoque lasciui cantarunt scripta Catulli,
> Lesbia quis ipsa notior est Helena;
> haec etiam docti confessa est pagina Calui,
> cum caneret miserae funera Quintiliae.
> et modo formosa quam multa Lycoride Gallus
> mortuus inferna uulnera lauit aqua!
> Cynthia quin uiuet uersu laudata Properti,
> hos inter si me ponere Fama uolet.

Propertius is here justifying his sort of love poetry after praising Vergil. It is possible that his praise of Vergil (particularly of Vergil's epic) was not totally unequivocal. He certainly now intends that his love poetry should appear at least arguably on a par. It too, says Propertius, gives pleasure (81–2); and it is better—because more artistic—than some more ambitious but crude productions (something like this I take to be the implication of 83 f.). And it has by now good authority and precedent: that is the purpose of citing this list (85 ff.). Propertius is showing his literary pedigree, he is demonstrating that the poetry of the immortalizing lover-poet devoted to one woman has become a genre in its own right with worthy exponents. In these circumstances he is unlikely to leave out any obvious name.

Varro of Atax,[33] born in 82 BC (and thus a contemporary of Catullus and Calvus), wrote an Ennianizing *Bellum Sequanicum*, presumably about Caesar's campaign in 58 BC—when he himself therefore was a young man. Subsequently, it seems, he turned to mythological epic (besides other works)—an *Argonautae*, possibly stimulated by Caesar's journey to Britain. *After* the *Argonautae*, as Propertius expressly tells us ('perfecto...Iasone') he turned to love poetry, about a girl he called Leucadia. The timing clearly suggests that Varro, who is not associated with the Catullan coterie in our sources, was one of those who imitated particularly *Catullus*—and wrote his own version of 'Lesbia' poetry, finding or fancying himself in a comparably enthralling situation.

I imagine that Varro is mentioned by Propertius before Catullus because he combined in his person both epic and love poetry, moving from the one to the other; and therefore, in the context, provided a particularly pertinent authority for the genre. After Varro comes Catullus and Lesbia—here too (possibly) a slight hit at epic is contrived: from one point of view Catullus was a more powerful poet than Homer. Then before Gallus, who, with his Lycoris, was

---

[33] Cf. Schanz and Hosius (1927), 312 f. On the chronology of Varro's works cf. too Hofmann (1927/8), 170–6.

the clear and immediate predecessor of Propertius, there is Calvus and Quintilia—or rather there is Calvus who sang of the *funera Quintiliae*; and that is something rather different. But at least Calvus gets a mention. What of the neoterics Caecilius, Cornificius, Cinna, and Cato? The last three of these we know wrote erotic verses (§IV).

Propertius is contriving so far as he can a canon of poets *like himself*, lover-poets devoted to and celebrating one woman. A woman's name *was* intimately connected with Calvus, and he was renowned for celebrating her; but the situation was a very particular one and Propertius' wording responds accordingly. Calvus in fact composed a well-known *epicedion* for his Quintilia. It forms the background to Catullus' poem 96, and Calvus frgs. 15 and 16 M are probably from it.[34] In the course of this epicedion—which may have been lengthy—Calvus seems to have regretted his acts of unfaithfulness to Quintilia: that seems definitely to be the implication of Catullus' 'atque olim missas flemus amicitias' (96. 4);[35] and (it seems to me) Propertius' 'haec etiam docti confessa est pagina Calui | cum caneret...' may also refer to affairs confessed *in the course* of the epicedion. As for Quintilia herself, it seems most likely that she was Calvus' wife—and that Calvus composed an epicedion for her partly under the stimulus of the epicedion composed by the influential Parthenius for his wife Arete.[36]

So: we know that Calvus was an erotic poet—'detexit uariis... sua furta modis' (Ov. *Trist.* 2. 432); we infer that he mentioned or alluded to these 'furta' in his epicedion; and his epicedion possibly included amorous allu-

---

[34] On Calvus' epicedion and Catullus 96 see Fraenkel (1956), 278–88 (cf. too the next note).

[35] Note the text is 'missas' not 'amissas'. Cf. Fraenkel (1956), 285–8. (Bringmann (1973) has an ingenious alternative explanation of the couplet 3–4—that it refers to a *mythological* section in Calvus' epicedion, to mythical *exempla* which Calvus adduced as a mirror and comfort for his suffering: 25–31. The existence of such a mythological section in Calvus is highly likely—as B. shows; but B.'s interpretation of Catullus seems to me to founder—chiefly on 'quo desiderio'. 'desiderium' is particularly the yearning one feels—it is the *vox propria*—for something personally dear that is parted from one or lost for always.)

[36] On Calvus' and Parthenius' epicedia see conveniently and interestingly Pfeiffer (1943), 23–32; further bibliography at Wiseman (1974), 50 n. 33. I am prepared now to reconsider my sceptical attitude (Lyne (1972), 36 n. 4) to Parthenius' influence on the neoterics—with qualifications however: see § IX. Pfeiffer's remarks in this connection ((1943), 30–1) are cogent; so too are Wiseman's (1974), 47 ff. See also the useful and cautious article of Crowther (1976), 66–71. I should have thought that the fact that no pseudonym (apparently) is used for Quintilia points to her status as wife rather than mistress. Certainly it seems that the poets in the 'Lesbia' tradition almost invariably used pseudonyms for lovers whether they were freedwomen or not (Camps on Prop. 2. 34. 89 suggests Quintilia might be a freedwoman of the Quintilii). It is certainly a very risqué act, to be specially remarked, when later on a married woman is celebrated under her real name (Ov. *Trist.* 2. 437–8). (The assumption that Quintilia was Calvus' wife is also attacked by Tränkle (1967), 93–9.)

sions to his relations with Quintilia.[37] But his fame as a celebrator of one beloved woman rests on the epicedion, his commemoration of the death of, in all probability, his wife. Now we see what Propertius must have had in mind at 2. 25. 4. Calvus therefore fits into the canon of lover-poets of Propertian type at 2. 34. 81 ff. only with difficulty. If Propertius could have drawn a clearer analogy, pointing to a single woman immortalized in life by a devoted and singing Calvus, he surely would have done so. In fact Propertius slips him in rather speciously—to swell the ranks, to add the lustre of this famous name to the poetry of erotic devotion.

And why no mention of Caecilius, Cornificius, Cinna, or Cato?—Cinna at least was a famous poet, worthy to grace any pedigree.[38] The answer I think is simple. No name at all consistently or prominently features in their love poetry.[39] By no stretch of the imagination could they be represented as 'Lesbia' poets and therefore they had no place in the Propertian canon. In so far as they were love poets they must have been poets of the erotic idle hour, producing precious *uersiculi* like (we may infer) Catullus' delightful poems to Ipsitilla, Ameana, and Juventius. Catullus the poet of Lesbia was unique in his time.

The impression we gathered above (p. 70) that it must be some or all of Catullus' 'longer poems' which represent his distinctly neoteric poetry has been confirmed. Not only are polymetric and elegiac versicles in general far from being an exclusively neoteric domain: the one really idiosyncratic, original, and striking feature of Catullus' own production was, at the time, uniquely his—not neoteric at all. We must now examine those 'longer poems' of Catullus which seemed to have parallels in other neoterics' *oeuvres* (poems 61–4; see above, §§ IV and V) to see what, if any, common motivations or other characteristics they share. In this way the nature of the neoteric

---

[37] Parthenius' epicedion for Arete possibly did: Pfeiffer (1943), 32.

[38] Cf. Verg. *Ecl.* 9. 35 'nam neque adhuc Vario uideor nec dicere Cinna | digna'; Valgius Rufus praises a fellow-poet by equating him with Cinna (Schol. Veron. on Verg. *Ecl.* 7. 22). The commentaries on Cinna's works, mentioned on pp. 67 and 84, testify to his continuing fame. Wiseman (1974), 53–8 argues for the primacy of Cinna among the neoterics (as he defines them).

[39] What (the question ought to be faced) of Valerius Cato and 'Lydia'? Suet. *gramm*. 11 writes that Cato wrote 'praeter grammaticos libellos etiam poemata ex quibus praecipue probantur Lydia et Diana. Lydiae Ticida meminit "Lydia doctorum maxima cura liber".' But this hardly sounds like a book of love poetry to a Lesbia-figure called Lydia. Perhaps the *liber* was more like Antimachus' *Lyde*: narrative elegiacs for, or in memory of, a girl; or perhaps Lydia in Asia Minor is meant (cf. Euphorion's *Thrax*?). At all events I imagine that the work was abstruse and mythological: there is a nice humour in calling such a book the 'cura' ('the beloved') of 'docti'. It is the sort of joke that was made about Cinna's *Zmyrna* and the 'doctus' Crassicius in the epigram reported by Suetonius (*gramm*. 18). Cato's *Lydia* was, incidentally, certainly not the *Lydia* of the *Appendix Vergiliana*, which is patently influenced by the Augustan Elegists.

programme should clarify itself. We must see too if any of the other extraordinary 'longer poems' of Catullus, which the niggardly remains of neoteric poetry do not happen to parallel, could also fit into the picture. Let us begin by looking at Catullus' *un*paralleled longer poems.

There appears to be no parallel for poems 66 (with 65), 67, and 68 in the neoteric fragments. At this point some stylistic features noted by Ross (115–37) are interesting. He argues that what he calls the 'neoteric elegiacs' (that is, poems 65–8) differ in technique, are more consciously and sophisticatedly wrought, than the distichs of the epigrams. There is a lot of truth in this; but it is some exceptions noted by Ross which are particularly interesting. Among other metrical laxities (so to call them) offered by poem 68, line 49 neglects Hermann's Bridge—the only example in the 'neoteric elegiacs' (against four examples in the epigrams), and not a rhythm that we should expect in highly wrought Grecizing poetry at this stage of Latin literary history.[40] More noticeable is poem 67: Ross remarks that Catullus employs twelve σπονδειάζοντες in his distichs and that all but three of these occur in the 'neoteric elegiacs'. To be more precise they occur in 65, 66, and 68 and not in 67.[41] Poem 67 too has considerably less artistic word-patterning than 65, 66, and 68 (and of course 64, where it is rife).[42] In short these two poems 67 and 68, in particular 67, seem to *neglect* niceties of neoteric style (according to Ross's own definition)—as well as being unparalleled from the point of view of form or subject in the other neoterics' *oeuvres*. Let us therefore leave them out of consideration for the moment.

Poem 66 (with its introduction) is by definition a Callimachean poem. I suggested earlier (above, p. 65) that the neoteric programme might in some way be 'Callimachean'.[43] Could poems 61–6, i.e. the poems paralleled in other neoterics plus 66 (with its introduction 65), present a common front as being in some way all 'Callimachean'? Is a common motivation to be found here?

I think so. Let us note that all these poems are in their own way *narratives*; they all rather extraordinarily or deviously convey an account of a more or less fictional incident or incidents. Poems 63 and 64 do so more obviously than 62, 66, and especially 61. Perhaps 61 ought to be left aside for the moment. The rest[44] do, in their own way, manage to communicate a fictional story or drama. And perhaps we could put it this way: they are the sort of poems an ancient poet might produce (given certain availabilities and certain circumscriptions) who wanted to tell a story but found the conventional way of doing so uncongenial. The conventional way of telling a story was in epic or

---

[40] Ross (1969), 129–30.   [41] Ibid. 130–1.   [42] Ibid. 135.

[43] Hardly a revolutionary thesis of course: but my view of what direction the neoterics' Callimacheanism took is much more defined and specific than, say, Clausen's (1964), 187 ff.

[44] On poem 62 as a narrative see above p. 69, referring to Fraenkel's article.

(as a second runner) in narrative elegy, like Antimachus' *Lyde*. And this of course takes us back to Callimachus.

On aesthetic grounds, as we know, Callimachus eschewed the continuation of epic (above, p. 64); he found Antimachus' *Lyde* παχὺ γράμμα καὶ οὐ τορόν (frg. 398 Pf.).[45] This left him, and poets of his aesthetic persuasion, an obvious problem. How then was one to tell stories, a main wish of most ancient poets? In what forms was Callimachus to communicate his delightfully idiosyncratic versions of myth? With considerable ingenuity Callimachus evolved *alternatives* to epic, alternative ways of telling stories. He popularized if not concocted the perversely ingenious alternative *epos* itself, the epyllion; he revived the naturally narrative Homeric Hymn; he revamped didactic and included allusive little narratives in it (e.g. 'Acontius and Cydippe' in the *Aetia*: frgs. 67–75 Pf.). And it was probably Callimachus, too, who took up the idea of telling a story from the orgiastic myth of the east (Cybele) in its own orgiastic metre, galliambics. It is a devious thought, worthy of an original scholar-poet casting about for alternatives to conventional forms of Greek narrative; and there is some (small) objective evidence pointing this way.[46] It is also worth noting that the bizarre shape which Catullus' own Attis story[47] takes could plausibly derive from the ironical and occasionally black-humoured Callimachus; Catullus is certainly I think following *some* Alexandrian source, at times closely, in poem 63.[48] But whatever the details of the matter, it seems to me certain that Callimachus

---

[45] I take it that Callimachus considered efforts to write long, consistent, and continuous narrative in elegiacs just as disastrous as efforts to write traditional epic—for much the same reasons. And *all* such efforts—not just Antimachus'. We should remember that there are good grounds for supposing that Callimachus criticized the long narrative elegies of even Philitas and Mimnermus (*Aetia praef.* 10 ff.: see conveniently Trypanis (Loeb. edn.) ad loc., Lesky (1966), 710 f.; Lesky is against this view, but he cites the evidence). Callimachus' own discontinuous, capriciously apportioned narrative episodes in elegiacs (e.g. in the *Aetia*) will have been as different from Antimachus' *Lyde* (and perhaps from Philitas' longer elegy and Mimnermus' *Nanno*) as his *Hecale* is from Apollonius' *Argonautica*—which is a lot, but not quite as much (perhaps) as Callimachus thought or would have us think. On Antimachus see further Lesky (1966), 638, Wilamowitz (1924), i. 101–3, also (though I disagree with the article in some quite important respects) Vessey (1971), 1–10.

[46] Hephaestion 12. 3 tells us that the very rare galliambic metre was particularly associated with the 'magna mater'; he quotes two 'famous' lines (reminiscent of parts of Catull. 63): Γαλλαὶ μητρὸς ὀρείης φιλόθυρσοι δρομάδες | αἷς ἔντεα παταγεῖται καὶ χάλκεα κρόταλα and the scholiast on this passage tells us that 'Callimachus also used the metre.' Cf. Elder (1947), 394 n. 2, 397 n. 9.

[47] Is the Attis of Catull. 63 supposed to recall and 'correct' the image of the original mythical lover of Cybele (for whom see Graillot (1912), e.g. p. 12)? Or is he meant just to be an (idiosyncratically Greek and repentant) eunuch priest (priests of Cybele were named eponymously Attis: cf. *Anth. Pal.* 6. 220, Graillot (1912), e.g. p. 19)? I rather infer the former; Wilamowitz (1924), ii. 292 seems to be on the side of the latter.

[48] Cf. Wilamowitz (1924), ii. 291–5, Fordyce (1961), 262. Elder (1947), 398, remarks on the 'Callimachean' narrative technique of the poem.

or some Callimachean poet nurtured the idea of galliambic versions of Cybele myth as a novel and striking alternative to *epos*.

And another Callimachean poet demonstrated yet another attractive method of narrative entertainment which did not involve one of the conventional, tedious forms. Theocritus' Callimacheanism is (virtually) expressly stated in *Idyll* 7. 43 ff.; he too had written his own epyllion (*Id.* 13). And as well as producing the Bucolics (rustic tales in recherché language for the *litterati*) as one fine way of alternative story-telling, he revived the idea of a fictional epithalamion. He may have done this most immediately under the stimulus of Sappho; for Sappho's narrative poem on the nuptials of Hector and Andromache (as it seems to be)[49] was probably partnered by other fictional, mythical epithalamia.[50] Anyway, in an epithalamion for Menelaus and Helen (*Id.* 18), Theocritus gives us a delightfully individual glimpse into heroic myth—though the general strategy and ethos of the poem is interestingly and significantly Callimachean.[51] We have in fact little or no evidence for other fictional epithalamia in the 'high' Alexandrian period,[52] but I think we are entitled to guess that such an attractive idea had other exponents.[53] And Parthenius, whose influence we have noticed (above, p. 74) probably wrote an epithalamion—but whether fictional or not we cannot tell.[54]

Some concluding comments on these 'Callimachean' narrative alternatives are necessary before we return to the neoterics. First we must observe that there is a certain common tendency in *content*. The oddly weighted *Hecale* of Callimachus, Erysicthon with his bourgeois-souled parents in *Hymn* 6, Menelaus familiarly addressed in his bridal bedroom, Heracles and Hylas in *Id.* 13—all suit an alternative narrative, reacting to a convention of epic and orthodox heroes behaving heroically. The Callimachean poets explored byways of myth or probed unexpected corners in well-known myths. The sex-lives of heroes were congenial. If the plots of later or more extreme Callimacheans became more erotic or more off-beat, that should not surprise us. Extremer or diverser tactics are still serving the same strategy: the cultivation of the unexpected and the unconventional, often with an eye directly

---

[49] Frg. 44 L–P. There is some doubt about the ascription as well as the nature of this poem: cf. Bowra (1961), 227–31.

[50] Cf. *RE* iA 2371 f. (We should note that Crusius, *RE* i. 1569.13 ff. detects reminiscences in Theoc. *Id.* 18 of Alcman—who was called by Leonidas (*Anth. Pal.* 7. 19) τὸν ὑμνητῆρ' ὑμεναίων).

[51] Cf. Maas in *RE* ix. 133.15 ff.

[52] Cf. *RE* ix. 133.4–38: the reported ἐπιθαλάμιον of Eratosthenes may have been for an actual wedding; those that Philodemus has in mind certainly are.

[53] The Alexandrians collected Sappho's epithalamia into a special book—while the rest of her poetry was organized according to metre (*RE* ix. 132. 24 ff.). This may betoken an especial popularity for the particular genre; it was surely likely to encourage imitation.

[54] Cf. Reitzenstein (1912), 3; also Wilamowitz (1924), ii. 279 n. 1. But note Crowther (1976), 67 f.

on affronting conventional expectations. It could be fun, for example, to make epics with heroines instead of heroes—and monstrous heroines at that.[55]

Secondly, though the common concentration of these poets on exquisiteness of *style* (more or less for style's sake) is well known, it ought to be stressed that it—and their allusive, often wilfully capricious method of unfolding events—serves the same ultimate strategy as the common tendency in content. All are part of one front of unorthodoxy—ranged against the ordered telling of an expected story in a consistent and standard idiom.

We look back now to the longer poems of Catullus, and first to those paralleled in the neoteric fragments. What emerges immediately is that Catull. 63 and 64, the epyllions of Calvus, Cinna, and Cato (or Cato's Hymn if that is what his *Diana* was: above, p. 68), Caecilius' inchoate 'magna mater', all have this in common: they are all versions of what one might call 'Callimachean' alternatives to conventional narrative. Of course Catullus' epyllion is very different in impact to Callimachus'; but the *genus*, the ultimate strategy of the poem is demonstrably the same. Likewise (we can take it) with the epyllions of Calvus and the rest.

Catullus' poem 62 should be seen in the same way. The epithalamial form takes us unexpectedly into a *story*, allusively and exquisitely told. This is Catullus' version of the 'Callimachean' alternative genre epithalamion. It is very much Catullus' *version*: the tactics—but not the strategy—are, especially in respect of content, very different from Theocritus'. Catullus has so far reacted to traditional narrative that he has fled beyond even a mythical domesticity and arrived in a domesticity of fiction. And we should I think consider Catullus' other epithalamion (poem 61) in the same context. It is essentially dramatic—things *happen* in the course of the poem—so that in its effect, or for part of its effect, it is a *narrative*—much of it Grecizing fancy.[56] But this poem Catullus seems to have composed with a definite marriage in mind and adapted it accordingly. One or other of Calvus' epithalamia (the lyric?) may have been comparable: an essentially literary and narrative epithalamion given particular relevance.

And poem 66 of course also slots into place. By definition, as a translation of a narrative episode of Callimachus' *Aetia* (a brilliant and witty piece of instant myth), it is a version of a Callimachean alternative to conventional narrative. We should note that plenty of lines in it could remind one of Cicero's parody in *Att.* 7. 2. 1—and poems 61, 63, and (to a lesser extent) 62 also offer example after example of comparably contrived and superb artifice. Whether or not

---

[55] The tendency of later epyllion's subject matter is probably fairly enough represented by Parthenius' collection of ἐρωτικὰ παθήματα, written for Cornelius Gallus to draw upon and put εἰς ἔπη (presumably what we should call epyllions) καὶ ἐλεγείας. Many of the stories derive from Euphorion. On Gallus and Euphorion see below, §VIII.

[56] Cf. Fordyce (1961), 236–8.

other neoterics imitated or translated episodes of the *Aetia* we cannot say, but the relation of poem 66 itself to the neoteric programme is clear. And so, in its own very particular way, is the relation of poem 68.

But first let me sum up (for it is now possible) what the neoteric programme was; or, to be most exact, I shall describe what the neoterics did which distinguished them from other writers and united them among themselves— and which I rather assume they consciously regarded as their programme. In one way or another they affected the typically and ostentatiously 'Callimachean' forms, forms evolved by Callimachus and like-minded poets to provide the means for a more or less provocatively alternative narrative literature. Cicero at *Att.* 7. 2. 1 seems to have had affectation of style particularly in mind. But the neoterics were aiming at idiosyncracy of style *and* content, for they were imitating genres that imposed both. They were imitating genres evolved by the Callimacheans to suit both new emphases in subject matter and a new (and concomitant) concentration on stylistic exquisiteness; and taking upon themselves the genres, the neoterics took upon themselves the whole strategy. If their content varied in the tactics or degree of its contrived unorthodoxy, that is what we should expect from our observations above (pp. 78–9) about the Greek Callimacheans.[57] Similarly with their style: that too could be more or less recherché according to the tactical wishes of the poet. But the common ground—the common strategy—is clear.

Now back to poem 68, or rather 68b. The allusive and individual account of Laodamia and Protesilaus (73 ff. and 105 ff.) which we find there could easily be a Catullan version of the sort of whimsically told mythological narrative which Callimachus fitted into the *Aetia*. And that I think is what, in essence, it is. The tenderly unheroic concentration of the Laodamia story suits the tenor of later 'alternative' narrative's subject matter;[58] and its style (and the style of the rest of the poem) displays all the features which we have associated (since analysing Cicero's parody) with the neoterics[59]—the few metrical licences noted by Ross (above, p. 76) are comfortably outweighed, and explicable besides, in view of the poem's unique personal endeavour. For what Catullus has done is (I submit) to put a neoteric narrative to personal service:[60] he has

---

[57] Wiseman (1974), 54 therefore makes too much of the difference between Catullus' subject matter in poem 64 and that of the other neoterics' epyllions. The tactics of unorthodoxy seem to be fairly different in all of them, but the strategy, and the orthodoxy being played against, is common to all.

[58] Cf. Moschus' *Europa* and e.g. Parthen. ἐρωτ. παθ. (cf. n. 55 above) 4 (Oenone and Paris).

[59] See conveniently Fordyce (1961), 344. As well as noting a plenitude of five-word hexameters, we should note three-word pentameters at 74 and 112. The extensive hypotaxis which Fordyce points to disapprovingly was probably intended by Catullus to be appreciated as mannered and contrived *ars*.

[60] Cf. how he has probably adapted a neoteric form to his particular use with poem 61; but the poetic achievement is not remotely comparable.

used it to adumbrate and amplify the complex and tragic ambivalences of his own current feelings. And he has then worked the whole into an amazing, elaborately structured ring-composition.[61] The result is something original and fascinating: a neoteric form consciously adapted to a particular and untypical, *personal* end. In its idea and execution the poem is the work of genius. It has the characteristics of genius too—at times touching the stars, at times falling flat on its face.

To conclude this section: we have now hazarded a description of the neoteric programme and located Catullus' particularly neoteric production in his longer poems. But we have not *identified* his longer poems with his neoteric production. 68a may introduce 68b or be as it were Part I of the same poem as many believe.[62] This would, either way, associate it with neoteric poetry; but it would not *be* neoteric poetry. It would have even less claim than the mannered poem 65 which introduces 66. And if in truth it has no relation to 68b at all,[63] then it has no relation to neoteric poetry either. And what of poem 67? This we saw lacked conspicuously neoteric features of style (above, p. 76); and its only allusiveness is the allusiveness of defamatory innuendo. It is not a version of a 'Callimachean' alternative narrative; it is not a fictional narrative at all. It employs a motif of epigram, the dialogue with a house-door, to indulge at length a medley of provincial scandal. It is in fact an overblown, occasional, delightful, brilliant epigram—nothing to do with neoteric poetry at all.

But this may seem curious: that Catullus should group completely unneoteric occasional poetry with ostentatiously neoteric poems. I think it would be curious. But I do not think he did. I think it likely that 67 and possibly 68a were grouped with other 'longer poems' by an editor, probably for no other reason than that they too were 'longer'.[64]

VIII

We have now identified a school of poets behind Cicero's remarks on οἱ νεώτεροι and established its programme. Does Cicero have in mind the

---

[61] Cf. Kroll (1960), 219.   [62] Cf. Williams (1968), 229 ff.

[63] This has been argued most recently by Wiseman (1974), 88–103. One does not have to accept the suggestion that Manlius had his eye on *sharing* Catullus' mistress (I imagine he simply wants Catullus to organize a girl for him) to appreciate the cogency of some of Wiseman's points.

[64] Our collection could not possibly have been produced by Catullus himself, and the degree to which the present order of poems still reflects any of his original wishes is largely speculation. Several factors suggest that the ordering of the 'longer poems' in particular is not his. Such are the unassailable conclusions to be drawn from Wheeler (1934), 1–32, esp. 22 ff.; also 39 f.

same poets when he talks in 45 BC of 'hi cantores Euphorionis' (*Tusc.* 3. 45)? Or rather (since individual poetic stars wax and wane in five years) does he have in mind the same sort of poets?

Probably. It has already seemed likely (above, pp. 60 and 68–9). And now we have recognized precisely how important Callimachus was for the neoteric programme, and in what ways. A neoteric's Callimacheanism should or could have endeared him to Euphorion.

Although the directness of the relation between Callimachus and Euphorion is debatable, it is clear that the latter's aesthetic sympathies would have been with Callimachus; and his poetic practice was consonant. Indeed in many ways—ways that should have appealed to a neoteric—he seems like a kind of extreme version of Callimachus.[65] The deviousness of his poetry—which included epyllions at least—was virtually unbeatable: deviousness manifesting itself in mannered obscurity of style *and* highly exotic, off-beat content. A devoted neoteric might well therefore have reason to study Euphorion. A fanatic might have reason to be an addict, a 'cantor'.

Perhaps some neoterics were more fanatical than others. Perhaps there were more fanatics among them when Cicero wrote 'hi cantores Euphorionis' than when he wrote about οἱ νεώτεροι five years earlier. We cannot say. But it seems likely that, although the school Cicero describes in 50 BC and then in 45 may be dynamic and evolving, it is substantially the same school. And perhaps there is no significance in the change of reference at all: it simply pleased Cicero to use a different slighting and exaggerative appellation on a different occasion. He may have had several. He may at times have referred to the school as simply the 'poetae noui'.

What of Cornelius Gallus? It is possible that Cicero had him, among others, in mind at *Tusc.* 3. 45:[66] by 45 BC or even earlier Gallus (a waxing star) could have been associated with 'cantores Euphorionis'—and with what we have established as the neoteric school. We have explicit information that he wrote (somehow) in the manner of Euphorion (cf. Verg. *Ecl.* 10. 50 with Servius and pseudo-Probus ad loc.; cf. too Serv. on *Ecl.* 6. 72 discussed below). It is, too, to him that Parthenius dedicates for use εἰς ἔπη (presumably epyllions) καὶ ἐλεγείας his collection of sometimes Euphorionic ἐρωτικὰ παθήματα. And it appears from Verg. *Ecl.* 6. 64–73 that Gallus wrote or was meditating an ambitious 'Hesiodic' poem—an epyllion presumably—on the origin of the 'Grynean Grove' (line 72: 'his tibi Grynei nemoris dicatur origo')—and Euphorion had apparently told one story connected with that grove, the contest of Calchas and Mopsus (Serv. on *Ecl.* 6. 72).[67]

---

[65] Cf. Webster (1964), 221 ff., esp. 221–3, Clausen (1964), 191 f.; Crowther (1970), 325–6.
[66] Cf. Crowther (1970), 326–7, Bramble (1974), 181.   [67] Cf. the following footnote.

The whole question of Gallus is of course too complex to raise here and so I confine myself to two qualifying observations.

(1) Gallus' subsequent fame was almost exclusively as a love poet of the stamp of Catullus and Propertius. There is for example no discernible sign that any poem by Gallus on the 'Grynean Grove' influenced poets of succeeding generations.

(2) If Gallus did complete such a poem, I doubt that its plot was the contest of Calchas and Mopsus, as Serv. at *Ecl.* 6. 72 may imply[68] and as most modern scholars assume; nor will Vergil have had this story in mind. It would hardly provide the *aetiological* slant we expect (note 'origo' in 72); and it is not the sort of story that particularly suits epyllion—or the tenor of the stories in *Ecl.* 6. Much more plausible is the story which we infer from Serv. *auct.*, commenting on 'Gryneus Apollo' at *Aen.* 4. 345: 'Clazomenae ciuitas est Asiae...iuxta hanc nemus est Gryneum, ubi Apollo colitur, qui traditur ibi Grynem Amazonem stuprasse...'. That sounds potentially aetiological; it could too make a very good, and indeed more typically, Euphorionic epyllion; and it fits the tenor of the other stories in *Ecl.* 6. The story's provenance may, interestingly, be Parthenius himself: we note that Vergil's 'Gryneus Apollo' at *Aen.* 4. 345, where the story is cited, seems an echo of Parthenius' poem *Delos*.[69]

IX

We have fitted two apparently individual Catullan poems (66 and 68b) into the neoteric programme. What of two individual and idiosyncratic poems that we know by other neoterics, namely Cinna's propempticon for Asinius Pollio (frgs. 1–5 M) and Calvus' epicedion for Quintilia (mentioned above, p. 74)? I have already suggested that Calvus' epicedion was probably written

---

[68] But Servius' note is vaguer than many admit. The crucial words are as follows: 'in quo ⟨!luco⟩ aliquando Calchas et Mopsus dicuntur de peritia diuinandi inter se habuisse certamen...hoc autem Euphorionis continent carmina, quae Gallus transtulit in sermonem latinum...' This seems to me to imply Servius' knowledge of, or belief in, two separate facts: (1) that somewhere in his works Euphorion had told of or referred to the story of Calchas' and Mopsus' contest; (2) that Gallus 'translated' (one knows incidentally how loosely *transfero* is used by Servius) Euphorionic poetry. Nothing preciser. He may wish to imply that Gallus 'translated' a poem by Euphorion about Calchas and Mopsus, i.e. that the two facts should be put together; but he certainly does not commit himself to saying so. I think, in fact, it is clear that he knows *at first hand* no poem by either Gallus or Euphorion on Calchas and Mopsus, or for that matter any poem at all by them connected with the Grynean Grove.

[69] Cf. Clausen (1964), 192.

under the influence of Parthenius (p. 74). And we have reason to believe that Cinna's propempticon (which, like his *Zmyrna*, subsequently merited a commentary) was also stimulated by an example of Parthenius'.[70] So: two poems written (presumably) along formal Greek lines, and under the stimulus of a Greek poet who we gather strongly influenced neoteric poets (above, p. 74); and the surviving fragments of Cinna's poem offer obvious instances of neoteric *ars*. Are these not to be counted neoteric poems? How are they to be fitted into the programme?

I would make the following points. First, there is actually no evidence for Parthenius' influence over *all* the neoteric poets. In particular it is slim for Catullus,[71] who explicitly recognizes only Callimachus as a Greek influence. In this connection it is worth noting that the neoteric poets seem more prone to complimenting *each other* as a coterie of equal talent than to acknowledging any one as master; I have the impression of a group of poets who fed each other ideas, took and gave advice where they could or wanted, and formed their own programme.[72] We might indeed provisionally conclude that Parthenius' influence among the neoterics—apart from Gallus—was particularly or only upon Cinna (for an obvious reason)[73] and Calvus. Secondly, the two poems, though idiosyncratic and Grecizing, do not fit into the general definition comfortably and honestly arrived at above (§VII) of the neoteric programme; and they are, also, very obviously *special* cases—in that they are written for specific and special occasions not likely to be too frequently repeated. I would therefore (at risk of seeming to draw too fine a distinction) class them as specially occasioned *tours de force* written by neoteric poets rather than poetry of the neoteric programme.

[70] Cf. Wiseman (1974), 48, with references.

[71] Cazzaniga (1961) compares some fragmentary lines of Parthenius with Catull. 68. 94–100 at 124–6.

[72] Cf. Catull. 14, 35, 50 etc. (above, § III), Cinna frg. 14. The idea of Valerius Cato as the 'Leader' of the school has once more (it should not have been necessary) been exposed by Wiseman (1974), 53 f.

[73] Wiseman (1974), 47 cogently supports the notion that it was 'Cinna the Poet' who captured Parthenius, brought him to Rome, and then freed him on account of his learning.

6

Seruitium Amoris[1] (1979)

In this paper I shall be examining the nature and provenance of what many people state or imply to be a traditional, conventional, even trite figure of speech: the Augustan Elegists' figure of the 'seruitium amoris'. It is indeed a very frequent image (so to call it for the moment) in the Elegists. As. F. O. Copley says:[2] 'Of all the figures used by the Roman elegists, probably none is quite so familiar as that of the lover as slave.' But frequency does not equal triteness nor traditionality. Copley himself argues that the frequency of 'seruitium amoris' and the way it was used in the Elegists was novel. It is my intention to confirm that conclusion and to argue further that the Elegiac image was effectively an Elegiac invention—more particularly probably Propertius'. It was also I think far more potentially earnest, immediate, and realistic in impact than Copley (or indeed most scholars) would allow,[3] and this too will be demonstrated. First a word of background is necessary.

It is important to realize that the poetry of Propertius and Tibullus, whose first books were published in the late 30s and early 20s BC[4], contains, indeed proclaims, a radically unconventional philosophy of life. In several carefully organized poems[5] they argue for a serious devotion to the arts and pleasure of 'otium', in particular to love and love poetry, to the exclusion of conventional and honourable 'negotium' and achievement. This philosophy was quite earnestly intended or at least earnestly intended to provoke. Much of it had in fact been implicit in the life and works of the Elegists' most important predecessor, Catullus; and Cicero for one had identified an idle society of pleasure, often alluding to it in his letters and on one famous occasion publicly attacking it.[6] But with the early Elegists the implicit is made explicit

---

[1] Jasper Griffin kindly read a draft of this paper and offered many acute and helpful suggestions. I owe the Plautine references on p. 92 to Mrs. N. Zagagi.

[2] Copley (1947), 285.

[3] 'By its very nature, therefore, the figure is romantic-sentimental, for it idealizes love out of all relation to reality, and... transports the poets into a phantasy-world created out of their own imagination.' Copley (1947), 285.

[4] Cf. Enk (1946), 16–19; Enk (1962), 34–45.

[5] Cf. in particular Prop. 1. 6 and 14, Tib. 1. 1 and 10.

[6] Cic. *Pro Sestio* 136 ff. (56 BC).

and a veritable 'alternative society' now emblazons itself. Propertius and Tibullus provocatively codify a way of life whose dishonourableness they are the first to avow: we may call it the 'life of love'.[7] This is the context in which the efflorescence of the 'seruitium amoris' image occurs, and the context helps to explain that efflorescence.

At the outset we ought to establish what, broadly, was the function of the figure of 'seruitium amoris' in the early Elegists. It expressed often quite subtly the lover's state or sense of degradation. The lover-poet who called himself or implied himself to be the slave of his beloved communicated thereby the humiliation and abasement to which, as subject–lover of that person, he was or felt himself exposed. Propertius and Tibullus may stress different aspects and have different attitudes to their situation. But both imply through the image that their love for the person in question involves *degradation*—and degradation, be it noted, for the party whom we should in fact expect to be the dominant one.[8] The crucially relevant aspect of slavery for the image is (to put it briefly) the *servility* of the slave as a social institution.[9]

If we look at the surviving occurrences of 'slavery of love' imagery in Greek literature we note at once not only its rarity, but also the comparatively simple function it usually performs. It tends to illustrate the power of love rather than the state or feelings of the lover: the overwhelming or miraculous power of love to enthrall or to keep in thrall. It is closely associable with, indeed not always separable from, another and common idea, the idea of love capturing or making prisoner—prisoners being *ipso facto* slaves. The *servility*, degradation, of the lover-slave is *not* usually at issue.

In Greek poetry Copley[10] refers us first of all to the Alexandrians' erotic versions of god–slave myths: Apollo and Admetus, Hercules and Omphale. The only example from these that substantially survives is Callimachus' account of Apollo's servitude to his beloved Admetus (*Hymn* 2. 47–54; cf. Rhianus fr. 10 Powell). Here we are presented with the miraculous spectacle of Apollo as a herdsman—a great tribute to the power of love and an amusing but very far from humiliating picture of Apollo.[11] An anonymous epigram (*Anth. Pal.* 5. 100) of uncertain date is also cited by Copley but is of doubtful

---

[7] For what I call the 'life of love' cf. Boucher (1965), ch. 1, 'La génération élégiaque'; Grimal (1963), ch. 6; Griffin (1976), 87–105.

[8] That of course is a key aspect of the Elegiac figure: the fact that the man is enslaved to the woman (or boy). It was a comparatively common idea for a woman either to appear as a 'slave in love' or to express willingness to be the literal slave of a beloved man. Cf. Nisbet and Hubbard (1970) on Hor. *Carm.* 1. 33. 14, with Catull. 64. 160 ff., Prop. 4. 4. 33 f., Ov. *Her.* 3. 69 ff.

[9] Cf. Copley (1947), 288.   [10] Copley (1947), 286 f.

[11] The slave-god, like the child-god, appeals to Alexandria because of the piquant incongruity (cf. Herter (1929/1975), 371 ff. on Callimachus' *Hymn to Artemis*, esp. 377 ff.).

relevance. A lover talks of himself as the slave of Love (λάτρις Ἔρωτος) *not* of another lover, and claims as excuse for his conduct the precedents of Zeus and Hades each of whom was the 'slave of violent desires' (μαλερῶν δοῦλον... πόθων). In effect the image here is of slavery to *emotions*—something very different in possible implications from an image of slavery to *people* and in its essence of course well paralleled.[12] There are in fact a couple of other more colourful, and definitely Hellenistic, epigrams to be cited which are based on the idea of slavery to *love* rather than a lover.[13]

I can make some few further additions to Copley's examples from Greek poetry. Most follow the simple 'power of love' pattern. At Menander fr. 568 (Sandbach) it is asked 'by what are lovers enslaved (τίνι δεδούλωνται ⟨sc. οἱ ἐρῶντες⟩ ποτέ;)'—to which it is answered that lovers are not enslaved by their faculty of sight nor by desire: the decisive factor is νόσος ψυχῆς. The image simply describes the catastrophic process of falling in love not the state (humiliating or otherwise) of being in love. At *Misumenus* fr. 2 the soldier Thrasonides exclaims 'the paltry little girl has enslaved me, a feat never achieved by any one of my foes in war.' From the allusion to foes and from the fact that we know the girl in question was Thrasonides' prisoner of war, we deduce that he is drawing attention to an ironic reversal. He who has always been victorious has been vanquished, vanquished and captivated by his defeated and female captive. The image of slavery is here not distinguishable from the image of capture and again denotes just the catastrophic (but here ironically catastrophic) action of falling in love. With this latter we may compare quite interestingly an epigram of Paulus Silentiarius[14] (*Anth. Pal.* 5. 230):

χρυσῆς εἰρύσσασα μίαν τρίχα Δωρὶς ἐθείρης,
οἷα δορικτήτους δῆσεν ἐμεῦ παλάμας ...

Cf. too the epitaph of Lais (*ap.* Athen. *Deipn.* 589b):

τῆσδέ ποθ' ἡ μεγάλαυχος ἀνίκητός τε πρὸς ἀλκὴν
Ἑλλὰς ἐδουλώθη κάλλεος ἰσοθέου,
Λαΐδος ...

---

[12] Cf. Plat. *Phaedr.* 238e (ἡδονή) etc., LSJ s.v. δοῦλος and δουλεύω 2, Hor. *Serm.* 2. 7, etc. A willing or at least unconquered (but not 'natural') slavery to a person, especially a man's to a woman or boy, has implications of actual and literal degradation and also, possibly, of masochism and sexual reversal which the quasi-philosophical metaphor cannot have.

[13] *Anth. Pal.* 12. 80 and 81 (Meleager).

[14] It seems, incidentally, unlikely that Paulus, or Agathias (see below), was familiar with the Augustan Elegists, though they did of course draw on Hellenistic and other earlier Greek epigram: cf. Enk (1946), 32 with bibliography; and on Agathias see Cameron (1970), esp. 12–29.

Here ἐδουλώθη has wider range but the same sort of colouring as in *Misumenus* fr. 2 above. Cf. finally *Anth. Pal.* 5. 302. 15 f. (Agathias Scholasticus):

ἢν δὲ μιγῇς ἰδίῃ θεραπαινίδι, τλῆθι καὶ αὐτὸς
δοῦλος ἐναλλάγδην δμωΐδι γινόμενος.

Ironic reversal again.

Not many examples remain to be cited from extant Greek literature. But in considering what do remain we must also consider an important area which is probably under-represented: colloquial speech. Copley remarks:[15] 'it is altogether likely that the popular mind, in Greek times, had seized on the similarity between the lover's fawning conduct, his humility and abasement, and the demeanor of the slave'; so that the image of the lover as slave, and the lover's degradation as slavery, i.e. something like the Elegiac 'seruitium', might well have been part of Greek *colloquial* speech.

There is of course one famous place in Greek (cited by Copley) where lovers' degradation is thus described. In Plato's *Symposium* (183a) lovers who are prepared even to sleep on the beloved's doorstep are said to be willing δουλείας δουλεύειν οἴας οὐδ' ἂν δοῦλος οὐδείς and the idea is taken up again in the dialogue (184b–c, 219e). The occasion and style of the *Symposium* might suggest that the image was colloquial; and Copley remarks: 'since there is little, if anything, in Greek literature that would have suggested the idea to Plato, then, unless Plato himself conceived it, it must have been derived from the speech of the people.' And it certainly would have been a comprehensible and natural idiom. Athenian society like any other society with slaves saw slavish acts as demeaning for free men and used 'slavish' instinctively to describe inappropriate or undignified actions. Demosthenes for example (57. 45) talks of 'poverty compelling free men to do many slavish (δουλικά) and lowly things'; and there are a great number of occasions (unnecessary to illustrate here) when other undignified behaviour is described in similar terms, obviously idiomatically. So it would be very surprising if Plato had been the only person to depict lovers' indignities in this way and we should probably infer a wider currency of the 'slavery of love' (used in the manner of the Roman 'seruitium' image) in Greek *popular* language than our sources suggest. There is in fact the implication of Aristotle *Eth. Nic.* 1157ª7 to digest; talking of the different aims of ἐραστής and ἐρώμενος he says: οὐ γὰρ ἐπὶ τοῖς αὐτοῖς ἥδονται οὗτοι, ἀλλ' ὃ μὲν ὁρῶν ἐκεῖνον, ὃ δὲ θεραπευόμενος ὑπὸ τοῦ ἐραστοῦ. And I can cite one Hellenistic (and one Imperial) epigram which certainly seems to reflect such a usage. *Anth. Pal.* 12. 169 (Dioscorides 8 Gow–Page):

---

[15] Copley (1947), 289.

ἐξέφυγον, Θεόδωρε, τὸ σὸν βάρος. ἀλλ' ὅσον εἶπας
'ἐξέφυγον τὸν ἐμὸν δαίμονα πικρότατον'
πικρότερός με κατέσχεν, Ἀριστοκράτει δὲ λατρεύων
μυρία δεσπόσυνον καὶ τρίτον ἐκδέχομαι.

Cf. too *Anth. Pal.* 5. 22 (Rufinus).

So: an image of 'slavery of love' in the mould of the Roman 'seruitium' probably had some currency in *colloquial* Greek. But this is *not* to say that it was ever actually a cliché in classical or Hellenistic speech, or even particularly common. For if it had been, we should expect to see some substantial reflection of it in the popular comedies—which we do not. Even in the Roman comedy which adapted Greek middle and new comedy there are very few signs.[16] As for Greek *literature*, slavery to illustrate the demeaning behaviour of lovers simply never caught on; it was never a topos. Writers seem to have found it unappealing or not to have considered it. This may sound a rash statement given the loss (in particular) of so much Alexandrian Greek. But if a slavery image of this type had been a popular literary topos we should expect to see some considerable sign of it in erotic epigram or idyll, quite a lot of which (after all) survives. We see almost none. And the absence in comedy should again be noted; it is in fact a remarkable statistic. In comedy astute slaves are forever counselling dotty, amorous young masters—and offering, one might have thought, nice ironic opportunities for the use of the motif. No such use or virtually no such use is made. We must infer from this silence that it was not prevalent—either in literature or speech.

Let us now survey the scene in Latin. Examples are in fact again very rare—until the Elegists. In Terence there is only *Eunuchus* 1026–7 to cite, where the Alexandrian erotic version of Hercules and Omphale is simply adduced as a comic *exemplum* with no elaboration, nor concentration on humiliation and degradation. A couple of instances in Plautus I shall come to soon. The image does not feature in Lutatius Catulus and the other Roman epigrammatists. In Catullus there is only (I think) 68. 136 to reckon with: 'rara uerecundae furta feremus erae'. But the main intention here is to anticipate the reversal of sexual roles implied in the following lines (Catullus will play Juno to Lesbia's Jupiter), and the effect is pathetic rather than shocking—Catullus is stressing forbearance not humiliation. And in general of course Catullus' ideals of love excluded acquiescence (let along glorying) in degradation; his was a very

---

[16] See below. It should of course be noted that the comic idea of a *husband* as slave to his *wife* (cf. Caecilius *ap.* Gell. 2. 23. 10) carries very different implications from those of either 'power of love' slave imagery or imagery in the mould of the Roman *seruitium*; and it is really irrelevant to this discussion.

different romanticism from the Elegists'.[17] It begins to look therefore as if it is *only* in the Augustan Elegy that the 'seruitium amoris' is developed into an elaborate image to illustrate the humiliation, the *servile* state of the lover. It begins to look indeed as if it is only in the Elegists that the image becomes frequent in any form. The picture in Latin *previous to the Elegists* is therefore looking, on the face of it, much like the picture in Greek. And this is corroborated by some further considerations: arguments from silence.

It is relevant to recall Lucr. 4. 1121 ff., where Lucretius satirizes the romantic lover. His scorn for such a lover's abject subjection and humiliation is complete and clear: 'alterius sub nutu degitur aetas...languent officia atque aegrotat fama uacillans'. But Lucretius does *not* liken such subjection to a slave's. And that I think has clear implications. If the picture of the lover as slave had been a familiar one to Lucretius—if the comparison had been common or fashionable in current literature or speech—surely Lucretius would have introduced it (particularly, we might note, if people had been more or less gladly confessing 'slavery', as the Elegists were to do). It is the purpose or effect of the 'seruitium' image to give concrete expression to despicable aspects of love; as such it offers a superb handle for the satirist and, if it had been available and tempting, Lucretius is unlikely to have passed it up.

Two other such arguments are worth consideration. An obvious candidate for the popularization or utilization of the 'seruitium' is the 'founder of Elegy', Cornelius Gallus. I doubt that he had any of it. Vergil's picture of Gallus in the tenth *Eclogue* seems in many respects a fun-poking parody—the pastoral poet, advocate of ordered Epicurean emotions, rallying the Elegiac tool of passion. It is for example part of Vergil's parody that Gallus, who no doubt many times represented himself as 'dying of love' ('pereo') in the emotional, colloquial (and Elegiac sense), is depicted in the *Eclogue* as *literally* dying: 'indigno cum Gallus amore peribat'. If Gallus had represented himself as the slave of a woman, I doubt whether Vergil could have resisted comparably parodying it. I would draw the same sort of conclusion from Hor. *Serm.* 1. 2, the satire on the ridiculous behaviour of romantic adulterers (and others), which is 'probably the earliest ...of Horace's satires' (Fraenkel): say, early 30s BC. If it had been fashionable or even common in colloquial parlance or erotic literature to talk of lovers as slaves, if Horace had *thought* of the image at the time of writing *Serm.* 1. 2, it is hard to imagine that he (any more than Lucretius) would have missed its satirical potential. But it does not feature at all in that satire.

[17] Witness for example the hoped-for *foedus amicitiae* (109. 6). At 68. 68 'isque domum nobis isque dedit dominae' (*dominae* Fröhlich), *domina* must, in conjunction with *domum* and in the context of an expanding fantasy of marriage, be referring to 'mistress *of the house*' (i.e. effectively *wife*) not 'mistress from the point of view of a slave'. (The transmitted *dominam* cannot I think work, but this is of course a notorious crux; *dominam* is defended by, among others, Wilkinson (1970), 290.)

Seruitium Amoris

At this point someone might well object that *Epod.* 11 vitiates my arguments from silence. Here in an erotic poem dating from approximately the same time as the *Sermones* Horace *does* allude to the slavery of lovers—in his own case.

> quodsi meis inaestuet praecordiis
> *libera* bilis...

he had protested, at the time of his love-affair with Inachia (15 f.). And

> nunc gloriantis quamlibet mulierculam
> uincere mollitie amor Lycisci me tenet,
> unde expedire non *amicorum* queant
> *libera consilia* nec contumeliae graues,
> sed alius ardor... (23–7)

The implication that his state was and is servile is clear; and there are, actually, obvious similarities in language to Propertius himself, especially to the first poem of the *monobiblos*.[18] So (the objection would run) *Epod.* 11 shows that, at the approximate time of writing *Serm.* 1. 2, Horace was able to think of and use the image of love's degrading slavery—but simply, for his own reasons, did not choose to in that satire.

I respond as follows. The inference from *Serm.* 1. 2 seems too plausible to be hastily discarded; *Epod.* 11 is rather a special poem; and 40–30 BC, the 'approximate' period of composition of the *Sermones* and *Epodes*, is a long and eventful time.

F. Leo called *Epod.* 11 'plane elegia iambis concepta' and showed that it has many resemblances to Hellenistic epigram—and to Propertius and Tibullus.[19] I would stress that there is a lot of humour to it; it seems in fact something of a *parody* of the attitudes and actions of Augustan Elegy. That is clear in Horace's treatment of the 'exclusus amator' (20 ff.), a crudely funny version in which the excluded lover exhausts himself in masturbation in the doorway instead of romantically singing a serenade.[20] And Horace, once upon a time in thrall to Inachia, now in thrall to Lyciscus and only able to be freed by 'alius ardor', is a slave to love in a very different way from the slaves of Elegy. Elegiac 'seruitium' implies (in amongst everything else) that the poet-lover's love is *inseparable* from the particular beloved: he must be in love all the time because he must be in love with one irresistible

---

[18] Cf. esp. Prop. 1. 1. 25–8: 'et uos, qui sero lapsum reuocatis, amici, | quaerite non sani pectoris auxilia. | fortiter et ferrum saeuos patiemur et ignis, | sit modo libertas quae uelit ira loqui.'
[19] Leo (1900), 9 ff.   [20] Cf. Aristoph. *Eccl.* 707–9; Grassmann (1966), 112–15.

person.[21] Horace must be in love all the time because he must be in love all the time—and it does not much matter with whom. His 'slavery of love' placed side by side with the Elegists' is amusing and cynical. It was meant to be. I think *Epod*. 11 was written in the *late* 30s in humorous response to (most probably) the early elegies of Propertius himself. That is the simplest and most satisfactory explanation of the uniambic tone of the poem, the impression of parody, and the close parallels with, specifically, Propertius.[22]

My conclusion therefore remains that the image of 'seruitium amoris' was *not* a literary *topos* in Latin any more than it was in Greek—until the Elegists, until (it seems) Propertius himself, in the late 30s. But neither was it, so far as we can tell, a very common or fashionable *colloquial* idiom. That is also implied by the *argumenta ex silentio* based on Lucretius and Horace. Even in the early 30s (i.e. the time of Horace's second satire) the association of lovers' humiliation with slavery still appears not to have been an immediately obvious one to make.

However, in Rome just as much as in Athens, the comparison was *potentially* a natural one to make in colloquial speech. Latin was strongly inclined in principle to refer generally to abject or dishonourable behaviour as 'servile' in the same way and for the same reasons as Greek—as I shall be exemplifying shortly. We must assume therefore that the comparison between abject lover and slave *was*, from time to time, colloquially drawn. We do not just have to assume. We have two incidental examples in Plautus and one very interesting one in Cicero.

At Plautus, *Bacchides* 92, Pistoclerus expresses the fact that he has become willing putty in the hands of a courtesan by saying 'mulier tibi me emancupo', 'I make myself over to you'—implying as a slave.[23] In the *Pseudolus* (14) Calidorus, desperately miserable in love, informs us that 'sub Veneris regno uapulo': he is taking a beating—a servile punishment[24]—under the jurisdiction of Venus. Here we see Plautus applying a colloquially metaphorical use of servile language—which elsewhere he applies to other people who have patently

---

[21] Cf. e.g. Prop. 1. 12. 18–20: 'sunt quoque translato gaudia seruitio. | mi neque amare aliam neque ab hac desistere fas est: | Cynthia prima fuit, Cynthia finis erit.' Tib. 1. 1. 55–60, 5. 39–40, etc. (Propertius' and Tibullus' inalienable beloved may of course from time to time change—but that is an eventuality they will not normally at any given time foresee. Prop. 2. 22 incidentally is a very uncharacteristic poem.)

[22] Elegiac romanticism demonstrably provokes Horace's amused criticism and parody in the *Odes*—and in ways which support the above interpretation of *Epod*. 11. In 3. 10 for example we find Horace as an unexpectedly acute, even cynical 'exclusus amator', and the poem depends for its effect on our recollection of woeful Elegiac 'exclusi'. In 1. 33 when Horace reads a lesson in love and life to Albius (Tibullus) he uses servile (Elegiac) terms ('me... grata detinuit compede Myrtale | libertina', 14–16) to make his unelegiac message the more pointed.

[23] Cf. Schulz (1951), 344 ff. on *mancipatio*.   [24] Cf. Wirszubski (1950), 25.

become the tools of others or are cruelly suffering[25]—for once particularly to lovers. But he does not suggest by it any very serious degradation, nor does it occur to him to develop what could be called a regular 'seruitium amoris' figure.

Cicero's example, occurring in his *Paradoxa Stoicorum*, is very striking but usually unremarked, and I quote it in full in a note.[26] In the *Paradoxa*, written in 46 BC, Cicero set out explicitly to *popularize* famous Stoic paradoxes;[27] and seeking popular *exempla* to illustrate the paradox ὅτι μόνος ὁ σοφὸς ἐλεύθερος καὶ πᾶς ἄφρων δοῦλος hit on the idea of instancing the *lover* (conventionally regarded as a fool) as a slave; he was (in effect) the humiliated slave of his beloved.[28] Cicero also therefore applied Latin's natural mode of designating a degraded state and conduct to a *lover's* state and conduct; and the passage is a highly remarkable example of an obvious colloquial *potential* being actually realized—much more remarkable indeed than Plautus'. But its isolation suggests that it is precisely a remarkable example; it is not a reflection of a colloquial cliché. This conclusion is confirmed by consideration of Cicero's purpose. He clearly selected the comparison as a potentially popular, vivid, and available one—but also as a striking and therefore *novel* one. And there is no sign that the comparison became popular subsequently—until the Elegists.

We conclude therefore that the Elegiac 'seruitium amoris' developed out of Latin colloquial speech—not out of Latin literary tradition, not out of Greek literary tradition. But equally it was not a Latin colloquial cliché. The evidence is firmly against any widespread habit of alluding to particularly *lovers'* behaviour (*vis-à-vis* the beloved) as servile—Plautus' examples are isolated and incidental, and Cicero's exceptional. The *general* idiom of labelling all sorts of abject behaviour 'servile' is the source of the Elegiac 'seruitium amoris'. The 'seruitium amoris' is a particular application of this general idiom, a particular application

---

[25] e.g. *Bacch.* 1205, *Poen.* 720.

[26] Cic. *Paradoxa* 36: 'si seruitus sit, sicut est, obedientia fracti animi et abiecti et arbitrio carentis suo, quis neget omnes leues omnes cupidos omnes denique improbos esse seruos? An ille mihi liber cui mulier imperat, cui leges imponit, praescribit iubet uetat quod uidetur, qui nihil imperanti negare potest, nihil recusare audet? poscit, dandum est; uocat, ueniendum; eiicit, abeundum; minatur, extimescendum. ego uero istum non modo seruum sed nequissimum seruum, etiam si in amplissima familia natus sit, appellandum puto.'

[27] *Paradoxa praef.* 3–4 'ego tibi illa ipsa quae uix in gymnasiis et in otio Stoici probant ludens conieci in communes locos. quae quia sunt admirabilia contraque opinionem omnium... tentare uolui possentne proferri in lucem, id est in forum, et ita dici ut probarentur... *etc.*' (the whole preface is interesting).

[28] Cicero's passage can be interestingly contrasted with Hor. *Serm.* 2. 7 which argues (humorously) the same Stoic paradox and similarly instances the behaviour of the romantic (adulterous) lover. But it is the lover's slavery to his passion that is castigated in Horace, not his slavery to a person. The satire draws, like the epigram mentioned above, pp. 86–7, on the old idiom of slavery to emotions and the picture presented is one very different in impact and implications from the 'seruitium amoris' of the Elegists—and Cicero; cf. n. 26 above.

which was at most rare, even in speech—until the late 30s, until (it seems) Propertius.

We must now look more closely at this underlying general idiom. We must acquire some idea of its frequency, its emotive power, the sort of ways in which it was used. Armed with this knowledge we shall be better placed to see the Elegiac 'seruitium amoris' in context, to understand its efflorescence and to feel the kind of immediacy and relevance that a contemporary reader might have felt in it.

It had for instance been common practice to depict the loss (real or apparent) of political freedom in the state, the subjection of the state to dynasts, as 'slavery'. This sort of language is something we are familiar enough with today. It was habitual in the Graeco-Roman world (issues were continually thus described in the Peloponnesian war). But whereas in the modern world 'slavery' tends to be a fairly vacuous propaganda term, in the ancient world where slaves and their condition were an ever present reality, when free populations *were* enslaved in war, it was much more emotive. 'agitur autem liberine uiuamus an mortem obeamus, quae seruituti anteponenda est', says Cicero in the *Philippics* (44 BC: *Phil.* 11. 24). The measure of hyperbole should not obscure from us that to an extent he means what he says and had some justification for it; and his audience would certainly not have considered this empty, bombastic propaganda.

More interestingly we find the loss of very personal freedoms similarly described. When Cicero's liberty of speech was effectively curbed by the Triumvirs, he can find no more emotive and real way to describe his situation than to call it slavery. He writes to Atticus thus (*Att.* 4. 6. 1–2; 56 BC): 'nam tu quidem... nullam habes propriam seruitutem... ego uero, qui si loquor de republica quod oportet, insanus, si quod opus est, seruus, existimor... quo dolore esse debeo.' In 54 BC he writes even more painfully to his brother (*Q. Fr.* 3. 5. 4) about how he has been constrained to defend his enemies: 'angor mi suauissime frater... meum non modo animum sed ne odium quidem esse liberum.' And Matius writes (*Fam.* 11. 28. 3) to Cicero in 44 BC along the same lines but more emphatically and in more detail—he regards his condition as in crucial respects even worse than a slave's: 'o superbiam inauditam alios in facinore [i.e. the death of Julius Caesar] gloriari, aliis ne dolere quidem impunite licere! at haec etiam seruis semper libera fuerunt, ut timerent, gauderent, dolerent suo potius quam alterius arbitrio; quae nunc, ut quidem isti dictitant "libertatis auctores" metu nobis extorquere conantur.'

Many more examples like this could be adduced. But these are striking and typical enough and I shall now simply stress certain points. First, they are all from private and intimate correspondence. Therefore there is no question that the feelings of servility expressed are empty rhetorical hyperbole. On the contrary, Cicero to Atticus and Matius to Cicero are making heartfelt and specific use of a natural mode of speech. This conclusion is reinforced by my second point. The items that Cicero and Matius describe as servile *are* in a way servile. To be unable to speak one's mind, to be compelled to order one's emotions to the whims of others *was* arguably not the condition of a free man—arguably was the condition of a slave, in part even worse than a slave's. Not only therefore do we not have to do with rhetorical hyperbole. We should perhaps not even talk of imagery. Cicero in a way *means* (at the time of writing) that in certain vital respects he was the *seruus* of Caesar, Pompey, and Crassus; Matius *means* that he was the super-*seruus* of the liberators. And to an extent—in certain respects—they were.

Now let me turn to Propertius, the first surviving proclaimer of the developed 'seruitium amoris' and very possibly the first of all. Actually Propertius does not really 'proclaim' the 'seruitium amoris'; he never actually presents or expounds it as a complete or general idea. Rather he cites *instances* of servility forced by love; or in *particular* circumstances, with a *particular* motivation, he will refer to his love as a 'seruitium'. I do not in fact get the impression that Propertius in the *monobiblos* sees himself as either manipulating or creating a self-contained *topos*. Significantly in his opening and more or less programmatic poem he pictures his initial subjection in terms of capture rather than slavery (1. 1. 1–3). The two ideas are as we have seen closely related. But it might seem surprising that Propertius does not take the opportunity to set in unequivocal and programmatic prominence what is arguably his most dramatic image. I return to this point.

The most obvious signs of 'seruitium' in the *monobiblos* are as follows. There are several references to Cynthia as 'domina' in which Propertius (unlike Catullus at 68. 68)[29] clearly does intend *slave*–mistress.[30] On three special occasions he refers with particular contextual motivation to his love as 'seruitium' (1. 4. 4, 5. 19, 12. 18).[31] Then there are the following.

---

[29] See above, p. 90 n. 17. [30] Prop. 1. 1. 21, 3. 17, 4. 2, 7. 6, etc.

[31] In the fourth poem Propertius talks of 'seruitium' in connection with his love, but is making neither a programmatic nor a general statement. Love with Cynthia at this time is humiliating and unpleasant as well as superb; Bassus (his addressee) suggests he try other girls; Propertius in these circumstances both does and does not want to quit. Bassus' advice is therefore at once both compelling and impossible. Hence 'quid cogis?' on the one hand and terms of *slavery* on the other. The paradox and ambivalence of Propertius' immediate situation and attitude is vividly and concretely caught. In the twelfth poem Propertius, despised by Cynthia who is (we take it) raving it up at Baiae, reflects on the possibilities open to some despised lovers to transfer their affections: 'felix...si despectus potuit mutare calores, | sunt quoque translato gaudia...'. But even as he speaks he realizes and acknowledges the impossibility of such a course in *his* case: 'translato gaudia seruitio.' It is scarcely easy for a slave 'transferre' his '*seruitium*'. The impossible dilemma that Cynthia has cast him into *at this time* (loyalty to a faithless and absent girl) is—again—concretely and vividly conveyed by paradoxical use of servile terminology. Finally at 1. 5. 19 very singular inflictions in very singular circumstances are graphically summed up as 'tam graue seruitium': cf. Lyne (1974) [= Ch. 3, this volume].

In poem 1 (after the opening allusion to capture) we find Propertius referring dramatically to a symptom of servile state. He will undergo drastic surgery (27 f.),[32] 'sit modo libertas quae uelit ira loqui': provided he gains the *liberty* to speak what his anger wants. He feels therefore a servile lack of 'libertas loquendi'. It is a topic to which he returns repeatedly. It seems in fact in Propertius' eyes to be the most characteristic part of love's degrading effect. In S. Lilja's words[33] 'The most difficult thing about the slavery of love, for Propertius, is the impossibility of speaking like a free man. His wish *sit modo libertas, quae uelit ira, loqui* (I, 1, 28) is only fulfilled when, alone in a forest, he is able to give vent to his grief—*hic licet occultos proferre impune dolores*, I, 18, 3.' As Propertius admits later in that poem (lines 25 f.), in Cynthia's presence 'omnia consueui timidus perferre superbae | iussa neque aruto facta dolore queri'.

The substance of his taunt to the proud Ponticus fallen into servile love follows the same lines (1. 9. 1–4):

> dicebam tibi uenturos irrisor amores
> nec tibi perpetuo *libera uerba* fore.
> ecce iaces supplexque uenis ad *iura* puellae,
> et tibi nunc quouis *imperat* empta modo.

As a slave Ponticus' speech is not his own and he himself is now in the legal control and under the orders of his girl. Note too Propertius' instructions to the newly fallen Gallus (1. 10. 21 ff.) which include 'neue ⟨cupias⟩ superba loqui' and conclude:

> at quo sis humilis magis et subiectus amori,
> hoc magis effectu saepe fruare bono.
> is poterit felix una remanere puella
> qui numquam uacuo pectore liber erit.

Propertius enjoins the surrender of free speech—and more. Only the lover who surrenders the freedom even of his heart, his emotions ('pectus'), is going to be happy in the Propertian type of love.

These are the most striking instances of love's slavery in the *monobiblos* (there are one or two more signs, to be mentioned below). The Propertian emphasis is on love's degrading effect on liberty of expression. That is clear. Something else should also be clear. *Propertius is drawing attention to feelings or manifestations of servility almost identical to those complained of by Cicero and Matius.* Cicero complained 'si loquor... quod opus est, seruus existimor' i.e. that he might be forced to a servile line of speech; even his spirit and hate were unfree: 'meum non modo animum sed ne odium quidem esse liberum'.

---

[32] On line 27 see too below, pp. 99–100.   [33] Lilja (1965), 83.

Now hear Propertius again: 'sit modo libertas quae uelit ira loqui'; 'nec tibi perpetuo libera uerba fore'. Matius complained 'o superbiam inauditam... aliis ne dolere quidem impunite licere'—a privilege which, he says, even slaves should have. Listen to Propertius: 'hic licet occultos proferre impune dolores' ('here, i.e. in desolate woods and *not* in Cynthia's presence, I may utter my hidden grievances with impunity'); in Cynthia's presence 'omnia consueui timidus perferre superbae | iussa neque arguto facta dolore queri'. The lover, Propertius says, is to be 'numquam uacuo pectore liber': never free, with his emotions his own: that is what Matius complained (in effect) *was* his situation. The similarities are almost uncanny, and more parallels between my quotations from Propertius and those from Cicero and Matius will be noticed. And actually the similarities are quite natural. That really is my point.

The conclusions I draw are clear and straightforward. Cicero and Matius were making heartfelt particular use of a general and natural colloquial idiom. What suggests that Propertius is in essence doing anything else? Cicero felt himself in painful respects to be the 'seruus' of the 'Triumvirs' and Matius felt the 'seruus' of the 'Liberators'. Propertius is implying that he feels *in those same respects* the 'seruus' of Cynthia. He is using a natural Latin mode of expression to describe particular conditions just as Cicero and Matius had done—albeit in different circumstances.

So we should not (after all) use the term imagery or metaphor of Propertius' 'seruitium amoris' without some thought. It seemed not quite appropriate to describe Cicero's and Matius' talk of servile constraint as imagery, for they complained of real conditions that *were*, in a sense, servile. Propertius complains of the same conditions. They are obviously just as potentially servile. Who is to say they are not just as real? His text certainly implies they are. Now of course the circumstances *are* different and it is shameful, shocking, outrageous, even unbelievable, that a mere woman should be able to exercise the same sort of power as autocrats. But that is precisely Propertius' point. That is the sort of paradox we are supposed to confront.[34]

Here is the reason why the 'image' of the 'seruitium amoris' is not programmatically proclaimed or expounded in the *monobiblos*. It is scarcely an image and does not need to be explained; and its programmatic significance is still developing. Propertius talks for the most part in specific terms that everyone would immediately understand, of specific conditions that everyone would understand, indeed would in the years during and after the civil wars rather painfully understand. His language connects directly with natural Latin modes of speech and evokes circumscriptions and humiliations that were to many only too familiar. What was *not* familiar of course was the avowal of such humiliations

---

[34] One of my main disagreements with Copley (1947) is now clear.

being imposed by a woman. That was appalling. Propertius meant to appal. He *therefore* chose this most real and concrete language to describe his humiliation—and not only pictured himself submitting to it but advocating it (ultimately) as part of a way of life.

My thesis is thus that the Elegiac *topos* of 'seruitium amoris' is still evolving in the *monobiblos*[35] and is basically the invention of Propertius. To view lovers' conduct as servile was, until Propertius, potentially natural enough but simply not commonly done. It required a stimulus. Cicero in the *Paradoxa* had one: he needed popularly to illustrate the Stoic slavery paradox and the risibly abject behaviour of lovers came happily to mind. And Propertius? His stimulus was partly or mainly his wish for concretely provocative terms to evoke the 'life of love'. The strategy of the Elegiac 'alternative philosophy' was openly to avow its dishonourable nature. Emotional and intellectual subjection to a woman was something that Lucretius and others had derided ('sub nutu degitur aetas'; above, p. 90); it was something that Propertius and the Elegists were prepared to proclaim. But Propertius hit upon the idea of proclaiming it in a particularly concrete and provocative way: as something servile. From this it was a natural step to express other aspects of the lover's life as servile and indeed love as servility. And so 'seruitium amoris' soon (and very naturally) developed a virtually programmatic function. The lover an avowed slave! Here was a focus for the appalled attentions of conventional sensibilities and a delightfully awful programme for the unconventional to rally to.

The formalization of 'seruitium amoris' happened quickly. By the time of Prop. Book 2 and certainly by Tib. Book 2 it seems a convention, albeit a fresh and challenging one.[36] In Ovid's *Amores* it is a conceit.[37] Even in Tib. Book 1 servile language is used (arguably) more systematically and conventionally than in the *monobiblos*. However, the concentration there is still on a *particular* aspect of 'seruitium', as it had been in the *monobiblos* (though it is a different one); it is not until Book 2 that Tibullus talks of his love generally as 'seruitium'.[38]

It is interesting (incidentally) to notice what this particular emphasis of Tibullus' was in Book 1, and how it works. We can see how he has probably

---

[35] This is another point upon which I radically disagree with Copley (1947), 290.

[36] Cf. e.g. Propertius' epitaph for himself at 2. 13. 35 f. 'qui nunc iacet horrida puluis | unius hic quondam seruus amoris erat'; at 2. 3. 11–32 Tibullus retells the story of Apollo's slavery to Admetus (above, p. 86) as an elaborately *humiliating* slavery; and in 2. 4 he talks explicitly, elaborately, and generally of his love affair with Nemesis as 'seruitium': 'hic mihi seruitium uideo dominamque paratam; | iam mihi, libertas illa paterna, uale ...' etc.

[37] Note e.g. *Amores* 1. 6 where Ovid plays with the idea of *seruitium* in an amusingly literal way; cf. too Lilja (1965), 86–9.

[38] In Book 1 he does not in fact use the word 'seruitium' or any of its cognates in contexts strictly of Elegiac 'seruitium amoris'. (1. 2. 99 'at mihi parce Venus: semper tibi dedita seruit | mens mea' is in line with other expressions of devotion to other gods (cf. Eur. *Bacch.* 366, *Or.* 418, *Ion* 152, Plat. *Apol.* 23c, *Phaedr.* 244e) and very different in effect from an expression of servility to a beloved human woman.)

taken up and developed a hint from Propertius; more interestingly, we can note the *difference* between the two poets' attitudes to love, neatly exemplified in their attitude to 'seruitium'.

Propertius at 1. 18. 8 describes or rather alludes to a specific experience in love in servile terms which we have not yet noted: 'nunc in amore tuo cogor habere notam'. What he is doing is assimilating the humiliating punishment to which Cynthia is subjecting him (and which he *must*, not wants to, accept) to the stigma ('nota') branded on and marking out offending slaves. This sort of mode of speech is actually a favourite one with Cicero,[39] and though much more rhetorical, more plainly metaphorical than the use of servile terms to evoke curtailed liberty of speech, it was still clearly an acute way of expressing an ignominious condition or disgrace. Hence Cicero uses it. Hence too Propertius uses it (also, allusively, at 1. 5. 16;[40] and cf. too 1. 1. 27 discussed below). But he utters the idea only incidentally and does not develop it. It appealed however very much to Tibullus (this is the aspect of 'seruitium' he stresses in Book 1), and in his hands the idea of the lover subject to servile punishments at the hands of love or the mistress is extensively exploited and embellished—and given a very different function from the Propertian one.

In general Tibullus projects an acquiescent, at times effectively masochistic attitude to the degradation of love as a whole, quite unlike Propertius'.[41] And he found this particular motif of servile punishment (possibly taken from Propertius) useful in communicating his unpropertian emphasis. Note for example his words to Marathus 1. 9. 19–22:

> diuitiis captus si quis uiolauit amorem,
> asperaque est illi difficilisque Venus.
> ure meum potius flamma caput et pete ferro
> corpus et intorto uerbere terga seca.

Perverse complaisance! Propertius rarely if ever *invites* humiliation. Note too Tib. 1. 5. 5 f.:

> ure ferum et torque, libeat ne dicere quicquam
> magnificum post haec: horrida uerba doma,

which is patently to be contrasted with Propertius' continual complainings about loss of liberty of speech (above, p. 96). But it is here especially interesting to recall Prop. 1. 1. 27 f.:

---

[39] Cf. *Sull.* 88, *Phil.* 13. 40, etc.   [40] Cf. Lyne (1974), 265 f. [= Ch. 3, p. 35 above].
[41] Tibullus' programmatic poem 1. 1 and Propertius' programmatic 1. 6 and 14 afford an immediate and interesting comparison.

> fortiter et ferrum saeuos patiemur et ignis,
> sit modo libertas quae uelit ira loqui.

Propertius writes with calculated ambiguity. On one level line 27 refers to healing surgery. On another it suggests—I think—servile punishment.[42] Propertius therefore implies his willingness to submit even to servile torture if it would restore his ability to speak freely (a nice, and expressive, paradox). Tibullus invites servile torture to *prevent* such licence, indulged and now deeply regretted. The two lover-poets, though so close in their final message, can indeed be neatly contrasted.

Ultimately, we take it, neither has liberty of tongue, nor any other liberty; and ultimately of course Propertius himself far from unequivocally wants any such thing. He, like Tibullus, ends up advocating the 'life of love', servility and all. But whereas Tibullus proclaims the philosophy with a bland acceptance, Propertius represents himself as arriving at it against the strenuous strivings of his own better inclinations. His more muscular method of coming to the same conclusion makes for a subtler and even perhaps more provocative statement.

A final point. I have said that the inventor of the Elegiac 'seruitium amoris' is probably Propertius himself and that his stimulus towards it lay (basically) in his desire concretely to codify aspects of the life of love. There is another possible stimulus. In the years preceding the publication of Propertius' *monobiblos* a very great and very romantic figure had been, perhaps, publicly arraigned as the slave of his own beloved woman. He had even possibly at times rather gloried in that role. It seems very possible that Propertius and other elegists were attracted to this romantically degraded figure and via the 'seruitium' mutely identified with him. Certainly the propaganda campaign against this figure's erotic 'seruitium' (if it took place) would have helped the 'seruitium amoris' to crystallize; and the memory of the campaign would have maintained the immediacy of the developing literary topos. The romantic figure in mind is Marcus Antonius, slave of Cleopatra—and the main source which might suggest that he was thus known and labelled is the history of Cassius Dio.[43]

---

[42] Cf. Tib. 1. 9. 21 quoted above.

[43] Dio 48. 24. 1, 49. 33. 4–34. 1, 50. 5. 1 οὕτω γάρ που αὐτὸν ἐδεδούλωτο ὥστε...βασιλίς τε αὐτὴ καὶ δέσποινα ὑπ' ἐκείνου καλεῖσθαι. On this question cf. Griffin (1977), 17–26. This theory has of course to assume (plausibly in fact) that such shrill propaganda was considered otiose or inappropriate or even self-defeating in the post-Actium period. Note how Horace in *Epod.* 9 will go as far as but no further than talking of the Roman soldiery as 'emancipatus feminae' (12); while Antony is the unromantically anonymous 'hostis' in line 27.

7

Introduction to C. Day Lewis's Translation of Vergil's *Eclogues* and *Georgics* (1983)

Vergil's model in the *Eclogues* is the Greek poet Theocritus, who wrote bucolic poems (the *Idylls*) in the first half of the third century BC. Vergil acknowledges his master at *Eclogue* 6. 1 ff. and his text is a mass of Theocritean echoes. He invites comparison.

Theocritus was a contemporary of the great Alexandrian poet Callimachus. Callimachus had strong views on literature, which he expressed aggressively; and these views Theocritus shared. It was an 'aesthetic' creed. Against a tradition that expected serious poetry to be morally or politically beneficial, Callimachus insisted simply that it should be pleasant, clever, and above all well written. Instead of (for instance) grand epic, Callimachus offered dainty, donnish exquisiteness in epigram, elegiacs, hymns, and a *miniature* 'epic'.

Theocritus offered among other things his bucolic *Idylls*. In these, shepherds, goatherds and other rustic folk converse and sing in a brilliantly artificial version of a Greek regional dialect (Doric), employing finely turned hexameters, the traditional metre of heroic epic. Paradox is entertainingly evident. His rustics may be characterized with—relative—naturalness. Note, for example, the banter at the opening of *Idyll* 4:

BATTUS: Tell me, Corydon, whose cows are these? Philondas'?
CORYDON: No. Aegon's; he gave me them to graze.
BATTUS: And you, maybe, milk them all on the sly in the evening?
CORYDON: Nay, the old man puts the calves beneath the dams and keeps his eye on me.

Or they may add to the general aura of paradox by displaying notable literacy. Here is a goatherd serenading Amaryllis (3. 40 ff.):

Hippomenes, when he would wed the maid, took apples in his hand and ran his course; and Atalanta saw, and frenzy seized her, and deep in love she plunged. The seer Melampus, too, from Othrys brought the herd to Pylus; and in Bias's arms was laid the gracious mother of wise Alphesiboea. And did not Adonis... etc.

The singer adduces various recherché lovers from mythology as persuasive examples in his own suit. The resources of this goatherd strike one as incongruous. The whole poem is indeed pleasantly incongruous and unreal, in that it transfers the obviously urban institution of the serenade to the countryside: the Amaryllis who receives this elaborate and sophisticated courtesy lives in a cave. So the poem may have its touching aspects, but in its total effect it is amusing. Other Theocritean bucolics have pathetic, even plangent moments. But none is ever disturbingly affecting, for the same basic reason: because of the unreality, the incongruousness of this Theocritean world. Theocritus, we may conclude, writes with the earnest wish to entertain. He entertains a sophisticated, urban audience by creating a world in which quaint rustics may utter chiselled, exquisite, and often learned verses.

Vergil, I have said, invites comparison. The opening of *Eclogue* 6 proclaims not only Theocritean lineage, but Callimachean aesthetics. And the *Eclogues* do in part seem to accord with the theory of the one, and the practice of the other. Vergil's shepherds employ finely turned hexameters. Vergil cannot reproduce the effect of Theocritus' artificial Doric, but he attributes to his shepherds a studied elegance of phrasing and some deftly placed colloquialism which gives a not unTheocritean impression. His shepherds may, like Theocritus', be presented with—relatively speaking—naturalistic characterization. The opening of *Eclogue* 3 is in fact based on Theocritus 4:

MENALCAS: Who owns that flock, Damoetas? Come tell me. Meliboeus?
DAMOETAS: No, it belongs to Aegon: he's just left me in charge.
MENALCAS: Those sheep have nothing but bad luck! So Aegon, he goes off
  To keep Neaera warm, for fear she prefers me
  To him, while a hired hand milks them twice an hour—
  Milks the ewes all dry, not a drop left for the lambs.

Note too the characterization at the start of *Eclogue* 5 where the astute Mopsus politely gets his way over the venue for the exchange of songs. And, on the other hand, Vergil's shepherds, like Theocritus', display sudden and surprising education. In *Eclogue* 3. 40 ff. Menalcas may fumble for the name of the fourth-century astronomer and scholar Eudoxus, but he knows about him and what he did—and he can name the third-century Alexandrian astronomer Conon. Vergil's shepherds, like Theocritus', sing plangent songs; for example Damon at 8. 37–42, 58–60:

> A child you were when I first beheld you—
>   our orchard fruit was chilled with dew—
> You and your mother both apple-gathering:
>   just twelve I was, but I took charge of you.
> On tiptoe reaching the laden branches,
>   one glance I gave you, and utterly
> My heart was ravished, my reason banished—
>   . . . .

> Farewell, O
> my woods. I'll hurl me into the sea
> From yonder peak. This last song for Nysa—

But again that fails to affect us disturbingly. For one thing, Vergil has carefully distanced it, it is an avowed fiction: Damon is *comfortably* (line 16) singing a temporarily adopted *part*. For another thing, Vergil's world, like Theocritus' world, may well seem basically unreal. There are indeed factors which increase the unreality of Vergil's world in comparison with Theocritus'. His landscape is less particularized than Theocritus'; and his shepherds have quaint Greek names, largely adopted from Theocritus himself. Theocritus' world is pretty remote from real Sicily or Cos; Vergil's Theocritean world is even more remote—it might be argued—from any contemporary Roman reality.

But we should begin at the beginning. *Eclogue* 1 is a rather different sort of poem from 3 and 8. Here are the first five lines:

> Tityrus, here you loll, your slim reed-pipe serenading
> The woodland spirit beneath a spread of sheltering beech,
> While I must leave my home place, the fields so dear to me.
> I'm driven from my home place: but you can take it easy
> In shade and teach the woods to repeat 'Fair Amaryllis'.

Let us try to imagine the reaction of an educated contemporary reader. He unrolls the book, and in the first two lines he may be supposed instantly to spot what Vergil is doing: he is producing a Latin imitation of Theocritean pastoral. An elegant treat is in store.

But line 3 may give him pause. Why is a Theocritean shepherd having to quit his country, native place, *patria* ('home place' in Day Lewis's translation)? This sort of dislocation is unheard of in Theocritus. It smacks of present Roman reality. And in the following lines a number of further allusions—to a god, to disruption in the country, to exemption, to Rome (the allusions are more specific in the Latin than in Day Lewis's English)—become insistent. While Latinizing Theocritus, Vergil is also referring to contemporary politics and events: to the land confiscations in Italy around the year 41 BC supervised by Octavian and designed to settle discharged soldiers.

By line 20 or so our contemporary reader may in fact have completely revised his assessment of what Vergil is doing: Vergil, he will think, is *using* Theocritean shepherds to mask contemporary events and issues; he is writing an allegory. Meliboeus stands for a dispossessed farmer, Tityrus stands for a farmer who has sought and won reprieve from dispossession at Rome; the god, subsequently referred to more precisely as a 'young man' ('young prince' in Day Lewis), is Octavian, who granted the reprieve. The allegory seems to work; the masks seem only a slight disguise. Indeed, when Tityrus refers to Rome, where the historical Octavian resided, rather than to a place suited to the world in which a Tityrus and a Meliboeus reside, the mask may even seem to slip.

And *Eclogue* 1 has of course been taken as an allegory by a legion of readers. The ancient commentary of Servius even sees Tityrus as standing for Vergil himself, landowner at Mantua. But the poem cannot simply be called an allegory. It is something more confusing and ambiguous than that.

The more a character is individualized, the less easy it is to say that he simply 'stands for' someone or something else. He demands attention in his own right. Thus it is with Tityrus. Tityrus turns out to be a slave, an old slave; after living with the spendthrift Galatea, he has found himself a sensible girl, Amaryllis; in consequence he has been able to save up enough money to go to the city to purchase his freedom from his servile status; he now resides on a poor and carefully described holding; he proceeds to display a certain insensitivity towards the plight of Meliboeus... This is an individualized Tityrus, who demands attention as Tityrus and is not easily seen merely or mainly as a cipher for a typical Italian freeholding farmer—or for Vergil.

And consider what happens at lines 26 ff.[1] At this stage the reader thinks he is reading an allegory, an allegory like this: shepherd Meliboeus forced to leave his 'native place' = an evicted farmer; shepherd Tityrus who is reprieved from a similar fate by a 'god' (in Rome it seems) = a farmer who has sought and found exemption from a powerful patron at the capital city. The reader has no reason to expect that the poem will not continue along the same lines. And it is a critical moment. Tityrus' answer to Meliboeus' interesting question in line 18, 'But tell me about that god of yours, my friend: who is he?', is deflected by the memories it arouses of Rome (lines 19–25). But when Meliboeus then asks 'What was the grand cause of your setting eyes on Rome, then?', Tityrus must surely be expected to get back to the point. He must be expected to answer 'To seek and appeal to the god'—and then get on to the interesting information about who this god is and why he reprieved him. Giving that sort of answer, Tityrus will continue to be an allegory for the reprieved farmer, his appeal to his god standing for the process of a farmer's appeal to Octavian.

It doesn't happen. The reader finds the surprising answer of lines 27 ff. Tityrus supplies a completely unexpected, unpredicted, and unpredictable reason for his visit to Rome, which is then amplified. Tityrus the *slave* went to Rome to be manumitted, to be freed from servile status. Not until line 45 does he include what seems to be an oblique reference to the expected topic: reprieve from confiscation. What is going on?

---

[1] It could not be claimed that my interpretation of these lines would command universal assent. Contrast the view of R. D. Williams in his note on line 27, Williams (1979), and that of Coleman (1977), 82.

The details of manumission and servile 'savings' (the Latin word is the prosaic *peculium*) seem Roman. But they do not help the Roman allegory. I have already remarked that the sheer detail helps Tityrus demand attention as Tityrus. This can now be put more particularly. Tityrus' answer is in effect an assertion of his fictional and independent status; it diminishes, indeed temporarily obscures, the possibility of reading him as an allegory for a type in contemporary Roman history. If that sounds paradoxical, it will only do so momentarily.

For where do we find slave shepherds? An answer to that would of course be: on real contemporary Roman estates. But where do we find slave shepherds with a name like Tityrus? Answer: in at least one *Idyll* of Theocritus (*Idyll* 5). And where we do not find slave shepherds is in possession of farms liable to confiscation. I argue therefore that when Vergil starts to stress and amplify servile status, motives, and adventures in his Greek named Tityrus, it is a fictional, indeed Theocritean, figure that he is elaborating, even though he may let Roman institutions affect some of that elaboration. He is certainly making the equation 'Tityrus = Roman freeholder' more and more difficult. So just at the point where we expect the easy allegory to continue and become interesting, Tityrus answers in a way which resists allegory and asserts his status as an independent fictional character.

Various puzzled questions are prompted. Why *is* Tityrus going to Rome? Is it to seek reprieve from confiscation, or manumission from slavery? (Which is the 'reality'?) Is the poem an allegory of contemporary events, or an entertaining fiction based on (Theocritean) slave shepherds? The simple answer is that there is no real resolution. The poem is oscillating (and continues to oscillate) between these alternatives, and doesn't commit itself. Though we may want to find *one* reality and *a* type of poem, we shall not be able to. Vergil will not allow us to reduce the poem in this satisfying way. He is writing *ambiguously*, showing in embryo a technique which he will perfect in the *Aeneid*. And the technique is symptomatic of an ambiguous attitude to the nature and function of his art which Vergil continues to maintain throughout his life. Vergil wants to probe the moral and political issues of his day, but declines to tie his poetry to such a tedious and perhaps imprudent thing as a poetical history or allegory. Vergil the moralist continues to love fancy and beauty, and sees the propagation of these qualities as a valid function of art.

Eclogue 9 alludes to the land confiscations in much the same way as *Eclogue* 1 and partners that poem. But it is more pessimistic—and has a sharper edge. In 1 the plight of Meliboeus is matched by the felicity of Tityrus. In 9 the emphasis is on a failed appeal by the singer Menalcas, and on Moeris' dispossession. Moeris quotes what seems to be that failed appeal (lines

27–9), a mordant gesture;[2] and he and Lycidas quote other fragments of Menalcas' songs.[3] Very interestingly the subject matter of the fragments invites us to see Vergil behind the mask of Menalcas.[4] Obviously therefore we look at these fragments with care. We find one in which Menalcas had once upon a time expressed confidence in a future under the star of the deified Julius Caesar. That in the present sad context, when Caesar's heir holds sway in Italy, must also be considered mordant. The fragments of song do, I say, invite us to see Vergil behind the mask of Menalcas. But they do not insist. And in general the context obscures and confuses the political and personal comment. Vergil oscillates between Italian, even Mantuan allusions and a pastoral, Theocritean fiction.

In *Eclogue* 5 Mopsus laments and celebrates a dead Daphnis while Menalcas sings of his apotheosis. In content and atmosphere the poem is a fair way from the dictator Julius Caesar, his assassination and supposed deification. And yet it is hard not to think of the one behind the other. Refusing to be tied down to allegory, the poem will not allow a reader to leave with a pure fiction. It is the familiar kind of ambiguous utterance. In the fantastic prophecy of *Eclogue* 4, a 'somewhat grander theme' than the other pastorals, there is, maybe, a celebration of a dynastic political marriage and its hoped for, hopeful offspring. But the extraordinary detail of the poem refuses to be reduced to any simply political allegory. Christian interpreters read in it a prophecy of the coming of Christ. Their reaction was not unjustified. The poem demonstrably draws material from Eastern 'saviour' stories, and the scope of its detail and fantasy seems clearly designed to be suggestive; to admit, not exclude, different ranges of interpretation. The poem is exuberant, imaginative, not as deadly serious as some take it, and above all not to be pinned down.

Eclogues 2, 3, 7, 8 are more purely Theocritean and pastoral than the other poems—though *Eclogue* 2 in particular forbids us to leave a statement like that unqualified. It is based in the main on Theocritus' *Idyll* 11. In the introduction to that poem, Theocritus told a poet–doctor Nicias that the only remedy for love was song. He cited the example of the Cyclops Polyphemus hopelessly in love with the sea-nymph Galatea, who through singing found solace and cure. Most of the poem is a quotation of the Cyclops' song. A two

---

[2] Many scholars do not want to associate the appeal in lines 27–9 with the failed appeal referred to in line 10. It seems to them *too* tactless. But they have to go into contortions to avoid the inference. Cf. Wilkinson (1969), 31, Williams (1968), 312 ff., esp. 322 ff.

[3] Lines 23–5, 27–9, 39–43, 46–50 are all *quotations* of Menalcas' songs. Day Lewis's translation is misleading in this respect.

[4] In particular lines 19–20 refer to *Eclogue* 5. 40, and lines 46–50 seem an allusion to Menalcas' song in *Eclogue* 5. 56 ff. At 5. 86–7 Menalcas virtually identifies himself as Vergil.

line epilogue confirms the success of the cure: 'Thus did Polyphemus shepherd his love with song, and found more ease than if he had spent gold.'

Vergil's *Eclogue* presents some striking modifications. Consider first the protagonists. The pathos of Theocritus' poem is balanced by a basic humour and incongruity: the yearning of a monstrous one-eyed pastoral Cyclops for a nymph who lives in the sea amuses rather than disturbs. Vergil's poem is less easily amusing. He assigns the passion of love to a shepherd far nearer reality than Polyphemus; and the love-object Alexis, 'his master's favourite', is even nearer: Vergil's language clearly suggests (more clearly than Day Lewis's translation) that he is a slave fancy-boy of recognizable Roman type. Secondly, we note that there is no clear suggestion that Corydon finds any help in his outpouring of song as Polyphemus did. No introduction assures us that it will be the case; and no epilogue confirms Corydon's unconvincing bravado in the last line—and line 5, 'with fruitless zeal' (misleadingly translated by Day Lewis as 'alone with his futile passion'), seems to suggest that the song was not efficacious in any way. Corydon's song is a song of unrequited love that achieves nothing—other than to reveal the lamentable state of mind of the singer. And finally we may note that Vergil has changed the love from heterosexual to homosexual.

The first and second of these modifications work to make the poem more affecting, more 'serious'. Somewhat in the manner of *Eclogues* 1 and 9, we can see Vergil Latinizing Theocritus, but letting his Latinized Theocritus attend to more serious issues more seriously than we should expect of such a genre. In 1 and 9 it was politics and dispossession, here it is the cruel, disruptive effects of passionate love—and the brand of passionate love (homosexual) which was, we can be pretty sure, of more acute concern to Vergil himself. The disruptive power of passionate love is a theme that haunts Vergil throughout his life (cf. below p. 111). But we may see the same ambiguity as in 1 and 9. Is the poem a paradigm of what violent love can do to real people—or a plangent, pastoral entertainment? The Theocritean atmosphere and echoes disallow complete commitment to the first description. The poem oscillates, even as we look at it. The nature of our reaction depends, it might be said, on whether we respond more powerfully to the relation or to the irrelation to Theocritus. Vergil's ambiguous mode is more artfully handled here than in 1 and 9.

Vergil's decision to extend the range of pastoral, giving to it the possibility of moral and political commitment, may have been cued by Theocritus himself. In *Idyll* 7 Theocritus too plays with allegory, though to deal with nothing more serious than literature. One figure in the *Idyll* (Simichidas) seems to stand for Theocritus himself and another (Lycidas) for another poet on whose identity scholars cannot agree; and at one point (lines 43 ff.) Lycidas speaks in terms which very obviously allude to literary controversies of

Theocritus' day. Vergil, as well as building on this hint and giving pastoral more serious commitment, used it as Theocritus did to mask literary controversy or instruction. Both *Eclogues* 6 and 10 seem to be poems of this type. Scholars are even more divided in their interpretations of these poems than they are of Theocritus' *Idyll* 7; and with the loss of so much contemporary literature, in particular of the works of Cornelius Gallus (for whom, see note on *Eclogue* 6. 64), certainty is impossible. I give my own views briefly.

At the start of *Eclogue* 6 Vergil declines to write laudatory epic in honour of Varus. His poem then stages the capture of Silenus by two boys and a nymph, and lists the songs Silenus then sang to them. Now besides his rustic (and Dionysiac) associations, Silenus had been given a role in philosophical tradition as someone who had revealed under restraint great wisdom and truth. All the subjects of which he sings in *Eclogue* 6 suit hexameter verse; in particular, many suit epyllion, the miniature 'epic' that poets of Callimachean persuasion evolved in the place of the traditional grand genre. I think Vergil is giving the wise old Silenus a new 'philosophical' function: to reveal the proper subjects of the 'epic' poet. The poem thus continues and amplifies the refusal to write a conventional epic with which Vergil began the poem. Vergil as a Theocritean–Callimachean poet cannot write epic, but through Silenus, a figure who doesn't jar in a pastoral context and who has a reputation for wise revelation, he could show the sort of thing a modern 'epic' poet would write. And it wouldn't be laudatory, 'historical', epic, but learned didactic, exquisite epyllions on romantic and grotesque themes—that sort of thing. Vergil can even refer to a contemporary example, neatly complimenting Gallus in the process (64–73). So (the underlying reasoning goes) even if Vergil were not a pastoral poet but a modern epicist, he still would not be able to oblige with the sort of thing that Varus wants.

In *Eclogue* 10 Vergil, advocate of ordered emotions (see e.g. *Eclogue* 2), is taking issue with Gallus the elegiac love poet, *soi-disant* slave of passion. In many respects the poem is, I think, a fun-poking parody. Gallus was complimented in 6; now with friendly humour he is taken to task. Vergil casts him in the role of Daphnis who died tragically and heroically of love (see Thyrsis' song in Theocritus' *Idyll* 1). Why? Because as an Elegist Gallus would often describe himself as 'dying of love' in the emotional, colloquial, metaphorical sense of that phrase; and it amused Vergil to take him at his word, to depict him as *literally* dying in this spectacular way. Similarly it amused him to have rustic figures like Pan earnestly counselling *modus*, 'due measure', to the incapacitated romantic poet who would characteristically scorn such a concept. It amused him too to fit fragments of Gallus' own verse to the moribund *Eclogue* Gallus. Many more items of parody and fun-poking can be suggested; but they are of course conjectural. We would need a text of Gallus himself fully to understand the friendly confrontation that takes place in the *Eclogue* between the passionate romantic and the cool Epicurean, between the elegist Gallus and the pastoral poet Vergil.

In the *Georgics* Vergil has many sources and influences, but the most signal is an archaic Greek poet. Having established himself as the Roman Theocritus, Vergil now aspires to be the Roman Hesiod. Hesiod's *Works and Days*, a medley of moral and religious advice and practical instruction on agriculture and other subjects, is the acknowledged model of the *Georgics*.

But the *Georgics* is even more different from its main model than the *Eclogues*. Vergil confines his practical advice to farming. Vergil is also little interested in the practicality of his practical advice. Seneca's judgement was that he 'wished not to teach farmers, but to delight readers' (*Epistles* 86. 15). This statement is largely true—but not the whole truth.

The glaring selectivity in what is treated (for example a whole book on bees, but no instruction on other important small animals like the chicken) suggests practical usefulness was not a primary aim. On the other hand Hesiod too had been selective. More significant is how out of date, even idealized, are the poem's presuppositions. A contemporary Roman farmer is unlikely to have built his own plough—and might in any case have found Vergil's impressionistic instructions unhelpful. And in general the smallholder that the *Georgics* apparently addresses was a vanishing figure. Italian agriculture was now a matter of great estates—worked by slaves. Slaves are not referred to at all in the *Georgics*. For a realistic and useful agricultural handbook Roman landowners could turn to the almost contemporary prose treatise of Varro (*Res Rusticae*). Vergil gives selective and often unhelpful advice to a type of farmer who was increasingly an irrelevance in contemporary Italy. Why?

'To delight readers', says Seneca. I shall revert to that statement. The *Georgics* has another function that must be discussed first. Like Hesiod's poem, Vergil's is a *moral* and *religious* didactic.

Vergil writes against the background of another round of civil wars—wars that threaten, happen, and then find their conclusion even as he writes. In reaction to the chaos and destruction of war, Vergil argues for the virtues of work, piety, and peace. He does so through the figure, we could say through the *metaphor*, of the farmer.

The small, independent farmer may have been a vanishing figure, but he was an important one for Roman sensibility. In the Roman mind rural life and the moral life were easily identified. In addition there was a feeling that the original, the *true* Italian way of life (when things were so much better) was agricultural. There was even a temptation to talk of the affinity of rural life to the Golden Age. The practical Varro himself can be found prey to this sort of thinking. The farmer, the traditional and perhaps rosily viewed smallholding farmer, was thus an emotive figure for Romans, a figure in whom reality merged with idealism and morality. If Vergil wanted to argue for general principles of morality and religion in a specific instance, the way of the farmer was an obvious choice, a ready enough 'metaphor'. The farmer exhibited or should exhibit the desired virtues directly and sympathetically. His specific actions (ploughing, sowing, planting, etc.) lent themselves to more detailed metaphors. Exhorting the Italian farmer to a good and successful life, Vergil could write a poem that was morally and religiously didactic in a more general and consistent way than Hesiod's didactic had ever been.

It is important to note that the *Georgics* does not maintain a consistent mood, or even a consistent message, throughout its four books. I am inclined to think that this reflects at least in part a development in Vergil's views or at least his emphases, as the circumstances around him changed during the eventful years of the poem's composition. The changes may be noted in summary. At the same time I can indicate how the 'metaphor' works.

In the first book Vergil describes Jove's Dispensation to man—tough but just (lines 121 ff.) The book as a whole is tough in tone. It insists, given this dispensation, on the constant need for work, piety, order. In terms of the poem, the farmer must for instance plough twice (line 48), respect the laws imposed by Nature on the soil (lines 60 ff.), venerate the gods (line 338), observe the divinely and beneficently given weather signs (line 352), and so on. We note that Vergil frequently uses military imagery of the farmer's occupation (as at line 160, 'I'll tell you too the armoury of the tough countryman'). We may infer, by paradox, Vergil's belief that the farmer's existence is an embodiment of the idea of 'swords into ploughshares': in other words, the moral life is peaceful. The imagery is also a warning. The farmer—man—does have violent instincts and must channel them, in peaceful work. But what does all this work, order, and piety lead to? To life, and peace. That is the reward. But the emphasis of this insistent book is negative. If we *neglect* these principles, we shall have chaos, war, and death. That is the implication of the tremendous description that concludes the book: the tumultuous reaction to the assassination of Caesar. Civil war, is presented as the alternative to the moral life. When we appreciate quite how appalling—and looming—the price of neglect is, we may appreciate why Vergil makes the tone of his first book so tough and insistent.

Book 2 is happier and more enticing. Vergil instructs on trees, with particular attention to that very warming tree, the vine. The need for the farmer to work is not forgotten, but the emphasis is on the fruitfulness and responsiveness of nature, especially Italian nature: the moral life (to interpret the 'metaphor') may be full and happy as well as peaceful. Vergil now allows himself to look more positively at the life he counsels. There is no radical shift of view here, just of emphasis. Set pieces like the praise of Italy (lines 136–76) and, in particular, the final 'praise of country life' (lines 458–542) confirm and elaborate this positive approach.

The third book attends to horses, cattle, sheep, and goats. The atmosphere is again gloomier. The most striking instruction to the farmer comes at lines 209 ff.: keeping horses and cattle away from females is the most efficacious method of reinforcing their strength, for work, war or whatever. This leads into a great set piece on the futile and destructive lengths to which the passion of sex will drive all creatures, mankind among them. Now Vergil's teaching here is very different from the brief and practical farm instruction which we find in Varro (2. 1. 18; 5. 12; cf. Aristotle, *History of Animals* 6. 21) to separate male animals from females for a short while before mating—which is simply designed to ensure the success of that mating. The set piece that then develops is derived, clearly, from Aristotle's great description of the excitement that sexual passion induces in animals (*History of Animals* 6. 18); but again it is very different in scope and impact. For it is not so much a *description* as a *denunciation*, and as such clearly and significantly recalls Lucretius' great denunciation of irrational sexual passion in mankind at the end of *De Rerum Natura* Book 4. In terms of practical agricultural didacticism the passage does not make much sense, or not a sense that one can scrutinize. It makes a great deal of sense when we start to interpret the 'metaphor'. Once more Vergil comes out against unreasoned passion. The message recalls *Eclogue* 2 (above p. 107), though here the voice is more strident and the context more significant. Passion, says Vergil, must be eliminated for the benefit of the peaceful and moral life. It is a thought that will engage him again.

The set piece that concludes Book 3 is a plague that devastates all animal life. This introduces a radical change of opinion—or it suggests a new perspective which radically affects the significance of what has been said so far. Hitherto it has been stated or implied that 'the farmer', working with the gods, is in charge of his destiny. Jove's Dispensation is tough, but *if* the farmer commits himself to work, piety, order, reason, then his life will be peaceful, productive, and indeed happy. Now it is revealed that there *are* occasions when this simply is not true. A cataclysm, a hellish (lines 551–2) plague may destroy the world of the farmer, for all his piety and work. Details like those of an animal dying when offered as sacrifice (lines 486 ff.) and of the ox collapsing harnessed to the plough, press the message ironically home. And of course we have to admit its truth. Sometimes piety and work are of no avail to the farmer. And the 'metaphor' contains a more general truth—for which readers who had recently witnessed a civil war might not find it difficult to supply an example. In the face of, say, rampant civil war and revolution, individual piety and effort is pretty powerless. 'From hell's black country came the pale Tisiphone', says Vergil. So what is man to do?

Book 4 attends to bees and sees a complete change of focus. After an initial series of instructions to the beekeeper, containing some more or less clear allegories, there is an interlude: the old Corycian with his garden (lines 116–48). Then a systematic description of bee society develops—and a systematic allegory. The *society* of bees clearly stands for a human *society* with many admirable qualities, especially to Roman eyes: the 'citizens' exhibit an absolute patriotism, a complete concord, total subordination of self to the common good, and so on. In fact when we realize quite how exactly these virtuous bees are virtuous in traditionally Roman civic ways, we must be tempted to conclude that Vergil's allegory stands for an ideal Roman society, a model for a Roman society (the bees are even called *Quirites*, Roman citizens, at line 201). And this is in a way true. But we should notice straightaway that this ideal state, its unity, justice, and order, is absolutely dependent on a *monarch*, whom the 'citizens' respect with a very unRoman and indeed more than oriental devotion (lines 210 ff.).

Vergil also presents his bee society as emphatically *passionless* (lines 197 ff.), a belief about bees' reproduction at least as old as Aristotle (*History of Animals* 5. 21). His model for a state therefore takes account of the great warning in *Georgics* 3. He points out too that the society, as opposed to the individual bees, is immortal (lines 206 ff.). We translate the metaphor: a state unlike its individual members may indeed presume to possess resilience, continuity, if not immortality. But more particularly and strikingly Vergil presents the bee society as something which can be *re-created* even after a *plague* has wiped it out: this is the invention of Aristaeus, whose story concludes the book. Again we perceive a response to *Georgics* 3. Again we can see how the metaphor might be translated, how a ruler and state might make an analogous claim. War or revolution may wipe out citizens, but the state may be regenerated: by a saviour, or a man of destiny. It might help if the man had divine parentage: like Aristaeus, like Octavian...

We can start to tie up the moral and political message of Book 4. A huge shift in focus has indeed taken place; and we can explain it. The individual farmer, master of his fate (Books 1–3), has been replaced by the image of a society in which the surrender of individuality is the vital prerequisite of a common efficiency. But we remember that at the end of Book 3 Vergil reached an *impasse*. A disaster may happen which upsets the best efforts of the farmer: there are calamities which any amount of individual morality and piety cannot prevent or cope with. We think, as I am sure Vergil was thinking, of civil war. And since the individual is ultimately so weak, Vergil has concluded, it seems, that it is best for the individual to think and work as part of a greater entity which subsumes his mere individuality, and which is powerful where he is weak. Hence the shift of focus. Vergil holds out for man a corporate solution: the model state. The model state should be immune to calamities like civil war. In any case, it, unlike individuals, can survive catastrophe: given a saviour, it can be regenerated. In Book 4 Vergil shows in allegorical form (Aristaeus and the regeneration of the bees) the need for, and action of, such a saviour. He also shows the model for the efficient, immortal state which should not again need the saviour: the allegorical society of bees. Much of the society is familiar, for it is based on traditional Roman views and traditional modes of thinking, which had been abandoned or forgotten. But it has the added characteristic Vergilian emphasis on passionlessness. And it has a 'king'. That is a modification which Vergil seems to think necessary in the new age. Certainly the new model state which was actually formed—was in the process of being formed even as Vergil wrote—adapted to it: there was a *princeps*.

I have talked of 'model' and 'ideal'. The society pictured in the society of the bees may not sound very attractive. It is not I think meant to. Vergil is offering us a hard choice, not glossing the sacrifices involved. We may note that not only does this society lack passion, it lacks art.[5] Bees are traditionally associated with poetry. Vergil's bees have no such association. It is a suggestive silence. The model state, for its efficiency and salvation, must be prepared to exclude even the Muses. Anchises is going to say something closely related to that in *Aeneid* 6. What Vergil is doing is showing the options available to man, given the state of the world and human nature. He suggests man has a choice—an exclusive choice—between ordered corporate peace and the dangerous vulnerability of individuality. The choice, and the difficulty of it, strikes us most acutely in the concluding Aristaeus episode, which involves the story of Orpheus. Aristaeus' regeneration of the bees is, as I have already implied, in some sense allegorical of the regeneration of the Roman state by the saviour Octavian, happening in and after the Battle of Actium. Vergil pictures the process as unpleasant but successful. He contrasts it with the intensely sympathetic story of the great singer and lover Orpheus, who so nearly succeeds in his attempt to regain Eurydice, but ultimately fails and dies. Orpheus may be seen to typify what the rising model state must exclude, what it *costs*: passion, individuality, art; the right to heroic self-indulgent failure, the right to Love and Death. Now of course it is Orpheus who attracts us, who commands our sympathy, and we may opt for him—for the precarious vulnerability of individuality, for the right to failure, Love, and Death. Or we may prefer to share in the endless Life of a successful, productive, efficient

---

[5] On this and other aspects of the Aristaeus story and *Georgics* 4 see Griffin (1979), 61–80.

state. The choice (Vergil implies) is open. Perhaps he shows which way his head if not his heart inclines, but his position is essentially ambiguous. The necessity for this choice and the problems it raises continue to preoccupy Vergil throughout the *Aeneid*.

What I have done in the above summary is reduce the *Georgics* to a moral and political metaphor, to an allegory. But, as always, Vergil refuses to be reduced. Like the *Eclogues*, the *Georgics* suggests allegories—and yet will not be confined or committed to them. The poem also pleases, as Seneca stressed. Many parts of the poem in fact *only* please, resisting attempts to 'interpret' them and making us a little unsure in consequence of the interpretations we have glibly foisted on other apparently amenable sections. Vergil the Hesiodic moral poet is still also Vergil the entertaining, aesthetic Callimachean.

The largest pleasure of the *Georgics* is the pleasure to be had simply from *descriptive* poetry:[6] often akin to the pleasure that is derived from landscape painting. I may see in the description of vines and the rural life in Book 2 a picture of the happiness that the moral life can bring. I also see a fine description, a beautiful picture, much of which resists and is ruined by 'interpretation'. I may see in the instructions on the management of sheep and goats in Book 3 a further insistence on the need to work, and so on. But the dominant and most important impression left by, say, the passage on Libyan and Scythian shepherds in lines 339–82 is of vivid poetical pictures constructed out of challengingly unpoetic material. The point need not be laboured. There is always this aspect, this *aesthetic* aspect, to the *Georgics*, and for a good deal of the time there is only this aspect—for which we are truly grateful. And, to conclude, I would return again to the Aristaeus story at the end of *Georgics* 4. It epitomizes the ambiguity of Vergilian art. I have talked of its political and moral significance: I have interpreted it. That significance is there. But the whole episode is also, irreducibly, a devious and beautiful mythical epyllion in the tradition of Callimachus: more aesthetically entertaining than (for example) any of the *Eclogues*.

---

[6] This aspect of the *Georgics* is admirably emphasized and illustrated by Wilkinson (1969).

8

Vergil and the Politics of War (1983)

The Romans had various ways of justifying their imperial aims and methods, some high-minded, some less so.[1] We find in particular that they could give honourable and satisfying explanations of their aims and methods in war. Here for example is Cicero:

quare suscipienda quidem bella sunt ob eam causam, ut sine iniuria in pace uiuatur; parta autem uictoria conseruandi ii, qui non crudeles in bello, non immanes fuerunt, ut maiores nostri Tusculanos, Aequos... in ciuitatem etiam acceperunt, at Carthaginem... funditus sustulerunt... mea quidem sententia paci, quae nihil habitura sit insidiarum, semper est consulendum. et cum iis, quos ui deuiceris, consulendum est, tum ii qui armis positis ad imperatorum fidem confugient, quamuis murum aries percusserit, recipiendi. (*Off.* 1. 35)

Cicero makes basically two points: (1) the aim of Roman war is peace and security; (2) the proper policy towards vanquished peoples is, where possible, magnanimity and mercy. These keynotes are easy to parallel.[2] Here is a passage later in the *De Officiis* (1. 62):

sed ea animi elatio, quae cernitur in periculis et laboribus, si iustitia uacat pugnatque non pro salute communi, sed pro suis commodis, in uitio est; non modo enim id uirtutis non est, sed est potius immanitatis omnem humanitatem repellentis. itaque probe definitur a Stoicis fortitudo, cum eam uirtutem esse dicunt propugnantem pro aequitate.

Note, among other things, *pro salute communi*. Rome's supposed clemency towards her enemies was virtually proverbial—among Romans (Cato *ap.* Gell. 6. 3. 52, Liv. 33. 12. 7, Caes. *B. G.* 2. 14, etc.); Sallust's reference to Rome's traditional magnanimity in victory (*Cat.* 12. 4) also implies that the aim of

---

Much has of course been written on most of the topics dealt with in this paper, and many articles and books are referred to in the notes. A high proportion of the articles are disappointing; one that is not and which I would single out for special mention is Williams (1967), 29–41. Messrs P. G. McC. Brown and D. P. Fowler have read and criticized the present paper. My thanks to them. It is not to be assumed they agree with it all.

[1] See the useful paper of Brunt (1978).
[2] Cf. too Brunt (1978), esp. 178 ff. and Norden on *Aen.* 6. 847–53. Be it noted, however, that we find some curious interpretations of what constituted 'mercy', and of what 'peace and security as the aim of war' involved or allowed. This is amply documented by Brunt.

war was 'peace':

neque uictis quicquam praeter iniuriae licentiam eripiebant [sc. maiores].

Let us turn now to Augustus. Long before he catalogues his imperial victories and gains in the *Res Gestae* (26–33, 'omnium prouinciarum populi Romani, quibus finitimae fuerunt gentes quae non parerent imperio nostro, fines auxi...'), he records his policy of imperial mercy towards the defeated (3):

externas gentes, quibus tuto ignosci potuit, conseruare quam excidere malui;

just previously to that he celebrates his slightly more ambiguous policy of mercy towards his defeated enemies in the civil wars:[3]

uictorque omnibus ueniam petentibus ciuibus peperci.

And, again long before that catalogue of imperial victories, he focuses on the peace that is to be attributed to those victories; proudly he records the solemn, ritual celebrations of his peace (13):

Ianum Quirinum, quem clausum esse maiores nostri uoluerunt, cum per totum imperium populi Romani terra marique esset parta uictoriis pax... ter me principe senatus claudendum esse censuit.

Horace, his poet laureate, hymns that same peace and the same ritual in his final Ode (4. 15. 4 ff.): 'tua, Caesar, aetas... uacuum duellis | Ianum Quirini clausit', etc.). And lines 49 ff. of Horace's *Carmen Saeculare* are perhaps particularly notable:

> quaeque uos bubus ueneratur albis
> clarus Anchisae Venerisque sanguis,
> impetret, bellante prior, iacentem
>   lenis in hostem.
> iam mari terraque manus potentis
> Medus Albanasque timet securis,
> iam Scythae responsa petunt superbi
>   nuper et Indi.

Military supremacy, magnanimity to defeated foes, peace and security *because* of military supremacy: Horace lyricizes the achievements of his patron. Horace reminds us of Cicero too, and the others—because Augustus phrased his achievements in traditional, idealizing ways.

The above passages suggest, then, certain ways in which Roman imperialists in idealizing mood liked to present Roman aims and methods in war. The authors in fact (in spite of their idealizing) speak in the main from a political standpoint;

---

[3] Cf. Sen. *Clem.* 2. 3. 1 'clementia est temperantia animi *in potestate ulciscendi* uel lenitas *superioris aduersus inferiorem* in constituendis poenis.' One can see why an offer of *clementia* might be resented. See the excellent comments of Earl (1967), 60. I return to the question of *clementia* below.

indeed, excluding Horace, they are politicians, active or retired.[4] Philosophers offered ways in which the presentation of Roman warfare could be further refined—as *Off.* 1. 62 (and 63) already indicates. It is of particular interest to consider Stoic ideas, because Stoic ethics had so much practical significance in Roman public life[5]—and of course for Vergil.[6] Stoic advocacy of self-denying duty, of subordination, *praebere se fato*, was in tune with traditional Roman and Vergilian ideas and ideals: with *pietas*, with *non sibi sed patriae natus*, and with Vergil's *fatum sequi*.[7] Of course the traditional Roman admiration for personal or familial *gloria* was less easily married with Stoicism; but *gloria* was far from beloved by Vergil—and much less in favour in the New Age of Augustus than formerly.[8]

Off. 1. 62 shows us that the Stoics had views on the proper nature of bravery. But on this topic a discussion in Cic. *Tusc.* 4. 43 ff. is more illuminating:

What of the contention of the Peripatetics that these selfsame disorders (*perturbationes*) which we (Stoics) think need extirpating are not only natural but also bestowed on us by nature for a useful end?... In the first place they praise irascibility (*iracundia*, i.e. one of the 'disorders') at great length; they name it the whetstone of bravery (*cotem fortitudinis*) and say that the assaults of angry men upon an enemy or disloyal citizen show greater vehemence (43)... The answer to the Peripatetics is given by the Stoics... 'disorder is an agitation of the soul alien from reason, contrary to nature' (47)... [Examples are then cited where bravery was quite clearly divorced from anger: e.g.]... I do not think either that the famous soldier who won the surname of Torquatus was angry when he dragged the torque off the Gaul, or that Marcellus at Clastidium was brave for the reason that he was angry (49). Of Africanus indeed, of whom we have better knowledge, because his memory is fresh in our minds, I can even take my oath that he was not in a blaze of irascibility (*non iracundia... inflammatum fuisse*) when on the field of battle he covered M. Allienus Pelignus with his shield and planted his sword in the breast of his enemy... Why then do you bring in anger here? Is it that bravery has no impulses of its own unless it begins to lose its wits (*nisi insanire coepit*)? Again, do you think that Hercules, who was raised to heaven by that selfsame bravery you would have to be irascibility, was angry when he struggled with the boar of Erymanthus...?... See to it that bravery is not the slightest bit frenzied, and that irascibility is wholly part of inconstancy; for there is no bravery that is devoid of reason (*quae rationis est expers*). (trans. J. E. King, with some changes)

---

[4] Cicero speaks (it seems to me) more as a Roman than as a Panaetian in *Off.* 1. 35; though the distinction is perhaps artificial: see below.

[5] See Arnold (1911), esp. 380 ff.

[6] See e.g. Heinze (1914), index *sub* 'Stoa', and see below.

[7] Sen. *Dial.* 1. 5. 8, Verg. *Aen.* 2. 701, 3. 114, etc.; Heinze (1914), 301 f. For the attitude 'non sibi sed patriae natus' (Cic. *Mur.* 83, etc.) see most usefully Griffin (1979), 73–4.

[8] See Earl (1967), 65–79. Cf. and contrast section iii of Brunt's paper (1978), 'The glory of imperial expansion'.

If we combine this passage with the earlier ones, we can gain an idea of how an idealizing imperialist with Stoic sympathies might view the aims and method of war. The proper *method* of war involves dispassionate, rational bravery and employs judicious, rational mercy; the *aim* of military action is seen solely as peace and security.

We may notice now that when Horace provides a rationale of, and an 'image' for, Augustus' military actions (*Odes* 3. 4) he talks of 'regulated force' (by implication Augustus') and 'irrational force' (the other side's); and clearly this notion of a rational force is allied to the Stoic ideal of a dispassionate, rational bravery. The key lines are 65–7:

> uis consili expers mole ruit sua:
> uim temperatam di quoque prouehunt
> in maius.[9]

We should remember, too, that in the *Aeneid* Vergil suggests the close association, even identity, of a whole range of apparently distinct violent emotions (rage, passionate love, despair), calling them *furor*, 'madness'; and that of course is in the Stoic manner.[10] Further, he represents all *furor* as the inimical polarity to everything that makes for peace, civilized Empire, and justice; in particular *furor* is the inimical polarity to the cardinal virtue of *pietas*. Note in the first place how Vergil phrases the conclusion to Jupiter's grand prophecy of Empire in Book 1 (lines 291 ff.)

> aspera tum positis mitescent saecula bellis:
> cana Fides et Vesta, Remo cum fratre Quirinus
> iura dabunt; dirae ferro et compagibus artis
> claudentur Belli portae; Furor impius intus
> saeua sedens super arma et centum uinctus aenis
> post tergum nodis fremet horridus ore cruento.

Consider too the implications of the prominent simile that concludes the great symbolic storm, the first manifestation of Juno's passion, 1. 148–52, esp. 151 f.:[11]

---

[9] There is an interesting comparison to be made between these lines and Cic. *Off*. 1. 50.

[10] Cf. e.g. Cic. *Tusc*. 4. 11 ff.: 'This then is Zeno's definition of "passion" (*perturbatio*)... that it is an agitation of the soul turning its back on right reason, contrary to nature.... (16)... numerous subdivisions of the same class are brought under the head of each emotion: ut "aegritudini" inuidentia...aemulatio, obtrectatio, misericordia, angor, luctus, maeror (etc.)..."libidini" ira, excandescentia, odium, inimicitia, discordia, indigentia, desiderium, et cetera eius modi...(21) quae autem libidini subiecta sunt ea sic definiunt ut "ira" sit libido poeniendi eius, qui uideatur laesisse iniuria (cf. 44 'ira...ulciscendi libido')...', etc.

[11] The relation between simile and narrative is the reverse of what we expect. We are invited to see the storm as a great symbolic overture: *pietas*, a virtue which involves supreme *subordination* of self to god, duty and the like and is thus Stoic as well as Roman in colour, is the quality

> ... furor arma ministrat;
> tum, pietate grauem ...

This, and much other evidence,[12] suggests that the imperialism of these two poets is coloured by a Stoic idealism. They appear to be imperialists of the type posited above.

Let us concentrate for a while on the *Aeneid*. It is possible to put the case a little more precisely. I do so charily, unwillingly: the application of labels ('Stoic', or whatever) to a poem as elusive as the *Aeneid* is bound to have a distorting effect. Nevertheless: *pius* Aeneas, who follows with difficulty (sometimes in confusion, sometimes in despair) a duty imposed upon him by fate, who finds that his human passions and feelings are in conflict with that duty and must therefore subordinate them ruthlessly to it, clearly bears a resemblance to an aspiring Stoic in a world of Stoic truths.[13] He is also a hero issuing from Homer. He is a hero with a Stoic role thrust upon him—against his nature. Aeneas has much of the traditional heroic impulse to subordinate himself to nothing and no one: remember, for example, Book 2. 314 'arma amens capio; nec sat rationis in armis'—after Hector's solemn instruction. And it is not just a Stoic role that is thrust upon him. The command of fate is to establish a nation and found an empire. He is a hero with a Stoic and imperial role thrust upon him. In obedience to this role he eventually, belatedly, turns his back on love, passion and Dido—in a very Stoic gesture suppressing that other irrational *perturbatio*, compassion, which to the Stoic is as pernicious a *perturbatio* as, say, anger,[14] 4. 393–6:

> at pius Aeneas, quamquam lenire dolentem
> solando cupit et dictis auertere curas,
> multa gemens magnoque animum labefactus amore
> iussa tamen diuum exsequitur classemque reuisit.

In this light, we must have certain clear expectations of Aeneas when he enters upon the war in the second half of the poem. They are quite different from our expectations of a traditional epic hero. Not for him the superb but egotistical ideal of heroic conflict: 'always to excel', in the passionate business of battle; not for him the paramount claim of his own individual glory and

---

which may prevail in all the passionate struggles which follow, struggles on the road to Rome. Cf. Otis (1963); *not* that I would subscribe to all Otis says.

[12] For Horace note e.g. *Odes* 3. 3. 1 ff. 'iustum et tenacem ...'.

[13] Cf. Bowra (1933–4), 8 ff.; but with important parts of Bowra's paper I am in disagreement.

[14] Cic. *Tusc.* 4. 16 (quoted in note 10), 56 'cur misereare potius quam feras opem ...? ... non enim suscipere ipsi aegritudines propter alios debemus, sed alios, si possumus, leuare aegritudine'; Sen. in the *De Clementia* distinguishes *clementia* and *misericordia* (see Motto's index *sub* 'pity'); note esp. *Clem.* 2. 6. 4 'misericordia uicina est miseriae ...'.

honour, or the overriding need to avenge the dishonour of an individual with particular claims on him.[15] His role is Stoic and imperial, Stoically imperial. The end of his war must be peace, the security of all the peoples destined to be his responsibility; he is bound to politic mercy, and his bravery should be cool and rational. These are our expectations; and of course Anchises spells most of it out explicitly to Aeneas himself in his famous summation of the Roman imperial mission, 6. 851 ff.:

> tu regere imperio populos, Romane, memento
> (hae tibi erunt artes), pacique imponere morem,
> parcere subiectis et debellare superbos.

This may be compared with, for example, Cic. *Off.* 1. 35. But Anchises is even more magnanimous: he has no 'exclusion clause' like Cicero's *qui non crudeles*... And we might think that Aeneas should feel more committed to mercy and magnanimity than some generals in some imperial wars, for the Italians are destined, as he knows, to be not a conquered province but part of the unified Roman people: one nation.[16] Another point: we may feel encouraged, perhaps indeed entitled, to believe that Aeneas will uphold Stoically imperial principles in the war in the light of his belated, anguished but finally successful adherence to Stoic imperial principles in other situations in the first half of the poem. Or to put it more specifically and bluntly: it would be curious to precipitate the death of Dido because of principle and duty and then jettison that same principle and duty on an arguably less demanding occasion.

Now Aeneas does on occasion exhibit the attitude we expect of him.[17] Indeed he even surpasses our expectations. Here is his response to a sign that war with the Italians is imminent, 8. 537 ff.:

> heu quantae miseris caedes Laurentibus instant!
> quas poenas mihi, Turne, dabis! quam multa sub undas
> scuta uirum galeasque et fortia corpora uolues,
> Thybri pater! poscant acies et foedera rumpant.

---

[15] Cf. e.g. αἰὲν ἀριστεύειν καὶ ὑπείροχον ἔμμεναι ἄλλων (*Il.* 6. 208, 11. 783) and Hector's words to Andromache at 6. 441–6 (but note Griffin (1980), 95–100, on Homer and glory); note the role of θυμός in heroic fighting (e.g. in the formula ὣς εἰπὼν ὤτρυνε μένος καὶ θυμὸν ἑκάστου, *Il.* 5. 470, etc.), and of χάρμη ('joy of battle', e.g. μνήσαντο δὲ χάρμης, 4. 222, etc.). Achilles' response to the death of Patroclus, for example, 18. 91–3 (and following), 19. 199–214, and of course in his actions in Books 21 and 22 (and following), shows how the greatest of heroes viewed his obligations to a dead and dishonoured friend.

[16] Cicero, it might be noted, did not view the Italian wars in this way (*Off.* 1. 35, quoted above).

[17] As well as the passages cited, cf. the beginning of Book 8, which describes Aeneas' concern at the prospect of war and concludes (line 29) 'tristi turbatus pectora bello': this is a far cry from the *Iliad*.

heu... miseris unquestionably suggests *sympathy* with the Italians whom great slaughter awaits—and, indeed, he might well have sympathy for those who are to be his people. This feeling of sympathy is highlighted by a striking echo, by the fact that line 539, *scuta uirum...*, virtually repeats his own words in Book 1 (line 101). Now in Book 1 the river in question is Simois, in Book 8 it is the Tiber. In Book 1 Aeneas recalls the devastation at Troy, thinking of Trojan bodies rolled in the river waters; in Book 8 he looks forward to the destruction that is going to ensue in Italy, and thinks primarily of Italian bodies, dead at the hand of victorious Trojans. Now it would have been understandable if Aeneas had rejoiced in his conviction that the Trojans will reverse the situation at Troy. Far from it. He has sympathy for the Italians: *heu quantae miseris*. He grieves (we could say) that history will repeat itself (the Italians are in a way his people) rather than rejoices in an imminent reversal of fortunes. Aeneas sympathizes: but he does not allow his sympathy to degenerate into the compassion that is a disruptive *perturbatio*, fogging reason (see above). Aeneas sees his duty clearly: *poscant acies...* They will get what is coming; he will do the killing that is necessary. Still, the hero who can thus sympathize with his foe will surely be able to show mercy at the appropriate moment. He will not be inflamed with a desire to slaughter the objects of his humane sympathy.

Book 11 also shows the magnanimous Aeneas, true to form. Here are his words to an embassy of Italians requesting a truce to bury the dead, 11. 108–19:

> quaenam uos tanto fortuna indigna, Latini,
> implicuit bello, qui nos fugiatis amicos?
> pacem me exanimis et Martis sorte peremptis
> oratis? equidem et uiuis concedere uellem.
> nec ueni, nisi fata locum sedemque dedissent,
> nec bellum cum gente gero; rex nostra reliquit
> hospitia et Turni potius se credidit armis.
> aequius huic Turnum fuerat se opponere morti.
> si bellum finire manu, si pellere Teucros
> apparat, his mecum decuit concurrere telis:
> uixet cui uitam deus aut sua dextra dedisset.
> nunc ite et miseris supponite ciuibus ignem.

Peace is his desire for the *living* Latins. His own role in Italy is imposed upon him by fate. The war, for which he professes no desire or enthusiasm, has occurred only because Latinus and Turnus abandoned the peace that had been agreed, and obstructed his fate-ordained role. He and Turnus (he suggests rationally) should fight it out in a duel—the fairest, most expeditious solution. Again, therefore, we have the Stoic–imperial hero—with that added ingredient, a measured sympathy: *miseris supponite ciuibus ignem*.

Now it cannot be said that Aeneas tells any lies here. But we could forgive the Italian embassy if they felt a little bewildered by these cool, moderate, humane words. In the previous book, as is well known, Aeneas reacted to Turnus' killing of Pallas by bursting into a frenzy of rage (*furor*), callously slaughtering victims who begged for mercy, and taking eight live prisoners with a view to sacrificing them at the funeral of Pallas. It was an orgy of rage, cruelty and destruction recalling, significantly, the fearful actions of Achilles when he engaged in battle in Book 21 of the *Iliad*. Not until the death of Lausus do things start to change (10. 811–32). When he finds himself impelled to kill that young hero, Aeneas is appalled—to be contrasted at last with Turnus, who reacted so callously to the death of the youthful Pallas.

An immediate thought suggests itself. At times, *in practice*, Aeneas seems to have difficulty in preserving his own and Anchises' high-minded principles. It is noticeable that when he displays qualities of mercy and Stoicism in Books 8 and 11 he is not actually occupied in battle. I return to this point.

What we should now establish is the cause of Aeneas' rage in Book 10. Of course, there are probably many contributory factors. Pallas was the son of a *hospes*; he was sent to learn the art of war under Aeneas as well as to assist him as an ally (8. 514–19; but there is no more suggestion than what is contained in *sub te ... magistro* that Evander expected Aeneas to protect Pallas); the youthful Pallas in death is on any account pathetically affecting, an ἄωρος.[18] But the heart of the matter seems to be the fact that Turnus despoils him, strips him of his baldrick: here seems to be the centre of Turnus' offence. It is accompanied by one of Vergil's most striking interventions in the narrative (10. 495–505):

> ... et laeuo pressit pede talia fatus
> exanimem rapiens immania pondera baltei
> impressumque nefas: una sub nocte iugali
> caesa manus iuuenum foede thalamique cruenti,
> quae Clonus Eurytides multo caelauerat auro;
> quo nunc Turnus ouat spolio gaudetque potitus.
> nescia mens hominum fati sortisque futurae
> et seruare modum rebus sublata secundis!
> Turno tempus erit magno cum optauerit emptum
> intactum Pallanta, et cum spolia ista diemque
> oderit.

---

[18] This aspect of Pallas' pathos, that he died 'before his time', is underlined by the myth engraved on his baldrick: so Conte (1980), 96 ff. demonstrates; his argument is summarized by myself in Lyne (1981), 222. On Aeneas' motives in Book 10 see too Beare (1964), 18 ff., Quinn (1968), 226.

Pallas is then carted off—and Aeneas' rampage is precipitated. 'Pallas, Euander, in ipsis omnia sunt oculis...' (515 ff.).

All however is not simple. It was Roman no less than Homeric custom to despoil a defeated enemy. The action brought nothing but *laus* to the perpetrator, who might hang such *spolia* proudly in his *atrium*. If indeed a Roman general killed and despoiled an opposing commander, the spoils then became the *spolia opima* consecrated in the temple of Jupiter Feretrius: an honour so signal that in the time of Augustus it had to be jealously guarded. Consider too Pallas: it was his stated intention to despoil Turnus in the event of his victory in their duel (10. 449 f.)—a fact that is sometimes curiously overlooked. All indeed is not simple: but the basic issue can be identified. Spoils were the tangible proof and token of triumph, in Rome as in the *Iliad*. As such they enhanced the fame and honour of the despoiler: κλέος, κῦδος, γέρας, *fama, laus, honor*—the same ethic essentially persists. But by the same token, of course, to *be* despoiled was to *be* dishonoured; and friends or family of the dishonoured might think that that necessitated action.[19]

Thus Aeneas. We could say therefore that his motives and conduct in Book 10 are more than defensible. In rage at the death and, most important, the *dishonouring* of Pallas, his noble youthful ally and pupil, Aeneas seeks some sort of revenge, albeit indiscriminate. High motives, large justification for a noble rage. But it is not the highest motive, nor perhaps a sufficient justification. And can rage be noble? Certainly none of it is what we have been led to expect. On three cardinal counts, involving both 'aims' and 'methods', Aeneas fails to uphold the principles of 'Stoic imperialism': he fights in a frenzy (the word *furor* and cognates is attached to him), not with dispassionate bravery; he fails to extend mercy to those who are patently defeated (*subiectus*). And, most important, for a time at least he loses sight of the final purpose of his war. To avenge the dishonour of Pallas is a high aim, but 'peace' is a higher

---

[19] On *spolia* see the useful article in *RE*, Zweite Reihe, Sechster Halbband (1929), 1843 ff. I cite a few useful references. For Romans despoiling defeated enemies after individual combat see e.g. Livy 5. 36. 7, Gell. 2. 11. 3. For the display of *spolia* in houses see Livy 23. 23. 6 (where those 'qui spolia ex hoste fixa domi haberent' are among specially selected categories designated to fill vacant places in the Senate; the principle of selection was 'ita...ut ordo ordini, non homo homini praelatus uideretur'), 38. 43. 10, Cic. *Phil*. 2. 68. For Roman soldiers trying to prevent the despoliation (dishonour) of their dead consul: Livy 22. 6. 4. Homer of course often describes such attempts to prevent despoliation. The dying Sarpedon's words are worth noting, eloquently appealing to Glaucus not to let the Greeks despoil him (*Il*. 16. 492–501): he clearly thinks Glaucus has a *duty* to him in this respect (σοὶ γὰρ ἐγὼ καὶ ἔπειτα κατηφείη καὶ ὄνειδος | ἔσσομαι...εἴ κέ μ' Ἀχαιοὶ | τεύχεα συλήσωσι...). On the *spolia opima* (and Augustus) see *Cambridge Ancient History* x. 125. Note too Verg. *Aen*. 1. 289 'hunc (Caesar) tu olim caelo spoliis Orientis onustum | accipies secura'. (*spolium* in the *Aeneid* repays study: there are 22 examples; Heinze (1914) offers some brief and largely sensible remarks.)

aim, *his* aim, and the former is arguably incompatible with the latter. These issues will concern us in more detail when we discuss Book 12.

Let us here spare a thought for Turnus. He kills Pallas; he is callous in victory, and exultant. But what is his basic *offence* (as I termed it above)? At heart, I suggested, it was the action of despoiling Pallas. Leave aside for the moment the detail that he subsequently chose to *wear* the despoiled baldrick (more on this anon), and leave aside his exultancy: Turnus' 'offence' turns out to be not so very large at all; many commentators mislead us here.[20] Turnus' conduct, like Aeneas', is defensible. His basic action accords with Roman no less than Homeric codes of honour. But what brings praise to one brings dishonour to another; in the eyes of his friends or family an offence to be avenged, to be furious about. That is how Aeneas sees the despoiling of Pallas. That is why Aeneas acts as he does in Book 10. We understand. But we also understand Turnus. And what we also understand, from another point of view, is that there is something disturbingly inconclusive about this 'morality'. If Pallas had beaten Turnus and, as he promised, despoiled him, Turnus' nearest and dearest might have gone on a rampage of vengeance with nearly as much justification as Aeneas. The 'morality' may be judged yet more harshly: a system of honour like this is relentless and sterile. It may lead to a never-ending cycle of honour and dishonour, vengeance and vengeance in return.

One begins in fact to see why in a heroic world, more particularly in the real Roman world, which maintained heroic ideas of honour, a policy of *clementia* might have a specific *practical* function. Towards prospective provincials or client states, the function of *clementia* is easy to discern.[21] But when equals in status were one's enemies (as in civil war) the function is perhaps subtler but no less practical. If lasting peace is to be made one side must (it could be argued) eventually draw a line, swallow an 'offence'. To parade one's *clementia* might have its offensive aspects (above, p. 116), but it was not as offensive as enforcing subjection, nor did it leave dead and dishonoured relations for relations to avenge. *Clementia* could break the cycle of honour and dishonour; it might be the only route to reconciliation and peace. This topic will engage us again.

Before I proceed, I must attend to Vergil's intervention in the narrative accompanying the despoliation (quoted above). Does not Vergil here explicitly condemn Turnus' action? I think not.[22] He remarks that 'a time will come when

---

[20] See e.g. Knauer (1964), 301 ff.; Otis (1963), 356; Quinn (1968), 223, 326. Misunderstanding the role of spoils leads to these misinterpretations.

[21] See Brunt (1978), 184.

[22] Cf. Quinn (1968), 326 (more non-committal than I am); and there are some very perceptive points—and interesting information—in Barchiesi (1980), 45–55; Barchiesi discusses *Aen.* 10. 501–5, but not specifically to make the point I am stressing. Other scholars (e.g. Otis, Williams, Klingner) are curiously silent on this question. Heinze (1914), 209 gets it wrong.

Turnus would give anything not to have touched Pallas and will hate the spoils'. Of course Turnus will: his actions here eventually bring about his death. Vergil predicts likely facts; he does not pass explicit moral judgment. More significant is *nescia mens... seruare modum...* 'how ignorant are men's hearts to keep within bounds when uplifted by success'. *seruare modum* does have moral overtones. But what does it apply to? It is uttered in response to the previous sentence, presumably therefore to the main action of the previous sentence; and the main action of the previous sentence should be contained in its main verbs, *ouat gaudetque*. So Vergil passes adverse judgment not on Turnus' triumph and the prosecution of his triumph (taking the spoils), but on his *exultation in* that triumph—his exultation 'when uplifted by success'. He passes judgment not on an act but an attitude, adverting in the spirit of Greek tragic poets to Turnus' attitude of foolish, immoderate, premature elation. Much therefore may be criticized in Turnus—callousness, confidence, arrogance even—but we must be quite clear that he commits no absolute offence against morality, divine or human; nor does Vergil say he does.

Of course Vergil's intervention permits the *inference* (so long as we are quite clear about what Vergil actually *says*) that he is *uneasy* about the ethic of spoils—unlike his contemporaries. We may choose to remember in this connection the fact that was instrumental in the tragic end of Euryalus (9. 373–4, 384)—a suggestive detail. But Vergil has another very obvious reason, besides a desire to express distaste at spoils, for intervening at this moment: simply to mark out the action that will eventually precipitate Turnus' death. Tragic foreshadowing is thereby achieved; and the accompanying tragic irony is enhanced by Turnus' joyful exultation in the action.

Finally, a very significant comparison can be made between Vergil's criticism of Turnus and a passage that must have been in his mind: Zeus' criticism of Hector in *Iliad* 17. 204–6. Zeus sees Hector arrayed in Achilles' armour and is moved to utter thus:

> τοῦ δὴ ἑταῖρον ἔπεφνες ἐνηέα τε κρατερόν τε,
> τεύχεα δ' οὐ κατὰ κόσμον ἀπὸ κρατός τε καὶ ὤμων
> εἴλευ·

This does seem an explicit criticism of an act of despoiling. It is in fact unique in the *Iliad*, out of key with the *Iliad*'s normal ethic—and requires special explanation.[23] But whatever its own explanation it might well have encouraged

---

[23] The *scholia* provide their own implausible explanations. Eustathius, ad loc. (backed by Bassett (1923), 117–27) ingeniously tries to settle the inconsistency with *Il.* 16. 791 ff. (where Apollo is responsible for Patroclus' loss of his armour) at the same time as interpret Zeus' comment: τὸ δὲ, "οὐ κατὰ κόσμον – εἴλευ", ἀντὶ τοῦ οὐκ ἐσκύλευσας ὡς ἔχρην, ἀλλὰ τοῦ Φοίβου τὸν Πάτροκλον ἀφοπλίσαντος, σὺ δῶρον εἷλου αὐτὰ ἢ καὶ ὡς εὕρημα... (and the point is

Vergil to a similar explicit statement, given that his inclinations ran that way. The fact that it does not is indeed remarkable. Vergil's cautious comment is revealed as a deliberate back-pedalling. He is most anxious that Turnus should *not* appear indicted for an absolute or indeed a concrete offence.

We proceed to Book 12. At the beginning of the book, the various obstacles in the way of a duel between Aeneas and Turnus (desired by Aeneas in Book 11) seem to have been cleared away. A truce is established, sanctified by solemn, religious rituals. The two leaders will fight, and the armies abide by the result. A climax along the lines of *Iliad* 22 seems imminent. Actually, the main source at the beginning of the book (where the truce is established and the duel seems set) is the duel between Paris and Menelaus in *Iliad* 3 and 4—a contamination which we shall mention again later.

What are the mood and motives of Aeneas, now and later in Book 12? These are what I want to follow, in the light of our comments above on 'aims' and 'methods'. As he prepares himself at the beginning of the book, on the eve of the contest, Aeneas seems disinclined to eschew anger; it is as if he sees a Peripatetic role for it (107–8):

> nec minus interea maternis saeuus in armis
> Aeneas acuit Martem et se suscitat ira...

But this is not the passion that merits the term *furor*—in contradistinction to Turnus who, in spite of much sympathetic treatment hereabouts, is described as being in the grip of monstrous, Homeric frenzy,[24] 101–2:

> his agitur furiis, totoque ardentis ab ore
> scintillae absistunt, oculis micat acribus ignis...

And Aeneas' mind is on peace, 109:

> oblato gaudens componi foedere bellum.

This is confirmed in his prefatory speech on the actual day of the duel, 176 ff. He solemnly binds the Trojans to accept the consequences if he is defeated; and in the event of his victory, 'sin nostrum adnuerit nobis uictoria Martem', 189–91:

---

amplified). But clearly one cannot disjoin οὐ from κατὰ κόσμον in the way Eustathius implies; the two books simply are inconsistent. I take it that Zeus' point lies in the excellence of *Achilles*, and in the fact that it was *Achilles*' armour that Hector gained (note σὺ δ' ἄμβροτα τεύχεα δύνεις | ἀνδρὸς ἀριστῆος). It would be one thing to strip the defeated Patroclus of Patroclus' arms; it was another to strip him *of the divine arms of Achilles*. This Zeus finds 'inappropriate', 'not quite in order', vel sim., οὐ κατὰ κόσμον.

[24] Cf. e.g. Hom. *Il.* 19. 365 f. τὼ δέ οἱ ὄσσε | λαμπέσθην ὡς εἴ τε πυρὸς σέλας. I choose the word 'monstrous' advisedly: Turnus reminds us of Cacus.

> non ego nec Teucris Italos parere iubebo
> nec mihi regna peto: paribus se legibus ambae
> inuictae gentes aeterna in foedera mittant.

That is to say: he intends his victory to be the route to peace, and a peace in which the 'vanquished' will have equal rights with the 'victors'. In other words, Aeneas sees the *aim* of his fighting as peace, and intends to secure it through a policy of magnanimous *clementia*. The Stoic imperialist presents himself—impeccably, but for that small indulgence in *ira*. We remember, however, that he was nearly as impeccable on two previous occasions when he was similarly disengaged from battle.

Various factors including the prompting of Juturna, the Italians' own inclinations, an untimely portent, and the Pandarus-like action of the augur Tolumnius (*Iliad* 4 still underlies this section of text), lead eventually to the breaking of the truce by the Italians. Note that the disguised Juturna's inflammatory speech misrepresents, it seems, Aeneas' intentions, 229–30 and 234–7:

> non pudet, o Rutuli, pro cunctis talibus unam
> obiectare animam?...
> ille quidem ad superos, quorum se deuouet aris,
> succedet fama uiuusque per ora feretur;
> nos patria amissa dominis parere superbis
> cogemur, qui nunc lenti consedimus aruis.

Contrast Aeneas' words at 189 ff. (above).

The truce is broken amidst and as a result of an explosion of emotion. Juturna's words 'inflame' the Italians (238). Tolumnius' action 'inflames' the wounded Arcadian's brothers with 'grief' (277), as a result of which they reach for their weapons—and rush headlong 'blindly' (277–9). Battle is joined: a 'love' of war possesses all. Messapus is described as 'greedy' (*auidus*) for the confounding of the truce. Vergil's Stoic sense that all passionate emotions are allied and all destructive and pernicious is evident here in his choice of vocabulary and imagery.[25] How does Aeneas respond to all this? Impeccably. He identifies the cause (or a cause)—passion—and seeks to stem it, 313 ff.:

> quo ruitis? quaeue ista repens discordia surgit?
> o cohibete iras!...

But then ill luck takes a hand. Even as he speaks, an anonymous arrow wounds him, and he has to retire. Whether his attempt to stem the tide might have succeeded if he had been able to remain, we cannot finally say.

---

[25] See n. 10 above.

Certainly it is over and failed now. Aeneas retires, leaving Turnus to indulge his passion (324 ff.) in a savage *aristeia*.

And now Aeneas' attitude starts to change. The galling frustration of his position—incapacitated while the unwanted, impious battle grows ever more fiercely apace (405 ff.)—has its natural effect. We know that Aeneas is susceptible to emotion (see indeed 108), and his emotions now start to be aroused. In his fury he starts to sound distinctly like those very warriors whose passions he has just previously tried to stem: *saeuit* (387), *stabat acerba fremens* (398); and, after he is miraculously healed, *auidus pugnae... oditque moras*. When he returns to the fray it is with motifs and violence that are designed to recall that superb grim hero of the old heroic order, Ajax.[26] Finally, after Juturna maddeningly keeps Turnus out of his reach and Messapus holds him up and clips his crest, we are given these remarkable lines, 494–9:

> tum uero adsurgunt irae, insidiisque subactus,
> diuersos ubi sensit equos currumque referri,
> multa Iouem et laesi testatus foederis aras
> iam tandem inuadit medios et Marte secundo
> terribilis saeuam nullo discrimine caedem
> suscitat, irarumque omnis effundit habenas.

And frightful slaughter ensues, conducted by both Aeneas and Turnus.

o cohibete iras: clearly the ideals of Stoic imperialism have been heavily compromised. Aeneas deals out indiscriminate slaughter: this ill coheres with magnanimity and is scarcely the rational *fortitudo* of the sage; *irarumque omnis effundit habenas* is quantitatively if not qualitatively a vast distance even from *se suscitat ira* (108). But two points must be made absolutely clear. First, Vergil has traced with extreme realism how Aeneas has under utmost provocation come to this very comprehensible state of mind. Secondly, and perhaps more importantly, though Aeneas has now lost from view the Stoic ideal of *methods*, he has not fundamentally—perhaps truer to say, not permanently—lost all sight of the ideal *aim*. However deplorably Aeneas is prepared now to counter enraged violence with enraged violence, his high-minded view of the final purpose of all this force is not yet lastingly or wholly abandoned. In this respect the situation is still different from the episodes referred to in Book 10 (before the death of Lausus). But the point needs clarifying.

The furious Ajax-like Aeneas returns to war. He has one clearly defined object: 'solum densa in caligine Turnum | uestigat lustrans, solum in certamina poscit' (466–7). Why? It must be:[27] to finish the work that was so rudely

---

[26] With *Aen.* 12. 435 f. cf. Soph. *Ajax* 550–1 (imitated by Accius (fr. 156) in the form *uirtuti sis par, dispar fortunis patris*). I shall cite more evidence for my assertion at another time. [Cf. Lyne (1987), 8–12.]

[27] Cf. Williams's commentary on 12. 497.

interrupted, to remove in a duel with Turnus the obstacle to peace. Vergil, who has so carefully catalogued the 'decline' (if so we must call it) in Aeneas' attitude to the *methods* of warfare, has not yet given us any hint that his *aim*, spelled out so specifically in 176 ff., has fundamentally or lastingly changed. In the present lines (494 ff.) Aeneas recalls the treaty in which he committed himself to a policy of peace as the end of fighting, and justifies his present lack of discrimination by the fact that the Italians have broken that treaty and thus thwarted the policy. And we have seen that it took time for him to succumb in this way. It happened only after the final goading provocation of Messapus and because Turnus, whom he still viewed as the key to peace, was kept out of his way.

And the text reassures us that Aeneas' high-minded aim, peace as the end of war, is not permanently or wholly abandoned. It is sadly modified but just about intact. In 554 ff. Aeneas has returned to the single pursuit of Turnus ('ille ut uestigans diuersa per agmina Turnum | huc atque huc acies circumtulit...'), when Venus prompts him to attack the Latin city. He responds to the idea, and speaks thus to his men, 565–73:

> ne qua meis esto dictis mora, Iuppiter hac stat,
> neu quis ob inceptum subitum mihi segnior ito.
> urbem hodie, causam belli, regna ipsa Latini,
> ni frenum accipere et uicti parere fatentur,
> eruam et aequa solo fumantia culmina ponam.
> scilicet exspectem libeat dum proelia Turno
> nostra pati rursusque uelit concurrere uictus?
> hoc caput, o ciues, haec belli summa nefandi.
> ferte faces propere foedusque reposcite flammis.

Fire breeds fire, indiscriminate methods are to be answered by indiscriminate methods. But Aeneas still sees the *aim* of war as peace—of a sort.[28] That imperial ideal is still there. *foedus reposcite flammis*: the aim of attacking the city, he says, is to re-establish the treaty, and the treaty is the route to peace. We must of course lament the methods to which Aeneas is now prepared to have recourse: *flammis*, more particularly 'eruam et aequa solo fumantia culmina ponam', said of a city which contains innocents; and Aeneas' heated portrayal of the 'city' as *causam belli* is of course hardly just. We must lament, too, the way in which he now sees and phrases his necessary victory: 'ni frenum accipere et uicti parere fatentur'. Contrast that with his promise of peace in 189; ironically, he seems to vindicate Juturna (above p. 127). But in a bloody, ugly way, Aeneas' aim is intact: 'pacique imponere morem'; 'ut sine iniuria in pace uiuatur'; 'foedusque reposcite flammis'. And much has changed

---

[28] Poe (1965), 334, gets this wrong.

since line 189 and the truce, by no means all of it to be laid to Aeneas' charge. On this point he himself is insistent. As in 496, so now, 579–82:

> ipse inter primos dextram sub moenia tendit
> Aeneas, magnaque incusat uoce Latinum
> testaturque deos iterum se ad proelia cogi,
> bis iam Italos hostis, haec altera foedera rumpi.

Aeneas sees the attack on the Latin city as an alternative to the duel with Turnus he cannot have (*scilicet expectem*..., 570 above). In fact it functions as a tactic to bring Turnus finally into single combat (620 ff., 643 ff., 653 ff., 669 ff.). As soon as that happens Aeneas—significantly, of course—abandons the attack (697 ff.). He has what he wants: the key to peace. The duel is finally to take place. A *de facto* truce is observed. The climax along the lines of *Iliad* 22 is finally to take place.

At this point it is vital for us to have one thing clear. Aeneas and Turnus are indeed embarking on a duel closely recalling and of course based on the climactic duel between Achilles and Hector. But Aeneas does not enter the duel with a motivation and purpose like that of Achilles (desire for vengeance owed to a friend); his *aim* is quite different.[29] Here is the reason (or a reason) why Vergil combined as sources the *Iliad* 3 and 4 duel (Menelaus and Paris) with the *Iliad* 22 duel: it allows him to provide Aeneas with this different initial aim. For Aeneas enters the final duel inspired by rage at the breaking of a treaty, to conclude the original business of that treaty, to establish *pax*: if not the rosy *pax* of 189, *pax* none the less. Turnus perceives the first point (694–5 'me uerius unum | pro uobis foedus luere et decernere ferro'), and Aeneas has recently reaffirmed the second. He attacked the city to force a peace; he attacked the city because he could not corner Turnus. Now he has Turnus.

This question of Aeneas' overriding aim is crucial to bear in mind in the final scene of the poem.[30] When Aeneas wounds Turnus (not mortally), Turnus begs for mercy, 930–8:

> ille humilis supplex oculos dextramque precantem
> protendens 'equidem merui nec deprecor' inquit;
> 'utere sorte tua. miseri te si qua parentis
> tangere cura potest, oro (fuit et tibi talis

---

[29] Quinn (1968), 273 misunderstands this.

[30] This scene has of course been much discussed. Some scholars are anxious to justify Aeneas' conduct in victory (e.g. Bowra (1933–4); Otis (1963), 379–82; Heinze (1914), 210–11; Binder (1971), 146); others are more critical (e.g. Quinn (1968), 272 ff.; Putnam (1965), 193 ff. ('It is Aeneas who loses at the end of Book XII...')). More cautious is Pöschl (1977), 81–4; cf. too Beare (1964), 18–30; these two, together with Quinn's discussion, are among the most helpful. None gets to the heart of the matter.

> Anchises genitor) Dauni miserere senectae
> et me, seu corpus spoliatum lumine mauis,
> redde meis. uicisti et uictum tendere palmas
> Ausonii uidere; tua est Lauinia coniunx,
> ulterius ne tende odiis.'

Turnus supplicates, he is defeated, he is humiliated. His time as a proud leader of men is finished; he knows it and he knows that everyone else knows it. There is no question about any of this; it is all quite explicit in the text. Note particularly *humilis, supplex*, and his words 'uicisti et uictum tendere palmas | Ausonii uidere'. Next (938–41):

> stetit acer in armis
> Aeneas uoluens oculos dextramque repressit;
> et iam iamque magis cunctantem flectere sermo
> coeperat, ...

Turnus begins to persuade Aeneas. Why? Because Aeneas sees that it is appropriate, perhaps more than appropriate, that he should be persuaded. The purpose for which he entered the duel with Turnus is achieved, and nothing—nothing to do with that purpose—can be lost and perhaps much can be won by sparing Turnus. His aim has been 'peace'; to establish peace it is necessary to war down the proud ('pacique imponere morem, debellare superbos'). The proud Turnus has been warred down and is emphatically no longer proud, unequivocally *subiectus*. He is a foe who should qualify for *clementia, parcere subiectis*. Perhaps we should put it more strongly. In wars which involve the honour of equals (like civil wars, or quasi-civil wars) *clementia* was not just woolly humanity. Unless (as I said above) a victor is prepared to extend tactical forgiveness, a sequence of honour, dishonour, vengeance and vengeance in return, may never end. Far from gratuitous largesse, *parcere subiectis* may have as vital a practical role in the business of establishing peace as *debellare superbos*. Aeneas has heard the words of Anchises and can see the course demanded by policy and humanity. And yet he is not in the final count persuaded. Why?

Because a *new* motive and aim succeeds the former aim, the aim of *pacique imponere morem*. He catches sight of the belt of Pallas which Turnus is wearing, the *spolia*, the token of Pallas' defeat and dishonour; and Turnus' chance to persuade him is over, 941 ff.:

> ... coeperat, infelix umero cum apparuit alto
> balteus et notis fulserunt cingula bullis
> Pallantis pueri, uictum quem uulnere Turnus
> strauerat atque umeris inimicum insigne gerebat.
> ille, oculis postquam saeui monimenta doloris

> exuuiasque hausit, furiis accensus et ira
> terribilis: 'tune hinc spoliis indute meorum
> eripiare mihi? Pallas te hoc uulnere, Pallas
> immolat et poenam scelerato ex sanguine sumit.'
> hoc dicens...

Now, a whole nexus of feelings may be seen working on Aeneas, helping to change his mind.[31] But one factor is basic and essential: the question of honour. An honourable impulse to avenge the dishonour of Pallas succeeds, and overrides, the claims of *pacique imponere morem*. Now, and only now, Aeneas' motives as well as his actions resemble those of Achilles in *Iliad* 22.

Before any hasty judgment is passed on Aeneas, some points need stressing. First, since Aeneas' motive in killing Turnus is basically to avenge Pallas' dishonour, that motive is not immoderately called honourable (to talk of 'primitive vendetta' is misleading). It should also be recalled that Aeneas' own impulse for revenge has the backing of Evander's compelling and touching plea in Book 11, lines 177–80:

> quod uitam moror inuisam Pallante perempto
> dextera causa tua est, Turnum gnatoque patrique
> quam debere uides. meritis uacat hic tibi solus
> fortunaeque locus.

Evander at any rate feels that Aeneas has a *duty* to him to kill Turnus; cf. the feelings of Sarpedon (see note 19). And (against Turnus) it is also right to remind ourselves that while despoiling a defeated enemy was part of heroic and Roman ethics, the *wearing* of such spoils infringed what seems to have been some kind of rather hazy taboo.[32] So Aeneas has honour and an ἄγραπτον νόμιμον and piety on his side. But his new motive replaces a grander one and (I would say) is in conflict with it (honour and piety conflict with a greater Piety—to destiny and Rome, as often in the *Aeneid*). An impulsive act of revenge, however ethically defensible, is not the best way to lay the foundations of reconciliation and peace. To avenge dishonour is to inflict dishonour; vengeance may provoke vengeance in return (cf. above p. 131). From certain points of view indeed Aeneas' action might be thought rather a mad action. Certainly Aeneas does it in a mad frenzy, 'furiis accensus et ira terribilis', emotions that the ideology of the *Aeneid* condemns.

We have by the end of the poem become used to the fact that Aeneas cannot uphold the ideal *methods* of a Stoic imperial warrior. We have seen Aeneas in

---

[31] Good discussion in Quinn (1968) and Beare (1964).
[32] See Reinach (1908), iii. 223 ff.; contrast what happens at *Aen.* 8. 562, 11. 5–11, 83–4, 193–6, and see n. 19 above.

the grip of *ira*, even of *furor*, many times, and perhaps it is no great surprise to see him thus now. But to see him lose sight of the *aims* enjoined upon the Stoically imperial warrior at the conclusion of the poem, at this moment of climactic political and historical importance—that surely is more surprising. It is obviously more striking and more significant than his temporary inclement abandonment of those aims in Book 10. Aeneas' aim at the end of the poem is human, even in its own way humane (remember Evander), honourable, heroic. But not only is it not the grand aim, it is (I assert once more) arguably in conflict with that aim. If Aeneas achieves his reconciliation and peace, it will *not* surely be due to this last act: rather, in spite of it.[33] And we do not of course hear anything about peace. Unlike the *Iliad*, the *Aeneid* does not proceed after its 'Book 22' into eventual hard-won harmony. Book 12 ends in an echoing silence.

A thought is worth taking up (see above p. 120). On one occasion Aeneas belatedly did not allow a human, humane, honourable impulse to override the great Pietas: in Carthage. The conclusion of the poem imparts further disturbing complexions to that episode.

Now in spite of all I have said I think it is misleading to talk baldly of 'Aeneas' failure' in the poem. Certainly I do not think that Aeneas *progresses* fundamentally as man or hero:[34] I do not think that the passion-prone Aeneas in Books 1–6 becomes a determined and controlled Aeneas in Books 7–12. On the contrary, we see Aeneas displaying the same vulnerability to passionate emotion in the second half as in the first. The theatre of course is different, and the emotions are superficially different. But (as I have said) in the view of the Stoics and, it seems, of Vergil—and indeed of many people—apparently distinct passionate emotions are closely interrelated, even perhaps identifiable.

---

[33] Cf. the very sensible comments of Beare (1964), 26. Beare p. 23 also reminds us of Priam's mercy towards Sinon and Anchises' towards Achaemenides, suggesting that mercy is, or should be, a particularly Trojan characteristic. But (it must be said) anyone who recalled Sinon might have felt justified in regarding mercy in a cynical light... At this point, I must concede that not all Romans would regard the argument in favour of a practical function to *clementia* as cut and dried. Cic. *ad M. Brutum* 6 (Shackleton Bailey). 2 = 1. 2a 2 (my attention was drawn to this letter by D. P. Fowler) is fascinating: 'scribis enim acrius prohibenda bella ciuilia esse quam in superatos iracundiam exercendam. uehementer a te, Brute, dissentio; nec clementiae tuae concedo, sed salutaris seueritas uincit inanem speciem clementiae, quod si clementes esse uolumus, numquam deerunt bella ciuilia.' Against this we should recall other Roman and Stoic views: not only the same Cicero's and others cited above, but also Sen. *De ira* 2. 32. 1 ff. 'non enim ut in beneficiis honestum est merita meritis repensare, ita iniurias iniuriis...', and *Clem.* 1. 21. 1–2 'si quos pares aliquando habuit, infra se uidet, satis uindicatus est... perdidit enim uitam qui debet, et quisquis ex alto ad inimici pedes abiectus alienam de capite regnoque sententiam exspectauit, in seruatoris sui gloriam uiuit plusque nomini eius confert incolumis, quam si ex oculis ablatus est.'

[34] But this of course is the common view: see e.g. Bowra (1933–4); Heinze (1914), 275 ff.; Otis (1963), index *sub* 'Aeneas—development of'.

To the Stoic, passion, despair, fear, anger and hatred are closely allied—and all pernicious; for Vergil they may all be lumped under the condemnatory title of *furor*. Aeneas succumbs at the end as in the beginning. But I should be hesitant about calling it failure.

If Aeneas, the son of a goddess, the hero of the epic, cannot 'succeed', then perhaps no one can. With great realism Vergil shows how an Aeneas who is genuinely in sympathy with Stoic imperial ideas of the appropriate *methods* of warfare cannot, under the relentless pressure of human reality, always uphold them. He shows Aeneas trying to keep in view the high-minded *aims* enjoined by a Stoic imperialism and finding again that sometimes it is simply not humanly feasible. Perhaps that is simply the truth of the matter.

And of course Vergil's Aeneas has great success, as an imperial hero: he reaches Italy, he establishes his people. But he is an honestly depicted imperial hero. Politicians and philosophers may present comforting, self-satisfying descriptions of, or prescriptions for, warfare. Leaders may laud themselves for having adhered to the high principles of such prescriptions. Such a one was Augustus—who also lauded himself for building a temple to Mars the Avenger (*Res Gestae* 21). Poet laureates may then echo the claims of their masters—like Horace, who hymned the *uis temperata* of the *princeps*, his *clementia* and the peace and security that was due to his victories. Horace also hymned Augustus as the avenger of Caesar (*Odes* 1. 2. 41 ff.), and was perhaps less sensitive than Augustus to the fact that there might be a clash between the virtue of vengeance and the virtue of clemency.[35] Vergil was different.

Let us speak bluntly. The notion that force employed on *our* side is rational and dispassionate, on the *other* side frenzied and irrational is of course close to nonsense. War is war and violence is violence, and to distinguish between *our* methods of fighting and *their* methods of fighting is pleasant and comforting but likely to be cant. What of aims? Of course one side's aims may be different from another's—but even here imperial spokesmen often fool themselves or others. Many of Rome's aggressive wars were designed to procure security for herself, but they *were* aggressive and 'peace' was hardly their only motivation or always their motivation—as indeed many Romans were happy enough to admit.[36]

There is therefore a certain amount of glibness in Horace's lyricizing of Augustan imperialism. Earlier I associated the two imperial poets, Horace and Vergil. Now they must be distinguished. For Vergil takes issue on the politics of war.

Vergil has constructed a hero with whom any founder or refounder of Rome must be and would no doubt like to be compared. Vergil's hero

---

[35] Note the careful wording of *Res Gestae* 2–3.
[36] See Brunt (1978), 176 ff. (esp. perhaps p. 176).

understands and espouses the high imperial ideals sung by Horace. But he finds that in practice *uis temperata* is a chimaera (*uis* is indivisible), *inclementia* is often irresistible, and High Motives clash with high motives; nor is it always possible to keep one's eye on the Highest. Vergil's hero demonstrates the truth (we might say) of imperial ideals, what actually happens to them in practice. The hero succeeds in laying the foundations of a new nation and a great empire; we must not obscure the measure of his success. But Vergil does not obscure the reality. The wars that gain empire involve ugly violence, and less than perfect motivations will sometimes direct even the greatest hero.

9

Lavinia's Blush: Vergil, *Aeneid* 12. 64–70 (1983)

In the *Aeneid* actions are consistent with character and psychology, indeed indicative of character and psychology. This statement has, I think, general if not universal truth. At any rate, one should not hastily assume otherwise.

Amata begs Turnus not to fight Aeneas. Lavinia is listening. She weeps, she blushes (*Aen.* 12. 64 ff.):

> accepit uocem lacrimis Lauinia matris
> flagrantis perfusa genas, cui plurimus ignem
> subiecit rubor et calefacta per ora cucurrit.
> Indum sanguineo ueluti uiolauerit ostro
> si quis ebur, aut mixta rubent ubi lilia multa
> alba rosa, talis uirgo dabat ore colores.
> illum turbat amor...

It is a famous blush, with a famous simile. Two similes, of course—but the second tends to get overlooked. Neither has been properly explained. Nor for that matter has Lavinia's weeping. Why does she weep? And why does she blush?

To most scholars Lavinia is not a character with feelings and emotions.[1] Naturally therefore her own state of mind cannot supply answers to these questions. But some scholars do have a sense of character—in particular, in these lines. Some scholars even sense that Lavinia is in love—but with whom?

If Lavinia were characterized enough to be in love, I would find this a welcome touch of colour, φάρμακον, in the outline of the μῦθος at this point.[2] The poem would be richer. If there was any suggestion that she was in love with, specifically, Turnus, this would be troubling. It would seriously complicate our emotional if not our moral response to the rapidly approaching dénouement. But that is not implausible. Our responses to the dénouement

---

[1] In an appendix I have collected together a range of comments, on Lavinia in general and our lines in particular. In an effort to keep my paper succinct and clear I have refrained from expressing agreement or disagreement with this or that aspect of this or that interpretation.

[2] Cf. Aristotle, *Poetics* 1450^{a}37–^{b}2.

are pretty complex already. And it is in fact the case. Lavinia comes alive in these lines. Lavinia, the text adumbrates, is in love with Turnus.

We should not expect such a disturbing revelation to be floodlit. The future wife of the founder of the Roman people cannot too explicitly have loved another man; it ill suits a proto-Roman *uirgo* to have such emotions at all. But disturbing insinuations, these are preeminently in the Vergilian manner. For example, the final victory of the *Aeneid*'s Augustan hero is marred—albeit by a human, honourable action:[3] an honourable, human impulse overrides the higher claims of the new *pietas*: *parcere subiectis* and, for that matter, *pacique imponere morem*. And the nubile Lavinia, 'plenis nubilis annis' (7. 53), had it seems set her heart on another man (a 'iuuenis praestans animi' in the opinion of an admirable judge, 12. 19): it is implicit in our lines. But let us start at line 55, with Amata.

The passionate Amata appears strangely devoted to Turnus, here and elsewhere; her relationship to him reminds us of other relationships besides that of possible future mother-in-law. In her pleading speech she recalls, of course, Hecuba pleading with her son in the analogous Iliadic scene (22. 82–9); and her words suggest a motherly love, and accord with a mother's circumstances—more than with her own: 'spes tu nunc una, senectae | tu requies miserae' (57 f.).[4] Her words, and Vergil's description of her, also suggest a more directly passionate emotion: 'flebat et ardentem generum moritura tenebat: | "Turne, per has ego te lacrimas... (55 f.) ... qui te cumque manent isto certamine casus | et me, Turne, manent..." (61 f.). With this, compare e.g. Prop. 2. 20. 18, 'ambos una fides auferet, una dies'; and, as so often, Amata recalls and exhibits the passion of Dido. Here she recalls the *moritura* Dido beseeching the parting Aeneas: 4. 307 ff., 'nec moritura tenet crudeli funere Dido?... per ego has lacrimas' (314) ... 'cui me moribundam | deseris...?' (323 f.).[5] Amata is an interesting creation. This is not the place to probe her psychology. But I can allow myself to say that she does have a coherent psychology. She is not merely a patchwork of characters from other

---

[3] This seems to me a reasonable description of Aeneas' killing of Turnus. His own understandable desire to avenge the death and dishonour of Pallas has been reinforced by the compelling and touching plea of Evander: 11. 177–81. Evander, at any rate, feels Aeneas has a *duty* to him in this respect. Note too that while it is part of heroic and indeed Roman ethics to despoil a defeated enemy (cf. Pallas at 10. 449, about to fight Turnus), the *wearing* of spoils breaks what one might call a taboo: cf. Reinach (1908), 223 ff.; also *Aen.* 8. 562, 11. 5–11, 83–4, 193–6. Aeneas, we could say, has honour on his side—and piety, and perhaps other things. But once more piety conflicts with Piety. Turnus is *subiectus* and no longer a threat to *pax*; from the grand point of view of Anchises (6. 851–3) he should have been spared.

[4] See my note on *Ciris* 293–4. The sentiment belongs most naturally to a parent or equivalent who loses or has the prospect of losing an only child. Amata exaggerates emotionally. The death of Turnus would not signify for her an ὀρφάνιον γῆρας.

[5] There are no other examples of an appeal *per has lacrimas* in Vergil.

books or poems uttering useful prompts at convenient places in the narrative. Vergil's description of her reflects his understanding of the close interrelation between, even identity of, many apparently distinct passionate emotions. It would be misleading to say that Amata is simply 'in love' with Turnus. But some of her language suggests she is. That fact must have repercussions.

One unexpected, incidental repercussion it has is for Lavinia and for the plot. Lavinia's sense of propriety, Vergil's sense of propriety, forbids Lavinia herself to speak. But Amata's words seem in some way to have spoken for her, to have caught her mood; anyway to have affected her.[6] She reacts to Amata's words, more particularly (as I would stress) she reacts *in line* with them. She weeps: *accepit uocem lacrimis*: like, and with, Amata (and like Dido—and like Delia: Tibull. 1. 3. 14). Why? A great many possible reasons suggest themselves. But one not to be excluded (among others) is the one already adumbrated. She weeps for the same general reason as Amata (and Dido, and Delia). She weeps in similar response to the same crisis: a person who arouses passionate emotion in her is meditating leaving on a dangerous enterprise. It is a natural interpretation. It is also a natural interpretation that she is weeping for the same person as Amata, with whom she weeps. And is it not plausible? 'praestans animi iuuenis' (12. 19), 'petit ante alios pulcherrimus omnis' (7. 55); 'iam matura uiro, iam plenis nubilis annis' (7. 53). And with Lavinia (and Delia, and perhaps Dido) the passionate emotion can be 'simply' defined: she is 'in love'. Harder evidence follows.

Lavinia blushes as well as weeps: 'flagrantis...rubor...calefacta per ora.' Why? Let us try following the interpretation of the previous paragraph. The psychology works, and a pleasant parallel offers itself. Passion for Turnus has been uttered (by Amata); Lavinia reveals her heartfelt sympathy with that utterance (in weeping). So she reveals her love—this anyway is what she thinks. In consequence she is embarrassed, guilty even: *conscia* and blushing—as modest girls are when caught in such a position: cf. Catull. 65. 19–24:

> ut missum sponsi furtiuo munere malum
>   procurrit casto uirginis e gremio,
> quod miserae oblitae molli sub ueste locatum
>   dum aduentu matris prosilit, excutitur,
> atque illud prono praeceps agitur decursu,
>   huic manat tristi conscius ore rubor.

---

[6] How useful for the modest Lavinia, and for Vergil! The fact that Amata is a plausible character speaking with plausible psychology does not of course *prevent* her advancing other people's action.

The parallel seems to me a most suggestive one. And from Hellenistic times on, of course, ἔρως has often provoked a maidenly blush, e.g. in Apollonius' Hypsipyle (1. 790 f.):

ἡ δ' ἐγκλιδὸν ὄσσε βάλουσα
παρθενικὰς ἐρύθηνε παρηίδας.

Such blushes are powered by ἔρως, but they also bespeak, to a greater or lesser extent, *pudor* (they are the reaction of a *pudibunda* to ἔρως);[7] and of course Lavinia will not voice her love or act on it—of that we may be even more sure now than before: *ubi enim rubor, obstat amori*. Contrast more brazen heroines, Scylla daughter of Nisus, for example: 'nullus in ore rubor: ubi enim rubor, obstat amori. | atque ... fertur' (*Ciris* 180 ff.).[8]

Let us concentrate a moment on the phrasing of *flagrantis genas, ignem subiecit rubor, calefacta ora*. It seems a tremendous amount of heat to attribute to a blush. But that is what Vergil seems to say:[9] 'cui plurimus ignem | subiecit rubor', 'in whom a great blush kindled fire'—and produced, presumably, the *flagrantis genas* and *calefacta ora* as well as the *ignem*. Of course Vergil helps to explain the amount of heat by stressing the huge size of the blush: *plurimus*. And we might (I think validly) infer from that that what was being blushed *for* was huge (at least in Lavinia's eyes)—causing the huge blush which caused the huge heat: ultimately, the love. So there is logic in the text—and food for thought. There is also a fine example of ἔμφασις, *significatio* (I am trying to avoid the word 'ambiguity').[10] For fire, as we shall soon recall, is a very significant image of love in the *Aeneid*. By emphasizing the depth of the

---

[7] Cf. Callimachus fr. 80. 10 with Pfeiffer ad loc., Musaeus, *Hero and Leander* 160–1 with Kost ad loc. (Apoll. 3. 297–98 (see below) is a little different.) Bömer collects many other blushes in his note on *Met.* 3. 423. It is interesting that Ovid depicts *rubor* on the face of the virginal Daphne (*Met.* 1. 484), and that his Phaedra perceives it on the face of Hippolytus (*Her.* 4. 72). Ovid may possibly mean to suggest that the two are virginal *in reaction* to stimuli they have at some time felt, or do in some way feel—they are not abhorring a completely unknown quantity. That would obviously be correct psychology; and the potential connotations of *rubor* would on this reading be fully exploited. I do not know whether *Met.* 1. 469–71 works against such an interpretation; note too that Ovid does sometimes (as some of Bömer's passages show) simply use *rubor* for the 'roses' part of a natural, unstimulated 'milk-and-roses' complexion. (Jasper Griffin reminds me that blushing is not Homeric. Vergil colours the epic according to a later sensibility. But note Enn. *Ann.* 352, 'et simul erubuit ceu lacte et purpura mixta'.)

[8] Cf. Ovid, *Am.* 1. 2. 32, *Ars* 1. 608, etc. for *pudor* as an obstacle to love.

[9] This is not an example of hypallage, pace Servius (Appendix (1)), who seems to have had influence on, among others, T. E. Page ad loc. Cf. Heyne on 64–9: 'non est hypallage ... utrumque dici et animo repraesentari potest; ut et ignis h. calor sanguinis ruborem faciat, et rubor, sanguine moto, calorem.' Bell's (1923) interesting discussion of Vergilian hypallage (esp. p. 320) does not, incidentally, include a subject–object interchange.

[10] *Rhet. Her* 4. 67: 'significatio est res quae plus in suspicione relinquit quam positum est in oratione' (cf. Cic. *Orat.* 139, 'significatio saepe erit maior quam oratio'); Quint. 8. 3. 83, 'amplior uirtus est ἔμφασις, altiorem praebens intellectum quam quem uerba per se ipsa declarant'.

blush in the symptoms and terminology of fire, Vergil suggests—he almost brings to the surface of his text—its erotic cause. Lavinia with *flagrantes genae*, with *ignis* kindled in her, with *calefacta ora*, is 'on fire'; and the repercussions of that sort of statement about a girl in a Vergilian text are obvious. It is tempting to use the word 'ambiguous'.

The source of the stained ivory simile is well known: the simile describing Menelaus' wound in *Iliad* 4. 141 ff.:

$$\dot{\omega}\varsigma\ \delta'\ \ddot{o}\tau\epsilon\ \tau\acute{\iota}\varsigma\ \tau'\ \dot{\epsilon}\lambda\acute{\epsilon}\phi\alpha\nu\tau\alpha\ \gamma\upsilon\nu\dot{\eta}\ \phi\sigma\acute{\iota}\nu\iota\kappa\iota\ \mu\iota\acute{\eta}\nu\eta$$
$$M\eta\sigma\nu\grave{\iota}\varsigma\ \mathring{\eta}\grave{\epsilon}\ K\acute{\alpha}\epsilon\iota\rho\alpha\ldots$$

No one can deny that Vergil's choice of simile is quite surprising, its literary purpose unobvious. Of course, the poet is shortly to base a whole scene (the breaking of the truce) on precisely this section of the *Iliad*; and some might maintain that he uses the simile simply because it is present to his mind and attractively decorative. On the other hand, Vergil usually displays profounder artistic principles than convenience, and seeks more in his similes than extrinsic ornament. In fact, the latest full discussion of Vergil's similes tells us that Book 12 exhibits the greatest interdependence between simile and narrative.[11] The same discussion fails, however, to elucidate ours.

Allusion is the key. Readers of Vergil know that the content and context of a Vergilian source are often (not always) to be borne in mind when reading the new fabrication. This is most clearly demonstrable over broad stretches of text. The content and context of Odysseus' wanderings focus and direct our reading of *Aen.* 1–6. But it can be clearly demonstrated in small and specific cases, as Knauer has frequently shown.[12] For example the full significance of *Aen.* 12. 896 ff. is not realized unless the Iliadic source or rather sources (primarily Diomedes material) are sensed through the Vergilian lines.[13]

Now the fact that 12. 896 ff. are part, indeed the climax, of a pattern of more or less well-marked Diomedes material helps us to pick up the allusion. The very unexpectedness of our simile prompts us to consider sources, and takes us back to Menelaus and *Iliad* 4. But what is the significance of the allusion, if such it be? What has Menelaus to do with Lavinia? Personally, nothing. The point lies elsewhere.

Two lexical details, in comparison with Homer, are significant. The epithet *sanguineus* is an addition to the Homeric source. *uiolo* is a much stronger word than $\mu\iota\alpha\acute{\iota}\nu\omega$. It has (among other things) a strong moral connotation ('defile')—but some moral connotation ('sully') is probably always present in the Greek word;[14] and *uiolo* signifies physical injuring in a way that $\mu\iota\alpha\acute{\iota}\nu\omega$

---

[11] Rieks (1981), 1087.   [12] Knauer (1964).   [13] Knauer (1964), 317–20.

[14] A neutral sense 'stain', 'dye', is a figment of lexicographical imagination (this point is pressed upon me by D. P. Fowler). It is *not* illustrated by Heliodorus 10. 15, pace LSJ; and in *Iliad*

does not; indeed, in four out of its eight other uses in the *Aeneid* (all Vergil's examples occur in the *Aeneid*) it makes up a formula *uiolauit uulnere, sim.*[15] We could say that, especially for Vergil, it was a 'wound' word. This nuance obviously works with *sanguineus*.[16] Thus, paradoxically, these variations from Homer assist the recall of Homer: they remind us that the simile originally applied to a wound (Menelaus' wound). And they also focus our attention upon what in the original context is relevant to our own: the *wound*.

The simile, in the first place illustrating Lavinia's blush, suggests by allusion (allusion assisted by diction: *sanguineus, uiolo*) that Lavinia is wounded. So, by a concatenation of emotions including love, is Turnus: 'Poenorum qualis in aruis | saucius ille...' (12. 4 ff.). So, preeminently, was Dido (suggestively linked to Turnus by the specification *Poenorum*). Wound, and fire, were dominant and striking images for Dido's love in Book 4: 'at regina graui iamdudum saucia cura | uulnus alit uenis et caeco carpitur igni' (1–2), and so on, at salient intervals in the book.[17] Wound and fire: *flagrantis, ignem, calefacta, sanguineo uiolauerit,* ὠτειλή. Discreetly but perceptibly Vergil reinforces the suggestion that Lavinia, like Dido, was in love: she was in love with (it must be) Turnus.

It is not, of course, in Vergil's way to say or suggest things objectively. His 'subjective style' (Otis's clumsy but now traditional phrase) instils into the narrative the feelings of the narrator—or one of the narrator's characters. Here we sense the narrator, Vergil himself. Wound imagery suggests sympathy. Wounds involve suffering, which we pity: remember how Dido's *tacitum uulnus* was amplified into the pitiable picture of the wounded hind, and finally realized in the frightful *uulnus stridens* of her suicide (4. 67, 69 ff., 689). Fire imagery is less sympathetic: we remember how Dido's *ignis* switched fluently to the *atri ignes* of her curse (4. 384). Vergil sees an antipathetic as well as a sympathetic aspect to Dido's violently passionate love. We perceive the same ambiguity in his delicate adumbration of Lavinia's more delicate passion: wound and fire. But in the final count, however sympathetic with its victims, Vergil condemns passionate love itself—he has done so (arguably consistently) since *Ecl.* 2: note especially *Georgics* 3. 209 ff.

---

4. 141 ff., μιήνῃ (141) is surely an example of 'intrusion' by a 'tenor' term (cf. 146, μιάνθην αἵματι μηροί) into the 'vehicle': cf. Silk (1974), 138–42. For other uses of μιαίνω in Homer, see *Iliad* 16. 795, μιάνθησαν δὲ ἔθειραι | αἵματι, 797, 17. 439, 23. 732: a sense 'sully' is clear in all of them.

[15] See Lewis and Short sub voc.; *Aen.* 11. 277, 591, 848, 12. 797.

[16] *sanguineus* might also be interpreted as the intrusion of 'tenor' terminology (the blood in Lavinia's cheeks) into the 'vehicle' (cf. n. 14). But this certainly does not preclude, nor is it as important as, the interpretation offered above.

[17] Cf. Otis (1963), 70 ff.

Vergilian disapprobation of love, his distaste, is evident here, in the moral connotation of *uiolauerit*.

Behind the second simile, 'aut mixta rubent ubi lilia...', is, probably, Apollonius' description of Medea, *Argonautica* 3. 297–8:

> ἁπαλὰς δὲ μετετρωπᾶτο παρειὰς
> ἐς χλόον, ἄλλοτ' ἔρευθος, ἀκηδείῃσι νόοιο.

The imagery itself reminds one (a) of a lover describing his beloved: cf. Prop. 2. 3. 10 ff.:

> lilia non domina sint magis alba mea;
> ut Maeotica nix minio si certet Hibero,
> utque rosae puro lacte natant folia...

It also recalls (b) Catullus' epithalamium, Catull. 61.185 ff.:

> uxor in thalamo tibi est,
> ore floridulo nitens,
> alba parthenice uelut
>   luteumue papauer.

The type of imagery was perhaps conventional in epithalamia. If it was, it would explain the way 'Lygdamus's' thought moves in the following ([Tibull.] 3. 4. 30 ff.):

> ...et color in niueo corpore purpureus,
> ut iuueni primum uirgo deducta marito
> inficitur teneras ore rubente genas,
> et cum contexunt amarantis alba puellae
> lilia et autumno candida mala rubent.

These are, I think, the most relevant parallels for our simile,[18] and they seem to me to guide its interpretation. It seems (a) a simile appropriately uttered *by* someone in love; it seems too (b) a simile appropriately uttered *of* somebody in love—by someone relatively detached. The erotic connotations, at least, seem indisputable; and the simile has I think a twofold suggestion, and a twofold 'subjectivity'. We detect quite distinctly I think (prompted by parallel (b)) *Vergil's* description of a girl in love; we detect too (following parallel (a)) *Turnus'* feelings for the girl he loves. That suggestion is confirmed by the next

---

[18] But note too the interesting passages cited by Enk on Prop. 2. 3. 11–12; also some of the passages listed by Bömer at Ov. *Met.* 3. 423. It should be observed that such imagery sometimes applies to a stimulated effect (Lavinia, Catullus' *uxor*), sometimes to a natural 'milk-and-roses' complexion (Propertius' Cynthia). But I do not think the distinction affects the point I am making, and so I have not encumbered the text with it.

movement of the text: 'illum turbat amor'. But I should like my emphasis to be on the first point: in the second simile, as in the first, Vergil suggests the love of Lavinia, Lavinia's love for Turnus.

'illum turbat amor...' The reference of *amor* is, I am inclined to think (in view of the above), ambiguous: Turnus' love for Lavinia—and *vice versa*. There is a point to be drawn out of this. 'illum turbat amor figitque in uirgine uultus; | ardet in arma magis...' In the opinion of Plato's Phaedrus love inspires bravery in a warrior.[19] Our text suggests a kindred idea, but with characteristic Vergilian colouring: passion inspires violence. And Phaedrus specified that not only loving, ἐρᾶν, but *being* loved, ἐρᾶσθαι, was inspiring.[20] Our ambiguity suggests the same sort of point in the new context.[21]

[19] Plato, *Symp.* 179a and following.
[20] Note the case of Achilles, *Symp.* 179e–180b.
[21] My best thanks are due to D. P. Fowler and Jasper Griffin for helpful contributions and criticisms.

Appendix

I collect here some comments on Lavinia in general and our passage in particular. Johnson's (12) is the most thoroughgoing, and has points of contact with my interpretation as well as radical differences from it.

1. Servius ⟨auct.⟩ on 12. 66: IGNEM SVBIECIT RVBOR 'hypallage est pro "cui ignis animi subiecit ruborem". mouebatur autem, intellegens se esse tantorum causam malorum, sic ⟨ut⟩ supra ⟨ipse⟩ [11. 480] causa mali tanti, oculos deiecta decoros.'

2. Tiberius Claudius Donatus on 12. 65: 'Lauinia, inquit, uocem matris lacrimantis accepit et uirginalis uerecundiae signa ipsius uultus sui permutatione monstrauit. nouerat enim se propter illa omnia geri...' (Donatus notices the stained ivory simile—'admirabilis parabola'—but has nothing to say—beyond enthusing and paraphrasing.)

3. C. G. Heyne, in the Heyne–Wagner edition of Vergil (1833) on 12. 64–9: 'Praeclare τὸ ἦθος in virgine servatum. Erubescit illa; animi sensa non eloquitur. Quandoquidem autem sive ex antiqui aevi more, sive ex carminis oeconomia, Laviniae nullae praecipuae partes esse in rerum actu poterant: multo magis in rubore puellae acquiescere debuit poeta... Erubuisse autem putanda est, cum praesente Turno nuptiarum esset facta mentio, quas mater cum ipso, non cum Aenea, factas esse vellet. Nam de amore Laviniae, in utrum illa animo inclinaret, nihil usquam, si bene memini, poeta meminit.'

4. J. Conington, in the Conington–Nettleship edition of 1883 on 12. 64: 'As Heyne observes, Virg. never informs us what were the feelings of Lavinia.' (As far as Heyne is concerned this is a little misleading.)

5. R. Heinze, *Virgils epische Technik* (3rd edn. Leipzig, 1914), 460: '...kein Versuch [wird] gemacht..., Lavinia aus dem Hintergrunde hervorzuziehen und zu einer handelnden Figur zu machen; die Ereignisse am Hofe des Latinus sind so gerade kompliziert genug, und der Dichter bedient sich gern des Vorwandes, dass die altrömische *filia familias* keinen Eigenwillen hat... Lavinia soll den Leser gar nicht als Individuum, sondern lediglich als Tochter des Latinus interessieren, mit deren Hand das Königreich vergeben wird.'

6. W. Warde Fowler, *The Death of Turnus* (Oxford, 1919), 49: 'Once and again Virgil has carried the Homeric simile of fact into the region of feeling and character; the blush reveals Lavinia as she is nowhere else revealed...' (But nothing more of substance is added.)

7. Schur in *RE* XII. 1. 1006. 45 ff. (article 'Lavinia', 1924): 'L. selbst ist bei dem ganzen Kampfe völlig passiv, wird nicht um ihre Meinung gefragt und lässt alles willig über sich ergehen.'

8. V. Pöschl, *The Art of Vergil* (English translation: University of Michigan, 1962), 201 n. 43 (= *Die Dichtkunst Virgils*, Innsbruck and Vienna, 1950, p. 145 n. 211): 'Lavinia's charm, doubled by her grief (XII.64f.), is one more reason for Turnus to fight. His love for Lavinia is treated with the same restraint as that of Aeneas for Dido.'

9. M. C. J. Putnam, *The Poetry of the Aeneid* (Cambridge, Mass., 1965), 159: 'Lavinia's blush, prompted by Amata's speech, is caused by Turnus' love for her.' (There is further comment on our lines, part fanciful, part stimulating.)

10. F. Klingner, *Virgil* (Zürich/Stuttgart, 1967), 591: 'Ein einziges Mal wird Lavinia als schönes Wesen gegenwärtig, das Liebe zu erregen vermag, dort, wo Turnus zum letzten Kampf aufzubrechen im Begriff ist (12,64–70). Lavinia ist nicht eine betörende Beute für den kühnen Mann, sie ist Macht und Anrecht, und Ursprung einer Ahnenreihe.'

11. W. S. Anderson, *The Art of the Aeneid* (Englewood Cliffs, NJ, 1969), 116 (a footnote on lines 64–70): 'Vergil never interprets Lavinia's feelings towards Turnus or Aeneas. It is clearly possible to explain her blush in several fashions, indeed to attribute it to her affection for Amata alone. We see how Turnus is moved, but his wild emotions may completely misinterpret the situation.'

12. W. R. Johnson, *Darkness Visible, A Study of Vergil's Aeneid* (University of California Press, 1976), 56 f.: 'But why does she blush? What is it that her mother says that conjures up this manifestation of simple embarrassment or of delicate, shy, turbulent eroticism? *Ardentem generum/generum Aenean*? We know nothing whatever of Lavinia's conscious thoughts, much less of her private fantasies. Does she respond to the passion of Turnus? Has she toyed with notions of the glamorous Asiatic barbarian...? One may speculate, but Vergil has seen to it that such speculation is as fruitless as it is boring. We are given nothing but a fleeting, tantalizing vision of possible erotic excitement, but that vision is as incisive and as artistic as anything Vergil wrote. Yet it was not imagined in order that we might understand something about Lavinia; it was imagined in order that we might understand something about Turnus... My point here is that we see Lavinia blush through Turnus' eyes, and it is Turnus' passion and his point of view that cause Vergil to select *uiolauerit*... *Violauerit* echoes the *uiolentia* of Turnus... The flawlessly mixed simile describes the confused manner in which Turnus see[s] Lavinia's blush...'

10

Ovid's *Metamorphoses*, Callimachus, and *l'art pour l'art* (1984)

I. Alcyone, pathetically devoted wife of Ceyx, has forebodings of her husband's death at sea (*Met.* 11. 421 ff.). We sense that these forebodings are not misplaced. They are not: the narrative conducts us remorselessly to the point where Alcyone sees their vindication. Ceyx's body is washed up on the shore before her eyes. The tragic *praxis* of the Ceyx and Alcyone episode seems unmistakeable.[1]

From Alcyone's forebodings to their terrible vindication: an action in which the heroine provides the principal point of focus. One's sense of tragedy is carefully heightened as the action proceeds. We (but not Alcyone) swiftly hear of the death of Ceyx. Throughout most of the story therefore we know that Alcyone must confront loss and suffering: the narrative proceeds with tragic inevitability. And our knowledge coupled with Alcyone's ignorance allows scope for tragic irony—resonantly in the scene succeeding Ceyx's death where Alcyone counts the time till Ceyx's return, and wonders what to wear on that day (573–6). Ceyx dies with words of devotion on his lips (566–7): this and many other signs of their reciprocal love give the tragedy pathos and humanity. Delay and foreshadowing (the dream image of Ceyx, 663 ff., Alcyone's first, 'anticipatory' lament, 676–707) render the disastrous climax more expected, more awaited and therefore more terrible. Ceyx's body is washed ashore. A last postponement: 'qui foret, ignorans, quia naufragus omine mota | ... "heu miser" inquit | "quisquis es ..."' (719 ff.). Then finally, it seems, the stark confrontation: *erat coniunx* (725).

But it isn't. And this is not a tragedy. At the last moment the actors and ourselves are, in a way, spared. Confrontation is side-stepped: by the metamorphosis.

My best thanks are due to Mrs. C. E. Clark and Professor E. J. Kenney for advice, information and criticism. It is not to be supposed that they agree with all my conclusions.

[1] From time to time I shall make use of phrases from Aristotle's *Poetics*. Like everybody else I do not understand all this treatise, and some of it I think is erroneous. But much of it is very and brilliantly true, and expressed in terse and down-to-earth language. Its terminology is therefore useful. I shall usually quote from it in Margaret Hubbard's lucid translation: see Russell and Winterbottom (1972), 85–132. I shall use this volume for other literary critical texts.

Alcyone becomes the halcyon bird even as she runs to the body. Ceyx too: 'tandem superis miserantibus ambo | alite mutantur.'

To talk of a happy ending here would not be apt. The impending tragedy simply *dissolves*. In the bulk of the narrative we have been concerned with *people*. It was the impending tragedy of 'someone like us'[2] which seemed appalling. The magically produced halcyons cannot affect us comparably. A *mimesis* of life (or rather of the *idea* of life)[3] slips into a world that is incontrovertibly fictional. The emotional demand upon us becomes quite different.

It happens that the transformed halcyons live lovingly forever together. They might have grieved apart in lonely nests, and still have had a comparable 'dissolving' effect on the imminently tragic story. The one is a sweet evasion rather than a happy ending: the other would be an evasion indulging something equally tolerable, a sentimental melancholy. The one does, the other would, avoid 'the sort of thing that would happen'[4]—avoid confrontation with the stark fact of tragedy. We are on the point of beholding the ineffaceable spectacle of Alcyone beholding the ineffaceable spectacle of her dead husband when reality and the spectacle fade into the warmth of a comfortable fiction. Ovid allows us to taste the ingredients of tragedy, but spares us the totality of the experience.

II. Here is probably the most important function of metamorphosis in the *Metamorphoses*.[5] It allows us to enter all manner of affecting experience—and to leave relatively unscathed. The 'Murra' episode, for example (*Met*. 10. 298–502), lays bare a story of incest. The reader encounters suggestive ironies ('"accipe" dixit | "ista tua est, Cinyra" deuotaque corpora iunxit. | accipit obsceno genitor sua uiscera lecto | uirgineosque metus leuat hortaturque timentem'). As the story proceeds the reader also develops sympathy for the heroine. And by the end the plot is disturbing. Murra pregnant, discovered and exiled. How will Ovid resolve it? A dénouement that squared with either morality or plausibility ('the sort of thing that would happen') would be

---

[2] Aristotle *Poetics* 13; cf. *Poetics* 15: characters 'should be life-like'. I realise I am using the phrase from *Poetics* 13 (and perhaps 15) in a context different from Aristotle's. But it seems to me a justifiable extension.

[3] Aristotle explains his conception of the nature of mimetic art (it seems to me to have wide validity) at *Poetics* 9. He has it in mind to counter Platonic criticism of art, and his own view can be conveniently stated in quasi-Platonic terms. Cf. Hubbard in Russell and Winterbottom (1972), 88. Of course Aristotle himself did not believe in substantive *ideai*; and I do not employ *idea* in its full Platonic sense above. By 'the *idea* of life' I mean (an episode of) life as it would be in a more economic and orderly world; a world where the fact of happiness or the fact of disaster is undiminished by coincidences und unobscured by inessentials, and where the consequences of actions follow. Cf. the fine comments of Jaeger (1945), 36–7 on the nature and significance of events in art compared with life; and of course Aristotle himself, the fount of all this: *Poetics* 9.

[4] *Poetics* 9.   [5] Cf. Galinsky (1975), 61–70.

bleak. 'crura loquentis | terra superuenit.' Reality, and with it the dilemma of the story, dissolves.

In 'Echo and Narcissus' (*Met.* 3. 339–510) we find a less melodramatic but perhaps more affecting dilemma. What is to become of the protagonists whose yearning is so piquantly quaint, so surprisingly touching, and so absolutely incapable of being satisfied?[6] The nymph Echo wastes away for love (395 ff.) and becomes echo. The nymph knew what frustration was and we pitied her, but our pity then dissipates in a comfortably plaintive fiction. Narcissus too wastes away for love (502 ff.), again pitiably. And this time Ovid toys with pathos longer. He takes us up and beyond an actual death: to the underworld. There Narcissus is still contemplating his reflection, in the river Styx. Already in this we sense a shift in the order of reality. Meanwhile, back on earth, 'nusquam corpus erat'. Instead of a body there is a flower: metamorphosis and fairytale again. And the flower becomes the final focus of all pitying feelings for Narcissus, transmuting them into something comfortable, even pleasurable—because the story is now a patent and undisturbing fiction.

Here, as I say, is probably the most important function of metamorphosis in the poem; and it is a standard tactic. We cannot feel the same for a supernaturally produced bird, tree or phenomenon as we do for a human character, a character 'like us'. Ovid knows this, and exploits it. By creating a story which starts, to a greater or lesser extent, as a *mimesis* of the *idea* of life and then letting it dissipate in unambiguous fantasy, Ovid permits us to taste life as it were *safely*. We can share the anguish of sorrow and the dilemma of perversity—and sample perversity as an excitant—without having to live with either dilemma or anguish thereafter.

So Ovid's purpose in the *Metamorphoses* should be seen as radically different from that of an artist—prose narrator, poet or playwright—whose *mimesis* is unflinching to the end, whose work concludes with 'a state that is the necessary or usual consequent of something else';[7] an artist whose stories are truthful in a way that Ovid's are not. When one sets aside a 'truthful' narrative or leaves a 'truthful' play, one does not easily shake off the pathos, tragedy or moral dilemma that the work has suggested. To witness a *mimesis* of the *idea* of life is in a way to be forced to live, intensely. Ovid works it so that we can sample life safely. He controls our dose. Some people might think it was, in a way, rather an immoral form of art.

III. Metamorphosis therefore insulates the reader from the full implications of an action imitated. Such is Ovid's continual aim; and metamorphosis is his

---

[6] Familiar elegiac motifs are transferred to Narcissus (see Bömer on lines 415 ff.), which makes the story more quaint—and the fact that it touches perhaps the more surprising.

[7] *Poetics* 7.

continual and most definable device. There is another, more or less apprehensible: his use of style, his manipulation of style in relation to content.

I know that critical discussion of form and content is beset by problems of definition, indeed of metaphysics. But at times we have no choice but to attempt it. Critics must often suggest where they cannot prove; and some poets clearly do have ideas of form and content distinct in their minds.

It seems to me that Ovid in the *Metamorphoses* sometimes deliberately contrives a discrepancy between content and form; and this, to an extent, insulates us. For example, rhetoric deployed obtrusively (even for Augustan taste) can interpose a kind of barrier between us and the action. We find our responses curiously and very importantly complicated. At *Met.* 8. 462 ff. there is a passage of over fifty outstandingly epigrammatical lines. Their ingenuity is of the sort to elicit cries of *euge, belle* and polite applause. It is a struggle to remember that Althaea is debating whether to kill her own son. The verbal ironies studding the 'Murra' are, incidentally, inclined to provoke an aesthetic pleasure hard to reconcile with the intrinsic earnestness of the subject matter.

Rhetoric complicates response to horrific violence; here is a favourite trick of Ovidian art.[8] Urbane hexameters and pointed conceits adorn the violence and gore of the battle of the Lapiths and Centaurs, e.g.

> nec dicere Rhoetus
> plura sinit, rutilasque ferox in aperta loquentis
> condidit ora uiri perque os in pectora flammas.   (12. 293–5)

> plenoque e gutture fluxit
> inque toros inque ipsa niger carchesia sanguis.   (12. 325–6)

In the brutally grotesque scene of the death of Niobe's sons a topos, reversed παρὰ προσδοκίαν, occupies us while Alphenor dies:[9]

> pars et pulmonis in hamis
> eruta cumque anima cruor est effusus in auras.   (6. 252–3)

And the following hyperbole grotesquely, and divertingly, decorates basic content:

> altera per iugulum pennis tenus acta sagitta est;
> expulit hanc sanguis seque eiaculatus in altum
> emicat et longe terebrata prosilit aura.   (6. 258–60)

In all these style and content are (arguably) discrepant. And this causes a kind of insulation. Basic subject matter (killing) is distanced by stylistic display—

---

[8] Cf. Galinsky's chapter 'Ovid's Humanity: Death and Suffering in the *Metamorphoses*', (1975), 110–53, a useful if unsympathetic discussion. The famous simile for Pyramus' wound (*Met.* 4. 120–4) is another example of what I am talking about.

[9] See Bömer ad loc.

just as Althaea's declamatory skills distanced us from the facts of her dilemma. We are diverted by stylistic invention. We find the episodes horrifying in their way but not finally harrowing: ultimately, we might even have to conclude, entertaining. A curious experience.

Ovid, we could say, is creating 'effects' rather than composing *mimeseis*. By 'effect' I mean something technical: an 'effect' is provided for our *aesthetic* senses. An 'effect' excludes moral or profoundly emotional involvement; we contemplate it rather than live it. Let me amplify that slightly (and see too below, pp. 154–5). According to normal criteria of experience the basic subject matter in the above passages is appalling. The *mimesis* of the *idea* of what is appalling would or should move us much as the appalling would do in life. But in the Ovidian passages this does not happen. By his manipulation of style in relation to content Ovid can present the appalling as an 'effect'; as something to be contemplated, to be sampled aesthetically. He permits an encounter with the appalling which does not truly appal. The broad policy of the *Metamorphoses* achieved by metamorphosis (§§ I and II) is discernible within the individual episodes.

In certain circumstances the appalling can be made into an 'effect' by emphatic *congruence* of style and content. This may sound paradoxical, but it isn't. Ovid stages[10] the death of two of Niobe's sons thus:

> transierant ad opus nitidae iuuenale palaestrae;
> et iam contulerant arto luctantia nexu
> *pecto*ra *pecto*ribus; *con*tento *con*cita neruo,
> sicut erant iuncti, traiecit utrumque sagitta.
> *in*gemuere *simul, simul in*curuata dolore
> membra solo posuere, *simul* suprema iacentes
> lumina uers*arunt*, animam *simul* exhal*arunt*.   (6. 241–7)

A series of rhetorical devices (homoiocatarcton, anaphora, homoioteleuton, etc.[11]) mirrors in style the grotesque facts of the context: the simultaneous, interlocked deaths of the two brothers.

Two questions ought to be asked. First, here is certainly a congruence of style and content: but is it a marriage, a perfect blending so that the one is no longer practically or conceptually distinguishable from the other? The answer to this is surely No. The congruence is so contrived that we know the two are still clearly distinct in the poet's mind. More tangibly and importantly, the components are still distinguishable on the page. We can see that Ovid has laid on homoiocatarcton and the rest to mirror, to elaborate (not *be*) the content. The description stands out; it is a virtuoso performance in the depiction of the grotesque. Ovid has contrived it and does not mind the

---

[10] And it is Ovid's original staging: see Bömer's introduction to the episode.
[11] See Bömer on lines 242 and ff.

means of contrivance being visible, indeed wants them to be visible. Form and content are in fact as distinct as when Ovid contrived actual discrepancy.[12] Our response is similarly complicated. Brilliant, flagrant artifice does not, cannot, affect us in the same way as a *mimesis* that marries form and content.

We might also ask: why? Why this grotesque picture, exactly and luminously elaborated by rhetoric? Context does not demand it. The sequence of hybris, vengeance and pathos which forms the *praxis* of the Niobe story (until it too dissipates in metamorphosis) has no need of it. Indeed it occurs oddly in context (so do the other grotesque descriptions). It is not 'the sort of thing that would happen'. It is an extrinsic virtuoso performance.

So the horror is Ovid's brilliant, gratuitous contrivance. Again it is 'effect'. It cannot elicit, nor does it mean to elicit, the same emotional response as horror integral to an engrossing, plausible *praxis* (a true *mimesis*).

'The appalling can be made into an "effect".' The poetic policy is now plain. But perhaps (the thought might again occur to us) this *is* rather an immoral sort of art.[13]

IV.1. The literary principles, indeed the genre, of the *Metamorphoses* seem to be indicated at *Met.* 1. 4:

> ad mea perpetuum deducite tempora carmen.

---

[12] Decision in any particular case as to whether there is distinction or actual discrepancy betwen form and content can be hard, even subjective (e.g. in the passages from the 'Lapiths and Centaurs' above). But it is not important. The vital fact common to both is that the poet is distinguishing form and content, in his mind and on the page. Cf. below pp. 161 f.

[13] With Ovid's practice here it is tempting to compare Boileau, *Art poétique*, Chant III 1–5: 'Il n'est point de Serpent, ni de Monstre odieux | Qui par l'art imité ne puisse plaire aux yeux. | D'un pinceau délicat l'artifice agréable | Du plus affreux objet fait un objet aimable. | Ainsi, pour nous charmer, la Tragédie en pleurs...'. But Ovid's procedure is more complex than anything envisaged by Boileau. Boileau's statement that art, by gracefully decking horrifying subject matter, can make it pleasing, is meant in all simplicity (note his views on *mimesis* quoted by the Pléiade editor ad loc.). He has no notion of the concept and piquant pleasure of an 'effect'. Still, despite the simplicity (indeed naiveté, implausibility) of what he actually means, Boileau's lines could have been suggestive to poets of 'Ovidian' inclination ('Ovidian' in the aspect that I have identified). See below §V.2.

Boileau has in mind Aristotle *Poetics* 4, but Aristotle of course meant something quite different: '*Mimesis* is innate in human beings from childhood... and pleasure in instances of *mimesis* is equally general. This we can see from the facts: we enjoy looking at the most exact portrayals of things we do not like to see in real life, the lowest animals, for instance, or corpses. This is because not only philosophers, but all men, enjoy getting to understand something, though it is true that most people feel this pleasure only to a slight degree; therefore they like to see these pictures, because in looking at them they come to understand something and can infer what each thing is, can say, for instance, "This man in the picture is so-and-so". If you happen not to have seen the original, the picture will not produce its pleasure *qua* instance of *mimesis*, but because of its technical finish or colour or for some such other reason.' Aristotle's point is his cardinal one that learning is pleasurable; and so *mimesis*, being instructive, give pleasure. The same argument is put forward (perhaps more suggestively) at *Rhetoric* 1. 11. 23.

'perpetuum carmen' unmistakeably recalls Callimachus' phrase ἓν ἄεισμα διηνεκές (*Aetia* fr. 1. 3 Pf.), 'a single continuous poem'. Ovid seems, therefore, to identify the *Metamorphoses* as an epic, an epic of traditional type; for that is what Callimachus has in mind—and rejects.[14] So Ovid is alluding to Callimachus' famous statement of poetics, the preface to the *Aetia*; and he seems to be declaring his apostasy.[15]

At this point we ought to clarify something perhaps not adequately clarified. What *are* Callimachus' poetics? And how are they reflected in practice? The preface, and Callimachus' other theoretical utterances, do sometimes verge on the oracular.

IV.2. Callimachus *Aetia, praef.* (fr. 1 Pf.):

The Telchines [spiteful, envious mythical figures cited here to typify literary enemies] often squeak at my poetry, ignoramuses who are not the Muses' friends; they complain that I have not finished off a single continuous poem [ἓν ἄεισμα διηνεκές] many thousand miles long in honour of kings or heroes of olden times, but unroll my verse only a little distance like a child, though the decades of my years are not few (6). I say this to them: '...all right, my lines are few; but Philetas' *Demeter* far outweighs his long old woman [i.e. Philetas' short poem in elegiacs is better than his long one], and of the two it is his poems that accord with fineness [αἱ κατὰ λεπτόν] that show Mimnermus delightful [γλυκύς], not his great girl [i.e., probably, his long elegiac poem *Nanno*] (12)... Nightingales [i.e. poems] are honeysweeter [μελιχρότεραι] thus (16)... Learn to judge poetic skill by art [τέχνῃ], not by its leagues of length (18). And do not look for me to breed a loud-sounding minstrelsy; thundering is Zeus' trade, not mine.' For when first I set my writing tablet on my knees, Apollo said to me, he of Lycia: 'Dearest of poets, feed your sacrificial offering as fat as may be, but keep your Muse, dear fellow, thin [λεπταλέην] (24). And this too I bid you, to tread where wagons do not trample, not drive your chariot on tracks that others share nor on the broad highway, but on unworn paths, even though the way you drive be rather narrow.' (M. Hubbard's translation,[16] with some changes and omissions).

Let us attempt a summary. Callimachus accepts an accusation that he does not write poems on a grand scale on kings and heroes: he is saying in fact that he does not write epic in the Homeric or historic tradition; and he also says that he eschews extended narrative elegy (9–12). Along with this there is an important point, not to be underestimated. Callimachus is admitting—and not overtly defending himself—that he neglects what most ancient critics,

---

[14] Cf. Herter (1948), 139–42; Kenney (1976), 51.
[15] Ovid had previously adopted a Callimachean stance—in his own irreverent way: *Am.* 1. 1; 2. 1; 1. 15 esp. lines 8 and 13. He is more assertively independent at *Rem.* 371 ff.
[16] Hubbard (1974), 73–4.

certainly Aristotle, would deem a cardinal virtue: unity of plot, continuity of narrative technique (διηνεκές (3), see below).

What else? Callimachus implies that bombast and pretension are inseparable from large-scale productions. Stylistic perfection seems to be a preoccupation of his—it almost seems to be the heart of the matter: his key word is λεπτός (11, and cf. 4 λεπταλέος), 'finely-woven', a metaphorical term which presupposes the common Greek image of 'weaving' literature.[17] He demands brief compass (9 etc.). And, finally, he lays great stress on originality (25 ff.).

The above paragraphs may sound familiar; and the analysis is not as yet very illuminating. I think we must get behind the polemic and the details to find the theoretical principles which unite and explain them. First of all, one thing must be made clear. Callimachus, whose diction bespeaks obsessive love of and familiarity with Homer, has no grudge against the master, the 'divine bard' as he himself calls him (Epigram 6 Pf.). It is the epigones whose epics are uncouth and filthily written; it is the fading post-Homeric epic tradition that he eschews. ἐχθαίρω τὸ ποίημα τὸ κυκλικόν ('I hate the cyclic poem'): Callimachus speaks more precisely in Epigram 28 Pf.[18] And Aratus, who is lauded for following Hesiod, for imitating 'probably the honeysweetest quality of poetry', has not imitated, presumably because one could not imitate, the 'supreme poet': Epigram 27 Pf.[19]

Homer we may conclude is inimitable. Is the grudge against the epigones simply that their work is unoriginal, its stylistic quality dreadful? Certainly Callimachus' positive utterances are preoccupied with style and originality. But the root issue I think lies a stage further back: Callimachus' view of the *function* of poetry. From this all, or virtually all, flows.

μελιχρότατον, 'honey-sweetest', in Epigram 27 is a revealing word. 'Sweetness' in poetry is clearly regarded as a mark of its excellence; pleasure therefore would seem a or the legitimate criterion by which to judge it. The same criterion of poetic excellence is forcefully implied in the *Aetia* preface: γλυκύς 'sweet' (11), μελιχρότεραι 'honey-sweeter' (16). Here we can scent a basic issue, a real point of divide. The profound and perennial orthodoxy among the Greeks was that the main function of serious poetry was a moral one: in some way to improve, to edify, to teach.[20] Callimachus seems to be aligning

---

[17] See LSJ s.vv. λεπτός 3, ὑφαίνω III 2. Vergil seems to have understood λεπτός as 'finespun'—or at least that is how he rendered it: *Ecl.* 6. 5. At *Aetia* fr. 1. 24 Callimachus is punning on λεπτ(αλε)ος 'thin' i.e. 'scrawny' and λεπτός 'fine'. For Callimachus' preoccupation with stylistic perfection see too *Hymn to Apollo*, 105 ff.

[18] On the sense of κυκλικός see Blumenthal (1978), 125–7.

[19] On the interpretation of this epigram see Reitzenstein (1931), 43 ff. Reitzenstein further illustrates the point that Homer was inimitable, not undesirable, in Callimachus' eyes.

[20] Cf. Jaeger (1945), i, Ch. 3 'Homer the Educator', also Index s.v. *Education, educational character of poetry*. 'The Greeks always felt that a poet was in the broadest and deepest sense the

himself with the smaller voices of hedonistic heterodoxy: the function, the only function, of poetry is to delight. 'Every poet aims at entertainment (ψυχαγωγία)' is the succinct view attributed to Eratosthenes.[21]

We can say more. It is surely unlikely that anyone maintained that poetry should be judged by the 'league' (*Aetia, praef.* 18).[22] I think that Callimachus is here humorously misrepresenting his opponents—a custom in scholarly or artistic argument. Such opponents may of course have pointed out that his poetry tended to be slight in compass; but their solid objection would have been that it was slight in content, more particularly slight in purpose; deficient in moral worth. Callimachus, they might have said, produced not a *mimesis* of 'serious action',[23] but a frivolous indulgence in abstruse peripherals: 'like a child' (*Aetia, praef.* 6) indeed, albeit a precocious one: in sum, his poetic criteria were all wrong. Callimachus clowns with his critics, misrepresents them; but he delivers a clear statement on the substantive issue: 'nightingales (poems) are *sweeter* thus; judge poetry by *art*'. His idea of the function of literature is unconventional, *different*.

And in fact he is implying a subtler poetic than one merely hedonistic. The final test of excellence in poetry, says Callimachus, must be not moral worth (the unspoken alternative) but 'art', τέχνη.[24] Callimachus is preaching an amoral poetic, *aesthetic* rather than hedonistic; and in fact his theoretical insistence upon formal perfection, an insistence which assumes such perfection will be pleasurable and by implication derides any edifying function for poetry, brings to mind the principles of *l'art pour l'art*.[25] So does his practice.

'The achievement of formal Beauty was the sole purpose of a work of art, . . . aesthetic—and never ulterior—value was what counted.' In this way the *Oxford Companion to French Literature* defines *l'art pour l'art*. Some amplification is in order. Art is solely for art: formal perfection has, as in Callimachus, overriding importance. But this pregnant phrase—*l'art pour l'art*—carries with it many other implications.[26] The aestheticism it demands

---

educator of his people' (p. 35). In Aristophanes' *Frogs* Euripides does not quarrel with the principle of Aeschylus' remark that 'poets alone are the teachers of youth' (1055). Strabo 1. 2. 3–9 (Russell and Winterbottom (1972), 300–5) give a Stoic's version of the moral orthodoxy.

[21] Strabo 1. 2. 3.

[22] But note Aristotle's interesting comments on 'amplitude', *Poetics* 7.

[23] Cf. Aristotle *Poetics* 5 μίμησις σπουδαίων (pace Miss Hubbard I take σπουδαίων to be neut., but the text here is in great dispute), μίμησις πράξεως σπουδαίας. σπουδαῖος can of course carry a moral implication, and perhaps does in these phrases. See the excellent discussion of Vahlen (1914), 267–8.

[24] Cf. n. 26.   [25] Cf. (and contrast) Jaeger (1945), i. 35 and 472 n. 4.

[26] 'Art' in the mouths of exponents of *l'art pour l'art* (French and English) is a wide and embracing term (poetry, painting etc.; formal skill in poetry, painting etc.). (When I translate Callimachus' *techne* as 'art', I do *not* intend to imply that it has comparable connotations: the word means rather art in the sense of craft, artifice, *ars*. We can demonstrate *l'art pour l'art* in Callimachus without the aid of speciousness.)

means that the artist must create not *mimeseis* but 'effects' (cf. above p. 150). Taking myth, fiction, life or whatever as his raw material, he must so compose it that it appeals only to aesthetic senses. The myth, fiction, life or whatever that he works with becomes something that we contemplate, that we sample aesthetically, but do not live: an 'effect'. Moral involvement is to be excluded. Emotional involvement (in a sense) likewise. The artist's sole purpose, we might conclude, is to produce 'beautiful effects'—accepting that the conceptions of beauty may be various and the effects manifold.[27] Indeed it is an amoral art—but perhaps it is an ideal which artists rarely, in actuality, wholly achieve.

Some quotations: 'La Poésie se rattache aux arts de la peinture, de la cuisine et du cosmétique par la possibilité d'exprimer toute sensation de suavité ou d'amertume, de béatitude ou d'horreur...'; 'Ce n'est pas pour mes femmes, mes filles ou mes soeurs que ce livre a été écrit; non plus que pour les femmes, les filles ou les soeurs de mon voisin. Je laisse cette fonction à ceux qui ont intérêt à confondre les bonnes actions avec le beau langage' (from Baudelaire, *Projets de Préfaces* III and I). Gautier:

> Sans prendre garde à l'ouragan
> Qui fouettait mes vitres fermées
> Moi, j'ai fait *Émaux et Camées*.

Note too Baudelaire's poem *La Beauté* ('Je suis belle, ô mortels...'). These, spiced with humour, irony and cheek, catch something of the spirit of *l'art pour l'art*.[28]

And note of course the English Oscar Wilde: 'The sphere of Art and the Sphere of Ethics are absolutely distinct....', 'Form is everything',[29] etc. Wilde of course is parasitic upon the French thinkers but Callimachus is not. Nor can they have been significantly influenced by him, particularly not by his

---

[27] 'Le beau est toujours bizarre', says Baudelaire (ed. Pléiade ii. 578). Note too the implications of 'Dans les plis sinueux des vieilles capitales, | Où tout, même l'horreur, tourne aux enchantements...' (Baudelaire, *Les Petites Vieilles*) and 'Dessins auxquels la gravité | Et le savoir d'un vieil artiste, | Bien que le sujet en soit triste, | Ont communiqué la Beauté...' (*Le Squelette laboureur*).

[28] Note too Gautier's prefaces to *Albertus* (1832) and to *Mademoiselle de Maupin* (1834) which are exuberant and provocative though hardly analytical statements of essential principles of *l'art pour l'art*. Baudelaire (on Baudelaire's position with regard to *l'art pour l'art* see below §V.2) reacts interestingly to Gautier's poetry (imagining a scholar of the future, a 'savant amoureux de beauté', perusing his works): 'Avec quelle *délice* son oeil se promènera dans tous ces poèmes si *purs* et si *précieusement* ornés!' (my emphases: from *L'Art romantique: Théophile Gautier*): i.e. τέχνη has produced poems that will be pleasurable, γλυκύς, μελιχρός. Cf. further, Cassagne (1906), especially *deuxième partie*, II and III. As one might expect, the literary historians give the best definitions of the theory, better than the practitioners.

[29] From *The Critic as Artist, Part II*.

theorising.[30] Valid literary impulses simply recur, independently. Sometimes the reappearance is striking. The 'Callimacheanism' of Barbey d'Aurevilly's remark 'les artistes écrivent pour leurs pairs, ou du moins pour ceux qui les comprennent'[31] is unmistakeable but trite. A different matter is Gautier's famous poem *L'Art*. I do not suppose that Gautier had pondered the question of Callimachus' style very deeply,[32] but this poem is a fair rationale of the Alexandrian poet's formal esotericism:

> Oui, l'oeuvre sort plus belle
> D'une forme au travail
>   Rebelle,
> Vers, marbre, onyx, émail.
> Point de contraintes fausses!
> Mais que pour marcher droit
>   Tu chausses,
> Muse, un cothurne étroit.
> Fi du rhythme commode,... etc.

Once we appreciate the basic attitude to poetry that underlies the *Aetia* preface, the reason for Callimachus' preoccupation with quality of style becomes explained. Other aspects of his polemic, and of his poetic practice, become similarly comprehensible. Of course Callimachus would not want to join the epicists: no doubt the genre vaunted itself as edifying, *engagé*, useful; to Callimachus it was tediously earnest and misunderstood the function of poetry in his time. (But what, we might ask, of the example of Homer, hailed as the great moral poet, the educator of Greece?[33] Callimachus might have tartly retorted that Homer had no such view of his own art—on the contrary.[34] Anyway Homer was inimitable.[35])

And Callimachus could not consider epic or any grand scale poetry for another reason. Concentration of energies, he must have thought, was essential to achieve stylistic perfection. It was prudent therefore to keep poems short. Homer might have achieved both ampleness of scale and quality of style. But Homer was inimitable. It was a lesson that the admired Mimnermus

---

[30] The most striking and explicit statement of Callimachean aesthetics, the *Aetia* preface (fr. 1 Pf.), was not yet discovered. The Roman poets do not state or imply a theory of *l'art pour l'art*; not even the *soi-disant* Roman Callimachus, Propertius, who actually held—he certainly professed—quite different ideas of the function of literature.

[31] Preface to *Une vieille maitresse*.

[32] Gautier's prowess in Latin rather than Greek attracted attention (he exhibited an eccentric and significant penchant for later Latin style): cf. Richardson (1958), 18–19; Grant (1975) 16.

[33] 'Encomiasts of Homer (say) that this poet has educated Greece...' Plato, *Republic* 606e. Cf. above n. 20. The claim was far from absurd.

[34] Cf. Sikes (1931), 2–3; Grube (1965), 3.   [35] Above, p. 153.

could have used: 'and of the two it is his poems that accord with fineness that show Mimnermus delightful, not his great girl'.[36]

And there is another point to be made—or we should express ourselves more precisely. For Callimachus did not believe that poems *necessarily, always,* had to be short. Here we must pick up the implication of ἓν διηνεκές, the question of unity: the question why Callimachus abandoned this basic literary virtue (see above pp. 152–3). What Callimachus was unwilling to contemplate was poetry on a grand scale if it was to be continuous, unified, if it committed him to telling a story 'from beginning to end', διηνεκέως ἀγορεύειν.[37] A certain ampleness of scale *and* quality could be achieved even by post-Homeric man if he adopted genres by nature discontinuous (i.e. genres that could be presented in short, self-contained sections); and/or if he did not feel bound by Aristotelian scruples over unity to tell a story 'from beginning to end', more particularly 'with a beginning, a middle (or "middle parts"), and an end':[38] if he could presuppose knowledge of a story in his readers, his *pairs*, and then focus on selected aspects of it. And this policy allowed him not just the chance to concentrate his stylistic energies as well as achieve ampleness. It facilitated his problem of originality.

Callimachus' practice supports the above account of Callimachus' theory. He constructs a catalogue 'didactic',[39] and exploits opportunities that this discontinuous genre offers for higly-wrought, independent, unusual narratives. He adopted a discontinuous narrative technique that allowed him to produce the comparatively large-scale 'epic' *Hecale* with exquisite quality in the parts, and originality in the extraordinary 'plot' of the 'whole'. Discontinuous narrative technique is in fact the rule in all his narratives, making those that are already small-scale (e.g. those in the *Aetia*) yet finer and more original. He tells his stories in sequences of tableaux or with Pindaric asymmetry: he wings his way silently over tracts of plot, then swoops suddenly and overwhelmingly on a chosen aspect. Often a very unexpected aspect: the narrative becomes virtually all unexpected periphery and no solid story at all. In this way he contrives to concentrate stylistic energies, spectacularly. And, spectacularly, he satisfies Apollo's demand for originality. Classical, Aristotelian, unity is sold for a good price.

---

[36] *Aetia* fr. 1. 11–12 (above p. 152).
[37] The basic sense of διηνεκής is 'continuous', 'unbroken'. Callimachus has in mind the phrase διηνεκέως ἀγορεύειν, 'to tell from beginning to end': Hom. *Od.* 4. 836; 7. 241; 12. 56, LSJ s.v.
[38] Aristotle *Poetics* 7 and 23. It goes without saying that if one was prepared to abandon genuine unity, one would be all the more prepared to abandon the quasi-unity offered by a plot 'like history' (*Poetics* 23)—which is probably in fact all that Callimachus' critics themselves achieved. Cf. below p. 159.
[39] Didactic in Callimachus' hands was not teaching in the traditional and profound sense (cf. n. 20 above); it offered the delightful spectacle of learning for learning's sake and art for art's sake.

158   *Ovid, Callimachus, and* l'art pour l'art

And subject matter had to be, and was, carefully selected or shaped, so as not to compromise basic aesthetic principles. Moralist traditionalists held such a view with regard to their subject matter. Callimachus was no different. The moralists thought that subject matter should be *engagé*, moral. Strabo, for example, implies that poets must select subject matter prudently;[40] and he and other interpreters were always at hand to explain what was going on if great 'moral' poets were misunderstood;[41] and Plato, who had a problem with Homer, considered solving it by censorship:[42] 'we shall ask Homer... not to be angry if we strike out these and similar lines [*Od.* 11. 489 ff. *et al.*]. Not that they're not poetical and pleasant hearing for the public: indeed, the more poetical they are, the less they should be presented to boys and men who ought to be free...'. Callimachus, wanting to provide his readers with purely aesthetic experiences, needed subject matter that was socially and morally *ir*relevant or untroublesome. He gave it to them. Love (as Callimachus and his ilk understood it) and antiquarian aetiology were two readily available topics. But it was more fun or more challenging to defuse potentially serious material. This too Callimachus does. A hymn to Artemis focusses on Artemis as a very human and plainly fictional child—and includes a picture of Minos as a combination of would-be ravisher and distraught Milanion; a hymn to Zeus becomes preoccupied with Zeus's possible birthplaces, birth and other unawesome aspects; an 'epic' on Theseus contains an epic adventure but demotes it in favour of Theseus' sojourn in an old woman's hut *en route* to that epic adventure; and so on. More daringly a magisterial demonstration of Demeter's power to punish becomes a grotesque and sometimes bourgeois quasi-comedy; an account of Artemis' power to ruin wrongdoers and bless others is the climactic stage in the goddess's precocious leap to maturity: offering a pleasing tonal contrast with what precedes, not a convincing and salutary *exemplum* of divine justice.[43] Callimachus' subject matter is or is made to be a vehicle for wit, intellect, art. Out of his subject matter Callimachus creates 'effects'.[44]

IV.3. Ovid announces a *carmen perpetuum*, implying apostasy and ἓν ἄεισμα διηνεκές. It does not take long to realise that we do not really have anything of

---

[40] Strabo 1. 2. 3: 'But it is *not* right to... prove poetry to be a mass of old wives' tales, in which any fiction suitable for entertainment is allowed.'
[41] Witness how Strabo deals with Homer: loc. cit.   [42] *Republic* 387b.
[43] Callimachus, *Hymn to Artemis, Hymn to Zeus, Hecale, Hymn to Demeter*.
[44] Cf. Cassagne (1906), 213 on the approach of poets of *l'art pour l'art* towards their subject matter: 'ou bien ils iront chercher cette matière dans le passé, ou bien ils la prendront dans le présent, mais pour en faire de simples représentations objectives, pleinement désintéressées, soigneusement purgées de toute considération morale ou sociale.'

the sort. The genre of the *Metamorphoses* is, whatever else, essentially discontinuous; the poem is 'species unius corporis',[45] the illusion being contrived by (among other things) ingenious transitions. The very ingenuity of these transitions emphasises that the constituent episodes are essentially disparate.

Implying ἓν ἄεισμα διηνεκές Ovid in fact implies a traditional and conventional epic (above p. 152). That arouses various expectations in the reader. One by one they are defeated. Ovid does not tell a plot 'from beginning to end', a plot with a 'beginning, middle parts and an end'; nor even does he offer us a plot 'like history'.[46] Logical sequence across episodes is virtually non-existent, chronological sequence an intermittent, unimpressive and unimportant gloss. Besides, metamorphosis is not a plot; at least it is not the plot of the *Metamorphoses*. The *Metamorphoses* is dozens of stories moulded by Ovidian magic into an *illusion* of wholeness. Most of these stories are, incidentally, not quite the *mimesis* of 'serious things'[47] or 'kings and heroes of olden times',[48] that we expect of epic.

Ovid does not narrate even the individual stories διηνεκέως, genuinely 'from beginning to end'. For example, Apollo lusts after Daphne (*Met.* 1. 497 ff.):

> spectat inornatos collo pendere capillos,
> et 'Quid, si comantur?' ait. uidet igne micantes
> sideribus similes oculos; uidet oscula, quae non
> est uidisse satis; laudat digitosque manusque
> bracchiaque et nudos media plus parte lacertos:
> siqua latent, meliora putat. fugit ocior aura
> illa leui neque ad haec reuocantis uerba resistit:
> 'Nympha, precor, Penei, mane! non insequor hostis:
> nympha, mane!...

Rudimentary plot is cut (Apollo's initial advance, Daphne's reaction) while Ovid dwells enthusiastically on the god's lust and discomfiture, his delightfully ludicrous declaration of love. And this is his continual tactic. Ovid adumbrates or assumes knowledge of the facts of his stories; he abandons unity, continuity, in favour of guiding his readers by original Ovidian paths or via Ovidian tableaux.[49]

This is, of course, narrative technique in the Callimachean manner. Ovid does not prosecute it as obtrusively as Callimachus, but it is the same essential type. And we might say that the *Metamorphoses* as a whole is a Callimachean catalogue: in its treatment of individual episodes and in its overall structure it

---

[45] Quint. 4. 1. 77.   [46] Cf. above n. 38.   [47] *Poetics* 5, above p. 154.
[48] Call. *Aetia* fr. 1. 3–4, above pp. 152–3.
[49] Cf. Galinsky (1975), 4 ff. (on p. 12 he talks of the 'jumpiness' of the narrative). Otis (1970), 334 still gets this wrong.

is akin to the *Aetia*. The genre of the *Metamorphoses* is certainly much more akin to Callimachean catalogue than it is to epic. The view of the function of literature that informs the poem is also Callimachean, and incompatible with epic. But on this, and on the question of subject matter, I shall have more to say in a moment.

We first ought briefly to consider why Ovid says he is going to do virtually the reverse of what he does do. I allude to just one or two of several motives. Ovid introduces the Callimachean phrase (*carmen perpetuum*, ἓν ἄεισμα διηνεκές) because, obviously, he wants us to recall the Callimachean dispute. He wants us to decide for ourselves which side of the divide he lies on. Our immediate conclusion, based on *perpetuum carmen*, is rapidly proved wrong—anyway it ignores *another* hint in that same line, *deducite*.[50] So our final decision on Ovid's literary allegiance is underlined by paradox and defeated expectations. But there is another point. Ovid wants us to dally over that notion of continuity. Of course the *Metamorphoses* is not διηνεκές in any Callimachean sense; but it gives an illusion of continuity, an appearance of unity, an impression indeed of being epic, such as Callimachus never contrived.[51] Ovid was proud of his ingenious links: in a way he has achieved the final victory of the short poem; it has usurped the position of ἓν ἄεισμα διηνεκές, of, more precisely, the epic: speciously, but what a brilliant *species*! So Ovid has trumped the champions of poetical orthodoxy. In a way he has capped Callimachus too.[52]

IV.4. According to what canons would Ovid have wanted his poetry to be judged? The Callimachean canons surely, art and delight. To be more particular: in the *Metamorphoses*, Ovid is guided by the principles of *l'art pour l'art*.

His commitment to form for its own sake is in fact manifest in most of his works; his unabashed love of form for form's sake is neatly illuminated by the elder Seneca's famous anecdote:[53]

> He used language by no means over-freely, except in his poetry, where he was well aware of his faults—and enjoyed them. What can make this clear is that once, when he was asked by his friends to suppress three of his lines, he asked in return to be allowed to make an exception of three over which they should have no rights. This seemed a fair condition. They wrote in private the lines they wanted removed, while he wrote the ones he wanted saved. The sheets of both contained the same verses...

---

[50] See Kenney (1976), 51–2; Gilbert (1976), 111–12.
[51] Callimachus' 'epic' *Hecale* was, comparatively speaking, ostentatiously un-epic; and it did not attempt monumental length.
[52] 'If Propertius is the Roman Callimachus, Ovid is Super-Callimachus', Kenney (1976) with other most apt comments in this connection.
[53] *Contr.* 2. 2. 12 (trans. M. Winterbottom).

The following are two of the lines in question:

> semibouemque uirum semiuirumque bouem;   (*Ars* 2. 24)
>
> et gelidum Borean egelidumque Notum.   (*Am.* 2. 11. 10)

They are so contrived that content, even sense, is clearly subordinate to formal conceit. Ovid's anticipation of what might be impugned attractively demonstrates how conscious he was of his fond devotion to art.

His exclusive devotion to entertaining his readers has already been demonstrated (§§ I–III); the *Metamorphoses* in fact proffers the multiform and curious entertainment of 'effects'. And this aestheticism of Ovid's is strikingly evident in his attitude and policy towards subject matter: here he is far more radical than Callimachus. Callimachus occasionally adapts or adjusts potentially sensitive subject matter: when he hymns the justice of Artemis and the punishment of Erysicthon we are amused and dazzled by 'effect', not edified by *exempla*. But in general (it seems) his sense of *l'art pour l'art* imposed on him a selective approach towards subject matter. Ovid tackles sensitive stuff constantly, indeed as a rule. He writes of any and every subject and contrives (principally by the device of metamorphosis) never to force upon us anything other than an aesthetic, ultimately entertaining experience. He enacts tragedy, perversions, suffering and horror, and allows us to taste such strong meat without paying for it. Amoral aesthetics are realised to their limit; genius offers human life in a series of samples, absolving us from responsibility or final involvement. Some might call such aggressively amoral aesthetics immoral. Ovid illustrates the principles and practices of *l'art pour l'art* much more strikingly, in an extremer form, than Callimachus. Further brief demonstration of this is in order.

V.1.

'Life then is a failure?'

'From the artistic point of view, certainly. And the chief thing that makes life a failure from this artistic point of view is the thing that lends to life its sordid security, the fact that one can never repeat exactly the same emotion. How different it is in the world of Art! On a shelf of the bookcase behind you stands the *Divine Comedy*, and I know that, if I open it at a certain place, I shall be filled with a fierce hatred of some one who has never wronged me, or stirred by a great love for some one whom I shall never see. There is no mood of passion that Art cannot give us, and those of us who have discovered her secret can settle beforehand what our experiences are going to be. We can choose our day and select our hour... And if we grow tired of an antique time, and desire to realise our own age in all its weariness and sin, are there not books that can make us live more in one single hour than life can make us live in a score of shameful years? Close to your hand lies a little volume, bound in some Nile-green skin... There is no passion that we cannot feel, no pleasure that we may not gratify, and we can choose the time of our initiation and the time of our freedom also. Life!... It is a thing narrowed by circumstances, incoherent in its utterance, and without that fine correspondence of form and spirit which is the only thing that can satisfy the artistic and critical temperament. It makes us pay too high a price for its wares, and we purchase the meanest of its secrets at a cost that is monstrous and infinite.'

'Must we go, then, to Art for everything?'

'For everything. Because Art does not hurt us. The tears that we shed at a play are à type of the exquisite sterile emotions that it is the function of Art to awaken. We weep, but we are not wounded... How can it matter with what pleasure life tries to tempt one, or with what pain it seeks to maim and mar one's soul, if in the spectacle of the lives of those who have never existed one has found the true secret of joy, and wept away one's tears over their deaths who, like Cordelia and the daughter of Brabantio, can never die?... All art is immoral.'

'All art?'

'Yes.'

Oscar Wilde on the superiority of Art over Life.[54] Much of this is clearly or nearly sometimes true. Much however is certainly not true of an art which is a committed *mimesis* of the *idea* of life:[55] of classic or indeed of much romantic art. Art which is an unflinching *mimesis* does not allow us to determine the mode and extent of our emotion. It does wound. We cannot shake off the passions of a truthful book or the tears of a truthful play simply by closing the book or leaving the theatre. In this respect a *mimesis* of the *idea* of life is like life. Cordelia and Desdemona do die.[56] Nor indeed can we exactly repeat emotions by going back to the same work of art.

The quoted passage reflects an extreme 'art for art's sake' aestheticism. It is no longer simply argued that Art is an independent kingdom where only its own rules apply. Life is judged according to those rules, and found wanting; life is compared as a mode of experiencing and pronounced inferior. Art is *better*, allowing one to sample a distillation of emotions unscathed, exquisitely.

Such views (allowing for their author's characteristic use of paradox and overstatement) would be agreeable enough to many 'aesthetic' artists.[57] To

---

[54] From *The Critic as Artist*, Pt. II.   [55] Above p. 147.

[56] With characteristic inconsistency Wilde makes (in effect) exactly this point elsewhere: 'One of the greatest tragedies of my life is the death of Lucien de Rubempré' (*The Decay of Lying*).

[57] e.g. Gautier; Baudelaire in some moods; Oscar himself of course. But not, I think, Callimachus.

cite Shakespearean tragedy in illustration is of course specious or malicious. To cite Ovid's *Metamorphoses* is more plausible. That Ovid held and practised certain of these views (or something like them) is what in effect I have already argued. Ovid allows us to sample; he allows us to taste the emotions of life without hurt. He works to that end, offering 'effects' not committed *mimeseis*.

V.2. Baudelaire is sometimes purely and often partially (i.e. considered from one point of view) a poet of *l'art pour l'art*. He expressed a belief in the indissolubility of form and content: 'L'idée et la forme sont deux êtres en un.'[58] Much of his poetry squares with this view; some of it does not. It is when it does not that it reveals most obviously the principles of *l'art pour l'art*. So it seems to me—but critical analysis of form and content is, as I have said, beset by problems of definition, indeed of metaphysics.

> Un cadavre sans tête épanche, comme un fleuve,
>   Sur l'oreiller désaltéré
> Un sang rouge et vivant, dont la toile s'abreuve
>   Avec l'avidité d'un pré.
>
> (*Une Martyre*, 9–12)

Here Baudelaire elaborates in precise verses and striking imagery the horrific facts of the scene. To my judgement form and content are congruent but easily distinguishable. The imagery elaborates exactly, but the contrivance of the poet is self-evident, and proud: we can sense the basic subject matter and see the careful formal elaboration. Because the elaboration is so evident, and brilliant, our response to the subject matter is complicated curiously: we are diverted, and inevitably (to an extent) insulated. Baudelaire is perceptibly working up an 'effect' (cf. above p. 150), one superbly contrived 'effect' in a poem that is very largely and purely 'effect'.

Note too the following passage, from *Une Charogne*:

> Rappelez-vous l'objet que nous vîmes, mon âme,
>   Ce beau matin d'été si doux:
> Au détour d'un sentier une charogne infâme
>   Sur un lit semé de cailloux,
> Les jambes en l'air, comme une femme lubrique,
>   Brûlante et suant les poisons,
> Ouvrait d'une façon nonchalante et cynique
>   Son ventre plein d'exhalaisons.
> Le soleil rayonnait sur cette pourriture,
>   Comme afin de la cuire à point,

---

[58] In *L'Art romantique: Auguste Barbier*.

> Et de rendre au centuple à la grande Nature
> Tout ce qu'ensemble elle avait joint... (1–12)

Again (it seems to me) we can observe the same technique. From one point of view we have an 'effect'. But the lines are also functional. *Une Charogne* is not purely *l'art pour l'art* (it enlightens, teaches, informs as well as proudly *is*) and the stanzas have a function within the function of the poem.

Let us consider some more lines from these two poems. First, from *La Charogne*:

> Et le ciel regardait la carcasse superbe
> Comme une fleur s'épanouir. (13–14)

And from *Une Martyre*:

> La tête, avec l'amas de sa crinière sombre
> Et de ses bijoux précieux,
> Sur la table de nuit, comme une renoncule,
> Repose; et, vide de pensers,
> Un regard vague et blanc comme le crépuscule
> S'échappe des yeux révulsés. (15–20)

Here form and content are patently distinguishable. Extraordinary imagery is laid on to adorn basic content. Euphonious metre and fair pictures illuminate (or perhaps we should say decorate) subject matter that naturally, instinctively and inevitably we find ugly. Form and content are not in fact just distinguishable, but discrepant.[59] Baudelaire creates a disharmony which we may (depending on our taste) call piquant, titillating, or shocking; but we shall have to admit, I think, that the disharmony is diverting. Our responses to the basic subject matter are curiously complicated. Again insulation, again 'effects'.

In *La Charogne* the lines ultimately have their function (implicit bitter irony)[60] within the function of the poem. But, not simply or purely 'effect', the lines are from one point of view 'effect'; the lines from *Une Martyre* are I think pure 'effect'. And the 'effects' have the same sort of ingredients—and resemble those mentioned above. Here in fact is a particular type of 'effect' that Baudelaire was fond of: choice and careful elaboration of what is repellent results in something no longer unequivocally or implacably repellent.

---

[59] The line between *clearly distinguishable* form and content and form and content actually *discordant* or *discrepant* is not a clear one and judgement is to an extent subjective; some critics may for example judge *Une Martyre* 9–12 as discrepant. However the important fact for the point I am making is simply the distinction in the poet's mind and on the page. Cf. above p. 150.

[60] *La Charogne* is succinctly and quite well discussed by Fairlie (1960), 41–2.

'L'horrible artistement exprimé', we might say.[61] Where form and content are actually discordant, we might label the lines 'séraphiquement purulents'; if the label were to be useful, it would be an engaging irony.[62]

This 'effect' was something contemporary critics noticed and articulated. Victor Hugo has it in mind I think in his phrase 'un frisson nouveau' (though the poems to which he attached the comment are not the best examples).[63] Sainte-Beuve alludes to it more fully (addressing Baudelaire): 'Vous avez pris l'enfer, vous vous êtes fait diable; vous avez voulu arracher leurs secrets aux démons de la nuit. En faisant cela avec subtilité, avec raffinement, avec un talent curieux et un abandon quasi *précieux* d'expression, en *perlant* le détail, en *pétraquisant* sur l'horrible, vous l'avez l'air de vous être joué; vous avez pourtant souffert' (author's emphases).[64] And Baudelaire's own keen awareness of the 'effect' is demonstrated in a pleasing anecdote. Jules Levallois recalls recitations by the poet 'dans quelque crémerie de la rue Saint-André-des-Arts ou dans quelque modeste café de la rue Dauphine': 'il nous récitait d'une voix précieuse, douce, flûtée, onctueuse, et cependant mordante, une énormité quelconque, le *Vin de l'Assassin* ou la *Charogne*. Le contraste était réellement saisissant entre la violence des images et la placidité affectée, l'accentuation suave et pointue du débit'.[65] Baudelaire was only emphasising a 'contraste' already there in the text: the distinction he observed between form and content (more or less patently), to disturb and change response; to create 'effects'.[66] It was the same general type of 'contraste' that Ovid observed in, for example,

---

[61] See below n. 66.

[62] The phrase I think graphically describes many Baudelairian lines and I am sure the poet would often have welcomed it. But it was in fact uttered pejoratively, in connection with a poem it doesn't suit. It comes from J. Habans' comment on *Le Flacon*, a poem which is truly a *mimesis* of the *idea* of life and in which form and content are more or less perfectly blended. The Pléiade edition of Baudelaire (1921) quotes: 'J. Habans, qui allait de nouveau accabler le poète alors que menaçait le procès, se venge par des sarcasmes de son peu de goût pour l'originalité: "Dans le *Flacon*, qu'il m'a fallu, après une heure de méditations, renoncer à comprendre, j'ai dû entrevoir, dans un jour douteux, une armoire *arachnéenne*, contenant un *cadavre spectral* embaumé dans un *amour ranci*. J'ai pris la fuite, mais sur le seuil je suis tombé, le nez le premier, sur cet alexandrin séraphiquement purulent: 'Je serai ton cercueil, AIMABLE pestilence!'" | (*Figaro*, 30 Avril 1857.)' Habans seems to have been moved by a preconceived notion of what the content of an Alexandrine should be; he is reacting to a discrepancy between content and his expectation of content. Certainly form and content are here indistinguishable.

[63] Hugo (1896–8), ii. 314.

[64] Sainte-Beuve (1881), iii. 141.   [65] Levallois (1896), 93–4.

[66] Cf. too Baudelaire's comment ('Théophile Gautier', *L'Artiste*, 13 mars 1859) 'C'est un des privilèges prodigieux de l'Art que l'horrible, artistement exprimé, devienne beauté et que la *douleur* rythmée et cadencée remplisse l'esprit d'une *joie* calme.' Baudelaire is here basing himself upon a distinction between form and content, and, in spite of 'devienne', would surely have to allow that the distinction would remain perceptible in the final work of art.

'Niobe'. And much of what I said in connection with Ovid in §III bears comparison with the conclusions of this sub-section.

VI. In the *Metamorphoses* Ovid adopts the aesthetic principles of Callimachus, which are close to *l'art pour l'art*. He pursues certain of their implications to their logical limit, and at times reminds one strikingly of the theory and practice of specific nineteenth-century writers in England and France. It is profitable to consider them all together: our understanding of a more perspicuous or better documented poet may throw light on his spiritually related but less accessible confrère. It is profitable for another reason. It reminds us that many artistic impulses are eternal artistic impulses, even some that are apparently artificial. A poet may be spiritually related to another without being significantly influenced by him or related in terms of tradition. Artistic impulses recur at different times and in different places, perhaps nursed by a definable set of socio-historical circumstances, and perhaps not.

11

Vergil's *Aeneid*: Subversion by Intertextuality. Catullus 66. 39–40 and Other Examples[1] (1994)

1. CATULLUS 66. 39–40 AND VERGIL *AENEID* 6. 458–60

I think we have to accept that the term *intertextuality* serves a purpose.[2] One of the terms it allows us to dispense with, *allusion*, has its disadvantages.

Up until recently I was happy with 'allusion': Vergil 'alludes' to Homer. The term was time-honoured, and, surely, unproblematical. Unproblematical, and not, so far as it went, and in the right hands, unsubtle. One meant that Vergil was not just using his source text (or his *significant* source text) as raw material. The source text became part of the new text, its characters and context were relevant to the new text. Thus, when in his opening speech Aeneas 'quotes' Homer's Odysseus, we sense that Vergil is casting Aeneas as a new Odysseus, comparing him and contrasting him with Odysseus, in a new *Odyssey*. And so the *Aeneid* proceeds: an allusive text, constantly alluding to Homer, re-forming Homer, remaking the Homeric characters, re-forming other texts in the same significant way... What texts? What texts does it not *significantly* re-form?

What texts does it merely 'echo' without significance, 'without any intention behind' the echo?[3]

The theoretical and practical problems begin. The trouble with the term 'allusion' is that it encourages us to evade such problems, for it smooths the path to a simple and sham solution. It encourages us to invoke the 'author's

---

[1] My colleague Jasper Griffin and my pupil Bruno Currie kindly read an earlier draft of this paper. I owe much to both of them, and made many changes in reaction to their suggestions. It is not however to be assumed that they agree with all that remains. An acute observation by another pupil, Michael Collins, has also been noted, and, I hope, absorbed.

[2] No one can accuse me of rude haste in making this statement. The term was coined by Julia Kristeva in the mid-1960s. See, for example, her work 'Word, Dialogue, and Novel' published in 1967, most easily available to English readers in Moi (1986). For bibliography on intertextual approaches to Latin Literature, see Appendix 2. The first time that I tentatively tried out the term in print was in 1987. Age and Anglo-Saxon empiricism may make one cautious.

[3] Cf. Camps quoted in Appendix 1 below.

intention' to settle any unwelcome facts or difficulties.[4] The process happens thus. Allusion has a verb, 'allude'. The verb favours a personal subject: *Vergil alludes*. We think we know about people and what they intend, especially our own favourite poets. And thus we feel licensed to say that Vergil significantly alludes in *this* echo, but—if we cannot seem to make sense of it—not in *that* one. And we retire contented. It will not do. We are making unjustifiable assumptions, we are forming preconceptions about an author's 'intentions' which we have no right or evidence to form. Let me illustrate the point practically, and try to settle an old crux, by considering *Aen.* 6. 458–60 and Catullus 66. 39–40.

To prepare the way, we should recall the passage I have already glanced at, Aeneas' opening speech, *Aen.* 1. 94 ff.:

> o terque quaterque beati,
> quis ante ora patrum Troiae sub moenibus altis
> contigit oppetere!...etc.

Oh thrice and four times blessed were they to whom it happened to die before the eyes of their fathers beneath the lofty wall of Troy...

Here there is *no* problem, no perceived problem anyway. Vergil, we can say,[5] is alluding to Homer, he makes Aeneas 'quote' Odysseus (*Od.* 5. 306 ff.), and it is a useful functional allusion: he casts Aeneas in the role of an Odysseus, an Odysseus with a difference, an Odysseus travelling *away from* not *to* his emotional focal centre... All this sort of thing has been said, and a certain measure of agreement secured.[6]

What then of this passage, Aeneas to Dido in the Underworld (6. 458–60)?

> per sidera iuro,
> per superos et si qua fides tellure sub ima est,
> inuitus, regina, tuo de litore cessi.

I swear by the stars, by the gods above, and by whatever faith there is beneath the earth, unwillingly o queen I departed from your shore.

The text brought inevitably to mind—it too is virtually 'quoted'—is Catullus' version of Callimachus, the 'sidus nouum' (66. 64) in the *Coma Berenices*, Catull. 66. 39–40:

---

[4] The object of my attack is, of course, the hoary old 'Intentional Fallacy': an ugly and not perfectly apt phrase, but it would waste time and the reader's patience to try to rename it. The body of my text illustrates why I think it wrong to appeal to an author's intentions, and Appendix 1 contains further reflections on the topic.

[5] I am of course self-consciously using the traditional language of Intentionalists.

[6] Cf. e.g. Otis (1963), 231 f., Clausen, (1966), 76 ff., Lyne (1987), 104 ff.

> inuita, o regina, tuo de uertice cessi,
>   inuita: adiuro teque tuumque caput.

Unwillingly, o queen, I departed from your crown, unwillingly: I swear by both you and your head.

Now here there is a problem. What is the function of this allusion? Why on earth should Vergil, at this tragic juncture, have Aeneas quote a witty but trivial piece of court poetry?[7] Attempts have been made to provide reasons, most of them unconvincing and none of them (I would argue) wholly adequate.[8] But a favourite device has been simply to say: Vergil is *not* alluding. At 1. 94 ff. Vergil significantly alludes to Homer, at 6. 458–60 he merely echoes a phrase that comes into his mind—raw material—and doesn't allude.[9] We can back this up with specious talk of 'significant' and 'nonsignificant' source texts.[10] But what we are basically doing, and we must face the fact, is taking the smooth path to an unjustifiable solution. We are making assumptions about Vergil's 'intentions', assumptions which we cannot possibly make. Vergil alludes in 1. 94 ff., but not in 6. 458–60. Who or what says so? Only our *preconceptions* about what Vergil's

---

[7] I do not mean to be dismissive either of Call. fr. 100 ff. or of Catull. 66 by this phrase. Both pieces are magnificent *tours de force*. Callimachus' conception is brilliantly original, and Catullus' translation is creative. But I would insist that the context and ethos of both poems is witty and trivial compared with the apparent high tragedy of the context of the *Aeneid* at this point. On Callimachus and on Catullus' version of Callimachus, see the excellent and succinct comments of Hutchinson (1988), 322–4; also the full discussion of Syndikus (1990), 199 ff. In his discussion of the lock's 'pain at parting' (lines 39–50), Syndikus, no frivolous critic, is moved to the word 'komisch' (p. 210). Hutchinson (p. 322) states 'In the second half of ⟨Catullus'⟩ poem the fundamental conception is fantastic and delightful.' Commenting on lines 79–88, which he believes Catullus has added to his Callimachean original, he remarks (p. 323): 'The strong moral language used of the unchaste makes the interplay with the fantasy the more preposterous.' Others (cf. e.g. Wiseman (1969), 21; Tatum (1984), 443; this article is mentioned again below, n. 8) might not share these views. I do. 'Trivial' incidentally is the word that comes to E. L. Harrison's mind when discussing Catullus 66. 39, and Vergil's use of it (Harrison (1970), 241 = (1990), 445).

[8] Harrison (1970), 241 f., with notes 2 and 3, reprinted in Harrison (1990), 445 f. Thornton's conclusion, Thornton (1962), 77–9, was independently arrived at by Wigodsky (1972), 127: 'Thornton is surely right to explain the echo as a deliberate allusion to Aeneas' destiny: he is ultimately to be enskied, like Berenice's lock, and it is to ensure this that the gods ordered him, unwilling and unaware, to leave Dido.' This gets part of the truth: see below p. 173. Besides this, a sequence of articles in *AJP* has made some progress: Tatum (1984), 434–52, esp. 444; Skulsky (1985), 447–55, esp. 451; Johnston (1987), 649–54.

[9] Austin, ad loc. (who however does not share the view): 'Modern susceptibilities are pained by Vergil's presumed indifference to the incongruity so produced, and suggest that his line is an unconscious reminiscence...'. Harrison (1970): 'Most commonly it is assumed that the reminiscence must be unconscious...'; he provides a bibliography of those who state such a view.

[10] I confess that my slightly cautious phrasing in Lyne (1987), 103 was leaving room for some sort of escape clause like this. I am slightly suspicious too when I read G. B. Conte distinguishing between 'modello-antigrafo' and 'modello-codice' (Conte (1984), 147; see Appendix 2), but I am not sure that I exactly understand C. at this point, so my suspicions may be unfounded. Cf. too Wigodsky (1972), 80–1 on Vergil's borrowings from Pacuvius and Accius.

intention might be—and the difficulty of interpreting the allusion. But we have no access to Vergil's intentions besides their actualization in the text itself; and the difficulty of interpretation is our problem, and not to be evaded.

So: we have no evidence about Vergil's intentions in the matter of allusion *beyond the evidence of the text*. It is only texts we can reasonably talk about. Since the term 'allusion' encourages us to appeal to an entirely chimerical 'authorial intention'—to turn away from the text—it is best abandoned. And we pick up the term *intertextuality*, along with its slightly repellent associate *intertext*. This terminology too is objectionable in a way I outline in Appendix 3. But at least it encourages us to state *facts* about a *text*; more precisely, it allows us to say relatively objective things about something which exists. And if we do this it becomes harder to dodge difficult or unwelcome implications. Therefore I adopt the terminology. Fact: *Aen.* 1. 94 ff. is intertextual with *Od.* 5. 306 ff. Fact: *Aen.* 6. 458–460 is intertextual with Catull. 66. 39–40. And these are equivalent facts, are they not? And so, if we interpret the one—if we assume there is or should be an interpretation for the one—then we should assume the same for the other. No fudge about what (by some divine inspiration) we decide to be Vergil's intentions. No fudge about 'significant' source texts.

I do not claim, by the by, that to talk of intertextuality rather than allusion brings total clarity to our theoretical vision. I suppose the largest theoretical difficulty that persists is to answer the following question. When is an intertext readable and identifiable enough actually to constitute an intertext? This seems to me to be a problem that the theoreticians evade, and indeed I think it submits to no theoretical solution. For my part I revert to my Anglo-Saxon empiricism. Judge each case on its merits. One thing seems to me certain. Catull. 66. 39–40:

> inuita, o regina, tuo de uertice cessi,
> inuita: adiuro teque tuumque caput...

Unwillingly, o queen, I departed from your crown, unwillingly: I swear by both you and your head...

is, surely, as readable and identifiable in the text of *Aen.* 6. 458–60 as *Od.* 5. 306 ff. is in *Aen.* 1. 94 ff. *Everybody* notices it. Here is an intertext that, however much we might wish it away, is there. And if *Od.* 5. 306 ff. merits interpretation at 1. 94 ff., so should Catull. 66. 39–50 at 6. 458–60.

So it is worth looking at it again. The Catullan intertext (poem 66) is, when we have hindsight, visible earlier in the *Aeneid*. For a start it can be detected in the great explanatory speech which Aeneas makes to Dido in Book 4. 333 ff., expounding the moral and religious imperatives of his departure. 'Adiuro teque tuumque caput', 'I swear both by you and your head' (Catull. 66. 40) underlies Aeneas' 'testor utrumque caput', 'I invoke both our two heads' at 4. 357. The interpretation of Aeneas' 'utrumque' is admittedly problematical. Servius offers three explanations, but I agree with Austin when he says that the first of these—'meum et tuum' ('mine' and 'yours, Dido's')—is the most natural. The idea therefore of *Dido's head* in Catullan '*Berenice*' *language* is already a discrete part of the text of the poem. At a morally crucial juncture Aeneas has appealed to Dido's head; and the appeal is quietly but (as will emerge) importantly intertextual with Catullus. Nor, by the by, should we miss the Catullan intertextuality in Dido's words to Anna, 4. 492 f.: 'testor, cara, deos et te, germana, tuumque | dulce caput', 'I call to witness, beloved sister, the gods, and you, and your sweet head.'

Let us now summon back *Aen.* 6. 458–60. In the Catullan intertext behind Aeneas' words a lock of hair addresses a head whence it had been severed. Discussion of these two passages tends to ignore[11] another absolutely vital piece of the *Aeneid*, and *the fact that Dido too had had a lock of hair severed.* 4. 693 ff.:

> tum Iuno omnipotens longum miserata dolorem
> difficilisque obitus Irim demisit Olympo
> quae luctantem animam nexosque resolueret artus.
> nam quia nec fato merita nec morte peribat,
> sed misera ante diem subitoque accensa furore,
> nondum illi *flauum* Proserpina *uertice crinem*
> abstulerat Stygioque *caput* damnauerat Orco.
> ergo Iris...
>   .   .   .   .
> ...et supra *caput* astitit. 'hunc ego Diti
> sacrum iussa fero teque isto corpore soluo';
> sic ait dextra *crinem* secat...

Then omnipotent Juno, pitying her long pain and difficult death, sent Iris down from Olympus to loose her struggling spirit and close-locked limbs. For, because she was perishing neither through fate nor by a deserved death, but pitiably before her day, inflamed by sudden madness, Proserpina had not yet taken a blonde lock from her crown and consigned her head/life to Orcus. And so Iris... stood above Dido's head and said: 'I take this lock, as ordered, consecrated to Dis, and I release you from your body.' So she spoke, and with her right hand cut the lock...

There is not only the parallel of motif. Given the clear intertextuality at 6. 458–60, we can detect further signs of Catullan intertextuality here. I recall for comparison 'tuo de uertice' and 'tuumque caput' from 66. 39–40, and I quote two more lines of the poem: 66. 62, 'deuotae flaui uerticis exuuiae', 'the votive spoil of a blonde head' (both Berenice and Dido are not only blondes[12] but 'flauae') and 66. 47, 'quid facient crines' 'what will locks achieve?'

---

[11] Honourable exceptions: Tatum, Skulsky, and Johnston in n. 8 above.

[12] Nothing too remarkable in this, however: fair hair conventionally belonged to heroes and heroines of legend (Fordyce on Catull. 64. 62), nor was 'the blond type in antiquity' that uncommon according to the massive note of Pease on *Aen.* 4. 590. But 'flauus' is not the only way to say 'blonde'.

Words and phrases from Catull. 66 therefore form quite a readable and *extensive* intertext in the *Aeneid*; a much more extensive intertext than has hitherto been admitted. And it is not just words. The words adumbrate a plot, and this plot has parallels and significances for our plot. Let me recall something we all agree on: the *Aeneid* casts Aeneas as a new Odysseus, the Trojan's journey as a new Odyssey, etc. And as with all such cases of intertextuality, the reader has the option of comparing and/or contrasting Aeneas and his situations with the figures and situations in the intertexts. What I am arguing is—in line with this—that the *Aeneid* compares and contrasts Dido, her lock, and her fate (text) with Berenice, her lock, and her fate (intertext). For Dido tragic contrasts emerge. Curious resonances for Aeneas emerge, too.

First consider Dido and the contrasts brought out by the intertext. The magnificent Queen of *Aen.* Book 1 is reduced to death agonies. Venus is causally involved in her death, as imagery, if nothing else, tells us.[13] In these death agonies a lock of Dido's fair hair has to be cut from her head and devoted to the god of Death, Dis, and thus and then she can die.

Now consider the fate of her intertextual counterpart, Berenice. A lock of her fair hair is also cut, but it is honoured by Venus, it is placed in the bosom of Venus (66. 56, 'et Veneris casto collocat in gremio'), and it is made a star in heaven by, if the text is correctly emended, the direct agency of Venus. 66. 59–62:

> inde Venus[14] uario ne solum in lumine caeli
>   ex Ariadnaeis aurea temporibus
> fixa corona foret, sed nos quoque fulgeremus
>   deuotae flaui uerticis exuuiae...

Then Venus, lest alone in the varied light of heaven the golden crown from Ariadne's temples should find a place, but that we also might shine forth, the votive spoil of a blonde head...

And the catasterized lock tells of all this fantastic felicity to the *living and reigning* Queen Berenice. The courtly dazzle of the intertext, Berenice's and her lock's magnificent triumph, the honouring of Berenice by Venus, underscores the tragedy of Dido's text, Dido destroyed by Venus, and the text of her death-dedicated lock; the intertext works here in a way comparable to a Homeric 'contrast simile'.[15]

We might also note in passing that Berenice's lock, in the passage quoted above, compares itself to the crown of Ariadne, that too a recipient of a blessed fate. At *Aen.* 4. 305 f. and 316 Dido recalls Catullus' Ariadne of 64.

---

[13] Lyne (1987), 18–27, 194–7.
[14] Postgate's correction of the corrupt *hi dii uen ibi*.
[15] On such 'contrast similes', see Porter (1972), 11–21; Macleod (1982), 48 f.; Moulton (1977), 31; Lyne (1989), 135–40 and ff.

132–5, 155 f., 141, Ariadne in her tragic aspect.[16] The Ariadne-intertext of poem 64 works (arguably) like a straightforward simile; the Ariadne-intertext of poem 66 (lines 59–61) contributes to the 'contrast simile' effect.

The resonances for Aeneas of all this are interesting too. It should not escape our notice that he, Aeneas, is in a sense to *share* the fate of that lucky Berenicean lock. He too will—owing to the intercession of Venus—end up in heaven. At 12. 794 f. Jupiter tells Juno:

> Indigetem Aenean scis ipsa, et scire fateris,
> deberi caelo, fatisque ad sidera tolli.

You yourself know and you confess that you know that Aeneas as a god *Indiges* is owed to heaven, and is raised to the stars by the fates.

Berenice and her lock functioned as a contrast simile for Dido; we could say that Berenice's lock functions as a simile for Aeneas. Disaster for one, stardom for the other, mirror-imaged and imaged in the intertext. Now, of course, a familiar theme in the *Aeneid* is that Trojan success seems inevitably to involve suffering for others:[17] here, the fact that the *same* intertext illuminates Dido's suffering and Aeneas' success underscores this point, that the one seems inevitably to entail the other. It is perhaps disquieting.

There is more to disquiet, disturbing textual ironies of detail which have their repercussions for our response to Aeneas. With hindsight we observed that Aeneas' appeal to Dido's head back at 4. 357—at that agonizing and critical juncture—invoked Dido's head with a reference to her happier intertextual counterpart: 'testor utrumque caput' / 'adiuro teque tuumque caput' ('I call to witness both our two heads' / 'I swear both by you and your head'). Then, at the final tragic climax, 6. 460, Aeneas 'quotes' the felicitous intertextual lock to the queen whose lock was dedicated to death. How do we feel about this? We remember that it was Aeneas as well as Venus who contributed causally to the death of Queen Dido.[18] And yet at 4. 357 we find him appealing to Dido's head with a reference to her happier intertextual counterpart, and at 6. 460 we find him parroting lines from the intertextual queen's lock whose happy fate *contrasts* bitterly with Dido's but which his own will in fact one day *resemble*. The character Aeneas cannot himself of course be aware of any of this irony. But there are ironies in his text, inescapably. By these ironies, the text insists upon the intertwining of Trojan success with other people's disaster, the familiar

---

[16] And there are further echoes. Cf., e.g., the two 'whither shall I turn?' passages, 4. 534 ff., 64. 177 ff., and the two imprecation passages, 4. 608 ff., 64. 188 ff.

[17] Cf., e.g., Griffin in Boardman, Griffin, and Murray (1986), 631–2; Lyne (1987), 200 (and the preceding pages).

[18] Lyne (1987), 173–6.

theme. By these ironies, the text underscores Aeneas' own involvement in this tragic chain of connection. And by these ironies, the text leaves Aeneas unwittingly speaking rather smugly, as he cites an intertext simultaneously radiating Dido's disaster and his own stardom.[19]

2. DISTURBING LUCRETIAN INTERTEXTS

One quite humorous—and subversive—use of a Lucretian intertext (Lucr. 1. 33 f. at *Aen.* 8. 394) I have discussed elsewhere.[20] And, of course, Lucretian intertextuality is everywhere in the *Aeneid*: a 'dialogue with Lucretius' starts in the *Georgics* and is maintained in the Epic.[21] Here are two more details.

(a) Consider the following lines of Lucretius, 5. 1127 ff. (we are mid-sentence):[22]

> inuidia quoniam, ceu fulmine, summa uaporant
> plerumque et quae sunt aliis magis edita cumque;
> ut satius multo iam sit parere quietum
> quam regere imperio res uelle et regna tenere.

... since by envy, as by lightning, topmost heights are most often set ablaze, and all places that rise high above others; so that it is far better to obey in peace than to desire to rule the world with power and hold kingly sway.

Since Envy incinerates the High Places, says Lucretius, it is much better to lead the quiet Epicurean life than to seek imperial or regal power. Munro on 5. 1130 tells us that 'regere imperio', 'to rule with power' is an expression found in *Aen.* 6. 851, Livy 3. 15. 7 (the consuls' inability to control a panic-stricken people in 46 BC, 'nec enim poterat pauida et consternata multitudo regi imperio', 'for the panic-stricken and terrified multitude could not be ruled by power'), 8. 23. 9 ('proinde inter Capuam Suessulamque castra castris conferamus, et Samnis Romanusne imperio Italiam regat decernamus', 'accordingly let us pit camp against camp between Capua and Suessula and determine whether Samnite or Roman is to rule by power'), and then in Seneca's tragedies and Pliny. Bailey on 5. 1130 says simply that 'regere imperio' is 'imitated by Virgil in *Aen.* vi.851'. *Aen.* 6. 851 occurs in Anchises'

---

[19] Dido too cites it (4. 492 f., above p. 171), offering a different—a pathetic—irony.
[20] Lyne (1987), 40–1. This was back in the days when I was using the term 'allusion'.
[21] There are vital pages on this topic in Hardie (1986), 33–50, 158 ff.
[22] I was put on the track of this example by D. P. Fowler.

famous imperial instruction to 'Romane' ('excudent alii spirantia mollius aera...', 'others will beat out breathing bronzes more delicately...'). It runs:

> tu regere imperio populos, Romane, memento
> (hae tibi erunt artes), pacique imponere morem,
> parcere subiectis et debellare superbos.

Do you, Roman, remember to rule nations with power (for these will be your arts), to add civilization to peace, to show clemency to the conquered, and to fight the proud into subjection.

Given the exact parallel of wording, syntax, and metrical position between the *DRN* and the *Aeneid*, Bailey's terseness is justified: it must surely be right to see the *Aeneid*'s 'regere imperio' as intertextual with Lucretius.[23]

So what do we do with this fact? We must interpret it, in one way or another. For here is an intertext that is certainly identifiable and readable in the new text.

The Lucretian text tells present-day[24] Romans to lead the quiet life: *not* to seek 'regere imperio'. Anchises in the *Aeneid* tells the Roman the opposite: that 'regere imperio' is, precisely, his duty. However, this crucial part of his message 'quotes' the quietist Lucretian passage. The fact must have implications.

And we have options of interpretation. Above, I said that intertexts may offer opportunities for comparison or contrast: they may function like similes or like contrast similes. They may also offer hints of ideology that agree with the new text—or disturb it. Here we may comfortably think of the 'dialogue with Lucretius' that I referred to, and simply infer that Anchises is, as it were, correcting Lucretian quietism. On the other hand, there are signs that the narrator at this point in the *Aeneid* is slightly at odds, in disagreement, with Anchises: for example, he makes Anchises, who is here keen to eschew and dismiss the arts, *quote* a line of Ennius (6. 846): a nice, undermining irony.[25] We have an option therefore of seeing the Lucretian quietist intertext as *reinforcing* this distance between narrator and character. We may see it as *not* corrected by Anchises; as, in fact, discreetly subverting his speech. It will surprise no-one which option I choose, but of course I would not insist upon it. What I would insist upon is that there are these options of interpretation, the intertext is there and readable; and the reader must confront it.

---

[23] Characteristically Norden on *Aen.* 6. 851 posits an Ennian source for both. This may be right. But the text whose ideology most recently and vividly attaches to the phrase must be the *DRN*.

[24] For an appropriate emphasis on the fact that the Lucretian text has significance *for the (then) present day* see Fowler (1989a), 143–4.

[25] See Lyne (1987), 214–15; but this quotation—and 6. 847–50 as a whole—raise further and complex questions: cf. Hine (1987), 173–83, esp. 179, 181–3.

(b) Consider the following lines from Book 3 of Lucretius:

> est igitur calor ac uentus uitalis in ipso
> corpore qui nobis moribundos deserit artus.   (3. 128–9)

There is therefore a heat and a life-giving wind in the very body which abandons our limbs as they die.

> mors omnia praestat
> uitalem praeter sensum calidumque uaporem.   (3. 214–15)

Death preserves all save the feeling of life and warm heat (i.e., Death leaves the body, but takes what gives us sentience, 'the warm heat').

> sed comes [sc. anima] insequitur [sc. animum] facile et discedit in auras
> et gelidos artus in leti frigore linquit.   (3. 400–1)

Soul follows in the train of mind with ease, and scatters into the breezes, and deserts the chill limbs in the cold of death.

> ergo dissolui quoque conuenit omnem animai
> naturam, ceu fumus, in altas aeris auras.   (3. 455–6)

And so it is natural that all the nature of the soul is also dissolved, even as is smoke, into the high breezes of the air.

Thus Lucretius on death. At death, the soul—*heat*, 'vital wind'—dissipates into the air or *breezes*, and that is *it*: you are dead and gone forever. No afterlife, ghosts or whatever.

We might note that at Lucr. 3. 455 f., at least, there is a Homeric intertext, *Iliad* 23. 100–1, the departure of the ghost of Patroclus:

His soul (*psyche*) went beneath the earth, like smoke, with shrill cry.

But the rewriting operated by the *DRN*, and those other quoted passages, 'correct' this Homeric text. Lucretius: 'like smoke', yes, but no soul going with 'shrill cry' 'beneath the earth'. An intertext that spoke of ghosts and mystery is transformed into a text that speaks of scientific comprehensibility and annihilation.

If we now return to the end of *Aen.* 4, the death of Dido, it seems clear to me that the line at the very end of the Book is a composite text based on the lines of Lucretius that I have quoted. At her death, Dido's life, her 'heat' dissipates into the 'breezes'. In short, *Aen.* 4. 704 f.:

> omnis et una
> dilapsus calor atque in uentos uita recessit.

And at once all the heat and life slipped away and receded into the winds

is intertextual with Lucretius.

Austin, ad loc., remarks as follows: 'So when Lausus died (x. 819 f.) "tum uita per auras | concessit maesta ad manis corpusque reliquit"; and at Turnus' death (xii. 952) "uitaque cum gemitu fugit indignata sub umbras".' But the vital point is that *Aen.* 4. 704 f. is *not* like those occasions. Those occasions suggest, in the Homeric manner,[26] some sort of ghostly existence after death. *Aen.* 4. 704 f. has Lucretian intertexts and lacks any rewriting that would return Lucretian annihilation to Homeric mystery. The concluding line therefore spells Dido's *death*: an annihilation with no possibility of ghosts.

This is one of those many occasions where the text of the *Aeneid* is in dialogue, one might say in conflict, with itself. In the previous lines an important intertext for the dying Dido has been Alcestis, as already Servius (on 3. 46) and Macrobius (*Sat.* 5. 19. 2 ff.) saw.[27] If we *interpret* the intertext, we must—besides seeing that it agrees with Dido's own view of herself as a wife—allow for the possibility that Dido, like Alcestis, may return from the dead. But then the last line of Book 4 seems to preclude even the possibility of a ghostly existence. And for a book and a bit she duly disappears until... we *see* her ghost, shatteringly, in Book 6. Or we think we do. We remember, too, that Dido promised to pursue Aeneas as a ghost after her death in 4. 384 ff. and that in more ways than one we may, if we wish, infer that she does so.[28] So what is the truth? Does Dido continue to exist, and to exist virulently, after death? Or does she suffer obliteration, are the implications of 4. 704 f. right, and are we the readers the victim of an illusion in, say, Book 6? We make up our own mind. One thing we cannot do is ignore the striking Lucretian intertext that concludes *Aen.* Book 4—an intertext that subverts some of our certainties.

---

[26] *Iliad* 16. 470, 22. 362 f., etc.

[27] Cf. Eur. *Alc.* 74 ff. and Austin on *Aen.* 4. 698. Cf. too Hor. *Odes* 1. 28.30 with Nisbet and Hubbard, ad loc. Eur. *Alc.* is already an intertext (we are already comparing—or contrasting— Alcestis with Dido) at *Aen.* 4. 648 ff.: cf. *Alc.* 175 ff.

[28] Note the elaboration of her curse at 4. 607 ff. with its promise of an *ultor* (Hannibal?) in 625 f.; note too 8. 18 ff. with Lyne (1987), 125–32. We might observe, however, that at 4. 379 f. Dido produced this opinion: 'scilicet is superis labor est, ea cura quietos | sollicat'; and her ironic point there was, as Servius saw, almost exactly the Epicurean first *Kuria Doxa*: 'The Blessed and Immortal Nature knows no trouble itself nor causes trouble to any other...'. One might wonder how an Epicurean Dido could promise to pursue Aeneas as a ghost; one might even reckon that an Epicurean Dido should (as it were) endorse the Epicurean description of her death at 4. 704 f. But inconsistency in a character's views are less disturbing than subversions built into the narrative. There is no psychological reason, for example, why Dido should not genuinely believe she can persecute Aeneas after death and yet, for ironic rhetorical purposes, proffer her sneering version of the Epicurean *Kuria Doxa* at 4. 379 f. Cf. her sister at 4. 34, 'id cinerem aut manis credis curare sepultos?': Epicurean stuff on the insensibility of the shades, for a rhetorical purpose.

3. AN AUDIENCE'S LIMITATIONS AND THE FALLACY OF AUDIENCE LIMITATION

I quote a couple of modern scholars. (1) David West dismissing an interpretation of the simile at *Aen.* 12. 67–9: 'Virgil was not writing for hyperintertextualists, for readers who would collate his text with Homer to decode the secrets of a young girl's heart.'[29] (2) E. J. Kenney, objecting to the suggestions of a sense 'tapeworm' in the background of the word 'taenia' at *Aen.* 7. 352: 'In any case, how much did those for whom ⟨Virgil⟩ wrote know about tapeworms? How many had seen one or read about them? The effectiveness of an image must be related to the reader's experience, actual or literary.'[30] The 'Intentional Fallacy'[31] is radiant in West's comment, and it glimmers behind Kenney's (his previous sentence starts 'Moreover, if this was what Virgil meant to convey...'). But there is another fallacy involved in these quotations which is widespread. In essence it runs as follows. *We know for whom our writer was writing, we know what sort of effects they could absorb and understand.*[32] *Therefore, if a scholar posits the sort of effect that the imagined audience could not have grasped, he must be in error.* To give it a name—no doubt it has been given names before[33]—I shall call it the Fallacy of Audience Limitation.[34] To apply the Fallacy to what I have written above in Sections 1 and 2. Vergil was not writing for hyperintertextualists; he could not have supposed that his readers would have collated, compared, and contrasted the relevant texts of Catullus and Lucretius. Therefore the interpretations offered are ruled out. People in Vergil's time didn't read that way.

---

[29] *Times Literary Supplement*, Jan. 19–25 (1990), 71.

[30] Kenney (1990), 211.

[31] I now use the more familiar, if not very pleasing term, as a shorthand. See my comments (above, pp. 167–70) on unjustified preconceptions about an author's intentions, and Appendix 1 below.

[32] Actually, I would dispute that we know this sort of thing—always or even often—but I let it stand for the moment. Cf. the thoughtful comments of Taplin in n. 42 below.

[33] Readers of Philip Larkin might like to call it the 'Fallacy of the Comparability of the Sale and Movement of Poultry (Domestic) Act, 1943'. Cf. his interesting remarks in Larkin (1983), 137, very interesting since they issue from someone who appears mainly to be victim to the Intentional Fallacy. What I call the 'Fallacy of Audience Limitation' is distantly related to the 'Affective Fallacy' (see Wimsatt (1970), 21 ff., and the entry in Preminger et al. (1986), 8), but only distantly related.

[34] I know that this sounds a bit pretentious. It also sounds more universally applicable than I perhaps intend; scholars will no doubt be able to think of instances where an audience's incapacities should be brought into the reckoning. I wish simply to get at a general (rather than, necessarily, an absolute) fact of literature, and to provoke thought. A portentous and catchy label may therefore be in order.

Vergil's Aeneid: Subversion by Intertextuality

'Virgil was not writing for hyperintertextualists'—and Aeschylus was not writing for A. Lebeck[35] or Oliver Taplin,[36] and Shakespeare was not writing for Caroline F. E. Spurgeon.[37] Let us consider for a moment those last two instances. It seems clear that Aeschylus wrote for dramatic performance at the City Dionysia, and, with luck, for re-performance, but with no expectation of being studied in texts: the practice of *reading* tragedies grows at the end of the fifth century.[38] In Shakespeare's day there were reasons why a playwright should not commit his plays to published texts, but Shakespeare seems to have been uninterested in the printed survival of his works to a remarkable degree, even allowing for those reasons. He was so much the man of the theatre (we might say) that he elected to be in the position that Aeschylus was in by virtual necessity. He wrote for a theatre audience.[39]

So: Aeschylus and Shakespeare wrote for theatre and audiences. We think we know about theatre audiences and what they can understand and absorb. And so, the Fallacy of Audience Limitation would say, this should set clear limitations on the interpreter. The critic should not 'extract from the text subtleties so tortuous that they could never reach the consciousness of an audience through a medium as fast moving and unhaltable as music'.[40] Well, I wonder. I wonder just how much of (for example) the subtle patterns of linked imagery in the *Agamemnon*, the sort of thing in fact that Lebeck and Taplin illuminate, would have reached the consciousness of the audience in the Theatre of Dionysus. I wonder how *un*necessary audiences at the Globe would have found Miss Spurgeon's illuminations. I am prepared to hazard a guess: Lebeck, Taplin, and Spurgeon would have proved pretty startling reading for most if not all such audiences. And yet is not what Lebeck, Taplin, and Miss Spurgeon claim (I have purposely picked on fairly tried and trusted critics)[41] by and large *true*? But Aeschylus was not writing for Lebeck and Taplin, nor Shakespeare for Miss Spurgeon. So it cannot be true...

---

[35] Lebeck (1971).   [36] e.g. Taplin (1977); note e.g., pp. 311–15.
[37] Spurgeon (1935).   [38] Taplin (1977), 12–18.
[39] See Wells and Taylor (1986), pp. xxx–xxxiii. The only works that Shakespeare himself seems to have cared about putting into print are the narrative poems *Venus and Adonis* and *The Rape of Lucrece*. The first efficient publication of his dramatic works was the First Folio, produced by John Heminges and Henry Condell in 1623, after Shakespeare's death. It is a sobering and revealing fact that, had it not been for their work, eighteen of Shakespeare's plays, including *The Tempest*, *Macbeth*, and *Antony and Cleopatra*, might, for all Shakespeare knew or apparently cared, have vanished. Wells and Taylor conclude on p. xxxii: 'John Marston, introducing the printed text of his play *The Malcontent* in 1604, wrote: "Only one thing afflicts me, to think that scenes invented merely to be spoken, should be enforcively published to be read." Perhaps Shakespeare was similarly afflicted.' Of the inaccurate Quartos produced in Shakespeare's lifetime, some at least were produced from the 'foul papers', another sign of Shakespeare's lack of interest in accurate textual survival: see Campbell and Quinn (1967), s.vv. 'foul papers', 'Quartos'.
[40] David (1961), 158, quoted by Taplin (1977), 18 with approval. But Taplin in fact shows much greater subtlety of critical position later. See below.
[41] The very title of Goldhill (1986) is of course indicative.

Clearly the reasoning is fallacious. Clearly, to limit interpretation to aesthetic effects which the imagined audience could supposedly grasp is wrong.

I think the simple fact is that a great artist does not confine the richness of his work to the intellectual capacity or physical circumstances of his audience, probably (simply) because he cannot. Of course he will provide *something* for that audience—if it is quantifiable and definable—especially if he wants to win prizes or make a living. But poetic creativity works at such incalculably multiple and profound levels, poetic genius is so rich, that the poet may pack his text with meaning and effects way beyond what his immediate audience can grasp, way beyond indeed what he himself may be consciously aware of.[42] These meanings are left to be unpacked, gradually by succeeding generations. Aeschylus may not have written in the immediate instance for Lebeck and Taplin, but there is a sense in which he did write for them. He created a work of art that would take, and will take generations totally to unpack, and here are Lebeck and Taplin patiently doing the job. Vergil did not write for hyperintertextualists. In a sense, he didn't. There is, of course, no word in Latin for intertextuality, not even for 'allusion' in the way that modern scholars use it. But few would deny that the text of the *Aeneid* is in fact allusive: intertextual. Few would deny the more general point that poets operate techniques and procedures which are only categorized and labelled a long time after the event. This is obviously in the nature of things: the artist creates, the scholar shuffles behind in his footsteps labelling. There is therefore a more important sense in which Vergil *did* write for intertextualists, if not hyperintertextualists, for he created a work which *is* intertextual—and which may take forever totally to unpack.

Some of the above is tendentious and speculative—and I am aware that I have indulged in the occasional 'intentionalist' sentence—but I hope that a clearly *wrong* way, a fallacious way, to approach the interpretation of texts— the Fallacy of Audience Limitation—has been indicated.[43]

---

[42] Cf. my remarks below on 'intention' in Appendix 1. Cf. too the perceptive comments of Taplin (1977), 18 f. After citing David with approval, he writes: 'But these are negative cautions, and one should take care in pressing them. Especially one should be careful not to dogmatize too confidently about what an author could or could not put into his work, for there are many levels of creative consciousness besides clearly formulated deliberation; and [Taplin continues, interestingly] similarly with what an audience could or could not register during a work in performance, for there are many degrees of apprehension beside the full and conscious recognition which it is the critic's task to formulate.' I, of course, would not accept that limitation on the critic's task in the last clause. But those who do not like to bypass the presumed capacities of the immediate audience (as I do) and yet wish to argue for, say, patterns of symbolism in Aeschylus or intertextuality in Vergil could exploit Taplin's (true) statement that 'there are many degrees of apprehension besides... full and conscious recognition' in an audience's response to a play or poem.

[43] In the Oxford *Honour School of Literae Humaniores* Latin Literature paper for 1990, there was the following question: 'Can we ever know that a Roman writer wished his readers to notice an allusion to earlier literature?' Radiating, as it does, the Intentional Fallacy and the Fallacy of Audience Limitation, it was presumably inviting the candidate to dispose of both.

APPENDIX 1

The 'Intentional Fallacy'

'Fallacy' is perhaps a misnomer, suggesting too tightly a *logical* error. Nevertheless there is much of value in the ancient essay of W. K. Wimsatt, written in collaboration with M. C. Beardsley, 'The Intentional Fallacy' (published in 1946 and reprinted in Wimsatt's *The Verbal Icon*, London, 1970) which has yet to be taken on board by some classical scholars. There is also a truly excellent article on the topic ('Intentions, problem of'). What I would argue is that an appeal to an 'author's intentions' is usually a sign of evasion: an evasion of responsibility to the text, an evasion of the responsibility to read as impartially and fully as possible. For, in the first place, we normally have no access to an author's intentions besides their actualization in the text; when scholars appeal to an author's 'intentions' in these cases, what they are really appealing to is their own preconception of what the author might or could intend. This may be a comfortable procedure, but it is hardly a tightly defensible one. In the second place, the very concept of 'intention' is a psychologically slippery one, not one to be invoked without the most careful thought. Thus (for example) I can intend something with full consciousness, or I can intend something in a subliminary kind of way ('preconsciously'); or I can intend something in an unconscious way, in the Freudian sense of 'unconscious' (Freudian slips being the most banal example of this): that is to say, I can intend something, I can then do or say it, but if challenged, I will deny that it was my intention. I can, of course, also simply lie about my intention... 'Intention' is indeed a slippery concept. It is lucky, in my opinion, that we have no statements by Vergil about his 'intentions'. They might be interesting historically, biographically, but as keys to unlock the secrets of the *Aeneid*? Best ignored. 'Authors in the main tend towards concealment of their secret intention... They obfuscate what their books are really all about...', Serjeant, loc. cit., with interesting examples. But suppose Vergil's statements were sapped by no such deviousness? There still remains the psychological slipperiness of the concept of 'intention', the depths and complexities involved in it. Vergil's statements would still be best ignored. But, of course, the problem does not arise. Vergil has left no statements of intention. And when scholars appeal to his 'intentions' they are indeed appealing to their own preconceptions.

I offer a couple of quotations in illustration of the preconceptions involved in such appeals to 'intention', and the deleterious evasions entailed. N. Horsfall, *CR* 38 (1988), 244 writes as follows of another scholar's interpretation of an 'allusion': 'I can see why he finds the Homeric plague god behind *Aen.* 4. 143 ff., but not there alone we might pause to ask "is that association actually relevant?"... and above all, "can we believe that that is what V(ergil) himself wanted us to conclude?"'. We have no evidence for what Vergil wanted us to conclude—beyond the text. The question is pointless and *evades* the interesting fact in the text. 'Is that association actually relevant?' Why shouldn't it be, unless we have preconceptions about what Vergil 'intends' to be relevant? Cf. too W. A. Camps, *An Introduction to Virgil's Aeneid* (Oxford, 1969), 106 ff.: 'But while some of the echoes and repetitions in the *Aeneid* can be seen to reflect an intention..., it is equally evident that many such echoes, whether of motif or of diction, occur without any intention behind them.' Comfortably buoyed by this sort of belief, we can evade the echo of, say, Catull. 66. 39–40.

I should conclude by admitting that avoidance of the Intentionalists' evasion leads to no objective and ever-applicable *Methode*. We still have to use our judgement, knowledge, and instinct. Inevitably, subjectivity cannot be completely expelled. As I wrote above, of the apparently more exact terminology of intertextuality: 'When is an intertext readable and identifiable enough to constitute an intertext? This is a problem that the theoreticians seem to me to evade...'. Another evasion. For my part, I fell back on Anglo-Saxon empiricism, faintly anti-climactically.

APPENDIX 2

Intertextuality and Latin Literature: Some Selected Bibliography

Many of us were modernized by the pioneering work of G. B. Conte, now appearing in English as *The Rhetoric of Imitation: Genre and Poetic Memory in Virgil and Other Latin Poets*, translated and edited with a foreword by Charles Segal (Ithaca and London, 1986): note esp. pp. 23 ff., 32 ff., esp. 38–9; see too Conte, *Il genere e i suoi confini* (Pisa, 1984), pp. 145–7, which is not included in the *The Rhetoric of Imitation*. Exemplary too is A. Barchiesi, *La Traccia del modello: Effetti omerici nella narrazione virgiliana* (Pisa, 1984); and cf. my offering in *Further Voices in Vergil's Aeneid* (Oxford, 1987), pp. 100 ff., with further bibliography. Conte to a small measure, and I to a large measure, were still in those days romantically attached to the term 'allusion'; Barchiesi is more systematic, modern, and exact. R. F. Thomas, 'Catullus and the Polemics of Poetic Reference (64. 1–18)', *AJP* 103 (1982), 144–64, J. E. G. Zetzel, 'Catullus, Ennius, and the Poetics of Allusion', *ICS* 8 (1983), 257–60, which productively takes issue with Thomas (1982), and Thomas, 'Virgil's *Georgics* and the Art of Reference', *HSCP* 90 (1986), 171–98 are other examples of works by intertextualists not yet systematically calling themselves intertextualists. J. Farrell's first chapter in *Vergil's Georgics and the Traditions of Ancient Epic: the Art of Allusion in Literary History* (New York and Oxford, 1991), 'Introduction: On Vergilian Intertextuality', is most stimulating and informative. One notes with interest his conclusion (p. 23): 'My own position, which is at odds with Conte's theory if not his practice, is that the student of allusion [that word again, significantly] is on some level concerned with a poet's intentions.' It is certainly true that one can observe intentionalism seeping back into some of Conte's discourse.

APPENDIX 3

Objections to the Term 'Intertextuality'

The objection is that it might imply, it might encourage an unhistorical approach to literature. Thus: T. S. Eliot is intertextual with Shakespeare. One must read Eliot conscious of the Shakespearian intertexts within it. But *inter*textuality perhaps implies a two-way process. Should one read the text of Shakespeare conscious of guest appearances by the intertext of Eliot? It must be stressed that Julia Kristeva herself, the inventor of the term intertextuality, encouraged no such unhistorical approaches. But (I infer) those who countenance Roland Barthes and his conception of intertextuality (see conveniently T. Eagleton, *Literary Theory: an Introduction* (Minneapolis, 1983), pp. 137–9) would be quite prepared to study Persse McGarrigle's thesis on the influence of T. S. Eliot on Shakespeare (David Lodge, *Small World* (London, 1984), p. 51 etc.). And there is a sense, of course, in which such a thesis need not be wholly without interest or point. After all, in a post-Eliot world it is virtually impossible to read Shakespeare without being influenced by Eliot as one reads, and to talk of Eliot as a Shakespearian intertext is, therefore, not wholly absurd. But we would have to be quite clear what we were doing. McGarrigle's thesis, if it were to have value, would be a study in reception: how our attitudes to Shakespeare have been affected by intervening poetry, how we the readers, by reason of our reading and experience, contribute to the making of a new Shakespearian text. Such a study would be highly legitimate (and historical); it could also be argued that it would not be illegitimate in this context to talk of Eliot as a Shakespearian intertext. On the other hand we must remain entirely clear, if we are to preserve our sanity, that the text of Eliot is historically compounded of Shakespeare in a way that Shakespeare's text is not compounded of Eliot. What, as an historicist, I radically object to is the sort of way *inter*textuality is interpreted and applied in the following quotation (from Carl A. Rubino, 'Lectio Difficilior Praeferenda est: Some Remarks on Contemporary French Thought and the Study of Classical Literature', *Arethusa* 10 (1977), 63–83; the quotation is from pp. 77 f.): 'since textuality is radically synchronic, it calls our accepted notions of literary history into question... It would be quite possible, therefore, to read a text that extends through and beyond Heidegger, Derrida... Plato, Hegel, Gorgias, Heisenberg, Vergil, Mallarmé, and Archilochus, *in that order*. Or perhaps we might conceive the whole of Western culture as one vast text—that can be read from end to end in any order...'. So: one finds oneself making a case for reading Eliot as a Shakespearian intertext (to serve the study of reception), but then one finds oneself in this sort of terminological company. One blushes, recoils—and wonders about the wisdom of a terminology that can accommodate, if it does not actively encourage, such lustrous folly.

12

Introductory Poems in Propertius: 1. 1 and 2. 12[1] (1998)

I wish to argue primarily that Propertius 2. 12 introduced the poet's original third book. 'Book 2b',[2] (Section III). On the way I examine Propertius' use of his various addresses (Section I), and I discuss strategies in his indisputably introductory poem 1. 1 (Section II). Similarities of strategy discernible in 2. 12 head my argument that 2. 12 was, like 1. 1, an introductory poem. The question of addresses in introductory poems raises the topic of Propertius' social status and his relations to great men, and this is briefly surveyed.

I. ADDRESSES AND THEIR USES

There is an astonishing change of tone between Propertius 1. 1 and 1. 2, under-remarked. In 1. 1, oppressed and hostile to love, Propertius talks of

---

[1] My thanks are due to the editors of *PCPS*, Dr P. R. Hardie and Dr S. P. Oakley, and to their scrupulous anonymous reader.

[2] Lachmann (in his edition of 1816) first made the suggestion, not universally accepted, that our 'Book 2 is a product of two ancient books.' I have surveyed the evidence in an article forthcoming in *JRS* ('Propertius 2.10 and 2.11 and the Structure of Books "2a" and "2b"' [Lyne 1998a]), arguing in favour of Lachmann; and so I shall content myself here with a bibliographical summary. Skutsch (1975), 229–33 offers a succinct defence of Lachmann's thesis; Heyworth (1995), 165–85, argues for Lachmann's basic thesis in convincing and minute detail. Cf. too the terse statement of facts by Hubbard (1974), 41–2 and the cautious survey in the commentary of Butler and Barber (1933), pp. xxviii–xxxv. Opponents have been (e.g.) Williams (1968), 481 (sufficiently rebutted by Hubbard and Skutsch), Camps (1967), 1, and, quite recently, though implicitly rather than explicitly, Wyke (1987), 47–61, esp. 48, 61, an article to which I attend in Lyne (1998a) [= Ch. 14]. Lachmann presented 2. 10 as the opening poem of Book 2b. Heyworth puts the case persuasively for believing (*a*) that 2. 10 was closural in Book 2a (following a point made by Hutchinson (1984), 100, who does not however believe in the division of 'Book 2'), and (*b*), following Richmond (1928), that 2. 13 was inceptive in Book 2b; cf. too Heyworth (1992), 45–9 on 213 discussing its unity, opening status, and so on. Heyworth thinks 2. 13 was actually the first poem in Book 2b, and here is where we differ. I accept its inceptive function, but think that 2. 12 actually opened the book. Birt (1882), 419–20 accepted Lachmann's suggestion that 2. 10 opened Book 2b, but also pointed out that both 2. 12 and 2. 13 belong in the front of a book;

madness, folly, bitter nights (6, 7 etc.); he confesses disease, degradation, desperation (27–8): 'fortiter et ferrum *saeuos* patiemur et ignis, | sit modo libertas quae uelit ira loqui', 'I shall endure iron and savage fire with bravery, provided that I get the liberty to speak what my anger wants.'[3] And so on. But then 1. 2. 'Quid iuuat ornato procedere, uita, capillo', 'my love, why does it please you to go out with coiffured hair...?' Here we find (on the face of it anyway) lightness and grace, delicate admonishment of Cynthia's use of cosmetics and finery, complimentary references to her natural beauty and artistic accomplishments. It seems a different world. This radical change in stance and mood requires explanation.

The answer lies in change of addressee, and a general Propertian strategy. Different people possess different ignorances, prejudices, and powers. To the love-poet bent on explaining his love they present different requirements. Propertius exploits precisely this fact. He chooses addresses with different characteristics in order to show different aspects of love. Thus, in 1. 4 Bassus is an iambic poet.[4] To judge by the ethos of Horace's *Epodes*, Bassus' published interests in love and sex will have lacked discrimination and subtlety. To Propertius he has counselled the safety and pleasure of numbers: *multas puellas*. He therefore requires Propertius to reveal something of what is so exclusively special about Cynthia—and something of her jealous vindictiveness. In 15, Gallus has a mind to cut in on Cynthia. He is a *nobilis*, a casual philanderer accustomed to easy girls (*uagae puellae*), with no knowledge of the defencelessness of masculinity and class in the face of a really strong woman: Propertius uses this fact to bring out other aspects of love and Cynthia. Two different addressees: different aspects revealed. Of course these and other male addressees addressed by the male Propertius can reveal only masculine perspectives. Addresses to Cynthia also tend to reveal a Propertian, male view. To reveal female views of his love, Propertius contrives at times to give them voice.[5] And what a different view of the love affair of Propertius

by Birt (1909), 398–9 and Birt (1915), 266 he is suggesting, in summary form, that 2. 10 and the 'epigram' 2. 11 closed Book 2a, and at Birt (1909), 399–400 he suggests in similar summary form that 2. 12 and 13a opened Book 2b; at Birt (1915), 266 he assumes that 2. 12 to 13. 1–16 is all one poem—and opened Book 2b. But on none of these occasions does he offer any substantive argument for his theses. My *JRS* article, Lyne (1998*a*) [=Ch. 14] argues that 2. 10/11 (all one poem) closed Book 2a.

[3] Line 27 plays between ideas of medical cure (surgery, cautery) and, paradoxically, servile punishments: cf. Lyne (1979), 129 [=Ch. 6, p. 100 below]. (Cairns (1974), 106, citing Celsus, sees a reference to cures for madness.) *Contactum* in line 2 already suggests disease: cf. Camps (1961) ad loc. and below n. 48. For the degradation involved in the absence of *libertas loquendi*, see below §II.1.iii.

[4] Ovid *Trist.* 4. 10. 47–8: Bassus the iambist is coupled as a friend of Ovid's with Ponticus the epic poet, addressee of Prop. 1. 7 and 9.

[5] Rosati (1992), 71–94 is heading in a different direction, but has very important things to say in this area.

and Cynthia is then produced! Cf. 1. 3. 35–46, 2. 29B. 31–8, 4. 7. 13–94; cf. too 4. 8. 73–80, 3. 6. 19–34. The truths of love are shown to be not only multifaceted but relative.

So what of 1. 2? We are not in a different world. The poem is addressed to a different person, to Cynthia. And this matters. Cynthia possesses power, especially over Propertius, as poem 1. 1 tells us. In particular we learn that Cynthia's power over him is such that he is slavishly unable to speak his mind to her (1. 1. 27 f.). Now 1. 2 is actually, at bottom, concerned with Propertius' fear of Cynthia's promiscuity, his fear that she may be casting her net after other lovers.[6] But Propertius does not come out and say so. Why not? Because he has not the *libertas loquendi* to do so. Instead, he must package the message in adjuncts, flattery, and humour. The different addressee shows a different aspect of this love affair. On certain topics, with certain people, with one person in particular, Propertius must walk on tiptoe.

But now we must take up the hostile, apparently despairing declarations of 1. 1.

II. POEM 1. 1

1. Propertius and the Public Roman World

Propertius chooses as the addressee of his introductory poem a friend called Tullus. Tullus is a man from the conventional equestrian world, nephew of the L. Volcacius Tullus who had been consul in 33 BC; we learn from 1. 6 that he proposes to form part of his uncle's proconsular entourage, a standard career move for an ambitious young equestrian.[7] Comparatively speaking therefore Tullus is—for the time being[8]—a public and political figure. Now the passions

---

[6] See Lyne (1980), 104–9.

[7] L. Volcacius Tullus' consulship in 33 BC is recorded in the *Fasti Venusini*, Degrassi *Inscriptiones Italiae* xiii. 1: text pp. 254 and 255, commentary p. 251. For his proconsulship in Asia, see Ehrenberg and Jones (1955), no. 98 (this proconsulship and its date are discussed in my forthcoming paper in *CQ* [Lyne 1998c = Ch. 15 in this volume]). For the well-documented institution of young equestrians serving in the entourage of a provincial governor, see Gelzer (1975), 101 f.; Cic. *Q. F.* 1. 1. 11–12 (a key text though Gelzer and Shackleton Bailey's commentary differ slightly in interpretation of detail); the racy but informative poems of Catullus (10, 28, 46); Hor. *Epist.* 1. 3; the amusing letters of Cicero to Trebatius Testa, *Ad fam.* 7. 6, 17, 18; and Cic. *Cael.* 73 on M. Caelius' service as *contubernalis* to Q. Pompeius Rufus proconsul of Africa in 61 BC (another key text) 'cum autem paulum iam roboris accessisset aetati, in Africam profectus est Q. Pompeio pro consule contubernalis. . . . usus quidam prouincialis non sine causa a maioribus huic aetati tributus.'

[8] Prop. 3. 22 suggests with some irony and *Schadenfreude* that Tullus discovered idleness and pleasure while in the East; cf. Griffin (1985), 56.

of love, carried to any extreme, tended to strike men of the conventional, public Roman world, as stupid, sick, mad, criminal, or worse. Cicero for example implies that love should merely be a passing, trivial amusement of youth, and it is tolerable if it is kept as such; but if love or the love-object starts to dominate, we find the sternest condemnation.[9] Or we can recall the anecdote of the Elder Cato, earthily expressing the same kind of view: a youth may, indeed should, seek summary satisfaction for his sexual urges, but must show no preoccupation with them.[10] The comic stage is the proper place for the hopeless infatuated lover.[11] Tullus, budding *comes* of the

---

[9] Cf. esp. Cic. *Cael.* 28 and 42. Cicero has to be indulgent of love affairs in this public speech, since he is defending the amorous Caelius, but his way of presenting and defending love is precisely as a mere *ludus*, quite tolerable if—and only if—important limiting rules are observed; cf. Lyne (1980), 1–2. (Cicero talks in fairly general terms, but his eye is clearly on the pleasures of *amor*.) From *Cael.* 28: 'datur enim concessu omnium huic aliqui ludus aetati' (i.e. youth), 'et ipsa natura profundit adulescentiae cupiditates. quae si ita erumpunt ut nullius uitam labefactent, nullius domum euertant, faciles et tolerabiles haberi solent.' From *Cael* 42: 'detur aliqui ludus aetati ... postremo cum paruerit uoluptatibus, dederit aliquid temporis ad ludum aetatis atque ad inanis hasce adulescentiae cupiditates, reuocet se aliquando ad curam rei domesticae, rei forensis reique publicae ...'. The limiting rules are clear. Condemnation when they are transgressed is crushing. A *meretrix* Chelidon played a dominant role in Verres' life. Damningly, Cicero so presents him as if she yielded the power when he was *praetor* (*Ver.* 1. 104, 135–40, 'praefuit, dominata est, eius mulieris arbitratu gessisse praeturam'; 5. 34, 'nutu atque arbitrio Chelidonis meretriculae gubernari'; 5. 38, 'non modo a domo tua Chelidonem in praetura excludere noluisti, sed in Chelidonis domum praeturam totam detulisti'). Cf. also on Antony's behaviour with Cytheris: *Att.* 10. 10. 5 'hic tamen Cytherida secum lectica aperta portat, alteram uxorem' (note the emphasis: treating a mere lover as a spouse); *Phil.* 2. 20 'a mima uxore'; Cic. *Phil.* 2. 58, *Att.* 10. 16. 5, and others. And cf. the denunciation of passionate love (which Cicero unwillingly calls *amor*) in Tusc. 4. 68–76: dominant words are *flagitium, leuitas, insania*, and terms indicative of disease and contempt ('sic igitur adfecto haec adhibenda curatio est, ut et illud quod cupiat ostendatur quam leue, quam contemnendum, quam nihili sit omnino'), and *furor*; Cicero concludes by saying that passionate love is against nature: 'etenim si naturalis amor esset, et amarent omnes et semper amarent et idem amarent, neque alium pudor, alium cogitatio, alium satietas deterreret.' Interestingly, Catullus uses comparable condemnatory terms when seeking finally to be *quit* of love (poem 76). Lucretius uses such condemnatory terms generally when he talks of 'love' (4. 1073 ff.); tolerant of sex, he is scornful of passion in ways remarkably similar to Cicero and Cato (see next note): Epicurean philosophy, Lucretius' version at least, here overlaps with conventional wisdom; Cicero, *Tusc.* 70 can spare some grudging words of praise for Epicurus in this regard. Note Lucretius' uses of *sanus* (1075), *rabies* (1083), *furor* (1117), and 'adde quod alterius sub nutu degitur aetas' (1122; cf. that with e.g. Cic. *Ver.* 5. 34 above); note too 1124 'languent officia atque aegrotat fama uacillans', fears that were clearly in Cicero's mind in the above *Cael.* quotations. (Many of the terms of condemnation are traditional: e.g. for love as sickness see Pease on Verg. *Aen.* 4. 1, and Barrett on Eur. *Hipp.* 476–7).

[10] Horace refers to the famous anecdote indicative of Catonian attitudes at *Serm.* 1. 2. 31–5. The whole anecdote is summarised by Horace's commentators on line 31. It catches, among other things, Roman apprehension lest 'love' should preoccupy, as well as the wish to see Roman freeborn women spared amorous attentions.

[11] Allen (1950), 255–77 at 262 f. with n. 26 observes the interesting and close parallels between Phaedria's slave's description of Phaedria at Ter. *Eunuchus* 56–63 and Propertius'

proconsul, may be presumed to share, or at least to be apprised of, these attitudes. To explain love to him therefore Propertius chooses to adapt to his position and prejudices: Tullus presents special requirements, and Propertius exploits this fact, as he exploits the special requirements made by Bassus and Gallus. But in 1. 1 he does not seek to adjust Tullus' presumed views. Rather he adopts his friend's kind of discourse, in order to show his love in these terms and to explain it in these terms. Propertius' path of life is (he agrees) stupid, diseased, mad, dominated by love and the lover—all sorts of overlap with the Ciceronian and other texts cited in n. 9 will be immediately noticed. But then he says: I can do nothing about it. The result is a striking and interestingly programmatic poem. The comparatively public addressee allows Propertius to make a public, radically dissociative statement. The poem positions Propertius the lover in, and in contrast to, the great world around him. The world may condemn, Propertius may accept the logic of the condemnation. But: 'caput impositis pressit Amor pedibus' (1. 1. 4), Love has trodden his head beneath his feet. Propertius simply *is* dominated by love and removed from the conventional world. Then, when his radical dissociation has been expressed, Propertius proceeds—in succeeding poems—to finer distinctions, positioning himself in relation to other lovers, loves, and poets.

Propertius 1. 1 has of course been much discussed,[12] and I shall concentrate on a few detailed ways in which Propertius shows his variance from the Roman world around him, in that world's terms. Some of the details I pick are disputed, and that is partly why I choose them. And a particular interest of mine is to show Propertius' dissociation not just from the public world but from the public world in its political aspect.

(i) *Consilium*. Love has taught Propertius 'nullo uiuere consilio', 'to live with no deliberation, judgement, prudence', 1. 1. 6. Three inadequate glosses are elicited from me in an attempt to catch this crucial word. Pages of Hellegouarc'h[13] swiftly illustrate how *consilium* is a recurring virtue, a *sine qua non*, of the public Roman man. Cf. e.g. Livy 6. 27. 1 'Camillus, consilio et uirtute...'; Cic. *Ad fam*. 5.7.3 (to Pompey) 'quae, cum ueneris, tanto consilio

---

self-description in 1. 1; with Prop. 1. 1. 6, 'nullo uiuere consilio', for example, he compares *Eun*. 57–8, 'quae res in se neque consilium neque modum | habet ullum, eam consilio regere non potes.'

[12] Allen (1950) is still stimulating and important; he sees that Propertius uses 'conventional' depreciatory language of love, but cites parallels from 'philosophy' (Cicero, Lucretius) and comedy. He neglects the fact that these condemnatory views are also, and most importantly, views that public Romans publicly espouse. For other views and emphases see Hubbard (1974), 14 ff.; Cairns (1974), 94–110; Ross (1975), 59–70; La Penna (1977), 32 ff., 228–9; Williams (1980), 34–40 (some very challenging ideas here, especially on points of detail); Stahl (1985), 22–47 with extensive notes.

[13] Hellegouarc'h (1963), 254–6.

Introductory Poems in Propertius: 1. 1 and 2. 12   189

tantaque animi magnitudine a me gesta esse cognosces, ut tibi... me... facile et in republica et in amicitia adiunctum esse patiare', 'when you return home, you will recognise that my achievements have been performed with such judgement and greatness of spirit that you will easily admit me into close association with yourself both in politics and in private friendship'.[14] We should note too in this connection *improbus*, the epithet of Amor, which, with *consilio*, frames line 6. Familiar as an epithet of love from Verg. *Ecl.* 8. 49 (then *Aen.* 4. 412), it is also part of Roman political discourse.[15] It is used typically of those who defy the laws of the state, act outside its order and restraint: *improbi* are the antithesis, for example, of Cicero's tendentious and embracing vision of *optimates*.[16] Coupled together, these two words will enhance each other's potentiality to convey values of social and political importance. So: Propertius declares himself imprudent and commanded by a power that defies good order: the sort of man who would be hopeless, indeed dangerous in public life. While we are noticing such language in this vicinity, we should not miss *furor* (7). This too is a *vox propria* of political–public discourse, the word with which one labels crazed revolutionary opponents of optimate order.[17] We find it combined with a cognate of *improbus*.[18]

(ii) *Castae puellae*. Love has taught him to hate 'chaste girls', *castas puellas*, 1. 1. 5. An informative, summarising note here is Fedeli's.[19] We can reject the

---

[14] Cf. further *TLL* iv. 455. 61 ff. Very illuminating are the *iuxta posita* cited under *consilium* at *TLL* iv. 456. 69 ff. (457. 12 f. '*persaepe coniunguntur* sapientia, prudentia, ratio, ingenium, animus, virtus, gravitas, constantia, gratia, mens, cogitatio, iudicium *al.*')

[15] Fedeli (1980), on line 6 traces epithets of Amor like *improbus* and *saeuus* to οὖλος and σχέτλιος in Apollonius, appropriately enough, but the path I suggest must also be followed.

[16] Cic. *Sest.* 97, 'omnes optimates sunt qui neque nocentes sunt nec natura improbi nec furiosi nec malis domesticis impediti'; 139, 'cum multis audacibus, improbis, non nunquam etiam potentibus dimicandum'. Cf. Hellegouarc'h (1963), 528–30 'Il faut d'ailleurs remarquer que, dans le domaine politique, le contraire de *bonus* n'est pas le plus souvent *malus*, comme dans le vocabulaire moral, mais *improbus*... *improbus* qualifie surtout ceux qui agissent contre les lois ou les règles d'ordre imposées par l'État...', with shoals of examples.

[17] Cf. Cic. *Sest.* 97 quoted n. 16, also 99, 'qui propter insitum quendam animi furorem discordiis ciuium ac seditione pascantur', Cic. *Cat.* 1. 1. Cf. further *TLL* vi. 1630. 80 ff. This political use of the word should not be forgotten when assessing the importance of *pietas / furor* in the *Aeneid*: indeed a political charge is given to *furor* (and *pietas*) by the most prominent first use in the *Aeneid*, in the Statesman simile, *Aen.* 1. 150.

[18] Cf. Cic. *Rab. Perd.* 22 'improbitas et furor L. Saturnini'. Cf. too Cic. *Sest.* 97 quoted n. 16.

[19] Fedeli (1980) ad loc. documents the following interpretations: (i) *castae puellae* refer to the Muses: (ii) *castas odisse puellas* alludes to a current partiality on Propertius' part for tarts (the *uiles* referred to in 2. 23 and 24); (iii) *castae puellae* are 'women of good family', the sort whom a Roman of good social position would choose to marry, women *unlike* Cynthia (cf. Fontenrose (1949), 378, followed by Enk (1956) ad loc., and others, most recently Holzberg (1990), 30); with some qualification this is the path I follow; (iv) *castae puellae* are women like Cynthia (at the moment) and Milanion's Atalanta who resist men's advances. Option (iv) is Fedeli's, and Allen's ((1950), 266 f.), choice; Fedeli cites *inter al.* Prop. 3. 12. 37 which might rather support

favoured interpretation of Fedeli himself (and Allen); we can be less Freudian than Sullivan's pages on 'Dirnenliebe'.[20] The epithet needs to be seen within the public language and strategy of the poem as a whole—and within the immediate context of the socio-political terms *consilium, improbus, furor*. Again, Propertius is positioning himself in, and against, the orthodox Roman world around him. It is a *sine qua non* of the women who are 'loved' and then married by men in this world that they are—and remain— 'chaste', *castae* (*castitas* does not necessarily have anything to do with technical virginity, let alone the ritual virginity of, say, Vestal Virgins). Consider Horace's horror, in his high 'Roman Odes' mode, at the unmarried Roman girl who 'incestos amores...meditatur' (*Ode* 3. 6. 23 f.: next stop adultery, 25); consider the oath sworn by the blood of the proto-typically chaste Roman married lady (Lucretia), Livy 1.59.1 'per hunc...castissimum sanguinem iuro'. The girls' wedding chorus call the bride at Catull. 62.23 'castam... puellam'. The word *castus* is very common in Cicero (37 examples) who uses it of men (e.g. *Cael.* 73) as well as married women (*Ver.* 6. 28, *Har.* 27, etc.). And here are a few more passages, which, of very varied type, capture the same fact with the same word: in Roman society a married or marriageable Roman woman should be *casta*. Publilius C9[21] 'casta ad uirum matrona parendo imperat'; Cic. *Ver.* 5. 28 (with irony) 'si quae castiores erant'; Verg. *Aen.* 8. 665 f. 'castae...matronae'; Ovid *Ars* 1. 623 'delectant etiam castas praeconia formae', *Fast.* 2. 139 (Caesar) 'castas...iubet esse maritas'; Propertius himself uses it of Postumus' *uxor* Galla at 3. 12. 15 and 37. Treggiari remarks that *castissimus, -a* is surprisingly uncommon in *CIL* as an epithet on the tombstones of spouses (perhaps not so surprisingly, when we find that the warmer *carissima* is common), but adds that 'literary sources abundantly confirm the central position of wifely chastity, *castitas* and *pudicitia*';[22] and, on the other hand, whatever the total comparative picture that leads Treggiari to her conclusion, *TLL* iii. 567. 5–22 records many *castae* deceased wives.

So, anti-social love has taught Propertius to live without the prudence and order necessary to a man in public affairs; and it has taught him to hate the sort of proper, moral women that Roman gentlemen 'love': here is the implication of *castas odisse puellas*. To such an extent is Propertius alienated from his own proper society (probably equestrian: Section III. 5). The inescapable (further) implication of line 5 is that Cynthia cannot be classed as a

---

option (iii). Allen puts it thus: '*castae puellae* are girls who, like Cynthia, coldly reject a lover... Propertius makes the bitter complaint that Love has taught him to hate the woman he loves.' *Castas* is also discussed e.g. by Stahl (1985), 36 ff.; he too favours something like option (iv); cf. too Shackleton Bailey (1956), 1 f.

[20] Sullivan (1976), 102–5.   [21] Line 108 in the Loeb *Minor Latin Poets* (1961).
[22] Treggiari (1991), 231–3.

casta. Now *castitas* involves high moral and social qualities, and no doubt should in theory be inseparable from high social status, inseparable even from free-born Roman status. But in practice it isn't. Consider the girl Horace has in mind, consider too Cicero's Clodia and other examples.[23] And consider Propertius himself. Just as he admits social behaviour inconsistent with his own social class in his own case, so he may imply social attitudes in Cynthia inconsistent with her social class, attitudes which (as in Cicero's Clodia's case) putatively remove her from that class. We simply cannot tell. We can make moral inferences from this line, but none regarding the official class of Cynthia.

It may be objected that Prop. 1. 11. 29 and even 2. 6. 28 imply that Cynthia is after all a *casta puella*. But Prop. 2. 6. 28 ff. is a general denunciation of obscene paintings in chaste houses, with perhaps little or no connection with Cynthia.[24] Prop. 1. 11 is addressed to Cynthia: Cynthia has power over Propertius, robs him of his *libertas loquendi*, moves him to careful flattery instead of vehement protest (1. 2, cf. above). Talking *to her* he is unlikely (yet) to call her *incesta*. More likely, flatteringly to suggest the opposite.

(iii) *Libertas loquendi*. 1. 1. 27 f. are Propertius' first clear reference to the condition called *seruitium amoris*.[25] Other love poets will profess their *seruitium* in their own ways. But, suiting the strategy of this introductory poem, Propertius expresses servility to Cynthia in a way which acutely positions himself within, and in contrast to, the conventional public world (Tullus' world) around him. He lacks, he suggests, the *liberty to speak his mind*.

---

[23] It is a major strategy of Cicero's to portray Clodia as a self-elected, de facto, *meretrix* (cf. esp. *Cael.* 38, 48–50): in this way Caelius' connections with her are explained and excused. Cicero's picture is not devoid of plausibility, nor indeed, one surmises, of truth. For other Roman ladies displaying an absence of *castitas*, see Lyne (1980), 13–17 ('the amateurs'). By contrast, observe the picture of a matronly *casta* Delia, who is in declared fact no *matrona* (1. 6. 67–8), which is imagined or wished for by Tibullus at 1. 3. 83 ff. (spinning in domestic surroundings).

[24] There is of course no reason why Propertius should not imply that Cynthia is not *casta* in one poem (1. 1) with one (public) context, and preach to her about the proper decorations of a *casta domus* in another poem (2. 6) and another context. I am not however persuaded of the integrity of 2. 6, and doubt in particular whether the *casta domus* of 28 relates in any immediate way to Cynthia. In 1 ff. Propertius complains that Cynthia's (presumably Cynthia's) house is thronged like the dwellings of famous women of pleasure (Lais, Thais, Phryne); in 28 ff. he denounces the deviser of obscene decorations in chaste houses. It is hard to see how these remarks on pictures improper for a *casta domus* (28 ff.) can bear upon Cynthia's *domus*, which has been compared in effect to a brothel; it is hard to see how they can coexist in the same poem. In addition, pictures *are* mentioned in 1 ff. but they are quite different ones from the obscene decorations of 28 ff. Propertius moans that he is prey to reasonable and unreasonable jealousy, and mentions (innocuous) pictures of young men, imagined as rivals (9). And anyway, do 15 ff. follow on from 1–14? In sum, I find it hard to suppose that we have one single poem here. As often in 'Book 2', I have the impression of excerpts, associatively or randomly joined.

[25] Cf. Lyne (1980), 78–81 with bibliography, also Lyne (1979) [=Ch. 6 in this volume].

On the one hand, the Roman upper classes frowned on the complete freedom of speech on which the Athenians had prided themselves (παρρησία). Cf. e.g. Cic. *Flacc.* 16; Athens in its great days, 'illa uetus quae quondam opibus, imperio, gloria floruit, hoc uno malo concidit, libertate immoderata ac licentia contionum', 'that Athens of old which once upon a time flourished in wealth, power and glory, failed through this one evil, the unrestrained freedom and licence of its public assemblies'. In the Athenian assembly any man had a right to speak; in Roman assemblies the appropriate magistrates spoke. 'Magistrates, leading senators and barristers enjoyed freedom of speech and made the most of it; but they cannot be identified with the Roman people.'[26] Freedom of speech was therefore, for the Romans, a class privilege; these top political and juridical positions were in the Roman system inalienable from class.

But among these top classes the privilege was keenly felt and jealously guarded. We can see this most vividly from the expressions of pain which its absence caused in exceptional, tyrannical circumstances—pain expressed in terms very relevant to our context. Consider Cic. *Ad fam.* 4. 14. 1 written in the oppressive days of 45 BC: 'mihi gratulabare quod audisses me meam pristinam dignitatem obtinere... si dignitas est, bene de republica sentire et bonis uiris probare quod sentias, obtineo dignitatem meam; sin autem in eo dignitas est, si, quod sentias, aut re efficere possis aut denique libera oratione defendere, ne uestigium quidem ullum est reliquum nobis dignitatis', 'you congratulate me because you heard that I preserved my former honour... If it is honourable to be of good opinion about the state and to commend your opinions to good men, I preserve my honour; but if honour exists upon this condition that either you can accomplish what you feel in action or at least defend it in *free (public) speech*, not even a trace of honour has been left me.' Cf. too Cic. *Att.* 4. 6. 1–2 (55 BC) 'nam tu quidem... nullam habes propriam seruitutem... ego uero, qui si loquor de republica quod oportet, insanus, si quod opus est, seruus existimor... quo dolore esse debeo', 'for you... have no peculiar servitude... But I, reckoned insane if I speak on politics as I ought, a slave if I say what is expedient... how pained ought I to feel?' I have collected elsewhere further such references in which inhibited speech seems unacceptably abject, indeed servile, to Cicero and others.[27]

So, Propertius admits to the infringement of a liberty that should have been his by right of class. As an equestrian (cf. Section III. 5), he had access to a juridical career, and the *cursus honorum* might have been open to him.

---

[26] Wirszubski (1950), 18–19 with n. 2; Wirszubski 13 ff. is particularly interesting and relevant here.
[27] Lyne (1979), 124 f. [=Ch. 6, pp. 94–5 above].

Libertas loquendi is the right of men of such rank. Not in Propertius' case. Whence this painful deprivation? Not, as with Cicero, exceptional political circumstances, but: Cynthia. It is Cynthia who disallows his behaving as a man of his class should. Propertius the lover continues to position himself within, and in contrast to, the society around him. What should be his by right, from the world's point of view, is not his because of Cynthia and love—and then follows 1. 2, the tiptoeing admonishments of an unfree man.

(iv) *Amici*. I add briefly a comment on Propertius' appeal to friends to help him in this predicament (25 ff.). Propertius' view of how friends might serve him—restore him to decency, sanity, freedom—shows familiarity with a conventional mode of high-minded thinking and practice. He is writing within a context.

Help with folly or weakness of spirit is one of the things that the better class of Roman likes to think his *amici* provide. Compare how Cicero presents one of the functions of friends in the discussion conducted among public men in the *De amicitia*. For example, *De am.* 44, 'haec igitur prima lex amicitiae sanciatur... consilium uerum dare audeamus libere. plurimum in amicitia amicorum bene suadentium ualeat auctoritas, eaque et adhibeatur ad monendum non modo aperte, sed etiam acriter, si res postulabit, et adhibitae pareatur', 'let the first law of friendship be fixed as follows... let us dare to give true advice freely. Let the authority of friends who urge well be of the greatest force, and let it be administered not only openly, but even vehemently if the facts demand it; and when it is administered, let it be obeyed'; 59 'tertius uero ille finis deterrimus, ut, quanti quisque se ipse faciat, tanti fiat ab amicis. saepe enim in quibusdam aut animus abiectior est aut spes amplificandae fortunae fractior. non est igitur amici talem esse in eum, qualis ille in se est, sed potius eniti et efficere ut amici iacentem animum excitet inducatque in spem cogitationemque meliorem', 'the third definition of the limits of friendship is the worst, namely that a man should be estimated by his friends as he estimates himself. In certain people in fact there is often a spirit that is too abject, a hope of ameliorating fortune that is too feeble. So it is not a friend's business to be towards another as he is towards himself, but rather to strive to bring it about that he arouses his friend's prostrate spirit, and leads him to hope and better habits of thought.' This is what Propertius needs, and this is what he seeks. Again, however, as in the earlier instances, although he can think and talk within the framework of conventional practices and values, he swiftly conveys their inapplicability to himself. For, if he is about to canvass surgery as a remedy for his condition (27), he can have little faith in the sort of *auxilia*—counselling and so on—which friends would conventionally provide and which Cicero, say, has in mind.

2. Propertius and a Greek View of Love

We now may proceed to another Propertian self-positioning in poem 1. 1: in relation to what we might see as Greek amorous spiritedness.

It is well known that the opening of Prop. 1.1 closely follows Meleager Gow–Page ciii = *Anth. Pal.* 12. 101. The whole of Meleager's poem is not always quoted, and it is vital that it should be:

> τόν με Πόθοις ἄτρωτον ὑπὸ στέρνοισι Μυΐσκος
> ὄμμασι τοξεύσας τοῦτ' ἐβόησεν ἔπος·
> 'τὸν θρασὺν εἷλον ἐγώ· τὸ δ' ἐπ' ὀφρύσι κεῖνο φρύαγμα
> σκηπτροφόρου σοφίας ἠνίδε ποσσὶ πατῶ.'
> τῷ δ' ὅσον ἀμπνεύσας τόδ' ἔφην· 'φίλε κοῦρε, τί θαμβεῖς;
> καὐτὸν ἀπ' Οὐλύμπου Ζῆνα καθεῖλεν Ἔρως'.

Myiscus shot me beneath the breast, unwounded by Desires, with <the arrows of> his eyes, and shouted out thus: 'I have captured the bold one; see, I tread with my feet upon that arrogance of princely wisdom that was on his brow.' But I, gathering breath as I could, said this: 'Dear boy, why are you amazed? Love (Eros) brought down even Zeus himself from Olympus.'

Other sources for Prop. 1. 1 may be found—e.g. Meleager Gow–Page XVI.1 = *Anth. Pal.* 12. 48. 1 has the detail of Love's foot actually on the lover's neck. But CIII = *Anth. Pal.* 12. 101 is the most vital text. And it is most important to realise that Propertius not just exploits but alludes to this poem of Meleager— and contrives thereby another programmatic dissociation. Incidental details of difference spring to mind (a girl not a boy...). But I choose something more important. In the wake of Myiscus' triumphant action and speech, Meleager may be winded, but he still manages spiritedly to respond: 'What's so special about you? What's so special about what you have done to me?' The special nature of Cynthia is of course, by contrast, beyond question, and a dominant feature of Propertius' poem. But what I would like to stress is simply: that Meleager responds, spiritedly, cheekily, wittily. Contrast Propertius: 'sit modo libertas quae uelit ira loqui'. No such possibility of spirited response for him. The poem, radically dissociating Propertius from public Roman liberties, also dissociates him from the game and chirpy bravado that Hellenistic lover-poets may evince.

3. Propertius and a Roman Lover's View of Love

While addressing Tullus in 1. 1, Propertius draws attention to an erotic myth of service, suffering, and reward. The legendary Milanion served and suffered for his beloved Atalanta and eventually won his prize, he 'subdued', 'mastered' her: 1. 1. 9–16. Propertius (by implication) has been comparably attentive to Cynthia, but without winning similar advantage.[28] Lines 17–18: 'in me tardus Amor non ullas cogitat artis | nec meminit notas, ut prius, ire uias', 'in my case Love is slow and contrives no arts nor remembers to proceed as before on his well-known way.' Propertius draws an emphatic contrast between himself and the mythical lover he adduces. It seems certain to me that he is in fact drawing Tullus' attention, through this myth, to the experience of a predecessor Roman lover-poet, Cornelius Gallus, and showing a contrast between himself and that lover-poet. Gallus had had to suffer for his beloved, but in time had been rewarded for his pains; and the myth which Gallus had notably used to capture this experience of service, suffering, and love had been Milanion–Atalanta: so we can reasonably infer.[29] From this myth and therefore from the experience of his predecessor lover-poet, Propertius dissociates himself in his opening poem: *in me tardus Amor*. His lot is even harder than another elegiac lover's.

[28] What exactly is Propertius implying here? Is he saying that he has not even managed to have sexual relations with Cynthia during the year of *furor*? One detects this question behind euphemistic discussions like Allen's ((1950), 255–7) referring to Lachmann, and Butler and Barber. And it is an important one for critics who would like—not unreasonably—to find a story behind these poems, fictional or real. If Propertius hasn't yet made love to Cynthia, when was the poem written or—a more realistic question—at what stage in the affair are we to suppose that the poem was written? And how then does it relate to, say, 1. 2? I think actually that Propertius' emphasis here is on the full reverberations of *domuisse*. Milanion–Gallus managed not just to sleep with, but to subdue, to master the woman. As Propertius stresses in this poem, and will stress time and again (*seruitium amoris*), it is Cynthia, who, though she grants sexual favours, masters: 1. 1. 28, 1. 4. 2 (Cynthia is the *domina*; *non domuit Propertius*), 1. 5. 12, etc. Miserable subjection is Propertius' lot: it is control and free access—mastery—that Amor has forgotten how to contrive for him. So, miserably subject though he be, there is no reason to suppose that Propertius has not already had sexual relations with Cynthia—at her, not his, convenience and pleasure—and this is what we would naturally infer from the book as a whole.

[29] For Gallus' identification with (rather than contrast with) Milanion, cf. Lyne (1980), 95 (and preceding) with n. 16; this insight stems from Skutsch (1901), 15–16, via Ross (1975), 89–91. A crucial fact is that this version of the Milanion–Atalanta story, which is unknown to us before Propertius, is well-known to Ovid: *Ars* 2. 185–96. And it is well-known to Ovid as a story that exemplifies the success that accrues to *obsequium* in love; for Ovid it is an *applicable* and valid story. For Propertius it is painfully inapplicable. We infer therefore that someone publicised the myth as an applicable and valid *exemplum* of *obsequium*, and was the source and authority for Ovid—but this same someone provided Propertius with an example from which to dissociate himself, i.e. provided him with yet another chance in this opening poem of showing his isolated position. Cornelius Gallus is the obvious candidate. The fact that Vergil includes the Propertian gloss *Parthenius* (Prop. 1. 1. 11) for 'Arcadian' in Gallus' speech in *Ecl.* 10 (line 57)—a speech which Servius (on *Ecl.* 10. 46) suggests contains multiple echoes of Gallus himself—supports the thesis that Propertius' Milanion–Atalanta alludes to a famous Gallus *exemplum*.

4. Summary

Propertius' introductory poem 1. 1 positions him within, but in contrast to, the standards of the public Roman world; to this end he addresses and responds to Tullus, nephew of the consul of 33 BC. His love for Cynthia is disorder, madness and so on, yes: but he can do nothing about it. By allusion the same poem divorces Propertius from the game and spirited world of Meleager: in Propertius all is subjection, no chance here of spirited ripostes. By allusion too the poem distinguishes Propertius from an elegiac predecessor who, to judge from Verg. *Ecl.* 10, regarded his own suffering with plangent pity. By contrast, Propertius: *in me* (17) . . . Things are even worse for him. So the poem is radically and extensively dissociative—from the public Roman world, from Greek erotic *brio*, and from established Roman romanticism too.

III. POEM 2. 12

1. Introduction and Text

The strategy of this poem too is dissociative. Like 1. 1 it positions Propertius in relation to other views of love. Again, I shall be selective in my comments. But, first, a text and translation. The text is Goold's;[30] the translation varies from his, on one occasion importantly.

> Quicumque ille fuit, puerum qui pinxit Amorem,
>   nonne putas miras hunc habuisse manus?
> is primum uidit sine sensu uiuere amantes,
>   et leuibus curis magna perire bona.
> 5 idem non frustra uentosas addidit alas,
>   fecit et humano corde uolare deum:
> scilicet alterna quoniam iactamur in unda,
>   nostraque non ullis permanet aura locis.
> et merito hamatis manus est armata sagittis,
> 10 et pharetra ex umero Cnosia utroque iacet:
> ante ferit quoniam tuti quam cernimus hostem,
>   nec quisquam ex illo uulnere sanus abit.
> in me tela manent, manet et puerilis imago:
>   sed certe pennas perdidit ille suas;
> 15 euolat heu nostro quoniam de pectore nusquam,
>   assiduusque meo sanguine bella gerit.

[30] Goold (1990), 152–5.

Introductory Poems in Propertius: 1. 1 and 2. 12

> quid tibi iucundumst siccis habitare medullis?
>   si pudor est, alio traice tela, puer!
> intactos isto satius temptare ueneno:
>   non ego, sed tenuis uapulat umbra mea. 20
> quam si perdideris, quis erit qui talia cantet,
>   (haec mea Musa leuis gloria magna tuast),
> qui caput et digitos et lumina nigra puellae
>   et canat ut soleant molliter ire pedes?

Whoever he was who painted Love as a boy, don't you think that he had marvellous skill? He first saw that lovers live without sense, and that great prosperity is lost for petty passions. Not to no purpose did this same person add windy (inconstant) wings, and made it so that the god flies from the human heart since, to be sure, we are tossed by waves this way and that, and with us the breeze never sits in the same quarter. And justly is his hand armed with barbed arrows and a Cretan quiver lies across his shoulders, since he strikes while we feel safe and before we see the enemy, and from that wound no one departs whole.

In my case (*in me*, 13), the weapons are still there, and the boyish image is still there, but he has certainly lost his wings, since nowhere, alas, does he fly from my heart and he wages constant war at the cost of my blood. What pleasure is there for you to lodge in my bloodless marrow? If you have any shame, shoot your arrows elsewhere. Better to assail those who are untouched with that poison of yours. It is not I, but an insubstantial shadow that you beat. If you destroy that, who will there be to sing such things (this my petty Muse is your great glory), to sing of the girl's head and fingers and black eyes, and how her feet are wont to proceed softly?

Some small points on text and interpretation.

Line 6. The text has been deemed corrupt (cf. e.g. Shackleton Bailey (1956), 84 f.) but I think it is sound. Goold translates *humano corde* 'in the human heart'. There may well be passing uncertainty or ambiguity about the force of the ablative; but from line 15 it emerges that Propertius is concerned with Cupid's normal habit of flying *out of* human hearts. As we shall see, he is contrasting the general behaviour of the god (1–12) with the god's behaviour in his own case (13 ff.). Line 15: Cupid does *not* fly from Propertius' heart. We look for the statement that he does normally fly from other hearts; the sense 'from' therefore asserts itself in line 6, anyway in retrospect.

Line 10. Cupid has a single quiver slung over his shoulders. By *umero utroque* Propertius means little more than 'shoulders', ὤμοισι.[31] An essential parallel is Hom. *Il.* 1. 45 and 46. But we might recall Latin's habit of putting in dual words, perhaps partly as a calque for the Greek dual number.[32]

---

[31] Shackleton Bailey (1956), 85 f. unnecessarily complicates this passage.

[32] Cf. Lucr. 1. 88, '(infula) ex utraque pari malarum parte profusast', Verg. *Aen.* 6. 685, 'palmas utrasque tetendit', and uses of *gemini*: *geminas aures* is transmitted at Catull. 63. 75, *aures*

Line 13. Camps's gloss is: 'i.e. in my case the conception of Love as archer and child remains applicable...'. The essential and concrete point to grasp (as Camps and others do not) is that Propertius is still thinking of painters and painting (note the word *imago*).[33] There is the standard painting, which is generally applicable (1–12); and there is an imaginable picture of the Cupid which fits Propertius (13–16). And Propertius imagines it. In his case Cupid would still be painted with weapons and a boyish form: they remain in the painting, *manent, manet*. But Cupid would not have wings.

Line 18. V^2 offers a reading of the line which is most attractive: 'si pudor est, alio traice tela, puer', which was defended by Housman *JPh* 22 (1894), 111–13 = *Classical Papers* (1972), 334–5; Goold (1990), 20 offers an ingenious explanation of how this might have been corrupted to the 'si puer est, alio traice puella tuo' of the main manuscript tradition. It is what, tentatively, I have adopted. But another Renaissance correction *bella* (instead of *tela*) has things to be said for it.[34] *Bella* are the most immediate point at issue. Cupid won't fly away, 'assiduusque meo sanguine bella gerit'; Propertius would be asking him to take those *bella* elsewhere. But the linguistic parallels are all in favour of *tela*: cf. Caes. *Civ.* 3. 19. 1 'neque ullum interim telum traiciebatur' and *OLD* s.v. *traicio* 1. We may infer from Propertius' instruction to Cupid to 'shoot his arrows elsewhere' that he wishes him to take his *bella* elsewhere.

2. Propertius and Greek Views of Love

In 2. 12, as in 1. 1, there is an allusion to Greek poetry and an accompanying dissociation from a Greek view of love. But in 2. 12 this aspect is more prominent, and I therefore take it first. Quintilian (2. 4. 26) tells us of a school exercise in which pupils were asked to expound why Cupid was imagined as a boy, winged, and armed with arrows and torch,[35] and some scholars see a rhetorical test like this as the most influential factor in our poem.[36] But, as was the case in 1. 1, I think that an important Propertian

---

geminae may be the right reading at Catull. 51. 11 (Schrader), and then see *TLL* vi. 2. 1742. 46 ff. But in some of these the sense 'both' is arguably more welcome than in our line.

[33] Shackleton Bailey (1956), 87 appears to grasp the point ('Since the portrait is confessedly allegorical...'), but it needs to be made explicitly and positively. Cf. e.g. Butler and Barber ad loc. as well as Camps.

[34] It is supported by Shackleton Bailey (1956), 88, but he also reads *tua* for *puer*.

[35] 'Solebant praeceptores mei neque inutili et nobis etiam iucundo genere exercitationis praeparare nos coniecturalibus causis cum quaerere atque exequi iuberent "cur armata apud Lacedaemonios Venus" et "quid ita crederetur Cupido puer atque uolucer et sagittis ac face armatus" et similia...'

[36] Hunter in his note on Eubulus below remarks: 'The most striking feature of this passage is, however, its similarity to Propertius 2. 12...Propertius derived this theme from Hellenistic epigram and the rhetorical schools: Quintilian 2. 4. 26...'.

dialogue is directly with a Greek poetic composition. The most interesting text to look at is a fragment of the comic poet Eubulus (cf. Butler and Barber (1933), ad loc.); Eubulus writes a passage like ours which directly exploits the idea of an artistic representation, indeed a painting of Cupid. I do not insist that it is exactly this piece of text which Propertius uses to position himself against, though I rather think it is; we may at least take it as representative. The piece is Eubulus fr. 41 Hunter, quoted by Athenaeus 13. 562c–d:

> τίς ἦν ὁ γράψας πρῶτος ἀνθρώπων ἄρα
> ἢ κηροπλαστήσας Ἔρωθ' ὑπόπτερον;
> ὡς οὐδὲν ᾔδει πλὴν χελιδόνας γράφειν,
> ἀλλ' ἦν ἄπειρος τῶν τρόπων τῶν τοῦ θεοῦ.
> ἐστὶν γὰρ οὔτε κοῦφος οὔτε ῥᾴδιος
> ἀπαλλαγῆναι τῶι φέροντι τὴν νόσον,
> βαρὺς δὲ κομιδῆι. πῶς ἂν οὖν ἔχοι πτερὰ
> τοιοῦτο πρᾶγμα; λῆρος, εἰ καὶ φησί τις.

Who was it of men who first painted or wax-moulded Eros with wings? How ignorant he was except at painting swallows; of the ways of the god he was inexperienced. For he is neither light nor easy to be rid of for the one who bears sickness; rather he is wholly heavy (grievous, burdensome). So how would a thing such as this have wings? It's nonsense, even if someone says it.

Propertius is in dialogue with this argument. No, he says, the comic character's denial hasn't got it right either. Subtler, more individual qualification is needed. He takes in particular, the question of wings. Whoever painted Amor in the way decried by Eubulus' character actually did so reasonably, he had 'marvellous hands'. For generally, Cupid flies from the human heart (2. 12. 5–6): one moment we are in love, the next we are not, as the different imagery of the next couplet (fair winds for sailing 7–8) unpacks. It is in *my* case, says Propertius, *in me*, that a correct depiction of Cupid would lack wings: Love never flies from *my* heart. Propertius adjusts the arguments staged by Eubulus to identify a special position for himself. In his own case, and perhaps only in his own case, are the comic character's objections applicable: *in me*. We should notice that exact phrase from 1. 1 (1. 1. 17). In both poems he uses it to isolate his idiosyncrasy.[37]

With other Greek texts, too, we can find agreement and disagreement on Propertius' part, and we may detect allusions which help to position him in

---

[37] We should not however read *in me* in 1. 1. 33. I am persuaded by Heyworth (1984), 394–7, that we should read *nam me*, with *me* as object of *exercet* ('harass', cf. e.g. Verg. *Aen.* 6. 739 which the unwary might take to support the paradosis), and *noctes amaras* as accusative of duration. Heyworth well explains the function of *nam* and *nostra*. (Housman had proposed *me non nostra*.)

regard to Greek views of love.[38] But the most important surviving text, with its motif of painted representations of Cupid and the question 'Winged or Not?', is Eubulus.

3. Propertius and the Public Roman World

In 1. 1 Propertius accepted that he lived a life which merited worldly criticism; it was a means of presenting his own position as a lover. In 2. 12 we find the same admission less prominently, but it is there. Most important is the second couplet:

> is primum uidit sine sensu uiuere amantis,
> et leuibus curis magna perire bona.

He first saw that lovers live without sense, and great prosperity is lost for petty passions.

From the depiction of Love as a child (*puerum qui pinxit Amorem*) Propertius infers the belief that lovers display childish behaviour: living without sense, and so on. And this is something from which in the dissociative section (13 ff., *in me*) he does not dissociate himself. Now, there is little difference between *sine sensu uiuere* of 2. 12. 3 and *nullo uiuere consilio* of 1. 1. 6.[39] In addition Propertius admits a yet more worldly criticism. Whatever else we may find in the word *bona*,[40] the meaning 'goods', 'wealth' is inescapable. Propertius is here acknowledging precisely the folly that socially responsible folk deride: lovers waste their wealth on the objects of their infatuation. Cf. Cicero *Cael.* 42 'ne effundat patrimonium, ne faenore trucidetur', 'let a young man not squander his patrimony <on love>, be crippled with debt...'; cf. too Cic. *Sest.* 97 (twice) on the necessity for home economic propriety among good citizens; and cf. too Lucretius 4. 1123–30 on lovers, in this respect quite conventional.[41] Not only does Propertius not dissociate himself from this

---

[38] Cf. Meleager Gow–Page X. 5–6 = *Anth. Pal.* 5. 212. 5–6 'O winged Loves, do you know how to fly to us, but have not the strength to fly away?' Cf. too e.g. Meleager Gow–Page XXXVII = *Anth. Pal.* 5. 177, and Moschus I. But these, all accepting the wings of Cupid as inalienable, lack the idea which Eubulus and Propertius exploit (and they lack the motif of the painting of Cupid).

[39] Shackleton Bailey (1956), 84 'Here it <*sine sensu*> is a stronger variant of *sine consilio*...'. He cites most relevantly Val. Max. 1. 6. Ext. 1 (of Xerxes' folly in the face of a *prodigium*) 'si quod uestigium in uecordi pectore sensus fuisset'. Cf. too Cic. *Cat.* 3.2, 'sine sensu nascimur', and see further *OLD* s.v. *sensus* 6.

[40] Goold (1990), hedging slightly and perhaps justifiably, translates 'great blessings'; Rothstein (1920; repr. 1966) ad loc. interprets the phrase to mean 'brilliant talents'.

[41] Cf. n. 9 above. See too Brown ad loc., esp. on 4. 1123 (Brown (1987), 254); Brown also well supports (252 f.) the transposition of 1123 and 1124 (Lambinus, who found this order in a manuscript now unknown).

folly, in other poems he give grounds to substantiate such an accusation: 2. 23. 17 f., 2. 8. 14.[42] In 1. 1 Propertius accepted the logic of the world's condemnation. Here too he accepts it, choosing to infer it from the artistic representation of Cupid as a boy; in 2. 12, as in 1. 1, Propertius the lover is positioned *vis-à-vis* the world, in the world's terms. But now as then the fact remains: he can do nothing about it. 'euolat heu nostro quoniam de pectore nusquam'; 'caput impositis pressit Amor pedibus.'

4. Propertius 2. 12 as an Introductory Poem

It seems to me likely, in view of the points of contact between 2. 12 and 1. 1, that 2. 12 was an introductory poem and opened Propertius' original third book (Book 2b).[43] There is more to be said.

First, let us consider 2. 12 in the context of further Propertian opening poems. The introductory poem of Book 1 positioned Propertius as a lover. The opening poem of the putative Book 2a (2. 1) positioned him as a love-poet: he answers the question, 'Whence comes his inspiration as a writer?' The opening poem of our Book 3 will again position him as a poet. My contention is that the opening poem of Book 2b returned to the task of placing Propertius as a lover, so that the opening poems of Propertius' first four books alternated in their emphasis of theme. Now, of course, all these distinctions between lover and poet are crude and approximate, inevitably so with a lover-poet like Propertius who likes to play upon the inextricability, even identity of the two activities, love and love-poetry.[44] Thus 2. 1 has a great deal to say about Propertius' love-life as well as his poetry, and the last four lines of 2. 12 concern Propertius' love-poetry. But I would argue that the essential alternation of emphases stands.

I now add further material to support the contention that 2. 12 opened Book 2b. First, I shall show how 2. 12 takes up yet another theme (and item of diction) from the introductory 1. 1. This does not prove the thesis of course, but it corroborates it; it is at least suggestively consonant with it.

Consider line 19 'intactos isto satius temptare ueneno'. Take your warfare elsewhere, Propertius tells Cupid, better to assail with your poison others who are *untouched*. This picks up 1. 1. Propertius himself was once upon a time

---

[42] Camps (1967) has a good note on this line.

[43] Cf. n. 2 above for the thesis (in origin, Lachmann's) that our 'Book 2' contains remnants of two ancient books, and for the various views on which poem concluded Book 2a and which opened Book 2b.

[44] Cf. e.g. 1. 7: being a lover involves and occasions love poetry; cf. 1. 11. 8: a rival may have carried off Cynthia out of Propertius'... poems.

untouched by love, untouched indeed by Cupid(s), 'contactum nullis ante Cupidinibus' (1. 1. 2).[45] But he was then devastatingly touched. Cynthia captured him, and Amor cast down his eyes, so that *contactum nullis* became a thing of the past and he was now most definitely *contactus*. 2. 12 takes up the motif. Cupid should now move on to the *un*touched, the *intactos*: 2. 12. 19. (Note how in 2.12 Propertius wishes Cupid onto someone else, as Horace in his introductory *Ode* 4. 1 will wish Venus.)

The connection between initial theme (1. 1.2) and reprise (2. 12. 19) is dense. In 1. 1 there is allusion to Meleager Gow–Page CIII = *Anth. Pal.* 12. 101 quoted above. In that epigram, Meleager quite plainly makes Myiscus' eyes perform the role of Cupid's arrows (ὄμμασι τοξεύσας). More discreetly (Cynthia is after all a female), Propertius (in 1. 1) does something similar. First, transient ambiguity of syntax in *deiecit* (1. 1. 3) suggests identity between Cynthia and Amor,[46] shadowing the more explicit identification between Myiscus and Eros in Meleager. Next, Cynthia's eyes play a similar role to Myiscus' in Meleager. There must therefore be an echo of Myiscus' *arrow*-eyes in Cynthia's *ocelli*.[47] This confirms that *contactum* (1. 1. 2) is ambiguous (as Camps says) between 'hit' by a missile and 'infected' with a disease.[48] A comparable ambiguity exists, I think, in the 2. 12 reprise (*intactos*): Cupid is wished away onto those 'uninfected' by poison (*ueneno*) and 'untouched' by the darts of Amor; whether we read *bella* or *tela* in line 18, a reference to Cupid's weapons is impossible to exclude from *intactos*. But I would not wish to talk simply of 'poisoned arrows' in 2. 12. 19, as Camps (and, in effect, Goold) does. We remember how Vergil talks darkly, generally, mysteriously of Cupid's operating with *uenenum* (*Aen.* 4. 688), and I would like to respect the productive imprecision of Propertius' text here. So, in both cases of 'touching' (1. 1. 2 and 2. 12. 19) a comparable ambiguity: infection and piercing.

Now consider the last four lines. Here Propertius turns to a matter which depends on his own continued tenuous existence: his ability to perform the duties of a love-poet. If Cupid destroys his remaining *umbra, quam <umbram> si perdideris,*

---

[45] The modern editor is forced either to capitalise *Cupidinibus* (Rothstein 1920) or to write *cupidinibus* (Barber 1960). The ancient poet could enjoy the ambiguity.

[46] Cf. Allen (1950), 265 f.

[47] The conceit is not wholly 'given up' as Allen loc. cit. says.

[48] *Contingo* of missiles: Livy 37. 40. 12 (*gladiis*); Verg. *Aen.* 5. 509, 'ipsam...auem contingere ferro | non ualuit', *OLD* s.v. 3a, and cf. Propertius' use of *tango* at 2. 34. 60 (of Cupid), 'quem tetigit iactu certus ad ossa deus'; of disease, Lucr. 2. 660 *religione*, Verg. *Georg.* 3. 566, 'contactos artus sacer ignis edebat', *OLD* s.v. 6.

> quis erit qui talia cantet,
> (haec mea Musa leuis gloria magna tua est),
> qui caput et digitos et lumina nigra puellae
> et canat ut soleant molliter ire pedes?

Who will there be to sing such things (this my petty Muse is your great glory), to sing of the girl's head and fingers and black eyes, and how her feet are wont to proceed softly?

We are clearly reminded of key items in three poems that explained the appearance of Propertius' second book (Book 2a). First, we should recall poem 2. 2. 'I intended to stay free of love', Propertius had said. 'But her *facies, coma, longaeque manus,* and her divine walk, *incessus*—all these were too much for me ('at me composita pace fefellit Amor'); love deceived me again' (2. 2. 1 ff.). Hence another book. Likewise 2. 3, trumping 2. 2. Again the list of dazzling physical features (9 ff.), Cynthia's *facies*, her *comae*, and her *oculi, geminae, sidera nostra, faces*. In this poem Propertius designates these features as only a part, indeed not the main part, of the entrapment: *non tantum... quantum*.[49] But as a result of the total package, a new book will result: 'iam liber alter erit' (2. 3. 4). Poems 2. 2 and 2. 3 are introductory, explanatory poems: explaining the new publication. The girl possesses features and other qualities which irresistibly inspire this second book of love-poetry. Note too 2. 1 which also cites Cynthia's hair (2. 1. 7–8) as inspirational for the new book ('quaeritis... unde meus ueniat mollis in ora liber', 1 f.), likewise her walk and other features, though here in more ancillary aspect (5, 9–10, 11). Poem 2. 12 picks up, with slight variation, all these very features (head, i.e. face and hair, fingers, eyes, gait). We may see here an introductory function, a tactic to introduce a third book (2b). The reasoning would be as follows. Such features inspired a book previously. If Cupid now destroys the last vestiges of Propertius, where will he get another book like 2a? And this should matter to Cupid since Propertius' Muse, though 'petty', is Cupid's 'great glory'. My conclusion therefore is that these suggestive recalls of introductory poems in Book 2a helped Propertius to construct a poem to introduce the third book (2b).

The last line of 2. 12 is a slight variation on the praise of stately, divine gait in 2. 2. 6 ff.; it gets at femininity and delicacy of walk.[50] There is one important reason for the variation, nothing to do with Cynthia's attractions. It allows Propertius a play on words, a neat possibility of metaliterary statement, suiting an introductory poem. We may find in the last line the punning

---

[49] I have discussed Prop. 2. 2 and 3 in 'Propertius and Tibullus: early exchanges', forthcoming in *CQ* [Lyne (1998*c*) = Ch. 15 in this volume].

[50] Cf. Shackleton Bailey ad loc. (1956), 89, who collects interesting passages on attractiveness of female gait.

sense 'who will there be to sing so that the metre may be wont to proceed in the love-elegiac manner?'[51]

(i) *Pedes* and pun. Propertius himself will pun on *pes, pedis*, foot / verse-foot / and (by synecdoche) metre in the opening poem to what I take to be his fourth book: 3. 1. 1 ff. 'Callimachi Manes et Coi sacra Philitae... dicite, quo pariter carmen tenuastis in antro quoue pede ingressi?'[52] Ovid will use *pes* with the sense verse-foot dominating in his programmatic *Am.* 1. 1 (vv. 4 and 30), and will pun on the metrical and literal senses in 3. 1. 8 (Elegia) 'et puto pes illi longior alter erat' (cf. 10) and elsewhere. In Tibullus 2. 5. 111–12 'sine qua uersus mihi nullus | uerba potest iustos aut reperire pedes' the sense verse-feet or metre predominates, but there is surely some suggestion of pun (though the commentators do not note it); and in Horace, *Serm.* 1. 10. 1 'nempe incomposito dixi pede currere uersus | Lucili' there is also a pun.[53] And there is a pun again in Horace, *Ars* 80 'hunc socci cepere pedem grandesque cothurni'.[54] Cf. too Ovid, *Trist.* 3. 1. 12 cited below, and see further the note of Fedeli on Prop. 3. 1. 6, and *OLD* s.v. *pes* 11.

(ii) *Mollis* and a double sense. Apt of Cynthia's soft motion, *mollis* is also is a *vox propria* of love elegy. Again an introductory poem of Propertius may provide our first example: Prop. 2. 1. 1–2 'quaeritis... unde meus ueniat mollis in ora liber'. The most important force in *mollis* for Propertius is perhaps 'gentle, *conciliatory*', *OLD* s.v. 11. Propertius had stressed love-elegy's soothing, wooing function: cf. his earlier example of *mollis*, 1. 7. 19 'et frustra cupies mollem componere uersum', his prediction for the epic poet Ponticus, in the poem in which he pictures his own occupation as the search after something 'duram... in dominam'.[55] Cf. too Dom. Mars., fr. 7 Courtney, the epitaph for Tibullus, 'te quoque Vergilio comitem... | mors... campos misit ad Elysios, | ne foret aut elegis molles qui fleret amores | aut caneret forti regia bella pede', where Domitius uses *mollis* in close connection with love-elegy (and also uses *pes* in the sense of metre). *mollis* is also used of light verse more generally; *Ciris* 20 provides us with an example of the epithet denoting 'soft' poetry in combination with *pes* = metre: 'gracilem molli liceat pede claudere uersum'.[56]

---

[51] Cf. Wyke (1987), 56. [52] So e.g. Camps (1966) and Fedeli (1985), ad loc.
[53] Thus Kiessling and Heinze (1886), ad loc.
[54] Unremarked, oddly, by Kiessling and Heinze (1889) or Brink (1971), ad loc., but noted by Rudd (1989), ad loc.
[55] Cf. Stroh (1971), 19; cf. too 3. 23. 5, recalling the conciliatory function of Propertian elegy; contrast, however, Fedeli (1980) on 1. 7. 19. But when all this has been said, we must admit that a seminal text for the elegiac use of *mollis* must be Hermesianax fr. 7. 35 f. Μίμνερμος δέ, τὸν ἡδὺν ὃς εὕρετο πολλὸν ἀνατλὰς | ἦχον καὶ μαλακοῦ πνεῦμα τὸ πενταμέτρου, 'Mimnermus... discovered the breath of the soft pentameter.'
[56] See further Lyne's note ad loc. Skutsch (1906), 20 thinks that the poet of the *Ciris*, like Hermesianax (quoted n. 55), is referring in line 20 to a pentameter (so that the reference is to elegy

(iii) The metaliterary metaphor punningly suggested by the whole phrase *molliter ire pedes* can be seen as the reverse of that in *scazon* (Mart. 1. 96. 1, 7. 26. 1), LSJ σκάζω I and χωλίαμβος; and we can contrast with it the image used by Ovid of the elegiac metre of his *Tristia* in 3. 1. 11 f. 'clauda quod alterno subsidunt carmina uersu, | uel pedis hoc ratio, uel uia longa facit', 'if the poems halt lame in every other verse, this is the effect of the foot / metre's nature, or the long journey', where again there must be some play in *pedis*. Cf. also Ov. *Am.* 2. 17. 19–22.

(iv) Finally, for the use of *soleant* in this metaliterary dimension, cf. Propertius' wish to restore or maintain the tried and practised elegiac manner in the introductory 3. 2. 1 f. 'carminis interea nostri redeamus in orbem | gaudeat ut solito tacta puella sono', 'let us return meanwhile to the wonted round, so that my girl may rejoice touched by the accustomed strain.' We might also compare 1. 7. 5 'nos ut consuemus nostros agitamus amores', 'I, as is my wont, am busy with my love (love-poetry).'

5. Propertius 2. 12, Introductory Poems, and the Question of Addressees. Remarks on Social Status and Ambience

If this last metaliterary interpretation is accepted, it may seem to corroborate the thesis that Prop. 2. 12 introduced 'Book 2b'. But there is a factor that might give pause. The poem is not addressed to Maecenas. Poem 2. 1 signalled that Propertius had entered the circle of Maecenas.[57] Why does not the opening poem of 2b address, at least acknowledge him, as the opening poem of 2a addressed him? Why is this opening poem, if it is an opening poem, not addressed to any real person at all? The following comments on Propertius' social status, his position regarding patronage,[58] and his consequent policy with addressees in his introductory poems, are meant to

---

and *pes* means 'foot'). But the poet is referring to his own wish occassionally to revert from philosophy to light verse, and there is no sign that the poet of the *Ciris* is an elegist. More likely therefore that line 20 refers generally to light verse (like the *Ciris*); and for such a use of *mollis* there are ample parallels, which the note on *Ciris* 20 provides. Another example of *mollis* of 'soft' poetry other than elegy: Catullus 16. 4. Provocatively, Catullus is prepared to see his love-poems (it must surely be poem 7 in particular), as opposed to himself, termed *molliculi*; for Catullus *mollis*, at least in social contexts, was not a term that had good connotations (25. 1 *cinaede Thalle, mollior...*).

[57] Cf. Griffin (1985), 29 with n. 243; Lyne (1980), 62, 147 f.; Hubbard (1974), 99; Syme (1978), 183.

[58] For discussion of Propertius' social status and position regarding patronage, cf., as well as the preceding note, Griffin (1985), 56–7; Hubbard (1974), 98 ff.; White (1993), 12 f.; Syme (1978), 182 f. Zetzel in Gold (1982), 86–102, esp. 89 and 97–9 generally downplays the influence from outside of patrons on Augustan poetry, to my mind excessively.

be no more than summarising and suggestive. They will allow me to maintain my belief that 2. 12 opened the original third book.

We may infer, though we cannot prove, that Propertius possessed equestrian status. In his first book he addresses the nephew of a proconsul on more or less equal terms. He refers in 4. 1. 129–30 to the reduction of previously extensive estates, presumably in the confiscations after Philippi (cf. 2. 34. 55). But nowhere do we discern the need to earn a living; we are reminded of Tibullus, certainly a knight (*Vita Tibulli*), whose estate had also been reduced (1. 1. 19 f., 41 f.) but whose *paupertas* (1. 1. 5) was merely comparative: a life of idleness is still open to him (1. 1. 5 f., 43 ff.), his claims to poverty are put in perspective by Hor. *Epist.* 1. 4, and he himself has the sense and wit finally to define his present and desired economic condition as a golden mean (1. 1. 77 f.).

For Propertius' class and his actual wealth we might also note the charming and witty funeral address, which he imagines his lover uttering over his bones, 2. 24B. 35–8:

> 'ossa, Properti,
> haec tua sunt. eheu tu mihi certus eras,
> certus eras eheu, quamuis nec sanguine auito
> nobilis et quamuis non ita diues eras.'

'These are your bones, Propertius. Alas, you were faithful to me, faithful to me, alas, although your ancestry was not noble and you were not so very rich.'

Propertius amusingly, quite touchingly too, imagines his lover finally disabused of a naive belief that somehow consular family, great wealth, and fidelity go together. Amusing, touching—and tactical: Propertius is having problems with, precisely a noble, wealthy rival (22 ff., 49). But for our immediate purposes we note that in terms of class Propertius falls short specifically only of consular (*nobilis*) family; and that he wasn't 'so very' rich.[59] Again we are reminded of the not so very rich Tibullus, rich enough however to do nothing if he should so choose. Not dissimilar in their implications are 2. 34. 55 f. A comfortably-off equestrian Propertius is compatible with all the evidence.

And we can bring into play the facts that a career in the Roman forum (?juridical) had clearly been open to Propertius (4. 1. 134), and for that matter a position in the *cohors* of the proconsul of Asia (1. 6); but he turned his back—and he was able to turn his back—on both these prospects in the public demesne. Here we are reminded of another well-to-do equestrian poet

---

[59] Camps (1967) has a succinct and useful note on *non ita* (in fact a correction of the manuscripts, but a certain one).

from outside Rome, Ovid (*Trist.* 4. 10, esp. 33 ff.; but Ovid is proud of his *ancient* equestrian status, 4. 10. 7 f.).

These three poets, Propertius, Tibullus, Ovid, are men of class and substance. Class and substance assist independence, if it is desired—social and political independence, as well as economic. Tibullus acknowledges a great public figure (M. Valerius Messalla) in 1. 1 and 3; but he does not get around to extensive praise of him until 1. 7. Ovid rarely gets round to sincere praise of great public figures—mainly addressing *sodales*—until the dark days of exile. His political independence, we may say insolence, is visible from the *Amores* on. Nor did he seem to require the social and artistic advantages of association with a particular great house which even Propertius was to seek or anyway accept.[60] And in Book 1 at least Propertius shows social, political, and economic independence. His main addressee (in 1. 1, 6, 14 and 22) is his *sodalis*, the young Tullus; no patron, no great man at all, is addressed.

But Propertius enters Maecenas' circle of poets before the existing 'Book 2', presumably to gain access to the salon society and to the best class of audience for his recitations; we know that the formal *recitatio* in a great house was an important medium of publication, its institution traditionally attributed to Asinius Pollio.[61] That is to say, Propertius entered the circle for social and artistic advantage. There is no sign that he needed economic support; and there are no expressions of gratitude for its receipt which would surely have been necessary, had it been received: another personal poet—Horace—who

---

[60] There is no convincing sign that Ovid enjoyed the special protection or advantages of the house of Messalla during the main part of his career. If he had done so, surely there would be some acknowledgement in his poetry of the time. But there is none. There are repeated references in letters from exile to Messalla's sons (*Trist.* 4. 4. 27 f., *Pont.* 1. 7. 27 f., 2. 2. 97, 2. 3. 69 ff.) concerning Messalla's supposed interest in and protection of him, but I think it is likely that Ovid retrospectively magnifies Messallan interest in order to exert pressure on these sons; Syme (1978), 76, 117 takes the suggestions of these exile letters too literally, I think.

[61] For Asinius Pollio and the *recitatio* see Sen. *Contr.* 4 *praef.* 2, 'primus enim omnium Romanorum aduocatis hominibus scripta sua recitauit'; T. F. Higham's treatment of the institution is still useful, in Herescu (1958), 45 f.; cf. too Quinn (1982), esp. 158–65, Woodman and Powell (1992), 204–6 (pages in the editors' own epilogue). One should note that the reference in Seneca is to the recitation of Pollio's own writings, but he or others must swiftly if not immediately have provided opportunity for other writers to publicise their work in this way. Such invitations (*aduocatis hominibus*) must have been more general, and the recitations more public and open, than, say, Sestius' in Catullus 44 (we should read *fecit* in line 21 with Baehrens) or those envisaged by Hor. *Ars* 419 ff. (for more examples of such private recitals see Higham 46); and this public nature of them was what was important. The importance of the more public *recitatio* as a medium, the publicity it conferred, is shown by Ovid, *Pont.* 1. 5. 57 f., 'gloria uos acuat, uos, ut recitata probentur | carmina, Pieriis inuigilate choris', and *Pont.* 4. 2. 33–8. Ovid seems to have heard Propertius and Horace, among others, giving recitations (*Trist.* 4. 10. 45 f., 49 f.), and to have made his own initial impact that way (4. 10. 57 f.). Horace does not seem to have enjoyed reciting, but already knows the institution in *Serm.* 1. 4. 73, 'nec recito cuiquam nisi

received bounty felt it incumbent upon him to make acknowledgement (e.g. *Serm.* 2. 6). So Propertius obtained social and artistic advantage from Maecenas; what Maecenas got out of him is open to question.

We now move to Propertius' procedure with addressees in the post-Maecenas introductory poems of Book 2a and following. When Propertius acknowledges his new relationship with Maecenas, addressing him in 2. 1, we note that there is a measure of relegation in it, a disappointment perhaps of our expectations. For to begin with he addresses his general public, his readers or listeners (2. 1. 1 ff. *quaeritis...*). Only then does he turn to Maecenas (17 ff.; the poem then becomes quite generally addressed after, say, 39 ff.; and address to Maecenas is reasserted in 73 ff.). Lines 17 ff., the delayed, first address to Maecenas, involve an amusingly irreverent '*recusatio*': not only does Propertius say that he is unable to sing heroic Augustan deeds, and that his Callimachean alignment anyway prohibits that sort of thing; in the course of saying what Augustan events he will not write about, he manages to mention a sequence of civil conflicts which more tactful men were busily forgetting: Mutina, Philippi, Perugia.[62] A pointed, designed tactlessness. When he returns to Maecenas in 73 ff., he compliments him certainly ('nostrae spes inuidiosa iuuentae, | et uitae et morti gloria iusta meae', 'envied hope of Roman youth, just glory for me in life and death'), but there is also surely some praise for Propertius too in this;[63] and the poem ends with Propertius imagining Maecenas deferring to him—stopping his chariot at his tomb, weeping, commiserating, and uttering a fitting epitaph for the tragically dead love poet ('"huic misero fatum dura puella fuit".')

In short, when Propertius does first address Maecenas, he does so with a certain amount of displacement, humour, intimacy, self-regard, and cheek—as well as honour. Poem 21 is not simply addressed to Maecenas as patron. The social and economic standing of Propertius, and his temperament, produces something much more interesting.

Let us turn now to 3. 1, the opening poem of Propertius' 'fourth' book. No living person is here addressed at all. Propertius addresses first *Callimachi Manes et Coi sacra Philitae* (1), then competitor-poets (13), then Rome (15), and the Muses (19)—and apostrophises too Ilion and Troia (31 f.). Maecenas gets no address until the sometimes teasing poem 3. 9. In short Maecenas is nowhere for eight poems, and the introductory 3. 1 itself is consumed with

---

amicis idque coactus | non ubiuis coramue quibuslibet...'; and the institution of *recitatio* is presumably behind the mocking lines *Epist.* 2. 2. 90 ff. (on which cf. Horsfall (1976), 83 ff., Brink (1982), 315 f., 322).

[62] Cf. Syme (1978), 184.
[63] Particularly in *iusta*. But the exact interpretation of the lines is not easy. Camps (1967) ad loc. is helpful.

figures not from the real Roman world, but conjured up by the requirements and concerns of Propertius' literature. Somewhat similarly 4. 1. The *hospes* addressee (1) has grown out of an epigrammatic passer-by: he exists to enable Propertius to describe the Rome of yester-year; and then follow apostrophes to Troy (39), the *lupa* (55), Bacchus (62), Rome and the citizens (67), before Horus takes over. So, the introductory poem 4. 1 is also, like 3. 1, taken up with figures conjured up by Propertius' literary concerns and requirements.

By the time of the existing Book 4, Maecenas has faded from political and literary view, and his place as a patron of the arts has been taken by Augustus.[64] But Augustus gets no attention until 4. 6, and that only in a not wholly earnest narrative. When the existing Book 3 was published—in the immediate aftermath of Horace *Odes* Books 1–3—Maecenas' decline, occurring in the wake of the conspiracy of 23 BC, had probably already started. He gets no address until the teasing 3. 9, but again no supplementary address to a great public figure—Augustus for example—takes initial place. 3. 4 talks about, but not to, Augustus, and with equivocation; it is undermined by its partner 3. 5.

Special factors are therefore at play or beginning to be at play in the existing Books 3 and 4 which are not operative in the existing Book 2. But the fact remains that not only is Maecenas not addressed in 3. 1 and 4. 1, but no other real public figure is honoured with address in these introductory poems. 4. 1 and 3. 1—and 3. 2 and 3. 3—have as addressees constructions from Propertius' literary world. We may attribute much of this state of affairs to Propertius' social and economic status—and to his temperament.

Prop. 2. 12 does not address Maecenas, it does not address any real great man. The thrust of my argument is to show that this is not as strange for an introductory Propertian poem as might have initially appeared. It addresses no real person from the Roman world; it too addresses constructions conjured up by and required in Propertius' literary world: 'you', the reader (line 2), and Cupid (17). In this it most resembles and is perhaps sufficiently paralleled by 3. 1 and 4. 1; and for 'you' the reader we can compare too the *quaeritis* of 2. 1. 1.

But of course Book 2b antedates the decline of Maecenas. We might still therefore expect Maecenas to feature in its opening poem as he had featured in the opening poem of 2a.

But we remember that Propertius' address to him in 2. 1 was in a comparatively restrained mode: humorous, displaced, not very respectful. It is not impossible to imagine that this tendency was accentuated to the point of exclusion in the

---

[64] This is my view (in particular, I believe, as I say below, that Maecenas loses influence because of indiscreet behaviour in the wake of the conspiracy of 23 BC), but the position is still controversial: cf. Lyne (1995), 189–92, 194–5, 136–8.

opening poem of Book 2b. Perhaps the advantages of the house of Maecenas had proved to be less than Propertius hoped or imagined. Perhaps indeed he had quit this house and salon for the time being. We should note that, if 2. 12–34 preserve more or less the substance of Book 2b,[65] Maecenas features nowhere else in the book. It is also a fact that the book (if 2. 12–34 represent it) is one remarkably lacking in respect to all great figures and events. Poems 31 and 34 provide very minor exceptions; by contrast 2. 14. 23 f., 2. 15. 41 ff., 2. 16. 37 ff., and 2. 30. 19–22 (if these lines are correctly interpreted by Camps) are remarkably insolent, even hostile towards events of great ideological significance; and most of the rest of the text is quite disengaged from public life. Book 2b seems a more provocative book of love-poetry even than Book 1.

In short, the absence of an address to Maecenas or to any public figure in 2. 12 hardly debars it from being an introductory poem to Book 2b, and many other considerations support the conclusion that it could be.

6. Summary

Poem 1. 1 declares Propertian love in terms that set it apart from public Roman views of sense and sanity; it also *inter alia* dissociates Propertius from Greek amorous spiritedness. In 2. 12 Propertius replays these strategies, again disjoining himself from the conventional Roman world around him, and again positioning himself in regard to Greek notions of love; he even resumes themes and key turns of expression from his first introductory poem. He ends 2. 12 with a skilful metaliterary ambiguity which strengthens its claim to be the introductory poem of a book. Propertius' policy with regard to addressees follows a pattern consonant with his social position and temperament, and nothing in the way in which 2. 12 is addressed upsets an assumption that it introduced a book. Propertius wrote five books of poetry; Book 2b was one of his most provocative, and it was opened (I maintain) by our poem 2. 12.

---

[65] I give some thought to the structure and contents of Books 2a and 2b in Lyne (1998*a*), section VI. 1 [pp. 241–3 below].

13

Love and Death: Laodamia and Protesilaus in Catullus, Propertius, and Others[1] (1998)

I. LOVE CONQUERS DEATH? PROTESILAUS AND LAODAMIA. CATULLUS 68

In one form or another an elevated, pleasure-transcending view of love is common, we might say natural. For readers of Latin poetry Catullus is perhaps the most impressive spokesman. In many respects, of course, Catullus is special. His particular values and choice of terminology, in his time and situation, mark him out from his crowd; in the Roman world indeed, 'whole love', perhaps rather its utterance, is hard to document before him.[2] But a belief that love is powerful and profound, an important if not the most important thing in life, this is not a rarity. Roman tombstones attest to love and devotion, and myths inherited from Greece enshrine love's power, endurance, and transcendence.

Hand in glove with such attitudes goes—often—something else: a belief, or a need to believe, that supreme love may in some way survive even death. At one end of the scale, the Roman tombstones: they can show an unwillingness to accept that death ends love—the reunion of devoted couples is imagined.[3] The myths: love's triumph over death is the climax of famous myths of love—for example, Orpheus, in his pre-Vergilian incarnation. The desolated and devoted Orpheus persuades the Lords of the Underworld to give back the breath of life

---

[1] I have profited much from the kindness and learning of Bruno Currie. My thanks are also due to *CQ*'s editor, Dr Stephen Heyworth, and to the journal's anonymous referee.

[2] For the definition of the quoted phrase, see Lyne (1980), pp. viii–ix. The claim made in this sentence is supported in chs 1 and 2; see esp. pp. 17–18.

[3] Griffin (1985), 157 f. Griffin quotes *CIL* 6. 11252, 'domine Oppi marite, ne doleas mei quod praecessi: sustineo in aeterno toro aduentum tuum', 'Oppius, lord, husband, do not grieve for me that I have gone before you: I endure (wait for) your arrival on an eternal bed'; *CE* 1325, 'Iulius cum Trebia bene uixit multosque per annos: | coniugio aeterno hic quoque nunc remanet', 'Julius lived with Trebia well and for many years: in eternal marriage he also now continues', and others; and he refers to Lattimore (1942), 247 ff. Cf. too Hopkins (1983), 226–9.

to his beloved: see Hermesianax fr. 7. 1–14, and cf. Eur. *Alc.* 357–62.[4] Or Alcestis. She so loved Admetus that she died for him. But 'when she had done this deed, it seemed so noble not only to men but to gods that, although among all the doers of noble deeds there are few to whom the gods have granted the honour of sending their souls up again from Hades, hers they sent up in admiration of the deed'. By another route (divine honour for courage and nobility shown in love), love again overcomes death (Plato, *Symp.* 179b–d).[5]

And there is the story of Protesilaus and Laodamia. But the development of this story should be summarized.

By the time of the action of the *Iliad* Protesilaus is dead. In the Catalogue of Ships we find a terse but pregnant summary of his tragic love, marriage and death (*Il.* 2. 698–702). He was the first Greek to be killed at Troy; he left behind him in Phylace a 'wife tearing both cheeks' (ἀμφιδρυφὴς ἄλοχος) and a 'half-complete house' (δόμος ἡμιτελής). The desperate grief in his wife's gesture is clear. The exact significance of 'half-complete' was disputed in antiquity;[6] I think it simply means 'half-built'. Protesilaus did not even have time to complete his house before the end of his marriage and life, a concrete but eloquent detail. Compare and contrast how Odysseus 'built his bridal-chamber, until he *finished* it', θάλαμον δέμον, ὄφρ' ἐτέλεσσα (*Od.* 23. 192). It was proper that a heroic bridegroom should build his own married quarters, and Protesilaus was called away and killed before being able to complete the task.[7] Anyway, this detail aside, the essence of Homer's story is perspicuous. With extreme economy and suggestiveness he gives us a picture of love cut down at its inception, and leaves us with an expressively grieving (unnamed) wife, poised perhaps on the brink of tragedy. What happened to her? Homer's

---

[4] Before Vergil, Orpheus was traditionally successful in his quest for the return of his beloved. Hermesianax calls this beloved Argiope. For the introduction of the name Eurydice, and for more information on the myth, see Mynors (1990) on *Georg.* 4. 453–527. Plato's Phaedrus has an amusing variant, *Symp.* 179d: the gods of the Underworld did not restore to Orpheus the actual woman, 'merely showing him a wraith (φάσμα) of the woman for whom he had come', since they regarded him as a mere musician and softy, a trickster and manipulator who did not dare actually to die for love as Alcestis had done (on whom, see above).

[5] Euripides in *Alcestis* offers a different version. Struck by the nobility of what Alcestis has done, Heracles canvasses the option of going to the Underworld to beg for her restoration, but in the event secures her return more immediately and physically, by fighting Death: *Alc.* 843–60, 1140–2. Cf. Lucian, *Dialogues of the Dead* 28 for the rejected option. Euripides' choice of version may rest on Satyric influence; see Dale (1954), p. xi.

[6] The scholia propose among other explanations of the 'half-complete' house: its childlessness, that it was deprived of (the masculine) one of the δεσπόται, that it was physically unfinished (which I favour). For this last, they suggest that Protesilaus was still in the process of building his wedding-chamber when he sailed away to war, which, in view of the parallels I cite, is interesting. See below for what Catullus and/or a predecessor make(s) of it.

[7] Cf. too how Menelaus was said to have made Hyperenor's wife a widow μυχῷ θαλάμοιο νέοιο, Hom. *Iliad* 17. 36.

Love and Death 213

restraint leaves this to our fearful imagination, or to our knowledge from other sources.

Other early epic: according to Pausanias, the composer of the *Cypria* identified Protesilaus' wife as Polydora, daughter of Meleager (Paus. 2. 4. = *Cypria* fr. XVII Allen = fr. 18 Davies); but the information in Pausanias that she and two others 'slew themselves over their husbands who died before them' seems Pausanias' comment rather than demonstrably attributable in any part to the *Cypria*; similarly, the clause saying that it was Protesilaus who first dared to land at Troy—a fact which is virtually but not quite explicit in Homer's account[8]—this too is Pausanias', and cannot with certainty be attributed to the *Cypria*. But Davies conjectures that a story that the first to land at Troy was fated to be the first to die was already in the *Cypria*.[9]

Euripides wrote a tragedy entitled *Protesilaus*, and it is here that a full romantic and tragic story of Protesilaus and Laodamia (as she was later called)[10] was developed and presumably became canonical. Nauck thinks that Hyginus *fab*. 103 and 104 closely mirror Euripides' plot.[11] In gist: Protesilaus, the first to land at Troy, was the first to be killed, in fulfilment of an oracle. Overcome with grief, Laodamia besought the gods that she might converse again with him for a brief time. Her entreaty was successful: Hermes brought Protesilaus back from the dead, and, for a short time, they were able to converse again together. Then, when Protesilaus was returned to the dead, Ladoamia could not bear the pain. As a substitute she secretly made a wax image of him, and embraced

---

[8] Hom. *Iliad* 2. 701 f. reads τὸν δ' ἔκτανε Δάρδανος ἀνὴρ | νηὸς ἀποθρῴσκοντα πολὺ πρώτιστον Ἀχαιῶν, which Lattimore translates 'A Dardanian man had killed him | as he leapt from his ship, far the first of all the Achaians'. As evidence in court, this could not be forced to mean more than that Protesilaus was the first to be killed. But there is certainly ambiguity in the reference of πρώτιστον. O'Hara (1996), 10 thinks that Homer is alluding to an etymology in Protesilaus' name, 'the first to leap' (πρῶτος, ἅλλομαι). I doubt this particular explanation, but would accept that Homer is etymologizing his name: πρώτιστον is surely picking out πρῶτος, and . . . Ἀχαιῶν may be pointing to the surely true etymological component λαός. For Homer's etymologizing in general, see O'Hara (1996), 7 ff. (with bibliography).

[9] Davies (1989), 47. Davies cites the version found in Apollodorus, *epit.* 3. 29: 'Thetis charged Achilles not to be the first to land from the ships, because the first to land would be the first to die.'

[10] We may infer from Dio Chrysostomus, who preserves Euripides fr. 655N², that Euripides named his heroine Λαοδάμεια; Hyginus too, who is assumed to be dependent on Euripides (see below), names her Laodamia, and so do Apollodorus and Philostratus. Lucian, *Dialogues of the Dead* 28 gives her no name. Eustathius also refers to Protesilaus' wife as Λαοδάμεια in his note on *Iliad* 2. 701 mentioned below n. 29. I have no example of the name of Laodamia, as the wife of Protesilaus and daughter of Acastus, actually written in Greek before the imperial writers cited; but another Λαοδάμεια was (for example) daughter of Bellerophon and mother of Sarpedon (Hom. *Iliad* 6. 196–205), and another was nurse of Orestes according to Stesichorus (*PMG* 218 Page). Protesilaus' wife is Laodamia in Latin as least as early as Laevius, for whom see below. I doubt she was ever called Laudamia: see below n. 20.

[11] Nauck (1964), 563: 'Euripidem potissimum sequi videtur Hyginus fab. 103 et 104.' Cf. too Webster (1967), 97–8 for a reconstruction of the play.

and adored it. This stratagem was discovered and condemned. Laodamia's father ordered the image to be burnt on a pyre, and Laodamia, finding her grief unendurable, committed suicide on the pyre. So: a story of tragic interruption, death for love, and, briefly, *love overcoming death*: Protesilaus returned from the dead because of the power and eloquence of Laodamia's devotion.[12]

We infer therefore that Euripides—with whatever preceding help was available and attractive to him—picked up and developed the tragedy which Homer had left suggestively suspended. But the most immediately important point for us to infer is that Euripides' presumably classic account of Protesilaus included and staged the conquest of death by love—something not in Homer at all. Once again a story of love so powerful and elevated that someone will die for it (cf. Alcestis) naturally encompasses the converse idea that love can overcome death. To reassure ourselves that we are indeed talking about a Euripidean element in the story, we may note that, among other items in Hyginus' summary which are seemingly paralleled in Euripides' own fragments (the motif of the substitute image, for example, fr. 655N^2),[13] is the motif of Protesilaus' return. Fr. 646a (in Snell's *Supplementum* to Nauck^2 (Hildesheim, 1964)), which is identified by Photius as coming from the *Protesilaus*, seem to be words of command by Hermes to Protesilaus on his journey back to the living:[14] ἔπου δὲ μοῦνον ἀμπρεύοντί μοι 'only follow me when I lead you'; the verb ἀμπρεύειν is recherché and befits a god (it is so recherché that it attracted the attention of the lexicographer).[15] We may envisage a scene in which Hermes leads back Protesilaus as Heracles leads

---

[12] Hyg. *fab.* 103 *Protesilaus*, 'Achiuis fuit responsum, qui primus litora Troianorum attigisset periturum. cum Achiui classes appliculssent, ceteris cunctantibus Iolaus Iphicli et Diomedeae filius primus e naui prosiluit, qui ab Hectore confestim est interfectus; quem cuncti appellarunt Protesilaum, quoniam primus ex omnibus perierat. quod uxor Laodamia Acasti filia cum audisset eum perisse, flens petit a diis ut sibi cum eo tres horas colloqui liceret. quo impetrato a Mercurio reductus tres horas cum eo collocuta est; quod iterum cum obisset Protesilaus, dolorem pati non potuit Laodamia.' *Fab.* 104 *Laodamia*, 'Laodamia Acasti filia amisso coniuge cum tres horas consumpsisset quas a diis petierat, fletum et dolorem pati non potuit. itaque fecit simulacrum cereum simile Protesilai coniugis et in thalamis posuit sub simulatione sacrorum, et eum colere coepit. quod cum famulus matutino tempore poma ei attulisset ad sacrificium, per rimam aspexit uiditque eam ab amplexu Protesilai simulacrum tenentem atque osculantem; aestimans eam adulterum habere Acasto patri nuntiauit. qui cum uenisset et in thalamos irrupisset, uidit effigiem Protesilai; quae ne diutius torqueretur, iussit signum et sacra pyra facta comburi, quo se Laodamia dolorem non sustinens immisit atque usta est.'

[13] Cf. too fr. 656N^2: Laodamia debates her method of suicide. Nauck and Webster seek to place other fragments.

[14] This interpretation of fr. 646a follows Snell who however places an obelus before μοῦνον. Webster (1964) 97, accepting μοῦνον, thinks that the fragment 'is perhaps more likely to be said by Hermes when he takes Protesilaos back again to Hades'.

[15] Photius' entry is: Ἀμπρεύοντι· Εὐριπίδης Πρωτεσιλάῳ· ἔπου δὲ μοῦνον ἀμπρεύοντί μοι. ἀντὶ τοῦ προηγουμένῳ καὶ ὁδηγοῦντί σε καὶ οἷον ἕλκοντι.

back Alcestis in *Alcestis*.[16] And the motif of Protesilaus' return endures in other accounts, corroborating our evidence that it featured in Euripides' classic and influential tragedy. It, and the stratagem of the waxen image, are registered by Apollodorus, *epit.* 3. 30[17] (with some variation of detail from, say, Hyginus). Cf. too Lucian *Dialogues of the Dead* 28, a dialogue of Protesilaus, Pluto, and Persephone: in Lucian's version it is Protesilaus who asks for a brief return to life, for love of his wife; he says he will persuade her to follow him back to death, and he appeals to the precedents of Alcestis and Eurydice; and Lucian thinks it worthwhile to spell out that Protesilaus will be allowed to return for his short sojourn in his beautiful bridegroom's form, not as the 'bare, unsightly skull' that he now is. In Philostratus' *Heroicus* (ed. Kayser ii. 130) Protesilaus 'died because of Helen in Troy, but came to life again in Phthia loving Laodamia' (he then returned to the dead, persuading his wife to follow him—cf. Lucian—but for the purposes of this dialogue he has returned to life yet again). We may note then that the scholia on Aelius Aristides, *On Behalf of the Four* 228 Jebb (printed in Dindorf, iii. 671 f.) know that Euripides wrote a drama *Protesilaus*; and they tell us among other things that the dead Protesilaus 'asked the gods below, and was released for one day, and was with his wife'. But whatever the probability we cannot quite extract from these scholia the explicit information that the motif of Protesilaus' return from the dead was in Euripides' play; I admit and state this point because I think that some who cite the scholia are misled.[18] And finally (before

---

[16] Eur. *Alc.* 1008 ff., climax 1097 ff. It is worth noticing that there is already contact between the two plays: *Alc.* 348–53 alludes to the substitute image of Protesilaus: cf. Dale (1954), citing Wilamowitz. It is hard to believe that Euripides resisted the drama of Protesilaus' entrance, led by Hermes. (Hermes speaks the prologue of Euripides' *Ion*.)

[17] '... his wife Laodamia loved him even after his death, and she made an image (εἴδωλον) very like Protesilaus and consorted with it (προσωμίλει). The gods had pity on her, and Hermes brought up Protesilaus from Hades. When she saw him, Laodamia thought it was himself returned from Troy, and she rejoiced; but when he was again carried back to Hades, she killed herself.'

[18] Indeed reference to the scholia is sometimes made which does not suggest acute inspection of them and their lemma. Aristides' lemma is: καθάπερ τὸν Πρωτεσίλαόν φασι, παραιτησάμενον τοὺς κάτω, γεγενῆσθαι μετὰ τῶν ζώντων]. The scholia comment: ὁ Πρωτεσίλαος δρᾶμα γέγραπται Εὐριπίδῃ. λέγει δὲ ὅτι γαμήσας καὶ μίαν ἡμέραν μόνην συγγενόμενος τῇ γυναικὶ αὐτοῦ, ἠναγκάσθη μετὰ τῶν Ἑλλήνων κατὰ τῆς Τροίας ἐλθεῖν, καὶ πρῶτος ἐπιβὰς τῆς Τροίας ἐτελεύτησε. καὶ φασὶν [φησὶν] ὅτι τοὺς κάτω δαίμονας ᾐτήσατο, καὶ ἀφείθη μίαν ἡμέραν, καὶ συνεγένετο τῇ γυναικὶ αὐτοῦ. '*Protesilaus* is a drama written by Euripides. He says that Protesilaus, having married and having been with his wife for one day only, was compelled to go with the Greeks to Troy; and having been the first to go on Trojan soil died; and they say [he says] that he asked the gods below, and was released for one day, and was together with his wife.' We have BDOxon versions of this scholion; it is only D which gives φησίν. Up to '... on Trojan soil died', it seems fair to assume that the note is drawing on knowledge of Euripides. But Aristides himself referred to the restoration to life of Protesilaus, in order to lay the scene for an imagined restoration of 'the four', to plead their case with Plato: καθάπερ τὸν Πρωτεσίλαον φασὶ..., 'just as they say Protesilaus, having pleaded with the gods of the underworld, came among the

Catullus) I should like to mention Laevius. Interesting fragments survive from Laevius' poem *Protesilaodamia* (frs. 13–19 in Courtney (1993), 130–5), including moments from the wedding and wedding night (14 and 15); but none bears directly on the topic most immediately concerning us. However Courtney (p. 119) conjectures plausibly that this pre-Catullan innovator drew on Euripides in his *Alcestis, Ino,* and *Protesilaodamia*. It is a notable and perhaps surprising fact that no Roman tragedian is known to have essayed a *Protesilaus*.

And now we come to Catullus. In poem 68 Catullus wishfully attributes love beyond description and compare to Lesbia. To this end he takes a great story of love, Laodamia and Protesilaus. He assimilates Lesbia to Laodamia, telling us Laodamia's story, and endeavouring to communicate to us Laodamia's love for Protesilaus.[19] Catullus directs his story of Protesilaus and Laodamia through Laodamia, since Laodamia is his focus—initially as a comparison for Lesbia. But it was open to him to include as much of the whole story as he wished (a point I shall take up below). 68. 70–86:

> quo mea se molli candida diua pede
> intulit et trito fulgentem in limine plantam
> innixa arguta constituit solea,
> coniugis ut quondam flagrans aduenit amore
> Protesilaeam Laodamia[20] domum

living...'. It looks to me as if the commentators may simply be expanding (φασίν) Aristides' reference to Protesilaus' return (φασί) with their own information. It is hard to prove otherwise. The D reading φησίν seems produced by a desire conscious or unconscious to attribute the information on the return to Euripides. We should finally note that Oxon reads λέγεται; and there are other more minor variations.

[19] I use the phrase 'beyond compare' advisedly, enlightened by Feeney (1992). The explosion of simile, the sequence of comparison within comparison, makes the point that what Catullus is talking about (Lesbia's imagined love, and so on) is beyond description and satisfactory comparison. In what follows I discuss only part of the significance of Catullus' use of the Protesilaus–Laodamia story, the part relevant to my present subject. There is more in Lyne (1980), 52–60, 87. Cf. too Syndikus (1990), 275–80, 283–7; Macleod (1982), 159–65; Williams (1980), 50–61. Macleod (pp. 161 f.) and Williams (p. 59) well bring out the way the Protesilaus myth also conveys the tragic effect on Catullus of his brother's death.

[20] Like Goold and Lee I cannot accept that Catullus wrote *Laudamia*, an orthography inspired by V; the influential Mynors prints *Laudamia*, though his note on line 74 reveals clear doubt. The etymology of Laodamia's name protected the spelling *Lao*- for those who, like Catullus, knew Greek (there are also metrical difficulties with -*au*-). It is worth noting that what OGR actually show in 74, 80, and 105 is *laudomia*. It is a habit of this manuscript tradition simply to find and write Latin words which it recognizes, regardless of the sense of the context (e.g. *sed michi ante* at 61. 213), and what V is finding at 68. 74, 80 and 105 is *laudo*. This habit of the tradition has encouraged editors, in particular Mynors, to find interesting but perhaps unwarranted orthographies elsewhere: e.g. at 63. 47 Mynors (and Lee) print Victorius' *rusum*; Mynors bases himself on V and appeals to Lucretian spelling. What V actually transmits is *usum*; it has simply found a word in a jumble of letters which it recognizes; Goold is rightly sceptical,

> inceptam frustra, nondum cum sanguine sacro
>   hostia caelestis pacificasset eros.
> nil mihi tam ualde placeat, Rhamnusia[21] uirgo,
>   quod temere inuitis suscipiatur eris.
> quam ieiuna pium desideret ara cruorem,
>   docta est amisso Laodamia uiro,
> coniugis ante coacta noui dimittere collum,
>   quam ueniens una atque altera rursus hiems
> noctibus in longis auidum saturasset amorem,
>   posset ut abrupto uiuere coniugio,
> quod scibant Parcae non longo tempore abesse,
>   si miles muros isset ad Iliacos.

And my fair goddess betook herself there with gentle step; she set her shining foot on the worn threshold, halting, her sandal sounding—just as once upon a time burning with love came Laodamia to the house of Protesilaus—a house that was begun vainly, for not yet with holy blood had a victim appeased the lords of heaven. May nothing, maid of Rhamnus (Nemesis), so mightily appeal to me that it be undertaken rashly with our lords unwilling. And how hungrily the altar desires the pious blood Laodamia learnt, losing her husband, compelled to loose her bridegroom from her arms before the coming of a first and a second winter had satisfied eager love in length of nights so that, her marriage sundered, she might bear to live. And *that* the Fates knew was close at hand if once Protesilaus went a soldier to the walls of Troy.

Then, in lines 105 ff. he develops the devastation wrought upon Laodamia by the death of her husband, and expands upon the depth of her love and passion (simile within simile):[22]

> quo tibi tum casu, pulcherrima Laodamia,
>   ereptum est uita dulcius atque anima
> coniugium: tanto te absorbens uertice amoris
>   aestus in abruptum detulerat barathrum,
> quale ferunt Grai Pheneum prope Cyllenaeum
>   siccare emulsa pingue palude solum,
> quod quondam caesis montis fodisse medullis

and prints *rursus* (we might prefer *rursum*). It is worth noting that Laevius' title *Protesilaodamia* clearly played on etymology, and Catullus may well allude to that title in 68. 74.

[21] Surely Catullus, not only knowledgeable of Greek, but sensitive to aspiration (poem 84), wrote *Rhamnusia* ('Ραμνούσια), as Goold prints. Mynors printed *Ramnusia* (*rammusia* O: *ranusia* GR). When Catullus wrote *Rhamnusia* at 66. 71 as again he surely did he was actually translating Callimachus, although that portion of the Callimachus papyrus does not survive.

[22] On which see Syndikus (1990), 283–5. See too Tuplin (1981), 119 ff. The story that Hercules built a drainage sink-hole at Pheneus is recorded by Pausanias 8. 14. 1 f.; Tuplin conjectures it figured in Euphorion. Tuplin has suggestive comment on the negative implications of the *barathrum* lines as an image of love (pp. 131 f.), suggestive comment too on Hercules and Hebe as figures which contrast with the other lovers in the poem (133–6).

> audit falsiparens Amphitryoniades...
> sed tuus altus amor barathro fuit altior illo,
> qui tamen indomitam ferre iugum docuit.

By that disaster, most beautiful Laodamia, marriage sweeter than life and soul was snatched from you: in such a whirlpool of love had passion engulfing you borne you down into a precipitous chasm, of the sort which the Greeks say dries the rich ground draining the marsh near Cyllenean Pheneus, which once upon a time the falsely-fathered son of Amphitryon (Hercules) is said to have dug, cutting out the vitals of a mountain.... But your profound love was deeper than that chasm, which taught you though untamed to bear the yoke (i.e. marriage).

Two more comparisons within the Laodamia comparison follow, one conveying non-physical love (119 ff., 'nam nec tam carum confecto aetate parenti...'),[23] the other passion (again), lines 125 ff.:[24]

> nec tantum niueo gauisa est ulla columbo
> compar, quae multo dicitur improbius
> oscula mordenti semper decerpere rostro,
> quam quae praecipue multiuola est mulier.
> sed tu horum magnos uicisti sola furores,
> ut semel es flauo conciliata uiro.

Not so much in the snowy dove has any (female) mate rejoiced, which is said to gather kisses with biting bill far more wantonly than any woman who is especially much-desiring. But you vanquished the great passion of these when once you were brought together with your fair husband.

This is Catullus' account of the story of Protesilaus and Laodamia. A comparison of the female Lesbia to Laodamia precipitates the narrative; and this is how Catullus rounds it off, though now he grants some slight discrepancy: 131 f., 'aut nihil aut paulo cui tum concedere digna | lux mea se nostrum contulit in gremium', 'in no wise or hardly worthy then to give place to her, she who is my light brought herself to my bosom'.

But it was of course in the main a wishful comparison. Superficial points of contact between Lesbia and Laodamia may be thought to abide (e.g. appearance and movement). But on the profound question, love, a sad truth emerges: it is Catullus' rather than Lesbia's devotion which is imaged in the devotion of Laodamia.[25] One simple and decisive point: Laodamia's inability to support life without her love (84, 'posset ut abrupto uiuere coniugio';

---

[23] Catullus gives his comparison Roman colouring, but the simile derives from Pindar, *Ol.* 10. 86–90; cf. Syndikus (1990), 286.

[24] For the dove as an illustration of passions (as well as devotion) see Syndikus (1990), 286–7.

[25] Cf. Macleod (1982), 160, though in my opinion he draws this conclusion prematurely, making late amends 163–4; Lyne (1980), 58.

106 f., 'ereptum est uita dulcius atque anima | coniugium') is effectively or virtually paralleled by Catullus, and certainly not by Lesbia: cf. lines 159–60, the last lines of the poem: 'mihi quae me carior ipso est, | lux mea, qua uiua uiuere dulce mihi est', 'she who is dearer to me than myself, my light of life; while she is alive, life is sweet for me'; contrast the sobered description of Lesbia and her affections at 135 ff.[26] The female mythical figure, advanced as an image of Lesbia, in fact more truthfully figures the male.[27] Other details might have alerted us to the idea that Catullus is moved more by his own feelings of love in his depiction of Laodamia than by enduring belief in a parity between Laodamia and Lesbia. But yet further details then forbid complete identification of Laodamia and Catullus.[28]

Anyway, embodying many Catullan feelings and only an imagined Lesbia's, the story of Laodamia in poem 68 is an example for Catullus of the power and potential of love. More particularly, it is a story of love and death. The way Catullus presents this story should allow insight into his views on love and death. We shall now set aside the similes within the simile, and consider Catullus' strategy regarding the bare story of Laodamia and Protesilaus. I repeat that it was open to Catullus to include, by allusion or whatever, any detail from the tradition that he chose. Who for example would have guessed that he would find room for the motif of neglected sacrifice?

The notion that Protesilaus was fated to die is not in Homer's reference to the story in *Iliad* 2. 698–702, but may in some form be as early as the *Cypria*

---

[26] Lyne (1980), 57 f.; Macleod (1982), 162–4 amplifies contrasts between Lesbia and Laodamia.

[27] Such interesting and suggestive sex role-reversal happens elsewhere in poem 68 and in other poems of Catullus: 68. 137–9, 11. 21–3, 65. 19–24. Cf. Macleod (1982), 160–1, who also cites poem 70 as an example, correctly I think. An important expressive device for Catullus, it has other but less devoted users: Propertius, for example, at 1. 11. 23–4, playing Andromache to Cynthia's Hector (noted by McKeown (1979), 75).

[28] Details showing similarity between Catullan love and the love of Laodamia: (i) The simile suggesting Laodamia's non-physical love (119 ff.) has a similar provenance, the area of Roman family bonds (but cf. n. 23 above), to Catullus' expression of his own non-physical devotion to Lesbia in 72. 3–4. (ii) The comparison suggesting Laodamia's passion (125 ff., the dove's mate 'quae multo dicitur improbius | oscula mordenti semper decerpere rostro | quam quae praecipue multiuola est mulier') might remind us of Catullus' own kisses poems, 5 and 7 and indeed 8 (8. 18, 'cui labella mordebis'). And see further Macleod (1982), 163–4. Details forbidding an assumption of complete identity: (i) Catullus, poem 7 in fact proclaims insatiability; in Laodamia's case Catullus admits (a perhaps surprising detail) that her love might eventually have been sated (83). (ii) Observe the fine wedge which careful wording in poem 68 itself puts between Laodamia and Catullus. Life without love for Laodamia *is* impossible and she does commit suicide: the narrator takes us to the imminence of that very event (84, 106 f.). For Catullus himself, Lesbia is dearer to him than himself, life is sweet if the light of his life lives (159–60). But if she doesn't? He dies? Or life is unsweet? Catullus' devotion is *virtually* the same as Laodamia's. But we cannot say that the two descriptions are *exactly* the same. (The question of death for love emerges again in Catullus' own poetical biography at 76. 17–20: another time, another mood.)

(see above). In Catullus we are told (68. 85–6) that Laodamia's felicitous marriage was condemned to be snatched from her, if Protesilaus went as a soldier to Troy. A sense of doom, even of supernatural opposition to the love is thereby given. A sense of divine hostility is certainly given by the motif of the neglected sacrifice, 68. 74 ff. This too is (apparently) not in Homer. The sacrifice that Catullus has in mind is simply, I think, an offering that should, in the gods' view, have been made before the construction of the married couple's house: the same sort of offering which the Greeks too neglected to make before building the wall round their ships (*Il.* 7. 449–50, 12. 3–9).[29] So the couple were guilty of a small ritual neglect. But because of it the gods contribute to the disaster of the marriage's destruction: this is the inescapable implication of 68. 79–81. Catullus is giving tragic colour to his story, a sense of inevitable and unmerited calamity. So far from blessing a marriage which we might say was 'made in heaven', divinity here is hostile: the Parcae have their conditional clause, and the gods react in brutal disproportion to the neglect of an ancillary sacrifice.

I say that the motif of neglected sacrifice is not apparently in Homer. But it is worth adding the thought (which has no doubt occurred to others) that Catullus, or, more likely, a Hellenistic predecessor, inventively found the germ of it in Homer. Catullus' *domus incepta frustra* is an echo, with variation, of Homer's disputed δόμος ἡμιτελής—which I am inclined to interpret simply as 'half-built' (see above). But an inventive poet could have glossed the epithet differently, finding in it an allusion to sacrifice. That is to say, just as 'Apollonius connects the disputed Homeric hapax ἀμφιλύκη, "morning twilight", with Lycia and derives κερτομέω from κέαρ, so another etymologizing poet may have found in -τελής an allusion to the many uses of τέλος and its cognates of

---

[29] Thus Van Sickle (1980), 91–5, following one of the paths offered by Ellis's commentary, and responding to another interesting, but not finally convincing, interpretation offered by Thomas (1978), 175–8 (the sacrifice at Aulis is in mind). A pre-building sacrificial offering is the simplest inference from the wording 'domum inceptam frustra, nondum cum ...'. The disproportion between the relative triviality of the sin and the devastating consequences smacks convincingly of the tragic tradition (Aristotelian ἁμαρτία), and contributes to Catullus' overall message (see text). Other ideas: Eustathius' note on Hom. *Iliad* 2. 701 (1. 507. 1 ff. in the edition of van der Valk) includes stories which refer to anger on Aphrodite's part. Syndikus (1990), 278 with n. 164 infers some sort of sacrificial omission in the pre-Catullan tradition (but not to do with building), of which he thinks Eustathius preserves relics. But it is to later events in the story, to (i) Protesilaus' continuing love for his wife after death and (ii) Laodamia's love for her dead husband, to which the wrath of Aphrodite is tied by Eustathius ('P. even after death loving his wife in accordance with μῆνις of Aphrodite ...'; 'others say that L. even when P. had died burnt with love because of the χόλος of A.'), and Macleod (n. 19), p. 164, thinks these stories are irrelevant to the *domus* sacrifice in Catullus' text. He thinks (as others e.g. Kroll on 75 (with useful information), and Ellis in his note on *hostia* in line 76 do) that the couple in Catullus neglected to placate the gods before their wedding (the customary προτέλεια to which Clytemnestra refers in Eur. *I.A.* 718), and Macleod concludes that 'this detail is, on the evidence as we have it, Catullus' invention'.

sacrifice.³⁰ As O'Hara and others note, Hellenistic poets enjoyed glossing and etymologizing disputed Homeric words, and ἡμιτελής was disputed. So I suggest that some poet found in Homer's ἡμιτελής an allusion to an unfinished sacrifice, τέλος, in connection with Protesilaus' δόμος, which Catullus then develops with the effect described above.³¹ Since Homer himself was already (arguably) etymologizing Protesilaus' name in *Il.* 2. 702 (above n. 8), a poet might have felt himself pressingly invited to etymologize the disputed adjective in the previous line.

Whatever germ for the motif of neglected sacrifice we may think to find in Homer, it and the motif of Protesilaus' fated death are substantially additions to Homer's account. In other essential respects Catullus' version of the story is a clear reversion to Homer.³² Catullus gives us a picture of love cut down at its inception, as Homer had; Homer left Protesilaus' wife 'poised perhaps on the brink of tragedy', as I put it above. Catullus develops this suggestively suspended text to the extent that it is surely clear in his account that Laodamia will commit suicide (84, 105–7); but still the suicide is not actually described, still Laodamia is on the brink of tragedy. And here is Catullus' climax and emphasis: the imminent suicide of Laodamia, death for love.

In this way Catullus narrates the story of Laodamia and Protesilaus, an instance for him of the power and potential of love. We may now summarize all the ingredients (bringing back the similes). A supernatural obstacle at the outset, more or less inscrutable (85–6); divine anger disproportionate to the possible offence (75–84). The lover's physical passion (73, 'coniugis... flagrans... amore', the similes at 107 ff., 125 ff.). Feelings of joy and love absolutely unphysical (119 ff.). Vast and engulfing profundity (107 ff.). And climactically, in spite of a surprising admission that satiety was imaginable (83), love turns out to be sweeter than life; life without love is not worth living: when the union is destroyed at its inception, we have, imminently, death-for-love, the lover's suicide, *Liebestod* (84, 105–7). Catullus' story of Protesilaus and Laodamia enshrines a view of love that is tragically romantic: love starts unblessed, exhibits huge intensity, and ends in death.

---

³⁰ Cf. προτέλεια in n. 29, LSJ τέλος 6 'services or offerings due to the gods', τελέω III.3 'also of sacred rites, perform, ἱερά...', the Homeric τελήεσσας ἑκατόμβας (e.g. *Iliad* 1. 315); and the LSJ entry for τέλειος opens 'perfect, of victims,' and we find e.g. Thuc. 5. 47. 8 ἱερῶν τελείων.

³¹ O'Hara (1996) is most concerned with the etymologizing of proper names, but pp. 38 ff. deals with Hellenistic poets' etymologizing of common words. The quotation in the text above comes from p. 38. O'Hara has extensive bibliography of course, and his book is now a most useful entry into the whole topic of etymologizing in antiquity. For Callimachus' enjoyment of effects in between pun and etymology, see too e.g. the indexes to Hopkinson (1984) and (1988) under 'etymologis(z)ing'.

³² Cf. Ellis (1889), 416; contrast Kroll's note (1960) on 68. 70–88, conjecturing that Catullus draws on a Hellenistic source dependent on Euripides.

To construct this story, Catullus' narrative strategy has been substantially to revert to Homer. He makes significant additions to it, but substantially he reverts to the summary in the Catalogue of Ships. Most noticeably, Catullus has cut out the entire post-Homeric development of the Protesilaus story, staged by the influential Euripides; in particular he has no hint of Protesilaus' return from the dead. This is a most remarkable silence, not something that can lack significance.[33] It is not just that Protesilaus' return must have been a star part of the story in the post-Euripidean world, and could easily have been incorporated in an allusion in poem 68. I said above that a belief that love may somehow overcome death goes almost hand in glove with a belief in a mighty power of love. The evidence ranged from tombstones to myths, from the wife of Oppius, from Julius and Trebia,[34] to Orpheus, Alcestis—and Protesilaus. But the two beliefs are not hand in glove in Catullus. That really is my point here. Catullus shows us in his Protesilaus and Laodamia a love so powerful that it can persuade a lover to commit suicide: romantic and powerful if you like. But he does not show us, he will not show us, he *excludes* the demonstration that love can overcome death. His view of love in 68 shows the hand without the glove. Love is powerful, love is life. But love cannot overcome death. For his time and place this is a distinct and stark romanticism. He takes issue on the question of love and death with exponents of love's power like Plato's Phaedrus and Euripides.

II. PROPERTIUS 1. 19 AND CATULLUS 68: DIALOGUE

And then Propertius takes issue with him.

In a poem (1. 19) which I have discussed elsewhere,[35] Propertius tries precisely to maintain the belief that love can overcome death: 'traicit et fati litora magnus amor', 'great love crosses even the shores of death' (12). But he tries to maintain this belief alongside a simultaneous belief in the destructive power of death. The poem is one of grim internal struggle. The attempt to believe in the power of love to overcome death generates—given Propertius'

---

[33] Syndikus (1990) passes by the fact in a footnote: p. 277 n. 163. Hutchinson (1988) gives it more weight, p. 316 'Catullus suppresses entirely the supernatural events of the myth (such as the brief resurrection of Protesilaus)', but without further comment.

[34] See n. 3.

[35] Lyne (1980), 100–2, 140–5. Propertius' treatment of love and death is brilliantly discussed by Papanghelis (1987), but he gives his most fruitful attention to poems in Book 2. I have considerable disagreement with Papanghelis (pp. 10–19) on Prop. 1. 19; and he has no inkling of a dialogue with Catullus.

views of death—powerful paradoxes: Propertius must envisage dust, ashes, and bones as capable of love: *puluis, ossa, fauilla* (6, 18, 19, 22). We can if we like see Propertius here in dialogue with a poem like Asclepiades II Gow–Page = *Anth. Pal.* 5. 85 in which it is the resonant and obvious *datum* that ὀστέα ('bones') and σποδιή ('ash') are the negation of love.[36] The more important dialogue is with Catullus. Propertius illustrates his belief that love conquers death with, of course, the myth of Protesilaus, restoring the motif that Catullus omitted: the hero's return from the dead. 1. 19. 5–12:

> non adeo leuiter nostris puer haesit ocellis,
>   ut meus oblito puluis amore uacet.
> illic Phylacides iucundae coniugis heros
>   non potuit caecis immemor esse locis,
> sed cupidus falsis attingere gaudia palmis
>   Thessalus[37] antiquam uenerat umbra domum.

Not so lightly had Cupid clung to my eyes that my dust could be void and forgetful of love. There in the regions of darkness the hero Protesilaus could not be unmindful of his sweet wife, but, desirous to reach his joy with false hands, the Thessalian came to his ancient home a shade.

And as it was for Protesilaus, so it will be for Propertius:

> illic quidquid ero, semper tua dicar imago;
>   traicit et fati litora magnus amor.

There, whatever I shall be, I shall always be called your image. Great love crosses even the shores of death.

Fedeli (1980) in his commentary sees echoes of Catullus 68 in Propertius' Protesilaus. He observes that *coniunx* reappears, transferred by Propertius to Laodamia; likewise the passion of Catullus' Laodamia (*coniugis flagrans amore*, etc.) is now transferred to the male (*cupidus attingere gaudia*); Fedeli also remarks the reappearance of the key word and concept *domus* (1. 19. 10, Catull. 68. 74, the *domum inceptam frustra*). Fedeli sees echoes—but senses no dialogue.

Dialogue and disagreement between the two poets there certainly is, focused on Protesilaus. But the disagreement is not clear-cut, and Propertius'

---

[36] Φείδῃ παρθενίης· καὶ τί πλέον; οὐ γὰρ ἐς Ἀίδην | ἐλθοῦσ' εὑρήσεις τὸν φιλέοντα, κόρη. | ἐν ζωοῖσι τὰ τερπνὰ τὰ Κύπριδος, ἐν δ' Ἀχέροντι | ὀστέα καὶ σποδιή, παρθένε, κεισόμεθα, 'You grudge your maidenhood. What does it profit you? When, girl, you go to Hades you will find no lover there. The delights of Aphrodite are among the living. In Acheron, maiden, we shall lie as bones and ashes.'

[37] Goold here adopts *Thessalis* of some *recc.* I would resist this. According to the inherited myth, Protesilaus did return a full man (a *Thessalus* therefore). Propertius' conviction of the truth of this myth falters in, so to speak, the telling, as I describe below. It is effective therefore that the final revelation of inadequacy (*umbra*) should be delayed until the last moment; it fits in with the strategy of the rest of the poem.

version of the story must be followed closely. He directs the story through Protesilaus, for it is Protesilaus who images Propertius himself and his belief that love, his love, can overcome death. He suggests a version of the return story, dissimilar to the one assumed to be Euripidean (if we follow Hyginus),[38] which is most suited to making his point. In Propertius it seems to be the sheer power of Protesilaus' love—no piteous weeping appeals—that overcame death: 'non potuit... sed cupidus... uenerat'.

That overcame death... But in the expression of the myth, Propertius shows his conviction faltering. 'False' or 'cheated' hands, a mere 'shade' or 'shadow' returned. The myth seeks to project belief, but betrays doubt. As Lucian's Persephone saw (see above), Protesilaus must return in full human form for the reunion to mean anything, and this is how it must traditionally have been shown, implicitly or explicitly. By admitting terms of deception and insubstantiality, Propertius shows incipient lack of confidence in the fact of Protesilaus' return. His belief that love can overcome death is rather an *attempt* to believe; his attempt to confute Catullus via Protesilaus is an attempt which as the poem progresses collapses. It collapses before the facts of ash and bones. Propertius too, in 1. 19, seems to find death finally triumphant. His sense of death's triumph is the most important justification for, it must be the essential logic behind, his conclusion (25 f.): '*wherefore*, while it is *possible*, let us love and be glad together....'.[39] Propertius 1. 19 is a dynamic attempt to confute Catullus. This time it retreats. There will be other attempts.[40]

We might note that Propertius' conclusion picks up and agrees with Catullus 5, and with the partner of that poem, Catullus 7. Prop. 1. 19. 25 f.:

> quare, dum licet, inter nos laetemur amantes
> non satis est ullo tempore longus amor.

Wherefore, while it is possible, let us love and be glad together: love is not long enough in any extent of time.

This is the Propertian version of Catullus 5, 'uiuamus, mea Lesbia, atque amemus... | nobis cum semel occidit breuis lux, | nox est perpetua una dormienda', 'let us live, Lesbia, and let us love... when once our brief light has set, there is just one everlasting night to be slept'; and it conveys too the insatiability of

---

[38] But cf. somewhat similar versions in Lucian and the scholia on Aristides, referred to above p. 215.

[39] This and other points made in this paragraph are unpacked in Lyne (1980), 101. Of course, other considerations may contribute to the 'wherefore' conclusion, as I grudgingly allow (loc. cit.); the other considerations are stressed by Jacoby (1961), ii. 163). But the fact of death and the end that it brings is by far the most important.

[40] One of the best is 2. 15: this poem clearly picks up 1. 19 and its themes, and engages not only with that poem but directly.

Catullus 7 'quam magnus numerus...tam...satis'. It is also the Propertian version of Asclepiades' 'the delights of Aphrodite are among the living', Gow–Page II = *Anth. Pal.* 5. 85 (n. 36). But Propertius emerges from a dense and morbid dialectic (can love overcome death?); he reaches this limpid conclusion with, surely, regret: *dum licet* is a sad retreat from *traicit et fati litora magnus amor*. Asclepiades endures no such conflict to come to the same result. Some would say that Catullus in poem 5 draws his conclusion with a facility similar to Asclepiades'.

From this view of Catullus 5 I would be inclined to dissent. Asclepiades—and, say, Horace in *Ode* 1. 11—have relatively limited, relatively hedonistic views on love, and the gist of their message is not so very terrible. We die, there are pleasures, love is one of them, death ends everything, so take pleasures while you can, love included. But Catullus has a huge and sublime view of love (shown in, say, poems 72, 87, and 109, not to mention 68): it is what we live for, it should be eternal (*aeternum foedus*). So when Catullus shows death ending love in poem 5, it ought perhaps, unless we keep this poem in hermetically sealed isolation, to seem more lamentable than the superficially similar message in Asclepiades and Horace—even if Catullus chooses not to spell out the gravity (as it were running away from it, *da mi basia mille...*).

III. PROP. 1. 19 CONT.; THE WAX IMAGE MOTIF

It is worth a final look at the details in which Propertius' conviction concerning Protesilaus' return seems to falter: the 'false hands' and so on (1. 19. 9–10):

> sed cupidus falsis attingere gaudia palmis
> Thessalus antiquam uenerat umbra domum.

but, desirous to reach his joy with false hands, the Thessalian came to his ancient home a shade.

Dubiety spills over into his own inference from the myth (11):

> illic quidquid ero, semper tua dicar imago.

'There, whatever I shall be, I shall always be called your image.' Matching the insubstantiality of the shadowy (*umbra*) Protesilaus is the mere semblance (*imago*) that the dead Propertius presents. Fedeli suggestively remarks that line 9 is influenced by the vain embraces of the dead in Homer (*Il.* 23. 99–101, etc.). I think there is another point.

In his account of the Protesilaus and Laodamia story Propertius restored the motif of Protesilaus' return, attempting to confute Catullus. He brings in echoes of another motif, to show that attempt faltering. Propertius' Protesilaus, returning from the dead, and Propertius' own reflection of Protesilaus in the Underworld, nudge memories of the waxen image of Protesilaus which Laodamia constructed in her vain and pathetic effort to cheat death. Hyginus' summary (*fab.* 103–4) talks of Laodamia 'embracing and kissing a *simulacrum* of Protesilaus'. Euripides' allusion to the image story in *Alc.* 348–53, where the idea of an image of Alcestis recalls Protesilaus' image (n. 16), runs thus:

> σοφῇ δὲ χειρὶ τεκτόνων δέμας τὸ σὸν
> εἰκασθὲν ἐν λέκτροισιν ἐκταθήσεται,
> ᾧ προσπεσοῦμαι καὶ περιπτύσσων χέρας
> ὄνομα καλῶν σὸν τὴν φίλην ἐν ἀγκάλαις
> δόξω γυναῖκα καίπερ οὐκ ἔχων ἔχειν·
> ψυχρὰν μέν, οἶμαι, τέρψιν...

a likeness of your body made by the skilled hands of craftsmen will be stretched out in our bed, and I will embrace it, clasping it in my hands. Calling your name, I will seem to have my beloved wife in my arms, yet not having her: a cold delight, I think...

Cf. in Prop. 1. 19 the cheated hands, the *umbra*, and Propertius' *imago*, a word whose meanings extend through 'image', 'apparition', 'likeness', and 'statue'. The embraces permitted to the *umbra* of Prop. 1. 19. 9 and 10 and permissible to the *imago* of 11 are if we think about it no more substantial than, indeed very similar to, the false embraces provided by Laodamia's waxen image of Protesilaus, referred to by Hyginus (and a fragment of Euripides himself, 655N[2]), and the cold embraces that the Alcestis image would provide. Propertius' narration of the return of Protesilaus prompts recollection of the waxen, false Protesilaus of Laodamia's construction, and the latter undermines the former.

IV. NACHLEBEN

Catullus' Laodamia dying for love seems to have had more influence on subsequent Roman poets than Propertius' Protesilaus essaying the conquest of death. For the former, cf. Verg. *Aen.* 6. 447, Ovid *Am.* 2. 18. 38, *Ars* 3. 17, *Trist.* 1. 6. 20, *Pont.* 3. 1. 109 f.; in Ov. *Her.* 13 Laodamia anticipates her suicide (80, 163 f.), and, too, brings forward in time the motif of the waxen image (151–8, an *imago* of *cera*); this motif is also mentioned in *Rem.* 723 f. On the other hand the dream fantasies of Laodamia in *Her.* 13. 105–10 recall Propertius' Protesilaus, aspiring to return (*gaudia falsa, imago,* cf. too 115 *cupidis amplexa lacertis*); and Statius, *Silv.* 5. 3. 273 is a direct echo of the returning Protesilaus of Propertius.

14

Propertius 2. 10 and 11 and the Structure of Books '2a' and '2b' (1998)

I. THE DIVISION OF 'BOOK 2'

The manuscripts of Propertius present us with a single, massive 'Book 2' over thirteen hundred and sixty lines long. Like many before me, I am convinced that this 'Book 2' is a mistake of transmission and actually preserves the remnants of *two* ancient books. In this article I identify and discuss the poem which I believe closed the first of the ancient books; for convenience's sake we can call this book 'Book 2a'. I shall be saying something, too, about the structure and content of both ancient books—of Book 2b as well as Book 2a.

It was Lachmann who first made the—to me—irresistible suggestion that our 'Book 2' is the product of two ancient books.[1] There has been strong support for this view. For example,[2] a succinct case is put forward by Otto Skutsch;[3] and highly convincing and detailed support has been offered in an important recent paper by Heyworth.[4] There are intricacies of evidence to consider (for example, Nonius Marcellus' citation of our 3. 21. 14), but I shall set these to one side.[5] I shall simply cite two crucial and probably familiar facts, which are in summary as follows. (i). 2. 13. 25–6. Propertius wishes to be accompanied to the underworld by the corpus of his poetry. He refers to this work as 'tres...libelli'. It is hard to see how this can appear in anything but a third book; indeed it seems to belong in the front of a third book, just as 2. 3. 4 'et turpis de te iam liber *alter* erit' clearly belongs in the front of a second book. (ii). The number of lines in 'Book 2'. According to Barber's Oxford text, the transmitted Book 2 contains 1,362 verses, almost 300 more than any other Augustan book. And consider this total within the context of Propertius' other books, as transmitted to us: Book 1, 706 lines, Book 3, 990,

---

[1] It was first made in his edition Lachmann (1816).
[2] Cf. too the terse statement of facts by Hubbard (1974), 41–2, and the cautious survey in the commentary of Butler and Barber (1933), pp. xxviii–xxxv.
[3] Skutsch (1975), 229–33.   [4] Heyworth (1995), 165–85.
[5] For Nonius Marcellus and Propertius, see esp. Heyworth (1995), 178–81. Further evidence is cited and discussed by Heyworth.

Book 4, 952. The anomaly of 'Book 2' stands out. It contains too many verses not only for a natural Augustan book, but for a natural Propertian book. Of course, it also contains too few for two Propertian books, and we cannot simply divide 'Book 2' somewhere and find the two original ancient books; but on this question see Section VI.1.

I cannot claim that the basic Lachmann view is an overwhelming orthodoxy, and I refer to some dissenting voices. Williams believed that Propertius wrote 2. 13. 25–6 'contemplating an act of publication which comprised three volumes',[6] like Horace's simultaneous publication of *Odes* Books 1–3; but I think this view is sufficiently rebutted by Hubbard and Skutsch.[7] Camps in his edition of Book 2[8] rejected Lachmann's division chiefly on the grounds that 'tres...libelli' in 2. 13. 25 'is not likely to be meant as a statistic'; but 'tres' is after all naturally a statistic, and the previous reference to 'iam liber alter' (2. 3. 4) rather encourages us to take it as a statistical reference to the number of Propertian books existing at that time. Wyke assumes the integrity of our 'Book 2', perceiving (a) framing motifs in 2. 1 and 2. 34, and, what is more, (b) understanding 2. 10–13 as 'not only interrelated' but 'also integrated with the second Propertian poetry-book'.[9] Regarding (a), I do not think that the motifs are particularly salient, not nearly so salient as those I shall cite between 2. 10/11 and 2. 1.[10] As for (b), my present paper will argue that 2. 10/11 is heavily and finally *closural*, and a forthcoming paper [Lyne (1998*d*) = Ch. 12] will argue that 2. 12 is inceptive and programmatic; so (in sum) I am prepared to see a certain 'interrelation', but must deny any 'integration' within a single 'Book 2'.

Lachmann presented 2. 10 as the opening poem of Book 2b. Heyworth puts the case persuasively for believing that 2. 10 was closural in Book 2a.[11] Much of Heyworth's argument regarding 2. 10 I accept, but I have much to add to what he says, and I also believe that our poems 2. 10 and 11 were a single concluding poem in Book 2a.[12]

---

[6] Williams (1968), 481.   [7] Hubbard (1974), and Skutsch (1975), 229–30.
[8] Camps (1967), 1.   [9] Wyke (1987), 47–61, esp. 48, 61.
[10] Wyke (1987), 48 summarizes, 'The second book is framed by the naming of Callimachus, by extensive borrowings from the Callimachean polemic in favour of writing elegy, and by references to the Elegiac Woman as Propertius' poetic material'. It seems to me that these quite general motifs could be exhibited by the opening poem of a second book and the closing poem of a third book without surprise. The devices of ring-composition that I cite (see below §VI.3, esp. VI.3.v) seem to me much more insistently to mark the beginning and end of a book.

[11] Heyworth (1995), 166–7, following a point made by Hutchinson (1984), 100, who does not, however, believe in the division of 'Book 2'.

[12] Birt (1882), 419–20, first accepted Lachmann's suggestion that 2. 10 opened Book 2b, but by Birt (1909), 398–9, and Birt (1915), 266, he suggested, in summary form, that 2. 10 and the 'epigram' 2. 11 closed Book 2a. On neither of these occasions did he offer any substantive argument for his thesis.

II. TEXT AND TRANSLATION OF 2. 10 AND 11

First I provide a text of 2. 10 and 11 together. Following one half of the manuscript tradition (FP) and, say, Scaliger, I believe they are one poem.

> sed tempus lustrare aliis Helicona choreis,
>   et campum Haemonio iam dare tempus equo.   2
> iam libet et fortis memorare ad proelia turmas
>   et Romana mei dicere castra ducis.   4
> quod si deficiant uires, audacia certe
>   laus erit: in magnis et uoluisse sat est.   6
>
> aetas prima canat Veneres, extrema tumultus:
>   bella canam, quando scripta puella meast.   8
> nunc uolo subducto grauior procedere uultu,
>   nunc aliam citharam me mea Musa docet.   10
> surge, anime, ex humili; iam, carmina, sumite uires;
>   Pierides, magni nunc erit oris opus.   12
>
> iam negat Euphrates equitem post terga tueri
>   Parthorum et Crassos se tenuisse dolet;   14
> India quin, Auguste, tuo dat colla triumpho,
>   et domus intactae te tremit Arabiae;   16
> et si qua extremis tellus se subtrahit oris,
>   sentiat illa tuas postmodo capta manus!   18
>
> haec ego castra sequar: uates tua castra canendo
>   magnus ero. seruent hunc mihi fata diem!   20
>
> ut caput in magnis ubi non est tangere signis,
>   ponitur his imos ante corona pedes,   22
> sic nos nunc, inopes laudis conscendere carmen,
>   pauperibus sacris uilia tura damus.   24
> nondum etiam Ascraeos norunt mea carmina fontes,
>   sed modo Permessi flumine lauit Amor.   26
>
> scribant de te alii uel sis ignota licebit:
>   laudet, qui sterili semina ponit humo.   2
> omnia, crede mihi, tecum uno munera lecto
>   auferet extremi funeris atra dies;   4
> et tua transibit contemnens ossa uiator,
>   nec dicet 'cinis hic docta puella fuit.'   6

But now it is time to traverse Helicon with other dances, and to give the field to the Thessalian horse. Now I am pleased to bring to remembrance squadrons brave for battle and to tell of the Roman camp of my leader. And if strength should fail me, certainly daring will bring me praise: in great matters, even to have wished is enough.

Let first years sing of Venuses, let the last of tumults. I shall sing of wars, since my girl has been written. Now I want to walk forth with serious mien, now my Muse teaches me another lyre. Ascend, my soul, from the lowly; now, my songs, take on strength; Pierians (Muses), now a grander voice will be needed.

No longer does the Euphrates allow the Parthian cavalrymen to look over their shoulders, and it grieves that it has kept possession of the Crassi; India, indeed, offers its neck to your triumph, Augustus, and the house of untouched Arabia trembles before you; and if any land withdraws to the furthest shores of the world, may it hereafter be captured and feel your hand!

This is the camp I shall follow: by singing of your camp I shall become a mighty bard. Oh that the fates may reserve this day for me!

Just as, when it is not possible to reach the head of tall statues, a garland is placed before the feet below, so I now, helpless to climb the poetry of praise, offer paltry incense in a poor man's sacrifice. Not yet do my songs know the Ascraean springs, but Love has merely bathed them in the river of Permessus.

Others may write about *you* (Cynthia) or you may be unknown: let him praise you, who sows seed in barren soil. Believe me, the black day of the final funeral will bear off all your gifts with you on one bier; and the traveller will pass by your bones in disdain, and will not say: 'This ash was an artful girl.'

I append some preliminary notes, adding to, highlighting, or adjusting the standard commentaries:

Line 1. 'sed': the justification of the adversative. Goold,[13] following Lachmann (who, however, believed 2. 10 opened Propertius' third book), signals missing text before 2. 10. 1. I see no reason for this. Propertius opposes the thrust of the present poem ('But it is time to write laudatory poetry...') to what has preceded (love poetry). Camps[14] ad loc. cites other Propertian elegies which begin with conjunctions (note especially 2. 27. 1 'at'), but the usefulness of the parallels is limited, since particular reasons obtain in each case. The 'at' of 2. 27. 1, for example, seems to me to be in anticipation of the contrast between the uncertainty of 'mortales' (1–10) and the certainty of lovers (11–12). The best parallel for our 'sed' is perhaps Verg. *Georg.* 2. 541. Vergil opens his dissociating, closural paragraph with 'sed' as Propertius opens his dissociating closural poem with the same adversative conjunction. We shall return to these lines of Vergil below: they are in Propertius' mind.

Line 2. 'Haemonio...equo'. Surprisingly the commentaries of Camps, Enk,[15] miss the point of the epithet 'Haemonian' = Thessalian. Heinsius

---

[13] Goold (1990).   [14] Camps (1967).
[15] Enk (1962) and Rothstein (1920).

wished to emend to 'campum et Maeonio'; Enk wanted to write 'Aonio'. Of course Thessalian horses were prized, as Camps and others who keep 'Haemonio' say; but that is hardly sufficient explanation for Propertius' choice. Propertius' main allusion is to his own Achilles' horses at 2. 8. 38 'fortem illum Haemoniis Hectora traxit equis'. We must recall Choerilus' literary imagery of untouched meadows and chariots of poetry;[16] likewise Vergil's horse image of composition at *Georg.* 2. 542 ('et iam tempus equum fumantia soluere colla'). Then, putting these together with Propertius' own quintessentially heroic horses ('Haemonian', 'Achillean'), we find a most effective image for the proposed epic poetry: 'giving the field of literature to the horse of epic'.

Line 11. 'humili' is neuter, I think: cf. Cic. *Tusc.* 2. 5 'atque oratorum quidem laus ita ducta ab humili uenit ad summum, ut...'. Propertius is quite close to saying 'get up off the ground'; the root of 'humilis' is 'humus', the ground, ground-level. (In Hor. *Odes* 3. 30. 12 'ex humili potens', 'humili' is masculine.)

Line 13. 'iam negat...' The interpretation of this line is troublesome. Camps offers two ways of taking it: (1) 'Euphrates declares that the Parthians' horsemen look behind their backs no more', (2) 'Euphrates refuses any more to keep the Parthians' horsemen safe behind him'; Goold plumps for something in the middle, which I have followed. It is certainly hard to imagine that 'post terga tueri' refers to anything other than the renowned Parthian method of shooting over the shoulder. The gist of the sentiment I take to be that the Euphrates, hitherto boundary and protection of Parthia, now repents of and withdraws its patronage.

Lines 15–16. 'India... Arabiae'. These references to the submission of India and to an impending expedition against Arabia date the poem (and Book 2a) to 26–25 BC: this I have discussed elsewhere (Lyne 1998c) [= Ch. 15 of this volume], but the evidence can be summarized.[17]

Line 23. I have kept 'carmen' tentatively. I am confident that 'currum' (Markland, followed by Camps and Goold) is wrong (though Lucr. 6. 47,

---

[16] Lloyd-Jones and Parsons (1983), 147, fr. 317; it is quoted by Enk (1962), in his note on line 2.

[17] Indian embassy in 26–25 BC: *Res Gestae* 31 records embassies from India; Orosius 6. 21. 19 tells us that 'legati Indorum' met Augustus at Tarraco in Spain; Dio 53. 22. 5 tells us that Augustus left Rome in 27 BC, 'lingered in Gaul', then proceeded to Spain; Suet. *Aug.* 26. 3 tells us that Augustus began his eighth and ninth consulships (26 and 25 BC) at Tarraco; another datable embassy from India falls in 20 BC (Dio 54. 9. 8), clearly too late for our poem. The date of the Arabian expedition (still impending in Prop. 2. 10, note 'intactae') is 25–24 BC, and the best evidence for this comes from Dio 53. 29. 3–8; but it needs careful interpreting. This it gets from Hardy (1923), 123; the essential points made by Hardy are quoted by Enk (1962), 152. Cf. too Rich's note (1990) on Dio 53. 29. 3–8, and La Penna (1977), 48 n. 1. Augustus himself refers to the Arabian expedition at *RG* 26. 5.

adduced by Camps, is initially enticing[18]). The important ascent metaphor at play here is ascent of a mountain: see below Section III.2, and a chariot at this point, by this stage,[19] is alien and intrusive. So the right reading may be 'culmen',[20] or 'in arcem' (Palmier); parablepsy ('carmina' in 25) could have ousted something with no resemblance to the paradosis in 23. But 'carmen' is justifiable as a 'trespassed' term—as the language of the 'tenor' (the ultimate thrust of the message) 'intruded' into the 'vehicle' (the imagery conveying it);[21] Shackleton Bailey supports 'carmen' citing Lucian, *Menipp.* 1 ('the metaphor in *conscendere carmen* is hardly bolder than in Lucian, *Menipp.* 1 λέγε οὑτωσί πως ἁπλῶς καταβὰς ἀπὸ τῶν ἰαμβείων').[22] And 'carmen' has an advantage over, say, 'culmen'. Propertius has adduced a simile in 21–2 to illustrate his failed attempt to ascend and its consequences; he will have a metaphor allied to, but not the same as, this simile in 24. To assert the ascent and hill metaphor too concretely in between, rather than imply it, is perhaps clumsy.

III. THE DOMINANT MESSAGE AND MOTIF IN '2. 10'[23]

(1) The Dominant Message: The Question of 'Recusatio'[24]

To be sure, Propertius appears to announce an imminent epic poem (1–4, 7–8 etc.); to be sure that intention falters (20–6). But to call this a 'recusatio', even

---

[18] Lucr. 6. 47 'quandoquidem semel insignem conscendere currum...' has to do with Lucretius' literary enterprise, but we are hampered by an immediately following lacuna. However, since he has just recalled how, in Book 5, he explained the workings of heaven and the heavenly bodies, and will now proceed to explain 'cetera quae fieri in terris caeloque tuentur | mortales', 50, cf. 83 etc., a chariot image (the sun is drawn in a chariot, and so on) is arguably appropriate to his context in a way that it is not in Prop. 2. 10. 23. (Propertius uses 'currum conscendere' of Aurora at 2. 18. 13.)

[19] Even in lines 1–2, where the precedent of Choerilus (referred to above) might have induced him, Propertius did not employ chariots.

[20] A manuscript reading according to Passerat: Barber, *uet. cod. Memmii teste Passeratio.* Sil. 3. 510 cited in its support is not cogent, since its context is not literary.

[21] 'Trespass' is the simple term I prefer for the analogous phenomenon in similes (when narrative terms appear in the simile): cf. Lyne (1989), 92–9 and index s.v. 'trespass'. 'Tenor' and 'vehicle', stemming from I. A. Richards, are terms employed by Silk (1974), who refers to this phenomenon as 'intrusion'. For 'tenor' language 'intruded' into the 'vehicle' see Silk (1974), 138–42.

[22] Rothstein (1920) ad loc. supports it too, but he thinks the concealed metaphor is ascent of a chariot.

[23] On this 'poem' see Wimmel (1960), 193–202 (with ample bibliography), a useful discussion.

[24] On 'recusatio' see Lyne (1995), 31–9 with bibliography.

in the derived category I have given it elsewhere,[25] is slightly misleading. The following quotation is certainly misleading:[26] '2. 10 is a proper *recusatio* (that is, the poet refuses on Callimachean grounds to relate epic themes or the deeds of Augustus).' My own verb was cannier (Propertius 'ducks' the epic). We should be yet cannier and more precise. Propertius alludes through Vergil and Gallus to Callimachus (see (2) below), but his primary ground for demurring here is, not Callimachean authority, but the panegyrically acceptable one of insufficient talent (5 'quod si deficiant uires...', 23 'inopes conscendere').[27] And we must choose the verb we use to describe Propertius' action with great care. Propertius does not 'refuse'. He demurs, he postpones the epic—at least he goes through the motions of postponing it (20 'seruent hunc mihi fata diem').[28] Most importantly, he compromises meanwhile, because—meanwhile—he offers his mite. He offers this piece of text. And this text is not the *praeteritio*-type of compromise to be found in e.g. 2. 1, which is a 'recusatio' ('were I to write of such things, I would write of...').[29] Lines 13–18 actually get under way, singing of Parthians etc.; the poem does involve some high poetry, however specious, however locked into elegiac metre. In short, in Propertius' imagery, this piece constitutes the offering at the foot of the statue, the 'ante corona pedes', the 'uilia tura', instead of (to drop the imagery) the whole twelve hexameter books. The expressed intention to write an epic falters and compromises, but this is not exactly a refusal.

(2) Motif: The Ascent of Helicon

There are minor motifs in 2. 10: e.g. 'it is time to traverse Helicon with other dances' (i.e. change type of literature), 'give the field to an epic horse' (see above Section II), but these need not detain us. I wish to concentrate on the motif of (failed) *ascent*.

First, the simple idea of ascent. There is line 11 'surge, anime, ex humili', 'ascend from the lowly', 'get up from ground level'. Then 23 'inopes laudis conscendere carmen', 'I am helpless to climb the poetry of praise'. The notion

---

[25] Lyne (1995), 36.   [26] Ross (1975), 118.

[27] For the panegyrical acceptability of demurring for this reason, see Lyne (1995), 38. Hor. *Serm.* 2. 1. 12–13 is perhaps Propertius' immediate source (where Horace plays tricks with Callimachean topoi in addition); cf. then *Epist.* 2. 1. 250–9, also (though not in a panegyrical context), Verg. *Georg.* 2. 483–4.

[28] Note the phrasing of Wimmel (1960), 194 and 201 ('compromise' etc.).

[29] We may also distinguish the 'inclusion' or 'incorporation' of disavowed genres performed by e.g. Horatian 'recusatio', and observed by e.g. Davis (1991), 28–36, and Putnam in Harrison (1995), 59. The poet shows potential mastery of the supposedly disavowed genres by such 'inclusion', but does not actually proffer a piece of encomiastic text as Propertius does in 2. 10.

of ascent again: but the poet is unequal to it. (Note too the simile in 21–2: the imagery describes reaching for the top, but having to be content with the base.)

A geographical location for this motif of ascent, and the key to understanding it, is clearly given in the first line: Mt. Helicon. True, in the confidence of that line, Propertius seems in command of the mountain. But in line 11 he instructs himself to ascend. The natural inference would be, I think, that he wishes to mount to the summit of Helicon.

And if he gets to the summit of the mountain, this will symbolize his command of the desired laudatory and epic poetry. But the attempt fails, or rather falters and finds compromise (see above). That the geography of Helicon and its summit is envisaged in the body of the text is confirmed by the references to allied geographical features, to Permessus and Hippocrene ('Ascraeos fontes'), in 25–6: cf. immediately Vergil, *Ecl.* 6. 64–73. But we must pursue this further.

Most influential upon the Propertian scene and action (Helicon, ascent, Permessus) is almost certainly a scene of poetic initiation in Cornelius Gallus. This we can reconstruct from Vergil.[30] I sketch it first with all possible brevity. From *Ecl.* 6. 64–73 we infer the following. In his poem on the 'Grynean Grove' Gallus pictured himself conducted from the river Permessus up to the summit of Mt. Helicon by one of the Muses ('errantem Permessi ad flumina Gallum | Aonas in montis ut duxerit una sororum'); he described himself being given 'calami' by Linus, on behalf of the Muses; and these reed-pipes were to enable him to compose a poem on the origin of the Grynean Grove, 'his tibi Grynei nemoris dicatur origo'. We note, of course, that Gallus succeeded in his ascent. Propertius fails.

Ultimately a scene of initiation like the Gallan one derives from Hesiod's initiation in *Theog.* 22–34 via, most influentially, Callimachus' 'Dream' preface, our fr. 2 Pf.[31] Another important contributor to Gallus' scene may well have been Ennius. At the beginning of Book 7 of the *Annales* (a new proem in which Ennius explained why he did not propose to dilate on the First Punic War), Ennius glanced at, perhaps dilated upon, some interaction between

---

[30] For the Gallan origin of *Ecl.* 6. 64–73, see Skutsch (1901), 34–8, Ross (1975), 34 with bibliography in his n. 1.

[31] Important adjunct texts for fr. 2 are fr. 2A, a commentary on the scene (which tells us among other things that Callimachus made reference to Permessus, fr. 2a. 20), and *Anth. Pal.* 7. 42. For discussion of Callimachus' 'Dream' scene, cf. e.g. Kambylis (1965), esp. 69–75, 89–109. But it has recently been subjected to fresh scrutiny by Cameron (1995), 127–32, also ch. 4, esp. 119–32, and many familiar assumptions challenged. I am still however persuaded that Callimachus' 'Dream' pictured his initiation by a draught of spring water (cf. Lyne (1995), 36–7 with n. 11).

himself and the Muses on one of the mountains of the Muses;[32] and most likely he spoke of ascent. Cf. *Ann.* 208–9 Sk. (with Skutsch's conjectured supplement)[33] '<nam> neque Musarum scopulos <escendit ad altos>, | nec dicti studiosus <fuit Romanus homo> ante hunc'; cf. too *Ann.* 210 'nos ausi reserare <... fontes? claustra?>'.[34] That 'ascent' was involved in Ennius is suggested by—as well as many of the texts that imitate or allude to him—the summit position at which Hesiod set the Muses's dances in *Theog.* 7 ἀκροτάτῳ Ἑλικῶνι χοροὺς ἐνεποιήσαντο, 'and they made their dances on topmost Helicon'.[35]

I now amplify a couple of points about the Vergilian and putatively Gallan Helicon scene (*Ecl.* 6. 64–73), points with which, I have to say, not all Gallan scholars would agree. (There is an appendix at the end of this paper containing supplementary notes on Permessus etc. as imagined by Vergil, Gallus, Propertius, and others.) Permessus, leastwise the part of Permessus Gallus knows, is situated for him at the foot of Helicon; and his 'wandering' there symbolizes the love elegy that he wrote for Cytheris/Lycoris. His ascent of Helicon and the bestowal of the pipes marks his ascent to an aetiological ('origo') and therefore more ambitious and truly Callimachean poem—his 'Grynean Grove'.[36] That

---

[32] Kambylis (1965), 194, insists that we cannot pin down the identity of the mountain—presumably Parnassus or Helicon—referred to in *Ann.* 208–9 Sk., and this is true; cf. Skutsch (1985), 374 and 149–50. (Kambylis, 196 thinks that, on the basis of Persius, *Prologus* 2 and its scholiast, we can identify the mountain on which Ennius' dream encounter with Homer—in Book 1—took place: Parnassus. Skutsch, 149–50, is more sceptical.)

[33] Skutsch (1985), 374.

[34] Skutsch (1985), 375 favours a door metaphor, 'claustra (Musarum)', or 'fores'; Kambylis (1965), 194–5, favours 'fontes'.

[35] More or less certain imitations of, or allusions to, Ennius' scene in Book 7 are, I think: Lucr. 1. 117–18; Verg. *Georg.* 2. 175–6, 3. 10–11; Prop. 2. 30b. 25–40, 3. 1. 15–18 and 20 (cf. 4. 10. 3–4), and possibly 3. 3. 6; and 2. 10 may allude directly to Ennius as well as indirectly via Gallus. I would even be tempted to include Catull. 105 'Mentula conatur Pipleium scandere montem: | Musae furcillis praecipitem eiciunt'. Those interested in trying further to reconstruct Ennius' scene can profitably exploit these texts. Cf. too Skutsch (1985), 367, 373–5 (Skutsch seems to imagine nothing extensive), Kambylis (1965), 191–204, esp. 194–5, 202. (It should be noted that Skutsch, 147–8, and Kambylis, esp. 198–201, convincingly argue *against* any meeting with, and initiation by, the Muses back in Book 1, within or in addition to the 'Dream' scene in that book in which Ennius encountered the ghost of Homer (*Ann.* 2–11 Sk.; this is modelled in some other respects on Callimachus' 'Dream' which did, according to most scholarly opinion, stage an initiation by the Muses).)

[36] Cf. Skutsch (1901), 36–8; Clausen (1994)'s note on Verg. *Ecl.* 6. 64. Contrast Ross (1975), 31–4, advancing a thoughtful, stubbornly defended minority opinion regarding Permessus, its situation, and significance, an opinion which needs to be considered carefully. Naturally, in the absence of Gallus' text scholars dispute what sort of poem the 'Grynean Grove' was, indeed whether Gallus ever wrote the poem. But there is broad agreement that the poem was written, and that it was aetiological and Callimachean. For a conjecture on its subject (Apollo's rape of the Amazon Gryne in the grove which then took her name: Serv. *auct.* on *Aen.* 4. 345) see Lyne (1978a), 186 [= Ch. 5, p. 83 above]. Most scholars assume that it was the story of the contest in divination between Calchas and Mopsus (Skutsch (1901), 34; cf. Servius on *Ecl.* 6. 72).

the river Permessus symbolizes love elegy is confirmed by among other things our present text of Propertius. The reference in Prop. 2. 10. 26 containing Permessus can only be to Propertius' love poetry.[37]

We may now return to Propertius, and to his use of the Permessus–ascent–Helicon motif. First, Permessus. We may assume that Permessus is for Propertius, as for Gallus, situated at the foot of Helicon. In his reference to Permessus in 26 ('Love has merely bathed my poems in the waters of Permessus'), he can only, as I say, be referring to love-elegy: he has not significantly or decisively progressed beyond such poetry. But the reference contains a joke, neglected by Propertius' commentators, and if we miss jokes we shall misappreciate the total message of the poem. The commentators undervalue, indeed they mistranslate, 'lauit' ('dipped', Goold; Permessus is 'a source of... poetic inspiration... i.e. that required for love-elegy', Camps). 'Lauo' means 'wash' or 'bath', and Propertius refers to the bath of the Muses in Hesiod, *Theog.* 5–7: καί τε λοεσσάμεναι τέρενα χρόα Περμησσοῖο | ἢ᾽ Ἵππου κρήνης ... | ἀκροτάτῳ Ἑλικῶνι χοροὺς ἐνεποιήσαντο | καλοὺς ἱμερόεντας, 'and having washed their tender skin in Permessus or Hippocrene..., the Muses made their fair, graceful dances on topmost Helicon'. Instead of the Muses bathing themselves in Permessus before their dances, Love baths Propertius' poems: the message is ultimately as, say, Camps sees it (Propertius' poetry has not seriously progressed beyond love elegy), but the poet handles the topic with wit, creating for us this funny picture.

Next we must explain exactly line 25, the reference to 'Ascraeos fontes': Propertius fails in his ascent, his poems have only been bathed in Permessus; 'not yet do they know the Ascraean springs'. These springs, named after Hesiod ('Ascraeus' denotes 'Hesiodic', *Ecl.* 6. 70 etc.),[38] must in the first place refer to Hippocrene; Hesiod is tied to Hippocrene by the canonical Call. *Aetia* fr. 2. 1–2 and (according to the traditional interpretation)[39] by the equally prominent fr. 112. 5–6. And Propertius must presumably picture Hippocrene high up, if not at the summit of Helicon: his poems would, we infer, 'have been able to know the springs', if he had succeeded in his ascent. Now (most importantly) 'Ascraean' *Hesiodic* springs must in the post-Callimachean, post-Gallan world supply inspiration for Callimachean, aetiological poetry. Hesiod's figure-head status for the aetiological Callimachus has been challenged,[40] but is borne out by, say, the *Aetia* 'Dream' preface (fr. 2) which draws on

---

[37] With relief I here find myself in some agreement with Ross (1975), 119–20.
[38] The epithet Ἀσκραῖος applied to Hesiod first appears in the Hellenistic period, in Nicander (*Ther.* 11) and in epigram; we may conjecture that Callimachus used it thus, but no instance survives. Cf. Thomas (1988) on Verg. *Georg.* 2. 176, and Clausen (1984) on Verg. *Ecl.* 6. 70.
[39] Cameron (1995) 371 challenges the usual interpretation of 112. 5–6, arguing that they refer to Callimachus himself, not Hesiod.
[40] Cameron (1995), 362–86.

Hesiod's initiation; it is borne out indeed by the *Aetia* lines just referred to; cf. too the praise of Aratus in Epigram 27 Pf.[41] His figurehead status for the aetiological Gallus is borne out by Verg. *Ecl.* 6. 70. When, therefore, Propertius says that 'his songs do not yet know the Ascraean springs', he must mean that he has 'not yet' essayed Gallan or Callimachean aetiology. 'Ascraeos fontes' can by no stretch of the imagination be made to refer to epic inspiration, although that would superficially fit the poem's logic better.[42] Propertius is joking again. The poem announces epic poetry, then it acknowledges that the time is not yet ripe for the full performance. But in lines 25–6, when admitting that the poet is stuck in love-elegy, it says, not the straightforward thing that the poet has not yet had epic inspiration: it says he has not yet even[43] ascended as far as Gallus, he has not even essayed an aetiological poem like the *Aetia* or the 'Grynean Grove'. Much less epic, we infer.

So, to sum up. These lines *compromise* on the statement that an epic is imminent, they falter and they offer a mite instead: this text. They admit that Propertius is not ready for the peak of poetry, exploiting imagery of ascent and Helicon which derives most immediately from Cornelius Gallus. And the whole topic is handled with wit, containing two clear jokes: the Bath of the Poems, and Propertius' unexpected confession that he has not even got as far as Gallus had.

IV. THE THRUST OF '2. 11'

There are two primary questions to answer: (1) What are these 'munera', these 'gifts' of Cynthia's? (2) Why is writing about Cynthia, praising her, now deemed effort wasted, 'sowing seed in barren soil'? I shall give swift and summary answers, in order to identify the essential thrust of '2. 11'; full explanation will come in stages.

(1) The 'munera' in question, now seen as mortal, must predominantly be the wonderful endowments of Cynthia, recounted in 2. 2 and 2. 3 and

---

[41] In spite of Cameron (1995), 374–9, which is convincing in some details, we must surely still see Callimachean veneration for Hesiod in this epigram.

[42] *Pace* e.g. Enk (1962) ad loc., following Skutsch (1901), 37 ('der Strom des Permessus bedeutet für Properz die niedere, die erotische Poesie, die Musenquellen aber die höhere, die heroische'), Goold (1990) ad loc. An attempt at explanation and compromise, to me not successful, is made by Wimmel (1960), 200. Camps (1967) ad loc. retreats into vagueness: 'higher up the mountain is another spring from which a higher inspiration could be drawn.'

[43] I am inclined to lean on 'etiam', in spite of Camps' (1967) note on 'nondum etiam' ('meaning the same as plain *nondum*; cf. 1. 3. 11, 9. 17, etc.').

summed up as 'caelestia munera' in 2. 3. 25: those 'heavenly gifts' which inspired Propertius' second book, and which, so Propertius insisted, must have been gifts from the gods.[44] We note: these 'munera' in 2. 3. 25 were really climactic. 2. 2 stressed the beauty of Cynthia, her face, hair, fingers, build, gait, all things which meant that Propertius could not be free of her. 2. 3 then trumped this poem by saying, 'yes, her face, hair and so on, all inspire me; but it is not so much physical attributes like these, as artistic accomplishments, to which my second book of poetry is owed'. And the climactic summary of the totality was 'caelestia munera', gifts of heaven. So: simple paradox and a total and convincing sense of reversal underline that it is to the 'munera' of 2. 3. 25 that Propertius now refers in 2. 11. 3. What was earlier seen as divine, artistically inspirational, and climactic is now seen as bathetic, paltry, and emphatically mortal. This is a topic to which we will return.

(2) 'laudet qui sterili...' It should be stressed first that Propertius does not deny the possibility that someone will write about Cynthia, indeed praise her: it may not happen, 'uel sis ignota', but it well may. The emphasis is that it will be effort wasted. Why? It must be because the material will be not worth praising. Of this there is immediate confirmation and indeed justification (3–4). The quintessential Cynthia material (her 'munera') is now stated to be emphatically mortal, as paltry as the corpse from which it will be inseparable: therefore not worth writing about.[45]

So here is the essential thrust of '2. 11'. Cynthia's 'munera' are after all merely paltry, their writing a worthless pursuit, something for others to do, if anyone. But we may observe two questions. One might expect this mere mortal, effort-wasting material (as it is now said to be) to be contrasted with something immortal and worth a poet's time and trouble. Second, we will wonder at the function of this reversal: from *raison d'être* of a book to waste of effort, 'munera' 2. 3. 25 to 'munera' 2. 11. 3.

---

[44] Rothstein (1920) on 2. 11. 3, sees the reference to 2. 3. 25 (and pertinently compares too 1. 2. 27), but does not appreciate how climactic 2. 3. 25 is. Camps (1967) on 2. 11. 3, who also sees the reference to 2. 3. 25, thinks that mercenary 'munera' 'in the sense of II, xvi, 15 and 21' may also be in mind. We could add 1. 16. 36, 2. 8. 11, 2. 16. 9, 2. 20. 25, 2. 23. 3 and 8 and others. But I think this sense is marginal and unimportant. The only uses of 'munus' in the remnants of the putative Book 2a (2. 1–11; cf. below §VI.1) are those in 2. 3, 2. 8, and 2. 11.

[45] Rothstein's extensive, paraphrasing efforts to explain the reasoning (in his notes on both 2. 11. 1 and 3 (1920)) boil down to: 'others may praise you, but I won't because there is no lasting fame in it for me' ('dauernder Ruhm ist auf diesem Gebiete doch nicht zu erreichen'). He sees an important connection to 2. 10 ('also *bella canam*'), but to harp on the question of Propertius' fame is not hitting the centre of the target. Enk (1962) has nothing helpful to offer ad loc. Camps (1967) ad loc. has nothing.

V. 2. 10/11: BASIC REASONS FOR UNITY

We will first remind ourselves that one of the two main halves of the manuscript tradition (FP) does not disjoin 2. 10 and 11. And from Scaliger to Rothstein the unity of the FP text has found defenders. In recent times (Butler and Barber, Enk, Camps, Goold) this has gone out of fashion.

Second, we will note that an unprepared apostrophe of Cynthia in the middle of a poem (as 'te' would be in 2. 11. 1) should cause no problems. In 'Book 2' Propertius is given to such apostrophes, making demands upon the reader: cf. e.g. 2. 3. 23–32 addressed to Cynthia, within a poem that first talks about her in the third person and contains other apostrophes; 2. 8. 13–16 to Cynthia, unnamed as yet, after 1–12 to 'amice', and then again 25–8 to Cynthia after 17–24 to Propertius himself; 2. 9. 15 to Achilles, with Enk ad loc. (though Housman and Goold reject this text); 2. 15. 11–30 to Cynthia, after an apostrophe to the bed, and followed by lines about Cynthia in the third person, followed eventually by yet more lines which apostrophize her (49–54).

But perhaps the main reason I see for asserting the unity of the piece is the convincing structure it offers.[46] It fits or rather reverses a conventional pattern. Once (incidentally) we observe this structure one of the questions left unanswered above will be disposed of.

There is a repeated rhythm, we may say structure, in the Roman 'recusatio'.[47] '*Others* will write the uncongenial epic material: *I* by contrast will write love poetry vel sim...' The ancestor of this is in Callimachus' 'Telchines' preface, *Aetia* fr. 1. 26 ἑτέρων and (especially) 32 ἄλλος, ἐγὼ δ'. Cf. Verg. *Ecl.* 6. 6–8 'nunc *ego* (namque super tibi *erunt qui* dicere laudes, | Vare, tuas...) | agrestem tenui meditabor harundine Musam', Prop. 2. 1. 43–5 '*nauita* de uentis... | enumerat *miles* uulnera... | *nos* contra...';[48] then (subsequent to our poem, but no doubt confirming the pattern of other lost 'recusationes'[49]), 2. 34. 59–62 '*me* iuuat hesternis positum languere corollis... || Actia *Vergilio*

---

[46] I think I make a convincing case in this article that 2. 10/11 closed Book 2a. But while much of what I say is consonant with, and is I think most comfortable with, the assumption that 2. 10/11 formed one poem, much is not incompatible with an assumption that Propertius closes with a pair of allied poems, 2. 10 and 11. But the argument on structure that I here give is very strong support for the contention that 2. 10/11 is indeed one single poem.

[47] Many examples are gathered in the discussion referred to above n. 25.

[48] Propertius here plays between the doing of the actions and the description of the actions in a way which I have discussed elsewhere ('Propertius 2. 30b' [not published]), but the message and the structure are essentially the same as in other 'recusationes'.

[49] For the likelihood of lost 'recusationes', see Lyne (1995), 34–6.

est[50] custodis litora Phoebi, | Caesaris et fortis dicere posse ratis…', 93 'Cynthia quin uiuet[51] uersu laudata *Properti*', 3. 1. 15–18 '*multi*, Roma, tuas laudes annalibus addent || sed quod pace legas…| detulit intacta *pagina nostra* uia', Hor. *Odes* 1. 6. 1–5 'scriberis *Vario*…|| *nos*, Agrippa…' What 2. 10 and 2. 11 combined (the FP text) give is a convincing reversal of this pattern: '*I* will write the epic material, *others* by contrast may write the Cynthia poetry': 'iam libet et fortis memorare ad proelia turmas…, nunc *uolo*' etc.; 'scribant de te *alii*'. To appreciate the completeness of the reversal of structure it is necessary to have absorbed a point made above: that Propertius falters in '2. 10', he postpones, compromises but does not 'refuse'; indeed he writes something in the way of epic material—his mite, 'uilia tura', lines 13–18: '2. 10' is not really a 'recusatio'. And now we have an answer for a question I left open above. The thrust of 2. 11 was that Cynthia was effort-wasting material for a poet, her 'munera' paltry and mortal. I said that we might expect Propertius to contrast this material with something immortal, worth a poet's time and trouble. He is doing so, in this very poem, if we see 2. 10 and 11 as one text. The immortal subject matter worthy of the poet's efforts are the achievements of Augustus—to which he accords some attention.

Now, granting that Propertius reverses the 'recusatio' structure and pays some attention to the achievements of Augustus, it may be timely to recall the humour in the piece. I would not wish to construct too ideologically obsequious a poet. We have lines 13–18, but—poems in baths, cheap offerings at the foot of statues, trying and failing to climb, the inability even to match Gallus' aetiological poetry—there is sport going on here, this is not the Horace of the Roman Odes. And, of course, this reversal of the 'recusatio' structure in 2. 10/11 will itself soon be reversed: in 2. 34 and 3. 1; it will simply be ignored in what I think are the opening poems of Book 2b (2. 12 and 13; see below Section VI.1). And there is another point we could include at this time, line 10 'nunc aliam citharam me mea Musa docet'. Talk of '*my* Muse' might take us back to the quirkily proprietary Callimachus with his talk of 'our Calliope' (*Aetia* fr. 75. 77). It will take us back more immediately to Prop. 2. 1 where Propertius offered us the delightful conceit that his Muse was not Calliope, who had been Callimachus' source of song (cf. too fr. 7. 22), nor any other recognized divinity, but Cynthia herself ('non haec Calliope, non haec mihi cantat Apollo. | ingenium nobis ipsa puella facit', 2. 1. 3–4). We might wonder whether Cynthia ('mea Musa') will be very adept at teaching the poet another, non-amatory lyre.

---

[50] I have adopted the text recommended by Heyworth (1984), 399; Goold (1990) follows Housman's 'mi lubet…posito'. Surely *iuuet* (NFL) cannot be right.

[51] 'uiuet' Barber followed by Goold (1990); *etiam* MSS.

VI. THE STRUCTURE OF BOOKS 2a AND 2b AND THE CLOSURAL FUNCTION OF 2. 10/11. MORE EVIDENCE OF UNITY

(1) The Structure of Books 2a and 2b

I offer some thoughts on the original form of 'Book 2' as context for my closing discussion of 2. 10/11.

'Book 2' opens with a clearly inceptive sequence. 2. 1, Cynthia is my Muse: hence more love poetry; 2. 2 and 3, more explanation of the second book, 'liber alter'. But I, like many editors from the Aldine edition of 1502 to Goold, feel 2. 3 ends at line 44; and the rest of '2. 3' and 2. 4 read to me like fragments and excerpts.

'Book 2' ends with patently closural lines. 2. 34. 25–94 proceed from the uselessness of the literary interests of Lynceus (who is now a lover in the Propertian mould), via Vergil, to praise of Propertius' own literary achievement: the lines set Propertius triumphantly at the conclusion of a canon of Latin love poets. Working backwards hence we find 2. 34. 1–24. Unless lines have dropped out, I find it hard to believe that this is the same poem as 25–94. So I would talk as Barber's *Oxford Classical Text* does of 2. 34a and 2. 34b. I am then prepared to believe that 2. 34a was paired with, and perhaps adjacent to, 2. 34b, as 1. 5 was paired with 1. 10: the presumptive rival has his come-uppance; the come-uppance of Lynceus leads neatly into the literary finale. But before 2. 34a I can detect no closing sequence like, say, poems 20–25 in 'Book 3', which can be argued to represent a tight-knit closing sequence to that book.[52] But 2. 30b can be argued to be a 'proemio al mezzo',[53] perhaps introducing the poems following it.

But, anyway, we have a convincing beginning for a Book 2a (a sequence of three poems, 2. 1–2. 3. 44) and a convincing end (2. 34b) for a book—most obviously for Book 2b, if we are accepting that two ancient books have been compressed into our Book 2. What may now occupy us is with what poem or poems Book 2a ended and with what poem or poems Book 2b began—always supposing that these poems survive.

---

[52] On 3. 22, 23, 24 and 25 cf. the brief but suggestive comments of Williams (1968), 490–1. Cf. how 1. 17–19 arguably form a closing sequence to the Cynthia poems of Book 1. But in 'Book 4', while 4. 11 has clearly closural force, 4. 9 and 10 seem to me to contribute in no obvious way to a closing sequence. Back in Book 1 again, 21 and 22 clearly pair as a mixture of closing *sphragis* and political statement; but 20 requires comment.

[53] See my forthcoming article 'Propertius 2. 30b' [not published]; the phrase is borrowed from Conte (1984), 121–33.

Heyworth argued that 2. 13 opened Book 2b.[54] I agree it is inceptive. 2. 14 is then a magnificent candidate for the next poem in a continuing opening sequence: containing the secret of successful love (11–20), it provocatively and publicly celebrates the triumph of *militia amoris* (1–10, 23–8,), and it suggests the conquest of death by love (10, 16), thus countering the death *for* love that 2. 13 suggested. And 2. 15 also plausibly maintains the progress. It works from a particular event, a 'nox candida' of love; this prompts Propertius to advocate love-making in light and nudity (12, 'si nescis, *oculi* sunt in amore duces'); and this then turns into a brilliantly concrete restatement of the 'life of love', of 'uiuamus...atque amemus...' and of Propertius' own 'quare, dum *licet*, inter nos laetemur amantes' (Catull. 5 and Prop. 1. 19. 25): note especially lines 23–4 'dum nos fata sinunt, *oculos* satiemus amore: | nox tibi longa uenit, nec reditura dies', 49 'tu modo, dum *lucet*, fructum ne desere uitae'. I have argued elsewhere[55] that it is 2. 12 which in fact opened Book 2b, while 2. 13 continues the process of introduction. And if we view 2. 12–15 as a whole we have an utterly convincing inceptive sequence, as convincing in its own way as 2. 1–3. 44.

But where did Book 2a end? 2. 8 and 9a[56] read to me as closural: 2. 8, Cynthia has been snatched away, and Propertius is shattered; 2. 9a, Propertius adverts to his supplanter, complains of Cynthia's faithlessness, compares her with faithful figures of myth—and, in spite of it all, promises his fidelity to her, 45–6 'nec domina ulla meo ponet uestigia lecto: | solus ero, quoniam non licet esse tuum'. A bitter little joke then rounds off the poem. Do we not have a sense of impending closure? And then comes 2. 10. Hutchinson and Heyworth have usefully argued for its closural force, rebutting Lachmann's belief that it opened Book 2b.[57] In many respects I am in agreement with them. But the biggest difference between us is that I join 2. 10 to 2. 11.[58] My belief is that we have a closural sequence 2. 8, 2. 9a, 2. 10/11.

Before I offer my final thoughts on 2. 10/11, we might try to take stock of what may be the two books, 2a and 2b, or rather their remnants.

Let us suppose that Book 2b opened with 2. 12–15 and closed with 2. 34b and contained the text in between. Book 1 contained 706 lines, our 'Book 3'

---

[54] Cf. Heyworth (1995), 167–8; cf. too Heyworth (1992), 45–9, discussing the unity of 2. 13, its opening status, etc.

[55] See Lyne (1998*d*) [= Ch. 12 in this volume].

[56] i.e. 2. 9. 1–48. With Goold (1990) and many before him I can find no place for 2. 9. 49–52 in 2. 9, even supposing a lacuna. This is one of the many floating fragments or excerpts that complicate our reading of 'Book 2'.

[57] Hutchinson (1984), 100, Heyworth (1995), 166–7. See further below subsection (2).

[58] Heyworth (1995), 168 wonders how 2. 11 and 2. 12 'intruded' between the end of Book 2a and the beginning of Book 2b.

has 990, and 'Book 4' 952 (cf. Section I). In 2. 12–34 there are 976 lines. *Prima facie* we may see here our Book 2b—though there is, among other numerous problems, the question of dislocation mentioned in the next paragraph.

2. 1–3. 44 opened Book 2a. 2. 8–10/11 are I think convincingly closural. But in 2. 1–11 there are only 386 lines *in toto*. So, for a start, we should have to suppose that there has been severe loss of text if 2. 1–11 are the remnant of Book 2a—but we are faced from time to time with what seem to be accidental fragments or intentional excerpts, so explanations for this can be found. Then, however, there is the question of dislocation of poems between our putative books. Heyworth thinks that the position in which some poems now stand suggests membership of the wrong book. He thinks for example that 2. 9. 25–28 (lines on Cynthia's illness), presumptively in Book 2a, may presuppose 2. 28, presumptively in Book 2b. I rather doubt this. The topic is one that is available enough (cf. e.g. Tibull. 1. 5. 9–18). More troublesome to me is 2. 23/24. 1–10: this piece surely belongs, as Heyworth sees (though he concentrates on 2. 24), in Propertius' second book.[59] Substantially, however, 2. 12–34 may reflect Propertius' original third book, and 2. 1–11 may be the residue of his second.

But now let me get to grips with 2. 10/11 as a closural poem.

(2) Propertius 2. 10/11 as Closural: '2. 10'

Working with 2. 10 alone, Hutchinson and Heyworth have shown its affinities with other closural texts. Hutchinson[60] compared the first couplet of 2. 10 with the closing lines (541–2) of Verg. *Georg.* Book 2: 'sed nos immensum spatiis confecimus aequor, | et iam tempus equum fumantia soluere colla'. It should be added that Propertius' allusion in 2. 10 is not just to the close of *Georg.* 2, but also to the opening of *Georg.* 3.[61] Vergil, who there looks forward to his epic, has the same idea of ascent: 8–9 'temptanda uia est, qua me quoque possim | *tollere humo*' (cf. Prop. 2. 10. 11) 'uictorque uirum uolitare per ora' (and in Vergil an allusion to Ennius is unmistakable);[62] and Vergil gives the same sense of his enterprise already beginning: 22 'iam nunc...' (cf. Prop. 2. 10. 13). I would see these further allusions not as marring the closural status of '2. 10', but as reinforcing points in it which I have mentioned above.

---

[59] For Heyworth's views on both 2. 9. 25–8 and 2. 24 see (1995), 169. I am accepting, provisionally, Scaliger's junction of 2. 23 and 2. 24. 1–10, adopted by Goold (1990).

[60] Hutchinson (1984).

[61] Wimmel (1960), 193, 195–6, 199, 201 already well brings out the influence on Prop. 2. 10 of the end of Verg. *Georg.* 2 and the beginning of *Georg.* 3.

[62] With 'uictorque uirum uolitare per ora', cf. Ennius' 'epitaph' *Varia* 18V = Epigrams 10 Warmington 'uolito uiuos per ora uirum'. Cf. above n. 36.

Propertius, talking of epic in this poem, is compromising and postponing (or at least wishing to give us this impression), as Vergil is in *Georg*. 3; indeed he is offering his interim mite, as Vergil does: he is not actually 'refusing'. The poem is closural, but also promissory. Propertius is closural and promissory in the one poem, where Vergil had been closural at the end of one book, and promissory at the beginning of the next. Vergil will go on to higher things. In the next book, in some other book, Propertius too will proceed to higher things. Maybe.

Heyworth[63] adduces among other pertinent texts the very relevant last line of Callimachus' *Aetia* epilogue, fr. 112. 9 αὐτὰρ ἐγὼ Μουσέων πεζὸν ἔπειμι νομόν, 'but I will pass on to the prose pasture of the Muses'. Whether this signalled a succeeding text of the *Iambi* in a collected edition of Callimachus' works (vel sim.), or whether it announced the imminence of *Iambi* not yet published,[64] it too is both closural and promissory, as Propertius '2. 10' wishes to appear. As, yet again, I use the word 'promissory', I should perhaps be quite explicit: unlike Vergil and Calllimachus, Propertius' feinting promise is no doubt insincere. Anything more than the interim mite which '2. 10' itself offers is unlikely even to be in the planning stages.

But let me now suggest how the whole text, 2. 11 with 2. 10, most convincingly and cleverly draws Book 2a to a close.

(3) 2. 10/11: The Contribution of '11' to Closure

(i). The *scribo* motif. We have seen that the total structure of 2. 10/11 reverses that of a 'recusatio': '*I* shall tell of Caesar (but not yet, not anyway in full), *others* may write of Cynthia.' The first part of the structure ('I shall tell of Caesar') is closural in the forward-looking ('promissory') mode of Callimachus (and cf. Verg. in *Georg*. 3 *init.*). The second part ('Others may write about you, Cynthia, and waste energy on paltry, mortal "munera"') closes in retrospective mode, surveying the preceding production, Book 2a.

---

[63] Heyworth (1995), 166–7.

[64] Pfeiffer (1949) on fr. 112. 9 briefly states the thesis of a later, collected edition of Callimachus' works in which the epilogue was added to the *Aetia*, its last line effecting the transition to the text of the *Iambi* (he likewise argued that the 'Telchines' preface, our fr. 1, was added to a second edition of the *Aetia* or to a collected edition of his works: Pfeiffer (1928), 302–41). Parsons (1977), 50 intrudes caution, elaboration, and refinement: he thinks that the epilogue was fitted (together with the new prologue, fr. 1) to a new edition of the *Aetia*, when Books 3–4, framed by honorific pieces to Berenice, were added to Books 1–2 (and at that point the *Iambi* would already have been published). But Knox (1985), 59–66 suggests that the epilogue was composed for the earlier issue of *Aetia* Books 1–2 and looked forward to *Iambi* not yet published. For a summary of the views of Pfeiffer, Parsons, and Knox, see Cameron (1995), 104, 112, 145, 157–8.

'Scribant de te alii' (2. 11. 1) picks up Propertius' statement in 2. 10. 8 'scripta puella mea est'; and both these close the dominant introductory motif of Book 2a: the *writing* of the book. The book opened with the interrogatory 'quaeritis, unde mihi totiens scribantur amores' (2. 1. 1)...How come all these love poems are *written*? Whence this *book* (2. 1. 2, cf. 2. 3. 4)? The answer: the inspirational Cynthia. In 2. 10/11 the closure: 'my girl has now been written by me; others can write about her and waste their time.' In short, the whole key conceit of the programmatic 2. 1 and following (Cynthia inspires writing) is now dismissed, denied, and closed.[65]

(ii). *Munera*. We should now affirm the full impact of 'munera' in 2. 11. 3 (cf. Section IV). In poems 2. 2 and 2. 3 Propertius praised Cynthia's inspirational physical features; in 2. 3 he said that it was not so much these physical attributes (though deserving further recital) that inspired his second book of poetry, but her artistic accomplishments. And the climactic summary of this totality was 2. 3. 25 'caelestia munera', 'heavenly gifts': 'haec tibi contulerunt caelestia munera diui, | haec tibi ne matrem forte dedisse putes. | non, non humani partus sunt talia dona...', 'these heavenly gifts the gods bestowed on you, lest you think your mother gave you them. No, no, such presents are no part of human parentage...'. Now we find that, just as the inceptive, positive presentation of Cynthia and writing was dismissed and abandoned, so too the divine and inspiring 'munera' of the opening sequence are conclusively dismissed as topics for poetry. These gifts are (Propertius now says) merely mortal, they will die with Cynthia, they are not—for Propertius—worth writing about. By contrast, the achievements of Caesar (2. 10. 4, 13–18): they, we infer, are immortal and worthwhile. (We may also infer an implied play on words. 'Munera', 'gifts', are also the 'duties' of statesmen.[66]) Further effective closure.

---

[65] 'Scribo' is used in a self-reflexive manner within the remnants of the putative Book 2a too: 2. 5. 27, Tibullus may knock his girl around, but Propertius will *write* his retaliation to bad behaviour on Cynthia's part (cf. Solmsen (1961), 273–89). The one other use of a 'scribo' cognate in this Book 2a is 2. 3. 21: Cynthia produces 'scripta'. In 2. 13. 12 'scripta' plays a leading role in the introduction of the putative Book 2b; it plays a prominent role in 3. 9. 45 in the description of 'Book 3', and in 3. 23. 2 it contributes to a closural motif. 'Scribo' and cognates occur often in other passages of Propertius, but not with quite the same key force as in Book 2a and perhaps 'Book 3'. Interesting from my present point of view (self-reflexive, or potentially self-reflexive) are 1. 18. 22, 2. 34. 87, 3. 9. 3, 3. 23. 19, 4. 1. 136 (and perhaps 3. 3. 21 deserves consideration in this context); less interesting (from this point of view) are 2. 23. 8, 2. 28. 44, 3. 8. 26, 3. 20. 16, 3. 23. 24, 4. 3. 72, 4. 5. 37, 4. 7. 83. There are 'scriptores' at 2. 34. 65 and 3. 1. 12. (This is I think a complete list of 'scribo' cognates in Propertius.)

[66] Cf. *OLD* s.v. 2 'A duty owed by a citizen to the State (e.g. military service, tenure of magistracies)...'. Cf. Cic. *Ver.* 3. 98 'multa sunt imposita huic ordini munera, multi labores', Livy 9. 3. 5 'is grauis annis non militaribus solum sed ciuilibus quoque abscesserat

(iii). *Docta puella*. Cynthia has been 'written', her 'gifts' are merely mortal, not worthy of poetry. What of the 'docta puella', the 'learned', 'artful' girl (2. 11. 6)? Here too we find closure, and in the same vein. 'Doctrina' had been a leading, indeed programmatic, Cynthia motif. Prop. 1. 7. 11 presented her as 'docta', in the cycle of poems explaining the source and purpose of love poetry to the epic poet Ponticus: 'me laudent doctae solum placuisse puellae', 'let them praise me that I alone found favour with a learned, artful girl' (where the sense is equivocal between Propertius the lover/poet and Cynthia the accomplished beloved/discerning critic); we heard about Cynthia's accomplishments, enough to merit the epithet 'docta', in 1. 2. 27–30. At the beginning of Book 2a (2. 1. 3–4) the inspirational Cynthia, in a nice play with Callimachus, is presented as Propertius' Muse (see above, Section V). We remember that way back in Hesiod's time the Muses are associated with teaching, they 'taught' Hesiod song (*Theog*. 22 ἐδίδαξαν ἀοιδήν), and for the post-Catullan poet (at least) the Muses are 'doctae':[67] Catullus 65. 2 refers to the 'doctis...uirginibus', and this is echoed in Prop. 2. 30b, where the Muses are 'uirginibus' (33) and the epithet 'docta' is transferred to the accompanying Bacchus' 'cuspis' (38). So, Cynthia presented as Muse in 2. 1. 3–4, has her aura of 'doctrina' reinforced. Then, among Cynthia's divine, inspirational accomplishments in 2. 3 is the fact that she is 'par Aganippaeae ludere docta lyrae', 'artful to play something to match Aganippe's lyre' (20); nor do we need the explicit word 'docta' to infer Cynthia's treasured artistic 'doctrina' from 2. 3 esp. 19–22. Cynthia, therefore, in these inceptive and programmatic poems, is 'docta'. But then in 2. 11. 6: a chilling closure. Looking forward to Cynthia's death, to the death of her 'munera', and to the disdain her bones will incur, Propertius says: 'the traveller will *not* say: "this ash was a *docta puella*".' This is closure, forceful and damning. The great inspirational characteristic that this book and the previous one had constructed for Cynthia is effectively undone. Her 'doctrina' will be lost to knowledge.

(iv). *Docta puella*, and the ironic mode. 'Her "doctrina" will be lost to knowledge.' But of course it won't. This is a brilliant, ironic, ambiguous closure. Maybe the 'uiator' will not say Cynthia was a 'docta puella', but it is being said. Propertius is saying it: 'cinis hic docta puella fuit'. And the words will last as long as literature lasts: and for the sanguine, this is forever, as Propertius will tell us in 3. 2, drawing on Horace and a long tradition.

muneribus'. The only other use of 'munus' in Book 2a is 2. 8. 11. For other uses of the word in Propertius (but not a complete list) see n. 45 above.

[67] Some post-Catullan examples are cited by Fordyce (1961) ad loc. See too *TLL* 5. 1. 1757. 34–44 which gives Catullus 65. 2 as the first instance of 'doctus' 'de deis'. In Greek culture, it is typically the poet who is σοφός: cf. e.g. Nisbet and Hubbard on Hor. *Odes* 1. 1. 29. The use of διδάσκω cited above in connection with the Muses in Hesiod is perhaps particularly interesting.

Propertius' ironic method of (ultimately) immortalizing Cynthia as 'docta' is—one might feel—related to the post-modern mode of expression that Umberto Eco talks about.[68]

We could say similar things about the whole tenor of 2. 11. 3–6. On the face of it they deny, they chillingly close the bright opening that is (for example) 2. 3. 29–32:[69] there Cynthia has a future, and it sounds like an immortal one, as consort of Jupiter. 2. 11. 3–6 tell us that she and everything about her will die (no sharing Jupiter's bed for example, her bed will be her bier). On the other hand the lines ensure precisely the opposite: that she will live. Here we are now reading about her and her accomplishments. The lines participate in the perpetuation of her future.

(v). More parallels with 2. 1; closural ring-composition. Cynthia inspires (2. 1), Cynthia doesn't inspire—it's all written etc. (2. 10/11). Augustus doesn't inspire (2. 1), Augustus does inspire (2. 10/11). 'Laus' has now been transferred from love and Cynthia (2. 1. 47 *bis*) to Augustan praise-poetry and its rewards (2. 10. 6 and 23); 'bella', refused as a subject of poetry in 2. 1. 25 and 28, are accepted in 2. 10. 8; likewise 'tumultus': refused in 2. 1. 39, accepted in 2. 10. 7.[70] On top of these thematic and lexical rings between the two poems, we will also note the theme of death, tomb, and epitaph.

In 2. 1 Propertius envisages his death, his death-for-love, 2. 1. 47–78 'laus in amore mori...'. He imagines his tomb. The great Maecenas, passing by on the road (75–6), is asked to pause, and (77–8),

> taliaque illacrimans mutae iace uerba fauillae:
> 'huic misero fatum dura puella fuit.'

and shedding a tear, let fall these words for my silent embers: 'a harsh girl was the death of this wretched man'.

---

[68] I refer to a well-known passage in the 'Postille a "Il nome della rosa" 1983' (see Eco (1995), 528–9: 'Il post-moderno... Ironia, gioco metalinguistico'). In Eco's now celebrated example, the post-modern lover is inhibited from saying 'ti amo disperatamente', since it has been said too often, it is the sort of thing that is said in the sentimental novels of Liala; and he says instead 'Come direbbe Liala, ti amo disperatamente'. In this way he is dissociated from the unsayable sentiment, but nevertheless manages to say it in an *ironic* mode. Comparably, Propertius is dissociated from saying 'cinis hic docta puella fuit', but in an ironic mode still manages to say it. (In the English version of the *Postille,* Eco (1984), 67–8, Barbara Cartland is used instead of Liala. The post-modern lover is unable to say 'I love you madly', but can say 'As Barbara Cartland would put it, I love you madly.') D. P. Fowler has already used the insight of Umberto Eco, and the quoted passage, to illuminate brilliantly Catullus 51: see Fowler (1989*b*), 112–13. Cf. too Fowler (1994), esp. 236–7, citing the same passage of Eco in an interpretation of Theognis 236–54.

[69] Goold (1990), prints Sterke's reordering of these lines (29, 32, 31, 30), correctly I think.

[70] These are the only examples of 'laus' and 'tumultus' in the putative Propertius Book 2a. 'Bellum' occurs in addition to the examples cited at 2. 3. 35 and 40, safely mythical.

And so poem 2. 1 ends. Romantic agony, *Liebestod*, and so on:[71] but also, of course, self-praise and fame in death: 'laus', attention from the great man, and Maecenas' succinct, commiserating *epitaphios*.

2. 11. 5–6 gathers up the theme of death and *epitaphios*, in neat closural ring-composition:

> et tua transibit contemnens ossa uiator,
> nec dicet 'cinis hic docta puella fuit'.

and the traveller will pass by your bones in disdain, and will not say: 'this ash was an artful girl.'

Propertius delivers chilling contrast to the close of 2. 1. Cynthia's death and tomb are envisaged, not his. And for her there will be no great man pausing at her tomb, and no *epitaphios*. Far from it, an anonymous traveller will pass on by in scorn, and will not bother to utter her commemoration. So: ring-composition, stark with contrasts, closes the book.

Unless, of course, you read the close in what we may call an Eco way. There is after all a great man at Cynthia's tomb, and there is an *epitaphios* to match Maecenas' *epitaphios* for Propertius. Propertius is there, and Propertius delivers the eulogy: 'cinis hic docta puella fuit'.

(vi). A final point is worth noting. Given that the ironic, Eco reading of the close of 2a is magnificently available—*Propertius* constructs an epitaphios, *Propertius* still assigns the key epithet 'docta'—this close is indeed not as devastating as it might at first sight seem, especially when we remember that death is an inseparable part of Propertius' erotic thinking.[72] There is therefore no great surprise that a third book of Cynthia poetry quite swiftly followed, nor that her lead epithet is 'docta' (2. 13. 11).

---

[71] Cf. the interesting comments on this poem of Papanghelis (1987), 47–9 (and see his Index of Passages for further comments).

[72] It is worth here referring the reader in a general way to the important book of Papanghelis (1987).

APPENDIX

Some Supplementary Notes on Permessus etc. as Imagined by Vergil, Gallus, and Others[73]

(i). A Low-lying River Permessus in Relation to Mt. Helicon

Callimachus made reference to Permessus in his Helicon scene (cf. *Aetia* fr. 2a. 20), but we cannot tell how he situated it. We can say more about Vergil and Gallus. If Gallus, wandering by the river Permessus, is led onto Helicon (*Ecl.* 6. 64–5), Permessus or the relevant stretch of Permessus is presumably imagined—by Vergil and Gallus—as situated at the foot of Helicon. This is plausible, in real terms. Strabo 9. 2. 19 (C 407) tells us that 'the Permessus and the Olmeius, flowing from Helicon, meet one another and empty into Lake Copais near Haliartus'; Pausanias 9. 29. 5 tells us that the Permessus (under its variant name Termessus) flows 'round Helicon'. West on Hesiod, *Theog.* 5 discusses modern brooks which might suit Strabo's quite detailed description and favours the stream Zagará 'which flows from the northern side of the same watershed [as a rival candidate, Archontitsa] near the top of the mountain [Helicon]'. More importantly for us (because more important for the key Roman poets), the text of Hesiod, *Theog.* 5–7 might imply that Permessus is low-lying compared with the summit of Helicon: 'having washed their tender skin in Permessus or Hippocrene or holy Olmeius, the Muses made their fair, graceful dances on topmost Helicon.'

(ii). Hippocrene and Helicon

This text (Hes. *Theog.* 5–7) would then also imply, of course, that *Hippocrene* is low-lying in relation to the summit of Helicon. And if one puts together Hesiod, *Theog.* 23 (Hesiod met the Muses while 'shepherding lambs beneath holy Helicon') and Callimachus fr. 2. 1–2 (Hesiod met the Muses while tending sheep by Hippocrene) and fr. 112. 5–6 (according to the conventional interpretation of these Callimachean lines which sees them again linking Hippocrene to Hesiod: but see above n. 40), one would make the same inference. We do not know what Gallus did with Hippocrene. But Prop. 2. 10. 25 seems to envisage Hippocrene high up, if not at the summit of Helicon. This actually accords with modern views of the identity and situation of Hippocrene (West on Hesiod, *Theog.* 6, Hippocrene 'can with some confidence be identified with the modern Kriopigádi, a perennial source of cold, clear water near the summit of

---

[73] Cf., most recently, Clausen's note (1984) on Vergil, *Ecl.* 6. 64.

Helicon'). But I doubt that Propertius' autoptic knowledge of the summit of Helicon would have survived a searching viva-voce examination; I imagine he suggests its summit position (if that is what he does) through a combination of luck and desire, and perhaps the precedent of Gallus and/or Ennius.

(iii). A Detail in Nicander

Another text to observe is Nicander, *Ther.* 11 εἰ ἐτεόν περ | Ἀσκραῖος μυχάτοιο Μελισσήεντος ἐπ' ὄχθαις | Ἡσίοδος κατέλεξε παρ' ὕδασι Περμησσοῖο, 'if indeed he spoke the truth, Ascraean Hesiod, on the rising ground (banks, heights) of secluded Melisseeis by the waters of Permessus.' The scholiast on Nicander tells us that Melisseeis was the part of Helicon where Hesiod received instruction from the Muses: 'beneath holy Helicon', according to *Theog.* 23. So Nicander's picture is not inconsistent, I suppose, with a Permessus low-lying at the foot of Helicon, as imagined by the sources already mentioned. But there is an important point of conflict with other texts (with Vergil–Gallus, Propertius 2. 10, perhaps Callimachus, Hesiod himself): the close association of Hesiod's own composition with Permessus. For Hesiod, Permessus (*Theog.* 5) is incidental to his own composition, in particular to his initiation (22–35); in Vergil–Gallus and Propertius, at least, Permessus is opposed to Hesiodic production. This reminds us that for these poets invention and variation could be a potent factor, and a predecessor's authority—even the master's—could be more or less important.

15

Propertius and Tibullus: Early Exchanges[1] (1998)

This paper sets out in Section I the most useful evidence we possess for the dating of Propertius Book 1, Tibullus Book 1, and Propertius Books 2a and 2b.[2] The evidence squares with a sequence of publication: Prop. 1, Tib. 1, Prop. 2a, Prop. 2b, which is what, in my view, literary considerations suggest. Most important, or at least most interesting, of these considerations are the

---

[1] Parallels between the two poets have of course been extensively noted: as well as the bibliography cited from time to time below (especially Jacoby 1961), see e.g. Murgatroyd (1980), 13–15, 50 f.; the apparatus of Lenz & Galinsky (1971); Enk (1962), 34–45; La Penna (1950), 209–36, La Penna (1951), 43–69, esp. La Penna (1950), 233–6, discussion of Propertius–Tibullus, and La Penna (1951), 56–9, an appendix listing some Prop.–Tib. parallels. But scholars underestimate or miss entirely the fact that the two poets are in amusing dialogue, delivering ripostes: e.g. Enk on p. 44: 'Si quis rogat, num Propertius e lectis elegiis Tibulli fructum ceperit, cum librum secundum scriberet, respondendum est cum viro docto D'Elia...: "Si può concludere, che gli incontri, certo interessanti, sono puramente superficiali"; cf. the summary of La Penna (1950), 235–6 and (1951), 55. There are exceptions to this kind of misappreciation. Solmsen (below n. 51) is a very notable one; Hubbard (1974), 61 ff. has interesting material, discussing e.g. Prop. 2. 16 which she sees as challenging comparison with Tib. 1. 9 and, in lines 43ff., not only echoing 1. 9. 11 f., but amusingly inverting Tib. 1. 4. 21 ff.; Cairns (1979), 53 f. argues that Tibullus' Elysium in 1. 3 supplies Prop. 4. 7. 59 ff.; Griffin (1985), 151 f. sees a relation between the heroines in the Underworld of Prop. 1. 19. 13–16 and Tib. 1. 3. 57 ff., reckoning that 'influence between the two, in either direction, is a possibility' (a Tibullan relation to Prop. 1. 19 is discussed below); further important information and acute comment in Griffin pp. 144 ff. There are of course many links between the two poets which I shall not be discussing in this paper, even between Tibullus Book 1 and Propertius 'Book 2', the books to which this paper attends.

[2] I put the primary evidence on view; in literary commentaries and books it can be hard to come by. In e.g. Enk (1946), 16–19, Murgatroyd (1980), 11 ff., Hubbard (1974), 42–4, Fedeli (1980), 10 and 168, the illumination is limited. As for Propertius Book 2a and Book 2b, I accept the basic thesis of Lachmann that the transmitted Book 2 of Propertius contains the remains of two original books. For a succinct argument in favour of Lachmann's view, see Skutsch (1975), 229–33. But see further Heyworth (1995), 165–85. I agree with Heyworth that 2. 10 is not a likely candidate for the introductory poem of Book 2b (Lachmann); Heyworth puts the case persuasively for believing (*a*) that 2. 10 was closural in Book 2a (following a point made by Hutchinson (1984), 100, who does not however believe in the division of 'Book 2'), and (*b*), following Richmond, that 2. 13 was inceptive in Book 2b; cf. too Heyworth (1992), 45–9 on 2. 13, discussing its unity, opening status, and so on. I have some reason to question whether 2. 13 was actually and precisely the *first* poem in Book 2b, but now is not the time to discuss this.

signs of response and counter-response between the two poets. I detect spirited ripostes by the poets, one to the other. Section II examines some Tibullan responses to Propertius Book 1, and Section III some Propertian responses, in 'Book 2', to Tibullus Book 1.

I. DATES

1. The Lowest Date in Propertius Book 1

We look for a hard fact. What is the latest date we can find, before which the book cannot have been published?

The most useful has to be extracted from Prop. 1. 6. Propertius' addressee Tullus proposes travelling to the East; Asia is given prominent mention (14); his uncle will deploy 'axes' (19 f.), emblems of a magistracy.

This uncle must be L. Volcacius Tullus, consul in 33 BC: his consulship is recorded in the *Fasti Venusini*, Degrassi *Inscriptiones Italiae* 13. 1: text pp. 254 and 255, commentary p. 251. Another inscription then testifies without ambiguity to the fact that L. Volcacius Tullus was proconsul of Asia: see Ehrenberg and Jones (1955), no. 98.[3]

Prop. 1. 6. 19–20 read:

> tu patrui meritas conare anteire securis,
> et uetera oblitis iura refer sociis.

Goold[4] translates: 'You must attempt to surpass your uncle's merited axes and to restore the old laws to forgetful allies.' When line 14 (*Asiae*) is included, we cannot but see here a reference to L. Volcacius Tullus' proconsulship in Asia. *Secures* preceded a proconsul as well as a consul (or praetor, dictator): cf. Cic. *Ver.* 4. 8 'mercatorem in prouinciam cum imperio ac securibus misimus...', 5. 39 'secuta prouincia est...fascis ac securis et tantam imperi uim'.[5] The situation

---

[3] A supplementary fragment from Apamea clinched the fact of L. Volcacius Tullus' Asian proconsulship: see Jones (1955), 244 f.; but the 2nd edn. of Ehrenberg and Jones incorporates it.

[4] In the Loeb edition Goold (1990) provides a challengingly independent text and useful notes and introduction, as well as translation.

[5] *Secures* ('axes') belong with the *fasces* ('bundles of rods'). The two are sometimes mentioned specifically and separately as a couple (cf. e.g. Lucr. 3. 996 as well as the Cicero quoted in the text), but often *secures* are—in prescribed circumstances—a physical but unspecified component of the 'bundles of rods', i.e. of the emblems, indeed instruments, of *imperium*, which lictors bore in front of magistrates (consuls, praetors, proconsuls, and others; *fasces* were originally inherited by the consuls from the kings (Livy 2. 1. 7 f.)). The word *fasces* is therefore slightly ambiguous: it depended on where the magistrate was operating whether the *fasces* 'bundles of rods' contained *secures* 'axes' or not, and *fasces* could apply to both—rods with axes

behind the poem is, I think, clear. The young Tullus is to be part of the governor's personally chosen entourage of well-to-do subordinates, his *cohors* of *amici*,[6] and has suggested that Propertius participate too. Goold's 'surpass' is a legitimate translation (cf. Propertius' other use of *anteire*, 2. 3. 41), though there is probably some play on a literal sense of 'precede' (for which see Camps ad loc.). But with 'surpass' Propertius indulges in chaffing hyperbole. It is surely wrong—dangerously over-literal—to infer from the suggestion of competition some independent command of the young Tullus: Tullus is a young man, he is the friend of a poet, he has a powerful uncle with a proconsular command, there is the institution of the governor's cohort, there are the close parallels of e.g. Catullus and Memmius, Propertius seems to have the option of participating: the conclusions that Tullus is to act as an *amicus* on L. Volcacius Tullus' proconsular staff, and that it is to this that Propertius refers, are irresistible.[7]

But when was this proconsulship? The Ehrenberg and Jones inscription, itself a later document (probably 9 BC, say E. and J.), does not date Volcacius Tullus' proconsulship. A decree that 'no-one, neither an ex-praetor nor an ex-consul, should assume a command abroad before five years had elapsed' had been proposed (δόγμα ἐποιήσαντο) by the consuls Cn. Domitius Calvinus and

and rods without axes. *Secures*, instruments of execution (see below), were present in the *fasces* of magistrates only outside the city. Cic. *Rep.* 2. 55 tells us that (in 509 BC) Valerius Publicola 'lege illa de prouocatione perlata statim secures de fascibus demi iussit'; Dionysius of Halicarnassus 5. 19. 3 makes it more explicit: Valerius Publicola 'desiring to give the plebeians a definite pledge of their liberty, took the axes from the rods (ἀφεῖλεν ἀπὸ τῶν ῥάβδων τοὺς πελέκεις) and established it as the custom for his successors in the consulship—which has lasted down until my day—that, whenever they are outside the city, they make use of the axes, but, within the city, they are distinguished by the rods (ῥάβδοι, i.e. the *fasces* in the narrower sense) only.' (Some modern scholars think this association of the removal of the axes with the law *de prouocatione* is false: they think that from the start *secures* were included in the *fasces* only *militiae* and not *domi*: this is discussed by Stavely (1963), 464–5; but all agree that in (say) Propertius' time *secures* were included in the *fasces* of magistrates only outside the city.) The *secures* signified the power to execute, sometimes directly: Livy 9. 16. 17 f., 28. 29. 11. Reference is made to proconsuls' lictors (ῥαβδοῦχοι) in Dio's account of Augustus' adjustments to senatorial provincial governors (53. 13. 4); for specific mention of *secures* preceding a proconsul, cf. the passages quoted in the text, and for a proconsul employing the *securis* in execution see Cicero's account of Dolabella in *Verr.* 1. 75–6.

[6] This institution is important and well-documented: cf. Gelzer (1975), 101 f.; Cic. *Q. F.* 1. 1. 11–12 (a key text, though Gelzer and Shackleton Bailey's commentary differ slightly in interpretation of detail); the racy but informative poems of Catullus (10, 28, 46); Hor. *Epist.* 1. 3; the amusing letters of Cicero to Trebatius Testa, *Fam.* 7. 6, 17, 18; and Cic. *Cael.* 73 on M. Caelius' service as *contubernalis* to Q. Pompeius Rufus proconsul of Africa in 61 BC is another key text: 'cum autem paulum iam roboris accessisset aetati, in Africam profectus est Q. Pompeio pro consule contubernalis.... usus quidam prouincialis non sine causa a maioribus huic aetati tributus'. And Cicero, like Propertius, refers to such service as *militia*. See n. 22 below.

[7] An over-literal view is recorded by Enk ad loc. More thoughtfully, but still unconvincingly to me, Cairns (1974), 161–2 works with the possibility of etymological play between *anteire* and *praeire* / *praetor* to suggest that the young Tullus had a position as *praetor* or *propraetor* or *legatus* / *quaestor pro praetore*.

M. Valerius Messalla in late 53 BC, and confirmed by Pompey (ἐπεκύρωσεν) in 52 BC: Cassius Dio 40. 46. 2 and 40. 56. 1. Presumably therefore a *lex Pompeia*, determining a five-year gap between consul- /praetor-ship and provincial governorship. But scholars doubt, surely correctly, that it was still applied in our period.[8] So: we are left with the hard date of Volcacius Tullus' consulship (33 BC), the hard fact of his proconsulship, the reference to it in Prop. 1. 6. 19 f. (and 14)—and the implications of Prop. 1. 6. 20: disaffection in the provinces (for the use of *socius* see *OLD* s.v. 4b). This line can surely only refer to a period immediately after Actium. We may infer a proconsulship in 30/29 BC—as many of course have done (e.g. Enk on 1. 6. 19). But it is as well to set out the evidence clearly.

The book cannot have been published earlier than 30 BC. Another suggestion: it is perhaps unlikely that Propertius would issue Book 1 when the events of 1. 6, relating directly to his addressee, were stale. Rather, when they were still topical.

2. The Lowest Date in Tibullus Book 1

The *Fasti triumphales Capitolini* (Degrassi 13. 1 p. 87) record Messalla's triumph *pro consule ex Gallia* on 25 September 27 BC. Tibullus refers to this triumph in 1. 7. 3–8. It is a certain date, and it is the latest certain date which we have in his first book.[9] The book cannot have been published before this.

One wonders whether Tibullus would issue his book when feats performed by his addressee were stale. But this kind of thought has less force, perhaps, in Tibullus' and Messalla's case, than in Propertius' and Tullus'. Prop. 1. 6 is, or poses as, a topical poem; Tibullus 1. 7 celebrates the birthday of one of Rome's illustrious statesmen, and the accomplishment of a triumph is hardly something to go out of fashion.

3. Propertius 'Book 2' and Relative Dating

So: hard dates suggest, or at least they concur with the inference, that Tibullus Book 1 follows Propertius 1; as most but not all scholars have assumed.[10] Now

---

[8] Richardson, *CAH*[2] ix. 575 thinks it lapsed in 49 BC. Hubbard (1974), 42 f. is certainly right to question whether it could be applied in our period, when many consulars were compromised as ex-Antonians. For further discussion of the law—how it was established and applied, its motives, and so on—see Marshall (1972), 887–921, esp. 891–3.

[9] Syme (1986), ch. 15 attempts a chronology of Messalla's career, seeking *inter alia* to place the other events mentioned in Tib. 1. 7; for the journey lying behind 1. 3 he suggests a date in the spring of 30 BC (pp. 209 f.).

[10] La Penna (1950), 234–6, and La Penna (1977), 17, Cairns (1979), 228. It should not be forgotten that Ov. *Trist.* 4. 10. 51–3 names Propertius as the successor to Tibullus, and *Trist.* 2. 447 ff. lists Tibullus before Propertius; but an operative factor here may be that Tibullus died

we look for dates in Propertius Books 2a and 2b. If we see 2. 10 as closural in 2a (and not as opening a Book 2b), then we have useful material for that book.[11] *Auguste* (2. 10. 15) post-dates 16 January 27 BC (the calendars cited by Ehrenberg and Jones, *Documents* p. 45 give the exactest date; then *Res Gestae* 34, etc.); the book could not have been published before then. The reference in 2. 10. 15 to the submission of India points to 26–25 BC; it is to this time that, if we pursue references in *Res Gestae*, Orosius, Dio and Suetonius, we can date one of the embassies from India. The reference to fear in an Arabia yet *intacta* in the next line suggests the same time: an expedition is impending but has not yet happened. The best date for the ill-starred Arabian expedition which actually ensued (that of Aelius Gallus) is to be inferred from Dio 53. 29. 3–8, and is 25–24 BC. Arabia could not have been termed *intacta* after the commencement of the campaign. So, a publication date for 2a not after 25 BC, but close to that time (embassy from India, Arabian expedition impending).[12] Looking at the rest of 'Book 2' we find one other fairly hard piece of dating. 2. 34. 91–2 refer to the death of the poet Cornelius Gallus, assigned by Jerome, *Chronicle* p. 164 H to 27 BC, and by Dio 53. 23. 5 to 26 BC;[13] Book 2(b) must post-date this event.

---

years before Propertius (for Tibullus' death in 19 BC see below; Propertius was alive at least long enough to compose a poem referring to the year 16 BC: see n. 19). Cairns and La Penna mention the possibility of pre-publication influence, via recitations, which is indeed something we should keep in mind (cf. Griffin 1985). It is quite possible in fact that there was a degree of two-way influence between the two poets during their respective first books: the periods of composition must have overlapped. I simply argue that the publication of Tibullus 1 postdates Propertius 1, and that the main one to deliver ripostes in this case is Tibullus. (If I wanted to argue for a Propertian response to Tibullus in Book 1, I would choose Prop. 1. 16. Plaut. *Curc.* 145 ff. assumes an animate, addressable door. Catull. 67 gives the door a voice. Prop. 1. 16 uses the door's voice to mimic (?mock) excluded lovers' songs: cf. Tib. 1. 2. 7 ff. But if Propertius is mocking such songs, there are other poets to canvass as his butts.)

[11] But further problems get in the way of any confidence we may feel. Not only is there insufficient text in 2. 1–10 to amount to a plausible book, so that we have to assume lacunae: confusions in the order of poems caused in the process of transmission may be complicating assignment of poems to 2a or 2b. For the closural status of 2. 10 and for these further problems, see Heyworth (1995).

[12] Indian embassy in 26–25 BC: *Res Gestae* 31 records embassies from India; Orosius 6. 21. 19 tells us that *legati Indorum* met Augustus at Tarraco in Spain; Dio 53. 22. 5 tells us that Augustus left Rome in 27 BC, 'lingered in Gaul', then proceeded to Spain; Suet. *Aug.* 26. 3 tells us that Augustus began his eighth and ninth consulships (26 and 25 BC) at Tarraco; another datable embassy from India falls in 20 BC (Dio 54. 9. 8), clearly too late for our poem. Arabian expedition: the best evidence for this (probably 25–24 BC) comes from Dio 53. 29. 3–8, but it needs careful interpreting. This it gets from Hardy (1923), 123 (Augustus himself refers to the expedition at *RG* 26. 5); the essential points made by Hardy are quoted by Enk (1962), 152. Cf. too Rich's note on Dio 53. 29. 3–8, and La Penna (1950), 48 n. 1. [A later note of Lyne's adds: 'I would now bring the date of Book 2b back a bit, say 25 BC. 2. 34 refers to the death of Gallus as "recently", *modo*.']

[13] Cf. Syme (1939), 309 favouring 27 BC.

We would be interested in any topical references which might suggest publication of any part of 'Book 2' *before* Tibullus Book 1. Poems which invite dating but which tease are: 2. 7 referring to abolished legislation, and 2. 31 referring to the opening of the portico attached to the Temple of Apollo. In the former, although we can perhaps date the abrogation with some plausibility (28 BC), it is not necessarily in close temporal proximity to the poem.[14] As for the latter, the dedication of the Temple itself can of course be dated: to 9 October 28 BC (again the exact date is given by calendars, Ehrenberg and Jones p. 53; then Cassius Dio 53. 1. 3 etc.), but Propertius seems to me to suggest the separation rather than the contemporaneity of the portico-opening and the dedication of the Temple. In short I see no topical reference anywhere in 'Book 2' that forces a date before Tibullus 1 for any of 'Book 2'.

Given the *terminus post quem* dates mentioned above, I would suggest the following order of publication (with approximate dates in brackets): Propertius 1 (28 BC), Tibullus 1 (27 BC), Prop. 2a (26 BC), Prop. 2b (24 BC).[15] This squares with datable facts and makes most sense of the literature, as—from one vantage point—I shall proceed to show. But the suggestion in 2. 3. 3 (however hyperbolic) that Propertius' second book came hard on the heels of his first may need further pondering. And the possibility, perhaps probability, of pre-publication influence by one poet on the other, via for example the medium of recitation, must always be borne in mind (cf. n. 10). (Then following the publication of Horace, *Odes* 1–3

---

[14] For the relevant legislation and its abrogation, see Badian (1985), 82–98. In sum. (i) The (*lex*) *de maritandis ordinibus* which Augustus 'prae tumultu recusantium perferre non potuit' (Suet. *Aug.* 34. 1) must, *pace* influential Propertian commentators, be the Lex Papia Poppaea of AD 9; the Suetonian passage has nothing to do with Prop. 2. 7 (note the dating implications of Suet. *Aug.* 34. 2 'accitos Germanici liberos'). (ii) Propertius' phrase *sublatam legem* must refer to a law actually enacted and then repealed; compromise interpretations which talk of 'proposals' for legislation cannot be accommodated. (iii) It is inconceivable that Augustus should have enacted a marriage law and then repealed it in say 28–27 BC, without this having an impact upon our historical sources. But there is no evidence at all of such legislation and repeal in the historical sources. (iii) So what *lex* does Propertius refer to? A solution (Badian's) is that in the Triumviral years, the cash-hungry Octavian imposed—among many other taxes—a tax on *caelibes* (no new device in fact), which, together with all outstanding debts incurred under it, was then cancelled in 28 BC: Dio 53. 2. 3 records that in that year Augustus 'burnt the old records of debts owed to the treasury', debts incurred in the Triumviral years. Propertius in 2. 7. 1 refers to the cancellation of the tax on *caelibes*, but sees it from his own point of view: as the cancellation of a law that was threatening to impose marriage and the sundering of lovers. Badian suspects a date of 27 BC for the composition of Prop. 2. 7. Possibly. But we should note that the poem suggests no especial immediacy. On the contrary, the tenses even of the lovers' *reactions* to the abrogation is past, and the first couplet is a cue for more general if provocative reflections (*at magnus Caesar: sed magnus Caesar in armis*...). Nor am I convinced by the emendation of *est* to *es* in 2. 7. 1; Postgate's note ad loc. is pertinent. And the third person ('at all events, at least, Cynthia was happy at...') suggests I think even less sense of immediacy. (I am certainly not convinced incidentally by the division that places 2. 6. 41–2 at the beginning of 2. 7.)

[15] I differ thus in one important respect from Hubbard (1974), 42–4 who puts Tibullus 1 between Propertius 2a and 2b 'on the most probable hypothesis' (note that she sees 2. 10 with its datable suggestions as opening 2b rather than closing 2a). For Enk's views see (1962), 34–5.

came Propertius 3;[16] Tibullus Book 2, according to M. D. Reeve's persuasive argument, is unfinished,[17] and was issued posthumously after Tibullus' death in, it seems, 19 BC;[18] Propertius 4 post-dates 16 BC.[19])

II. TIBULLUS RESPONDS TO PROPERTIUS BOOK 1[20]

1. The 'life of love':[21] until Death. Introduction

In his first book of elegies, Tibullus makes declarations concerning love and life which obviously overlap with Propertius'. The two poets shared views and a tradition; but there were differences of substance and emphasis. There was motive for Tibullus to expose such differences. Coming so soon after Propertius (and after Gallus, and Catullus) he would wish to show novelty as well as contiguity. And so he does: he adds, trumps and responds, amusingly smug (for example) instead of riven by *Angst*. Compared with Propertius Book 1, Tibullus can strike one as really quite funny—on topics on which many readers, perhaps not altogether rightly, have detected no Propertian humour or self-irony at all. Tibullan wit is something to emphasize.

Tibullus' opening poem argues a life of leisure in contrast to service in the entourage of a soldier and statesman (*militia*);[22] he disdains the wealth and honour that such service might bring: Tib. 1. 1. 1–6, 41 ff., 49–58. This is much the same message as that delivered by Propertius in 1. 6 and 14.[23] Not

---

[16] For succinct and true comment on the dating of Book 3 see Hubbard (1974), 44.

[17] Reeve (1984), 235–9.

[18] An epigram of Domitius Marsus (7 Courtney), despite efforts to interpret it in different ways, ties Tibullus' death closely in time to Vergil's (Sept. 19 BC). The epigram is correctly interpreted by Courtney and by Murgatroyd (1980), 5 f.

[19] Prop. 4. 11. 66 refers to the consulship of P. Cornelius Scipio in 16 BC. Prop. 4. 6. 77 refers to the submission of the Sygambri, who caused a much exaggerated difficulty in 17 BC: Syme (1933), 17–18.

[20] I am most concerned in this section with Tibullus 1. 1. A seminal article is Jacoby (1909), 601–22 and Jacoby (1910), 22–87 = Jacoby (1961), ii. 122–205; references below will be to the pages of the *KlphS* 1961 edition. Jacoby documents debts of Tibullus in 1. 1 to Propertius (to poems 1. 6, 17, 19, but not 14) and to others (e.g. to Horace). But (i) he has no high opinion of Tibullus' resulting poem (note e.g. ii. 170); (ii) he has no sense of Tibullus responding to, trumping, having fun with, Propertius; what he maps is a Tibullan piecing-together of source material (his 'Arbeitsweise'). Nevertheless, this is still a most important work. Important too is Wimmel (1976), 93–111, discussing the relation of Tibullus to Prop. 1. 6, 17 and 19.

[21] For amplification of this phrase, should it be wanted, see Lyne (1980), 66–81.

[22] For service in the entourage of a provincial governor, see n. 6. Cicero (*Fam.* 7. 18. 1, twice) as well as Propertius (1. 6. 30) uses the actual word *militia* of such service.

[23] Cf. Jacoby (1961), 149 ff.; but he misses Tibullus' relation to Propertius 1. 14 here. Wimmel (1976), 95 ff., discussing Tibullus' relation to Prop. 1. 6, also brings Tibullus 1. 3 into play.

however until Tib. 1. 1. 46, and then esp. 55 f., do we hear of love as a constituent of this life of leisure, not until then do we hear that love gets in the way of Tibullus' honourable and profitable *militia*. And not until 57 is Delia named. These delays tease the reader; this is a calculatedly different introduction from Propertius' self-presentation.[24] Meantime Tibullus asserts a major un-Propertian and idiosyncratic point: the life which, with greater insolence than Propertius, he has called *iners*, 'indolent' (5), is to be rustic (7 ff.). There is additional provocation as well as difference here. Initially Tibullus makes his desired rustic life sound strenuous and moral: so it would seem to most readers, to readers of the *Georgics*, for example (*ipse seram*, and so forth). In fact the life he actually envisages, far from that of a *Georgics* farmer, is the life of the leisured gentleman proprietor, the life which, say, Horace exhibits in *Serm.* 2. 6 or *Epist.* 1. 14. He will merely toy with the work; those strenuously active verbs are just play with the world and language of the *Georgics*.[25]

This rustic situation of Tibullus' dream of love and leisure provides a source of romantic woe unavailable to Propertius—though Propertius found plenty of others. Love in the country can only be a dream beyond realization, given that the habitat of girls like Delia is the city (1. 1. 55 f.).[26] Tibullus' country estate exists, of course (e.g. 1. 1. 19 ff.), but to imagine the urban Delia domiciled there is the purest fantasy.[27] Tibullus structures his first book in two halves,[28] and the last poem of the first half of Tibullus' book (1. 5) elaborately exposes the fact that his dream is and must stay a mere fantasy

[24] From Propertius' self-presentation in 1. 6 and 14 themselves; and these poems are of course preceded by Prop. 1. 1 and ff. with their love and Cynthia emphases.

[25] Cf. further Lyne (1980), 149 ff. The tease in Tibullus' rustic vision (initially he makes this life of leisure sound moral and hardy) is missed by many of his commentators: e.g. Jacoby (1961), 138, 148, Murgatroyd (1980), 55 and 298. Tibullus includes echoes of the bogus Alfius' vision of country life (Hor. *Epod.* 2) in his vision, documented by Jacoby (1961), 136, and Wimmel (1976), 108, 111–13. But these scholars rather misappreciate the effect. Hearing echoes of the fraud Alfius, we should be alerted to the fact that Tibullus' is *not*, ultimately, a *Georgics* moral-rustic vision.

[26] In fact of course *two* considerations prevent Tibullus simply upping and going full-time to the country estate: the urban-domiciled Delia, but also the demands of Messalla—more potent in Tibullus' case, than Tullus' in Propertius' case: see Tib. 1. 3 and 1. 7. 9 ff., cf. also 1. 10. 13 f., 25; but, in 1. 1 and 5 Tibullus chooses not to stress this. (It may be that 1. 1. 41 ff. are Tibullus' discreet reply, negative at this point, to a specific suggestion by Messalla that if Tibullus serves with him, he may restore the family economic fortunes: *diuitiae* may be acquired. Lines 53–4 then take up the topic yet more discreetly, viewing such service from Messalla's point of view: the honour of *exuuiae*; on this cf. Jacoby (1961), 134.)

[27] The point is developed Lyne (loc. cit.), but there are new emphases in the above summary.

[28] 1. 5 is closural: *discidium*, this was the dream ('haec mihi fingebam'), 'heu canimus frustra'. 1. 6 is inceptive: 'semper, ut inducar, blandos offers mihi uultus...Amor. quid tibi saeuitiae mecum est?' etc. (*saeuitiae* is the MS text, which some doubt); cf. e.g. Hor. *Odes* 4. 1. Some too might see the strange intrusion of the priestess of Bellona in 1. 6. 43 ff. as having metaliterary implications: war, and love and war, play a larger part in the second half of the book: 1. 7 and 10. For further comment on the structure of Tibullus, Book 1 see below n. 69.

(cf. too 1. 2. 71–6). Delia as the country spouse is pictured at length (1. 5. 21–34), but prefaced and concluded with words confessing the fanciful invention: 'fingebam demens' (20) '... haec mihi fingebam' (35). It is because his life of love and leisure can only be a wish that we find wishful subjunctives predominating in Tibullus' first poem: e.g. 'hoc mihi contingat' (1. 1. 49).[29] From 'hoc mihi contingat' to 'fingebam demens': we can see a ring-composition here.

Compared with Cynthia, Delia has a carefully delayed entry. But, like Cynthia, it is she who prevents the poet-lover's participation in *militia*. Here are Tibullus' lines, 1. 1. 55 f., 'But the fetters of a beautiful girl hold me back in bonds, and I sit in front of her harsh doors, her door-keeper':

> me retinent uinctum formosae uincla puellae,
> et sedeo duras ianitor ante fores.

These recall and surely allude to parallel lines in Propertius, 1. 6. 5 f., 'But the words of my girl embracing me hold me back, and her frequent grievous entreaties, her changing complexions':

> sed me complexae remorantur uerba puellae,
> mutatoque graues saepe colore preces.

Propertius focusses on affective constraints, pressurizing words and so on; this emotional self-presentation is quite plausible. In Tibullus, bonds that could have been expressively metaphorical are given a concrete possibility. He toys with the picture of himself as a slavishly fettered *ianitor*.[30] In comparison

---

[29] Wishful subjunctives: 'Oh, may I sow the vine, a countryman..., may I be able to live content with a little...', 7 ff., etc. I translate the subjunctives of 7 ff. as optative subjunctives; sooner or later (e.g. 29), a hypothetical subjunctive seems more appropriate ('but I would not be ashamed sometimes...'). Commentators hedge and differ as to which if any of these subjunctives are optative. Perhaps justifiably, reflecting an ambiguity: modern scholars feel bound to parse *seram* etc.; Tibullus writes simply a non-fact, a non-indicative.

Are 15–18 subjunctive as transmitted ('sit... ponatur') or indicative as some emend? Tibullus' talk of country-life shifts between the estate which exists and his practices on it when he is there (indicatives, e.g. 19–24, 35–6) and his dreams of passing his whole life there (subjunctives, e.g. 7 ff., 25–32). The transmitted subjunctives of 15–18 intrude a not impossible but perhaps unwelcome interruption of indicative descriptions of the estate and Tibullus' country habits: 11–14 (his customary religious habits which justify 9–10 'nec Spes destituat...') and 19–24 (more religious observances). If emendation is wanted, the renaissance *fit* in 15 serves, but *ornatur* in 17 is perhaps better than the *donatur* which several scholars have excogitated: cf. 2. 1. 54. Thus emended, all lines 11–24 then describe Tibullus' present religious scrupulousness, which justifies his hope (9–10) for a successful full-time life spent on the country estate. (Others find so much to trouble them in Tibullus' text hereabouts that they transpose: cf. e.g. Murgatroyd's critical appendix (1980), 298 f.; one thing that troubles Murgatroyd—'the work in 7 f.... seems odd and abrupt so soon after the wish for *inertia* in 5'—is a non-problem if the tease mentioned above is appreciated.)

[30] The prosaic word and figure *ianitor* occurs in Propertius only at 4. 5. 47, a revealing context: the *lena* talks. He will reappear, relocated, in Ovid's *exclusus amator* poem, Am. 1. 6.

with Propertius, there are elements of farce here, even of parody. With this humorously concrete self-depiction and humorously concrete allusion to *seruitium amoris*, cf. Tibullus' treatment of *militia amoris* (Section II.4).

Tibullus then declares his 'life of love' for Delia, 1. 1. 57–60, 'I do not care about glory, Delia. Provided that I am with you, I court the name lazy and inactive. May I gaze upon you when my last hour comes; may I hold you as I die in my failing grasp':

> non ego laudari curo, mea Delia; tecum
>   dum modo sim, quaeso segnis inersque uocer.
> te spectem suprema mihi cum uenerit hora;
>   te teneam moriens deficiente manu.

The first couplet quoted is Tibullus' more insolently assertive version of Propertius' resigned and conquered 1. 6. 25 ff. 'me sine, quem semper uoluit fortuna iacere.... non ego sum laudi, non natus idoneus armis...' ('allow me, whom fortune always wished to be prostrate... I was not born suited for glory and arms...'). Tibullus has then noticed that Propertius' characteristic emphasis in his proclamation of the 'life of love'[31] is: love *until death* (1. 6. 25–8, which catches the ideas both of loving until death and dying for love, 1. 14. 14).[32] Indeed in 1. 19 Propertius pushes the idea even further. He will love Cynthia in death, and after death, will he not?[33] Accordingly Tibullus also phrases his commitment to a 'life of love' morbidly: love until death, 59 f. 'te spectem suprema mihi...'.

2. A Concern: Funerals[34]

In 1. 19 Propertius raises another issue. Here are some key lines. 1–4:

> non ego nunc tristis uereor, mea Cynthia, Manis,
>   nec moror extremo debita fata rogo;

---

[31] Already implied in Catullus, e.g. 5 and 109. It is phrased in relatively simple form too by Propertius at 1. 12. 19–20. Cf. n. 21.

[32] Cf. Gallus in Verg. *Ecl.* 10. 33 f., 43, Damagetus 10 Gow–Page (= *Anth. Pal.* 7. 735). 5–6 where the dying Theano addresses her absent husband thus: ὡς ὄφελόν γε | χειρὶ φίλῃ τὴν σὴν χεῖρα λαβοῦσα θανεῖν 'oh that I had been able to die taking your dear hand in mine'.

[33] More on 1. 19 below, Section II.3. The theme of love in and after death is pursued by Propertius in 'Book 2'. Papanghelis (1987) discusses these poems splendidly; readers will not agree with everything in his book, but they will hardly fail to be inspired. Jacoby (1961), 165 suggestively raises the question of what 'death fantasies' there may have been in Gallus. The emphasis love *until death* there surely was: cf. previous note. But perhaps more. Prop. 2. 34. 91 f. seem to me, in spite of the tortuous note of Camps, to imply that Gallus died of love. Is Propertius mixing history with a fantasy of Gallus? The couplet recalls a fragment of Euphorion on Adonis (fr. 43 Powell = 47 van Groningen), and a common source in the 'Euphorionic' (*Ecl.* 10. 50) Gallus himself is therefore a strong possibility. Cf. Rothstein on 2. 34. 91, Papanghelis (1987), 68 n. 46.

[34] On Propertian and Tibullan funerals, cf. Jacoby (1961), esp. 162 ff., Wimmel (1976), 93 ff. esp. 99–106 (usefully, he brings Tib. 1. 3 into play); but they have little or no sense of

> sed ne forte tuo careat mihi funus amore,
> hic timor est ipsis durior exsequiis.

I have no fear now of the gloomy Spirits, Cynthia, nor do I mind about the destiny that is owed to the final pyre. But that perchance my funeral may lack your love—this fear I find harsher than the rites of death themselves.

Lines 21–4:

> quam uereor, ne te contempto, Cynthia, busto
> abstrahat a nostro puluere iniquus Amor,
> cogat et inuitam lacrimas siccare cadentis!
> flectitur assiduis certa puella minis.

How I fear that, my pyre <or tomb> despised, unfriendly Love may drag you away from my dust and compel you against your will to dry your falling tears. A loyal girl is swayed by constant threats.

Propertius himself will love up to, even beyond, death, but betrays agonized anxiety lest Cynthia's devotion be so slight that she neglect his funeral and tomb: not bother with his obsequies, exhibit dry eyes and so on.

A similar anxiety obtrudes in 1. 17. The setting: Propertius pictures himself marooned by a storm; he has sailed abroad to escape Cynthia's harshness (15–18), and has been cast up *en route* on a thankless, deserted shore. He imputes not only the undertaking of the voyage to Cynthia, but also his present marooned and dangerous predicament: for he sees the hostile winds that trap him as expressions of Cynthia's pursuing hostility (5 f., 9); the poem exploits old motifs: love as seafaring (storms, etc.), woman as the (stormy) sea.[35]

From this situation comes the anxiety. If his present predicament can be imputed to Cynthia, and if as seems likely it may lead to his lonely and unregarded death, this again raises the thought that Cynthia does not care about what happens to his dead body. Lines 5–12:

> quin etiam absenti prosunt tibi, Cynthia, uenti:
> aspice, quam saeuas increpat aura minas.
> nullane placatae ueniet fortuna procellae?
> haecine parua meum funus harena teget?
> tu tamen in melius saeuas conuerte querelas:

dialogue and riposte. Papanghelis (1987), excellent on the general topic of Propertian funerals, largely avoids the question of the relation between Propertian and Tibullan funerals: pp. 14 n. 14, 100; such a relation is superficially glanced at by Murgatroyd (1980), 14, 50 f., also in his nn. on Tib. 1. 1. 61–8).

[35] For love as seafaring, the storms of love and so on, cf. Gow–Page, *Hellenistic Epigrams* anonymous XXII = *Anth. Pal.* 12. 156, Meleager LXIV Gow–Page = *Anth. Pal.* 5. 190, CXIX Gow–Page = *Anth. Pal.* 12. 157; for woman as the sea (calm, stormy, changeable and so on), Semonides 7. 27–42.

> sat tibi sit poenae nox et iniqua uada.
> an poteris siccis mea fata reponere[36] ocellis,
> ossaque nulla tuo nostra tenere sinu?

Furthermore, Cynthia, the winds benefit you in your absence: see with what savage threats the blast resounds. Will the good luck of an appeased storm not come? Will this scanty sand cover my dead body? Do you rather give your complaints a kindlier turn: let the night and hostile shoals be sufficient punishment for you. Or will you be able to put away my fate with dry eyes and to clasp no bones of mine in your bosom?

Cynthia's temper *is* these winds that threaten him with an untended death (5, 9), and if she will not abate her temper, it suggests she can think with equanimity of his dying without her loving attention: no clasping of his bones, dry eyes (again).

So Propertius should, he concludes, have stayed in Rome and endured her hard treatment. For then, in the event of his death, she would—he hopes, he imagines—have paid all due and tender respect. Lines 19–24:

> illic si qua meum sepelissent fata dolorem,
> ultimus et posito staret amore lapis,
> illa meo caros donasset funere crinis,
> molliter et tenera poneret ossa rosa;
> illa meum extremo clamasset puluere nomen,
> ut mihi non ullo pondere terra foret.

There, if any fate had buried my pain, and the final stone stood on my interred love, she would have offered her dear hair at my funeral, and would gently place my bones in tender roses; she would at my last dust have called my name, that the earth might be weightless on me.

So, in two poems, we observe a matter of acute concern to Propertius. Cynthia should exhibit love at his funeral, weep, embrace his bones, offer a lock of her hair, make ritual prayer... As Griffin notes, part of the power here derives from the fact that Propertius desires the lover and only the lover to fulfil the obligations and rituals which a dead Roman's family would normally and dutifully perform.[37] Another part of the power stems from his clear and acute anxiety lest Cynthia may in fact be loveless and negligent at his death.

Tibullus professed his 'life of love', love until death, in terms reminiscent of Propertius': Tibullus 1. 1. 55–60 (see above). Then (61–8):

> flebis et arsuro positum me, Delia, lecto,

---

[36] I keep the MSS *reponere*; Goold prints Baehrens' *reposcere*. The phrase *fata reponere* seems to me to contain suggestive and plausible ambiguities: note e.g. *OLD* s.v. *repono* 9 'store away', 10b 'to lay (a body) to rest'.

[37] Griffin (1985), 144, 148. Documentation on gestures of mourning (weeping, locks of hair and so on) is provided in notes 39, 61, 63.

> tristibus et lacrimis oscula mixta dabis.
> flebis: non tua sunt duro praecordia ferro
>   uincta, neque in tenero stat tibi corde silex.
> illo non iuuenis poterit de funere quisquam
>   lumina, non uirgo, sicca referre domum.
> tu Manes ne laede meos, sed parce solutis
>   crinibus et teneris, Delia, parce genis.

You will weep for me, Delia, laid on the bier that will burn, and you will give me kisses mixed with sorrowing tears. You will weep: your heart is not bound with iron, nor is there flint in your tender breast. From that funeral there will be no young man, there will be no girl who will be able to return home dry-eyed. But you, Delia, do not injure my Spirits; rather, spare your loosened hair and spare your tender cheeks.

Love-until-death suggests thoughts of death, and funerals: Propertius' anxious concern. But Tibullus washes away Propertian *Angst* on a tide of tears, confidence and security. The devotion of Delia at Tibullus' funeral is not in the slightest doubt. There is an emphasis to be found in Tibullus' second person singulars, *flebis, dabis*, and, especially, the repeated *flebis* and *tua, tibi*: '*you* will weep, *your* heart is not bound in iron, no flint in *your* tender breast.' With amusing smugness Tibullus draws an implicit contrast between Delia and the Cynthia of Propertius' anxieties. As for dry eyes (*siccus*), feared twice in Cynthia's case, not only Delia but no-one will leave Tibullus' funeral dry-eyed. And the offering of the lock of hair, a cause of anxiety to Propertius: Tibullus is so secure in his conviction of Delia's devoted mourning, that he imagines his departed spirit may actually be pained by this particular exhibition,[38] and, magnanimously, he asks her to spare her hair, not rend or cut it: 'parce solutis crinibus'.[39]

Acute Propertian anxieties are replaced by smug Tibullan confidences: this is surely funny.[40]

---

[38] For the idea that mourning can cause distress to the dead (as well as being profitless, a burden to the mourner, etc.), see Nisbet and Hubbard's note on Hor. *Ode* 2. 9. 9, Murgatroyd on Tib. 1. 1. 66–8. The secure and proper Propertian Cornelia will say (4. 11. 1) 'desine, Paulle, meum lacrimis urgere sepulcrum'.

[39] The rending or offering of hair was, like weeping, a gesture of mourning embedded in Graeco-Roman tradition: cf. Hom. *Od.* 4. 197–8 τοῦτό νυ καὶ γέρας οἶον ὀϊζυροῖσι βροτοῖσι, | κείρασθαί τε κόμην βαλέειν τ' ἀπὸ δάκρυ παρειῶν, 'this is the only honour we pay to miserable men <at death>, to cut the hair and let the tear fall from the cheek', and see Murgatroyd on 1. 1. 67–8. For further on tears at funerals see n. 63. As for 'teneris...parce genis' (Tib. 1. 1. 68), this may be a memory of Prop. 1. 6. 16 'insanis ora notet manibus', imagined passion on Cynthia's part on a different occasion. For the rending of cheeks at a funeral, and for Propertius' reply to this detail, see below pp. 272–3 with n. 61.

[40] Further consideration might be given to Tibullus' thoughts of funeral when stranded in 'Phaeacia' in 1. 3. 5–9: he exhibits a more bourgeois and sentimental concern than expressed by Propertius (*mater, soror, Delia*), and the poem holds out every prospect of a happy outcome (89 ff., a happy and bourgeois version of an Odyssean return). We can see here further amusingly complacent glances at Propertius' funeral agonizing in 1. 17 and 19—and, also, at his tougher

3. ...until Death. Meanwhile...?

Propertius protests love until death (1. 6. 25–8 etc.). His nineteenth poem, as well as agonizing over funerals, pushes this idea further: can Love conquer Death? Death's power to reduce to ash and bones delivers an answer which is ultimately negative. For this and other reasons Propertius concludes as follows (1. 19. 25–6):

> quare, dum licet, inter nos laetemur amantes:
> non satis est ullo tempore longus amor.

Wherefore, while it is possible, let us love and be glad together: love is not long enough in any extent of time.

This is his version of Catullus 5 (and 7); cf. too e.g. Asclepiades II Gow–Page = Anth. Pal. 5. 85, Hor. Odes 1. 11. The basic message is of course commonplace. But in Propertius it strikes one, after the dense and romantic dialectic of the poem (can Love conquer Death?), as a compromise full of pathos and tension, an arresting end.[41]

Tibullus 1. 1. 59 f. protests love until death (cf. Prop. 1. 6 etc.). Then, cued by Prop. 1. 19 (and 17), he imagines Delia's unhesitating devotion at his funeral; no *Angst* or problematics for him. And he concludes (1. 1. 69–70), in obvious recollection of Prop. 1. 19. 25–6, and indeed of Catullus 5:

> interea, dum fata sinunt, iungamus amores:
> iam ueniet tenebris mors adoperta caput...

Meanwhile, while the fates allow, let us join our love. Tomorrow death will come, head shrouded in darkness...

Propertius arrives at his conclusion regretfully, after morbid, internal debate; the sentiment strikes one in consequence, in context, as far from banal. Tibullus coasts with smooth and contented melancholy to the same conclusion. But I would not call the conclusion in Tibullus banal:[42] rather I would argue that his unruffled, unruffling progress towards it, and his consequent ease of inference (*interea...*), trumps for a certain taste his predecessor. Where Propertius found

---

stranded condition in 1. 17. Wimmel (1976), 99–103 discusses the relation between these poems to considerable effect, but without finding any humour. Papanghelis (1987), 100 on the relation of Tib. 1. 3 and these Propertian poems is uncharacteristically disappointing.

[41] Propertius' reasoning which leads to this conclusion is discussed by Lyne (1980), 101 f.; cf. too my recent article Lyne (1998b) [= Ch. 13, this volume], Section II. Other reasons why Propertius concludes thus exist, and are focussed on by Jacoby (1961), 163. But the fact of death and the end that it brings is by far the most important of them.

[42] Contrast Jacoby (1961), 163, 168 f. He argues that Propertius' argument in 1. 19 gives the conclusion (25 f.) special significance (clearly correct), but that Tibullus' version (1. 1. 69–70), in his unproblematic context, is merely banal. This is to misappreciate humour, above all to misappreciate the dialogue that Tibullus is essaying.

an agonized terminus, Tibullus finds in the same sentiment an unforced and placid resolution. The comparison should amuse. It may not have amused Propertius to see his text so tamed and accommodated.

Propertius ends 1. 19 with 'non satis est ullo tempore longus amor', amplifying *dum licet*. This is a summary and suggestive version of Catullus 7, a romantic claim that love can never be satisfied. In the Tibullan couplet just quoted satisfaction already seems, I think, far from unrealizable. But of course Tibullus does not end here. He has more to say in riposte to his romantic, insatiable colleague. After *mors adoperta caput* he continues (71–4):

> iam subrepet iners aetas, nec amare decebit,
>   dicere nec cano blanditias capite.
> nunc leuis est tractanda Venus dum frangere postes
>   non pudet et rixas inseruisse iuuat.

Tomorrow indolent age will creep up, and it will not be seemly to love, nor to talk sweet nothings with white hair. Light Venus must be carried on now, while there is no disgrace in breaking doors, and brawling is pleasurable.

Propertius broadened out to proclaim insatiability. Far from broadening out, Tibullus limits and adjusts something which he has apparently granted. These lines adjust his own 'dum fata sinunt': love, he now says, is for youth. It is an adjustment that is most unexpected. Given the poems which Tibullus recalls, we will have expected him to mean by 'dum fata sinunt' simply 'for life'—the sense of Catullus' 'uiuamus atque amemus' and the sense of Propertius' 'dum licet'. The adjustment is unexpected from another and general point of view: we do not expect a love poet in the orbit of Catullus and Propertius to concern himself with the impropriety of amorous conduct in old age. Such a view belongs to conventional Roman society, to Cicero for example, and to Horace too.[43] The romantic generally disregarded bothersome detail like ageing: 'tota...uita, aeternum... foedus' (Catull. 109. 5 f.); 'Cynthia prima fuit, Cynthia finis erit' (Prop. 1. 12. 20); 'dum me fata perire uolent' (Prop. 1. 14. 14); 'te spectem suprema mihi cum uenerit hora; | te teneam moriens' (Tib. 1. 1. 59 f.).[44] Most unexpectedly therefore, in sober or Horatian mode, Tibullus adjusts his own 'dum fata sinunt'. In so doing he adjusts and as it were corrects Propertius 1. 19. 25–6 'quare dum licet...'. Propertius 1. 19. 25–6 offered a particularly tempting target, proclaiming not just love-for-life ('dum licet') but insatiability: 'love is not long enough in any extent of time'. Tibullus' sudden insistence on youth, adjusting his own 'dum fata sinunt' and 'correcting' Propertius' 'dum licet', is even more devastating in its

---

[43] Cf. Hor. *Epodes* 8, 12, *Odes* 1. 25, 3. 15, 4. 13, Cic. *Cael.* 42.
[44] Cf. Lyne (1980), 66; I here pick up an embryonic suggestion from p. 67 (with n. 4). Some apparent exceptions to the statement in the present text ('The romantic generally disregarded bothersome detail like ageing') are discussed loc. cit.

implications for Propertius' insatiably romantic last line. So: unexpected limitation and 'correction', based on an unpredictable intrusion of Ciceronian or Horatian ethics. The effect will have been amusing (surely) to some.

But what of Tibullus' own 'te spectem suprema mihi cum uenerit hora' and so on: love is for life? We could fudge here, and find consistency, and say that Tibullus envisages a domesticated and proper love for his old age. Far more probably: Tibullus writes in a post-Propertian world, to respond, to guy, even to parody. To score points and to amuse. And of course to add and construct on his part. But I stress: to score points. Consistency is not I think a huge issue. His Horatian qualification 'iam subrepet iners aetas' simply sits inconsistently, better to say unexpectedly, with the romanticism of 'te spectem...'. Guying the romantic lover, he passes to a surprising adjustment. Adjusting his own persona, 'correcting' Propertius.

Observe how he concludes the introductory poem of the second half of Book 1. A woman who has been faithful to no lover is condemned to a dismal old age. By contrast, 1. 6. 85 f. 'You and I, Delia, must be a paradigm of love when we are both white-haired,'

> nos, Delia, amoris
> exemplum cana simus uterque coma.

That breaks Catullan–Propertian taboo (Don't Mention Decrepitude)—and flouts his own injunctions in 1. 1, unless we excogitate high-minded distinctions in the senses of *amare* and *amor*. I prefer to think of spirited and amusing inconsistency.[45]

4. The 'Life of Love': in Particular, the Issues of *militia, diuitiae*

The last lines of Tibullus' first poem are as follows (1. 1. 75–8); they pick up the couplet on *leuis Venus*, door-breaking and brawls, quoted above:

> hic ego dux milesque bonus: uos, signa tubaeque,
>   ite procul, cupidis uulnera ferte uiris,
> ferte et opes: ego composito securus aceruo
>   dites despiciam despiciamque famem.[46]

Here I am good general and soldier. You standards and trumpets hence far away! Take wounds to greedy men, take wealth too. Let me, free from care, with my store laid up, despise the rich and despise hunger.

---

[45] Other passages in Tibullus suggest Ciceronian–Horatian belief that love is for youth, and distaste at love in old age: 1. 2. 89–98, 1. 8. 47–8, 2. 1. 73–4. Cf. too Priapus at 1. 4. 27 ff.

[46] I do not understand why some editors (Luck's Teubner, Murgatroyd, defending his decision (1980), 301) prefer to lose this neat chiasmus, following a minority of the manuscript tradition (*despiciam dites...*).

Tibullus reverts to his dissociation from active life, from honourable and profitable *militia* (Section II.1), exploiting the figure of *militia amoris*. He gives more literal, and novel, expression to the figure than Propertius, his immediate model, had done. In 1. 6. 29 f. Propertius phrased his dissociation expressively, with (even) an appearance of dignity, in the abstract noun: 'non ego sum laudi, non natus idoneus armis: hanc me militiam fata subire uolunt', 'I was not born suited for glory and arms: the fates want me to undergo *this* military service (i.e. love)'. Tibullus sees things more concretely, puts it more funnily. Brawls occur in love, doors are broken in. Tibullus is good at this sort of spicy violence, here he can 'soldier' and be a good 'general'; but not in real wars which actually kill people. There is considerable anticipation here of the humorously literal treatment of *militia amoris* that we will find in Ovid; in intended contrast to Propertius, Tibullus is comic and innovative.[47] It is worth reflecting too that Tibullus' use of *dux milesque bonus* shows disrespect to a potentially august title.[48]

Tibullus' disdain of riches in these lines picks up 1. 1. 1–6, 41–44, 49–52. We should note that *paupertas* in line 5 is subsequently qualified, by e.g. line 43: a small sufficiency, not (of course) actual poverty, 'parua seges satis est', 'a small crop is enough'; he may not yearn for the *diuitiae patrum* (41), but this is after all a Roman Knight talking. The Roman Knight is then careful to define his disdain for rich people in the last couplet of the poem: 'let me despise the rich *and* despise hunger, let me despise the rich with a store laid up.' His disdain of *diuitiae* is cautiously gauged, he deploys that verb *despicere* with prudence.

Contrast the grand, romantic statements that it is possible to find in Propertius 1. 14. This is the poem that particularly attends to Tullus' Roman esteem for wealth, showing Propertian scorn for *diuitiae* compared with love.[49] Line 8, 'Love does not know how to yield to great wealth':

nescit Amor magnis cedere *diuitiis*.

And the conclusion (23 f.), 'I shall fear to despise no kingdoms nor wealth of Alcinous':

---

[47] Indeed Tibullus, finding his concrete figures of *dux* and *miles* of love, is innovative and comic even compared with the comic poets, as Murgatroyd in his note on 1. 1. 75–6 recognizes. M. can find (only) Plaut. *As.* 656 'amorisque imperator' as direct precedent, and *Pers.* 24 'saucius factus sum in Veneris proelio' is more typical of the (not very frequent) usage in Roman comedy: cf. Duckworth (1952), 337, Fantham (1972), 26 ff. On *militia amoris* and its use in Propertius and Tibullus, see Lyne (1980), 71–8; for Ovid's use see esp. *Am.* 1. 9, and Lyne (1980), 251–2. Tibullus now seems to me to be funnier—more Ovidian—than he did in 1980.

[48] *Bonus*, as Murgatroyd ad loc. sees, relates to *dux* as well as *miles*. Horace's address to Augustus as *dux bone* in *Ode* 4. 5. 5 is built on a dignified and well-parallelled collocation: cf. e.g. Cic. *Off.* 3. 100, Sall. *Hist. fr.* 1. 77 (= *oratio Philippi in senatu*). 21, Liv. 7. 40. 15.

[49] A contributor to Tibullus 1. 1 curiously neglected by Jacoby (1961), and barely glanced at by Wimmel (1976), 106. It also stimulates 1. 2. 77–80, as Murgatroyd on Tib. 1. 2. 76–6 observes.

> non ulla uerebor
> regna uel Alcinoi munera *despicere.*

The attentive reader of 1. 14 notices, of course, that Propertius' opening, unconditional and absolute scorn for wealth compared with love (which lasts down to line 14 and contains 'nescit Amor magnis cedere diuitiis') undergoes a complication. Love must be favourable to see off wealth. Line 15 reads 'nam quis diuitiis aduerso gaudet Amore?', 'for who rejoices in wealth when Love is hostile?', rather than, say, 'for who rejoices in wealth without or as opposed to Love?' And that last, splendidly delivered *despicere* is actually prefaced by a qualification: 'quae mihi dum placata aderit', 'so long as Venus attends me appeased...'. Nevertheless it is Propertius who provides us with the huge romantic scorn of 'nescit Amor magnis cedere diuitiis' and 'non ulla uerebor regna uel Alcinoi munera despicere'—into which he characteristically intrudes anxious presentiments. And to this romanticism Tibullus responds with plump, complacent, almost bourgeois, and certainly funny prudence: 'ego composito securus aceruo | dites despiciam despiciamque famem'.[50]

III. PROPERTIUS COUNTERS...

1. *Militia amoris,* and Violence

Tibullus, the boisterous soldier, brawling and breaking doors in 1. 1, defines and develops a picture of what seems acceptable violence in the *militia* of love in 1. 10. 51 ff.:

> rusticus e luco reuehit, male sobrius ille,
>   uxorem plaustro progeniemque domum.
> sed Veneris tunc bella calent, scissosque capillos
>   femina perfractas conqueriturque fores;
> flet teneras obtusa genas, sed uictor et ipse
>   flet sibi dementes tam ualuisse manus.
> at lasciuus Amor rixae mala uerba ministrat,
>   inter et iratum lentus utrumque sedet.
> a lapis est ferrumque, suam quicumque puellam
>   uerberat: e caelo deripit ille deos.
> sit satis e membris tenuem rescindere uestem,
>   sit satis ornatus dissoluisse comae,

---

[50] To Pholoe, by contrast—when he has a case to make, when he has the interests of his favoured boy at heart—he can counsel grand 'Propertian' romanticism, 1. 8. 33 f. 'huic tu candentes umero suppone lacertos, | et regum magnae despiciantur opes'.

> sit lacrimas mouisse satis. quater ille beatus
> > cui tenera irato flere puella potest.
> sed manibus qui saeuus erit, scutumque sudemque
> > is gerat et miti sit procul a Venere.

Home from a sacred grove the rustic, far from sober himself, carries wife and children in the wagon. But then Venus' wars blaze up, and the woman laments her torn hair and broken door. She weeps for the bruises to her soft cheeks, but the victor, he too weeps that his mad hands were so strong. But petulant Love supplies abuse for the brawl, and sits immovable between the angry pair. Ah stone is he and iron who beats his girl: he drags down gods from heaven. Let it be enough to tear off the fine dress, let it be enough to disarrange the hair's coiffure, let it be enough to move her tears. Four times blessed is he at whose anger a tender woman can weep. But he who will be savage with his hands, let him carry shield and stake <i.e. real military soldiers' kit>, and be far away from gentle Venus.

F. Solmsen[51] has noted that Propertius replies to this manifesto, delivering a splendid put-down; I develop the point slightly. Prop. 2. 5. 21 ff.:

> nec tibi periuro scindam de corpore uestis,
> > nec mea praeclusas fregerit ira fores,
> nec tibi conexos iratus carpere crinis,
> > nec duris ausim laedere pollicibus:
> rusticus haec aliquis tam turpia proelia quaerat,
> > cuius non hederae circuiere caput.
> scribam igitur, quod non umquam tua deleat aetas:
> > 'Cynthia, forma potens: Cynthia uerba leuis.'

But *I* shall not tear the clothes from your perjured body, nor shall my anger break down barred doors;[52] I should not dare in my wrath to injure you with harsh thumbs, or tear at your plaited hair: let some rustic or other seek battles so base, a man whose head the ivy has not wreathed.[53] So I shall *write*, something which your lifetime can never blot out: 'Cynthia, a powerful beauty: Cynthia, fickle in words.'

The riposte matches detail for detail. The violence that Tibullus seems to accept, tearing girls' clothes, mussing their hair, even breaking in doors (cf. too 1. 1. 73): that's bumpkin behaviour, says Propertius, it belongs to a *rusticus*, not a poet. A poet retaliates to his mistress's provocation, not with crude violence, but artistically, with verse, a devastating epigram, a cutting one-liner. Solmsen observes that Tibullus is actually talking about a generalized *rusticus*

---

[51] Solmsen (1961), 273 ff. = *Kleine Schriften* ii. 299 ff.

[52] I take *scribam* and *fregerit* as future and future perfect indicative like e.g. Camps and Rothstein, and, I infer, Goold; in Guy Lee's translation (Lee 1994) they are taken as subjunctive (cf. *ausim*), which is thought-provoking.

[53] The point as Solmsen brings out (if it needs to be brought out) is not that a country fellow is no poet, but that a poet will not sink to this low level of bumpkin behaviour.

in 1. 10, not himself. But (as Solmsen also sees) this is no obstacle to Propertius, who clearly identifies Tibullus with this rustic behaviour: this riposte has Tibullus himself in view, it is Tibullus who is being attacked through Propertius' *rusticus*. And not wholly unreasonably. After all Tibullus himself finds the actions in 1. 10. 61 ff. acceptable, i.e. most of Propertius' items. And did not his own programmatic self-presentation in 1. 1 rely upon, precisely, the adjective *rusticus* (1. 1. 8)? We remember too how in the opening poems of the two halves of the book (1. 1. 73–5, 1. 6. 73–4) violence—breaking in doors, brawls, beating—was canvassed and in the major part advocated. So, to assume an identity between rustic Tibullus and the *rusticus* and violence in Tib. 1. 10 was pretty irresistible—and not wholly unreasonable. And, in the word *rusticus* itself, it was witty. A complimentary word to some (Cicero in some contexts, Vergil, Varro, Tibullus),[54] *rusticus* was a pejorative word to others (Cicero in other contexts,[55] Catullus, and clearly Propertius).[56] Propertius turns Tibullus' favoured epithet on its head. So: Tibullus is the crude and violent bumpkin. Meantime Propertius will act as the ivy-wreathed poet acts, as Tibullus should act but doesn't. The joke is not absolutely fair, but it is a good one. Most unfair perhaps is the mention of injury with thumbs (referring to tightness of grip?); in 1. 10 no such action is mentioned, and actual blows at least are excluded.

We should observe, while we are talking about fairness and fun in good part, that Propertius is amusing at his own expense too. One cannot imagine Cynthia quaking with fear at the threat of Propertius' devastating one-liner. It is hardly a major deterrent. And, showing his hand, revealing what is in his armoury, actually quoting the unterrifying one-liner, Propertius must be aware of, and want us to see, the impotence of the poet's retaliation. He mocks Tibullus' coarse violence; but he exposes the limpness of the aesthete's alternative. Goold's suspicions of the text of 'Cynthia forma potens, Cynthia uerba leuis' are probably misplaced. Propertius' retaliation is seen to lack punch in every sense.[57]

---

[54] Cic. *Rosc. Amer.* 75 'praetereo illud... in rusticis moribus... istius modi maleficia gigni non solere... uita autem haec rustica quam tu agrestem uocas [he acknowleges a hostile point of view] parsimoniae, diligentiae, iustitiae magistra est'; Varr. *Rust.* 3. 1. 4; Verg. *Georg.* 1. 168 'diuini gloria ruris'.

[55] Cic. *Orat.* 2. 25 where *rusticus* is equivalent to *indoctissimus*, 3. 44 'rusticam asperitatem', 45 'non aspere..., non uaste, non rustice, non hiulce'.

[56] Cf. e.g. Catullus 22. 14 'idem inficeto est inficetior rure', 36. 19 f. 'pleni ruris et inficetiarum | annales Volusi, cacata carta'. *Rusticus* only elsewhere in Prop. at 4. 1. 12.

[57] Goold (1990), 134 'The inconcinnity spoils what the poet intended as a devastating line and raises a doubt about the accuracy of the manuscript tradition.' The objection is to the syntactical disharmony: *Cynthia* in apposition to a noun, *Cynthia leuis* as to a noun in the accusative of respect. Aspiring to concinnity Scaliger suggested *formipotens* and Richards *lingua* (for *uerba*); *alii alia*. But (we could argue) a weakness in the epigrammatic construction reinforces Propertius' humour at his own expense: as I say, his weapon of retaliation lacks punch in every way. We might

Prop. 2. 5. 21 ff. is a Propertian retort, in presumably Book 2a. But it is a retort to a retort. Tibullus writes (1. 10. 63 f.): 'four times blessed is he at whose anger a tender woman can weep',

> quater ille beatus
> quo tenera irato flere puella potest.

That was in response to Propertius 1. 12. 15 f.:

> felix qui potuit praesenti flere puellae;
>   non nihil aspersus gaudet Amor lacrimis.

Fortunate is he who has been able to weep to his present sweetheart. Love takes some considerable pleasure in being sprinkled with tears.

We may find pathos in the Propertius who, sundered from Cynthia, would wish to weep in Cynthia's presence, and is moved to utter: 'fortunate is he...'. Our sometimes passive-seeming Tibullus writes a robust retort: *'four* times blessed he who *makes* a woman cry.'

2. Funerals

Propertius constructs an aesthete's response to Tibullus' presentation of amorous violence. Consider now the funeral that Propertius imagines for himself in 2. 13,[58] and compare it with Tib. 1. 1. 61–8. Part of Propertius' inspiration in 2. 13 is again a desire to respond to Tibullus, and with comparable superior aestheticism. Tibullus' smug confidence had pictured Delia's tears and homely devotions; Propertius now imagines wild demonstrations of grief beyond tears, gestures of disturbing eroticism, and funeral honours befitting the poet. Stung by Tibullus' trumping of his early funeral anxieties, he constructs these magnificent obsequies, sensual and artistic, something to supersede mere sentimental devotion, a mélange of lover-poet's aestheticism. 2. 13. 25–38:

> sat mea sat magna est, si tres sint pompa libelli,
>   quos ego Persephonae maxima dona feram.
> tu uero nudum pectus lacerata sequeris,
>   nec fueris nomen lassa uocare meum,

note that in what is probably another book (2b) Propertius is provoked to threaten Tibullan violence—and more: torn clothes and bruised arms, 2. 15. 17–20.

[58] If Richmond and Heyworth are right, this poem is initial in Book 2b. See Heyworth (1995); cf. Heyworth (1992) for convincing arguments for the unity of 2. 13 as well as its inceptive status, and for general literary exposition. Fine discussion too in Papanghelis (1987), ch. 4 (and elsewhere).

272 *Propertius and Tibullus: Early Exchanges*

> osculaque in gelidis pones suprema labellis,
>   cum dabitur Syrio munere plenus onyx.
> deinde, ubi suppositus cinerem me fecerit ardor,
>   accipiat Manis paruula testa meos,
> et sit in exiguo laurus super addita busto,
>   quae tegat exstincti funeris umbra locum,
> et duo sint uersus: 'qui nunc iacet horrida puluis,
>   unius hic quondam seruus amoris erat.'
> nec minus haec nostri notescet fama sepulcri,
>   quam fuerant Pthii busta cruenta uiri.

My procession would be sufficiently costly, if my three books of poetry should comprise it; these books I should bear as most great gifts to Persephone. But you will follow with your breast naked and torn, nor will you be wearied to call my name. You will place last kisses on my cold lips, when the jar full of Syrian offering is given me. Then when fire has been put under me and made me ash, let a little earthen jar receive my Spirits, and let a bay tree be added at my meagre tomb, its shade to cover the site of my extinguished pyre. And let there be two verses: 'he who now lies here unkempt dust, was once upon a time the slave of a single love.' Nor will this fame of my tomb become less known than the bloody pyre of the Pthian hero.

Here we have been better served by the critics (who do not however generally see Tibullan response and Propertian counter-response),[59] and I shall comment selectively. Note first Cynthia's lacerated, naked breast. Here is a spectacular trumping of Tibullus,[60] a riposte to the torn cheeks which Tibullus could magnanimously excuse Delia (1. 1. 68). Even to tear the cheeks was theoretically unRoman. Propertius not only admits, he leapfrogs such demonstration. Tearing the breast, predicted and/or prescribed for Cynthia, introduces the huge and uninhibited grief of the epic and captive Briseis.[61] Next, Papanghelis observes the inescapable sexuality, the gruesome touches of love-in-death provided by the kisses on the cold but erotically worded lips,

---

[59] But an unexpected and productive glance at interplay between Prop. 2. 13 and Tibullus 1. 1 in Jacoby (1961), 163 n. 75.

[60] Griffin (1985), 148, talking of Cynthia's lacerated breast, observes that 'the gentler spirit of Tibullus...shrank from this...detail.'

[61] The Twelve Tables forbade Roman women even to scratch their cheeks at funerals: for this fact and for other facts and conjectures about actual practice at Roman funerals, see Treggiari (1991), 489 f. But back in the *Iliad* Briseis χερσὶ δ' ἄμυσσε | στήθεα..., 'tore at her breasts with her hands, and her soft throat, and her beautiful face' (*Il.* 19. 284 f.), over the body of Patroclus; we should note that the gesture is extravagant even in that epic world; elsewhere in Homer, 'heroic mourners do not go farther than tearing their hair' (Leaf ad loc.). Huge and special heroic despair—rather than eroticism—is provided by *nudum pectus lacerata*. Papanghelis (1987), 64 sees (I infer) an erotic colour in the detail; there is certainly eroticism in the vicinity, as (following P.) I remark in the text.

labella (the tone of this word is impossible to convey in translation).[62] Compare and contrast Propertius' line 29 with the sentimental and unsexual devotion of Tib. 1. 1. 62 'tristibus et lacrimis oscula mixta dabis'. And we should note that Propertius now has no time or wish for the tears which once upon a time (to Tibullus' delight) had caused him such anxiety (1. 17. 11, 19. 23). With the spectacular and unorthodox devotions that he now envisages, it is no wonder, indeed it is significant, that he finds no room for this most conventional of offerings;[63] and anyway (it might appear) the funeral text of Tibullus became so tediously awash with tears (*flebis, lacrimis, flebis, lumina non sicca*), that Propertius now scorns them. But he will have the attentions that a *poet* warrants: a procession provided by his own three books of poetry, and a bay tree, the tree sacred to Apollo (Tib. 2. 5. 5 etc.), to shade his tomb (33). We observe that in mundane respects his imagined funeral will be modest and his tomb exiguous (19 ff., 32, 33); but this sits well with Propertius' self-presentation as a Callimachean poet (cf. esp. 3. 9. 21–44, 4. 1. 59), though it reflects a tendentious and self-serving view of Callimachus, rather than a true one. Cf. 3. 16. 21 ff.: Propertius imagines his tomb and devotions even more in accordance with this self-view as Propertius' kind of Callimachus—a most amusing piece.[64]

More funeral recognition in 2. 13 befitting the *poet*: a verse epitaph (35 f.) recording his status as lover and poet: 'unius seruus amoris' suggests both of course.[65] In high and funny contrast with the sort of epitaph a conventional equestrian might construct for himself,[66] Propertius' epitaph glances too at the epitaph Tibullus imagines for himself in 1. 3. 55 f. ('hic iacet immiti consumptus morte Tibullus, | Messallam terra dum sequiturque mari', 'here lies Tibullus consumed by savage death, while he followed Messalla by land and sea'); Propertius' total commitment to love and poetry exposes Tibullus' worldly collaboration.[67] And then: his, a lover-poet's, tomb will be as famous

---

[62] Papanghelis (1987), 64. Propertius does not elsewhere use this diminutive. Catullus was fond of it: cf. most pertinently Catull. 8. 18 'quem basiabis? cui labella mordebis?' Cf. too Papanghelis 78 f.

[63] A conventional offering: this hardly needs documenting, but cf. at one end of history, in the grand heroic world, Hom. *Il.* 24. 712–14, 746, 760, 776, 786 (tears for Hector), *Od.* 4. 198 quoted above n. 39, at the other end, in the aristocratic Roman world, Paullus' tears for Cornelia in Propertius himself: 4. 11. 1. See further Treggiari loc. cit. (n. 61). Interestingly, Propertius eschews tears in his other arty burial scene, 3. 16. 21 ff. (mentioned below)—but not, be it noted, the grand Maecenas' at 2. 1. 76. We may note too that the offering of a lock of hair is now no longer of importance to Propertius: contrast 1. 17. 21 and above p. 262.

[64] Solmsen (1961), 277 ff. = ii. 303 ff. pursues a relation between 3. 16. 11–20 and Tib. 1. 2. 25 ff., an interesting one, but Solmsen misses the humour in it.

[65] The assumption that the two activities are identical is a common motif in Prop., with which he makes much play. In a simple form we find it in 1. 7. 5 ff.

[66] Cf. Griffin (1985), 149 with n. 26, quoting the real life epitaph of Q. Varius Geminus.

[67] Cf. how Propertius' triumphant dedication to Venus in 2. 14. 27–8 (an initial poem in Book 2b) may trump the wearied resignation of Tibullus' in 1. 9. 83–4 (closural in Tibullus: see n. 69).

as the tomb of the great Pthian hero, Achilles. The *miles amoris* will be as famous in death as the *miles* of violence, though Propertius does nothing so obvious as to call himself *miles* as Tibullus (above Section II.4) had done; other suggestions may be found in this expressive detail.[68]

Now here we have a funeral and tomb of class. Wild, unorthodox, sexual, above all a *poet*'s. Something to trump the plump, sentimental self-confidence of Tibullus, who had trumped the vulnerable anxieties of Prop. 1. 17 and 19.

3. *Puellae*

In the last poem of the first half of Book 1 (*discidium*), Tibullus reveals his dream of Delia.[69] In this important poem we find Tibullus' most detailed and devoted exposition of his first female beloved. The dream is that she will be the country wife, the guardian of the grain, and so on (21 ff.).

It is worth pausing on the name *Delia*. It will have been chosen, surely, because 'like Propertius' Cynthia,... it suggested the sister of Apollo, god of poetry...';[70] Gallus had also chosen a pseudonym (*Lycoris*) evocative of Apollo.[71] Propertius' Cynthia had displayed the talents her name might seem to require: e.g. Prop. 1. 2. 27–8 ('especially since Apollo bestows on you his songs, and Calliope willingly her Aonian lyre...'). From a Propertian point of view, Delia emphatically does not display such talents, not even, indeed especially, in the 1. 5 dream vision, where she will guard the grain, count the sheep, and so on: hardly poetic. It is I think partly to show the

---

[68] e.g. the parity of Elegy with Epic as a commemorative medium. Two elegiac verses (lines 35 f.) or, if one chooses to see it another way, this elegy itself, commemorate Propertius' tomb (and funeral); the hugely spectacular—but, arguably, in Propertius' view no more effective—*Od.* 24. 43–94 commemorate Achilles' funeral and tomb. Another interesting idea is to be found in Heyworth's paper (1992), 55: he suggests some allusive play with Cynthia / Polyxena. Propertius' inclusion of *cruenta* certainly encourages such a line of thinking (cf. Enk ad loc.).

[69] Cf. above pp. 258–9 on the structure of Tibullus Book 1. Some more detail on Tibullan structure and on Delia's appearances. Delia was programmatically presented in 1. 1, as discussed above, but without development. Her exclusion of the lover-poet precipitates the laments, reflections and other characters of 1. 2. She plays a quite large part in 1. 3, but no part in 1. 4, a poem concerned with homosexual love, at the end of which the name Marathus surfaces. Then come the revelations of the closural 1. 5. 1. 6, the introductory poem of the second half of the book, leads with Delia, and exploits her in that poem, but mainly as a vehicle for other characters, novel ideas and situations. And then, surprisingly, she appears no more. 1. 6, if read programmatically (cf. above n. 28), tricks one; novelty is in store. 1. 7 is devoted to Messalla; the boy whose name surfaced at the end of 1. 4 dominates 1. 8 and 9; 1. 9 is then closural, but of this homosexual love affair ('haec ego dicebam' 29, 'canebam' 47 ff., the concluding dedication to Venus 'resolutus amore Tibullus', Murgatroyd (1980), 256 on 1. 9 and 'end of affair' poems); and 1. 10 is phrased generally.

[70] Murgatroyd (1980), 7. Cf. Wimmel (1976), 107.   [71] Courtney (1993), 262.

difference—the superiority—of his taste in women that Propertius so assertively shows Cynthia's affiliations with art in his programmatic 2. 1.[72] His girl is the inspiration of his poetry, a Muse, the equal to or superior of Calliope and Apollo (2. 1. 1 ff.).[73]

But Tibullus 1. 5 also contains a fascinating and unequalled exposure of Delia's physical charms and powers.[74] In context Tibullus is describing his attempts to diversify with other girls, given Delia's desertion of him. When he cannot satisfactorily complete the act of love, the substitute girl goes off saying that Delia has used the black arts and bewitched him. Tibullus responds (1. 5. 43–4), 'no, she doesn't do this with magic herbs, she bewitches me with her face, soft arms, and fair hair':

> non facit hoc herbis,[75] facie tenerisque lacertis
> deuouet et flauis nostra puella comis.

An amazing moment: we catch Tibullus defining Delia's magic. But lest she seem so limitable, Tibullus adds, uniquely,[76] an expansive romantic myth (45–6), 'like the blue-eyed[77] Nereid Thetis who once upon a time rode a bridled dolphin to Haemonian Peleus':

> talis ad Haemonium Nereis Pelea quondam
> uecta est frenato caerula pisce Thetis.

The described, defined Delia is enlarged by this comparison to (another) goddess who came to a mortal.

Tibullus essays to convey the magical beauty of his girl. Propertius pounces. In 2. 2 he explains his succumbing to love again, and the poem picks up and

---

[72] It is an interesting fact that Propertius does not name, does not feel the need to name, Cynthia in the three opening programmatic poems (2. 1–3), if these were the three opening poems of Book 2a (which seems plausible). Her first naming in the transmitted Book 2 is in 2. 5. 1. Her fame speaks for itself? We should infer Cynthia from her Cynthian attributes in 2. 1?

[73] Propertius here trumps Tibullus' Delian girl, and at the same time asserts contact with, but a witty difference from Callimachus, whom Apollo set on the right road, and to whom Calliope and the other Muses revealed the first two books of the *Aetia* (fr. 1. 22 f., 7. 22 ff., cf. Cameron (1995), 107–8).

[74] From other passages we gain the guarded information that she is *formosa* (1. 1. 55), and has long hair (1. 3. 91); and besides 1. 5. 43–6, the passage to which I attend here, there is line 66 mentioned below referring to a *niueus pes*. Of course we do not expect the romantic love poets often to attempt to describe the indescribable (Lyne (1980), 262–4); but when they do attempt it, we expect them to do so with extreme care; and other love poets, aware of the difficulties, will read with professional and challenged interest.

[75] This reading, printed by Luck, is arguably superior to the *uerbis* of the main manuscript tradition, not least because (an interesting fact) Delia is not much given to words in any context—very unlike Cynthia. In his apparatus Luck compares 1. 8. 17, Prop. 3. 6. 25.

[76] Cf. Murgatroyd ad loc.

[77] Lee translates *caerula* 'blue-eyed'; Murgatroyd has a useful note on the adjective.

outdoes Tib. 1. 5. 43–6.[78] So does poem 2. 3, another explanation of Propertius' second book. First, Prop. 2. 2. 1–8, 13–14:

> liber eram et uacuo meditabar uiuere lecto;
>   at me composita pace fefellit Amor.
> cur haec in terris facies humana moratur?
>   Iuppiter, ignosco pristina furta tua.
> fulua coma est longaeque manus, et maxima toto
>   corpore, et incedit uel Ioue digna soror,
> aut cum Dulichias[79] Pallas spatiatur ad aras,
>   Gorgonis anguiferae pectus operta comis
>   .   .   .   .
> cedite iam, diuae,[80] quas pastor uiderat olim
>   Idaeis tunicas ponere uerticibus!

I was free, and I intended to live and sleep alone; but Love deceived me when peace was made. Why does this mortal face dally on earth? Jupiter, I pardon your stolen loves in olden times. Her hair is golden, her fingers long, her whole size majestic, and she moves even worthy of Jupiter himself, his sister, or when Pallas Athene strides to Dulichian altars, her breast covered with the snake-locks of the Gorgon... Yield now, goddesses, whom once upon a time the shepherd (Paris) saw set aside your clothes on the summits of Ida.

Propertius goes straight for the *facies*, as Tibullus had done, but instantly suggests Cynthia's face's superiority to other girls' faces: it would tempt Jupiter, how is it still among mortals?[81] Long hands (fingers)[82] replace the

---

[78] La Penna (1950), 234 observes interestingly that Prop. 2. 2. 1 echoes (but he would *not* say alludes to) Tib. 1. 5. 1 f.: 2. 2. 1 f. 'liber eram et... | at', 1. 5. 1 f. 'asper eram et... | at'. An opening poem in Propertius 2a alludes to a closural poem in Tibullus 1 (first half).

[79] *Dulichias* is suspect. Why should Athene stride to altars in Dulichium? Dulichium is one of the distinct group of four islands in the *Odyssey* which include Ithaca: Ithaca, Dulichium, Same and Zacynthos: *Od.* 1. 246 f., 9. 24, 16. 123 f. etc.; Dulichium is where the suitor Amphinomus came from in Homer. At 2. 14. 4 Prop. seems to identify the *litora Dulichiae* with Ithaca, and this is perhaps sufficient to justify the reading in 2. 2. 7 (Athene had of course a special affection for Odysseus). Goold adopts Heinsius' *Munychias*, which would signify 'Athenian': cf. Ov. *Met.* 2. 709 where Mercury flies over 'Munychios... agros gratamque Mineruae... humum'. The transmitted *cum* is replaced with *ceu* by Baehrens, followed by Goold; I think that Camps' note (quoted in part below n. 85) is here useful, and I would retain *cum*.

[80] The reference is of course to the Judgement of Paris. Either we infer a reference to Venus, to complete the trio Juno (6), Athena (7 f.), and Venus, or we assume that a Venus couplet has dropped out—and radically but attractively we can also transpose the mythical but mortal comparisons transmitted in lines 9–12 to follow 2. 29. 28 (surely some myths have indeed dropped out from 2. 29, as comparison with 1. 3 shows). This whole package is Housman's solution, followed by Goold. It would, I suppose, be a possible option to supply a Venus couplet and retain the mortal comparisons 9–12.

[81] Propertius unexpectedly reverts to Cynthia's *facies* in the last couplet of 2. 2 (cf. Lyne (1980), 97–8).

[82] Contrast the disfavoured girl of Catullus 43. 3 'nec longis digitis'.

Tibullan soft arms. And, very notably, Delia's standard-glamorous fair hair becomes more exquisitely and rarely gold-coloured, as *flauae comae* is trumped by *fulua coma*. The choice of adjective is all-important here: by contrast with Tibullus, Propertius finds a most distinctive epithet to dignify *his* blonde.[83] Propertius then specifies that his is a big girl, a splendidly heroic taste; it should be stressed that he is not talking merely about tallness.[84] And then, as in Tibullus, we find myth, but in Propertius more than one myth; and we find (initially) actual equation rather than comparison.[85]

[83] Since fair hair was not actually common among Greeks or Romans, but was on the other hand quite conventionally heroic (the ξανθὴ κόμη of Achilles *Il.* 1. 196, ξανθὸς Μενέλαος *Il.* 3. 284, ξανθὴν Ἀγαμήδην *Il.* 11. 740, etc.; Pease on Verg. *Aen.* 4. 590), it was admired by Romans and Greeks, and occurrences were multiplied with the aid of imagination and other artifices. Murgatroyd in his note on Tib. 1. 5. 43–4, commenting on Delia's *flauae comae*, remarks on the popularity of fair hair among the Elegists' mistresses. But he includes here, without further comment, Prop. 2. 2. 5. This misses an important nuance. Latin colour terms are of course notoriously difficult to pin down, but I would hazard the following. There is not, I think, on the one hand, very much denotative difference between *flauus* and *fuluus*: note among the passages cited below how chrysolite, *aureo fulgore tralucentes* for Plin. *N.H.* 37. 126, is *flauus* for Prop. and gold is *fuluus* for Tib.; cf. further Aul. Gell. 2. 26. 8, 11–12, and André (1949), 128–32 on *flauus* and cognates, 132–35 on *fuluus*. But, on the other hand, there is a difference between the two in habits of usage, a difference therefore of connotation. (i) *Flauus* and cognates are common of the admired and imagined fair hair: see the passages quoted by Murgatroyd on Tib. 1. 5. 43–4, and *TLL* vi. 1. 888. 48–72 *flauus* 'de crinibus sim.', and 72 ff. of people, but with reference to their hair, 886. 32–41 *flaueo* similarly; note e.g. Catull. 66. 62 of Berenice's hair, Verg. *Georg.* 4. 352 of Arethusa's *caput*, *Aen.* 4. 590, 698 of Dido, Horace *Ode* 1. 5. 4 of Pyrrha, and Ov. *Am.* 2. 4. 43 *seu flauent* (*capilli*), where Ovid uses the common term as, significantly, he expresses his indifference to hair colour. By contrast (ii) *fuluus* is not commonly used of hair: *TLL* vi. 1. 1535. 44–50: Prop. 2. 2. 5 is the first of the few cited; the slightly eccentric note of Carter (1900) cited by Goold (1990) ad loc. is in this respect on target. Propertius puts a wedge between Cynthia's and Delia's hair, if only in diction. He selects a choice, not a common word, for fair hair in Cynthia's case. This is Propertius' only use of *fuluus* in any of his books, a significant and interesting fact: for him the word itself is choice. Meantime Tibullus uses *flauus* four more times in Books 1 and 2, at 2. 1. 48 of the *comae* of crops. Tibullus' epithet is not a choice word, not even for him. Propertius uses *flauus* at 2. 16. 44 of chrysolite, and at 4. 4. 20 of Tatius' horse's mane. The only thing that is *fuluus* in Tibullus, Book 1 is gold in his opening line; I suspect that this is relevant to Propertius' use; *fuluus* also in Tib. 2. 1. 88 of *sidera*. (It will be remembered that there is talk of Cynthia's dyeing her hair in 2. 18. 27–8; but since I am not persuaded of the integrity of the piece of text that is marked 2. 18c in Barber and Camps, and 2. 18d in Goold, I cannot pronounce on what colour is involved.)

[84] Cf. Hom. *Od.* 5. 217 and the passages collected by Heubeck, West, and Hainsworth (1988) ad loc., but it is wrong to restrict the sense of μέγεθος, 'magnitude', to height; Stanford's note (London, 1961) on *Od.* 6. 107–8 is here most useful. Heroically beautiful women were generously built, big ladies. Bacchylides' Heracles (5. 168) asks the shade of Meleager in the Underworld if there is a sister of his whom he could marry σοὶ φυὰν ἀλιγκία, 'like you in stature' (and there is of course: Deianeira); Heracles' taste would clearly not favour the Kate Moss type. This is not merely heroic taste: note the appearance of μέγεθος in Dicaearchus' list of favourable attributes among Theban women, below n. 88, but note too Müller's erroneous translation. Enk (n. 12) in his note on Prop. 2. 2. 5, similarly misunderstands what Propertius is saying ('Antiqui admirabantur longas feminas...').

[85] The comparison is so compressed that Propertius effectively expresses identity between Cynthia and Juno, as my translation brings out; cf. Goold 'and she walks worthy even of Jove, as his sister'. Shackleton Bailey (1956), 64 has misplaced suspicion of the genuineness of the text, though ultimately he retains it. So much does Propertius suggest identity that Vergil can echo

Propertius' myths are cued by the quality of Cynthia's gait: *incedit, spatiatur*...[86] This is not only an observant, it is an aggrandizing addition to Tibullus. Everybody knows that girls should have pretty feet, and Tibullus gives us such a detail later in 1. 5 for Delia (line 66).[87] But the discerning prescribe more exactly: women should walk with grace.[88] There is a yet more significant factor. It could seem to some that a god revealed divinity by sheer impressiveness of movement. We will think straight away of Venus at Verg. *Aen.* 1. 405 'et uera incessu patuit dea', but there is interesting precedent for such an idea.[89] This is Propertius' main reason for focussing on the detail. Not just graceful movement but the divine movement that can so distinctively impress is being attributed to Cynthia: she shares the verb *incedit* with Juno, and her divine progress is then confirmed in Athena's matching and illustrating *spatiatur*. Here we have a deft and potent trumping of Tibullus and Delia. We heard nothing of Delia's gait, and her divine counterpart travelled fancifully, dolphin-borne, in Hellenistic manner,[90] suggesting nothing useful.

the line in a speech by Juno herself: *Aen.* 1. 46–7 'ast ego, quae divum incedo regina Iouisque | et soror et coniunx'. Camps underestimates the implication of identity, but unpacks the line well, and his comment on the syntax is useful ('...the word *digna* (especially) compensates the absence of a comparative conjunction; in the following line 7 the syntax continues as if such a conjunction were felt to have been already introduced').

[86] When Housman composed a Venus couplet *exempli gratia* (printed in Goold's text), he built it round *ponit uestigia*.

[87] Contrast the disfavoured girl of Catullus 43. 2 'nec bello pede'; Tibullus in 1. 5. 66 implies or states Delia's *pes* to be *niueus*.

[88] Interesting passages on attractiveness of female gait are collected by Shackleton Bailey (1956), 89 in his note on 2. 12. 24. Note too Dicaearchus of Messana praising Theban women (text in Müller (1848), 259 or Müller (1855), i. 103): αἱ δὲ γυναῖκες αὐτῶν τοῖς μεγέθεσι, πορείαις, ῥυθμοῖς εὐσχημονέσταταί τε καὶ εὐπρεπέσταται τῶν ἐν τῇ Ἑλλάδι γυναικῶν, 'their women, in magnitude, gait, and concinnity, are the most graceful and comely of women in Greece.' Müller's translation of the key nouns is *proceritate, incessu, corporis concinnitate*. The first of these is wrong (see n. 84 above), the second and third interesting and probably right. The way a woman walked (*incessus*) could be not just attractive, but inappropriately tarty: Cic. *Cael.* 49 on Clodia, Sen. *Contr.* 2. 7. 4. (2. 7. 3–4 give an interesting if tendentious view of how a modest *matrona* should conduct herself in public.)

[89] Cf. too the phrasing of Juno in *Aen.* 1. 46–7 quoted above n. 85, also 5. 649. At Hom. *Il.* 13. 71–2 Ajax son of Oileus says that he recognized Poseidon thus: ἴχνια γὰρ μετόπισθε ποδῶν ἠδὲ κνημάων | ῥεῖ' ἔγνων ἀπιόντος, 'I recognized easily from behind as he went away the ⟨?⟩ of his feet and legs.' As Leaf, says ἴχνια can hardly here have its normal sense of footprints; 'movement' would make good sense: such good sense that a variant reading ἴθματα arose. It may be that Vergil read ἴθματα or interpreted ἴχνια as movement; likewise Propertius, and perhaps a host of intervening writers.

[90] For Thetis' dolphin transport, Murgatroyd compares Ov. *Met.* 11. 236 f. and Val. Flacc. 1. 131 ff. and conjectures a Hellenistic source. This is surely right. Strong corroboration comes from Moschus, *Europa* 117 f. where we find the Nereids riding on the backs of unspecified sea-creatures in the company of a specified dolphin: γηθόσυνος δ' ὑπὲρ οἶδμα κυβίστεε βυσσόθε δελφίς· | Νηρεΐδες δ' ἀνέδυσαν ὑπὲξ ἁλός, αἱ δ' ἄρα πᾶσαι | κητείοις νώτοισιν ἐφήμεναι ἐστιχόωντο.

Propertius and Tibullus: Early Exchanges 279

And if we move to Tibullus' elevating, enlarging myth as a whole (blue-eyed Thetis on her dolphin) and compare it to Propertius' myths (Juno and so on), it might to some tastes, Propertius' for example, seem merely winsome, a little rococo, prettily Hellenistic:[91] not in fact very enlarging. But no-one could so disdain Propertius' aggrandizing equation of the striding Cynthia with Juno, no-one could so disdain the comparison of her to the fearsome and ferocious Athena, and, implicitly or explicitly, to Venus.[92] These myths surely outstrip Tibullus' blue-eyed Thetis.

In 2. 3 Propertius responds to an interlocutor who has said, in gist (1–4): 'You said you were girl-proof now, but barely a month goes by, "et turpis de te iam liber alter erit", and now there will be a second disgraceful book about you. How come?' Propertius: 'I was trying to attempt the impossible; no love is ever removed.' And then he explains the irresistible attractions, lines 9 ff. These lines build on and in a sense trump his own poem 2. 2; and again they glance at and trump that other irresistible attraction, Tibullus' Delia:

> nec me tam facies, quamuis sit candida, cepit
>   (lilia non domina sint magis alba mea;
> ut Maeotica nix minio si certet Hibero,
>   utque rosae puro lacte natant folia),[93]
> nec de more comae per leuia colla fluentes,
>   non oculi, geminae, sidera nostra, faces,
> nec si qua Arabio lucet bombyce puella
>   (non sum de nihilo blandus amator ego):
> quantum quod posito formose saltat Iaccho,
>   egit ut euhantis dux Ariadna choros,
> et quantum, Aeolio cum temptat carmina plectro,
>   par Aganippaeae ludere docta lyrae;
> et sua cum antiquae committit scripta Corinnae,

---

[91] Cf. Moschus cited in the previous note, Catullus 64. 1 ff., Verg. *Georg.* 4. 388–9.
[92] See n. 80 above.
[93] Transposition of 11–12 to follow 16, proposed by Housman and accepted by Goold, is wrong. The red-lead & snow, roses & milk comparisons are more naturally prompted by reference to Cynthia's complexion, even if in the narrative only one colour (*candida*) in her complexion is specifically mentioned, than by a reference to a girl in a silk garment. For girls' complexions giving rise to red & white similes, cf. Catull. 61. 187 with Fordyce ad loc.; cf. too esp. Prop. 3. 24. 7–8 where Cynthia's false *candor* prompted Propertius to comparisons with rosy dawn; and Verg. *Aen.* 12. 68–9 seems to me a clear echo and confirmation of our transmitted text. Transposition also spoils Propertius' rhetoric, especially his rhetorical interchange with Tibullus. It is the *facies* of Cynthia that is important, that is an attraction—a better *facies* than Delia's—although it is not now for Propertius (in 2. 3) the main attraction; so it merits much stylistic attention. The *bombyx* dress by contrast is emphatically unimportant, dismissed in the line 'non sum de nihilo blandus amator ego' and by the non-specific attribution *si qua*: it hardly merits a couple of similes. (It will also be seen that I am happy with the text *si qua Arabio*, replaced with *si quando Arabo* (Pucci and Garrod) by Goold; cf. further below.)

> carminaque Erinnae[94] non putat aequa suis.
> non tibi nascenti primis, mea uita, diebus
> candidus argutum sternuit omen Amor?
> haec tibi contulerunt caelestia munera diui,
> haec tibi ne matrem forte dedisse putes...

It is not so much her face, although it is fair, that has captured me—lilies are not whiter than my mistress; as if Scythian snow should vie with Iberian red-lead, and as rose petals float on milk; it is not so much her hair flowing in order over her smooth neck, nor her eyes, two torches, my stars; nor if a girl shines in Arabian silk (I am no lover who flatters for no reason);[95] <not so much these things> as the fact that she dances beautifully when the wine is put out, even as Ariadne led the troupe of Dionysus; as when she essays songs with Aeolian plectrum, skilled to play, a match[96] for the Aganippean[97] lyre; and as when she pits her writings against ancient Corinna's, and reckons the songs of Erinna unequal to hers. Surely, my life, a fair and favourable Love sneezed a clear omen in those first days, when you were born. The gods bestowed these heavenly gifts upon you, lest perchance you think your mother gave them to you...

Tibullus in 1. 5. 43 f. was bewitched by Delia's *facies*, arms and hair. In 2. 2 Propertius trumped that presentation. Now, challenged again in 2. 3 to find explanation for his infatuated behaviour, he picks up his trumping 2. 2 and carries it further. It is not so much Cynthia's *facies*, although he can find four more lines for it in amplification of 2. 2;[98] nor is it so much those *comae*, for which he had found a choice and distinguishing epithet in 2. 2; nor is it her eyes, which have not been mentioned by the poet in these opening poems of Book 2, but deserve mention and praise by the poet who opened his first work 'miserum me cepit ocellis'; nor is it any fancy dress a girl might wear—of this kind of attraction he is very dismissive.[99] The heart of Cynthia's attraction and irresistibility lies in her accomplishments and art: her dancing, song, lyre-playing, and poetry. We are back—with more detail—in the same area of

---

[94] I adopt this attractive conjecture (Butrica following Beroaldus), but without conviction of its certainty.

[95] The translation of the parenthesis is Goold's, who has taken *blandus* with *de nihilo*, as Rothstein advises. I remain uncertain about this.

[96] I have taken *par* to be nominative; Goold and others take it as an accusative object of *ludere*.

[97] For Aganippe, one of the springs of inspiration on Callimachus' Mt. Helicon, see *Aetia* fr. 2A. 16 with Pfeiffer ad loc. and on line 30, comparing Cat. 61. 28 ff. and Verg. *Ecl.* 10. 12; note too Pfeiffer on fr. 696.

[98] On the text, see n. 93 above.

[99] He does not now, if the transmitted text is right (cf. n. 93), even tie this particular attraction to Cynthia (*si qua*); and it merits a line of outright disdain, 'non sum de nihilo'... In the past in Cynthia's case finery of dress, though not bombyx itself, was disapproved in 1. 2, admired in 2. 1. Such finery does not explicitly characterize Delia anywhere, so it does not look as if she is the butt here. I suspect Propertius glances here at another poet-lover, who had a taste for sensuously dressed women. Perhaps, in view of what is said about 43–4, Cornelius Gallus.

inspired artistic endowment which distinguished the Cynthia of 2. 1 from the Delia of Tibullus, Book 1. The cycle of trumping is complete.

Or nearly so. We may see Propertius' scorn at any contribution by Cynthia's mother as partly stimulated by Tibullus' glowing, sentimental tribute to Delia's mother in the opening poem of the second half of Book 1: 1. 6. 57 ff. More interestingly, in the lines that follow, Propertius reverts to the topic of a *facies*. Cynthia will be Jupiter's first Roman girlfriend, she is a second Helen; she would have been a fairer cause of Troy's destruction; now Propertius can at least understand why the Trojan war was fought (29–38). Then (39–40), 'her face is worthy indeed even for Achilles to die for it; it had been judged a worthy reason for war even by Priam':

> digna quidem facies, pro qua uel obiret Achilles;
> uel Priamo belli causa probanda fuit.

So, from talk of Cynthia's divine gifts (25–9), the poem has worked back to praise of Cynthia's *facies*; I think it is clear that the face in 39 is (in the first place) Cynthia's.[100] Achilles might have died for it, Priam would have approved it as a cause of war. More trumping of the original card played by Tibullus. And something more. Lines 41–4:

> si quis uult fama tabulas anteire uetustas,
>   hic dominam exemplo ponat in arte meam:
> siue illam Hesperiis, siue illam ostendet Eois,
>   uret et Eoos, uret et Hesperios.

If anyone wants to surpass the Old Masters' pictures, let him set my mistress before him as his model when he works: if he displays her to the people of the Occident, if he displays her to the people of the Orient, he will inflame the people of the Orient, inflame the Occidentals.

From the Aldine edition of 1502 down to Goold, these climactically closural couplets have been seen—from time to time, and correctly I think—as the end of the poem. The key to this final flourish is Gallus.

If, says Propertius, a painter should want to outdo the Old Masters, let him take Cynthia as his model for a portrait, and then he will set the world afire from East to West. The last couplet stresses two Grecisms (*Hesperius*, *Eous*), which Neoteric poets had affected.[101] Ovid celebrates Gallus at *Am.* 1. 15. 29 f.

---

[100] So Camps and Enk; oddly Rothstein takes *digna facies* as a predicate and supplies Cynthia as subject. I infer from Goold's translation that he takes *facies* as belonging to Helen. The text admits some (profitable) ambiguity. It is certainly possible to take the couplet as referring to Helen; but then we refer it to the second Helen. For the 'actualizing indicative' involved in referring *fuit* to Cynthia's face, see Hor. *Ode* 2. 17. 28 with Nisbet and Hubbard ad loc.

[101] Cinna fr. 6 Courtney, Cat. 62. 35, and see *Ciris* 352 with Lyne ad loc.

in a couplet 'Gallus et Hesperiis et Gallus notus Eois | et sua cum Gallo nota Lycoris erit', also containing those Grecisms, 'where the context makes it probable that a line of Gallus' elegies is being echoed'.[102] Much makes sense if we suppose that Gallus had celebrated his beloved in a line which was dominated by those neoteric Grecisms for East and West, which Ovid then echoed, and which Propertius echoes too.[103] Ovid, praising Gallus' poetry, echoes Gallus' own praise for Lycoris, indicating a salient feature of Gallus' poetry. Propertius: if a painter merely has Cynthia as a sitter, his picture will have an impact like Gallus' Lycoris. Without Gallus' text, we can of course only guess at Propertius' precise point, but we may feel sure that he works round to *facies* again not just to outdo Tibullus once more, but to trump that other great Elegist. What the face of Lycoris could achieve, a mere likeness of the face of Cynthia could match.

[102] Camps on Prop. 2. 3. 43.
[103] Cf. Boucher (1966), 98 and Ross (1975), 118 who (surely rightly) see Gallus echoed not only in Ov. *Am.* 1. 15. 29 f. and Prop. 2. 3. 43 f., but in Ov. *Ars* 3. 537 'Vesper et Eoae nouere Lycorida terrae' (reference misprinted as 527 in Boucher).

16

Notes on Catullus[1] (2002)

Nearly all these thoughts originated in a seminar which Don Fowler and I gave together some years ago. I include one conjecture which is specifically his. Characteristically, he delivered this off the cuff in conversation. Equally characteristically, and endearingly, he never bothered to lay claim to it, and so I shall make the attribution for him, and provide some back-up argument. The other notes, such as they are, are indebted to his presence and stimulus.

I. POEMS 10 AND 28

Both these poems dramatize financially unprofitable experience in a provincial governor's *cohors*.[2] In 10 a girl exposes Catullus' attempts to make the best of his dismal experience under his *praetor* in Bithynia. In 28 Catullus addresses friends whom he presumes to have fared just as badly under their governor (Piso), and ruefully recalls his own provincial episode. Poem 28 identifies Catullus' 'praetor' in 10 as (C.) Memmius, praetor in 58 BC.[3]

Poem 28 alludes to and builds on 10, and this is important to see. At 10. 12–13 Catullus refers to Memmius as an *irrumator* ('praesertim quibus esset

---

[1] My thanks to Jasper Griffin for helpful comments on this paper. Editions and commentaries cited by name alone: Bardon (2nd edn., 1973), Eisenhut (1983), Ellis (1876, 1878), Goold (1983), Fordyce (1961), Kroll (4th edn., 1960), Lee (1990a), Mynors (1958), Quinn (3rd edn., 1973), Syndikus (1984, 1987, 1990), Thomson (1997).

[2] For the well-documented institution of young equestrians' serving in the entourage of a provincial governor, see Gelzer (1975), 101–2; Cic. *Q. Fr.* 1. 1. 11–12 (a key text, though Gelzer and Shackleton Bailey's commentary differ slightly in interpretation of detail); Hor. *Epist.* 1. 3; the amusing letters of Cicero to Trebatius Testa, *Ad Fam.* 7. 6, 17, 18; and Cic. *Cael.* 73 on M. Caelius' service as *contubernalis* to Q. Pompeius Rufus proconsul of Africa in 61 BC (another key text) 'cum autem paulum iam roboris accessisset aetati, in Africam profectus est Q. Pompeio pro consule contubernalis...usus quidam prouincialis non sine causa a maioribus huic aetati tributus'. Catullus 46 dramatizes his leaving Memmius' province of Bithynia. Such service might be the first stage towards the *cursus honorum*; as we gather from Catullus and others, it was (also) hoped that enrichment would ensue: further excellent references on the financial aspect to service in a provincial governor's *cohors* in Kroll's note on 10. 8.

[3] On this C. Memmius, see Fordyce on 10. 13, Syndikus (1984–90), i. 117–18.

irrumator | praetor'): the reader will infer that he exploits the obscenity as a passing and casual term of abuse (as English might say 'a bugger of a praetor', 'a praetor who screwed us', which catches the gist though not of course the literal sense of *irrumator*).[4] But with surprise and wit Catullus picks up, expands, and makes concrete the abusive term at 28. 9–10 when he returns to the topic of Memmius: 'o Memmi, bene me ac diu supinum | tota ista trabe lentus irrumasti'.[5] So the two poems co-operate. With amusement we see that 28. 9–10 realize the potential of 10. 12–13. Re-reading 10. 12–13, we should find the lines funnier, latently witty, and original.

The actual topic of making money—and failing to do so—emerges in both poems in questions, direct and indirect. In 28 it surfaces in Catullus' paradoxical question to the *Pisonis comites* at 6–10 'ecquidnam in tabulis patet lucelli, | expensum...?'[6] The indirect interrogative *ecquidnam*[7] ('Is there anything which...?', *TLL* v. 2. 52. 26 ff., *OLD* s.v. *ecquis*, Kühner and Stegmann i. 656, ii. 515) introduces the prosaic topic with an amusing sense of obliqueness and insinuation. It is the more amusing if Catullus is *repeating* the question insinuatingly asked of himself—there in *oratio obliqua*—in the earlier poem, 10. 5–9 'incidere nobis | sermones uarii, in quibus... | | *ecquonam* mihi profuisset aere'. We get the impression that it is the sort of question that has to surface: '... *and did you make any money?*' Given the interrelation of *irrumator* and *irrumasti*, it seems likely that the poems allude to each other here too, and that Statius' conjecture in 10. 8 is right: *ecquonam* Statius: *et quoniam* OGR: *al. quonam* G¹R², whence the vulgate *et quonam*. Many recent editors print Statius' conjecture (Eisenhut, Goold, Kroll, Thomson, *fortasse recte* in Mynors's *app. crit.*) but only Kroll discusses the choice, and the argument from the co-operative relationship between the two poems may not be otiose.[8]

II. POEM 30

Poem 30 to an Alfenus is Catullus' only essay in the greater asclepiadean metre. Horace uses it twice in his first book of *Odes*: 1. 11 to Leuconoe, and

---

[4] Cf. Adams (1982), 124–30, esp. 124 and 130.

[5] *trabs* itself is used sens. obsc. only here, but there are similar metaphors: Adams (1982), 23.

[6] 'In your profit columns are there any... *debts?*' *vel sim.* The same paradox in 7–8. Cf. Syndikus (1984–90), i. 175–6.

[7] This is an uncontroversial adjustment of *et quid nam* transmitted by OGR.

[8] Kroll—as indeed Mynors in his *app. crit.*—cites 28. 6 as a parallel, but suggests no functional interaction between the poems. On the corruption and for further brief argument, see Luck (1966), 281.

1. 18 to Varus, and then in 4. 10. It seems a likely guess that Catullus' Alfenus and Horace's Varus are one and the same: the P. Alfenus Varus whom Vergil addresses as Varus in *Eclogue* 6 and 9. 26–9.[9] Catullus catches him young, as he caught the young Asinius Pollio (12. 6), and Horace metrically alludes to his predecessor's poem to the same addressee.

The poem is written in a high style, as well as an elaborate metre.[10] Whether or not the purported sentiments are entirely serious, there is no doubt about the poetic register: the Ennian compound *caelicolis* (4) and the Grecism *aerias* (10) are immediate stylistic indexes.[11]

In line 11 Catullus surely wrote 'si tu oblitus es, at di meminere, at meminit Fides...' which supports the high style. Muretus apparently read this in a manuscript. No such manuscript survives, and one wonders whether Muretus was creatively and wishfully misremembering the reading of—in Thomson's siglum—(ζ) 'meminerunt at'....[12] How this Renaissance manuscript came to offer an unmetrical text with an important component of truth is an interesting question. Muretus' text is curiously neglected by modern editors. Only Bardon of those listed above prints it. Muretus' expressed belief 'quae lectio quanto sit elegantior, nemo non videt' was wide of the mark.

Muretus' text gives us the rhetorical figure of anaphora, and on top of that the stately structure of anaphoric *at* in an apodosis to a *si* clause. For *at* in anaphora, see *TLL* i. 992. 79 ff., for *at* in apodosis, 1011. 8 ff. (and Mynors's note on Verg. G. 2. 467), and for the complete stucture of anaphoric *at* in an apodosis, cf. Verg. G. 2. 461–71 '<u>si</u> non ingentem foribus domus alta superbis | ... uomit ... | nec uarios inhiant ... || nec casia liquidi corrumpitur usus oliui; | *at* secura quies et nescia fallere uita, | ... *at* latis otia fundis, | speluncae uiuique lacus, *at*[13] frigida tempe... || non absunt'. Horace has a comparable structure, but without the formality of the regular *si* protasis at *Serm.* 1. 3. 341–2. Cf. too Philodemus, *Anth. Pal.* 11. 44. 1–6 = Gow and Page XXIII. 1–6 Αὔριον εἰς

---

[9] For P. Alfenus Varus, see the introductory note in Nisbet and Hubbard on *Odes* 1. 18.
[10] There is a useful summary history of the metre in Fordyce's introductory note to poem 30.
[11] *caelicolae* at Ennius *Ann.* 445; in Catullus also at 64. 386 and 68. 138; in between Ennius and Catullus the only instance of *caelicola* to survive is Lucilius 28 Marx = 21 Warmington, clearly parodic. *aerius* transliterates ἀέριος: *TLL* s.v. 'voc. poeticum (primi utuntur VARRO AT. CATULL. LUCR.), ex scriptoribus acceperunt CIC. phil. (semel), APVL....'. Cf. Lucr. 1. 12, etc., Varro Atacinus fr. 14. 6 Courtney, Catull. also at 64. 142, 240, 291, 66. 6, 68. 57. We note that Catullus' other uses of both *aerius* and *caelicola* are in his longer, high-style poems. (Perversely Mynors adopts the spelling *aereas* in 30. 10: Catullus is likely to have transliterated the Greek word accurately. Mynors prints *aere-* again at 64. 240, 291, 66. 6, but *aeri-* at 64. 142 and 68. 57.)
[12] Muretus' note (Venice, 1554) suggests that he was relying on memory: 'In meo illo libro, cujus bonitatem nunquam tantopere perspexi, quam cum haec scriberem (eo autem magis memini, quod eo urens, totum Catullum etiam tum puerulus, saepe relegendo edidiceram) in eo igitur versus hic ita scriptus erat....'.
[13] *et* has good manuscript authority, but Mynors prints *at*, clearly rightly.

λιτήν σε καλιάδα, φίλτατε Πείσων, | ἐξ ἐνάτης ἕλκει λουσοφιλὴς ἕταρος | εἰκάδα δειπνίζων ἐνιαύσιον· εἰδ᾽ ἀπολείψῃς | οὔθατα καὶ Βρομίου Χιογενά πρόποσιν | ἀλλ᾽ ἑτάρους ὄψει παναληθέας, ἀλλ᾽ ἐπακούσῃ | Φαιήκων γαίης πουλὺ μελιχρότερα...

The perfect form *meminere* may seem attractive in itself. *meminere* was plausibly conjectured by Czwalina at 64. 148[14] in a similar sort of context, and the *-ere* termination may seem to marry better with the surrounding poetic style[15]—though Catullus' practice with *-ere* and *-erunt* suggests no great stylistic distinction in his mind.

In lines 4–5 there is something seriously wrong:

> nec facta impia fallacum hominum caelicolis placent.
> quae tu neglegis ac me miserum deseris in malis.

A single *nec* makes little sense as a connective here: hence *nunc* (Baehrens), *num...?* (Schwabe); and the relative *quae* has no natural antecedent: hence *quos* (B. Guarinus) and other suggestions. Economically Ellis proposed to solve the problems together, positing a lacuna after line 3: 'That something is lost after 3 is probable partly from the unintelligible *Nec*, partly from *Quae*, which seems to refer to *several* considerations, perhaps the sense of shame, as well as the vengeance of the celestials.'

The economy of a lacuna as a solution is attractive, but I wonder whether it should not be placed after line 4 rather than line 3. Line 4 seems to allude to Homer, *Od.* 14. 83:

> οὐ μὲν σχέτλια ἔργα θεοὶ μάκαρες φιλέουσιν

but Eumaeus (the speaker) also puts the point positively in the next line:

> ἀλλὰ δίκην τίουσι καὶ αἴσιμα ἔργ᾽ ἀνθρώπων.

Did Catullus do the same? For, while a single *nec* is an unacceptable connective in the context, a *nec* followed by a *sed*—translating Eumaeus' ἀλλά—produces an idiomatic pattern: cf. Cic. *Phil.* 6. 7 'nec uero de illo sicut de homine aliquo debemus, sed ut de importunissima belua cogitare', 7. 19 'nec ego pacem nolo, sed pacis nomine bellum inuolutum reformido'; Verg. *G.* 3. 404–6 'nec tibi cura canum fuerit postrema, sed una | uelocis Spartae catulos acremque Molossum | pasce sero pingui', *G.* 3. 471–2; *Aen.* 2. 314–15 'nec sat rationis in armis, | sed glomerare manum bello...ardent animi'. And in such a *sed* clause we can easily imagine a suitable antecedent for *quae*. Exempli gratia:

---

[14] Cf. Goold (1958), 105.
[15] On the third-person plural perfect in *-ere*, see Coleman (1999), 44.

> nec facta impia fallacum hominum caelicolis placent
> sed grata officia et foedera seruata fideliter,
> quae tu neglegis ac me miserum deseris in malis.

A serious problem remains, however. Catullus' polymetrics do not follow any systematic pattern of even numbers of lines, let alone Meineke's law for Horace's *Odes* (Horace composed in multiples of four lines: the exception, 4. 8, suffers from interpolation).[16] But a glance at the transmitted text of poem 30 suggests that Catullus is thinking in terms of couplets, and the acute Ellis posited a lacuna of *two* lines. I can see nothing else that needs to be said between the transmitted lines 4 and 5. The best way I can see of restoring a couplet structure is to posit another, single line lacuna after line 3: another line beginning with *iam*.

In line 6 OGR transmit the unidiomatic *o heu*. Palladius corrected this to *eheu*. *heu heu* is just as available. Investigation suggests that *eheu* is more colloquial than *heu*, and an iterated *heu* may be more suitable in the high style of this poem. On *heu* and *eheu*, see my note on *Ciris* 264—a single telling fact is that the good manuscript tradition of Vergil preserves forty-five examples of *heu*, none at all of *eheu*. For iterated *heu* see, for example, *Ecl.* 2. 58, 3. 100. Horace presents an editor with some nice judgements in this respect.[17] Catullus 64. 61, 77. 5 and 6 likewise.

III. POEM 34

These are the last two stanzas of Catullus' Hymn to Diana, 34. 17–24:

> tu *cursu*, dea, *menstruo*
> metiens iter annuum,
> rustica agricolae *bonis*
> tecta *frugibus* exples.
> sis quocumque tibi placet
> sancta nomine, Romulamque,
> antique ut solita es, *bona*
> sospites *ope* gentem.

Romulam *Fowler* : Romuli *OGR*

---

[16] Lachmann irresistibly proposed the excision of 4. 8. 15b–19a: see the excellent summary of Syndikus (2001), ii. 346–8. Lachmann also proposed the excision of 28 and 33 to achieve a line-number divisible by four, but about this Syndikus (ii. 348) is sceptical.

[17] Horace, *Odes* 1. 15. 9, 1. 35. 33, and 2. 14. 1. Shackleton Bailey's Teubner (Stuttgart, 1985) gets it right on all three occasions, I think (*heu heu, heu heu, eheu*); the Wickham–Garrod Oxford text (1922) prints *eheu* at 1. 35. 33: this is surely out of keeping with the high style of the Ode?

The adjective form *Romulam* is a convincing improvement on the transmitted *Romuli* (which itself is an easy normalization). On this text, we have an ablative noun–epithet and an accusative noun–epithet in the participial (*metiens*) clause; we then have an accusative epithet–noun and an ablative epithet–noun in the succeeding main clause and in the the next sentence. What is more, in these last two, we have the pattern epithet–epithet/noun–noun (abAB in the first, abBA in the second). Catullus shows himself highly interested in word-patterning especially in poems 64 and 65–8.[18] The precise phrase *Romula gens* is picked up by Horace at *Ode* 4. 5. 1–2 'diuis orte bonis, optime Romulae | custos gentis...' and most significantly in another hymn at *Carmen Saeculare* 47 'di,... Romulae genti date remque prolemque | et decus omne'.

IV. POEM 61 (AND 68, AND OTHERS)

Poem 61 is the wedding poem for Manlius Torquatus. At 61. 31–2 'ac domum dominam uoca | coniugis cupidam noui', the text is guaranteed against attempts to make the bride less passionate and interesting[19] by the description of the mythical bride Laodamia, 68. 73–4 'coniugis ut quondam flagrans aduenit amore | Protesilaeam Laodamia domum'. Catullus conceives Junia Aurunculeia in similar terms to Laodamia. Whether poem 68 was composed before 61—that is, whether we have to do with a chronological allusion—we cannot of course tell; if 68 was composed after 61, Catullus makes explicit the implicit way he was thinking of Junia. Before noting other cross-references to Catullan poems that spice up 61, we should observe that poem 68 benefits from observing this parallel. At 68. 68 'isque domum nobis isque dedit dominae' (*dominae* Froehlich : *dominam* OGR), *domina* is combined with *domus* as it is at 61. 31 'domum dominam uoca', and the obvious inference would be that in the former as in the latter *domina* refers to the 'mistress, lady of the house',[20] and not to a mistress as seen from a slave's perspective (this is *not* an anticipation of the Elegiac use of *domina*).[21] Even less plausible than

---

[18] Cf. Ross (1969), 132–7; cf. too Conrad (1965), 195–258; Pearce (1966), 140 ff. and 168 ff.; Norden (4th edn., 1957), 391–404.

[19] Pleitner conjectured *coniugi*. Wilamowitz punctuated after *uoca* and took *cupidam* with *mentem*: see Fordyce's note ad loc.

[20] Briefly noted by Quinn in his note on line 68, countering current trends. But neither in that note nor in his large book Quinn (1972), 83, 90, 182, does he develop the point. In the commentary indeed Quinn then instantly equivocates: 'Perhaps also the first allusion to the concept... of the lover as his mistress's slave.'

[21] But to find a sense 'mistress of a slave' in 68. 68 is popular: see e.g. Syndikus (1984–90), ii. 271–2; Wiseman (1985), 160–1; Garrison (1991), n. ad loc.

seeing a reference to a slave's mistress is to retain the transmitted *dominam* and find a reference to a 'châtelaine' or 'housekeeper'—a sense which its advocates are slow to parallel[22]—or to the goddess Venus,[23] or to an unnamed girl provided by Allius.[24] In this vicinity of poem 68 Catullus is showing us a complex of fantasies that he built around Lesbia, fantasies stimulated by the exhilaration of expectation.[25] An index of his wishful fantasizing is provided by *candida diua* in line 70. In the Laodamia myth he will try, vainly, to maintain an image of Lesbia as a devoted bride arriving at the *domus* (74) of her husband: these fantasies begin in line 68, as Catullus gives her the terminology of wife and lady, *domina. nobis* is transiently ambiguous between true plural and plural for singular. The effect of this ambiguity is perhaps to lend weight to the final revelation of the fantasy contained in *dominae*. Problems have been seen in the interpretation of *ad quam*, if *dominae* is read (the antecedent must now be *domum*), but these are not I think real.[26] Nor do I find any difficulty in the juxtaposition of *domina* in line 156 with *lux mea* in 160, both referring to Lesbia.[27]

There seems a clear intention in poem 61 to talk of Torquatus' bride and marriage in spicier terms than was conventional.[28] There is, as well as the

---

[22] Cf. Fordyce ad loc.; Wilkinson (1970), 290; Feeney (1992), 34.

[23] Macleod (1983), 163 n. 8.

[24] This seems to be the view of Muretus (Venice, 1554). His note on line 74 reads 'Laodamiae comparat puellam illam, cujus sibi usum concesserat Manlius...'.

[25] Cf. Lyne (1980), 52–60, 87. For further discussion of the Laodamia myth, cf. e.g. Feeney (1992), 33–44; Syndikus (1984–90), ii. 275–80, 283–7; Macleod (1983), 159–65; Williams (1980), 50–61.

[26] Fordyce sternly remarks that 'The Latin for "the house in which" is not *domus ad quam* but *domus in qua*'. Similarly Wilkinson (1970), 290 points out that, on the other side of the coin, *ad* with an accusative of a person *is* idiomatic for 'at someone's (house)'; and on this positive point Wilkinson is of course right (*OLD ad* 16a). But there are plenty of examples of *ad* with an accusative of a place, effectively equivalent to *in* plus ablative. Note phrases like *ad forum, ad aedem*, and especially *ad uillam*, Cic. *Rosc. Am.* 44, Kühner and Stegmann i. 520. For a relative pronoun jumping to a remoter antecedent, cf. e.g. Cic. *Arch.* 25.

[27] Wilkinson (1970), 290 thought that *lux mea*, the last of the subjects following *sitis*, referred to Lesbia (correctly) and that therefore *domina* could not. But there is no need to suppose that *domina* is another subject of the optative *sitis*, which would indeed make it difficult for *domina* to refer to Lesbia. In 155 ff. Catullus wishes felicity to Allius, to Allius' lover, to the house in which he and Lesbia (*domina*) 'played', to a figure concealed by textual corruption, and, finally, to Lesbia (*lux mea*). It is the all-important *domus* that is the subject in 156. I take *lusimus* to be transiently ambiguous between true plural and plural for singular (cf. *nobis* in 68) and both Catullus (*lusimus*) and Lesbia (*domina*) to be relegated to the subordinate, relative clause. On this interpretation there is no problem in *domina* and *lux mea* both referring to Lesbia.

[28] In judging what was 'conventional' there is of course a large amount of (informed) guesswork. But see Griffin (1985), 119–21, paying special attention to note 31. The rather heavy-footed prescriptions of Menander the Rhetorician may, for example, give us some index of conventional taste: see Russell and Wilson (1981), 134–59 for Menander's advice both for the 'epithalamium' (also called the 'wedding speech', γαμήλιος λόγος), and for the 'bedroom speech',

parallel with 68. 73–4, the comparison of the bride to the Venus of the Judgement of Paris (61. 17–20). And there is overlap with Catullus' own shorter love poems.[29] Note first 61. 199–203:

> ille pulueris Africi
> siderumque micantium
> subducat numerum prius,
> qui uestri numerare uolt
> multa milia ludi.

These lines clearly recall the sand and stars comparison of 7. 3–8, and the 'basia... quae nec per*numerare* curiosi | possint' of 7. 9–11; also the *milia* of kisses in poems 5 and 48. Interaction between these poems will cause the romance of Catullus' lighter love moments to spill over into the wedding poem.

ludus at 61. 203 should also catch our attention, as should *ludite* at 61. 204 'ludite ut lubet, et breui | liberos date'. *ludus* is a key word for Cicero in his urbane defence of the amorous Caelius' youthful flings: *Cael.* 28 'datur enim concessu omnium huic aliqui ludus aetati [i.e. youth], et ipsa natura profundit adulescentiae cupiditates. quae si ita erumpunt ut nullius uitam labefactent, nullius domum euertant, faciles et tolerabiles haberi solent'; cf. too *Cael.* 39, 42, and elsewhere. Love is seen as a game. For Cicero's defensive purposes love is *only* a game, but *ludus* involves a view of love shared, say, by Horace (cf. *Odes* 3. 12. 1 and 3. 15. 12)—and not normally by Catullus. But in this wedding poem it serves the purpose of showing that married sex is not just functional but fun. Catullus may exhort Manlius and Junia Aurunculeia to procreate, but he is also assuming that they will enjoy the process. Contrast, say, Lucr. 4. 1274–7 and other publicly expressed views.[30]

Given these strategies of spice and allusion, we can protect another reading in poem 61. With 61. 109–12 '(o cubile...) quae tuo ueniunt ero, | quanta gaudia, quae uaga | nocte, quae *medio die* | gaudeat!', compare 32. 1–3 'Amabo, mea dulcis Ipsitilla, | meae deliciae, mei lepores, | iube ad te ueniam *meridiatum*', and so on. *uaga* may be debatable, but surely *medio die* is right. Both romantics and moralists were squeamish about sex at lunchtime, but this is not a wedding poem for the severe, and Catullus, choosing the erotics

---

κατευναστικὸς λόγος. Philodemus tells us that wedding *songs* (ἐπιθαλάμια with μουσική) were in Catullus' time virtually obsolete, but attests poems, ποιήματα. He gives no clue to the content of these poems, but does not seem to rate them highly, bracketing them with cooks and other handymen that make up the celebration: see Neubecker (1986), ch. 3, 43–4 and 96.

[29] *Mutatis mutandis*, the comment above on allusion and chronology applies to what follows.
[30] Lyne (1980), 2–3.

of *ludus* for Torquatus, plausibly adds to 61 the atmosphere of the Ipsitilla poem 32, even though for his own Lesbia poetry he favours exclusive focus on the romantic *tacita nox* as the right time for love-making.[31]

Finally, I add some support for a disputed punctuation. 61. 5–9:

> o Hymen Hymenaee,
> cinge tempora floribus
> suaue olentis amaraci,
> flammeum cape, *laetus* huc,
> huc *ueni*...

Thus Kroll, Eisenhut, Syndikus, Goold, and Thomson.[32] Other editions punctuate after *laetus*, taking the epithet with *cape* not *ueni*. The text as printed is surely to be preferred. It is a small matter that Catullus does not elsewhere in the poem start a colon at the | *huc* metrical position; and the usual division of the line is indeed after the third or fifth syllable. What is significant is that an epithet conveying the desired mood of the god in question naturally accompanies the summoning verb in a cletic hymn or a poem in that vein. Kroll cites Greek parallels (Plato, *Laws* 4. 712b, *h. Orph.* 6. 10, and more in Syndikus (1984–90), ii. 16, n. 85). Note the continuing pattern in Latin following Catullus: Verg. *G.* 1. 17–18 'Pan, ouium custos... *adsis*, o Tegeaee, *fauens*'; Tibull. 1. 7. 63–4 'at tu, Natalis multos celebrande per annos, | candidior semper *candidiorque ueni*'; Hor. *Ode* 3. 18. 1–4 'Faune... | per meos finis et aprica rura | *lenis incedas abeasque* paruis | *aequus* alumnis'. Cf. too the hymnic address to Mercury/Augustus at Hor. *Ode* 1. 2. 45 ff. '*serus in caelum redeas*', that is the other side of the cletic coin; and this continues: 'diuque *laetus intersis* populo'.

---

[31] For Catullus in romantic mood ('night time is the right time | to be with the one you love'), cf. 7. 7 *cum tacet nox*, and note the whole setting of poem 68b, esp. 145 where I think Lain's *tacita* for the transmitted *mira* is probably right (Lain (1986), 155–80). More examples of night as the special and romantic time of love: Prop. 1. 10. 3, 2. 14. 9, 15. 1. Contrast the calculatedly sensuous and fun effect of sex after lunch, not only in Catullus 32, but in Ovid *Am.* 1. 5. Note too the persuasively expansive *seu... totum... diem* option in Prop. 1. 14. 10 (this is a man of the world he is talking to). For discussion of the sexology and text of 61. 111, see Nisbet (1978), 99; Mayer (1979), 69; Harrison (1985), 11–12. Plut. *Quaest. Conv.* 655a on Paris in *Il.* 3, quoted by Nisbet, catches well the tone of the moralist: ὡς οὐκ ἀνδρὸς ἀλλὰ μοιχοῦ λυσσῶντος οὖσαν τὴν μεθημερινὴν ἀκρασίαν. Nisbet challenged *medio die* on grounds of both moral propriety and style. Mayer and Harrison correctly judge the sex to be acceptable, but underestimate the degree to which there is a strategy of spiciness in the poem. Harrison agrees with Nisbet that there is a stylistic objection (which I do not feel) to the pairing of *uaga* (110) with *medio* (111), and proposes *caua*.

[32] Also Fedeli (1972), 22 n. 1. See further Fedeli, 25–6 for the anadiplosis *huc huc* and for the cletic *huc ueni*.

V. 68. 89

Troia (nefas!) commune sepulcrum Asiae Europaeque

Horace, *Serm.* 1. 8. 8–10:

> huc prius angustis eiecta cadauera cellis
> conseruus uili portanda locabat in arca;
> hoc miserae plebi stabat *commune sepulcrum*...

By 'common tomb' Horace refers to mass-burial pits for the poor which had existed on the Esquiline (cf. line 14) just outside the city of Rome. Varro, *Ling.* 5. 25 calls such pits, which he says, exist *extra oppida*, 'puticuli', etymologizing the word from *puteus* 'well' or *putescere* 'rot'; the latter etymology is also in Festus 216M s.v. *puticuli*; as well as generally citing such pits *extra oppida*, Varro also localizes them in the *locus publicus ultra Esquilias*, and tells us that the Afranius played on their name in a *Togata*.[33] Pseudo-Acro on Hor. *Serm.* 1. 8. 10 thinks of the victims of executioners: 'soliti enim erant carnifices puteos in Esquilina uia facere, in quos corpora mittebant'. Nineteenth-century excavations of the Esquiline graphically confirmed references to burial pits there.[34]

A resonance like this gives powerful ironic point to *commune sepulcrum* in Catull. 68. 89, Catullus' reference to the burial ground of the great heroes of the *Iliad*. The resonance of a pauper's common graveyard may be at play in the only other poetical example of the phrase before Ausonius: Lucretius 5. 259 'et quoniam dubio procul esse uidetur | omniparens eadem rerum commune sepulcrum...|...terra'. It should be noted, however, that this resonance is not exclusive. Cicero (*Off.* 1. 55) can use the phrase of upper-class family tombs; but, according to Hopkins,[35] long-term family burial chambers were not frequent. The phrase *commune sepulcrum* is overall rare: *TLL* iii. 1969. 71–5.

---

[33] 'eum Afranius putilucos in Togata appellat, quod inde suspiciunt per puteos lumen' (though both key words, *putilucos* and *puteos*, are the result of emendation).

[34] For this evidence and for the institution of mass burial of the Roman poor, see Hopkins (1983), 207–11.

[35] Hopkins (1983), 206.

17

Horace *Odes* Book 1 and the Alexandrian Edition of Alcaeus[1] (2005)

The prime purpose of this paper is to show how our small knowledge of Alcaeus' Book 1 can give much more illumination to Horace *Odes* 1 than we at present permit it to. And Horace's first book may reflect back some little light on Alcaeus.

I. EDITIONS OF *ODES* 1 AND ALCAEUS BOOK 1

I first give some basic information about these books, in order to make a preliminary point.

The traditional view of Horace's *Odes* is that the first three books were issued together as a unit in 23 BC.[2] *Odes* 1. 4, addressed to the suffect consul of that year,[3] still inclines me to believe in a joint publication in 23 BC. But there is much to support the view that the books were at least written in sequence; and it has been argued that the books were not just written but published sequentially in the 20s BC.[4]

When we open Book 1, Horace quickly offers a literary alignment:

>   ...si neque tibias
> Euterpe cohibet nec Polyhymnia
> *Lesboum* refugit tendere barbiton.   (1. 1. 32–4)

---

[1] For Alcaeus' fragments I generally use the edition of Voigt (1971). For the most part Voigt's numeration overlaps with the useful and accessible Loeb of Campbell (1982), who followed the numeration of Lobel and Page (1955). Occasionally Campbell provides fuller citations of testimonia, and on these and other special occasions when it is necessary to cite his edition, his name is appended to the reference. Professor G. O. Hutchinson has throughout advised me, and his remarks on an early draft of this paper caused it to be radically reshaped. The expertise of Dr Bruno Currie and Dr Obbink was also indispensable. It is not of course to be supposed that these scholars agree with all I say. I delivered a version of the paper to the Corpus Christi Graduate Seminar, and owe thanks to that company—in particular to Claudia Strobel—for incisive comment as well as for organizing the occasion.

[2] See the summarizing remarks of Nisbet and Hubbard (1970), pp. xxxv–xxxvi.

[3] Cf. Lyne (1995), 73–5.   [4] See Hutchinson (2002), a piece to be reckoned with.

But the reference to the Lesbian lyre is not conclusive. There were two outstanding Lesbian poets, and an interesting paper has even argued for a 'biformis uates' with Sappho and Alcaeus jointly forming Horace's lyric model.[5] But the most probable alignment that looms is between Horace and the Lesbian male Alcaeus, and *Odes* 1. 32, *Epist.* 1. 19. 32–3, and indeed *Odes* 1. 9 and other evidence which I will adduce, will fix this latter alignment (at 1. 26. 11 'Lesbio... plectro', any ambiguity of implication is gone). First and foremost Horace emerges as the 'Roman Alcaeus'. So how did he read his Greek Alcaeus? We may assume that his text followed the sequence and book divisions of the 'standard edition', however customized by commentary his own copies may have been.[6] Coincidence of facts will bear this assumption out.

We know that there was a standard edition, dating from the great period of Hellenistic scholarship, and we know something about it.[7] Hephaestion in his work 'On Critical Signs', writing about peculiarities in the way strophes and poems are marked off in texts of Alcaeus, distinguishes between the edition of Aristophanes (c.257–180 BC), and 'the now current edition of Aristarchus' (c.216–144 BC).[8] So, in the second century AD there was a standard edition, Aristarchus', and this had presumably long prevailed, offering a canonical sequence of poems. Should we feel haunted by Aristophanes' edition, and the

---

[5] Woodman (2002) argues for Sapphic allusions in *Odes* 1. 32 where, as he admits, 'the reference is exclusively to Alcaeus' (54). Not too much should be built on the fact that Horace writes in the 'Sapphic' metre, which was very popular with Alcaeus, as I document below.

[6] It is educational to see—in my case, thanks to Professor Hutchinson—how inescapable commentary in some texts was. In Alcaeus fr. 71V (*POxy.* 1234 fr. 2), for example, the commentary, including the fascinatingly specific τὸν τοῦ Ἀλκαίου ἐρώμ(εν)ον, is alongside the text on the right hand side, in generously available space, a characteristic of the whole papyrus. The way such 'scholia' are now relegated to the apparatus gives a misleading impression of the impact commentary might have made.

[7] I am indebted in all my remarks on Alcaeus' Aristarchan edition to Professor P. J. Parsons (in correspondence) and to Pardini (1991), esp. 260 ff. See too Porro (1994), 239–41, summarizing, reviewing, and adding slightly to Pardini.

[8] T11 Campbell = Hephaestion 'On Critical Signs' 2s. (p. 73s. Consbruch). The essential phrase is κατὰ δὲ τὴν νῦν (sc. ἔκδοσιν) τὴν Ἀριστάρχειον, but the whole passage of Hephaestion is interesting. Hephaestion tells us (i) that in the lyric poets, if the poem is monstrophic, the *paragraphos* is placed after each strophe, (ii) that the *coronis* is placed at the end of each poem, (iii) that the *asteriskos* is usually employed if the next poem is in a different metre, 'which happens in the monostrophic poems of Sappho, Anacreon and Alcaeus'. And he concludes (iv) 'The poems of Alcaeus are peculiar in this, that in the edition of Aristophanes the asterisk was used only to mark a change of metre (ἑτερομετρία), but in the now current Aristarchan edition it marks every fresh poem.' Papyri do not suggest that Aristarchus' precise selection of the asterisk swept the board, but Hephaestion is testimony to a standard edition. We infer too that adjacent Alcaean poems in the *same* metre did occur: not every change of poem was accompanied by ἑτερομετρία; see further n. 11 below. ('Ἑτερομετρία could not have occurred in the first three books of Sappho, each of which was written in the same metre: T29 and 30 Campbell. For Sappho's edition in nine books, ordered by metre, see Pardini (1991), 261–2, and n. 10 below.)

possibility of a rival ordering of poems, an authoritative opinion is that Aristarchus did not change Aristophanes' sequence.[9]

It is clear that Alcaeus' books were not, like Sappho's, arranged by metre.[10] Papyrus remains show this, as well as one aspect of the information provided by Hephaestion.[11] The influential Bergk, back in 1883, suggested a clear generic scheme of arrangement (ὕμνοι, στασιωτικά, ἐρωτικά, and σκόλια), and was followed by Crusius in 1894 who assigned these categories to the supposed ten books (for which see below): Hymns in Books 1–2 and so on.[12] The evidence for a number of poems with the designation *stasiotica* is quite firm (see for a start, T1 Campbell [Strabo 13. 2. 3] τὰ στασιωτικὰ καλούμενα). But the evidence is against a book or books actually entitled Στασιωτικά,[13] and twentieth-century papyrus discoveries confute in particular the most enduring part of Bergk's legacy, a 'Book of Hymns'.[14] And a single, important fact is that all ancient citations of Alcaeus (collected in fr. 453V) which make any specification do so not by generic titles but by book numbers; on three occasions it is added these are books of Alcaeus' 'songs' (μέλη). The highest book number known to us is Book 10. A chance reference to a receptacle that contained Alcaeus' works supports the conclusion that there were no more than ten books in all. They were contained in a 'a triangular case, of wood':[15] 4, 3, 2, 1 fits a triangle nicely.

There is a simple but important point to emphasize here. Alcaeus' standard edition was in *numbered* books of 'songs'. 'Alcaeus Book 1' is therefore a way of thinking that Horace would share with us, and with select Roman

---

[9] Pardini (1991), 259; cf. too Fraser (1972), 462–3. In the section following his remarks on Aristarchus' and Aristophanes' order, Pardini begins: 'In ogni caso, il riscontro dei nostri dati, dove possibile, ci conferma l'esistenza di un ordinamento stabilizzato dell' opera alcaica...' etc., with evidence.

[10] On Sappho's books, see Pardini (1991), 261–2, Page (1955), 112–16.

[11] Hephaestion in n. 8 above. Papyri of Alcaeus show a high incidence of change of metre with change of poem; on one occasion (only) poems in the same metre are certainly collocated (*POxy.* 1234 fr. 1. 1–6 and 7–14, frr. 68V and 69); on many occasions, however, we are not in a position to judge: Pardini (1991) 265–6. Hephaestion (n. 8 above) clearly knows both ἑτερομετρία and ὁμοιομετρία in adjacent Alcaean poems.

[12] Bergk (1883), ii. 277 ff.; O. Crusius, *RE* 1. 1501: Books 1–2 *Hymnoi*, 3–4 *stasiotika*, 4–6, *erotica*, 7–10 *skolia*.

[13] See Pardini (1991), 267–9 for an assessment of Strabo's and other evidence, and for the reasons for rejecting the proposal of a book or books actually entitled Στασιωτικά.

[14] The evidence against the Book of Hymns is provided *in primis* by Lobel-Page's B (*POxy.* 1233): this collocates the sympotic B6A = 38a V and the hymnic B2 = 34 and 34A V (Pardini (1991), 279). Pardini infers that the diverse types of poem covered by POxy. 2734 all came from Book 1; on the fascinating *POxy.* 2734 see the text below. Horace seems to refer to (in effect) the *stasiotica* at *Odes* 2. 13. 26–8, and to sympotic and erotic poems at 1. 32. 9–11, but there need be no implication that he read them in a group, let alone a book.

[15] T10 Campbell, an inscription in Delos, talking it seems of the treasury of Andros and listing its 'wooden objects': among them, τρίγωνον θήκην ἔχουσαν βυβλία Ἀλκαίου.

readers.[16] We can phrase this point more exactly. References show that Horace's own title for his Odes was 'Songs', *carmina*;[17] and his sense of synonymity between Alcaeus' μέλη and his own *carmina* is suggested by his summarizing reference to Alcaeus' (stasiotic) songs as *carmina* at Odes 2. 13. 13. When therefore he came to write his *liber primus carminum*, 'Alcaeus in libro primo', 'Alcaeus ἐν πρώτῳ', indeed Alcaeus 'ἐν πρώτῳ μελῶν, in libro primo carminum'[18] would have been both a ready text and concept: invitingly and challengingly there. But not it seems for his later commentators, a fact worth bringing out into the open.[19]

II. THE 'PARADE ODES', 1. 1–9: DISORIENTATION BEFORE ORIENTATION

In the first nine odes in Book 1, known to us as the 'Parade Odes',[20] Horace displays his astonishing metrical dexterity. All nine poems are composed in

[16] Cicero, unless we take him too literally, had not been one: see the famously contemptuous opinion attributed to him at Sen. *Ep.* 49. 5: 'negat Cicero, si duplicetur sibi aetas, habiturum se tempus, quo legat lyricos.'

[17] e.g. *Ep.* 1. 13. 17, 2. 2. 25, 59, 91, cf. 2. 1. 138, 227; *Odes* 4. 2. 32, 4. 8. 11; cf. *Odes* 3. 1. 2, 2. 19. 1.

[18] Cf. references like ἐν τῷ πρώτῳ Ἀλκαίου, Ἀλκαῖος ἐν πρώτῳ, ἐν δευτέρῳ μελῶν, ἐν ἐνάτῳ μέλει, ἐνδεκάτῳ, to be found in 453 V. Cf. Porphyrio's methods of citation in his commentary on Horace's *Odes*: at 1. 12. 46, 'Vergilius in libro sexto'; 1. 22. 10, 'scilicet et liber Lucilii XVI'; 1. 27 pr. '...cuius sensus sumptus est ab Anacreonte ex libro tertio'; 3. 30 pr. 'ha⟨e⟩c ὠ⟨ι⟩δή, qua tertius liber consummatur'.

[19] Porphyrio refers to no book numbers of Alcaeus. Indeed, his tentative method of referring to Alcaeus, on the rare occasions that he does so, suggests to me that he had no text of the poet available, certainly that he consulted none, and this is a fact worth bringing out into the open. The closest he gets in his references is 1. 10 pr., 'hymnus est in Mercurium ab Alcaeo lyrico poeta', 1. 10. 9, 'fabula haec autem ab Alcaeo ficta', 1. 32. 11, 'hunc Lycum puerum Alcaeus dilexit', 3. 30. 13–14, 'Aeolid[a]e dialecto Alcaeus lyricus poeta usus est'. For an invaluable condensation of material on Porphyrio, see Nisbet and Hubbard (1970), pp. xlvii–xlix, who point out conspicuous deficiencies in his knowledge of Alcaeus: 'He fails to record fundamental Greek influences, Alcaeus on 1. 9, 1. 14, 1. 18, 1. 37'. There might be many reasons why Porphyrio—c. AD 200?; living in a province less favoured than Egypt?—might not have a text of Alcaeus, but it is perhaps strange that he carries no tralatician references: for earlier, non-extant scholarly work on Horace, see Nisbet and Hubbard (1970), p. xlvii. Porphyrio can however tell us on Ode 1. 15 'hac ode Bacchylidem imitatur. nam ut ille Cassandram facit uaticinari futuri belli Troiani ita hic Proteum', a slip, as N.–H. say, for 'Nereum'. As for pseudo-Acro (N.–H., pp. xlix–li), 'There is even less than in Porphyrio on Horace's Greek models.'

[20] This useful way of talking about *Odes* 1. 1–9 goes back, it appears, to Christ (1868), esp. 36 n. 12. The reference, which rather surprisingly I have not been able to check, comes from Santirocco (1986), who defends (14–41, and 42–3) the limitation of the term to the first nine odes. Rightly. Others have sought to seek a close to the 'Parade' in 1. 12: Port (1925–6), 301, referring back to Keissling; Porter (1987), 15, 58–77. Others, to ring the changes, have sought to close the main Parade Odes at 1. 10 or 11: Porter (1987), 15 n. 5.

different metres, a feat he will not attempt again.[21] 'Metrical dexterity', yes; but he provides us with a considerable tease too.[22] We are waiting for a firm alignment with a Greek poet, the poet who will provide his new image, as well as a basis for his text: what Theocritus had been to Vergil, and Archilochus and Hipponax to the younger Horace. An alignment between Horace and Alcaeus may seem to be in prospect (*Lesboum*, the not conclusive hint at 1. 1. 34), and we are accustomed to delay before alignments are made explicit.[23] But the opening of *Odes* 1 provides a particularly dazzling and surely bemusing postponement. When and how will this metrical gymnast settle down?

We can try to recreate the reader's sense of orientation, or lack of it, as the Parade Odes progress. 'nec...Lesboum refugit tendere barbiton...quodsi me lyricis uatibus inseres...' (1. 1. 34–5). A new Alcaeus? Sappho? The first ode is in stichic asclepiads: used by Alcaeus (112, 117(b). 1–12, and so on),[24] but hardly Alcaeus' metrical blazon.[25] The second ode is in sapphics: Alcaeus prominently used sapphics (34V, 68, 69, and so on), but so of course did Sappho.[26] No sure examples of the asclepiad stanzas of *Odes* 1. 3 and 1. 5 are known in Alcaeus or Sappho, but this may well be due to the paltry nature of fragments left to us, for Alcaeus certainly liked asclepiad metres: we know, for example, that the asclepiad stanza of *Odes* 1. 6 was used by him (5V, ?67). But none of these metres—to our knowledge—actually anchors us in Alcaeus. Jumping to *Odes* 1. 8 for a moment, no example of the so-called 'greater sapphic'[27] (*Odes* 1. 8), nor of either of its two component lines, survives in the fragments of Alcaeus, or indeed of Sappho; Latin *grammatici* supposedly attributing the second and longer line (a regular Sapphic line with choriambic expansion) to Alcaeus have been misinterpreted, by very influential

---

[21] There is a useful overview of Horace's metres in Book 1 in Nisbet and Hubbard (1970), pp. xxxviii–xlvi.

[22] Differently in Santirocco (1986), 14: 'these poems [1. 1–9] are an elaborate attempt to place the *Odes* both within Horace's oeuvre and within a larger poetic tradition'.

[23] Vergil in *Eclogue* 6, Horace in *Epode* 6.

[24] A full list of examples of Alcaeus' uses of each metre that he employs is given by Voigt (1971), 20–3.

[25] This, for the Romans at least, was what is legitimately termed the 'alcaic stanza': cf. Lyne (1995), 98–9; cf. too Hutchinson (2002), 530. The fact that Aristarchus put a poem in alcaics at the head of his edition of Alcaeus (see below) suggests that he had the same opinion of the metre.

[26] Hephaestion (citing Alcaeus fr. 308V) points out that 'the so-called sapphic eleven-syllable line' is found in Alcaeus too, and even says that 'it is uncertain which of the two invented it, even if it is called Sapphic'. This is where he cites the whole first stanza of Alcaeus' hymn to Hermes, on which more below. While Alcaeus used sapphics, it is unlikely that Sappho used alcaics: see West (1982), 33; possibilities are: 103A V, 137, and 168C. On the metrical relations of Alcaeus and Sappho—on what they do and do not share—see Voigt's note at Alcaeus 137, and Hutchinson (2001), 141. On the 'sapphic stanza', Hutchinson comments 'Neither poet is likely to be deriving this whole metrical system from the other; there is evidently...some poetic tradition.'

[27] This aeolic compound is well analysed by Raven (1965), 145.

scholars.[28] It may be, however, that Archilochus used the first and shorter measure, the 'aristophanean'.[29] And mention of Archilochus can move us to *Odes* 1. 4 and 7 and the most striking fact about the Parade metres. The ambitiously lyric (1. 1. 35) Horace uses epodic metres with definite Archilochean imprint. *Odes* 1. 7 is written in the first Archilochean: cf. Hor. *Epod.* 12, Archilochus fr. 195 W, also anon. *GLP* 91. The third Archilochean of 1. 4 is known from Archilochus 188–192W, and Theocritus suggests it had a particularly Archilochean stamp;[30] it has indeed been argued that Horace alludes to the text of 188–92W.[31] These clearly and exactly Archilochean metres are the most disconcerting and teasing in the Parade, even if the belief existed that Lesbian metres derived from Archilochean elements.[32] But then,

[28] At Alcaeus 455, Voigt lists passages from the *grammatici* supposedly attributing the pair of lines, or the second of them, to Alcaeus. These and other 'evidence' can be all tracked back to a metrical discussion by the lyric poet and metrician of the Neronian Age, Caesius Bassus, Keil, *GL* 6. 270. 3 ff.; Voigt has Bassus third in her list, but omits the important part. Discussing *Odes* 1. 8. 2 ('te deos oro...'), easily analysed as a regular sapphic line with choriambic expansion, Bassus says that Horace has erroneously *tampered with* an Alcaean metrical colon consisting of three choriambs and an 'antibacchius' (for him, ⌣--), by turning the iamb in the first foot into a spondee. Whether he is right or not about Horace's tampering (I very much doubt it, unlike Garrod below: surely Horace found this metre somewhere), Bassus is *not* evidence for Alcaeus' using this line: on the contrary. The whole of Bassus' section must then be read carefully. To push his point home, Bassus concocted a metrically 'correct' version of Horace's line ('hoc, dea, uere, Sybarim...', line 15 K). This then infected later tradition. It infected Bassus' own text too: at line 14 K, he is surely quoting Horace as he found him ('te deos oro'), and as the text still stands in his own initial quotation (line 5 K), but the quotation in line 14 has been infected in transmission by the nearby line of Bassus' own composition. Atilius Fortunatianus 6. 300. 19 ff. effectively repeats Bassus. Dependent on Bassus, too, is Marius Victorinus 6. 165. 25 ff. K, Voigt's lead *testimonium*, but with him the nuance of Horace's 'tampering' with Alcaeus' metrical colon has been lost: but his dependence on Bassus is suggested by his infected text ('hoc deos uere'). Diomedes 1. 520. 25–7 calls *Odes* 1. 8. 2 a 'metrum alcaicum', but he too quotes it with 'uere' and is surely dependent ultimately on Bassus. A full and clear discussion of Caesius Bassus and his effects on the text of Horace is that by Garrod (1921), 102–3. Page (1955), 326 also gives a wrong impression of the 'evidence' provided by Diomedes loc. cit.

[29] Fr. 318 W, which is among West's 'Testimonia de metris fide minus digna'. 'Lydia dic per omnes' is called an 'Anacreonteum metrum' by Diomedes, 1. 520. 20–1 K.

[30] In Epigram 21 Theocritus writes in praise of Archilochus. The metre he employs can be seen as the third Archilochean with an iambic trimeter inserted between the greater Archilochean line and the iambic trimeter catalectic. Theocritus' triplet combination itself 'does not occur elsewhere and there is no evidence that it was used by Archilochus himself though it may well have been so...' (Gow ad loc.). Caesius Bassus 6. 306. 9 cites the first lines of *Odes* 1. 4. 1 and says: 'alcaicon ἑπτακαιδεκασύλλαβον commissum est ex heroice et ithyphallico': Alcaeus may have used the line (in what combination?), but the Archilochean hue of the epodic pair will surely have blocked out any colour which that may have imparted.

[31] For the supposition of allusion to the *text* of Archilochus 188–92W in *Odes* 1. 4 and 5, see Bowie (1987), 13–23, esp. 21–3.

[32] Cf. *Ep.* 1. 19. 26–9 with Fraenkel (1957), 342–7. I think Fraenkel's interpretation is convincing; but cf. too Mayer (1994), 264–5, a different route to (substantially) the point I need; Marius Victorinus 6. 141. 143 ff., cited by Mayer, is useful. For further confirmation of the sense of Archilochean imprint on the 'Archilochean' metres just mentioned, we may remember the ancient belief that Archilochus *invented* epodic systems: see T47 and T50 in Gerber (1999).

at the end and climax of the Parade, at 1. 9, we can feel a sense of arrival: an alcaic stanza, Alcaeus' blazon metre.[33] There is a recall of Alcaeus' actual text too (on which I shall comment below), giving us a further sense of orientation and alignment: Horace as a Roman Alcaeus.

III. THE ARISTARCHAN ALCAEUS. THE FIRST THREE POEMS

At *Odes* 1. 9, therefore, Alcaeus looks set to be Horace's top model. We should now return to what we know about the standard edition of Alcaeus Book 1.

Fragment 307aV is the first line of the poem that opened Alcaeus' first book: this information is clearly given to us by a scholiast on Hephaestion.[34] The poem was a hymn to Apollo, in, it must have been, alcaic strophes. The surviving first line is: ὦναξ Ἄπολλον, παῖ μεγάλω Δίος. The second poem in the book is equally well known, its position identified by the same source. It is a hymn to Hermes of which we have the first stanza: 308V.[35] This time the poem is in sapphics, a more 'Alcaean' metre than the name implies (see above).

> χαῖρε, Κυλλάνας ὁ μέδεις, σὲ γάρ μοι
> θῦμος ὔμνην, τὸν κορύφαισ' ἐν αὔταις
> Μαῖα γέννατο Κρονίδᾳ μίγεισα
> παμβασίληϊ.

A text was then given to the world in 1968 which should have caused Horatian scholars much more excitement than it did: *POxy.* 2734 (= 306C Campbell), edited by E. Lobel.[36] Fragment 1 of this papyrus gives summaries of Alcaean poems, with citation by first line. Lines 5 and 11–12 of fr. 1 of the papyrus are remnants of 307aV and 308V line 1, that is, the first lines of the first two poems. We then hear of 'the third' (ἡ δὲ τρίτη), and the lemma in line 21 is recognizably fr. 343V. So we now know what the first *three* poems in Alcaeus' Book 1 were like. If a reasonable emendation to fr. 343 is accepted, this poem was a hymn to Nymphs:

> Νύμφαι,[37] ταῖς Δίος ἐξ αἰγιόχω φαῖσι τετυγμέναις

[33] See above n. 25.
[34] See the *testimonium* listed with Alcaeus fr. 307V and Pardini (1991), 259.
[35] The *testimonium* is cited again with fr. 308V; see too Pardini loc. cit. The text printed adopts Meineke's correction of the MSS κορύφαισιν αὐγαῖς.
[36] *Oxyrhynchus Papyri* 35 (1968), 2 ff. The economic reporting of the papyrus by Voigt (at fr. 343) and Pardini (1991), 259–60 should not obscure how fascinating it is. Lobel's edition is well worth looking up still. Supporting evidence for the sequence suggested by this papyrus can be inferred in Hephaestion: Pardini (1991), 260.
[37] Edmonds; Νύμφαις codd. Voigt prints Edmonds's correction.

The metre is the 'greater asclepiad'. Hephaestion provides the information that 'the whole of Book 3 of Sappho is written in this metre and many songs of Alcaeus too'.[38] And indeed there are many surviving Alcaean examples: 50V, 340–8, 349b, and others.[39]

We can see why an Alexandrian editor should have placed these hymns—if such they be—at the head of Alcaeus' first book, otherwise heterogeneous. They honour deities special to a lyric poet. Extensive information is provided on Alcaeus' extraordinary hymn to Apollo by Plutarch and especially—to the extent that he can be trusted—by Himerius: this material is most fully cited by Campbell under his frr. 307(b) and (c);[40] the five-line *H. hymn* 21 to Apollo should also be noted. If anyone wonders why a lyric poet in particular should write a hymn to Nymphs (to take the poems out of order), the Homeric Hymn to Pan is enlightening,[41] and so indeed is Horace *Odes* 1. 1. 31. The surviving passage of Alcaeus' Hermes hymn overlaps with the amusing *H. hymn* 4 to Hermes: this almost certainly post-dates Alcaeus, but will contain traditional material known to him.[42] There are specific glints of information about Alcaeus' poem in *POxy.* 2734 = 306C Campbell, fr. 1. Fragment 447V should perhaps not be neglected (where Hermes is wine-pourer, οἰνόχοος, of the gods). And a lot more information is provided by the passages listed under fr. 308V, more fully by Campbell at his 308(a)–(d), which include of course Horace *Odes* 1. 10 and Porphyrio.[43] A star item in Alcaeus' hymn was certainly Hermes' theft of Apollo's cattle. The additional theft of the quiver and Apollo's laughter, which we find in Horace, is also probably owed to Alcaeus.[44]

IV. HORACE'S ALCAEAN 'SIGNATURE SEQUENCE', *ODES* 1. 9–11

At the end of the Parade Odes, we at last arrive at an anchor poem: *Odes* 1. 9, an ode written in Alcaeus' blazon metre and alluding to an Alcaean text. There will be an abundance of further models for individual poems, and further

---

[38] Hephaestion, *Ench.* 10. 6, cited at fr. 343V. Cf. too Sappho T30 Campbell. Hephaestion calls the 'greater asclepiad' the 'Sapphic sixteen-syllable'. Theocritus 28 is in stichic greater asclepiads, and he uses the metre elsewhere: see Gow (1950), 495. Catullus uses it in poem 30.

[39] Cf. Voigt (1971), 23.

[40] Cf. too Page (1955), 244–52.

[41] Note especially *H. hymn* 19. 3, 19 ff. The nymphs in Pan's company are χοροήθεις, λιγύμολποι, they μέλπονται, and so on.

[42] Cf. Page (1955), 252–8; a summary in West (2003), 12–14.

[43] Cf. too Page (1955), 252–8.

[44] Nisbet and Hubbard (1970), 132 citing, besides Porphyrio, the scholium on *Iliad* 15. 256 and Philostr. *Imag.* 1. 26.

allusions, but *Odes* 1. 32 reaffirms the impression for the time being at least:[45] Horace is the Roman Alcaeus. It is therefore a fascinating and under-remarked fact that, when we arrive at this identifying poem (1. 9), Horace then mirrors not only the metre of Alcaeus' first poem in the Aristarchan book (alcaic stanza), but the metres of the second and third poems too. 1. 9, 10 and 11: alcaic stanza, sapphics, and the 'greater asclepiad': the metres of Alcaeus' 'Apollo', 'Hermes', and 'Nymphs'. If we are inclined to miss this, the last metre mentioned should hit us in the face: the 'greater asclepiad', common in Alcaeus, rare in Horace[46] and occurring here for the first time, is one of only three instances in all of *Odes* 1–3 where a metre is *not* introduced in the Parade Odes.[47] Meshing, therefore, with the Parade Odes (1. 1–9), which dazzle and bemuse until their last poem, there is a small and more specific Alcaean Signature Sequence (1. 9–11), a sequence of metres mirroring the opening of the standard edition of Alcaeus Book 1. The very conspicuous appearance of Pindar in *Odes* 1. 12 (*Ol.* 2, also *Isthm.* 7, *Nem.* 10, and so on)[48] suggests that this twinning relationship with Alcaeus ends, for the time being, with *Odes* 1. 11. The three poems obviously deserve closer inspection, individually, but then as a putative group.

V. THE SIGNATURE SEQUENCE: SOME DETAILS

The first of the sequence, 1. 9, gives us both alcaic metre and Alcaean text. But not, in any overt way, the text of the Apollo hymn. Horace employs another poem. 'The first two stanzas, perhaps the first three, are modelled on an ode by Alcaeus',[49] which is in fact the sympotic 338V. But 1. 9 contains an *allusion* to Apollo. Here is an important reason why Horace chose precisely Soracte as his location. At Verg. *Aen.* 11. 785 Arruns prays 'summe deum, sancti custos Soractis Apollo'. Arruns then refers to firewalking performed in Apollo's honour (786–8), a ritual among the Hirpi attested elsewhere, but not necessarily linked to Apollo.[50] But in Pliny both fire-walking and Soracte are linked to Apollo: *HN* 7. 19, 'haud procul urbe Roma in Faliscorum agro familiae sunt paucae quae uocantur Hirpi. hae sacrificio annuo, quod fit ad montem Soractem Apollini, super ambustam ligni struem ambulantes non aduruntur...'. Incidentally, as 1. 9 is inceptive, we may be justified in seeing a metapoetic allusion in the way

---

[45] On *Odes* 1. 32 (significantly paired with 1. 33), see Lyne (1980), 201–3; a slightly different view in Hutchinson (2002), 530 ('a relation of contrast as well as similarity').
[46] Thee occurrences in all: *Odes* 1. 11, 1. 18, 4. 10.   [47] The others are *Odes* 2. 18 and 3. 12.
[48] Cf. Syndikus (2001), i. 137 and ff., Fraenkel (1957), 395 291 ff.
[49] Nisbet and Hubbard (1970), 116.
[50] For example, Strabo 5. 2. 9 describes the ritual in detail, places it below Soracte, but ascribes it to Feronia.

the wine is described ('deprome quadrimum Sabina, | o Thaliarche, merum diota'); cf. 1. 20, the poem that opens the second half of the entire sequence of 38 odes, where there is surely some such play (1. 20. 1–2 'uile...Sabinum... Graeca... testa'). Thaliarchus, 'beginning of blooming', also bears reflection.

The second in the sequence, 1. 10, repeats both metre and subject matter of Alcaeus' second poem ('Hermes'): Horace's hymn to Mercury features the story of Mercury's theft of Apollo's cattle which we know to have been in Alcaeus' hymn. The third, 1. 11, repeats the metre, but not the content, of Alcaeus' number three, the Hymn to the Nymphs. Indeed it relates in content to no discernible text of Alcaeus at all. But like Horace's Soracte ode it makes, I think, an allusion to the Alcaean text it does not substantially employ.

The puzzlingly named addressee Leuconoe in *Odes* 1. 11 is passed over in silence by some, given honest and lavish discussion by Nisbet and Hubbard,[51] but no explanation for the choice of name is found. In myth the name was given to one of the daughters of Minyas, and to a daughter of Lucifer, mother of Philammon by Apollo.[52] But rather than these figures, we should think of nymphs. Catalogues of nymphs are constructed with freedom and invention: see for example the Nereids at Homer, *Il.* 18. 38–51, at Hesiod, *Theog.* 243–62, which has overlaps, but only overlaps, with Homer, and at Verg. *G.* 4. 334–44. Four of Hesiod's end in -*noe* (none of Homer's does), suggesting qualities of νόος: Hipponoe, Poulynoe, Autonoe, and Pronoe. I suggest that a propitious-minded, fresh-water nymph named Leuconoe, unknown to us,[53] was available to, or invented by, Alcaeus and featured in his 'Nymphs'. Horace, by his choice of the nymph's name, would be alluding to the poem whose content he is not actually following. Cf. LSJ s.v. λευκός v, 3 'bright', 'fortunate', 'happy', Aesch. *Pers.* 301... καὶ λευκὸν ἦμαρ νυκτὸς ἐκ μελαγχίμου, *Ag.* 668, Callim. fr. 178. 2 ἦμαρ Ὀρέστειοι λευκὸν ἄγουσι χόες, and uses of λευκός of clear (spring-) water: Hom. *Il.* 23. 282, *Od.* 5. 70 κρῆναι... ῥέον ὕδατι λευκῷ, Aesch. *Supp.* 23 ὦ πόλις, ὦ γῆ καὶ λευκὸν ὕδωρ, Eur. *Herc.* 573 Δίρκης τε νᾶμα λευκόν, Callim. fr. 546 κρήνη | λευκὸν ὕδωρ ἀνέβαλλεν.[54] Note too Virgil's candid nymph, *Ecl.* 2. 46 'candida Nais'. It may be relevant that Leuconoe was also the name of an Attic deme.[55]

---

[51] Nisbet and Hubbard (1970), 136–8.

[52] See Ov. *Met.* 4. 168 for the Minyad (the majority MSS reading *Leucothoe* is corrupt), Hyg. *Fab.* 161 for the daughter of Lucifer and mother of Philammon.

[53] See Larson (2001), 359–64 for a catalogue of nymphs which is 'necessarily incomplete'. No sign of Leuconoe (but Larson does not include—for example—Hesiod's Nereids).

[54] But the force of the Leuco- element in the name prompts much inconclusive discussion in Nisbet and Hubbard, loc. cit. As they say, it cannot have any connection with whatever Pindar derogatorily means by λευκαῖς... φρασίν at *Pyth.* 4. 109. If Nisbet and Hubbard's canvass of a force 'guileless' has any weight, then cf. Hor. *Odes* 2. 8. 14 'simplices Nymphae'.

[55] Cf. Oinoe which was both Attic deme and the name of an Arcadian nymph: see Larson's catalogue (2001) for Oinoe, the nymph. Most of the names of the Attic demes are argued to be pre-Cleisthenic and old: cf. Whitehead (1986), 24–5, 27.

Horace has one further surprise waiting. The 'greater asclepiad' of 1. 11 stands out on various accounts, as we have seen: common in Alcaeus, very rare in Horace himself, and highlighted by its lack of preparation in the Parade Odes. It is given its second of three exposures—in Horace's entire *oeuvre*—at *Odes* 1. 18. And 1. 18. 1 is a virtually verbatim translation of Alcaeus fr. 342V, also in the 'greater asclepiad':

μηδ' ἓν ἄλλο φυτεύσῃς πρότερον δένδριον ἀμπέλω
nullam, Vare, sacra uite prius seueris arborem

How Alcaeus then progressed we do not know, but Horace swiftly locates his poem, following a favoured policy of his,[56] in the Roman world of Tibur and P. Alfenus Varus.[57] By a metrical link, therefore, Ode 1. 11 eventually (in 1. 18) takes us to Alcaean text as well as metre, and our sense that this is an *Alcaean Signature Sequence* is again strengthened.

Horace treats and teases for eight poems, and then the Roman Alcaeus proper gets going. There is a particular reason why he chooses a light Alcaean poem for his first alcaic and does not, for example, calque Alcaeus' Apollo hymn in *Odes* 1. 9 (see Section VII below). But for the moment it will suffice to say that, generally, he wants to play the part of Alcaeus entertainingly, allusively, unexpectedly, keeping us on our toes. After 1. 11, in spite of the now almost exclusively Alcaean metres, he embarks on a series of allusions to different poets; starting, as we said, with Pindar.[58]

VI. THE SIGNATURE SEQUENCE AS A GROUP

Alcaeus 1. 1–3 give us three hymns: 'Apollo', 'Hermes', 'Nymphs'. In Horace, two 'Enjoy the day' poems centre one hymn, 'Mercury' (1. 10).

If one hymn only was to be selected, why Hermes–Mercury? Mercury was two special things to Horace. In the second poem of the whole book, the god had

---

[56] When Horace alludes to or quotes Alcaean text, he then very swiftly situates himself and the poem firmly in Italy. Think of *Soracte* in line 2 of *Odes* 1. 9, of *Saliaribus* in line 2 of 1. 37, as well as *Vare* and *Tibur* in lines 1 and 2 of 1. 18. And whatever else may be happening in 1. 10, the words *facundus* and *catus* are pretty uncompromisingly Latin, indeed prosaically so.

[57] Nisbet and Hubbard (1970), 227–8 are surely right in their identification of Horace's Varus in 1. 18: P. Alfenus Varus, the jurist and suffect consul of 39 BC. Among the most decisive arguments is that Horace decides to put Varus into this very distinctive metre, and Catullus, who had also once employed it, wrote in it to Alfenus (poem 30). One family of MSS heads *Odes* 1. 18 'Varus Quintilius', but one suspects that this is infection from the illustrious and disastrous Quintilius Varus who lost Germany for Augustus. The manuscripts' Q. V. is defended by Syndikus (2001), 195.

[58] Cf. Lowrie 49 (1995), 33–48. I should put it much less potently than Lowrie—but Lowrie 35 is more cautious than her title—or indeed than Hutchinson (2002), 529 'conspicuous imitations of different poets'. Allusions, glances, witty plays (esp. in 1. 13, and with Catullus as well as Sappho), but no parades.

achieved Augustan dignity as the emperor incarnate: 1. 2. 43–4 'filius Maiae patiens uocari | Caesaris ultor'. He was also Horace's personal protector: the 'Mercurialis uir' of *Odes* 2. 17. 29–30 had attributed his good fortune to Mercury back in *Serm.* 2. 6. 4–5 'nil amplius oro, | Maia nate', and does so again in *Odes* 2. 7. 13. And of course Horace exploits interplay between these two Mercurial roles—in for example *Odes* 2. 7. If only one of Alcaeus' gods was to be hymned, here are two pressing reasons why it should be the son of Maia (*Maia nate, filius Maiae*, τὸν ... Μαῖα γέννατο), now given a different genealogy, to ring the changes: grandson of Atlas, *nepos Atlantis*. And, to mark Mercury's selection and pride of place in the centre poem of the Signature Sequence, he is here given his own name, in the vocative first word, *Mercuri*.

But why the light content for this important and honoured god? The *testimonia* guarantee that the theft of Apollo's cattle was in Alcaeus' hymn, and we may be fairly sure that the theft of the quiver and Apollo's laughter was there too; but there was no compulsion to repeat Alcaeus' subject-matter. Horace is performing a tactical shift in tone, compared with the loudly Augustan *Odes* 1. 2. In the Mercury poem of his own Signature Sequence he decides to give this august *and* personal god impeccably civilian and sophisticated advertisement, a pleasing and quite characteristic move. And so we have the witty story (Mercury and Apollo), and we are informed of Mercury's enlightened and enlightening talents: 'facunde', 'feros cultus uoce formasti... et decorae | more palaestrae', 'curuaeque lyrae parentem'. Even as ψυχοπομπός Mercury's duties are phrased benignly: 1. 10. 17–18 'tu pias *laetis* animas reponis | sedibus...'; no troubling mention of anything other than the 'happy abodes'. The shift in tone from 1. 2 is acutely focused by the repetition of the phrase 'duce te'. Applied to Augustus–Mercury at the end of 1. 2, it was climactically military: 'te duce Caesar' (1. 2. 52). In 1. 10. 13 Mercury as *dux* ('duce te') is a kindly conductor in a mythical context.

We may now say that Horace fixes on only *one* of Alcaeus' hymned gods *because* of Mercury's outstanding personal and political importance to him; while the flanking poems merely allude to 'Apollo' and 'Nymphs'. And one centred god sets in relief the brevity of human life, key theme in the flanking 'Enjoy the day' poems, 1. 9 and 1. 11.

Background Alcaean texts enhance both these poems. In 1. 11 we may recall the conjectured allusion in 'Leuconoe'.[59] Horace's short-lived Leuconoe tellingly separates from her presumed counterpart among Alcaeus' Nymphs. Cf. for example *H. hymn* (5) *to Aphrodite* 259 ff., of mountain-nymphs, 'They belong with neither mortals nor gods. They have long lives, δηρὸν μὲν ζώουσι, and eat divine food, and ply the beautiful dance with the immortals; Sileni and the keen-sighted Slayer of Argus unite with

---

[59] The point that follows springs from a suggestion of Professor Hutchinson.

them in love, μίσγοντ' ἐν φιλότητι. In 1. 9 Horace alludes to Alcaeus' 'Apollo' via Soracte, but does not actively use Alcaeus' hymn. But we may see an effect of separation here too. Horace's icily winter setting massively contrasts with what appears to be a heavy and joyous summer emphasis in Alcaeus' poem, and the cold-of-*death* subtext[60] of this 'Enjoy the day' poem is underscored thereby. Himerius' summary (*Or.* 48, lines 120 ff., fr. 307 (c) Campbell) includes the following: 'Now it was summer and indeed the very middle of summer when Alcaeus brings back Apollo from the Hyperboreans: so, what with the blaze of summer and the presence of Apollo, the poet's lyre has a summer delicacy in the account of the god: nightingales sing for him... [*et cetera*].'[61]

There are links between 1. 9 and 11, giving a sense of ring-composition in the Sequence. Both focus 'day', 'quem Fors *dierum* cumque dabit...' (1. 9. 14), 'carpe *diem* quam minimum credula postero' (1. 11. 8); they both advise to 'seek' no further, 'fuge *quaerere*' (1. 9. 13), 'ne quaesieris' (1. 11. 1). There is a clear pointer in both poems to enjoy Love. In 1. 11. 4–5 'winters', 'storms' (*hiemes*) adumbrate 'years', far from obviously; and they are storms *at sea*. This recalls 1. 9. 9–11, where Horace's example of gods' omnipotence is their power to still the stormy oceans. Both passages stand out enough to attract commentators' attention.[62] And 1. 11 as well as 1. 9 alludes to Alcaeus 338V: the most clearly documented parallels are between 1. 9 and 338,[63] but Horace has brought 338. 1 ὔει μὲν ὁ Ζεῦς, ἐκ δ' ὀράνω ... | χείμων down to 1. 11. 4.

And 1. 11 meshes with 1. 10. In the last stanza of 1. 10, Horace opens up a huge perspective, conjuring up, albeit benignly, the realm of the mortal dead (see above). The conclusive sense of *finem* in 1. 11. 2, its clear intimation of death (cf. *OLD finis* 10a), links with the final place reached in 1. 10. 17–20 before, we hope, being eliminated from serious consideration.

All in all this trio of poems makes a co-operating sequence, with more than merely formal relations to Alcaeus' opening trio.

VII. THIRTY ODES: 1. 9–38

There is another reward for the realization that Horace mirrors the opening metres of Alcaeus' Book 1 in 1. 9, 10, and 11. After the fireworks and diversions

---

[60] The way Horace summarizes the opening winter stanza is pregnantly expressed: 'dissolue frigus...'. Cf. Lucr. 4. 924, etc., *OLD* s.v. *frigus* 4a.

[61] ἦν μὲν οὖν θέρος καὶ τοῦ θέρους τὸ μέσον αὐτό, ὅτε ἐξ Ὑπερβορέων Ἀλκαῖος ἄγει τὸν Ἀπόλλωνα. ὅθεν δὴ θέρους ἐκλάμποντος καὶ ἐπιδημοῦντος Ἀπόλλωνος θερινόν τι καὶ ἡ λύρα περὶ τὸν θεὸν ἁβρύνεται. ᾄδουσι μὲν ἀηδόνες αὐτῷ...

[62] See Nisbet and Hubbard (1970), 117, 121, 139. Alcaeus is suspected behind both passages.

[63] 338. 2 πεπάγαισιν δ' ὑδάτων ῥόαι (1. 9. 3–4), 338. 5–6 κάββαλλε τὸν χείμων', ἐπὶ μὲν τίθεις | πῦρ (1. 9. 5–6), 338. 6 ἐν δὲ κέρναις οἶνον ἀφειδέως | μέλιχρον (1. 9. 6–7).

of the Parade Odes, the Signature Sequence marks a determined beginning. The total number of odes in Book 1—thirty-eight—has caused some puzzlement, as I shall discuss below. But if we count from *Odes* 1. 9 we find that we have a preferred Roman type of total, a decimal number: thirty. Indeed, from the Signature Sequence on, we have thirty odes in Book 1, we have twenty in Book 2, and then thirty again in Book 3. It is worth briefly considering the structure of this group of thirty odes in the first book. I shall be selective, since this sort of discussion is always more persuasive and interesting to the writer than to the reader.

Consider the first poem again, 1. 9. Throughout his lyric career, Horace subscribes to a continuing, disingenuous self-presentation, and for this 1. 9 is an invaluable opener. The poet claims the position of Roman Alcaeus, but in passage after passage he urges the point that essentially, deep down, he is the sympotic, erotic rather than the *engagé* version of Alcaeus, and this constructed image served him well.[64] It was therefore suitable for the *Roman* Alcaeus, unlike the original item, to parade a sympotic, erotic poem as his first essay in alcaics—and even more pointed for him to put such a poem where his Alcaean Signature starts.

The first decade of the thirty odes closes (1. 18) with Horace's second essay in the 'greater asclepiad', the metre which was common for Alcaeus, rare for Horace. 1. 18 starts, as we saw, with a clear quotation of Alcaeus 342V. So the first ten poems of the thirty open and close with odes (1. 9 and 18) which allude to Alcaeus metrically *and* textually. *Odes* 1. 18 is also the poem to which the second ode in Horace's Signature Sequence (1. 11) is linked. Since it is the one that actually takes us from 1. 11 to a substantial piece of Alcaeus' text, it merits a focused place on this account alone.

The poem that opens the second decade (1. 19) is a parody *recusatio*: perfectly good closure of the first half of the total 1–38 structure, it can also suitably stand at the head of a group. Cf. Propertius' programmatic use of *recusatio* in 2. 1, and Horace himself will playfully feint a replay of 1. 19 in *Odes* 4. 1.[65]

The poem that closes the decade (28) is a box of surprises, among other things a masterpiece of generic *Kreuzung* (two types of sepulchral epigram, diatribe) and reader-manipulation.[66] It is not until you have read the poem a couple of times that you have some sense of what is going on, of ground beneath your feet. A sentence from Nisbet and Hubbard[67] gives a flavour of the complexity that awaits: 'The structure of the poem causes perplexity because we do not know

---

[64] Cf. Lyne (1995), 95–7, 78.
[65] The exact repetition of 1. 19. 1 at 4. 1. 5 underscores the mischievously misleading impression given by 4. 1 that it is declining a grander literary project in favour of love poetry.
[66] It is excellently introduced and explained by Nisbet and Hubbard (1970), 317 ff.
[67] Nisbet and Hubbard (1970), 318.

till 21 that the speaker is not Horace but a corpse.' And back now comes for the second and last time the first Archilochean metre, paraded at *Odes* 1. 7, reinforcing one's sense of exhibitionism and *Kreuzung*; the other strongly Archilochean metre in the Parade, that of 1. 4, never recurs. All this technical dazzle befits a position of structural importance, and its generic display recalls the tactics of the 'falsely' closural *Epode* 13.[68] The ode is also the second of the 'series of actual deaths' which confront us in the book[69]—the first opens the second half of the structure of thirty (1. 24)—and death is this time in a more obvious closural position; the third and last of the series is Cleopatra in the *penultimate* poem of both the structures operative in *Odes* Book 1. Horace is fond of exploiting penultimacy where we might have expect him to choose the actual last place.[70]

The third decade opens with two poems that engage great public events (1. 29 and 31), wrapped around a poem, the second in the decade, of apparent erotic triviality (1. 30, 'O Venus...'). The public events are: the impending Augustan expedition into Arabia under Aelius Gallus (26–25 BC, 1. 29) and the recent dedication of the Temple of Apollo (28 BC, 1. 31). But both these events are approached from a very personal angle, allowing a highly unexpected view of them. By the third decade Horace may feel it timely to open with Augustan poems that, unlike 1. 2 and 1. 12, treat their topics with witty independence. *Odes* 1. 29[71] joshes the apparently intellectual Iccius on his participation in a military affair unsuited to, and indeed *beneath*, a person of his quality, 'pollicitus meliora' (29. 16): we are given a disconcerting view, we may infer a disconcertingly unofficial opinion, of an event of which Augustus will boastingly present a very different picture in the *Res Gestae* (26). The details are interesting.[72]

---

[68] I illustrate and explain 'false' closure in *Epode* 13 in Lyne 2005*b* [= Ch. 18, this volume].
[69] Hutchinson (2002), 531.
[70] On Horace's displacement of apparently important poems from an expected position of closure to penultimacy, see Lyne (1995), index s.v. 'penultimacy'; on 1. 37 and 38, see 88. On the closural function of 1. 38 itself, Fraenkel (1957), 297–9 is not to be missed. More recently, Oliensis (1998), 176–7 has interesting discussion of the same topic. Cf. too Lowrie (1997), 164–75, overdoing the metapoetics for my taste; Syndikus (2001), 332–4, esp. 332; Fowler (2000), 259–60, in trenchant mode. Port (1925–6), 303 and Santirocco (1986), 79–81 discuss 1. 36–8 as a closural sequence.
[71] For excellent information on the historical background to 1. 29 and discussion of the poem, see Nisbet and Hubbard (1970), 337 ff. See too Syndikus (2001), 264–9: Syndikus well brings out the joshing irony of Horace in 1. 29, but underestimates the amusingly unofficial window which Horace opens on the great Augustan expedition.
[72] Augustus, *Res Gestae* 26 includes the Arabian expedition in his section on imperial expansion. Extension of empire was, we may assume, the justification for the expedition publicly given at the time, and a grand and Roman reason to conquer; cf. Verg. *Aen.* 6. 851–3 'tu regere imperio populos...'etc. Augustus also presents the campaign as a resounding success, which it was not (Dio 53. 29. 4, Strabo 16. 4. 24). *Res Gestae* 6: 'omnium prouinciarum populi Romani, quibus finitimae fuerunt gentes quae non parerent imperio nostro, *fines auxi*. meo

Then, 1. 31.[73] After the impressive and misleadingly grand opening 'quid dedicatum poscit Apollinem | uates?', bringing to mind both Horace the public poet and Augustus' dedication of his great showcase and ideologically loaded Palatine Temple of Apollo,[74] we find no Roman state request, which might match such a start. Instead, the ode turns to consider what Horace personally is to ask of Apollo—and not on the Augustan day (9 October), the anniversary of the Temple's dedication, but on a day close to it (11 October), the homely festival of the Meditrinalia. And his prayer is first for something which a self-regarding philosopher, particularly the anti-political Epicurus, might wish: simple self-sufficient enjoyment (3–17); and then for things which any ordinary fellow would wish: health of body and mind, a decent and musical old age (17–20). The *cithara* is of course in Apollo's gift: the cult statue of Augustus' Apollo temple was indeed Apollo *Citharoedus*, but one doubts that the imperial image-maker was much concerned with the old age of a self-indulgent poet when he erected this temple and statue.[75] Health too is in Apollo's gift, but there is quite probably a designed inappropriateness in asking the *Palatine* Apollo for this.[76] One doubts most particularly that

iussu et auspicio ducti sunt duo exercitus eodem fere tempore in Aethiopiam *et in Arabiam, quae appellatur Eudaemon,* maximaeque hostium gentis utriusque copiae caesae sunt in acie et complura oppida capta... in Arabiam usque in fines Sabaeorum processit exercitus ad oppidum Mariba. Aegyptum imperio populi Romani adieci...' Horace is careful to include a reference to the official motive for the campaign (extension of empire): 'non ante deuictis...' (3–5), but he alludes too to a less salubrious motive, anyway on Iccius' part, namely profit ('Icci, beatis nunc Arabum inuides | gazis...'), which is the one that the poem develops. The poem does not impose the interpretation that profit was the motive of anyone besides Iccius, but the ode gets close to the bone. For, as Nisbet and Hubbard (1970), 338 say, 'Strabo, who was a friend of Aelius Gallus...gives the show away': on top of strategic reasons moving Augustus, Strabo mentions the Arabians' reputation for huge wealth (16. 4. 22).

[73] For historical background and discussion, see Nisbet and Hubbard (1970), 347 ff., also Syndikus (2001), 274–81.

[74] The misleading effect of *uates* (pointing to the *public* poet Horace) is excellently observed by Nisbet and Hubbard (1970), 347. *Dedicatum* is unmistakable in its reference: there was only one temple that had been 'dedicated' to Apollo which was of any contemporary moment, Augustus' temple on the Palatine in 28 BC. On this masterpiece of visual propaganda, the showcase of the early reign, see Zanker (1987), 90–6 and (1988), 85–9; also Galinsky (1996), 213 ff.

[75] For the cult statue in the Temple of Apollo being particularly *citharoedus*, see Prop. 2. 31. 15–15, surely unequivocal, also 4. 6. 69. Tibullus 2. 5. 1 ff. is an under-advertised piece of evidence: this cletic address is not likely to picture Apollo in a guise that does not reflect the cult figure of the Temple in question. See too Zanker (1987), 90 and (1988), 85. The sculpture was, incidentally, by Scopas (Pliny, *HN* 36. 25).

[76] See Syndikus (2001), esp. 278–81, particularly enlightening on the prayer for health, and so on; also Lefèvre (1993), 219. But there is an impishness here that they miss. The festival of 11 October, the Meditrinalia, which closed the vintage with offerings of new and old wine, was cognate with health (Varro, *Ling.* 6. 21), and Apollo as the Healer had a cult title *Medicus*. But *Apollo Medicus* was actually honoured in *another* temple, one primarily associated with another Roman benefactor and not Augustus. See Wissowa (1912), 294–5; Latte (1960), 222–3;

Augustus' Apollo was quite the right god to ask for Epicurean contentment.[77] And overall it might seem amusing that Horace should so personally presume upon the god's time, when he might have asked, indeed we expected him to ask, for the safety of the empire or the like. Or is this a fitting acknowledgement of the Peace that allows such private interests to make themselves heard?—an interpretation open to us.[78] Horace likes to hedge his bets, but we can imagine how (say) Propertius would have read the poem. We should note incidentally that here finally is a Horatian Apollo poem in alcaics: much domesticated compared with Alcaeus' Apollo hymn, we may surmise, as well as with the expectations that it itself arouses.

That apparently trivial poem (1. 30) inserted between 1. 29 and 31 may remind us of the Pyrrha ode (1. 5), placed among much more serious company in the Parade Odes. But it has two interesting details. Second in its decade, it brings back Mercury ('Mercuriusque') in its last line, the recipient of the second poem in the Signature Sequence, and the Augustan god of the second poem in the whole book. Mercury is mentioned in 1. 30 among the desired companions of Venus, among whom are also the *Nymphae* (1. 30. 6), allusively behind the third poem of the Signature Sequence, 1. 11.[79]

Self-denyingly, I shall call a halt to this section. The structural positions I point to in the sequence of thirty (*Odes* 1. 9–38), and the arguments I make about the poems favoured to occupy them, do I think make plausible sense—more plausible sense than some of the suggestions made for the book of thirty-eight, even more sense than some made for the overarching 'unit' of eighty-eight.[80] But

---

Viscogliosi in Steinby (1993), 1. 49–54 The temple to Apollo Medicus was vowed in 433 BC following plague (Livy 4. 25. 3, 29. 7), and consecrated in 431 BC. It was the only temple of Apollo in Rome until Augustus (Asconius, *Tog. Cand.* 81). The consul who consecrated the temple was a Cn. Iulius, but it was repeatedly renewed during the centuries, and rebuilt in 32 BC or a little later by C. Sosius. After this rebuilding, it was so attached to Sosius' name that Plin. *HN* 36. 28 calls the Apollo of the temple *Apollo Sosianus*, and Latte assumes this was the general appellation after Sosius. (The title *Apollo Medicus* comes from Macrobius 1. 17. 15 who tells us that the Vestal virgins appealed to *Apollo Medice, Apollo Paean.* The appellation is assumed to date right back to the foundation of the temple.) C. Sosius was consul in 32 BC, but Antonian in sympathy, absconding to Antonius for the Battle of Actium, and becoming one of his two principal admirals. He was spared by Octavian after the victory, and gained position in the Augustan state: Syme (1939), 296, 349, etc. (index *sub nom.*, also index to Syme (1986)). But however much Augustus annexed Sosius and this other temple (Syme, and esp. Viscogliosi 50–1), it was a man ingenuous in politics who mentioned health in a request to the Apollo of the Palatine Temple. And Horace was not ingenuous.

[77] See Nisbet and Hubbard (1970), 357–8 on the meaning and philosophical tone of *paratis* (17), and on the sense of the last stanza, necessitating Lambinus' *et precor*.

[78] Cf. Syndikus (2001), 274.

[79] 'Nymphae' in *Odes* 1 also at 1. 1. 31 (in poetic function) and 1. 4. 6.

[80] For suggestions on structural patterns in the larger Book 1, see e.g. Port (1925–6) 296–304; Santirocco (1986), 42–82; Porter (1987), 56 ff. Hutchinson (2002), 529–32 surveys contents and organization with brevity, sense, and sensibility. Dettmer (1983) is more concerned to demonstrate ring-composition structure over Books 1–3 as a whole: see e.g. preface and 141 ff.

the book of thirty-eight, at least, is a structure that Horace exploits, at the beginning as well as the end, and at the close of the first half, and the opening of the second, to mention the most obvious places. Book 1 of the *Odes* offers two chances of structure: one based on the total number of poems, one based on a decimal block which started with Horace's Signature Sequence. Horace likes chameleon structures, as he has already shown in the *Epodes*.[81]

VIII. THE ARISTARCHAN ALCAEUS BOOK 1

Working back from Horace, I can draw two possible inferences about the edition of Alcaeus which Horace used.

The first concerns the number of poems in Alcaeus Book 1. It often strikes scholars that the thirty-eight poems of Horace's first book of Odes is a strange number.[82] Ten Vergilian *Eclogues*, ten poems in Horace's first book of satires, ten elegies in Tibullus Book 1. A decimal trend seems to be under way. Playing on this, Propertius organizes two sequences of ten elegies in his first book, with main but 'false' closure in what would have been his 1. 20.[83] There are of course only eight poems in Horace's second book of satires, but the total number of lines in the book is 1083, slightly above the total for *Satires* 1 (1030); the abnormal length of *Serm.* 2. 3, which serves a clear literary purpose, so to speak precludes Horace's proceeding beyond eight, and the closure at eight may productively draw attention to the obtruding and amusing length of 2. 3.[84] Then, twenty

---

[81] This is a topic that I treat in Lyne 2005*b* [= Ch. 18, this volume].

[82] After noting the decimal numbers in *Odes* Books 2 and 3, Port (1925–6), 297 remarks, 'fallt die Zahl 38 im ersten Buch auf', and he refers to the 'merkwürdige Zahl' later on the page; but he offers no satisfactory explanation. Santirocco (1986), 81 says 'an irregular number... as opposed to the other books' multiples of ten'; S. also notes that the number of poems is much larger in 1 than in 2 and 3, 43 per cent of the total in the three books. Fraenkel (1957), 112 with n. 1 notes the decimal trend which I outline below (the *Eclogues* 'ushered in a new era... ten, or a multiple of it, seems to have been considered by Horace, and by some contemporary poets as well, the ideal number for the poems of a book'); 'in the case of Book I', he says, 'there was an overflow,' hardly a sufficient explanation of an anomaly. Fowler (2000), 259–60 observes the odd total, and 'know[s] no reason' for it.

[83] I am using what would have been the ancient numeration: poems 8a and b are rightly divided, so that our poem 19 would have been 20 in Propertius' edition. So, Book 1 contained a sequence of twenty 'Cynthia' poems, and, in the final poem, Propertius squarely confronts the question 'Can Love Conquer *Death*?', a heavily closural topic, and ends the poem with a superbly final couplet. And then we get a coda of completely different, non-Cynthia material. Poem 10 (= 11 in the ancient edition) takes on new significances when one absorbs the fact that it opened the second half of the Cynthia sequence.

[84] To explain eight instead of ten poems in *Satires* Book 2, I think we should try 'to avoid the conclusion that Horace, as he went on writing *sermones*, began to run out of suitable subjects and settings' (Fraenkel (1957) 137). In the dialogue of the third satire, 326 lines long, we are

odes in Book 2, thirty in Book 3, fifteen—half thirty—in Book 4 to ring the changes. And twenty *Epistles* in Book 1. The strange total of *Epodes* has its own explanation, to which I shall attend in another paper. As I have shown, from the point where the Signature Sequence starts we have thirty structured odes (30, then 20 and 30 in Books 2 and 3). But why the strange total in Book 1?

A heroic effort has been made to cut down this total number in order to produce a more rational-seeming number:[85] adjacent poems in the same metre (1. 16 and 17, 26 and 27, 34 and 35, all alcaics) should be regarded as one poem, a simple expedient. But it disregards evidence for adjacent poems in the same metre in Alcaeus (see note 11), and more importantly defies sensible reading. We have a total of thirty-eight to explain, irreducibly.

The random-seeming total of poems is strange for an Augustan book, but not for an Alexandrian book. Aristophanes of Byzantium was content with fourteen *Olympians*, twelve *Pythians*, and perhaps eleven *Isthmians*. Eight *Nemeans*, giving a book of merely 908 verses, had three more non-*Nemeans* (as later ancient scholars noted) added, to produce a total of 1,273 lines (more in keeping with standard Alexandrian book length), and eleven poems.[86] Callimachus produced his own *Gedichtbuch* of *Iambi*, most probably thirteen in number, though seventeen has its adherents. If it was thirteen, then Callimachus or someone else subsequently bulked out the book to seventeen.[87] And seventeen was the number of *Aetia* in Book 4 of Callimachus'

---

swiftly informed that Horace is struck by incapacity to write: as a dramatic and humorous reflection of this he utters extremely few lines in the poem in his own voice. Damasippus dominates the dialogue, and he in turn is dominated by a huge speech which he quotes from the Stoic philosopher Stertinius (38–295). The Stoicism uttered by Damasippus–Stertinius is not as extreme as that sharply put down in *Satires* Book 1 (*Serm.* 1. 3. 77 ff., summed up in 96–8); following tactics of Book 2 Horace allows figures to make their own case and leaves us to assess. But there is a joke in the length of the speech quoted from Stertinius, especially in relation to the number of lines Horace gives to himself. Crispinus was not the only philosopher who could go on and on (1. 1. 120–1), and both Stertinius' wordiness *and* poor Horace's lack of words are emphasized by the inordinate span of the satire and its distribution. In his other works, including *Odes* 1 as this paper shows, Horace proves himself so aware of structure and number that we will reasonably seek a literary explanation of the *apparent* shortfall of poems in *Satires* 2, and our search swiftly takes us to the great length of 2. 3 and to the function of that great length.

[85] See Griffiths (2002). Stirring stuff, but some decisive contrary points are made in advance by Hutchinson (2002), 520 n. 14. Griffiths carries his metrical policy through to the Roman Odes (which become one 'monster mega-poem'), and thus cuts Book 3 to twenty-five odes, still obedient to what he engagingly calls the 'five and dime' principle (66). He does not tell us what he would do with 2. 13–15 and 19–20, all alcaics. The same sort of procedure would wreck the nicely decimal total at present in that book.

[86] See Irigoin (1952), 31–50, esp. 40–2; see too Pfeiffer (1968), 183 ff. and Fraser (1972), i. 459–60.

[87] For the thirteen Callimachean *Iambi*, see Kerkhecker (1999), esp. 272–6. Cameron (1995), 163–73 argues for seventeen Callimachean *Iambi* (the number of poems between *Aetia* and

Aetia.⁸⁸ Why not therefore a Book 1 of Alcaeus with thirty-eight poems, with an average of, say thirty-two lines each?⁸⁹ When the lyric Horace confirms that it is Alcaeus with whom he most especially wishes to align himself, he might have liked his readers to discover that the total number of poems in his Book 1 equalled the number of the master's poems in his standard edition Book 1. We remember that 'Alcaeus Book 1' was a way of thinking which Horace could share with his readers, ancient and modern (Section I).

The second inference I draw concerns the provenance of Horace's Alcaean models. Horace matches the metres of Alcaeus' first three poems in the Signature Sequence 1. 9, 10 and 11, but he only matches metre *and* content in 1. 10. However, he picks up a replacement Alcaean text in 1. 9 for content, and alludes to another Alcaean text, via the metre of 1. 18 and *its* quoted Alcaean line, in 1. 11. I think it more likely than not, considering Horace's apparent preoccupation with 'Alcaeus Book 1'—for him, both a ready text and way of thinking—that these replacements came from that Book 1. I would make the same suggestion for any other poems of Alcaeus that may be behind odes in Book 1. The most promising candidates are as follows. Fragment 208V, a main model of *Odes* 1. 14: this is a good candidate for pride of place in Alcaeus in its own right, since it appears to have been well known: it attracted (correctly) an allegorical interpretation from Heraclitus, *Quaestiones Homericae* 5, and is the subject of commentary/summary in two surviving papyri (*POxy.* 2306 col. II = 305bV and *POxy.* 2734 fr. 6 = 306C (c) Campbell). I infer from Pardini that he thinks the summary of 208V in *POxy.* 2734 is argument in itself for a position in Book 1 for that poem.⁹⁰ Then, fr. 6V also behind *Odes* 1. 14,⁹¹ fr. 332V the model at the start of *Odes* 1. 37, and fr. 286V, quite probably a model for *Odes* 1. 4.⁹²

Hecale in the Milan *Diegeseis*). Clayman (1980) supposes the thirteen *Iambi* were filled out with four more poems, by Callimachus himself or a copyist.

⁸⁸ Cameron (1995), 170 n. 39.

⁸⁹ Sappho's first book apparently contained 1,320 lines, and we have stichometric signs in 800 Alcaean papyri compatible with this sort of total. For the stichometric subscription in Sappho, see fr. 30V (*POxy.* 1231) and Irigoin (1952), 39. In an Alcaean papyrus, there is a marginal kappa beside fr. 120. 4V marking line 1,000 of its book; at 143. 12 there is a marginal theta, marking the 800th line in its book, perhaps the same book, perhaps another. This suggests at least one book of Alcaeus in excess of 1,000 lines, and in all probability Alcaeus' books met the Alexandrian norm in number of lines (like Sappho Book 1). But Dr Obbink warns against trusting stichometric markers *per se*, since they may have been carried over from non-colometrically written editions of the poems. He refers to Blanchard and Bataille (1964), 162; Kassel (1991), 283, bibliographical items also referred to by Arnott (2000), 198 n. 5, making this same sceptical point about stichometric numbers in Menander papyri. The bibliographical *POxy.* 2294 1/4 fr. 103V seems to point to a Sappho Book 8 of almost incredible brevity: ten poems and between 130 and 140 lines *in toto*: cf. Page (1955), 116–19. But since Sappho was ordered by metre (above n. 10), it is possible that strange bibliographical things happened.

⁹⁰ Pardini (1991), 283.   ⁹¹ Nisbet and Hubbard (1970), 179.   ⁹² Ibid. 58.

'Imitations of Alcaeus... are concentrated in Horace's first book (except for the metrical tour de force 3. 12)', say Nisbet and Hubbard.[93] If the papyrus evidence is representative in this respect, and I am right that the poems which Horace imitated were in Alcaeus Book 1, it opens an interesting window on Horace's strategy and his reading.

---

[93] Ibid. p. xxix.

18

Structure and Allusion in Horace's Book of *Epodes* (2005)

I. THE SPECIAL PLACE OF *EPODE* 13

First, a text.[1] The one I print differs significantly in two places from the Oxford Classical Text of Wickham and Garrod (1901) and Shackleton Bailey's Teubner (1985). I adopt Bentley's *amice* for *amici* in line 3, but reserve discussion of this for Section IV. In line 13 the manuscripts describe Homer's 'great', 'deep-eddying', 'fair-flowing' Scamander,[2] which gives Achilles such a tremendous battle in *Iliad* 21, as 'small', *parui*, and nothing can defend this corruption.[3] For Heinsius' *flaui*, *Odes* 1. 2. 13 *flauum Tiberim* is of small moment; the crucial point is that it calques Scamander's other designation Ξάνθος, which is in fact the one most used in *Iliad* 21. Horace is fond of bilingual plays,[4]

---

[1] References to Archilochus and Hipponax follow West (1989); West's numeration is preserved in the Loeb of D. E. Gerber, *Greek Iambic Poetry* (1999); testimonia (T) to Archilochus are in Gerber. For Alcaeus' fragments, I refer to the accessible Loeb of Campbell (1982), and for Anacreon to Campbell (1988); Campbell's numeration for the most part follows Lobel and Page (1955) and Page (1962), and (for Alcaeus) it virtually overlaps with the edition of Voigt (1971). The following commentaries on the *Epodes* have proved most useful: Watson (2003), Mankin (1995), and Cavarzere (1992). Watson's immensely scholarly work was still in proof when I did most of my work on this article, and he generously sent me a preview of his notes on *Epodes* 13 and 14. I owe great thanks to Professor G. O. Hutchinson, who read a draft of my article and offered his usual acute criticisms and suggestions. He will observe and I hope forgive that I have resisted some of his scepticism.

[2] *Iliad* 20. 73, 21. 1, 15, 603, and other similar passages. Cf. [δινâ]ντα in the passage of Bacchylides cited below.

[3] *parui* is printed by Wickham-Garrod, obelized by Shackleton Bailey. There is a balanced discussion of the textual problem in Mankin (1995) ad loc., but his text too prints *parui*. *parui* is also defended by e.g. Giarratano (1930), 93. The context at Lucan 9. 974 f., 'inscius in sicco serpentem puluere riuum | transierat, qui Xanthus erat' needs to be noted: Caesar is visiting the miserable present-day remnants of great Troy, and the unnoticed stream that he crosses is what great Xanthus *was*. I argue against one of the main 'defences' of *parui* in n. 45 below. Davis (1991) provides a predictable late twentieth-century argument from genre, 15: a 'contradiction of Homer—the deliberate inversion of scale from "great" to "small"'. Why should Horace do this and make nonsense in dramatic terms of Chiron's speech? A scholiast's variant *praui* is printed and defended by Cavarzere (1992) and Watson (2003) ad loc.

[4] *exilis Plutonia* (πλοῦτος) at *Odes* 1. 4. 17, 'dulces... Licymniae | cantus' ([γ]λυκ-, ὕμνος) at 2. 12. 13 f. (with Nisbet and Hubbard (1978) ad loc.), 2. 16. 17 (Nisbet and Hubbard). Cf. Lucretius'

a shrouded allusion suits the prophet Chiron, and a reference to this more overtly divine twin-name[5] suits the rhetoric of the passage. Chiron's purpose here is to allude to an outstanding example of Achilles' invincibility, as I shall amplify below; so the more his foe is built up, the more that point is made. Bentley in his edition of 1711 proposed *proni*, objecting to the sound of *frigida flaui* ('scabre & dure exibit'), but the alliterative pattern *fr fl f... fl* suits Horace's virtual addiction to this figure, an addiction which this very poem evidences.

> horrida tempestas caelum contraxit et imbres
>   niuesque deducunt Iouem; nunc mare, nunc siluae
> Threicio Aquilone sonant. rapiamus, amice,
>   occasionem de die, dumque uirent genua
> et decet, obducta soluatur fronte senectus.   5
>   tu uina Torquato moue consule pressa meo.
> cetera mitte loqui: deus haec fortasse benigna
>   reducet in sedem uice. nunc et Achaemenio
> perfundi nardo iuuat et fide Cyllenaea
>   leuare diris pectora sollicitudinibus,   10
> nobilis ut grandi cecinit Centaurus alumno:
>   'inuicte mortalis dea nate puer Thetide,
> te manet Assaraci tellus, quam frigida flaui
>   findunt Scamandri flumina lubricus et Simois,
> unde tibi reditum certo subtemine Parcae   15
>   rupere, nec mater domum caerula te reuehet.
> illic omne malum uino cantuque leuato,
>   deformis aegrimoniae dulcibus alloquiis.'

There is already much bibliography on this atypical epode.[6] My discussion will be selective, and its thrust will be to show that the poem is not only

---

Scipiades, belli fulmen at 3. 1034, picked up by Vergil at *Aen.* 6. 842–3 (owed ultimately to Ennius?). Cf. too Vergil's own *Ceraunia* (κεραυνός) *telo* at *Georg.* 1. 332, and so on.

[5] At *Iliad* 20. 74 we hear of the river 'whom the gods call Xanthos, but men call Scamander', and it is as Xanthus that he is known when we learn that 'Zeus bore him' (14. 434, 21. 2).

[6] A good place to start is with Watson (2003), 417–37, Mankin (1995), 214 ff., and Cavarzere (1992), 199 ff. Differences in interpretation between Mankin and the author, especially as regards the point of the *exemplum*, will be manifest. I shall point to some detailed points where we differ, but some only. On many occasions our differences may co-exist: a Horatian text is very open. The commentary of Tescari (1936) is still worth consulting. Rudd (1960), 373–92 is not solely devoted to *Epode* 13 of course, but is a classic article with much to say on our poem. See too Giarratano (1930), 89 ff. Commager (1962), 173 is brief in his comments, but highly suggestive. Cf. too Kilpatrick (1970), 135–41; Kilpatrick has a curious idea about the occasion of the poem (see below), but other interesting things to say; Babcock (1978), 107–18; Traina (1986), 227–51; Lowrie (1992), 413–33, a very helpful piece; Oliensis (1998), 96 offers brief comment, entirely different from anything I say.

special, but special in such a way as to merit an important structural position in the book. More exactly, if it had been a closing poem, it would have performed that role admirably.

I shall talk of 'Horace' as the speaker in the sympotic setting, since there is a very clear invitation to do so. I gather my comments under headings.

1. Genre and Symposium

The poem is a striking example of generic 'crossing', *Kreuzung*. In the *Epodes* book as a whole, Horace makes his official literary descent clear. He writes in the genre of *iambi*, and his models are Archilochus and Hipponax; *iambi* is indeed the title he gave to his collection ('Epodes' is grammarians' talk, though since it is conventional I shall use it).[7] Alignment with both Archilochus and Hipponax is advertised in *Epode* 6. 13–14, while Archilochus is focused upon in *Epist.* 1. 19. 23–5. Of available models, Archilochus does indeed seem to have been the most important. If we consider text, it is Archilochus', so far as we can tell, that is more frequently echoed than Hipponax's; *Epode* 2 perhaps owes a debt to Archilochus that has not been spotted.[8] Hipponax is, however, recognized as the author of the 'First Strasbourg Epode' by West (fr. 115) and others, and this poem seems to be behind *Epode* 10. As for metre, nearly all Horace's are demonstrably Archilochean,[9] and he eschews choliambics, Hipponax's metrical blazon.[10]

An Archilochean iambist he may be, but *Epode* 13 is clearly sympotic in its setting, the first and only epode to be so, and neither Archilochus nor

---

[7] See below and n. 77 for the title *iambi*. The genre of *iambi* is of course to be distinguished from metrical iambics: West (1974), 22 ff., e.g. 'Iambic metre got its name from being particularly characteristic of ἴαμβοι, not vice versa'. Our first occurrence of the word ἴαμβος itself is in Archilochus fr. 215 καί μ' οὔτ' ἰάμβων οὔτε τερπωλέων μέλει, where certainly more than metre is meant: West (p. 25) thinks that Archilochus' ἴαμβοι, coupled with τερπωλαί, points to an occasion; I might have said, with conscious and perhaps suggestive anachronism, to a genre.

[8] On Horace's use of Archilochus see Hutchinson (forthcoming [now 2007]); Mankin (1995) and Watson (2003) indexes s.v. 'Archilochus'. As for *Epode* 2, when Archilochus in fr. 19 makes 'Charon the carpenter' express in direct speech indifference to the wealth of Gyges etc., it seems to me likely that he is setting him up for an ironic revelation of hypocrisy just as Horace sets up Alfius in *Epode* 2; but it must be admitted that neither Aristotle, *Rhetoric* 1418^{b}23–31 nor Plutarch, *Moralia* 470b–c point to any such denouement in their references to the piece.

[9] See Mankin (1995), 14–22.

[10] Hipponax and choliambics: see Hipponax T8, T12, T13, and the fragments themselves; Theocritus' *Epigram* 19 Gow = *Anth. Pal.* 13. 3 on Hipponax is, significantly, written in choliambics. In contrast to Horace, Callimachus parades choliambics in his *Iambi*. While Callimachus presents himself as a genially reborn Hipponax (*Iambus* I), Horace gives more the impression of a relatively genial Archilochus: cf. Kerkhecker (1999), 275–6, but note too Hutchinson (2007), 37–9.

Hipponax, so far as we can tell, situate poems in this way.[11] *Epode* 13 is not only sympotically situated, but follows a well-known sympotic pattern. Taking stimulus from an external event, the poet issues convivial instructions in the first person, and these instructions then merge with moralizing. Here we are on familiar but uniambic ground. Indeed, apart from its epodic Archilochean metre, *Epode* 13 most resembles a sympotic type from monostrophic lyric.[12] It anticipates *Ode* 1. 9 in particular, and shows affinities to the Alcaean sympotic poem behind that ode (fr. 338), and to other Alcaean sympotic poems besides: cf. frr. 38A, 346, 347(a),[13] 352, 367.[14]

Issuing instructions, Horace is modelling his voice on that of the symposiarch, $συμποσίαρχος$.[15] The sense of generic intrusion is, as we shall see, thereby reinforced. But since the use of the symposiarch voice is not appreciated in *Epode* 13[16] and in other lyric, sympotic poems, and since material on the role of the symposiarch is not as easy to come by as one might have thought, the point is worth elaborating.

The fullest texts on the role of the symposiarch are Plutarch, *Moralia* 620a–622b (*Quaestiones Conuiuales*) and Plato, *Laws* 639d–641, and another fascinating snippet occurs in Plato's *Symposium*. The first two are, of course, tendentious, especially Plato's, but we can identify important emphases. In Plutarch it is an assumption that one *chooses* the symposiarch ($αἱρεῖσθαι$,

---

[11] Mankin (1995), 8 and 214 is misleading, likewise Cavarzere (1992), 33. In the elegiac fr. 4. 6–9 drinking on board ship is envisaged, as in *Epode* 9 (Nisbet in Woodman and West (1984), 10–18, esp. 17; Nisbet's note 62 is useful for Archilochus 4). Hipponax fr. 60 seems to refer to a sympotic occasion, but in the past tense. For a reconstruction of the occasion when archaic *iambi* were delivered (nothing to do with symposium), see West (1974), 23 ff.

[12] Pardini (1991), 271 f. argues plausibly that there was no Greek term for a 'sympotic' poem in the way that that term is used now, i.e. to describe a poem that brings to the fore its sympotic occasion and talks of the typical concerns of symposia—pouring the wine, celebrating an event, enjoying the moment, etc. When Aristotle talks of Alcaeus' 'drinking songs' ($σκολιὰ μέλη$) at *Pol.* 1285^{a}38, he is referring (says Pardini) to *all* Alcaeus' poems, on the assumption that all were destined to be uttered at symposia. But the absence of a limiting and technical term for a type of poem does not mean that that type of poem did not exist. Labelling lags behind creation. Page (1955), 299 f. argues against employing a separate modern label, but usefully groups and comments upon sympotic fragments, at 299–310.

[13] This is closely based on Hesiod, *Op.* 582 ff., which allows us to conjecture how Alcaeus' fragment continued.

[14] With this fr., cf. Horace, *Odes* 4. 12.

[15] For other titles of the symposiarch ($ἄρχων$, $βασιλεύς$ of the symposium), see Pellizer in Murray (1990), 178 n. 7. When the Romans adapted the symposium to their culture, the Latin terms reflected the Greek: Varro in Book 20 of his *Res Humanae* (Nonius Marcellus p. 142 M, 206 L), 'in conuiuiis qui sunt instituti potandi modimperatores magistri'; Hor. *Odes* 2. 7. 25, 'arbiter bibendi'; *Odes* 1. 4. 18, 'rex (regnum) uini'.

[16] Kilpatrick (1970), 136, citing little evidence, and repeated by Mankin (1995) ad loc., explains Horace's instructions regarding the wine in *Epode* 13 thus: it seems 'proper etiquette for a guest to specify the vintage to his host'. Watson (2003) on *Epode* 13. 6 assumes that Horace's addressee (*tu*) is 'the host or symposiarch' and quotes the same remark of Kilpatrick's.

620b): the location and its owner do not dictate who it is. For the purposes of his discussion on the symposiarch's function, itself convivially set, Plutarch accepts pressure and 'chooses himself' (620a); he appears to be at his own house, but the role clearly does not automatically go with the territory. True to the title, the symposiarch is, according to Plutarch, to take authority and give orders, prescribe (κελεύειν, προστάττειν, 620b); but he must know and understand his συμπόται so that he can, for example, get the right strength of wine for each drinker.[17] In Plato, a symposium's need for a ruler is (no surprise) very emphatically stressed: οὐκοῦν πρῶτον μὲν καὶ τούτοις ἄρχοντος δεῖ (640c). For Plato too the identity of the symposiarch does not go with the location: in his words, he must be 'provided', 'appointed' (ἐκπορίζεσθαι, καθιστάναι 640c and d). We hear again the need to understand the company: καὶ μὴν περί γε συνουσίας, ὡς ἔοικεν αὐτὸν φρόνιμον εἶναι δεῖ (640c). Particularly vivid then is Plato, *Symp*. 213e: here the tipsy, late arrival, Alcibiades, perceives an excess of sobriety in the assembled company, appoints himself ἄρχων τῆς πόσεως, and, in Agathon's house, gives an order for drink to be produced, and generally takes over. Alcibiades' self-appointment as symposiarch is funnily narrated, but the comparative material from Plato and especially Plutarch shows that it is not essentially transgressive. And once we have appreciated this point, we can appreciate that the conventional punctuation of Alcibiades' order for drink in Plato is importantly wrong.[18] In sum, Plato, *Laws*, Plutarch, and indeed by implication Plato, *Symp*. all suggest that an authoritative symposiarch, holding sway, who is neither the host nor on home turf, may be quite normal practice.

The symposiarch's voice is part of lyric sympotic poetry. In several odes we find Horace issuing advice and orders for present or imminent sympotic occasions, not necessarily at his own domicile, and to his social superiors

---

[17] ἔτι τοίνυν αὐτῷ δεῖ προσεῖναι τὸ μάλιστα μὲν ἑκάστου τῶν συμποτῶν ἐμπείρως ἔχειν τίνα λαμβάνει μεταβολὴν ἐν οἴνῳ καὶ πρὸς τί πάθος ἀκροσφαλής ἐστι καὶ πῶς φέρει τὸν ἄκρατον ... ἀνθρώπου δὲ πρὸς οἶνον οὐκ ἔστ' ἰδία κρᾶσις, ἣν τῷ συμποσιάρχῳ γιγνώσκειν προσήκει καὶ γιγνώσκοντι φυλάττειν ... etc. (620e).

[18] The text of Alcibiades' order for drink is conventionally printed with the following punctuation, ἀλλὰ φερέτω, Ἀγάθων, εἴ τι ἐστὶν ἔκπωμα μέγα..., and the sense abstracted is 'Agathon, let <some slave> bring...'. But this is very forced, especially in view of the 'abnormal' (Dover, ad loc.) omission of τις to indicate a slave; and, enlightened by comparative material on the symposiarch, we can correct it. Editors punctuate thus, avoiding Ἀγάθων as subject of φερέτω, because 'even when drunk Alcibiades would not give orders to his host as if to a slave' (Dover). But there must be some transgressive behaviour to indicate Alcibiades' tipsiness; his taking over the role of symposiarch does *not*, as we have seen, sufficiently constitute it; and it is precisely in his issuing of orders to Agathon that the amusing presumption of the drunk is revealed. The text should precisely show him ordering Agathon about: ἀλλὰ φερέτω Ἀγάθων... He then supplants this order with one to a *slave*, and the sentence as a whole is, or should be, unambiguous: ἀλλὰ φερέτω Ἀγάθων εἴ τι ἔστιν ἔκπωμα μέγα. μᾶλλον δὲ οὐδὲν δεῖ ἀλλὰ φέρε, παῖ, φάναι, τὸν ψυκτῆρα ἐκεῖνον ... (213e).

as well as equals and inferiors: 1. 4 (the consul Sestius); 1. 9, 11, 36, 2. 3 (Q. Dellius); 2. 14 (Postumus,[19] and the implied sympotic setting there is clearly Postumus' own gardens: note '*harum* quas colis arborum'); 3. 19 (to 'Telephus'; a party for the 'augur Murena'); 3. 28. The situations vary and are more or less blurred, but the role of the elected and authoritative *symposiarchus* is the one to which Horace most approximates. So too in *Epode* 13. A forerunner of this symposiarch voice may be sensed in many fragments of Alcaeus: see most obviously frr. 338, 346, 347, 352, also (though the context is often beyond certainty) 38A, 335, 362, 367, etc. In some of Horace's odes, and some of Alcaeus', we may get the impression of a party for two, as we do in *Epode* 13 (*Odes* 1. 9, 11, for example)—how consonant with reality, we cannot tell.

The poem also employs a mythical *exemplum*. Again this is like Alcaeus' sympotic lyric. In the sympotic 38A Alcaeus uses a mythical paraenesis (Sisyphus), and he features myth elsewhere.[20] Fable, αἶνος, is much more typical of Archilochus than myth; about Hipponax in this respect little can be said.[21] Horace does not use mythical paraenesis in *Odes* 1. 9, but he does in the generically related *Odes* 1. 7 (Teucer) and *Odes* 4. 11 (Phaethon); cf. too Itys in *Odes* 4. 12.

Horace brings the lyric symposium into *iambi*, an arresting innovation, enough to make us pause.

2. The Special Nature of the Symposium

The symposium set in motion is very much out of the ordinary. The wine (13. 6) is a vintage from the year of Horace's birth, a fact that we will note

---

[19] Nisbet and Hubbard (1978), 223 document the plausible identification of this Postumus with the successful magistrate (*ILS* 914) Propertius (Postumus) identified behind Prop. 3. 12.

[20] In fr. 42 he contrasts the stories of Helen and Troy on the one hand and Peleus and Thetis on the other: our fr. starts 'as the story goes', ὡς λόγος. Fr. 283—a fine piece—tells the story of Helen and her disastrous elopement to Troy. In fr. 298 the story of Locrian Ajax's impious rape of Cassandra is told, as, it seems, an *exemplum* in a political poem. These together with fr. 44 are given commentary and discussion as 'the principal examples of a practice seldom observable in the remains of Sappho and Alcaeus, the adaptation of Homeric themes to Lesbian dialect and metre' by Page (1955), 275–85. 'Seldom' perhaps gives the wrong emphasis: these poems certainly leave a lasting impression. At 387, too, there is a reference to the other Ajax and to Achilles.

[21] For (Aesopian) fable in Archilochus, see T44, frr. 172–81 (fox and eagle), 185–7 (fox and monkey), 201 (fox and hedgehog): Archilochus actually uses the word αἶνος in frs 174 and 185. Cf. Fraser (1972), 743–4. References are, however, made to Archilochus' telling the story of Hercules, Nessus, and Deianeira, frr. 286–9, but there is no hint that it provided some sort of paraenesis at a symposium. There is no trace left of fable in Hipponax (Fraser, ibid. 744); myth in an unknown context in Hipponax fr. 72 (Rhesus) and 75, 77 ('Odysseus', as a title apparently, fr. 74), perhaps in the context of Bupalus.

again below. For now we may make two inferences. A vintage *circa* thirty years old must be a very good vintage, implying grand status in the *amicus*:[22] it is one that in *Odes* 3. 21 will be deemed worthy of the great M. Valerius Messalla Corvinus (3. 21. 6: 'moueri digna bono die'). The choice by Horace of a vintage precisely from the year of his birth also implies a special relationship between him and the friend: it must have a sentimental value which would not be shared with just any (grand) person. Then too the balsam deemed proper in lines 8 f. is ostentatiously luxurious.[23] The verb *moue* (13. 6) is also important. The imperative ultimately denotes 'bring out', 'move from its storage place' (cf. *deprome* in *Odes* 1. 9. 7), but it is not an obvious word for the context, and the only parallel to be adduced is *Odes* 3. 21. 6. In that ode (a hymnic parody) many see, and Syndikus documents, a play on uses of (*com*)*moueo* for the moving of a sacred object for a ceremony on a religious day. This is a most effective connotation, even more effective in *Epode* 13 than in *Ode* 3. 21.[24] The verb *ceremoniously* marks both wine and occasion. So Horace presides over a rich and singular symposium, with a friend who seems both grand and intimate: a climactic occasion and poem. The identity of the *amicus* will be discussed in Section IV, where the reading *amice* is defended.

3. More Generic 'Mixing'. Other Contributors

The mythical story in *Epode* 13 is couched explicitly as (Chiron's) *prophecy*, unlike Alcaeus' *exemplum* in 38A and unlike Horace's later mythical examples. A Chiron prophecy about Achilles is reported, in direct speech, by the Centaurs who are said to have come to the marriage of Peleus and Thetis at Eur. *IA* 1062–75. Prophetic direct speech is a feature of choral lyric,[25] and Pindar, *Pyth.* 9. 39–65 stages a prophecy by Chiron to Apollo, of all characters (and Chiron is conscious of the incongruity). But most relevant to us is a fragment of Bacchylides (*Dithyramb* 27. 34–45 Maehler), in which someone reports in indirect speech what Chiron is prophesying concerning Achilles himself. It seems plain that Horace actually alludes to, even merges with, this choral lyric poem:

---

[22] Contrast the drinking companion and the wine deemed suitable in *Odes* 1. 9. Note the apologetics and wine snobbery, fitted to the greatness of Maecenas, in the invitation poem to him, *Odes* 1. 20.

[23] See Watson and Mankin ad loc.

[24] Syndikus (2001), 183, on 3. 21. 6, with references and bibliography; Syndikus compares *Epode* 13. 6. In the hymnic parody of *Odes* 3. 21, I am inclined to think that a play on the sense 'influence', 'move to softer feelings', *OLD* s.v. *moveo* 14 and 15, is more likely.

[25] See Führer (1967), 112 ff., esp. 117–29.

ξανθᾶς νιν εὔβ[ο]υλ[ο]ς θαμ[ὰ Φ]ιλλυρί[δας
ψαύων κεφ[αλ]ᾶς ἐνέπει·   35
φατί νιν [δινᾶ]ντα φοινίξειν Σκά[μανδρον
κτείνον[τα φιλ]οπτολέμους
Τρῶας· π.[....].´.....´. ·ι..α[]ματ[
ξείναι τ.[   ][
ἀλκίμουσ[   ]τ' ἐπ[40
Μυσῶν τ' α[   ][
ταῦτ' ἐνέπ[
καρδίαν π[
———
φίλα[ι]ς δεχ[45
δ' εὐφυλλ[ο

(when I remember what?) the wise son of Philyra (Chiron) often says of him, touching his fair head: he declares that he will crimson eddying Scamander as he kills the battle-loving Trojans;...and (will lie in a) foreign (land)...valiant... Mysians...That is what he says...(?his) heart...in loving (hands?)...leafy...

Note in particular that Bacchylides' Chiron focuses upon the battle by the river Scamander, unlike Euripides' Chiron, but in the same area as Horace's: in Horace the lack of detail like φοινίξειν allows us to think of Achilles' duel with Scamander himself, rather than the initial fouling of his waters with mortal corpses. And Bacchylides' Chiron not only prophesies to Achilles in person, but with affection, as does Horace's: in Bacchylides the affection is conveyed clearly by gesture (lines 34 f., touching his head),[26] in Horace by the mode of address (most obviously, line 12, *puer*). My hunch would be that the 'heart' in question (line 43) is Achilles': so that Chiron's 'encouragement' of Achilles was actually mentioned, picking up the opening affectionate gesture. Other material can be conjectured.[27]

The presentation of Chiron *instructing* Achilles may also engage— who knows, may allude to—the Hesiodic Χείρωνος Ὑποθῆκαι. But if so,

---

[26] Cf. how, a little more intimately, a parent may stroke her child's head (Hdt. 6. 61. 5 τὴν δὲ καταψῶσαν τοῦ παιδίου τὴν κεφαλήν), or a teacher a pupil's (Plato, *Phaedo* 89b καταψήσας οὖν μου τὴν κεφαλήν). The Homeric formula χειρί τέ μιν κατέρεξεν in comparably intimate situations probably signifies the same gesture (*Iliad* 1. 361, *Odyssey* 5. 181 etc.). More information in Sittl (1890), 33 f.

[27] See Maehler (1997), 47–8, 280–2. Maehler, after Barrett, suggests that Thetis or Peleus is calling to mind this prophecy ('Ich erinnere mich daran, was...') to help explain the two adjacent verbs of saying in lines 35 f.; Hutchinson (2001), 428 n. 3 thinks that this takes too little account of the present tenses. Maehler also thinks that the reference to Mysians accords with a possible implication of *Iliad* 2. 858–61: that Mysians were slain in the waters of Scamander, though this is not explicitly stated in *Iliad* 21. Snell's φίλαις δὲ χερσίν in line 44 is attractive.

there is likely to be some irony in an interchange with a seemingly grave and moral text.[28]

The incorporation of Bacchylides (at least) is another arresting display.

4. The Occasion for the Symposium

The occasion is apparently a storm (lines 1–3). But the appearance in the storm's description of images of human frowning (lines 1–2)[29] suggests straight away that we are concerned with less literal circumstances; and the symbolic possibilities of storm were manifold. For example, storms at sea in Alcaeus and Archilochus were read in antiquity as political allegories, and were surely designed as such.[30] But the suggestiveness in *Epode* 13 is open: I see nothing in the text to limit the suggestion to a political situation, much less to a specific event, or even day of the month.[31] As Nisbet and Hubbard say on *Odes* 2. 9. 1, with documentation worthy of true scholars, 'The vicissitudes of human happiness are often compared with the weather':[32] storms figure trouble,

---

[28] The surviving fragments are Hesiod frr. 283–5 Merkelbach and West; fr. 285 is Quintilian, *Inst.* 1. 1. 15 attributing to this work the view that boys should not be taught to read before the age of seven, but also recording that the Alexandrian scholar Aristophanes denied that Hesiod was the author. Fr. 283 preserves the first three lines, and it is indeed a grave opening (e.g. 2–3, πρῶτον μέν, ὅτ᾽ ἂν δόμον εἰσαφίκηαι | ἔρδειν ἱερὰ καλὰ θεοῖς αἰειγενέτῃσι; Pindar, *Pyth.* 6. 19–27 may give us a further sense of its tone (so Davis (1991), 13). For more references and bibliography on the Ὑποθῆκαι, see Watson (2003), 431, Lowrie (1992), 420.

[29] For the images of frowning, see Rudd (1960), 384, referring to Hor. *Serm.* 2. 2. 125, Quint. 11. 3. 79; cf. too Lowrie (1992), 416, and Watson (2003) ad loc., Ov. *Am.* 2. 2. 33, Sen. *Ben.* 1. The 'frowning' in the weather is then matched by weather imagery in the human description of line 5: Horace talks of a 'clouded brow', 'obducta...fronte': see Watson ad loc. With 'niuesque deducunt Iouem', Lowrie, like many, compares Anacreon fr. 362 μεὶς μὲν δὴ Ποσιδηίων | ἕστηκεν †νεφέλη δ᾽ ὕδωρ | <> βαρὺ δ᾽ ἄγριοι | χειμῶνες κατάγουσι†, a corrupt text, cited by Schol. T on *Iliad* 15. 192, which Bergk corrected and filled out (with Δία) on the assumption that Horace was using it. The verb κατάγουσι is certainly interesting. (Eustathius rewrites it, employing παταγοῦσι). The passage could well be noting an occasion for a symposium like ours, but we have no context, the crucial part must remain between obeloi, and a connection with Horace a matter of conjecture.

[30] Alcaeus frr. 6, 208, Archil. 105; for political symbolism in the epode storm, see further Lowrie (1992), 416 with n. 13, Watson (2003), 417 ff.

[31] Some are keen to fix the poem on the eve of Philippi: Giarratano (1930), 89–90 puts arguments for and against. Kilpatrick (1970), n. 8 places it at the headquarters of C. Cassius Longinus on 2 October 42 BC. By contrast Hierche (1974), 22 has Horace 'parmi ses compagnons d'armes' before Actium, and groups *Epode* 13 with 7 and 16. Mankin (1995), 214 favours a setting in 'the time of uncertainty after Actium and before the Alexandrian war,' maybe indeed on 31 December 31 BC. More sensitive to the generality of the imagery was Fraenkel (1957), 66. Watson (2003), 417–20 well criticizes such attempts to pin the poem too specifically, but favours the inference of 'a contemporary war setting'. He provides much useful material: his splendid n. 13 allowing for a 'symbolic import' without necessarily 'a political reference' should have found a place in the text!

[32] Nisbet and Hubbard (1978), 139.

and this is a mysterious and general suggestiveness. The poem looks outwards, rather than inwards to something specific. Trouble, anxiety, and, as we shall see, death are in the air.

5. The Chiron Prophecy

Factors strongly encourage us, *pace* e.g. Mankin,[33] to see the mythical *exemplum* as *like*, and enlarging upon, Horace's own paraenesis. The syntax is tight: *ut* (line 11), 'just as', relates in the immediate instance to *iuuat* (line 9), 'it is helpful... just as the Centaur sang...' (Mankin himself compares *Epode* 1. 19 etc.), and the natural inference is that the following myth provides authority for, and illumination of, what has just been said: cf., for example, how Bacchylides supports his proposition at 3. 7 ff. with the speech of Apollo to Admetus, in his case paratactically. Since Chiron is a seer and prophesies as well as advises, we should expect his utterance to be denser than the symposiarch's and to adumbrate points not explicitly made in it. In fact, the 'just as Chiron...' section works in Horace's context rather like a Homeric simile in the *Iliad*. Horace's paraenesis is taken up and 'runs on in' the Chiron–Achilles story.[34] There could indeed be contrasts in the story, as in Homeric simile, but our first expectation should be for justification and enlargement.

The phrase 'dumque uirent genua' (line 4), which puzzles some, also urges likeness. It recalls Homeric images of mortal vigour,[35] so that the present symposium is linked in advance into the world and truths of Chiron's Achilles; this is akin to 'interaction in poetic imagery'.[36] And there is the verb *cecinit* of Chiron (line 11). It obviously suits the *prophesying* Chiron (Catull. 64. 383 etc., *OLD* s.v. *cano* 8). But it also suggests a kind of twinning between Chiron—and therefore his whole message—and Horace. Horace is not yet (explicitly) the singing bard of the *Odes*, but he seems a potential lyrist

---

[33] Mankin (1995), 214 f.: 'the differences may be as important as the similarities', referring to Mankin (1989). A full survey of the question, inclining finally towards Mankin's view, in Watson (2003), 420–2.

[34] The unmatched book on the way Homeric similes work is still Fränkel (1921): summarizing remarks at 98 f., 104–7. Fränkel, 77 n. 22 remarks that *Iliad* 15. 263–8 is another example 'wie die Erz<ählung> im Gl<eichnis> weiter läuft'. It is hard to imagine a more succinct and penetrating statement of the truth. Fränkel (1921), 99–114 are translated into English in Wright and Jones (1997), 103–23, as 'Essence and Nature of the Homeric Similes'.

[35] The strength and activity of the knees was almost synonymous with being alive in the *Iliad*: note Achilles' phrases at *Iliad* 9. 610 εἰς ὅ κ᾽ ... μοι φίλα γούνατ᾽ ὀρώρῃ, and 22. 388. The speed of Hector's knees is focused on to demonstrate his restored health at 15. 269. In death, one's knees are 'loosed' (5. 176, 11. 579, 13. 360, etc.), and so on. Theocritus picks up the idiom at 14. 70 and adds the notion of greenness (γόνυ χλωρόν).

[36] Cf. Silk (1974), 138 ff., Lyne (1989), 92 ff. Cf. lines 1 f. and 5 of this *Epode* with n. 29 above.

at *Epode* 13. 9; he can call himself, with suggestive ambiguity, *uates* in 16. 66;[37] and he calls his book of *iambi* a *carmen* at 14. 7 (see below).

A myth in support of a sympotic paraenesis not only makes it denser, but increases our sense that the poem looks outwards (line 4) rather than being limited in what it addresses.

6. Death

Chiron is above all stressing death and its inevitability, indeed imminence. Not even the great son of a goddess will escape, and the beginning of the prophecy is already pregnant with the message: note especially the oxymora, centring upon *mortalis*, in the first three words ('inuicte mortalis dea nate puer Thetide', line 12). Horace's direct paraenesis (lines 1–10) 'runs on' in the myth, and the imminence of death is added to his direct words, despite the apparent allowance of lines 7 f. In this way the conventional preoccupation of symposium with death emerges: cf. Alcaeus 38A, Asceplciades Gow–Page XVI = *Anth. Pal.* 12. 50, Lucr. 3. 912–15.[38] And what of 'deus haec fortasse benigna | reducet in sedem uice' (lines 7–8)? Compare what Chiron says at lines 15 f., 'unde tibi reditum certo subtemine Parcae | rupere': no home-coming. In line 8 there is a play on the sense 'bring home' in *reduco* and *sedes* 'home', as Mankin ad loc. documents. He infers a suggestion that the *deus* may grant the symposiasts a metaphorical 'home-coming', denied by the Fates to Achilles. Temporarily, perhaps. But Chiron's larger message intrudes into lines 7 f. in retrospect, and his language reconfigures Horace's language. Whatever passing turns for the good there may be, there will be a time when none of us 'reducetur in sedem'.[39] There is something whence, for Horace, his *amicus*, and for all of us, 'reditum certo subtemine Parcae | rupere'. Death stops all change, ends everything, 'unde negant redire quemquam' (Catull. 3. 12).

7. Beginning, *Middle* as well as End

So, via Chiron's prophecy and its reverberations, Horace is—in the symposiast's frequent way—introducing the gloom of The End to drink away, a weighty and conclusive topic. But the poem refers to 'beginning' and 'middle' as well as the end. The 'middle' is especially interesting.

---

[37] *Vates* was a term used disparagingly by Ennius of Naevius (*Ann.* 206–7 Sk.), but resuscitated by Vergil for the elevated poet: *Ecl.* 7. 28, 9. 33 f., *Aen.* 7. 41; Horace uses it of Stesichorus at *Epode* 17. 44 and for the canon of lyric poets at *Odes* 1. 1. 35. Cf. Lyne (1995), 185.

[38] See further Lyne (1995), 66. A very different view of the relevance of death in the Chiron myth in Mankin (1995), 214 f.

[39] Cf. Rudd (1960), 385 f., bringing 'nec mater domum te reuehet' into the discussion.

In the middle, the meanwhile, there will be the sympotic comfort of music and wine, and so on (lines 8–10, 17–18). But Achilles' 'middle' is much more significant: it will be glorious. The opening word of Chiron's prophecy— *inuicte*, 'invincible', 'undefeated'—must presage, in spite of the immediate oxymoron (*mortalis*), some glorious event(s) in which the Centaur's illustrious fosterling will indeed be unconquered. As Mankin ad loc. says, 'since Achilles is still a "child", the epithet [*inuicte*] is proleptic... or, rather, prophetic'. We should expect Chiron to complement *inuicte* by prophetically alluding to an episode of invincibility. 'Te manet Assaraci tellus...' looks forward—in a loaded way (below)—to Troy, but by the end of the Trojan War Achilles will not be unconquered, as Chiron is swiftly going to say. An appropriate event is brought to mind by the relative clause, 'quam frigida flaui | findunt Scamandri flumina lubricus et Simois' (lines 13 f.), especially if we do not allow textual corruption to mar it (*parui*, pp. 314–15): Achilles' duel with Xanthus–Scamander, narrated in *Iliad* 21, with an interesting bit-part role for Simois. This was indeed an example of Achilles' glorious invincibility, arguably his greatest triumph: a unique scene in which the hero actually takes on a *god* and *prevails*, even if with eventual divine assistance.[40]

Bacchylides' Chiron also centred Scamander, but brought to mind the earlier scenes of corpses in the river ([δινᾶ]ντα φοινίξειν Σκά[μανδρον). Horace's Chiron allows us to think mostly of the duel with the god, but not entirely. His wording *subtemine Parcae* (line 15) and *Scamandri flumina* (line 14) recalls another prophecy of the earlier scenes, that of the *Parcae* in Catull. 64:[41]

---

[40] The status given to Xanthus contributes to the glory of Achilles in this episode: in the prelude scene of the *Theomachia*, Xanthus is ranged on the Trojan side with the Olympians Ares, Apollo, Artemis, Leto, and Aphrodite (*Iliad* 20. 38–40). *Iliad* 21. 212–382 sees the great confrontation in speech and action between Achilles and Xanthus–Scamander; for a sample of the heroic scale of the Scamander–Achilles combat, see 21. 233 ff. Divine assistance: Poseidon and Athena encourage a dismayed Achilles at 21. 284–97; Hera brings in Hephaestus to actually assist at 21. 330, but calls him off at 382 when Scamander backs down. At 21. 264 the narrator reminded us that 'gods are better than men'. Simois' bit-part: at 21. 307 ff. Scamander appeals emphatically to his brother river Simois to assist him against Achilles. The text does not state that he in fact does so. One inference might be that he does not. *Lubricus* could contain a covert allusion to this (Chiron is given to occult utterance): one of its senses is 'shifty', 'deceitful'. *Iliad* 5. 330 ff. offers interesting comparative material for Achilles' battle with the male divinity Xanthus–Scamander. Diomedes wounds and drives off a relatively unwarlike goddess, Aphrodite; Dione tells her stories of gods—outside the narrative of the *Iliad*—who have been temporarily discomfited by heroes; back in the narrative Diomedes then confronts a god, Apollo, and finds his come-uppance. Cf. too Apollo and the more conclusive defeat of Patroclus in *Iliad* 16.

[41] cf. Lowrie (1992), 426 f. The plural *flumina* in both calques Homer's καλὰ ῥέεθρα (*Iliad* 21. 361); Catullus' prosody *unda Scamandri* is ostentatiously Homeric.

306   ueridicos *Parcae* coeperunt edere cantus

                 . . . .

357   testis erit magnis uirtutibus unda *Scamandri*,
                 quae passim rapido diffunditur Hellesponto,
                 cuius iter densis angustans corporum aceruis
                 alta tepefaciet permixta *flumina* caede.
                 currite ducentes *subtemina*, currite, fusi.

The Parcae too conceived of Scamander as the climactic witness to the living prowess of Achilles. But they too—and with greater gusto—concentrate on the early scenes of human carnage, in which Achilles chokes the river's waters with corpses.[42] The final episode they cite in Achilles' career is the sacrifice of Polyxena on his tomb (lines 362 ff.). Once memory of Catullus' Parcae is triggered, this tragic scene is available for recall too.

In Chiron's prophecy of a glorious 'middle' for Achilles—as well as the end—we can see Horace's paraenesis being enlarged, 'running on'. Horace and his 'friend's' future may too have glory—and carnage and tragedy.

Spare a thought for Achilles. All the above information is available to Horace's *amicus* and to us. For the young Achilles there was, beyond *inuicte* and sympotic comforts,[43] nothing but death and topography. Chiron does not even grant the gruesomely available point that Achilles will 'warm' (*tepefaciet* of the Parcae) the 'chill' (Chiron's own *frigida*)[44] waters of Scamander with corpses, or, more graphically, 'redden' them, φοινίξειν as Bacchylides' Chiron. Chiron's policy of withholding such hints from Achilles renders one popular but unacceptable defence of the mss. *parui* in line 13 unlikely from the start.[45] (Chiron also withholds one item of bad news available to us: he alludes to the successor kingdom which will one day conquer Greece, the line of Assaracus.[46])

---

[42] Scamander sums this up in *Iliad* 21. 218–20. It is to these lines that Catullus alludes.

[43] Achilles does not neglect them. The embassy finds him playing the lyre and singing at *Iliad* 9. 186 ff. After welcoming the visitors Achilles instructs Patroclus to bring a bigger bowl of wine, 9. 202.

[44] At *Iliad* 22. 147 ff. Scamander's *springs* are both hot and icy cold.

[45] I refer to the attempt to defend *parui* by seeing it as an allusion to the 'narrowing' (Catull. 64. 359 angustans, *Iliad* 21. 219 στεινόμενος) of Scamander's waters with corpses: Vox (1993), 190–1 sees an allusion most immediately to Alcaeus 395 στενω.[.] Ξάνθω ῥό[ος] ἐς θάλασσαν ἴκανε, cited by a papyrus scholion on *Iliad* 21. 219. This approach entails seeing a reference to Achilles' triumphant slaughter, but Chiron is elsewhere withholding any such hint, and in any case neither Homer nor Catullus' Parcae talk of a Scamander made 'smaller', but, precisely, narrowed and yet still deep (*alta*) and, in Homer, awesome. In the huge individual combat that takes place with Achilles after his 'narrowing', Scamander is hardly 'small'! See e.g. *Iliad* 21. 233 ff., and at 21. 268 the μέγα κῦμα διπετέος ποταμοῖο beats down on Achilles' shoulders.

[46] Assaracus features in Aeneas' long genealogical self-description (*Iliad* 20. 232 ff.) delivered, ironically and tellingly—for Horace's context—to Achilles. Assaracus is then a surprisingly

8. Beginnings

Lines 11 f. reach back to the beginnings of Achilles. In 'grandis...alumnus' (line 11), the epithet shows—whatever it may imply about Achilles' size[47]— that Achilles is now on the threshold of manhood, 'grown-up' (*OLD* s.v. 1a), but for Chiron he is still a child, *puer* (line 12), and the noun *alumnus*, 'fosterling', reminds us that Chiron has brought him up since he was a baby.[48] In the present, Roman time Horace reaches back to his own beginning: he orders the wine of the year of his birth to be produced.[49]

9. Sympotic Comfort. But No Talk, *Locutio*

The prophetic Chiron—with a suitable future imperative—tells Achilles 'illic omne malum uino cantuque *leuato*...'(line 17), 'lighten every ill with wine and song'. This injunction is in a dark position, just following the prophecy of Achilles' death: its power to cheer is therefore severely limited. Chiron's phrasing reflects back on Horace's own '*iuuat...leuare* diris pectora sollicitudinibus' (lines 9 f.), and his context, especially the defined temporariness of the cheer offered, colours Horace's context.[50] At the time of utterance, lines 9 f. might have seemed quite hopeful; but we could have made inferences from the extraordinary way in which 'disquiets', *sollicitudinibus*, dominate line 10.[51]

There is a further fascinating connection between the two passages. 'Cetera mitte *loqui*' (line 7), says Horace, 'forbear to talk of other things', with *cetera* referring to what may be symbolized by the storm, to what is causing *sollicitudines*. 'Deformis aegrimoniae dulcibus *alloquiis*',[52] says Chiron in the closing line (line 18). 'Forebear to talk': we may note that Horace nowhere makes any provision for talk in the present time of the epode *at all*: wine (line 6),

---

resonant figure in the Trojan past and future in the *Aeneid*: Verg. *Aen.* 1. 284, 6. 650, 6. 778, 9. 259, and others.

[47] Mankin (1995), ad loc.

[48] Pind. *Pyth.* 6. 21 ff., *Nem.* 3. 43 ff.; Eur. *IA* 708–10, 926–7; Apoll. Rhod. 1. 554–8; cf. Hom. *Il.* 11. 832.

[49] He does so more explicitly in *Odes* 3. 21. 1, 'o nata mecum consule Manlio [Torquato]...'. The Suetonian life puts his birth in the year in which L. Cotta and L. Torquatus were consuls (65 BC), and that year is indicated by *Epist.* 1. 20. 27–8.

[50] There is a change in the way the ablatives are construed with *leuo* in lines 10 and 17, but this does not allow the optimist a great deal of room for manoeuvre, *pace* Mankin (1995) on line 17.

[51] *Sollicitudinibus* fills the entire hemiepes, a metrical event unparalled in surviving epodic verse, and rare in general. It is also—unsurprisingly—a prosaic word. See Mankin (1995) on line 10.

[52] I have followed conventional punctuation. Shackleton Bailey's Teubner puts the comma, not at the end of line 17, but after *aegrimoniae*.

balsam and music (line 9): maybe song therefore, but no *talk*. What of Chiron and his 'sweet consolations (*alloquiis*) of ugly melancholy'? It is vital to see that, unless we add *ac* before *dulcibus* with Bentley, *alloquiis* is in *apposition* to *uino cantuque*. Now this is in fact the first occurrence of the word in surviving Latin: we infer the sense 'consolation' and it 'ought to involve "conversation"', as etymology and later references suggest;[53] and most critics seem to assume that Chiron does indeed refer to conversation.[54] But at the top level of the text, at any rate, the appositional construction *excludes* that: the wine and song *are* the 'sweet-talk', the consolations of melancholy.

So Horace in his present and Chiron in Achilles' future close down talk. The poem ends with a word, *alloquiis*, which paradoxically ousts *locutio*. *Loquor* had been the defining term of utterance of *Epode* 2, given to Horace's surrogate narrator: 'haec ubi locutus' (line 67), the only other parallel for a *loquor* or cognate in the book.

II. *EPODE* 13 AND CLOSURE

The intention of Section I was in the first place to show that *Epode* 13 was special enough to merit an important structural position. I hope I have fulfilled the more particular aim which was to show that the poem might well have been closural. It may not actively assert itself as closural, and I have phrased myself tendentiously at times, but the factors are there. The extraordinary generic surprises (Sections I.1 and I.3) are, so to speak, a hard act to follow. After much iambic specificness (*Epodes* 8–12), the poem has a generality that lifts us up and potentially out: 'horrida tempestas...' (Section I.4), '*cetera* mitte loqui', and then the most significant and extended departure in the *Epodes* into the world of myth (Section I.5),[55] from which the poem does not return. It is a poem of beginnings, middles, and ends (Section I.6, 7, 8). In the beginning is birth, in the middle is the darkened glimpse of glory; the prophesied death of Achilles picks up links in the Horatian present, and infuses the whole poem with that most closural of all signs (Section I.5–8). And finally, though music (*fide* | *cantu*)

---

[53] Cf. Varro, *Ling.* 6. 57, cited by Mankin (1995), in his note on line 18, whence the quotation comes. Mankin has a very suggestive comment on the word. Mueller (1900) ad loc. compares Catullus' use of *allocutio* at 38. 4.

[54] Cf. notably Lowrie (1992), 430–2: e.g. '*Dulcibus alloquiis* (18), the last two words of Chiron's song, and of the poem as a whole, highlight the importance of talking in consolation...'.

[55] *Epode* 3 amusingly adduces Medea and Jason at lines 9–14, similarly Deianira and Hercules at lines 17–18; and *Epode* 10. 12–14 does the same with Athena and Ajax son of Oileus.

may linger, talk (*locutio*) the key term in *Epode* 2, is here explicitly sidelined (Section I.9). When all is taken into account, it will not overstate the case to say that *Epode* 13 encourages expectations of closure.

There is also a metrical pattern to notice.[56] The first ten poems of the book are all in the same epodic combination of iambic trimeter and dimeter. *Epodes* 11–16 employ more complex Archilochean systems (*Epode* 17 is then in stichic iambics). The shift to the more complex metres is interestingly managed, and a structure over *Epodes* 11–13 reinforces the sense of closure at *Epode* 13. To make my point I shall have to touch on material familiar to many.

The 'Third Archilochean' of *Epode* 11 consists of an iambic trimeter, and then a hemiepes plus iambic dimeter. The hemiepes–dimeter combination is conventionally printed as one line, and is so written in the Cologne papyrus (fr. 196a West) where Archilochus uses this same system, but the whole may be seen as a three-line strophe. The fact is that the hemiepes–dimeter elements are, in the ancient metrician's word, *asynarteta*, i.e. the first element is treated as a separate measure.[57] In Archilochus, and in Horace who imitates him, we find hiatus after the hemiepes or a *breuis in longo* to close it: in Horace, at *Epode* 11. 6, 10, 14, 24. From this we should note the following. Since the iambic trimeter of 11. 1 signals no change at all from *Epode* 10, the hemiepes which then follows does so with surprise. Should the reader have any sense of the asynartete nature of the line, that surprise is focused. It may be focused too by the fact that *uersiculos* in the hemiepes flirts with a different type of poetry (elegy),[58] though the amorous Horace poses as disinclined to write anything at all at the moment (see further below).

The metre of *Epode* 12 ('First Archilochean', cf. Archilochus fr. 195 West) is then wholly in essence dactylic—as it were, picking up the hemiepes: dactylic hexameter plus tetrameter. The metre of *Epode* 13 ('Second Archilochean',

---

[56] There is useful information on Horace's epodic metres at Mankin (1995), 14–22, to which I am indebted.

[57] For the publication of the Cologne Archilochus, see Merkelbach and West (1974), 97–113, with pl. V. Merkelbach (102) expresses the belief that we have actually to do with a short three-line strophe, and that the practice of writing the second two elements as one line was due precisely to the ancient theory of 'asynartete' verses. Hephaestion attributes the invention of 'asynartete' junctions to Archilochus (*Encheiridion* 15. 1–3), quoted by West at the head of frr. 168–71.

[58] The diminutive may suggest elegy, whose metre the hemiepes 'invades' (the graphic word is from Hutchinson (2007), 40). Horace is, of course, toying with Roman elegy's subject matter (*amor*). Diminutives are used judiciously, and in varying degrees by the Latin elegists: see R. Maltby in Adams and Mayer (1999), 387–8, building on Axelson (1945), 41–3. But *uersiculus* itself is not specific in its implications (cf. Hor. *Serm.* 1. 10. 58 as well as Catull. 16. 3 and 6, 50. 4). Heyworth (1993), 85–96, at 87 f., sees continuing attention being (metatextually) drawn to the metrical shift at 11. 20 *incerto pede*.

cf. frr. 199 and 193 West)[59] then seems to continue this dactylic pattern: its first line is also a dactylic hexameter. But its second line is a combination of an iambic dimeter plus hemiepes, also asynartete: see lines 8, 10, 14.

There is, therefore, a kind of metrical ring-composition from 11. 2, where the surprise starts, through to *Epode* 13: hemiepes, iambic dimeter (*Epode* 11. 2), dactylic hexameters and tetrameters, picking up the hemiepes (*Epode* 12), dactylic hexameter, iambic dimeter, and finally hemiepes again (*Epode* 13). The sense of ring is strengthened by the fact that *Epode* 12, the centre poem, stands out as the only epode with no iambics at all. It is worth adding too that the metrical shape of the words comprising the hemiepes in 13. 18 is exactly the same as in 11. 2, and other lines in *Epode* 11, but has no precursor in *Epode* 13 itself. The end of the metrical ring is affirmed. Ring-composition gives an obvious effect of closure.[60]

It should be noted finally that the metre of *Epode* 13 may have been a rarity, something special: we can point to the suggestive fragments of Archilochus above, but we cannot actually show the whole system in surviving Archilochus.

III. *EPODE* 14, THE *EPODES* AND CALLIMACHUS

Epode 13 is suited to closure, but the book does not close. *Epode* 14 therefore needs special attention. I shall keep my comments to the minimum.[61]

    mollis inertia cur tantam diffuderit imis
     obliuionem sensibus,
    pocula Lethaeos ut si ducentia somnos
     arente fauce traxerim,
5   candide Maecenas, occidis saepe rogando:
     deus, deus nam me uetat

---

[59] Fr. 199: Diomedes testifies to Archilochus' use of the iambelegus. In fr. 193 we find a dactylic hexameter combined with iambic dimeter.

[60] Cf. Call. *Aetia* frs 2 and 112, the prologue and epilogue with the same motifs, Mealeager I Gow–Page = *Anth. Pal.* 4. 1 and CXXIX = *Anth. Pal.* 12. 257, the opening and close of the *Garland* (note esp. 1. 3 and 129. 5), Catull. 16, 36, 52 etc., Williams (1980), 98–9 ('Ring-composition was frequently used by Roman poets of the late Republic and of the Augustan Age to effect poetic closure'), and index, s.v., Kenney (1971), 79 f.

[61] A very useful discussion of this poem is offered by Grassmann (1966), 122–44, though we differ on many points. See too especially Watson (2003), 438–57. Cavarzere (1992), 206–7 offers a heterodox view. The poem is in iambic character, aimed at Maecenas: Horace is not actually having any problems with love; it is Maecenas who is (and 'recusatio' has no part here); interesting, but I cannot subscribe to it.

> inceptos olim, promissum carmen, iambos
>   ad umbilicum adducere.
> non aliter Samio dicunt arsisse Bathyllo
>   Anacreonta Teium, 10
> qui persaepe caua testudine fleuit amorem
>   non elaboratum ad pedem.
> ureris ipse miser. quodsi non pulchrior ignis
>   accendit obsessam Ilion,
> gaude sorte tua: me libertina nec uno 15
>   contenta Phryne macerat.

Besides allowing Horace his arch allusions to Maecenas' love affair with the actor Bathyllus (for which, besides the name, note the torch imagery and the neglected feminine gender in lines 13–14),[62] the poem has two main thrusts, parodying 'recusatio'. The key component of the parody is the *deus, deus* who *uetat*, 'forbids': as the poem soon confirms, this *deus* is Love,[63] and he is substituting for the admonishing Apollo of Vergil's 'recusatio' in *Eclogue* 6. 3–9 (and Callimachus' Apollo behind Vergil).[64] By Horace's time the 'recusatio' had wider currency than surviving examples show,[65] and its standard functions are to *excuse* the poet from the duty to do one thing (epic), and *license* him to do another (essentially, to continue his present course; in Vergil's case, bucolic). Horace's parody 'recusatio' naturally has twists. Rather than excuse him from attempting another type of poetry, Horace's 'recusatio'

---

[62] For Maecenas' Bathyllus, see Tacitus, *Ann.* 1. 54. 2, Griffin (1985), 25; Watson (2003), 449 with bibliography; and excellent argument and bibliography in Cavarzere (1992), 206, 208–9. Grassmann (1966), 131–2 correctly sees an allusion to Maecenas' Bathyllus, but at 138–9 interprets the imagery of *ignis* etc. (14. 13–14) as referring to Helen, and talks in those lines of a female lover of Maecenas; cf. Watson, 449 and 452–3. The usual assumption concerning the imagery of line 13 (*pulchrior ignis*) is indeed that in one way or another it refers to Helen: Mueller (1900), ad loc.; Giarratano (1930), 98; Dettmer (1983), 93; Cavarzere (1992), 206; Mankin (1995), ad loc. hedges. But many do see that *ignis* most immediately evokes torches, and therefore better suits Paris (the dream of Hecuba) than Helen; see Watson (2003), 453 for references, though he himself prefers an allusion to Helen. Lines 13–16 therefore not only permit but encourage an allusion to a *male* lover of Maecenas: Bathyllus himself, more beautiful than Paris. Following these suggestions of Paris and a male lover, we should pay attention to 'obsess*am* Ilion'. 'H. seems to be the first in Latin to use the fem. *Ilios*...', Mankin, ad loc. Giarratano (1930), 98 points out that no metrical advantage accrues—as in Horace's other sure example of the fem., *Odes* 4. 9. 18. This latter example incidentally protects the reading *-am* in *Epode* 13. 14. It is surprising that no-one appears to see the additional innuendo (passivity in the affair, cf. Catullus 16 etc.) which the feminine gender of the object adds.

[63] Some play too on the Caesarian *dei*: cf. Verg. *Ecl.* 5. 64 'deus, deus ille Menalca', also 1. 6–7.

[64] On 'recusatio', the Roman practical adaptation of Callimachus' Apollo preface (*Aetia* fr. 1), see Lyne (1995), 31–9. Horace parodies the topos elsewhere, e.g. *Serm.* 1. 10. 31 ff., where he also uses the verb *ueto* (again at *Odes* 1. 6. 10). The parody in *Epode* 14 is like Propertius' in 2. 13. 3–8. (For Cavarzere (1992) ad loc., any thought of Apollo is 'fuorviante', because the *Epode* is not a 'recusatio'; cf. n. 61.)

[65] Cf. Lyne (1995), 34–5.

seeks to explain why he does not finish the present ongoing book (lines 7–8 clarify the vaguer lines 1–4), and hand it over for production in publishable form. The cause: Love (not Apollo). Horace's 'recusatio' does then, in an amusingly unexpected way,[66] appear to seek to *license* a path of poetry. When Horace first adduces Anacreon as a parallel to himself (*non aliter*, line 9), we expect the Greek lyrist to be matching his literary inaction. We are in fact shown how Anacreon's love (line 9, *arsisse*) was accompanied by, if not led to, frequent love poems. Our natural inference now must be that Horace is himself seeking to license love poems on his own part. But what love poems? Not some 'erotic lyric' outside the *Epodes*, I think.[67] 'Recusatio' licenses something in progress, and a ready deduction would be that Horace is licensing a shift into love poetry *within* the *Epodes* which has already begun, and which could I suppose be seen as a threat to the conclusion of a book of 'real' *iambi*, be they of the aggressive Archilochean–Hipponactean sort (e.g. *Epodes* 8, 10, and 12) or of the new-wave type suited to the patronized Roman iambist (*Epodes* 1 and 9). Love interest had already appeared in *Epode* 11, where Horace feigned in consequence a disinclination to write at all, while simultaneously flirting with thoughts of elegy (lines 1–2 and *uersiculos*, see above). *Epode* 14 more decisively declares erotic involvement, literary and biographical, and an inability to complete a book of (real) *iambi*.

The new erotic direction is very much a humorous feint: love surfaces again in *Epode* 15, but not thereafter. And Horace's alignment (*non aliter*) with Anacreon is funnily fleeting, indeed specious. Anacreon himself was, of course, a desirable introduction because of the convenient overlap between the name of one of his lovers and Maecenas' Bathyllus—permitting innuendo. But how much of an Anacreontic Horace do we actually sense and for how long? Nothing that bears serious scrutiny.[68] The formal alignment itself is neatly but tenuously based. The facts which Horace exploited and to which he refers are as follows. Anacreon wrote love poems, matching the supposed new Horace, and some were about Bathyllus, though none of these survive.[69] Anacreon wrote metrical iambics, as Horace did in much of

---

[66] Watson (2003), 447–9 makes much of this 'inconsequentiality', giving three possible explanations of it. His second and favoured explanation is quite close to the account I give above.

[67] Cf. Watson (2003), 448.

[68] Watson (2003), 440 f. finds features from Anacreon's lyric in *Epode* 14 itself, but they are not to me impressive. Nor is there significant evidence of an Anacreontic Horace in the *Epodes* outside *Epode* 14 (cf. n. 29). But, in view of *Epode* 14. 11 *fleuit amorem*, Dioscorides XIX. 3–4 Gow–Page (*Anth. Pal.* 7. 31. 3–4) is slightly interesting: ὦ 'πὶ Βαθύλλῳ | ... πολλάκι δάκρυ χέας.

[69] These are known to us only by the (many) later testimonia and epigrams devoted to Anacreon and his loves; e.g. Maximus of Tyre cited at Anacreon 402, 'His poems are full of the hair of Smerdies and the eyes of Cleobulus and the youthful beauty of Bathyllus'. Bathyllus also occurs frequently in the *Anacreontea*. See Campbell's index (1988), n. 1, s.v. 'Bathyllus'.

his *Iambi*, and some at least of Anacreon's iambics were love poems:[70] the relative simplicity of the iambic *metron* is surely what Horace refers to with 'non elaboratum ad pedem'.[71] And presumably some of Anacreon's Bathyllus love poems were in iambics. Horace taking a temporary amorous turn in his often iambic *Iambi* could passingly pretend an alliance with Anacreon—and be constrained to mention Anacreon's conveniently named lover.

Love causing *iambus*-block, Horace in the *Epodes* lining up with Anacreon, innuendos, these are amusing enough, but the wit is more fundamental. How seriously can we take a poem which stands in a finished book which explains why the poet cannot finish that same book? Catullus expresses difficulty in writing in 65, and at the same time introduces 66 as compensation for something notionally more desirable, and Pindar at *Ol.* 1. 17 issues an instruction to take the lyre from the hook seventeen lines into the song, but apologetics and circumstantial references like these have nothing to match the delightful implausibility of *Epode* 14.[72] We should note just how concretely

---

[70] For iambic metre in Anacreon, see fr. 427 (four stichic iambic dimeters), 428 (two dimeters), 425 (two trimeters), 426 (trimeter), and, in combinations, 424, 431, 432. Hephaestion, *Ench.* 5. 3 says that 'the (iambic) dimeter catalectic is the so-called anacreontean (τὸ καλούμενον Ἀνακρεόντειον)', citing fr. 429. (Anacreon also arguably wrote *Iambi* in the generic sense, poems of abuse and invective: this is an additional, complicating factor, and not I think very relevant to our context. The Suda A 1916 (T 1 Gerber) reports ἔγραψεν ἐλεγεῖα καὶ ἰάμβους, Ἰάδι πάντα διαλέκτῳ, but it is hard to know if that reference is generic rather than metrical. See Brown (1983), 1–15, interpreting Anacreon's Artemon poem 388, whose metrical system is two choriambic tetrameters anaclastic and an iambic dimeter, and other frr. in this way.)

[71] Tescari (1936), ad loc. takes 'non elaboratum ad pedem' to mean 'in versi non perfetti', as many do: Grassmann 'nicht ausgefeilt', discussed at length (1966), 134–6; Cavarzere (1992), ad loc. It is unlikely that Horace would gratuitously criticize Anacreon like this: in the *Odes* (1. 23) he elegantly and honorifically adapts him. A long discussion of this 'verso oscuro' in Giarratano (1930), 90; my own view is close to Nauck's. *TLL* v. 2. 321. 7 ff. on the use of the perf. part. *elaboratus* as an adjective is informative. It can be paired with *ornatus, elegans, perfectus* (Cic. *Verr.* 4. 126, *Orat.* 36 (of Pacuvius' verses)) and there can be degrees of *elaboratus* (Tac. *Dial.* 18 'Cicerone mitior Coruinus et dulcior et in uersibus magis elaboratus'): the negation would not therefore necessarily be 'imperfect'; it could just be 'not ornate', 'simple'. And this fits iambics very well, whose proximity to speech is remarked upon (and makes them suitable to drama): Aristotle, *Rhet.* 1408ᵇ34–5, discussing appropriate prose rhythms, calls the iambus 'the actual speech of the many', ὁ δ' ἴαμβος αὐτή ἐστιν ἡ λέξις τῶν πολλῶν; in consequence 'of all metres iambics are what people most use when they talk', μάλιστα πάντων τῶν μέτρων ἰαμβεῖα φθέγγονται λέγοντες. Most scholars assume that Callimachus, *Aetia Epilogue*, fr. 112. 9 Μουσέων πεζὸν...νομόν, 'the prose pasture of the Muses', refers to his often (chol-)iambic *Iambi*, but Hutchinson has argued strongly and succinctly that the reference there is simply to prose works: see Hutchinson (2003), 58 with n. 31.

[72] And yet Lefèvre (1993), 82 says of *Epode* 14 'Die Epode ist im übrigen ein seltenes Zeugnis dafür, in welchem Mass Horaz von Maecenas zur Veröffentlichung gedrängt wurde'. Cf. too Mueller (1900), ad loc.; Grassmann (1966), 122, 126 f., and elsewhere. Watson (2003), 438 ff. has excellent material on published literary apologetics, but nothing parallels a poet in a book explaining that he cannot finish that book. For an appreciation of the humour in Horace's position, see Hutchinson (2007).

Horace brings to mind *published books* by the phrase he uses for 'finishing', 'ad umbilicum adducere'.[73] To take *Epode* 14 at its face value, we have to assume a reader-attitude of truly extreme ingenuousness: we have to turn our attention away from books and from the object in our hands, and buy into a dramatic illusion that the composition of *iambi* is happening actually in front of us, and, at the dramatic moment of the fourteenth poem, is encountering deep trouble because of love. And Horace apologizes for the delay.

The witty implausibility of this, plus the other literary feints, pushes us to find a more sophisticated explanation of the poem. We go back to *Epode* 13. Horace gave many signs that *Epode* 13 was closural. And now: 'I'm sorry I cannot finish.' This witty apology metatextually draws attention to the fact that he has not closed with the 'closing' poem: it is a metapoetic acknowledgement that he has not finished his book of *Iambi* at the point, where, we infer, he both ought and (as it were) intended to. The reference to physical books of poetry and publication actually encourages us to think out beyond the supposed dramatic circumstances to a literary question and answer. Why doesn't the book close at *Epode* 13?

There is a pleasing little detail contributing to the undoing of closure. The sombre end of death in *Epode* 13 is now dissolved, first in the non-deathly forgetfulness of *Lethaeos* (14. 3, 'Lethaeos *ut* si...'),[74] and then, completely, in the jokingly colloquial use of *occidis* (14. 5) 'you'll be the death of me with your questions'.[75]

Well, why doesn't Horace finish his *iambi* with *Epode* 13? 'Love' is hardly the answer, with the implied diversion into erotic, uniambic *iambi*: we only get one more 'love' poem, and two others that are completely different. And

---

[73] The phrase seems to be Horace's own concoction, but it is built around a technical term. Watson's (2003) note here is very useful. The *umbilici* refer strictly or originally to the knobs on the ends of the rod around which the end-product, the physical papyrus roll book, was wound, though the exact details of how this was done are disputed. But *umbilicus* seems to be used, here and elsewhere, by synecdoche, for the rod itself. Cf. Catullus 22. 7, Ovid, *Trist.* 1. 18, Tränkle on [Tib.] 3. 1. 13, as well as Watson. Martial loves making reference to the physical object of the book, and in the last poem of Book 4 (4. 89. 1–2) writes 'ohe, iam satis est, ohe, libelle, | iam peruenimus usque ad umbilicos'—what Horace is unable yet to say. Cf. referring to the reader, Sen. *Suas.* 6. 27, 'ergo, ut librum uelitis usque ad umbilicum reuoluere...'. *Carmen* incidentally—within the 'Schema Cornelianum' appositional pattern of 'inceptos, olim promissum carmen, iambos' (I prefer this punctuation to a comma after *olim*)—must surely refer to the *Gedichtbuch* of *Epodes*, as Bentley already affirmed. Mankin (1995), 229–30 (good notes on lines 7 and 8) and Grassmann (1966), 130 question the interpretation.

[74] Lethe had been situated in the Underworld since Theognis (705, 1215): see Mankin (1995), note on line 3.

[75] For the colloquial use of *occido*, cf. Plaut. *Pseud.* 931, Horace, *Ars Poetica* 475, etc. Mueller (1900), ad loc. compares Horace's use of *exanimo* at *Odes* 2. 17. 1: an interesting passage, because here too we may see Horace defusing the topic of death with a similar colloquialism. Cf. uses of ἀπόλλυμι, LSJ. s.v. 2.

why did Horace encourage expectations of closure (now seen to be 'false closure')[76] at the thirteenth poem, and allow us to deduce that this was the 'right' place to close?

At *Epode* 14. 7 Horace for the first and only time within the body of this text suggests the *title* for what we call the 'Epodes': *Iambi*.[77] Previously he has advertised alignment with Hipponax and, especially, Archilochus. What editions of these poets Horace used, and with what titles, is hard to say. Archilochus had referred to his ἴαμβοι[78] but there is no sign of an Archilochean Book entitled by scholars *Iambi*. Archilochus' works were, where specified, cited by metre: elegiacs, trimeters, tetrameters, and epodes.[79] Two of Hipponax's books seem to have borne the title ἴαμβοι in later times at any rate.[80] But there were of course well-known *Iambi* which we know to have been composed as a book by their author and actually entitled Ἴαμβοι by him: the *Iambi* of Callimachus. Now with this Hellenistic book Horace surreptitiously aligns himself at *Epod*. 1. 16. He makes very little use of Callimachus' text itself, indeed takes steps *not* to be identified with the Hellenistic rather than the archaic iambists besides this allusion[81]—and the matter of structure, to which I attend. But when *iambi* is floated as the designation of

---

[76] On 'false closure', cf. Fowler (2000), 259–63; Roberts, Dunn, and Fowler (1997), index s.v. 'closure', 'false'.

[77] Cf. elsewhere, with varying degrees of directness, *Ode* 1. 16. 3 and 24 (though not all agree about the point of this ode), *Epist*. 1. 19. 23, 2. 2. 59. Horace surely officially titled the book thus. 'Epodes' is grammarians' metrical talk. Cf. Mankin (1995), 12. But Cavarzere (1992), 9–14 is much more cautious.

[78] For the alignment with Archilochus and Hipponax, see *Epode* 6 (above Section I.1). For Archilochus' use of ἴαμβοι, see fr. 215 and n. 7.

[79] We have glimpses of scholarly work on Archilochus by Apollonius of Rhodes, and, more substantially by Aristarchus: Fraser (1972), 452, 462. For citations from Archilochus' 'elegiacs' (ἐν ἐλεγείοις), see West at the head of frs 1–17; for citations from his 'trimeters', the head of 18–87; trochaic 'tetrameters', 88–167; 'epodes', 168–204.

[80] See West at the head of frs 1–114a: ἐν τῷ πρώτῳ (τῶν) ἰάμβων, ἐν τῷ δευτέρῳ τῶν ἰάμβων; metrically, Hipponax also wrote epodes, tetrameters, and dactylic hexameters besides choliambics.

[81] In Callimachus' opening and programmatic poem, Hipponax *rediuiuus* returns 'bearing an *iambus* that does not'—paradoxically—'sing of battle (with Bupalus)', οὐ μάχην ἀείδοντα ... 1. 3). Horace alludes to the unexpectedly genial iambic Callimachus in his opening poem, when he calls himself *imbellis* (*Epode* 1. 16). This idea, surely unassailable, belongs to Denis Feeney, and is as yet unpublished. But besides this, a possible connection between *Epode* 15. 7–9 and *Iamb* XII = fr. 202 Pf. 69–70 (Fraenkel (1957), 67; Heyworth (1993), 86), and the allusions in *Epode* 13 and, conceivably 14, suggested below, Horace avoids the Callimachean text (but Heyworth, loc. cit. sees an allusion to Callimachus' *Ibis* in the opening word of the book; cf. too Hutchinson (2007), 37–8). Most noticeably, indeed ostentatiously, he does not use Callimachus' metres, in particular Callimachus' favoured Hipponactean choliambics. By contrast he makes noticeable use of Archilochus' metres and text: see above p. 329. Publicly he is no Roman Callimachus: rather, Archilochus. But a public face does not preclude the surreptitious alignment mentioned; nor does it preclude play with Callimachean structure.

Horace's book at 14. 7, this may re-stir memory of Callimachus' book. Kerkhecker's dauntingly authoritative edition of Callimachus' *Iambi* presents us with *thirteen* poems and argues forcefully for this total. There is a mass of evidence to be weighed, but an outstanding factor is the impression of closure provided by *Iambus* XIII, in ring-composition with *Iambus* I.[82]

Thirteen *Iambi* and closure provided by *Iambus* XIII. Here is why Horace provides a closural poem in *Epode* 13. But why is it *false* closure? What game is he playing?

Here we must acknowledge the debate about the extent of Callimachus' *Iambi*, and register the bare minimum of facts. The Milan *Diegeseis* of Callimachus' work, the papyrus of which dates from c. AD 100, are summaries of *Aetia*, *Iambi*, *Hecale*, *Hymns* in that order, and they show *seventeen* poems between the *Aetia* and *Hecale* without differentiation, Kerkhecker's I–XIII and four more, a potential 14–17, frr. 226–9 Pf.; the *Diegeseis* provide lemmata as well as summaries, and other papyri have supplemented 227–9. It is a natural inference that the *Diegeseis* summarized a papyrus roll with I–XIII plus 14–17. More evidence: a second-century AD papyrus roll also contained the *Iambi* (frr. of IV, V, VI, and VII survive) and concluded with '17'.[83] So a book containing I–XIII and 14–17 was early in existence. But was this a book of seventeen Callimachean *Iambi*? Long before Kerkhecker, Pfeiffer,[84] though he believed in the existence of the seventeen-poem book, did not believe that the 'lyric' frr. 226–9 belonged to Callimachus' *Iambi*, and his edition conjecturally entitles them Μέλη. The possibility that frr. 227–9 had their own titles quite early on ('Pannychis', 'Apotheosis of Arsinoe', 'Branchus') may increase support for their separation.[85] But there is room for debate. A collection of Callimachus' 'Lyrics' is not reliably known from any source (the Suda's testimony is insubstantial).[86] While the content of '14–17' may seem uniambic, the content of the core I–XIII is not iambic in any way resembling Callimachus' formal model (Hipponax), indeed is very various.[87] The 'lyric' metres of '14–17' may likewise seem unsuited to *Iambi*, but this can be argued to and fro,[88] and it must be remembered that 'iambic' originally referred to a

---

[82] See Kerkhecker (1999), 255 ff., 272–82, esp. 269, 278 f. Kerkhecker argues the case for thirteen *Iambi*, and argues against the supposition of seventeen (see below). Cf. too Dawson (1950), 1–168, esp. 132–3.

[83] The papyrus book is *POxy.* 2171 + 2172. See Pfeiffer (1949), pp. xi and xxxvii for the evidence of this papyrus and of the *Diegeseis*.

[84] Pfeiffer (1949), esp. ii. p. xxxvii.

[85] Cameron (1995), 164 argues against the titles having such force, even granted they are genuine. (For Pannychis we rely on Athenaeus, for Branchus on Hephaestion, but Ἐκθέωσις Ἀρσινόης heads the entry in the *Diegeseis*.)

[86] Cameron (1995), 163 with n. 107, more mutedly Kerkhecker (1999), 276 f.

[87] Kerkhecker (1999), 278 and 291 ff.

[88] Kerkhecker (1999), 278, Cameron (1995), 164–5.

type of poetry rather than a metre.[89] There is indeed room therefore for debate. Thirteen or seventeen poems in Callimachus' *Iambi*? Four miscellaneous 'lyrics' or not? Pfeiffer's and Kerkhecker's authority has not, one suspects, stilled all discussion forever. Cameron deploys forceful arguments in the contrary direction.[90]

The parallel between Horace's seventeen *Epodes*, a strange total by all accounts, and the seventeen Callimachean poems has of course been seen, and assistance with the Callimachean problem sought therein. And there has surely to be some relation between the two totals of seventeen and some explanation of Horace's number.[91] Cameron championed the simple answer: seventeen *Iambi* mirrored by seventeen *Epodes*, with Horace's total deployed as part of the evidence for a Callimachean seventeen; the polemically literary XIII may be seen 'warning of' surprises to follow.[92] Another way of dealing with the facts: Callimachus' book of thirteen *Iambi* was later 'filled out' with four poems before Roman times, by the poet himself or a copyist, and Horace's seventeen mirrors this expanded book.[93] But the thirteen *Iambi* are calculated to have provided sufficient text for a Hellenistic book (*c.*1,000 lines),[94] so that there was no actual stimulus for padding.

But let us focus on Horace. There is a very interesting explanation of what he might be up to. Horace saw that *Iambus* XIII provided satisfying closure for a book of *Iambi*. But the edition he read, like the one summarized by the *Diegeseis*, continued on, and gave four more poems. A puzzle. Is XIII 'closure' followed by heterogeneous material or 'false closure' followed by more *Iambi*? Unlike an editor, Horace did not have to declare himself. He could transform the puzzle into art, and self-consciously replay what he found in front of him. He provides a sense of closure in *Epode* 13, but starts up again in *Epode* 14, and metapoetically advertises the fact that he had not closed the book; and he then provides three more poems to make up the total of seventeen that he found in his edition. Perhaps there was debate about the number of *Iambi* among *cognoscenti* in Horace's time, to match that of, say, Cameron and Kerkhecker. The creatively non-committal mimicry of the *Epodes* would be an amusing contribution to it.

[89] See above n. 7.   [90] Cameron's main discussion is 163–73.
[91] It is hardly sufficient explanation of the relation to say that seventeen is chosen as the next prime number after Callimachus' thirteen: Heyworth (1993), 86.
[92] For the idea that XIII 'warns of' what is to follow, see Cameron (1995), 167; cf. too Gallavotti (1946), 12, and a rebuttal in Kerkhecker (1999), 279 f. Cameron (1995), 170 n. 139 also interestingly points out that there were (probably) seventeen Aetia in Book 4 of the *Aetia*. It is perhaps worth focusing the interesting fact that Branchus (Call. fr. 229) occurs in Hipponax fr. 105.
[93] Clayman (1980), 7.
[94] Dawson (1950), 133–6 calculated a minimum of 800 lines in I–XIII, a probable 950–75, and a possible 1100–25.

What is Horace's foundational principle, a unit of thirteen or seventeen? Both. And there is a third: see Section V. How many *Iambi* did Horace think Callimachus wrote? He sits on the fence, making art of it. How many *Iambi* did Callimachus write? That is for Callimachean scholars to decide.

I have said that Horace makes little use of the text itself of Callimachus' *Iambi*. But there are two ways in which we can see *Epode* 13 and *Iambus* XIII related, in spite of the general complete difference of their subject matter. First, *Epode* 13 is the first and only poem in the book that is sympotic in setting, and, as I have said, this does not seem to be in the manner of the archaic iambists. But it is in the manner of Callimachus, *Iambus* XIII, also sympotically situated.[95] Second, Callimachus is defending himself in XIII against the charge, *inter alia*, of composing in too many genres, of, as the *Diegeseis* put it, πολυείδεια.[96] Now 'Kreuzung der Gattungen' is not πολυείδεια, but in his masterly merging of contributing genres and texts in *Epode* 13 (Sections I.1 and I.3), Horace may wish to parade a versatility analogous to the one which Callimachus defends. And Callimachus himself was of course a magician of *Kreuzung*.

The Diegeseis say that in *Iambus* 14 πρὸς τοὺς ὡραίους φησί, 'Callimachus speaks to boys blooming with youthful beauty'. There could have been some interesting Callimachean background for *Epode* 14 and Bathyllus.

IV. THE ADDRESSEE OF *EPODE* 13

The manuscripts offer *amici* in *Epode* 13. 3; the reading is surely corrupt. The movement from plural to singular (*tu*, line 6) is hard to make good sense of, and the supposed parallels in Horace and others do not stand up.[97] It is natural to seek a proper name in place of the corruption, since it is Horace's later practice to name addressees in sympotic poetry, unless the addressee be (we infer) a slave;[98] we might indeed seek a grand name, since the symposium

---

[95] See Kerkhecker (1999), 252 on the sympotic setting of *Iambus* XIII.

[96] Ibid. 251 ff. on the charges against and the defences made by Callimachus in *Iambus* XIII.

[97] In *Ode* 1. 27. 10 the change to singular is fully explained by the unfolding drama. In *Ode* 3. 14. 17 the address is to a slave conveying orders for the private party that is to follow the public celebration which Horace has, as it were, been directing. In Archilochus' elegiac fr. 13 the movement of the paraenesis is from singular to plural (1 Περίκλεες, 6 ὦ φίλ', 10 τλῆτε) in a piece that is firmly contextualized in, and makes earlier references to, the surrounding civic group. These are the supposed parallels for *amici*... *tu* cited by Mankin (1995), 217. Cavarzere (1992), ad loc. cites Alcaeus 346 in favour of *amici*: if anything, it supports *amice*.

[98] A slave boy may be inferred in *Odes* 1. 38. See Mueller (1900), n. on line 3, for the naming of addressees in *Odes*. Writing before Housman, whose suggestion is cited in the text above, Mueller offers in place of *amici* Scheibe's *Apici* or his own *Anici*.

planned is very special (Section I.2). Horace's later practice with vocative *tu* might also lead us to expect a named person, but not irresistibly.[99] Housman ingeniously advanced an Amicius, hence *Amici*, printed by Shackleton Bailey. But Nisbet points to the inartistic and surely unacceptable ambiguity this would produce in an ancient text;[100] nor is any grand Amicius known. Bentley's *amice* is I think right, cf. incidentally Alcaeus' αἴτα in fr. 346. 2, though this seems to have amorous flavour. But this is not a proper name. Nor does it visibly accompany a proper name, Horace's later practice when he does use a vocative *amice*.[101] So what is going on?

If we set the problem of the reading in the context of 'false closure', we can see that *amice* functions as a designed tease. The End impends, the party is special, the *poem* is special, and yet: To whom is it addressed? Who is this 'friend'? But of course the final close is actually four poems away: *Epode* 14 wittily restarts the book. And in *Epode* 14 the mystery identity is revealed, though still tantalizingly postponed until line 5: 'amice... Maecenas'. Here at last is the proper name and the specification for *amice*. And, across the *Epode* that appears to close the book and the *Epode* that then amusingly restarts it, we have the same pattern of address that opened the *Epodes* book: *Epode* 1. 2–4, 'amice... || Maecenas'.

V. STRUCTURES IN THE BOOK OF *EPODES*[102]

Horace plays with at least two co-existing structures in *Odes* Book 1 (1–38 and 9–38), as I show in another paper (Lyne 2005a [= Ch. 17, this volume]). In *Epodes* he operates with at least three:[103] we can read a book of ten (plus seven), a book of thirteen (plus four) or a book of seventeen.

[99] Vocative *tu* occurs in sympotic or similar contexts with a named addressee at *Odes* 1. 7. 17, 1. 9. 16, 1. 11. 1, 3. 29. 25. But at 1. 28. 25 the unnamed dead person addresses the unnamed passing sailor as 'at tu, nauta...'. At 2. 18. 17 the unidentified nominative *tu* may in fact be aimed at Maecenas: cf. Nisbet and Hubbard (1978), 289; Lyne (1995), 126 ff., overstating his case.

[100] The proper name vocative *Amici* is proposed by Housman (1972), 1087, and defended by Lowrie (1992), 417 n. 14. Two other proper name vocatives that have been suggested are cited in n. 98. Nisbet (1986), 232 raises the question of ambiguity, discounted by Brink (see next note). For plural addresses to companions in the *Odes*, Horace uses *sodales*: 1. 27. 7, 1. 37. 4.

[101] An objection to Bentley's *amice* made by Brink (1982a), 41–2.

[102] For different ways of looking at the structure of the *Epodes* book, see Port (1925–6), 291–6; Dettmer (1983), 77–109 (for comments on the place of *Epode* 13—no sense of closure—see 93); Heyworth (1993), esp. 91; Mankin (1995), 10–12; Oliensis (1998), 91 ff.

[103] As Professor Hutchinson points out to me, *Epode* 11 also plays with closure (touched on above). See esp. 11. 1–2 'Petti, nihil me sicut antea iuuat | scribere uersiculos', 5 'destiti', but then 23 'nunc', and the witty thought (25 ff.) that ending can only be achieved by new beginning, 'sed alius ardor'.

The first ten poems are distinct, forming a decimal group like the *Eclogues*. Each is written in exactly the same epodic metre, iambic trimeter and iambic dimeter; with *Epode* 11 comes radical metrical change, as we have seen. Here is the first unit. Roman poets who wrote even-numbered sequences considered the opening of the second half a position of importance. Thus Vergil in the *Aeneid* and Lucretius in the *DRN*—granted that the placing of 4. 1–25 reflects Lucretius' final intention—give us 'Proems in the Middle' at this point.[104] In Vergil's ten *Eclogues*, the sixth poem sets out Vergil's literary images and programmes: Vergil as the first Roman Theocritus, the Callimachean who must refuse epic, and, through the surrogate figure of Silenus, the arbiter of modern employment of the epic metre. Similarly *Epode* 6 sets out Horace's image and supposed programme: Horace the real Roman Archilochus and (here) Hipponax.

'Closure' at *Epode* 13 then gives us a sense of a group of thirteen to match Callimachus' thirteen *Iambi*. Odd-numbered collections put focus on the centred poem, whose topic may patently reflect the importance of such a position: Prop. 4. 6 (Apollo and Actium) for example, or *Eclogue* 5 (the apotheosis of Daphnis–Caesar) in Vergil's competing concentric structure built out of *Ecl.* 1–9.[105] *Epodes* 1–13 centre the important political *Epode* 7, the first to reflect serious political concerns since the opening *Epode* 1.

And finally, taking *Epode* 13 as 'false' closure, we have seventeen poems, from *Ibis* to *exitus*, as Heyworth sees.[106] This encompassing structure centres the even more important Augustan victory poem, *Epode* 9.

[104] 'Proemi al Mezzo'. For phrase and discussion, see Conte (1984), 121 ff., and (1992), 147–59. See too Barchiesi's interesting reflections on the proem to *Fasti* Book 4 in Barchiesi (1997), 56, and esp. 265–6 with n. 6.
[105] The most sensible discussion of this unmistakable structure is Skutsch (1969), 153 ff., esp. 158 f.
[106] The first and last words of the book: Heyworth (1993), 92.

19

[Tibullus] Book 3 and Sulpicia[1] (2004–5)

I. OVERVIEW OF, AND VIEWS ON, THE BOOK AS A WHOLE[2]

The contents would today be stated as: 3. 1–6 'Lygdamus', 3. 7 *'Panegyricus Messallae'*, 3. 8–12 'Sulpicia Cycle', 3. 13–18 'Sulpicia'; and 3. 19 explicitly and 3. 20 perhaps implicitly pose as 'Tibullus'. Numbers of lines: 'Lygdamus', 290; 'Panegyricus', 211; 'Cycle', 114; 'Sulpicia', 46; 'Tibullus', 28. Total: 685, a plausible length for an Augustan papyrus roll book (Prop. 1. 706; Tibull. 1. 812, 2 (unfinished). 432).

Theories to Cope with the Disparate Material in One Book

Norden (1954), 71 suggested the attractive idea of a Messalla 'Hauspoetenbuch'. This probably falls down on the dating of individual components (see below). Holzberg (1999) argues that the whole book was composed by one man (*sic*), indeed by someone posing as the young Tibullus. He builds on the already voiced idea that 'Lygdamus' points to λύγδινος, marble-white, which points to Albius Tibullus, but accepts the late dating of Lygdamus, the *Panegyricus*, and the Cycle mentioned below.

The Components and their Actual Dating

'Lygdamus'. Lee (1958–9) and Axelson (1960*a*, 1960*b*) persuasively date 'Lygdamus' to the later part of the first century AD.

---

[1] [This draft, which includes something of a commentary on the Sulpicia poems 3. 13–18, was found on Oliver Lyne's laptop computer after his death. It is substantially footnoted, but has not been fully written up for publication. It has been minimally edited in matters of presentation and one or two references have been added, but it is otherwise unaltered].

[2] The commentary of Tränkle (1990) on the *Appendix Tibulliana* is fundamental to study of Sulpicia and all Book 3. Holzberg (1998) has compiled a very full *Bibliographie zum Corpus Tibullianum* (for the online version see http://www.psms.homepage.t-online.de/bibliographien.htm). I work below with the apparatus of Luck (1988) but the text of Sulpicia cited is closer to Lee (1990*b*). The most interesting article I have come across is Lowe (1988). There is a basic on-line commentary on the elegies of Sulpicia at http://www.hnet.uci.edu/classics/cane/sulpicia.html by James R. Bradley, Trinity College, Hartford; Note: in the notes below I have occasionally performed searches in the list Catullus, Propertius, Tibullus, Ovid. I refer to this list with a ghastly inaccurate shorthand as 'Elegy' (in quotation marks).

Panegyricus. This poem is believed by Syme and others to have been composed in 31 BC in honour of Messalla Corvinus, consul in that year.[3] But literary scholars (e.g. Tränkle (1990), 172–84) tell us that it contains imitations of later poets which suggest a date of the early second century AD.

Sulpicia material. Lowe (1988), 194 provides a summary of views on the authorship of 3. 8–18 going back to Scaliger, who thought they were all written by Tibullus (a minor version of Holzberg above!); see also Skoie (2002) for the history of the question back to the Renaissance. 3. 8–18 were first divided into (i) the 'Cycle' (a—male—poet alternating the persona of an *amicus Sulpiciae* and of Sulpicia herself) and (ii) poems by a genuine female poet Sulpicia by Gruppe (1838), 27 ff., included 3. 13 in the 'Cycle'. Rossbach (1855), pp. vi and 55 added 3. 13 to Sulpicia and surely this is right (see below on style). Tränkle (1990), 258 collects the references that convincingly show the Cycle's indebtedness to Ovid (especially to *Heroides*, including the double letters). He dates 'genuine Sulpicia' to 25–20 BC.

'*Tibullus*' 3. 19 Tränkle (1990) 324 convincingly argues that this is fake Tibullus (but its quality at times is very high!); on 3. 20 Heyne, quoted by Tränkle (ibid.), remarked : 'Miri leporis et urbanitatis epigramma... An Tibullum auctorem habeat, credere licet et non licet.'

Conclusion on the Book as a Whole

It presents very disparate material. How—and when, and why—it was assembled into one book is beyond discovery. The *Appendix Vergiliana* provides a good parallel.

The Collection of Sulpicia Poems, 3. 13–18

13. A publication poem (that it is a publication poem is argued below)
14. Sulpicia 'de'-celebrates her birthday (a nice twist on the birthday poem tradition): prospect of separation (revelation of the names Cerinthus and Messalla)
15. The journey called off, the removal of prospect of separation
16. Jealousy poem: revelation of name Sulpicia
17. Illness
18. On her regret at dissimulation.

Is there any rationale to this sequence? Tränkle (1990), 300 argues against a simple chronological order. In particular, he thinks 3. 13 must post-date 3. 18.

---

[3] Syme (1986), 200, 203, Momigliano (1950).

So does Smith (1913), 81–5, who kindly reorders the poems for us. Both see 3. 13 as referring to consummation, and *therefore* it must be last in the list! Smith in particular is governed by unnecessarily prudish assumptions.[4] More interesting than chronology: is it a satisfactory *artistic* order? Yes, according to Lowe (1988), 203, who sees a 'deliberate narrative sequence'. In my eyes 3. 13 *is* a good *introductory* poem (indeed I argue that it is an opening and *publishing* poem), and the others follow well enough, but 3. 18 is not effectively closural—it would better belong in the earlier part of a sequence—though Bradley thinks that the way 'the poet affirms the shame of concealing a worthy lover' frames 'the collection'. Perhaps someone has excerpted from a much larger collection? If Sulpicia published poems, she presumably published more than six.

II. OTHER WOMEN POETS IN ROME[5]

(i) Cornificia, sister of Q. Cornificius, poet and statesmen in the 40s BC, on whom see Courtney (1993), 225–7; Jerome, *Chronicle* under 41 BC 'huius (i.e. Cornificii) soror Cornificia, cuius insignia exstant epigrammata'; she appears on an inscription as the wife of a Camerius, 'doubtless the Camerius of Catull. 55', Courtney 225 with references and bibliography.

(ii) 'Perilla', addressee of Ov. *Trist.* 3. 7, which gives us pretty fascinating information about her. Goold's Loeb maintains she is Ovid's stepdaughter, daughter of his third wife, the name being a pseudonym; this seems to me improbable. Strange and interesting that 'Perilla' is (?also) the pseudonym of a Metella, love-object of Roman love poets.

(iii) 'Cynthia'. Prop. 1. 2. 27, 2. 3. 21–2.

(iv) A Sulpicia, who wrote love poetry that was spicy stuff, but about her love with her husband Calenus: Martial 10. 35 and 38; she has just died—or they are just celebrating their fifteenth wedding anniversary, depending on your interpretation of the epigram—at the time of 10. 38. Two (spicy) iambic trimeters survive: see Courtney (1993), 361, who suggests that there is evidence she also wrote scazons and hendecasyllables, and notes that 'In late antiquity someone assumed Sulpicia's name to write the *Sulpiciae conquestio de statu rei p. et temporibus Domitiani* (*Epigr. Bob.* 37), taking care to bring in Calenus...'. It is a (?troubling) coincidence that she has the same name as our poetess.

---

[4] It ill befits a collection of love poems by a young girl to *start* with a poem that might imply intercourse: in all decency it must be the *last* composed (and the others be from a period of courtship). Voss (1810), 317 f. put 3. 13 at the end of the collection, reading it as a poem of happy *married* sex resulting from a sequence of courtship poems.

[5] See further Santirocco (1979) and now Stevenson (2005), 29–82.

(v) Persius, *Prol.* 13 talks of 'coruos poetas et poetridas picas', 'magpie poetesses'.

III. SULPICIA

Who does she suggest she is? The common assumption[6] is that she is a niece of M. Valerius Messalla Corvinus (*RE* Valerius 261, patron of Tibullus, consul 31 BC), daughter of Servius Sulpicius Rufus (*RE* Sulpicius 96) and granddaughter of the great jurist of the same name (*RE* 95, consul eventually in 51 BC, friend of Cicero) and of Valeria, sister of Messalla. Servius Sulpicius junior is praised by Cicero in letters to his father of the 40s BC (*Fam.* 4. 3. 4 for his culture, 'in omnibus ingenuis artibus', 4. 4. 5, 4. 6. 1, 13. 37. 4 'ego cum tuo Seruio iucundissime et coniunctissime uiuo magnamque ex ingenio eius singularique studio tum ex uirtute et probitate uoluptatem capio', cf. too *Phil.* 9. 12 etc.); at *Att.* 5. 4. 1 (51 BC), Cicero is canvassing him as a husband for Tullia (this came to nothing).

The evidence.

(i) Sulpicia and Messalla: Sulpicia [Tib.] 3. 14. 4 addresses a Messalla 'nimium Messalla mei studiose' as 3. 14. 5 *propinque*: but the text of the latter is far from certain.

(ii) Sulpicia and Sulpicius: At 3. 16. 4 she calls herself 'Serui filia Sulpicia', and Servius Sulpicius, father and son, are the ones well known to us (above). As the daughter of a Servius Sulpicius, it would be natural for her to call herself 'Serui filia', i.e. after her patrician father's distinctive *praenomen*.[7]

(iii) Servius Sulpicius and Valeria: Jerome *Adv. Iouinian.* 1. 46 'Mulieres Romanae insignes.—Ad Romanas feminas transeam; et primam ponam Lucretiam.... Valeria Messalarum soror, amisso Seruio uiro, nulli uolebat nubere. Quae interrogata cur faceret, ait, sibi semper maritum Seruium uiuere'; Jerome is supposedly quoting Seneca (*De Matrimonio* frg. 28 Bickel). The Valeria is assumed to be sister of M. Valerius Messalla Corvinus, not improbably, and the Servius, who cannot be the great jurist,[8] is assumed to be

---

[6] The identification is at least as old as Haupt (1871), 32–4.

[7] Cf. how her supposed father is referred to as 'Serui filius' at *Att.* 9. 18 (SB *Select Letters* 38).2. When *praenomina* were almost exclusively confined to patrician families (like Servius, Appius, Faustus), they could be used to identify a person on their own: cf. Appius at *Att.* 3. 13. 3, SB *Select Letters* ad loc. For the usual practice with nomenclature, see Balsdon (1979), 156.

[8] The jurist Servius Sulpicius Rufus is known to have married the patrician Postumia (and only her, so far as we know): Syme (1986), 198 and index; Syme identifies this Postumia with that of Catull. 27. 3.

his son S. Sulpicius Rufus (*RE* 96); the dating fits.[9] Their daughter would of course be Sulpicia, but no such daughter is with certainty independently attested.[10] It is worth adding that—accepting all the above identifications— if Valeria's re-marriage was an issue, it suggests that Servius Sulpicius her husband died young; and that therefore Messalla may have had to play a prominent role in his niece's life.[11]

IV. CERINTHUS (Sulpicia's lover, so named in 3. 14. 2)

Presumably a pseudonym (see *TLL Onomasticon* ii. 347. 27 ff.). Literary examples: Hor. *Serm.* 1. 2. 81[12] (Porph. ad loc. 'Cerinthus nomine prostitutus dicitur fuisse insigni specie atque candore'); then the Corp. Tib. A Cerinthus was 'haereticus saec. primi, magister Ebionis' (many examples). Most importantly, it is quite a common slave name on inscriptions: e.g. *CIL* vi. 3996

---

[9] Servius Sulpicius (father) consular candidate (legal age at least 42) for 62 BC, born *c*.102 BC? His son sounds in Cicero's letters in the 40s BC to be quite young, though this is merely an impression. If he was born when his father was, say, 30 (in *c*.70 BC), he would have been between 20 and 30 or so in the 40s BC; some think he was old enough to assist his father in the prosecution of 63 BC: cf. Münzer, *RE* iv a. 860 f. (there was *an*other Servius Sulpicius prosecuting): that would shove his birth date back a bit. He is a prospective bridegroom in 51 BC (above for Tullia). Valerius Messalla Corvinus was born in 64 BC; his sister is plausibly a young woman when Servius junior came to marry.

[10] Syme (1986), 206 accepts that the Sulpicia of the poems is the daughter of the sister of the great Messalla and of the son of the great jurist Servius Sulpicius. On p. 46 he conjectures that a M. Caecilius Cornutus listed as one of the *Arvales* in an inscription of 21/20 BC may be the Cornutus of Tibullus' marriage poem 2. 2, and conceivably the husband of Sulpicia (see Section IV below on Cerinthus). Back on p. 206 Syme notes that 'Another Sulpicia Ser. f. married a Cassius (*ILS* 3103)' and suggests that she is our Sulpicia's sister rather than a daughter of the great jurist. I am not quite sure why she could not be one and the same as our Sulpicia—unless we are committed to marrying her to Cornutus (and only to Cornutus).

[11] More on Servius (Sulpicius): a Servius is among the cultivated men whose approval for his poems Horace would like (*Serm.* 1. 10. 86); Ovid appeals to the saucy poems of a Servius at *Trist.* 2. 441; Pliny *Epist.* 5. 3. 5 defends his writing of *uersiculi* by appeal to the *lusus* of dignitaries, among whom is a Servius Sulpicius ('M. Tullium, C. Caluum, Asinium Pollionem, M. Messallam, Q. Hortensium, M. Brutum, L. Sullam, Q. Catulum, Q. Scaeuolam, Seruium Sulpicium...'). Many assume that all three refer to the son Servius Sulpicius, and the idea that Sulpicia's father was a poet as well as a noble—and talented and so on—is attractive. (The nobility of the Sulpicii: S.S.R. *RE* 95 had been consul in 51 BC; S. S. Galba consul 108 BC; and Servius the son was patrician on both sides of his family, Shackleton Bailey on *Att.* 5. 21.[= SB114]. 9)

[12] See Fraenkel (1957), 84 for text and interpretation (and a good understanding of a Horatian satiric practice). Read: 'nec magis huic, inter niueos uiridisque lapillos | sit licet, hoc, Cerinthe, tuo tenerum est femur aut crus | rectius...'. *Hoc* = *ideo, magis* goes with *tenerum*, and *tuo* is abl. of comparison: 'nor is this matrona's thigh softer or her leg straighter than yours, Cerinthus, though it be sited midst pearls and emeralds'.

(on the *monumentum Liviae*[13]) 'Cerinthus C. Caesaris ostiarius'; or iv. 4371 'T(hraex) m(urmillo) Cerinthus'. *Circa* twenty instances. It is suggested it may be a pseudonym for the Cornutus of Tibull. 2. 2 and 3, following Bentley's principle: the two names are metrically equivalent. (Syme—not however invoking this theory—thought Sulpicia might have married (M. Caecilius) Cornutus, one of the first Augustan Arvales.[14]

Whoever is covered by this pseudonym, why is this particular pseudonym used ? It is possibly a tease on the lover's comparatively low social status (low only in comparison with the noble Sulpicia), which Sulpicia explicitly refers to in embittered and still probably exaggerated terms in 3. 16. 6 'ignoto toro'; note the concern with social status suggested by the pun in 3. 16. 4 'Serui filia Sulpicia'. But the Cerinthus of the 'Cycle' hunts (3. 9. 1 ff.), a pursuit which, when followed for entertainment, was an indulgence of the leisured classes (e.g. Hor. *Epist.* 1. 18. 40 ff., 'a Hellenistic importation to Rome', Griffin (1985), 7.

Other (far-fetched?) ideas are assembled by Bradley (see n. 2 above). In Greek, $K\acute{\eta}\rho\iota\nu\theta os$ is a Euboean town (Hom. *Iliad* 2. 538, Theognis 1. 891, Apoll. Rhod. 1. 79, Strabo 10. 1. 3, etc.), while the common noun $\kappa\acute{\eta}\rho\iota\nu\theta os$ = 'bee-bread' (a compound of honey and pollen). Perhaps the most important fact that we should take hence is this: a pseudonym indicates literary affinity and *publishing* interests (cf. Clodia / Lesbia, Plania / Delia ...).

V. THE SULPICIA POEMS, 3. 13-18: THE PROBLEM OF AUTHENTICITY AND HOW TO APPROACH IT

How do we set about (dis)proving authenticity? It is comparatively easy to expose a fake, virtually impossible to *prove* genuineness in a case like this. The first thing we must do is avoid gender assumptions, indeed sexism.[15] The phrase 'feminine Latin' has dogged us since Gruppe (1838), 49, 'weibliches Latein'): the less than pellucid syntax on the one hand and the emotional simplicity etc. on the other hand adds up to a 'slip of a girl' for many—see the now hilarious pages of Smith (1913), 80–6, also his notes on 3. 13. 7–8 (which are mistranslated). But hilarity should not blind us to two facts: (i) Sulpicia's syntax is idiosyncratic (see below); (ii) female *speech* was said to be different

---

[13] A *columbarium* of slaves and freedmen in the household of Livia, chiefly Livia's own personal staff, dating from the first decade AD; see Treggiari (1975).
[14] See n. 10 above and Lowe (1988), 196 n. 21.
[15] For the gendered aspect of scholarship on Sulpicia see especially Skoie (2002).

from men's by Cicero, but *not* in ways that explain Sulpicia's poetical style.[16] Just as bad as naïve sexism is the rebound which sees the poetry 'as a feminist statement': bibliography for both these views in Holzberg (1999), 174–5. My own procedure regarding authenticity is to make the assumption that these poems are what they seem to present themselves as: love poems by Sulpicia, a girl of noble and patrician family, and niece of Messalla, written in the 20s BC—and then see if anything conflicts with this, or supports it. To date I find (i) nothing that conflicts with such an assumption, (ii) things that are not only consistent with but perhaps support such an assumption (especially the idiosyncrasy), and (iii) certainly nothing that clearly suggest a forger like the Ovidian echoes detectable in the 'Cycle'; nor (iv) do I get a sense— though here things get subjective—of a male writer writing the sort of thing he thinks females say, as I do e.g. in Propertius' 'Arethusa', 4. 3.

Alignment with other Poets. There are no marked borrowings from or allusions to other poems: contrast e.g. the 'Cycle's' echoes of Ovid. But note the definite resemblance in syntax and structure—and some in wording—to some epigrams of Catullus; it is with Catullus only that we find some affiliation, especially in 3. 18. This is consistent with, perhaps supports, an assumption of authenticity.

Language. We find colloquialism and prosaism of an unselfconscious nature, that does not suggest a pose: see especially 3. 16 and 17. This is at least consistent with authenticity. The degree of hypotaxis is even more interesting: see notes on 3. 18 (below).

Metre. The practice in these poems largely squares with the Augustan age, again cohering with assumption of authenticity. Elisions are rare; hexameter endings are constructed out of trisyllables or disyllables in such a way as to provide coincidence of word accent and metrical ictus, with the exception of 3. 16. 1 and 3. 17. 5, which are not startling exceptions. Pentameters all end in disyllables except 3. 16. 4 *Sulpicia* = the practice of more than 90 per cent of Tibullus, and virtually a rule of late Prop. and Ovid. However three pentameters end with a short vowel (3. 13. 6 *sua*, 16. 4 *Sulpicia*, 17. 6 *mala*), a high proportion in a tiny corpus: a practice avoided by Tibullus and esp. Ovid (the dilettante betrays herself, says Tränkle (1990), 301). Caesuras in the hexameters are regular, but varied: after the first long of 2 and 4 as well as of 3; and one arguable Greek caesura (3. 17. 1 'estne tibi, Cerinthe').

---

[16] Cic. *De Orat.* 3. 45. Cicero's point is that women's speech is more conservative than men's, since they have less interaction with the rough and tumble of *sermo*. But his emphasis seems to me to be largely on accent. For a theoretical perspective see e.g. Coates (1998).

VI. SPECULATION ON DATE

Composition: 25–20 BC (see especially Tränkle (1990), 300 ff.). This fits with literary considerations. Tränkle dates her birth to *c.*45 BC (which is compatible I suppose with what we can infer about the age of Servius Sulpicius junior— see Section III above). But note that, in dating the poems, Tränkle takes *tota... iuuenta* (3. 18. 3) curiously literally, inferring that she must be at the end of her *iuuenta*, at least twenty perhaps: but one can say 'in all my youth' at any stage of one's youth? We could agree with a Sulpicia composing *c.*25 BC, and suppose that she was still in her teens—if we wanted to.

VII. COMMENTARY ON 3. 13–18

I shall now look more closely at the poems and their language and affiliation, to show that at least 3. 16–18 are consistent with Sulpician authenticity.

3. 13 Introduction

Surely 3. 13 is an opening and *publishing* poem, designed to introduce love poems by Sulpicia to the public (and not a concluding poem, as some suggest—e.g Voss (1810), Smith (1913)). Tränkle (1990), 300 does not think Sulpicia thought of publication; compared with Catullus, her poems are 'real occasional poems of refreshing immediacy' (302, my translation). For Smith (1913), 504 this poem reads 'more like an extract as it were from her own diary'. Santirocco (1979) is very cautious in the area of talking about publishing; I cannot really make out where Lowe (1988) stands on this question.

In this apparent monologue, we find a sequence of bravado statements (1–2, 5–6, 7–8, 9–10), resulting from the triumph and elation of love achieved (1, 3–4, 5). The wording and potential symbolism of 7–8 should be scrutinised.

Sealing of letters and books is a natural move when the material is confidential, or for some other reason to be preserved for one reader only: cf. e.g. Cic. *Att.* 11. 1. 1 'Accepi a te signatum libellum[17] quem Anteros attulerat; ex quo nihil scire potui de nostris domesticis rebus', 15. 29. 3 'Obsecro te, quid

---

[17] This *libellus* could be a letter, but probably refers to some larger 'memorandum': see Shackleton Bailey ad loc.

est hoc? signata iam epistula...', 'my dear fellow, what's going on? I had already sealed this letter, when...'), Hor. *Epist.* 1. 13. 2 'Augusto reddes signata uolumina...'. Within the drama of the poem, Sulpicia's gesture of bravado here is that she doesn't care if her messages to her lover get read in transit. But we must remember the established use of physical media of writing (books, tablets, pages) to emblematise poetry. Catullus is very fond of this practice. He plays between the physical book (*libellus*) and the poetry it contains in poem 1 'cui dono lepidum nouum libellum | arido modo pumice expolitum', etc., creatively alluding to a similar punning example in Callimachus *Aetia* fr. 7;[18] meanwhile in Catull. 1. 6 f. Nepos' *Chronica* are 'chartis doctis...et laboriosis'. In poem 42, the wax tablets, *codicilli*, which are the objects of Catullus' pursuit in the poem, are best understood as standing for poetry that Catullus wants back. And there is further play between poetry and the physical constituents of books in Catullus 22 (unlike Catullus' poetry— see poem 1—Suffenus' poetry does not match the deluxe materials it is written on) and 36 'annales Volusi, cacata charta' (Volusius' writing is *merda*).[19] So another inference can be made from 7–8, besides the dramatic bravado: Sulpicia *will* write 'non signatae tabellae', 'unsealed tablets', which, following Catullus' puns on poetry and their physical media, would suggest an open i.e. *published book* of poetry. And the reader envisaged in *legat*— within the drama, a snooping messenger—now becomes the implied reader of this poetry book. Propertius in 3. 23 uses the exact word *tabellae* with the same symbolism, in a poem *closing down* love poetry. For Propertius, as for Sulpicia, the everyday nature of the waxed tablets symbolically catches the supposed impromptu nature of love elegy.

Prop. 3. 23. 1–11 is worth a closer glance:

> Ergo tam doctae nobis periere tabellae,
> scripta quibus pariter tot periere bona!
> has quondam nostris manibus detriuerat usus,

---

[18] Callimachus asks the Graces to 'come now and wipe your anointed hands upon my elegies that they may live for many a year'. Callimachus puns between asking the Graces to grace his poetry, and to preserve his book with oil. Catullus concocts his own book/poetry pun (deluxe book, polished poetry), and disjoins the wish for long life ('that they may live for many a year' 'plus uno maneat perenne saeclo'). Cf. Fowler (2000), 29 n. 46, a characteristically glancing reference to a point that others would have spent several pages on. I have benefited in the above paragraph from my conversations with Fowler.

[19] *Cacata charta* is a much discussed phrase, but as often the basic sense is quickly grasped— and delicately put—by Kroll (1960), 67 '*cacata* nicht in dem Sinne, in dem wir Papier damit in Zusammenhang zu bringen pflegen, sondern = *concacata*... Es ist "beschmiertes Papier"'. But the punning imagery needs a little more elucidation. *Charta* refers to the pages of Volusius' poetry book (cf. 1. 6, 22. 6, 68. 46). If Volusius' *Annals* are *cacata charta*, then on the pages, instead of beautiful pen and ink writing, symbolising deathless verse, there is: shit symbolising, well, shit.

qui *non signatas* iussit habere fidem.
5 illae iam sine me norant placare puellas,
et quaedam sine me uerba diserta loqui.
non illas fixum caras effecerat aurum:
uulgari buxo sordida cera fuit.
qualescumque mihi semper mansere fideles,
10 semper et effectus promeruere bonos.
forsitan haec illis fuerunt *mandata tabellis*:

Within the drama of the poem the 'seal' motif has slender dramatic justification. This, plus the fact that the phraseology common to both (italicized) occurs in one line in Sulpicia, suggest Sulpicia's priority, indeed that Propertius is alluding to her. Which is interesting.

Further evidence can be advanced that 3. 13 is a publishing poem:

(i) The poem has been read, not unreasonably, as a monologue (see e.g. Tränkle (1990), 300). But Sulpicia's other poems have dramatic addressees. Epigrams do naturally have addressees (cf. Catullus). 3. 13 has a natural addressee, perhaps rather a natural meta-addressee: the reader.

(ii) *Nudasse alicui* likewise works both within the drama ('I'm going to noise my love abroad') and metatextually ('I'm going to write about it').

(iii) Note 10 *ferar* (future, I think, 'I shall be spoken of'; Smith (1913), 508 interprets as subjunctive): cf. the proud public, publishing futures (more or less) of Prop. 1. 7. 22 'tunc ego Romanis praeferar ingeniis', Hor. *Odes* 2. 20. 1 'non usitata nec tenui ferar | penna' and futures throughout that poem), 3. 30. 6 'non omnis moriar' etc.... 10 'dicar', Ov. *Am.* 3. 15. 8 'Paelignae dicar gloria gentis ego', *Ars* 1. 8 'Tiphys et Automedon dicar Amoris ego', *Trist.* 3. 7. 51 f. 'dumque suis uictrix omnem de montibus orbem | prospiciet domitum Martia Roma, legar', *Pont.* 5. 14. 5, *Met.* 15. 876–9, etc. (going back to the sentiment of Ennius fr. 46 Courtney).

(iv) With 1 'tandem uenit amor...' cf. the introductory poems Prop. 1. 1, Ov. *Am.* 1. 2. On the other hand *illum* (3) and *meus* (8) are curiously non-committal for an introductory, publishing poem—or a designed inducement to the reader to proceed further. And see further notes below.

3. 13 Text and Notes

Tandem uenit amor, qualem texisse pudore
quam nudasse alicui sit mihi fama magis.
exorata meis illum Cytherea Camenis
attulit in nostrum deposuitque sinum.

[Tibullus] Book 3 and Sulpicia   351

> exsoluit promissa Venus: mea gaudia narret,   5
> dicetur siquis non habuisse sua.
> *non ego signatis quicquam mandare tabellis,*
>   *ne legat id nemo quam meus ante, uelim,*
> sed peccasse iuuat, uultus componere famae
>   taedet: cum digno digna fuisse ferar.   10

At last a love has come which it would disgrace me more to hide out of shame than to expose to someone. The Cytherean, prevailed upon by my Muses, has delivered him into my arms on trust. Venus has carried out her promises: let anyone who's had no love-life of his own gossip about my joys. I would not want to entrust a message to sealed tablets so that no-one could read it before my man, but I am glad to do wrong, I'm tired of putting on reputation's mask. I shall be spoken of as having been in a worthy love match.

1–2. text: (i) MS variant *pudori* printed by e.g. Luck (1988). On this text *fama* is subject, *pudori* predicative dative, 'of such a sort that the reputation that I had concealed it would be a greater cause of shame to me than (the reputation) that I had revealed it to someone'. Objections: word order and possibly a slight inappropriateness of *fama* with *nudasse* (we might expect 'than *the fact that*'). (ii) The translation above (essentially Lee) assumes that *texisse* (with *pudore*) and *nudasse* are subject infinitives: 'of the sort which it would disgrace me more to hide out of shame than expose it to someone'. For *fama* = *infamia* (a different sense from that in line 9, be it noted; some find this an objection), cf. Cic. *Planc.* 71 etc. (Tränkle), and for the construction of *fama* (instead of a predicative dative), cf. 3. 18. 1, Verg. *Ecl.* 2. 101, Löfstedt (1956), i. 194ff. (Other thoughts: *at* for *quam*, Scaliger (*et* in C); *cura* Heyne; *minor* E, Broukhusius, allowing us to keep *fama* = (good) reputation.)

Some puns in 1–2 on Cupid/Amor? (i) *tandem uenit amor*... sounds like the statement that a cletic hymn summons (to Amor) has worked: e.g. Catull. 61. 9 'huc huc ueni...', Tibull. 1. 7. 63 f. 'at tu Natalis... ueni'. (ii) Allusion to and play with *naked* Cupid? The nudity of Cupid/Amor is selected as a characteristic (γυμνός) by Nonnus 7. 275, 48. 107; also *Anth. Pal.* 207. 1, the fifth century AD (Palladas) and therefore, we can infer, by Hellenistic poets, and *Amor* is termed *nudus* by Prop. 1. 2. 8, Ov. *Am.* 1. 10. 15. These poets lean on some point or metaphor in γυμνός / *nudus*: hence their choice of an unobvious characteristic. Sulpicia would be playing with the thought of clothing as well as unclothing Amor: *tego* is the opposite of *nudo*, an idiomatic way of saying *uestio*. The thought of clothing *Amor* in *pudor* is wittily paradoxical (Ov. *Am.* 1. 2. 32 '... et Pudor et castris quidquid Amoris obest'); and the wit produced is further support for *pudore* rather than *pudori* (see below). Propertius goes down this sort of witty path (1. 2. 24 'illis ampla satis forma pudicitia').

tandem uenit amor... Camenis: some memory also of the incantation of Daphnis in *Ecl.* 8? The female *persona* asks (9. 72) 'ducite ab urbe domum, mea carmina, ducite Daphnin' and ends (109) 'parcite, ab urbe *uenit*, iam parcite *carmina*, Daphnis'. With this compare Sulpicia's 'tandem *uenit* amor... exorata... *Camenis*'. Though *amor* in Sulpicia cannot of course mean lover. 'tandem... uenit' at Tibull. 2. 5. 46.

3–4.   *illum* = the man who will be revealed as Cerinthus, but with some play on *Amor*. The delay of the identity of Cerinthus could be seen as artless- or artfulness. The content of 3–4: I want more parallels than I can find! Asking Venus, in poetry, for help in bringing a lover: Tränkle supposes an allusion to Sappho poem 1 (Sappho entreats Aphrodite and has done so in past). For the delivery of the beloved, perhaps cf. too Hom. *Il.* 3. 380–2 (Aphrodite rescues Paris). Some relation to Prop. 1. 11. 7f. 'an te nescio quis... | sustulit e nostris, Cynthia, carminibus?'

exorata: TLL cites our example (1585. 42) in the vicinity of Ov. *Her.* 21 (20).128 'exoranda tibi, non capienda fui', *Ars* 1. 37 'proximus huic labor est placitam exorare puellam', etc. ('win over by entreaty'); it has a different section (not really justifiably?, 1586. 79 ff., under 'praeualet notio placandi') where gods appear as the object: Ov. *Trist.* 2. 22 'exorant magnos *carmina* saepe deos', *Met.* 9. 699 f. (Io/Isis) 'dea sum auxiliaris opemque / *exorata* fero', Quint. *Decl.* 326. 6 'exorare posse sollemnibus sacris existimabamus deos', etc.; in 'Elegy' the verb occurs in all (besides our example) twice in Prop. and ten times in Ovid.

sinus as in e.g. Tibull. 1. 1. 46 or Ov. *Her.* 16. 266 'uenit ut in Phrygios Hippodamia sinus'; and the Cycle-poet perhaps alludes to our line in 3. 9. 24 'celer in nostros ipse recurre sinus'.

Cytherea: Aphrodite is Κυθέρεια since the *Odyssey*, *Cytherea* in Latin from 20s BC on (besides *Catal.* 14. 11), *TLL Onomasticon* ii. 811. 32 ff. Prop. 2. 14. 25, Hor. *Odes* 3. 12. 4, Verg. *Aen.* 1. 257, Ov. *Am.* 1. 3. 4 etc. Note the abAB pattern of adjectives and nouns in line 3.

Camenis: the Camenae had been relegated in favour of the Muses by Ennius, but there was considerable reinstatement from Verg. *Ecl.* 3. 59 on. Tränkle dates metonymic use of *Camena* from 20s BC on; cf. his n. on 3. 7. 24 and *TLL Onomasticon* ii. 117. 55 ff., which starts with Hor. *Odes* 1. 12. 39, but as *TLL* says 'sed non ubique discerni potest, utrum res an persona significetur', and perhaps we should give the *Camenae* as personages play in our context?

5–6.   *exsoluit promissa Venus...* Sulpicia supposes the interesting notion that Venus has *promised* her success in love / success with Cerinthus. For *exsoluere promissa* see *TLL* (*exsoluo*) v 1878. 63 ff. For *uotum, promissum, fidem exsoluere*: closest parallels Cic. *Off.* 3. 7, Tac. *Dial.* 27. 1; under *TLL* (*promissum*) x. 1879. 1 the only exact parallel given is Tac. just cited, but see also 1878. 72 ff. for *promissum* (*soluo* and *per-, ab- soluo*). Interpretation of *mea gaudia narret*... is not straightforward or easy. On any interpretation, I think, *dicetur habuisse* is not going to mean much more than *habuit* (Tränkle); cf. paragraph (17) item (v). Tränkle thinks the gist of the sense must be, to follow on from 3–4, 'anyone who after their own experience does not believe in the possibility of real fulfilment of love, can deduce from Sulpicia's experience the certainty that it exists, i.e. he can refer to it, cite it.' I don't think I can get this out of the Latin. Heyne and Dissen thought it referred to envious people. Bradley: 'Sulpicia can invite all and sundry whose lot it will be to lack their own (*sua*) to tell of the joys of love that are hers (*mea gaudia*)'. I think Sulpicia is saying something like Catullus 5. 2 'rumoresque senum seueriorum | omnes unius aestimemus assis' or Prop. 2. 30. 14 'ista senes licet accusent conuiuia duri', i.e. 'let the old fogies talk, I don't care'. This sense then goes well with what follows (7–8), and follows *exsoluit promissa Venus* well: 'My love life is up and running. I don't care what people say.' For the sense of *narro* ('make the subject of (hostile) talk', 'gossip about'), cf. Prop. 2. 18. 37 'credam ego narranti, noli committere, famae', Tibull. 1. 5. 42 'narrat scire nefanda meam'. Line 6 is a way of saying *senes seueriores*, 'old fogies': Sulpicia equates censorious Oldies with people who have had no love-life. We need to read *sua* FG²(*suam* AVX, *suum* G).

7–8. See above. *ne... nemo*. Colloquial double negative: see Fordyce on Catull. 76. 3 for comedy examples, and Löfstedt (1956), ii. 210. Of the examples cited by Tränkle from higher literature, Catull. 76. 3 and Prop. 2. 19. 32 don't stand up, but Cic. *Verr.* 2. 60 does ('debebat Epicrates nummum nullum nemini'). For *meus* on its own ('my lover'), cf. Ov. *Ars* 1. 322 (Hollis, 'lovers' language'), and more material in Tränkle.

9–10. *peccasse* generally of extra-marital sex, Hor. *Serm.* 1. 2. 63 etc. *uultus componere famae*: *TLL compono* 2114. 49 ff. cites our line, then Ov. *Met.* 13. 767 'et spectare feros in aqua et componere uultus', of Polyphemus' composing his expression, *Fast.* 5. 30 'omne uideres | numen ad hanc uoltus composuisse suos', 'compose, model their features on hers', Plin. *Epist.* 2. 20. 3 'componit uultum', 'composed his face', 'put on a grave look', *Lat. Paneg.* V (8). 9. 3, Manil. 3. 214, and a couple of later examples; add Tac. *Ann.* 1. 7 'uultuque composito', 'his expression adjusted'. Tränkle takes *famae* as predicative dative, following *TLL*, but finds it 'singular'; rather, genitive? (Lee 'I'm... tired of wearing reputation's mask'). One thing seems clear: Sulpicia works with a phrase that naturally has no further addition (she adds *famae* against normal idiom). *Cum digno digna*... recalls proverbial utterances,

354   *[Tibullus] Book 3 and Sulpicia*

Plaut. *Poen.* 1270 'eueniunt digna dignis' and more references in Tränkle; but no close parallel to Sulpicia's sentiment in 'Elegy'. Sulpicia's *digno digna* here stimulates the Cycle poet at 3. 12. 9–10. The euphemism *esse cum aliquo*: Plaut. *Amph.* 817, Ov. *Ars* 3. 664, and more references in Tränkle.

3. 14 Introduction

The poem is a *Genethliakon* (birthday-poem): cf. 3. 11, Tibull. 1. 7, 2. 2, Prop. 3. 10, Cairns (1972), 113 ff. and index. Sulpicia 'de'-celebrates her own birthday, a nice twist on the tradition of celebrating girlfriends' birthdays. The identity of *illum* (3. 13. 3) is clarified in so far as it is going to be clarified. The great man Messalla is introduced. A plausible second poem in a published sequence?

The birthday must be Sulpicia's, as is surely instantly clear (*pace* Bradley). The sequence of thought is easy enough. Messalla must be supposed to have invited her to celebrate the event on a country estate, in a way hard for her to refuse; she doesn't want to go; hence the birthday is *inuisus*. She adumbrates her real motive for wishing to stay in Rome (Cerinthus, line 2), but, suiting realism—and humour—gives prominence to other reasons for her wish not to leave the city. I think we are to imagine the poem as addressed *in toto* to Messalla.

For the motif of a girl out of reach in a country villa, cf. (though the reason is different) Tibull. 2. 3. 1 'rura meam, Cornute, tenent uillaeque puellam', 61, 65, 67. For birthdays in the Elegists, cf. Prop. 3. 10 and the birthdays of Cerinthus and Sulpicia in the Cycle, [Tibull.] 3. 11 and 12.

3. 14 Text and Notes

          Inuisus natalis adest qui rure molesto
            et sine Cerintho tristis agendus erit.
          dulcius urbe quid est? an uilla sit apta puellae
            atque Arretino frigidus amnis agro?
5   iam, nimium Messalla mei studiose, quiescas.
            non tempestiuae saepe, propinque, uiae.
          hic animum sensusque meos abducta relinquo,
            arbitrio quamuis non sinis esse meo.

[no translation given in author's original]

1. I find no parallel for *rus molestum* in all classical Latin (PHI CD-ROM). Luck conjectures *moleste*. Sulpicia's phrase is pointed in view of the use of *rus* to mean country estate (e.g. Cic. *Att.* 4. 18. 2 and others cited below).

3. For the turn from *tristis* to *dulcis*, cf. Gallus fr. 2. I can find no parallel in all Latin (PHI) for *dulcius urbe* or *dulcis urbs*. Livy 4. 12. 7 has 'dulcedine contionum et urbis'. Has *puellis* (H) anything going for it? Fitting Sulpicia's (humorously) indirect argumentation, esp. if we are to imagine this as *in toto* addressed to Messalla? Perhaps cf. how Tibullus, thinking about a *puella*, talks about *puellae* at 2. 3. 66 'o ualeant fruges, ne sint modo rure puellae'.

4. *Arretino* Z+, edd. : *Reatino* Huschke. Atticus had an Arretine villa: Nepos, *Att.* 14. 3 'nullos habuit hortos, nullam suburbanam aut maritimam sumptuosam uillam, neque in Italia,[20] praeter Arretinum et Nomentanum, rusticum praedium, omnisque eius pecuniae reditus constabat in Epiroticis et urbanis possessionibus.' Cf. too Sallust, *Catiline* 36. 1 using the actual phrase *agro Arretino*: 'Sed ipse paucos dies conmoratus apud C. Flaminium in agro Arretino, dum vicinitatem antea sollicitatam armis exornat, cum fascibus atque aliis imperi insignibus in castra ad Manlium contendit.' There are two or three examples of *Arretinus* in Martial (depending on whether titles of *Apophoreta* are Martial), but referring to Arretine pots: these besides Sulpicia are the only examples in verse. Nor are there other references to Arretine villas to be found in a search of *Arretinus* in all classical Latin (PHI). Tränkle makes a case for the attractiveness of the Arretine district. I see no reason to emend, but one might perhaps have supposed the *uilla* of Messalla to be either nearer to Rome than Arezzo (thus a convenient *suburbana*) and/or fashionable and/or known to be Messallan. Reate (*Reatino* Huschke) was in the Sabine territory (Varro, who would know, *Rust.* 6) and so is close to Rome, but surely not flash enough for Messalla; and *atque* before a consonant would be contrary to elegiac practice (Nisbet and Hubbard on *Odes* 2. 19. 11). The unobviousness of Arezzo might be an argument in favour of its and Sulpicia's genuineness.

amnis Z+ : *Arnus* Heinsius : *annus* Scaliger. One sees Scaliger's point: why should S. pick on a river? No parallel shown up by a PHI search of all classical Latin. For *frigidus annus*, cf. Hor. *Epod.* 2. 29 *annus hibernus*, 'winter (season of the) year', with Mankin ad loc.; *frigidus annus* itself at Verg. *Aen.* 6. 611. Another passage (the only other) turned up by a PHI search of all classical Latin is (quite interestingly) Sen. *Epist.* 114. 19 'Arruntius in primo libro Belli Punici ait "repente hiemavit tempestas", et alio loco cum dicere vellet frigidum annum fuisse ait "totus hiemavit annus", et alio loco "inde sexaginta onerarias leves praeter militem et necessarios nautarum hiemante aquilone misit".'

5–6. *studiose*: *OLD* s.v. 3, Cic. *Att.* 3. 22. 4 'mei studiosos habeo Dyrrachinos'. For 6 Lee et al. write '... quiescas. | non tempestiuae saepe, propinque,

---

[20] In context, *Italia* seems opposed to 'suburban' and 'maritime'.

356   *[Tibullus] Book 3 and Sulpicia*

uiae', 'Messalla, you worry too much about me. Stay put now ("be quiet", "leave it alone", "do be still"). Journeys, kinsman, are often ill-timed'. For an absolute *quiescas*, cf. *OLD* s.v. 4, Hor. *Serm.* 2. 1. 4 f. 'Trebati, | quid faciam praescribe'. On *quiescas* cf. Smith, 'a colloquial use of the word frequent e.g., in Plautus (*Most.* 1173; etc.) but not found elsewhere in the elegy'. We lack parallels for *propinque* as a form of address 'of an uncle or other close relative', and why should S. use such a general term (in spite of Servius' comments on *auunculus* at *Aen.* 3. 343)? No (other) example of the singular vocative *propinque* is shown by a PHI-CD ROM search of all classical Latin. But cf. Catull. 41. 5 (to the relatives of Ameana/Anneiana) 'propinqui [vocative], quibus est puella curae'; then cf. e.g. Prop. 1. 22. 7 'tu proiecta mei perpessa es membra propinqui', 2. 6. 7 'quin etiam falsos fingis tibi saepe propinquos'. Tränkle says Scaliger read the same text as Lee in the hexameter (but presumably a comma after 5), but took *non tempestiuae uiae* as dative singular with *propinque*, and gave it the sense 'qui saepe te accingis itineri intempestivo'; parallels for such a sense of *propinquus* are lacking, and the resultant construction of the couplet is ghastly; Smith assumes the same sense but with *uiae* genitive on the analogy of Greek ἐγγύς. Luck puts comma after *quiescas*, and obelises 6. Heyne: 'non tempestiuam sic properare uiam', with *quiescas* governing the infinitive, 'desist from' (a construction paralleled only at Plaut. *Most.* 1173, Gell. 2. 28. 2), and *properare* transitive (Tränkle on 3. 7. 205). Other ideas for line 6 in Luck's apparatus. *tempestiuus* in 'Elegy' only otherwise three times in Ovid.

7. Parallels for the quasi-reduplication of *animum sensusque* in Cicero (Tränkle); cf. too (in 'Elegy') Ov. *Met.* 14. 178 'nisi si timor abstulit omnem | sensum animumque'. For the idea (my thoughts are elsewhere), cf. Cic. *Ad M. Brutum* 1. 3 'te uelim habere cognitum, meum quidem animum in acie esse', Prop. 4. 8. 48 'Lanuuii ad portas, ei mihi, totus eram', possibly Petron. 65. 9, depending on interpretation; and this may be the explanation of Verg. *Ecl.* 10. 44 f. (Servius 'ex affectu amantis ibi se esse putat, ubi amica est, ut "me" sit "meum animum"'), and passages in Plautus cited by Smith. For the colour of *abducta*, cf. Catull. 68B. 103 'ne Paris abducta gauisus libera moecha | otia...degeret', Prop. 2. 20. 1 'quid fles abducta gravius Briseide?' Some humour in Sulpicia's expression.

8. The paradosis is: *arbitrio quamuis* (AVX+ : *quoniam* G) *non sinis esse meo*, which, like Lee, I would probably accept. (i) *Sinis*, addressed to Messalla like 5 f., looks pretty unimpeachable (though Luck writes *quam uis non satis*, 'whom you do not wish' and Statius wrote *sinit* with *uis* subject = 'force'— not, surely, something that S. is going to charge her uncle with). (ii) The case of *arbitrium*. Normal idiom is genitive with *esse*, thus *mei* etc. *arbitrii esse*, 'to be under (my) control, within (my) competence', *OLD arbitrium* 4b, but abl.

with active verbs, thus *meo* etc. *arbitrio facere* (vel sim.), 'to do something on (my own) initiative', *OLD* s.v. 4c. Hence the emendation *arbitrii... mei*, '... you do not allow me to be under my own control'. But I would be loath to distinguish the constructions quite so rigorously, and Tränkle produces two ablatives with *esse* from the Jurists (in addition the form *arbitrii*, i.e. the *-ii* genitive of neuters in *-ium* gives pause: see Tränkle; but while Verg., Hor., and Tibull. may avoid this genitive, there is Prop. 1. 6. 34 *imperii* etc., so this is hardly very substantial as an objection). Keep therefore *arbitrio... meo*. (iii) *quamuis* or *quoniam*. *quoniam* (G, conjectured by Heinsius, adopted by e.g. Tränkle; corruption easy via abbreviations): 'I leave my heart here *since* you do not allow me to be under my own control, you won't allow me to do what I want and stay in Rome'. *quamuis* (paradosis, Lee) 'If dragged away, I leave my heart and senses here, even though you don't allow me charge of them'; this interpretation, to justify *quamuis*, changes the sphere of reference of *arbitrium*. For *quamuis* with indicative, on analogy of *quamquam*, see Kühner-Stegmann ii. 2. 443, Lucr. 3. 403 and others, Verg. *Ecl.* 3. 84, etc.

3. 15 Introduction

This poem is clearly in 'chronological' sequel to 3. 14, and a very plausible third poem in a published sequence. It is presumably addressed to Cerinthus.

3. 15 Text and Notes

Scis iter ex animo sublatum triste puellae?
   natali Romae iam licet esse suo.
omnibus ille dies nobis natalis agatur,   3
   qui necopinanti nunc tibi forte uenit.

[no translation given in author's original]

1. The *iter* is surely the journey to Messalla's villa; the *iter triste* picks up the *natalis... tristis* of 3. 14. 1 f. The usual, and correct, translation/interpretation is as Lee 'the dreary journey's lifted from your girl's heart', i.e. the burdensome care caused by the imminent journey had been lifted from her. Sulpicia presupposes, or alludes to, an image which Catullus 31. 8 'cum mens onus reponit', Hor. *Epist.* 1. 5. 18 '(uinum) sollicitis animis onus eximit' make clear. Cf. too Plaut. *Cas.* 23 'eicite ex animo curam atque alienum aes', *Truc.* 454 'quanta est cura in animo', Catull. 2. 10 'tristis animi leuare curas', Lucr. 4. 908 'animi curas e pectore soluit', and for the construction *ex... sublatum* cf. Hor. *Serm.* 1. 1. 51 'at suaue est ex magno tollere aceruo', *tollere a* at Tibull. 1. 8. 45.

But I have no exact parallel for *ex animo tollere*: I cannot find one in *TLL animus*; but I cannot find our passage cited! Némethy took *ex animo* to mean 'to the liking' (of your girl), i.e. = *ex sententia*, and *sublatum* absolutely = 'lift', 'end'; Tränkle followed him, though taking *puellae* as dative rather than genitive; the supposed use of *tollo* is fine (see Tränkle), but *ex animo* on its own does not mean *ex sententia*; rather = 'sincerely', cf. Ter. *Eun.* 175, Catull. 109. 4, *OLD animus* 8b, *TLL animus* 99. 43 ff.[21]

2. (i) *iam licet* Scaliger's Fragmentum Cuiacianum (for F see Luck, pp. xxxvii, xiii, and, most usefully, Rouse and Reeve (1983), 424); also read by *excerpta Petrei* (for which see Luck, p. xviii = readings or conjectures of the Renaissance scholar Petreius): *non sinet* Z+. *iam licet* makes good sense (and is paralleled not surprisingly in 'Elegy'), and *non sinet* could be parablepsy from the last line of previous epigram, *non sinis*. (ii) *tuo* MSS including F, and Luck. Since the journey of 3. 15 presumably = the journey of 3. 14 (n. on line 1), we should expect the two birthdays to be one and the same (Sulpicia's); but *natali... tuo* could only refer to Cerinthus' birthday. This is accepted by Luck, but is surely wrong? *suo* Ald. and e.g. Lee: *meo* Huschke: *tuae* (codex Regius, acc. Luck = Renaissance MS? Not in his list). Tränkle obelises *tuo*, but thinks *tuae* is simplest. For *tuus* = 'your lover', cf. *meus* in 3. 13. 8 and other parallels in Tränkle's note here. But it gives us two different datives (*natali* and *tuae*). Tränkle finds *suo* much harder: because of absence of *ei* and the following *nobis*. But note *puellae* in preceding verse. Surely *suo* is the best correction? *meo* also possible, obviously.

3–4. Z+ read *omnibus ille dies nobis natalis agatur, | qui necopinanti nunc tibi forte uenit*. Lee accepts, 'Let the day that chance now brings you unexpectedly be spent as a birthday by us all'. At the moment I would go along with this.

In 3, objections have been felt since the Renaissance to *omnibus* (obelised by Luck; 'languet uersus', Heyne). I am not sure how strongly I feel this objection. Objection has also been felt to the repetition of *natali* (2) by *ille dies... natalis* (*ille dies* would be quite sufficient); and some indication of *how* the birthday is to be spent has been desired: both these points are met by reading *genialis*: cf. Juv. 4. 66 f. 'genialis agatur | iste dies', where *genialis* is predicative, as it would have to be here. But for repetition cf. how Sulpicia repeats *euincere morbos* in 3. 17.

---

[21] *Ex animi sententia* also means 'sincerely', *OLD sententia* 1c; on one occasion a sense *ex sententia* was punningly extracted from this phrase, Cic. *De Orat.* 2. 260, but that is hardly relevant to us, though Tränkle tries to make it so.

In 4 the objection to *necopinanti* is that Cerinthus *is* expecting the birthday; the defence is that he isn't in the sense that he doesn't expect Sulpicia to be around, he doesn't expect to be able to celebrate it with her. (*genialis* removes all objection.) Heyne thought this latter sense was better brought out by *necopinata... sorte*; Tränkle, accepting *necopinata*, defends *forte* as the true ablative of the subst. *fors* (rather than the adverbial *forte*), and compares *fors inopina* in Verg. *Aen.* 8. 476 f. Note that *necopinans* is, *necopinatus* is not, familiar in poetry (Tränkle; for the former cf. Lucr. 3. 959 'et nec opinanti mors ad caput adstitit ante';[22] but neither, be it noted, occurs in 'Elegy'; *necopinus, inopinus* in Ovid). Other conjectures: *quod* and *quam* for *qui*, neither of which is helpful. At the present I favour *necopinanti*.

3. 16 Text and Notes

> gratum est, securus multum quod iam tibi de me
>   permittis, subito ne male inepta cadam.
> sit tibi cura togae potior pressumque quasillo
>   scortum quam Serui filia Sulpicia:
> solliciti sunt pro nobis, quibus illa dolori est,
>   ne cedam ignoto maxima causa toro.

I'm glad you feel free and are so permissive to yourself about me—so that I don't fall into disgrace in my folly. Let toga-love and a tart weighed down by her wool basket be more powerful for you than Sulpicia daughter of Servius. People are concerned for me, those for whom this is the greatest cause of pain, namely that I should fall to the lot of a low-born bedmate.

1–2. For the two monosyllables at the end of line 1, see n. on 3. 17. 5. *gratum est... quod*, used ironically by Sulpicia, is a frequent formula in Cicero's letters. Cic. has *gratum est* more than thirty times in his letters (*TLL* s.v. 2261. 35 ff.), and very frequently constructed with the conj. *quod* (all the initial examples in *TLL*): cf. *Att.* 3. 20. 2, 4. 5. 3, etc., elliptically at 15. 7. 1 'gratum quod mihi epistulas'. Acc. to *TLL* it is rarely found outside this mass of examples in Cicero's letters (2261. 45 ff.). Cf. also Catull. 68. 1–11: but note the formality, disjunction, and artistry with which Catullus transmutes the construction. Sulpicia writes in authentic colloquialism, not a colloquialism colonised by poetry.

Cicero's uses cited in previous section obviously suggest Sulpicia's *quod* = conj., 'the fact that', and that makes good sense (but it is possible

---

[22] In a PHI check of all classical Latin, this is the only parallel for the dative form in dactylic verse.

that *quod* = relative, *Att.* 14. 20. 2 'quae de re mea gesta... grata', *Fam.* 13. 16. 4). *multum tibi de me* | *permittis* (*tibi* H, and conjectured by Heinsius : *mihi* Z+). *permitto* plus dative, 'allow, grant something to someone', *OLD* s.v. 6; it is used reflexively at Ov. *Her.* 8. 39, *Trist.* 2. 356, and there is a full list in Tränkle: this gives a good sense ('you're so permissive to yourself'), though the reflexive usage seems more natural to Ovid and Silver Latin. The construction with *de me* is not easy to parallel, though easy to understand (Lee '*re* me'): Tränkle compares Cic. *Att.* 12. 27. 2 'ipsi (sc. Marco) permittam de tempore', which is not quite the same. Is it the difficulty of *de me* which stimulates the reading/conjecture *promittis* which on the face of it looks less attractive than *permittis*? *promittis* then requires taking *securus* with *ne*, I suppose (see next para).

The final clause *subito ne*... This is I think best taken, not with *securus* (as Lee takes it; for this construction cf. Livy 39. 16. 6; and *subito* might incline us this way), but as an ironic 'pseudo-final' clause with *permittis*. Ironically Sulpicia interprets a *consequence* of Cerinthus' action as his *intention*: namely, that she should not fall into the error, disgrace... of marrying him, a person of lower social status than herself, the topic that is picked up in the last couplet. For *cado* in this sense see *OLD* s.v. 11 'be ruined, fall into disgrace, come to grief', and *male* intensifies *inepta*, cf. Catull. 10. 33 and other passages in Tränkle, and Fordyce on Catullus 10. 33 ('colloquial use... to reinforce a pejorative expression'). Note that Tränkle perhaps makes heavy weather of the sense of *cado*, but he is right that there is no overlap *cado* = *pecco* in sense of 'to make a sexual error' which is rather demanded by taking *ne*... with *securus*.

3–4. First the socio-sexology. The *toga* was 'worn by prostitutes and other *infames* to whom the *stola* was denied', *OLD* s.v. 2c; a prostitute could be called an (*ancilla*) *togata*, Hor. *Serm.* 1. 2. 63, 82 etc. *toga* in our poem (whether emended to *togae* or not) is more or less a metonymy; as Tränkle says, it is very like some metonymies in modern vernaculars; he cites uses of *stola* as metonymy for posh ladies. Spinstresses were often lowly slaves: cf. Petron. 132. 3 'non contenta mulier tam graui iniuria mea, conuocat omnes quasillarias familiaeque sordidissimam partem ac me conspui iubet'. For *scortum*, a symposiastic tart, see Lyne (1980), 197–8.

So: Sulpicia characterises her rival as a whore engaged in spinning. Tränkle wonders whether we are to imagine her practising both occupations at the same time, or as an ex- (spinning) slave who now practises the profession of prostitute as a freedwoman. Let's not get too literal-minded! We should allow in all this for the exaggeration and rhetoric of the embittered S., and the illogicality that that brings (as it were, 'your new girlfriend's just a servant and a tart'). And the underlying reality to this snobbery and abuse may merely be that the rival is not actually noble like Sulpicia, but who knows.

sit Z+, Lee, Tränkle. New sentence. 'Let your care for a prostitute... be greater than...' Renaissance manuscripts read, and Heinsius conjectured, *si... toga est.* This gives us equivalence between the substantives (*toga, scortum, filia*, with *cura* now predicative, for which cf. *fama* in 3. 13. 2); with the paradosis, *cura* lines up as subject nominative with *scortum* and *filia*, a slight asymmetry (*toga, scortum, filia* is logical, and so would be *cura togae... scorti*, but the latter doesn't help given the following unchangeable *filia*). *toga est* demands that *sit* go of course. Luck reads *si* even though he keeps *togae*. Surely *sit* is better in tune with the bitterness and irony of the poem, and see notes on 3. 18 for Sulpicia's fondness for jussive subjunctives. Plenty of parallels for the slight asymmetry of pairing (*cura togae, scortum...*) in Tränkle, and the desirability of *sit* is decisive for me in rejecting Heinsius. Tränkle also thinks the elision *toga est* is unlikely in Sulpicia. *Serui* does pun nicely on *seruus*: see Hinds (1987).

quasillus was the basket in which the unspun wool was kept. Cf. Prop. 4. 7. 41 'et grauiora rependit iniquis pensa quasillis'. Sulpicia means *pressum* in sense of 'oppressed', 'burdened'; she is not thinking of the girl physically carrying it—that wasn't its burdensome aspect. No other example of *quasillum/-us* besides ours and Prop. in poetry (but found e.g. 4 times in Cato *Rust.*, at Cic. *Phil.* 3. 10): too real for poetry, which preferred the Grecism *calathus*. Sulpicia is using arrestingly real diction, as she does even more strikingly with *scortum* (twice in Catullus, not otherwise in 'Elegy'; in Horace exceptionally at *Carm.* 2. 11. 21, less strikingly at *Epist.* 1. 18. 34), and, in this sense, with *toga* (not thus in 'Elegy', nor, besides the examples mentioned above, in Horace).

5–6. *ne* (Q) and *cedam* (M, and Statius) are essential. *solliciti sunt* refers surely to the *boni* in Sulpicia's family; though it has been an orthodoxy (says Tränkle) that rivals of Cerinthus are referred to. *sollicitus pro*: Cic. *Amic.* 45 etc., but prosaic. Construction of the couplet: *illa* subject of the relative clause (attracted to predicate), *maxima causa* predicate in the relative clause, and the *ne cedam* clause unpacking *illa* (Scaliger). Plenty of parallels for the hyperbaton of *maxima causa* in Housman (1972), i. 140 f., 415 ff., (Lucr., Catull. Verg., Ovid, etc.). So (literally): 'people are concerned for me, for whom this is the greatest cause of pain, namely that I should fall to the lot of a low-born bedmate.' *doloris* is proposed in place of the transmitted *dolori est* to avoid the two datives *quibus* and *dolori*; discussed by Tränkle. (Others construe *ne cedam* with *solliciti sunt*, have *maxima causa* in apposition to the subject of the *ne* clause, i.e. = Sulpicia, and comma off *quibus illa* [= the *scortum*] *dolori est*. Not possible—which is why we find the *maxima cura* of G[2] and the Aldine: there was a desire to read the text in this way.)

ignoto toro refers surely to Cerinthus (but see below); but *ignoto* (*OLD* 3 'obscure', 'inconspicuous') may, like *toga* etc., be the exaggeration of an embittered, jilted girl; see above under Section IV 'Cerinthus' he may simply be not as flash as the niece of Messalla and the daughter of Servius Sulpicius. The phrase *ignotus torus* recurs at 3. 6. 60: the only parallel cited by *TLL ignotus* 322. 70, and the only parallel I can find from a PHI search of all classical Latin. For the metonymy in *torus* cf. Ov. *Her.* 8. 26, Val. 5. 444.

Sense of *cedam*: 'fall to' 'pass to' 'become the property of', *OLD* 15, normally obviously of things, but also of women in, say, time of war (cf. Verg. *Aen.* 12. 17, also 3. 297). Some think: 'yield', 'give place to', and think the *ignotus torus* refers, not to Cerinthus, but to the *scortum*. Surely the former is preferable, and forceful writing.

3. 17 Introduction

For the theme of the girl's illness in Elegy see Tibull. 1. 5. 9–18, Prop. 2. 9. 25–8, 2. 28, Ov. *Ars* 2. 315–36 (321 'tunc amor et pietas tua sit manifesta puellae'), cf. too Ov. *Her.* 20 and 21 (Acontius and Cydippe); 3. 17 seems to have prompted the Cycle poet to 3. 10.

3. 17 Text and Notes

> Estne tibi, Cerinthe, tuae pia cura puellae,
>   quod mea nunc uexat corpora fessa calor?
> a, ego non aliter tristes euincere morbos
>   optarim, quam te si quoque uelle putem.
> at mihi quid prosit morbos euincere, si tu
>   nostra potes lento pectore ferre mala?

Do you feel real concern, Cerinthus for your girl, that a fever afflicts my wearied body? Ah, I would not wish to cure this woeful illness, unless I thought that you wanted it too. What would it profit me to cure the illness, if you can bear my suffering with a cold heart?

1. *Estne tibi* is a line-beginning unparalleled in PHI, but *estne* occurs at Catullus 66. 15 (as a line-beginning), at Hor. *Serm.* 2. 7. 61, in Silver Latin poetry, and frequently in prose. Note that the important phrase *pia cura* is in fact an emendation, a Renaissance MS reading, also independently conjectured by Heinsius (Luck's irritatingly unexplained abbreviation 'Voss. 4' = a Leidensis, the penultimate entry on p. xxix); the paradosis is *placitura*, emended to *placiture* by G²V², to give a semblance of sense. The only parallels

for the phrase before 4th cent. AD are (says Tränkle):[23] Ov. *Am.* 2. 16. 47 'si qua mei tamen est in te pia cura relicti' (Ovid is in Sulmo without his girl), where the phrase occurs in same metrical position and construction; *Her.* 8. 15 (Hermione to Orestes) 'at tu, cura mei si te pia tangit, Oreste...'. And cf. *Ars* above. The sense is good in Sulpicia, as *Ars* 2. 321 shows (*pia*, 'faithful', 'dutiful'), and I can see no necessary dependence on Ovid, or vice versa.

2. *quod* (Z) OK (see introduction to 3. 18, below): there are variants, and Heinsius proposed *dum calor* of fever is a medical term (Celsus), only thus in poetry at Juv. 12. 98, says Tränkle: see indeed *TLL* s.v. 181. 29 ff. 'de febre' which cites first our line, then 'Celsus 3. 3 (20^{ies}), Sen. *Dial.* 5. 10. 3', and so on, incl. the Juvenal. Sulpicia uses what was probably technical–medical and thence everyday language (cf. *euincere morbos* in next line, and say 'temperature' for fever in English: technical, everyday, but not very poetical). *corpora fessa*: cf. 3. 10. 10, in the Cycle poem this one prompts (*TLL corpus* 1008. 55), and at Cic. *Arat.* 68, Catull. 64. 189, and others (*TLL* 1016. 45–9). *uexat corpora*: under verbs meaning 'affligere, debilitare, uexare...' 1012. 10 ff., *TLL corpus* in fact cites NO example of *uexo*! A search of all classical Latin in PHI turns up the following: Livy 45. 39. 19 'ego hoc ferro saepe uexatum corpus uetus miles adulescentibus militibus ostendi', Cic. *Tusc.* 4. 18. 10 'sollicitudo aegritudo cum cogitatione, molestia aegritudo permanens, adflictatio aegritudo cum vexatione corporis, desperatio aegritudo sine ulla rerum expectatione meliorum', Sen. *Epist.* 78. 10. 3, and Columela, *RR* 6. 2. 11 of *corporis uexationem* of animals. Sulpicia's phrase is slightly prosy. Pity it is not in Celsus!

3. *a ego.* Same verse-beginning at 3. 4. 82 (Lygdamus again: see paragraph 14 for 3. 16. 6); see Tränkle ad loc. No other example in 'Elegy', nor can I find any in all classical Latin in PHI, but my search failed to produce the two examples in Corp. Tib. *o ego* at Tibull. 2. 3. 5, 2. 4. 7, Ov. *Her.* 6. 15, *Met.* 2. 520, 8. 51, 9. 487, *Pont.* 1. 4. 49, *Nux* 159; all these are verse-beginnings. For *o* and *a*, see Ross (1969), 49–53 (better on *a* than *o*). *euincere morbos* (*-um*) is only to be found otherwise (Tränkle) at Celsus 3. 22. 8, Colum. 6. 5. 2, and Vegetius, *Mulomedicina* 4. 3. 6; further similar phrases with *euincere* in Celsus and Vegetius. Again Sulpicia uses a technical–medical/everyday phrase? The verb *euinco* in 'Elegy' at Ov. *Her.* 19. 155, *Met.* 1. 685, *Pont.* 3. 1. 31, and others in Ovid. In 'Elegy' I find only Tibull. 1. 5. 9 as a parallel for the collocatation *tristis morbus*: '*ille ego*, cum tristi morbo *defessa* iaceres...', which has other (underlined) points of contact with our poem. *TLL morbus* citing our line (1479. 33) is uninterested in the epithet, and doesn't seem to cite 1. 5. 9.

---

[23] Cf. *TLL cura* 1462. 12 f.; Tränkle cleans up some errors here. My own PHI search for the exact phrase *pia cura* produced only the *Amores* 2. 16. 47 example.

3–4. *aliter... quam.* In 'Elegy' I find this example, and twenty-one in Ovid.
4. *optarim* in 'Elegy' at Tibull. 1. 6. 74 and Ov. *Her.* 17. 109. Hyperbaton of *quoque.* Tränkle finds examples in Lucretius, but that otherwise it is 'extraordinarily rare' (one example cited in Ovid, one in Martial).
5. *at* F (= Cuiacianum, see above): *a(h)* vel *ha* Z, and *nam* and *an* are conjectured.

si G²V², Heinsius and others : *quid* AFVX : *quod* CG : *ubi* Scaliger : *quom* Baehrens from a MS of the second half of the fifteenth century, the Bernensis. I think we must prefer *si*, in spite of the *quom* in the 'new' Gallus (below); *quid* arose through dittography. Tränkle: in elegiac poetry, two monosyllables at the end of hexameter, with sense pause before, occur 'otherwise almost exclusively in the first three books of Propertius and in the new Gallus fragment'; Gallus fr. 2. 2 Courtney 'fata mihi, Caesar, tum erunt mea dulcia, quom tu | maxima Romanae pars eris historiae...'. Best figures in Norden (1957), 448, though Norden does not bother about preceding sense pause. Here we learn e.g. that Tibullus in Books 1 and 2 only has one example of hexameter ending in two monosyllables (1. 4. 63; Lygdamus none; Sulpicia here, and 3. 16. 1), while Propertius has thirty-two examples.

6. *lento pectore.* The same phrase at [Ovid] *Her.* 15. 169 f. The sense of *lentus* is well paralleled: *OLD* 8, 'slow to feel emotion', cf. too the *TLL* entries at 1163. 14 ff. 'quietus', 'remissus', including Verg. *Ecl.* 1. 4 'tu Tityre lentus in umbra', Prop. 1. 6. 12 'pereat si quis lentus amare potest', 3. 8. 20 'hostibus eueniat lenta puella meis'); but the only exact parallel for the collocation in *TLL* is *Her.* 15. 169 f. (*TLL* 1163. 78).

3. 18 Introduction

The paradosis joins this to the previous poem; also, most MSS contributing to the paradosis transmit the poem twice, here and after 3. 6, i.e. at the end of the Lygdamus collection. In neither place do we find, I think, manuscripts offering any serious challenge to the received text of 3. 18. 3. 17 and 18 cannot be one poem. Are the two oddities of transmission connected?

This poem shows many unusual syntactical features (cf. Lowe (1988), 198), which—when we compare other poems—we see Sulpicia has an idiosyncratic fondness for. (i) (Sub-) subordination of syntax (in the other poems, except 3. 14 and 15). This is not syntax that a forger would obviously attribute to a female poet, I think. (ii) A liking for comparative constructions: 3. 18. 1–2 *aeque... ac*, 13. 1–2 *magis... quam*, 16. 3–4 *potior... quam*, 17. 3–4 *aliter... quam*, and cf. the tmesis *ante... quam* in 3. 13. 8. (iii) Jussive subjunctives (3. 18. 1, 13. 5, 14. 5, 15. 3, 16. 3). (iii) the ('focusing') use of *iam* (and *nunc*) 3. 18. 1, 14. 5, 15. 2, 16. 1,

17. 2. (iv) The *quod* noun clause 3. 18. 5, 16. 1, 17. 2. (v) Fondness for infinitives as penultimate word in pentameter (perfects at 3. 18. 2, 4, 13. 6, 10, presents with trochee shape at 3. 18. 6, 14. 8, 15. 2, 17. 4, 6. Perfect infinitive as penultimate word in hexameter in 3. 13. 1. Other perfect infinitives: 3. 13. 2, 9. Elegiac poets are fond of perfect infinitive, straying into areas where we might expect present infinitive (Platnauer (1951), 109–12). One suspects that the way in which, and the degree to which, Sulpicia uses infinitives is influenced by metrical convenience. At 3. 13. 6 it looks as if the periphrasis *dicetur...habuisse* is there simply to contrive the metrically convenient penult *-isse*. Tibullus can be indicted on the same grounds: he has *dicitur* (useful dactyl) plus penult perf. infinitive at: 1. 2. 53 f., 1. 3. 10, 2. 3. 18, 2. 5. 20, with (esp. in last) no pressing semantic need for the construction. Also *dicor...eripuisse* at Tibull. 1. 5. 10. Remember too Tibullus' hyperbaton of *-que*, also *-ue*, a metrical cheat.

The overall syntax of the poem, *ne tibi sim...si*, 3. 18. 1 ff. follows a colloquial type: Cic. *Att.* 4. 17. 5 'ne uiuam, <si> scio', 12. 3. 1 'ne uiuam, mi Attice, si...', 16. 13a. 1 'ne sim saluus, si aliter scribo ac sentio', *Fam.* 7. 23. 4 'ne uiuam, si tibi concedo...'; these are the examples of the *ne...si* locution cited under *OLD ne* 4. The construction looks colloquial. Further investigation confirms this. Kühner–Stegmann i. 190 f. include these Ciceronian *ne...* examples under the heading 'subjunctive in asseverations, in old Latin esp. in the formula *ita me di ament* vel sim.': K–S kick off with Plaut. *Poen.* 1258 'ita me di seruent, ut hic pater est noster'. They then have many such positive examples in Comedy, then more positive ones in Cicero's letters, then the negative examples cited above, then yet more positive ones in Cic. letters, and positive examples in Hor. *Serm.* 2. 1. 6, and other works of Cicero besides the letters. The positive examples so far cited by K–S are either plain subjunctive or (usually) with *ita*. They finally say: 'poetic also with *sic*, as Verg. *Ecl.* 9. 30 etc., Hor. *Odes* 1. 3. 1, and so on'. So it looks as if Sulpicia, with her *ne tibi sim...si* is again using a real colloquialism, one not colonised by poetry: cf. *gratum est...quod* above.

The poem also has strong Catullan affiliations. Structurally (one long sentence), the poem recalls Catull. 75, 81, 82, 96, 102, 103; note too that the line-beginning of 96. 1, 102. 1, also 107. 1 *si quicquam* = the line-beginning of 3. 18. 3. See further below on line 3.

> *Si quicquam* mutis gratum acceptumue sepulcris
>   accidere a nostro, Calue, dolore potest,
> quo desiderio ueteres renouamus amores
>   atque olim iunctas flemus amicitias,
> certe non tanto mors immatura dolorist
>   Quintiliae, quantum gaudet amore tuo.
>
>   (Catullus 96)

Si quicquam tacito commissumst fido ab amico,
    cuius sit penitus nota fides animi,
me aeque esse inuenies illorum iure sacratum,
    Corneli, et factum me esse puta Harpocraten.

(Catullus 102)

3. 18 Text and Notes

ne tibi sim, mea lux, aeque iam feruida cura
    ac uideor paucos ante fuisse dies,
si quicquam tota commisi stulta iuuenta,
    cuius me fatear paenituisse magis,
hesterna quam te solum quod nocte reliqui,
    ardorem cupiens dissimulare meum.

Let me no more, my love, be as fervent a care to you as I seem to have been a few days past, if in all my youth I have committed any folly which I should confess I more regretted than leaving you alone yesterday night, desiring to keep my passion secret.

1. In regular prose *cura* would be dative, but cf. 3. 13. 1–2 and n.; *TLL cura* 1456. 43 ff. gives many examples of *curae est, aliquis alicui*, starting with Turpil. *com.* 156 'cui ego sim curae', and citing both prose and verse. At 1455. 10 ff. *cura est, aliquis alicui* it cites only *Epic. Drusi* 196 'nos erimus magno maxima cura Ioui' and 302 (it does not cite our line); under (13 ff.) *aliquid alicui*, it cites Cic. *Att.* 10. 8. 4 'naualis apparatus ei semper antiquissima cura fuit', Tibull. 1. 9. 34 (incorrectly), and two or three later examples. The combination *feruida cura* occurs only here (Tränkle; I have confirmed this by a PHI search; *TLL cura, epitheta,* 1461. 45 ff. does not cite *feruidus* at all), but cf. Hor. *Odes* 1. 30. 5 'feruidus puer' of Cupid. For the phrase *mea lux, lux mea*, see *TLL lux* 1915. 8 ff. Catull. 68. 132 and 160 etc., most usually as a vocative form of address like ours: other instances (of the voc.) Cic. *Fam.* 14. 2. 2 and Ov. *Trist.* 3. 3. 52 both to wives, Prop. 2. 14. 29, 2. 28. 59, 2. 29. 1, then examples in Ovid and others (note Phaedr. ref. should be *Appendix* 29. 7); all addressed to women. Addressed to a man, only elsewhere at Ov. *Ars* 3. 523–4 'scilicet Aiaci mulier maestissima dixit | "lux mea" quaeque solent uerba iuuare uiros', and the probable imitation of our line in the Cycle, 3. 9. 15.

3. On *si quicquam* see above. Note esp. Catull. 102. 1 f. 'si quicquam... | cuius' although there the relative *cuius* does not refer to *quicquam*. *tota iuuenta*: *iuuenta* 'legitur maxime in poesi inde a Cic. ... Catull. ..., in prosa inde a Liv., Val. Max.' *TLL* cites neither our line nor any parallel for

tota... iuuenta, but cf. Cic. *Carm.* fr. 11. 1 Courtney 'prima a parte iuuentae', Verg. *Aen.* 4. 32 'perpetua... iuuenta', Catull. 109. 5 'tota... uita'. A PHI search of all classical Latin reveals only Val. Flacc. 3. 682 as a variant for the phrase *tota iuuentus* for 'all the youth'.

4. *paenituisse* (*sic*) occurs otherwise in 'Elegy' six times in Ovid.

5. *hesterna... nocte*: poetical. *TLL hesternus* cites the phrase (i.q. nox modo praeterlapsa) otherwise at Tibull. 2. 1. 12 'discedat ab aris | cui tulit hesterna gaudia nocte Venus', Lygdamus [Tibull.] 3. 4. 2, Prop. 2. 29. 1 'hesterna, *mea lux*, cum potus nocte uagarer' (note also *m. lux*), Ov. *Her.* 19 (18). 72 and 193 'hesternae confundor imagine noctis', Mart. 1. 27. 1, Gell. 8. 1. title *h. noctu*. Cf. Prop. 3. 8. 1 'hesternas... lucernas'. The phrase *hesterno die* i.q. heri is a regular prose phrase, *TLL hesternus* 2668. 15 ff. For *te solum... reliqui*, cf. Catull. 64. 200 'quali solam Theseus me mente reliquit', Lygdamus [Tibull.] 3. 6. 40 'Cnosia, Theseae quondam periuria linguae | fleuisti ignoto sola relicta mari' (a direct allusion to Catullus 64, as the next line shows), Prop. 2. 24b. 46 'sola relicta' (Medea), etc. (We could think about gender role-reversal.)

6. *ardor* of the fire of love is 'fairly common since Lucretius and Catullus' (Tränkle). Cf. Catull. 2. 8, Prop. 1. 7. 24, 1. 10. 10 and other examples cited by Pichon s.v. The verb *dissimulo* is used otherwise in 'Elegy' twice in Tibullus (1. 8. 7 and 44) and 49 times in Ovid. 3. 18. 6 is a climactic (?) four-word pentameter (6 words in line 2, 5 words in 4, 4 in 6), though I don't know what to build on this. Cf. the three-word pentameter in Catull. 68. 74.

Bibliography of Oliver Lyne

(* = included in this volume ; ‡ = books)

1. 'Horace, *Epod.* 5.95 and *Ciris* 268 ff.', *Latomus* 28 (1969), 694–6.
2. 'The Constraints of Metre and the *Ciris*: a brief note', *Latomus* 28 (1969), 1065–7.
3. * 'Propertius and Cynthia: *Elegy* I.3', *PCPS* 16 (1970), 60–78.
4. 'Prop. IV,4,65 sqq. and Pind., *Pyth.* IX,23 sqq.', *Hermes* 99 (1971), 376–8.
5. 'The Dating of the *Ciris*', *CQ* 21 (1971), 233–53.
6. '*Ciris* 85–6', *CR* 21 (1971), 323–4.
7. 'The *recentiores* of the *Ciris*', *PCPS* 18 (1972), 43–9.
8. 'A New Collation of the Graz Fragment (Steiermärkisches Landesarchiv Hs. 1814)', *WS* 6 (1972), 79–92.
9. *Lyne, R. O. A. M. and Morwood, J. H. W., 'Critical Appreciations: I: Propertius III,10', *G&R* 20 (1973), 38–48.
10. * 'Propertius I,5', *Mnemosyne* 27 (1974), 262–9.
11. * '*Scilicet et tempus veniet*... Virgil, *Georgics* 1.463–514', in T. Woodman and D. West (eds.), *Quality and Pleasure in Latin Poetry* (Cambridge, 1974), 47–66.
12. '*Ciris* 89–91', *CQ* 25 (1975), 156–7.
13. ‡ *Selections from Catullus: Handbook* (Cambridge, 1975).
14. ‡ (ed./comm./introd.), *Ciris. A Poem Attributed to Vergil* (Cambridge, 1978).
15. * 'The Neoteric Poets', *CQ* 28 (1978), 167–87.
16. * '*Servitium Amoris*', *CQ* 29 (1979), 117–30.
17. ‡ *The Latin Love Poets from Catullus to Horace* (Oxford, 1980).
18. * *Virgil: The* Eclogues, *the* Georgics, trans. C. Day Lewis; with introduction (pp. i–xx) and notes by R. O. A. M. Lyne (Oxford, 1983).
19. * 'Vergil and the Politics of War', *CQ* 33 (1983), 188–203.
20. * 'Lavinia's Blush: Vergil, *Aeneid* 12.64–70', *G&R* 30 (1983), 55–64.
21. 'La voce privata di Virgilio nell'*Eneide*', *MusPat* 2 (1984), 5–21.
22. 'The Text of Catullus CVII', *Hermes* 113 (1985), 498–500.
23. * 'Ovid's *Metamorphoses*, Callimachus, and *l'art pour l'art*', *MD* 12 (1984), 9–34.
24. 'Diction and Poetry in Virgil's *Aeneid*', *Atti del convegno mondiale scientifico di studi su Virgilio* (Milan, 1984), ii. 64–88.
25. 'Augustan Poetry and Society', in J. Boardman, J. Griffin, and J. Murray (eds.), *The Oxford History of the Classical World* (Oxford, 1986), 592–615.
26. ‡ *Further Voices in Vergil's Aeneid* (Oxford, 1987).
27. ‡ *Words and the Poet. Characteristic Techniques of Style in Vergil's Aeneid* (Oxford, 1989).
28. 'Words and The Poet: Characteristic Techniques of Style in Vergil's *Aeneid*', *SIFC* 10 (1992), 255–70.

29. * 'Vergil's *Aeneid*: Subversion by Intertextuality: Catullus 66.39–40 and Other Examples', *G&R* 41 (1994), 187–204.
30. ‡ *Horace: Behind the Public Poetry* (London and New Haven, Conn., 1995).
31. *Propertius, The Poems*; trans. with notes by G. Lee.; with an introduction by R. O. A. M. Lyne (New York, 1994), pp. ix–xxiii.
32. 'Propertius, Sextus', in S. Hornblower and A. Spawforth (eds.), *Oxford Classical Dictionary*, 3rd edn. (Oxford, 1996), 1258–9.
33. 'Tibullus, Albius', in S. Hornblower and A. Spawforth (eds.), *Oxford Classical Dictionary*, 3rd edn. (Oxford, 1996), 1524.
34. * 'Introductory Poems in Propertius: 1.1 and 2.12', *PCPS* 44 (1998), 158–81.
35. * 'Love and Death: Laodamia and Protesilaus in Catullus, Propertius, and Others', *CQ* 48 (1998), 200–12.
36. * 'Propertius 2.10 and 11 and the Structure of Books "2a" and "2b"', *JRS* 88 (1998), 21–36.
37. * 'Propertius and Tibullus: Early Exchanges', *CQ* 48 (1998), 519–44.
38. 'Don Paul Fowler', *MD* 43 (1999), 11–13.
39. 'Don Paul Fowler †', *Gnomon* 73 (2001), 186–8.
40. * 'Notes on Catullus', *CQ* 52 (2002), 600–8.
41. * 'Horace *Odes* Book 1 and the Alexandrian Edition of Alcaeus', *CQ* 55 (2005), 542–58.
42. * 'Structure and Allusion in Horace's Book of *Epodes*', *JRS* 95 (2005), 1–19.
43. * '[Tibullus] Book III and Sulpicia' [unpublished paper, 2004–5].

References

ADAMS, J. N. (1982), *The Latin Sexual Vocabulary* (London).
—— and MAYER, R. G. (eds.) (1999), *Aspects of the Language of Latin Poetry* (Oxford).
ALLEN, A. W. (1950), 'Elegy and the classical attitude toward love: Propertius I.1', *YCS* 11: 255–77.
—— (1962), '*Sunt qui Propertium malint*', in Sullivan (1962).
ALLEN, W. (1972), 'Ovid's *Cantare* and Cicero's *Cantores Euphorionis*', *TAPA* 103: 1–14.
ANDRÉ, J. (1949), *Étude sur les termes de couleur dans la langue latine* (Paris).
ARNOLD, E. V. (1911), *Roman Stoicism* (London).
ARNOTT, W. G. (2000), *Menander: Volume III* (Cambridge, Mass.).
AUSTIN, R. G. (1964), *P. Vergili Maronis Aeneidos Liber Secundus* (Oxford).
AXELSON, B. (1945), *Unpoetische Wörter* (Lund).
—— (1960a), 'Lygdamus und Ovid', *Eranos* 58: 92–11.
—— (1960b), 'Das Geburtsjahr des Lygdamus', *Eranos* 58: 281–97.
BABCOCK, C. (1978), '*Epodes* 13. Some Comments on Language and Meaning', in Riechel (1978), 107–18.
BADIAN, E. (1985), 'A Phantom Marriage Law', *Philologus* 129: 82–98.
BALSDON, J. P. V. D. (1962), *Roman Women* (London).
—— (1979), *Romans and Aliens* (London).
BARCHIESI, A. (1980), 'Le molte voci di Omero. Intertestualità e trasformazione del modello epico nel decimo dell'*Eneide*', *MD* 4: 9–58.
—— (1997), *The Poet and the Prince* (Berkeley and London).
BARDON, H. (1952–6), *La Littérature latine inconnue*. 2 vols. (Paris).
—— (1973), *Catullus* (Stuttgart).
BASSETT, S. E. (1923), 'Hector's Fault in Honor', *TAPA* 54: 117–27.
BEARE, R. (1964), 'Invidious Success: Some Thoughts on the End of the *Aeneid*', *PVS* 4: 18–30.
BELL, A. J. (1923), *The Latin Dual and Poetic Diction* (Oxford).
BERGK, Th. (1883), *Griechische Literaturgeschichte* (Berlin).
BINDER, G. (1971), *Aeneas und Augustus* (Meisenheim).
BIRT, T. (1882), *Das antike Buchwesen in seinem Verhältnis zur Litteratur* (Berlin).
—— (1909), 'Zur Monobiblos und zum Codex N des Properz', *RhM* 64: 393–411.
—— (1915), 'Die Funfzahl und die Properzchronologie', *Rheinisches Museum* 70: 253–314.
BLANCHARD, A., and BATAILLE, A. (1964), 'Fragments sur papyrus du *CIKYΩNIOC* de Ménandre', *Recherches de Papyrologie* 3: 103–67.
BLUMENTHAL, H. J. (1978), 'Callimachus, Epigram 28, Numenius Fr. 20, and the Meaning of κυκλικός', *CQ* 28: 125–7.

BOARDMAN, J., GRIFFIN, J., and MURRAY, O. (eds.) (1986), *The Oxford History of the Classical World* (Oxford).
BOUCHER, J.-P. (1965), *Études sur Properce* (Paris).
—— (1966), *Caius Cornélius Gallus* (Paris).
BOWIE, E. L. (1987), 'One that Got Away', in Whitby et al. (1987), 13–23.
BOWRA, C. M. (1933–4), 'Aeneas and the Stoic Ideal', *G&R* 3: 8–21.
—— (1961), *Greek Lyric Poetry* (Oxford).
—— (1964), *Pindar* (Oxford).
BRAMBLE, J. C. (1974), *Persius and the Programmatic Satire* (Cambridge).
BRINGMANN, K. (1973), 'Catulls Carmen 96 und die Quintilia-Elegie des Calvus', *MH* 30: 25–31.
BRINK, C. O. (1982a), 'Horatian Notes' *PCPS* 37: 30–56.
—— (1982b), *Horace on Poetry*. Epistles Book II (Cambridge).
BRINK, K. O. (1946), 'Callimachus and Aristotle: An Inquiry into Callimachus' *ΠΡΟΣ ΠΡΑΞΙΦΑΝΗΝ*', *CQ* 40: 11–26.
BROWN, C. (1983), 'From Rags to Riches: Anacreon's Artemon', *Phoenix* 37: 1–15.
BROWN, R. D. (1987), *Lucretius on Love and Sex* (Leiden).
BRUNT P. (1971a), *Social Conflicts in the Roman Republic* (London).
—— (1971b), *Italian Manpower 225 B.C.–A.D. 14* (Oxford).
—— (1978), 'Laus Imperii', in Garnsey and Whittaker (1978), 159–91.
BÜHLER, W. (1960), *Die Europa des Moschos* (Wiesbaden).
BUTLER, H. E., and BARBER, E. A. (1933), *The Elegies of Propertius* (Oxford).
CAIRNS, F. (1972), *Generic Composition in Greek and Roman Poetry* (Edinburgh).
—— (1974), 'Some Observations on Propertius 1.1', *CQ* 24: 94–110.
—— (1979), *Tibullus: A Hellenistic Poet at Rome* (Cambridge).
CAMERON, A. (1970), *Agathias* (Oxford).
—— (1980), 'Poetae Novelli', *HSCP* 84: 167–72.
—— (1995), *Callimachus and his Critics* (Princeton).
CAMPBELL, D. A. (1982), *Greek Lyric: Vol. I* (Cambridge, Mass.).
—— (1988), *Greek Lyric: Vol. II* (Cambridge, Mass.).
CAMPBELL, O. J., and QUINN, E. G. (1967), *A Shakespeare Encyclopaedia* (London).
CAMPS, W. A. (1961), *Propertius Elegies Book I* (Cambridge).
—— (1966), *Propertius Elegies Book III* (Cambridge).
—— (1967), *Propertius Elegies Book II* (Cambridge).
CARCOPINO, J. (1941), *Daily Life in Ancient Rome* (London).
CASSAGNE, A. (1906), *La Théorie de l'art pour l'art en France* (Paris).
CAVARZERE, A. (1992), *Il libro degli* Epodi (Venice).
CAZZANIGA, I. (1961), 'Catullo 68b, 50–60 e i vv. 1–7 del papiro Lond. di Partenio di Nicea', *PP* 16: 124–6.
CHARLESWORTH, M. P. (1952), 'The Avenging of Caesar', in Cook et al. (1952), 1–30.
CHRIST, W. VON (1868), 'Die Verskunst des Horaz', *Sitzungsberichte der Königlichen bayerischen Akademie der Wissenschaften zu München*: 1–44.
CLAUSEN, W. (1964), 'Callimachus and Roman Poetry', *GRBS* 5: 181–96.
—— (1966), 'An Interpretation of the *Aeneid*' in Commager (1966), 75–88.

CLAUSEN, W. (1994), *A Commentary on Virgil's* Eclogues (Oxford).
CLAYMAN, D. L. (1980), *Callimachus's* Iambi (Leiden).
COATES, J. (ed.) (1998), *Language and Gender: A Reader* (Oxford).
COLEMAN, R. (1977), *Vergil:* Eclogues (Cambridge).
COLEMAN, R. G. G. (1999), 'Poetic Diction and the Poetic Registers', in Adams and Mayer (1999), 21–96.
COMMAGER, S. (1962), *The Odes of Horace* (New Haven and London).
—— (1966), *Virgil, a Collection of Critical Essays* (Englewood Cliffs, NJ).
CONINGTON, J., and NETTLESHIP, H. (1963), *The Works of Virgil.* 3 vols., repr. (Hildesheim).
CONRAD, C. (1965), 'Traditional Patterns of Word Order in Latin Epic from Ennius to Vergil', *HSCP* 69: 195–258.
CONTE, G. B. (1980), *Il genere e i suoi confini* (Turin; 2nd edn. 1984).
—— (1992), 'Proems in the Middle', in Dunn and Cole (1992), 147–59.
COOK, S. A., ADCOCK, F. E., and CHARLESWORTH, M. P. (1952), *The Cambridge Ancient History X: The Augustan Empire, 44 B.C.–A.D. 70* (Cambridge).
COPLEY, F. O. (1947), '"Seruitium amoris" in the Roman Elegists', *TAPA* 78: 285–300.
—— (1956), *Exclusus Amator: A Study in Latin Love Poetry* (Madison, Wis.).
COURTNEY, E. (1993), *The Fragmentary Latin Poets* (Oxford).
CROWTHER, N. B. (1970), '*OI NEΩTEPOI, Poetae Novi,* and *Cantores Euphorionis*', *CQ* 20: 322–7.
—— (1971), 'Catullus and the Traditions of Latin Poetry', *CP* 66: 246–9.
—— (1976), 'Parthenius and Roman Poetry', *Mnemosyne* 29: 65–71.
CRUMP, M. M. (1931), *The Epyllion from Theocritus to Ovid* (Oxford).
CURRAN, L. C. (1966), 'Vision and Reality in Propertius 1.3' *YCS* 19: 189–207.
DALE, A. M. (1954), Euripides, Alcestis (Oxford).
DAVIES, M. (1989), *The Epic Cycle* (Bristol).
DAVIS, G. (1991), *Polyhymnia: The Rhetoric of Horatian Lyric Discourse* (Oxford).
DAWSON, C. M. (1950), 'The *Iambi* of Callimachus', *YCS* 11: 1–168.
DE JONG, I. J. F., and SULLIVAN, J. P. (eds.) (1994), *Modern Critical Theory and Classical Literature* (Leiden).
DETTMER, H. (1983), *Horace: A Study in Structure* (New York).
DISSEN, L. (1835), *Albii Tibulli Carmina* (Göttingen).
DUCKWORTH, G. E. (1952), *The Nature of Roman Comedy* (Princeton).
DUFF, J. W., and DUFF, A. M. (1961), *Minor Latin Poets* (Cambridge, Mass.).
DUNN, F. M. and COLE, T. (eds.) (1992), *Beginnings in Classical Literature* (Cambridge).
EARL, D. C. (1967), *The Moral and Political Tradition of Rome* (London).
ECO, U. (1984), *Postille a 'Il nome della rosa'* (Milan).
—— (1995), *Il nome della rosa* (Milan).
EDWARDS, M. W. (1961), 'Intensification of Meaning in Propertius and Others', *TAPA* 92: 128–44.
EHRENBERG, V., and JONES, A. H. M. (1955), *Documents Illustrating the Reigns of Augustus and Tiberius* (Oxford).
EISENHUT, W. (1983), *Catullus* (Leipzig).
ELDER, J. P. (1947), 'Catullus' *Attis*', *AJP* 68: 394–403.

ELLIS, R. (1876), *Catullus* (Oxford).
—— (1878), *Catulli Veronensis Liber* (Oxford).
—— (1889), *A Commentary on Catullus* (Oxford).
ENK, P. J. (1946), *Sex. Propertii Elegiarum Liber I, Pars Prior* (Leiden).
—— (1962), *Sex. Propertii Elegiarum, Liber Secundus, Pars Prior* (Leiden).
FAIRLIE, A. (1960), *Baudelaire:* Les Fleurs du Mal (London).
FANTHAM, E. (1972), *Comparative Studies in Republican Latin Imagery* (Toronto and Buffalo).
FEDELI, P. (1972), *Il carme 61 di Catullo* (Freibourg).
—— (1980), *Sesto Properzio, Il primo libro delle Elegie* (Florence).
—— (1985), *Properzio. Il libro terzo delle Elegie* (Bari).
FEENEY, D. C. (1992), 'Shall I compare thee...?: Catullus 68B and the Limits of Analogy', in Woodman and Powell (1992), 33–44.
FONTENROSE, J. (1949), 'Propertius and the Roman Career', *University of California Publications in Classical Philology* 13: 371–88.
FORDYCE, C. J. (1961), *Catullus: A Commentary* (Oxford).
FOWLER, D. P. (1989*a*), 'Lucretius and Politics', in Griffin and Barnes (1989), 120–50.
—— (1989*b*), 'First Thoughts on Closure: Problems and Perspectives', *MD* 22: 75–122.
—— (1994), 'Postmodernism, Romantic Irony, and Classical Closure', in De Jong and Sullivan (1994), 231–56.
—— (2000), *Roman Constructions: Readings in Postmodern Latin* (Oxford).
FRAENKEL, E. (1956), 'Catulls Trostgedicht für Calvus', *WS* 69: 278–88.
—— (1957), *Horace* (Oxford).
—— (1958), '*Vesper Adest* (Catullus LXII)', *JRS* 45: 1–8.
—— et al. (eds.) (1931), *Festschrift Richard Reitzenstein* (Leipzig and Berlin).
FRÄNKEL, H. (1921), *Die Homerischen Gleichnisse* (Göttingen).
FRASER, P. M. (1972), *Ptolemaic Alexandria* (Oxford).
FÜHRER, R. (1967), *Formproblem: Untersuchungen zu der Reden in der frühgriechischen Lyrik* (Munich).
GALINSKY, K. (1975), *Ovid's* Metamorphoses (Oxford).
—— (1996), *Augustan Culture* (Princeton).
GALLAVOTTI, C. (1946), 'Il libro dei *Giambi* di Callimaco', *Antiquitas* 1: 11–22.
GARNSEY, P. D. A., and Whittaker, C. A. (eds.) (1978), *Imperialism in the Ancient World* (Cambridge).
GARRISON, D. H. (1991), *The Student's Catullus* (London).
GARROD, H. W. (1921), 'Horace *Odes* I.viii.1–2', *CR* 35: 102–3.
GELZER, M. (1975), *The Roman Nobility* (Oxford).
GERBER, D. E. (1999), *Greek Iambic Poetry* (Cambridge, Mass.).
GIARRATANO, C. (1930), *Q. Orazio Flacco. Il libro degli* Epodi (Turin).
GILBERT, C. D. (1976), 'Horace, *Epistles* 1. 19. 37–40', *CQ* 26: 110.
GOLD, B. K. (ed.) (1982), *Literary and Artistic Patronage in Ancient Rome* (Austin).
GOLDHILL, S. (1986), *Reading Greek Tragedy* (Cambridge).
GOOLD, G. P. (1958), 'A New Text of Catullus', *Phoenix* 12: 93–116.
—— (1983), *Catullus* (London).

GOOLD, G. P. (1990), *Propertius: Elegies* (Cambridge, Mass.).
GOW, A. S. F. (1950), *Theocritus* (Cambridge).
GRAILLOT, P. (1912), *Le Culte de Cybèle* (Paris).
GRANT, R. B. (1975), *Théophile Gautier* (Boston).
GRASSMANN, V. (1966), *Die erotischen Epoden des Horaz* (Munich).
GRIFFIN, J. (1976), 'Augustan Poetry and the Life of Luxury', *JRS* 66: 87–105.
—— (1977), 'Propertius and Antony', *JRS* 67: 17–26.
—— (1979), 'The Fourth *Georgic*, Virgil, and Rome', *G&R* 26: 61–80.
—— (1980), *Homer on Life and Death* (Oxford).
—— (1985), *Latin Poets and Roman Life* (London).
GRIFFIN, M., and BARNES, J. (eds.) (1989), *Philosophia Togata: Essays on Philosophy and Roman Society* (Oxford).
GRIFFITHS, A. (2002), 'Just Where do you Draw the Line?', in Woodman and Feeney (2002), 65–79.
GRIMAL, P. (1963), *L'Amour à Rome* (Paris).
GRUBE, G. M. A. (1965), *The Greek and Roman Critics* (London).
GRUPPE, O. (1838), *Die römische Liebeselegie* (Leipzig).
HARDIE, P. R. (1986), *Virgil's* Aeneid: *Cosmos and Imperium* (Oxford).
—— (1998), *Virgil*, *G&R* New Surveys in the Classics no. 28 (Oxford).
HARDY, G. (1923), *The Monumentum Ancyranum* (Oxford).
HARRISON, E. L. (1970), 'Cleverness in Virgilian Imitation', *CP* 65: 241–3.
HARRISON, S. J. (1985), 'Catullus 61. 109–113 (again)', *PCPS* 31: 11–12.
—— (ed.) (1990), *Oxford Readings in Vergil's* Aeneid (Oxford).
—— (ed.) (1995), *Homage to Horace: A Bimillenary Celebration* (Oxford).
HAUPT, M. (1871), 'Varia', *Hermes* 5: 32–4 = Haupt (1876), iii. 489–517.
—— (1876), *Opuscula* (Leipzig).
HEINZE, R. (1914), *Virgils epische Technik* (Leipzig, 1914).
HELLEGOUARC'H, J. (1963), *Le Vocabulaire latin des relations et des partis politiques sous la République* (Paris).
HERESCU, N. I. (ed.) (1958), *Ovidiana. Recherches sur Ovide* (Paris).
HERTER, H. (1929/1975), *Kallimachos und Homer* (Bonn); repr. in his *Kleine Schriften* (Munich, 1975), 371–416.
—— (1948), 'Ovids Kunstprinzip in den Metamorphosen', *AJP* 69: 129–48.
HEUBECK, A., WEST, S., and HAINSWORTH J. B. (1988), *A Commentary on Homer's Odyssey: Introduction and Commentary Books 1–8* (Oxford).
HEYNE, C. G. (1755), *Albii Tibulli carmina libri tres cum quarto Sulpiciae et aliorum* (Leipzig).
HEYWORTH, S. J. (1984), 'Notes on Propertius Books I and II', *CQ* 34: 394–405.
—— (1992), 'Propertius 2. 13', *Mnemosyne* 45: 45–59.
—— (1993), 'Horace's *Ibis*: On the Titles, Unity, and Contents of the Epodes', *Proceedings of the Leeds Latin Seminar* 7: 85–96.
—— (1995), 'Propertius: Division, Transmission, and the Editor's Task', *Proceedings of the Leeds Latin Seminar* 8: 165–85.
HIERCHE, H. (1974), *Les Épodes d'Horace. Art et signification* (Brussels).

HINDS, S. (1987), 'The Poetess and the Reader: Further Steps Toward Sulpicia', *Hermathena* 143: 29–46.
—— (1998), *Allusion and Intertext: Dynamics of Appropriation in Roman Poetry* (Cambridge).
HINE, H. M. (1987), 'Aeneas and the Arts (Vergil, *Aeneid* 6.847–50)', in Whitby et al. (1987), 173–83.
HOFMANN, E. (1927/28), 'Die literarische Persönlichkeit des Publius Terentius Varro Atacinus', *WS* 46: 159–75.
HOLZBERG, N. (1990), *Die römische Liebeselegie: eine Einführung* (Darmstadt).
—— (1998), *Bibliographie zum Corpus Tibullianum* (Munich).
—— (1999), 'Four Poets and a Poetess or Portrait of a Poet as a Young Man? Thoughts on Book 3 of the *Corpus Tibullianum*', *CJ* 94: 169–91.
HOPKINS, K. (1983), *Death and Renewal* (Cambridge).
HOPKINSON, N. (1984), *Callimachus*: Hymn to Demeter (Cambridge).
—— (1988), *A Hellenistic Anthology* (Cambridge).
HORSFALL, N. (1976), 'The *Collegium Poetarum*', *BICS* 23: 79–95.
HOUSMAN, A. E. (1972), *Classical Papers*. 3 vols. (Cambridge).
HUBBARD, M. (1974), *Propertius* (London).
HUGO, V. (1896–8), *Correspondance*, ed. P. Meurice and J. Simon, 2 vols. (Paris).
HUTCHINSON, G. O. (1984), 'Propertius and the Unity of the Book', *JRS* 74: 99–106.
—— (1988), *Hellenistic Poetry* (Oxford).
—— (2001), *Greek Lyric Poetry: A Commentary on Selected Larger Pieces* (Oxford).
—— (2002), 'The Publication and Individuality of Horace's *Odes* Books 1–3', *CQ* 52: 517–37.
—— (2003), 'The *Aetia*: Callimachus' Poem of Knowledge', *ZPE* 145: 47–59.
—— (2007), 'Horace and Archaic Greek Poetry', in S. Harrison (ed.), *The Cambridge Companion to Horace* (Cambridge), 36–49.
HUXLEY, H. H. (1963), *Virgil. Georgics I and IV* (London).
IRIGOIN, J. (1952), *Histoire du texte de Pindare* (Paris).
JACOBY, F. (1909, 1910), 'Tibulls erste Elegie', *RhM* 64: 601–22 and 65: 22–87.
—— (1961), *Kleine philologische Schriften*, ed. Mette (Berlin).
JAEGER, W. (1945), *Paideia: The Ideals of Greek Culture* (Oxford).
JOHNSTON, P. A. (1987), 'Dido, Berenice, and Arsinoe: *Aeneid* 6.460', *AJP* 108: 649–54.
JONES, A. H. M. (1955), 'L. Volcacius Tullus, Proconsul of Asia', *CR* 5: 244–5.
KAMBYLIS, A. (1965), *Die Dichterweihe und ihre Symbolik* (Heidelberg).
KASSEL, R. (1991), *Kleine Schriften* (Berlin and New York).
KENNEY, E. J. (1971), *Lucretius* De Rerum Natura *Book III* (Cambridge).
—— (1976), '*Ovidius prooemians*', *PCPS* ns 22: 46–53.
—— (1990), 'Words and the Poet: Characteristic Techniques of Style in Vergil's *Aeneid*', *JRS* 80: 211–12.
KERKHECKER, A. (1999), *Callimachus' Book of Iambi* (Oxford).
KIESSLING, A., and HEINZE, R. (1886), *Quintus Horatius Flaccus, Satiren*.
———— (1889), *Quintus Horatius Flaccus, Briefe*.
KILPATRICK, R. S. (1970), 'An Interpretation of Horace, *Epodes* 13', *CQ* 20: 135–41.

KLINGNER, F. (1961), *Römische Geisteswelt* (Munich).
—— (1967), *Bucolica, Georgica, Aeneis* (Zürich).
KNAUER, G. N. (1964), *Die Aeneis und Homer* (Göttingen).
KNOX, P. E. (1985), 'The Epilogue to the "Aetia"', *GRBS* 26: 59–66.
—— (2005), 'Milestones in the Career of Tibullus', *CQ* 55: 204–16.
KROLL, W. (1960), *C. Valerius Catullus* (Stuttgart).
LA PENNA, A. (1950 / 1951), 'Properzio e i poeti latini dell'età aurea', *Maia* 3: 209–36, 4: 43–69.
—— (1977), *L'integrazione difficile. Un profilo di Properzio* (Turin).
LACHMANN, K. (1816), *Sex. Aurelii Propertii Carmina* (Lepizig).
LAIN, N. F. (1986), 'Catullus 68.145', *HSCP* 90: 155–8.
LARKIN, P. (1983), *Required Writing: Miscellaneous Pieces 1955–1982* (London).
LARSON, J. (2001), *Greek Nymphs* (Oxford).
LATTE, K. (1960), *Römische Religionsgeschichte* (Munich).
LATTIMORE, R. (1942), *Themes in Greek and Roman Epitaphs* (Urbana, Ill.).
LEBECK, A. (1971), *The Oresteia: A Study in Language and Structure* (Washington, DC).
LEE, G. (1958–9), 'The Date of Lygdamus, and his Relationship to Ovid', *PCPS* NS 5: 15–22.
—— (1962), 'Tenerorum Lusor Amorum', in Sullivan (1962), 149–80.
—— (1974), 'Otium cum dignitate: Tibullus 1.1', in T. Woodman and D. West (eds.), *Quality and Pleasure in Latin Poetry* (Cambridge), 94–114.
—— (1990*a*), *Catullus* (Oxford).
—— (1990*b*), *Tibullus: Elegies*. 3rd edn. (Leeds).
—— (1994), *Propertius* (Oxford).
LEFÈVRE, E. (1993), *Horaz: Dichter in augusteischen Rom* (Munich).
LENZ, F. W., and GALINSKY, K. (1971), *Albii Tibulli Aliorumque Carminum Libri Tres* (Leiden).
LEO, F. (1900), *De Horatio et Archilocho* (Göttingen).
LESKY, A. (1966), *A History of Greek Literature* (London).
LEVALLOIS, J. (1896), *Milieu de siècle: mémoires d'un critique* (Paris).
LILJA, S. (1965), *The Roman Elegists' Attitude to Women* (Helsinki).
LLOYD-JONES, H., and PARSONS, P. J. (1983), *Supplementum Hellenisticum* (New York).
LOBEL, E., and PAGE, D. L. (1955), *Poetarum Lesbiorum Fragmenta* (Oxford).
LÖFSTEDT, E. (1956), *Syntactica*. 2nd edn., 2 vols. (Lund).
LOWE, N. J. (1988), 'Sulpicia's Syntax', *CQ* 38: 193–205.
LOWRIE, M. (1992), 'A Sympotic Achilles, Horace *Epode* 13', *AJP* 113: 413–33.
—— (1995), 'A Parade of Lyric Predecessors: Horace *C.* 1.12–1.18', *Phoenix* 49: 33–48.
—— (1997), *Horace's Narrative Odes* (Oxford).
LUCK, G. (1966), 'Notes on Catullus', *Latomus* 25: 278–86.
—— (1969), *The Latin Love Elegy*, 2nd edn. (London).
—— (1988), *Albi Tibulli Aliorumque Carmina* (Stuttgart).

LYNE, R. O. A. M. (1970), 'Propertius and Cynthia: *Elegy* I.3', *PCPS* 16: 60–78 [= Ch. 1 in this volume].
—— (1972), 'A Hard Look at Catullus', review of Ross (1969), *CR* 22: 34–7.
—— (1974), 'Propertius I,5', *Mnemosyne* Ser. N 27: 1262–9 [= Ch. 3 in this volume].
—— (1975), *Selections from Catullus: Handbook* (Cambridge).
—— (1978*a*), 'The Neoteric Poets', *CQ* 28: 167–87 [= Ch. 5 in this volume].
—— (1978*b*), *Ciris: A Poem Attributed to Vergil* (Cambridge).
—— (1979), '*Servitium Amoris*', *CQ* 29: 117–30 [= Ch. 6 in this volume].
—— (1980), *The Latin Love Poets: From Catullus to Horace* (Oxford).
—— (1981), Review of Conte (1980), *JRS* 71: 221–2.
—— (1984), 'Diction and Poetry in Vergil's *Aeneid*', *Atti del convegno mondiale scientifico di studi su Virgilio* (Milan), 2. 64–88.
—— (1987), *Further Voices in Vergil's* Aeneid (Oxford).
—— (1989), *Words and the Poet: Characteristic Techniques of Style in Vergil's* Aeneid (Oxford).
—— (1992), 'Preface to the Paperback Edition', *Further Voices in Vergil's* Aeneid (paperback edn.; Oxford), pp. vii–viii.
—— (1995), *Horace: Behind the Public Poetry* (London and New Haven, Conn.).
—— (1996), 'Preface 1996', *The Latin Love Poets: From Catullus to Horace* (paperback edn.; Oxford).
—— (1998*a*), 'Propertius 2.10 and 11 and the Structure of Books "2a" and "2b"', *JRS* 88: 21–36 [= Ch. 14 in this volume].
—— (1998*b*), 'Love and Death: Laodamia and Protesilaus in Catullus, Propertius, and Others', *CQ* 48: 200–12 [= Ch. 13 in this volume].
—— (1998*c*), 'Propertius and Tibullus: Early Exchanges', *CQ* 48: 519–44 [= Ch. 15 in this volume].
—— (1998*d*), 'Introductory Poems in Propertius: 1.1 and 2.12', *PCPS* 44: 158–81 [= Ch. 12 in this volume].
—— (2005*a*), 'Horace *Odes* Book 1 and the Alexandrian Edition of Alcaeus', *CQ* 55: 542–58 [= Ch. 17 in this volume].
—— (2005*b*), 'Structure and Allusion in Horace's Book of *Epodes*', *JRS* 95: 1–19 [= Ch. 18 in this volume].
MACLEOD, C. W. (1973), 'Parody and Personalities in Catullus', *CQ* 23: 294–303.
—— (1982), *Homer, Iliad Book XXIV* (Cambridge).
—— (1983), *Collected Essays* (Oxford).
MAEHLER, H. (1997), *Die Lieder des Bakchylides, Zweiter Teil. Die Dithyramben und Fragmente* (Leiden).
MALTBY, R. (1999), 'Tibullus and the Language of Latin Elegy', in Adams and Mayer (1999), 377–98.
MANKIN, D. (1989), 'Achilles in Horace's 13th *Epode*', *WS* 102: 133–401.
—— (1995), *Horace*: Epodes (Cambridge).
MARSHALL, A. J. (1972), 'The Lex Pompeia de provinciis (52 B.C.) and Cicero's Imperium in 51–50 B.C.: Constitutional Aspects', *ANRW* I.1: 887–921.
MAYER, R. (1979), 'On Catullus 61.116–19', *PCPS* 25: 69–70.

MAYER, R. (1994), *Horace*: Epistles *Book I* (Cambridge).
MCKEOWN, J. C. (1979), 'Augustan Elegy and Mime', *PCPS* 25: 71–84.
MERGUET, H. (1912), *Lexikon zu Vergilius* (Leipzig).
MERKELBACH, R., and WEST, M. L. (1974), 'Ein Archilochos-Papyrus', *ZPE* 14: 97–113.
MOI, T. (ed.) (1986), *The Kristeva Reader* (Oxford).
MOMIGLIANO, A. (1950), 'Panegyricus Messallae and Panegyricus Vespasiani', *JRS* 40: 39–42.
MOREL, W. (1927), *Fragmenta Poetarum Latinorum* (Leipzig).
MORITZ, L. A. (1967), 'Well-Matched Lovers (Propertius i,5)', *CP* 62: 106–8.
MOULTON, C. (1977), *Similes in the Homeric Poems* (Göttingen).
MUELLER, L. (1900), *Quintus Horatius Flaccus, Oden und Epoden*.
MÜLLER, C. (1848), *Fragmenta Historicorum Graecorum* (Paris).
—— (1855), *Geographi Graeci Minores* (Paris).
MÜNZER, F. (1914), 'Hortensius und Cicero bei historischen Studien', *Hermes* 49: 196–213.
MURGATROYD, P. (1980), *Tibullus, Book 1* (Pietermaritzburg).
MURRAY, O. (ed.), (1990), *Sympotica: A Symposium on the Symposion* (Oxford).
MYNORS, R. A. B. (1958), *C. Valerii Catulli Carmina* (Oxford).
—— (1990), *Virgil: The Georgics* (Oxford).
NAUCK, A. (1964), *Tragicorum Graecorum Fragmenta*. 2nd edn. with supplement by B. Snell (Hildesheim).
NEUBECKER, A. J. (1986), *Philodemus, Über die Musik. IV. Buch* (Naples).
NISBET, R. G. M. (1978), 'Notes on the Text of Catullus', *PCPS* 24 : 92–115.
—— (1986), Review of Shackleton Bailey (1984), *CR* 36: 227–34.
—— and HUBBARD, M. (1970), *A Commentary on Horace*: Odes, *Book I* (Oxford).
—— —— (1978), *A Commentary on Horace*: Odes, *Book II* (Oxford).
NORDEN, E. (1954), *Die römische Literatur*. 5th edn. (Leipzig).
—— (1957), *P. Vergilius Maro Aeneis Buch VI* (Darmstadt).
O'HARA, J. (1996), *True Names: Vergil and the Alexandrian Tradition of Etymological Wordplay* (Ann Arbor).
OLIENSIS, E. (1998), *Horace and the Rhetoric of Authority* (Cambridge).
OTIS, B. (1963), *Virgil: A Study in Civilized Poetry* (Oxford).
—— (1970), *Ovid as an Epic Poet* (Cambridge).
PAGE, D. L. (1955), *Sappho and Alcaeus* (Oxford).
—— (1962), *Poetae Melici Graeci* (Oxford).
PAGE, T. E. (1898), *P. Vergili Maronis Bucolica et Georgica* (London).
PAPANGHELIS, T. D. (1987), *Propertius: A Hellenistic Poet on Love and Death* (Cambridge).
PARDINI, A. (1991), 'La ripartizione in libri dell'opera di Alceo: per un riesame della questione', *RFIC* 119: 257–84.
PARRY, A. (1963), 'The Two Voices of Virgil's *Aeneid*', *Arion* 2.4: 66–80.
PARSONS, P. J. (1977), 'Callimachus. Victoria Berenices', *ZPE* 25: 1–50.
PEARCE, T. E. V. (1966), 'Enclosing Word Order in the Latin Hexameter', *CQ* 16: 140–71.
PEASE, A. S. (1920), *M. Tulli Ciceronis De Divinatione Liber Primus* (Urbana, Ill.).

—— (1923), *M. Tulli Ciceronis De Divinatione Liber Secundus* (Urbana, Ill.).
—— (1935), *P. Vergili Maronis Aeneidos Liber Quartus* (Cambridge, Mass.).
PELLIZER, E. (1990), 'Outlines of a Morphology of Sympotic Entertainment', in Murray (1990), 177–84.
PFEIFFER, R. (1928), 'Ein neues Altersgedicht des Kallimachos', *Hermes* 63: 302–41.
—— (1943), 'A Fragment of Parthenios' *Arete*', *CQ* 37: 23–32.
—— (1949), *Callimachus* (Oxford).
—— (1968), *History of Classical Scholarship I* (Oxford).
PHILLIMORE, J. (1905), *Index Verborum Propertianus* (Oxford).
PICHON, R. (1902), *De Sermone Amatorio apud Latinos Elegiarum Scriptores* (Paris).
PLATNAUER, M. (1951), *Latin Elegiac Verse* (Cambridge).
POE, J. P. (1965), 'Success and Failure in the Mission of Aeneas', *TAPA* 96: 321–36.
PORRO, A. (1994), *Vetera alcaica: l'esegesi di Alceo dagli Alessandrini all'età' imperiale* (Milan).
PORT, W. (1925–6), 'Die Anordnung in Gedichtbüchern augusteischer Zeit', *Philologus* 81: 291–6.
PORTER, D. H. (1972), 'Violent Juxtaposition in the Similes of the *Iliad*', *CJ* 68: 11–21.
—— (1987), *Horace's Poetic Journey* (Princeton).
PÖSCHL, V. (1962), *The Art of Vergil* (Ann Arbor).
—— (1977), *Die Dichtkunst Virgils*. 3rd edn. (Berlin and New York).
PREMINGER, A. et al. (eds.) (1986), *The Princeton Encyclopedia of Poetry and Poetics* (Princeton).
PUTNAM, M. C. J. (1965), *The Poetry of the* Aeneid (Cambridge, Mass.).
QUINN, K. (1959), *The Catullan Revolution* (Melbourne).
—— (1968), *Virgil's* Aeneid (London).
—— (1972), *Catullus: An Interpretation* (London).
—— (1973), *Catullus: The Poems* (London).
—— (1982), 'The Poet and his Audience in the Augustan Age', *ANRW* II.30.1: 75–180.
RAVEN, D. S. (1965), *Latin Metre* (London).
RAWSON, E. (1978), 'The Identity Problem of Q. Cornificius', *CQ* 28: 189–201.
REEVE, M. D. (1984), 'Tibullus 2.6', *Phoenix* 38: 235–9.
REINACH, S. (1908), *Cultes, mythes et religions* (Paris).
REITZENSTEIN, R. (1912), *Zur Sprache der lateinischen Erotik* (Heidelberg).
REITZENSTEIN, E. (1931), 'Zur Stiltheorie des Kallimachos' in Fraenkel et al. (1931), 21–69.
REYNOLDS, L. D. (ed.) (1983), *Texts and Transmission* (Oxford).
RICH, J. W. (1990), *Cassius Dio: The Augustan Settlement*, Roman History 53–55.9 (Warminster).
RICHARDSON, J. (1958), *Théophile Gautier, his Life and Times* (London).
RICHMOND, O. L. (1928), *Sexti Properti opera* (Cambridge).
RICHTER, W. (1957), *Vergil. Georgica* (Munich).
RIECHEL, D. C. (1978), *Wege der Worte. Festschrift für Wolfgang Fleischhauer* (Cologne).
RIEKS, R. (1981), 'Die Gleichnisse Vergils', *ANRW* II.31.2: 1011–110.
ROBERTS, D. H., DUNN, F. M., and FOWLER, D. (1997), *Classical Closure* (Princeton).

ROBINSON, R. P. (1923), 'Valerius Cato', *TAPA* 54: 98–116.
ROSATI, G. (1992), 'L'elegia al femminile: le *Heroides* di Ovidio (e altre heroides)', *MD* 29: 71–94.
ROSCHER, W. H. (1884–1937), *Ausführliches Lexikon der griechischen und römischen Mythologie* (Leipzig).
ROSS, D. O. (1969), *Style and Tradition in Catullus* (Cambridge, Mass.).
—— (1975), *Backgrounds to Augustan Poetry. Gallus, Elegy and Rome* (Cambridge, Mass.).
ROSSBACH, A. (1855), *Albii Tibulli libri quattuor* (Leipzig).
ROTHSTEIN, M. (1920), *Propertius, Sextus: Elegien, erster Teil* (Berlin).
ROUSE, R. H., and REEVE, M. D. (1983), 'Tibullus', in Reynolds (1983), 420–5.
RUDD, N. (1960), 'Patterns in Horatian Lyric', *AJP* 81: 373–92.
—— (1966), *The* Satires *of Horace* (Cambridge).
—— (1989), *Horace. The* Epistles *Book II and* Epistle to the Pisones ('Ars poetica'), *(Cambridge)*.
RUSSELL, D. A., and WINTERBOTTOM, M. (1972), *Ancient Literary Criticism* (Oxford).
—— and WILSON, N. G. (1981), *Menander Rhetor* (Oxford).
SAINTE-BEUVE, C. A. (1881), *Les Grands Écrivains français: XIXe siècle, les poètes* (Paris).
SANTIROCCO, M. (1979), 'Sulpicia Reconsidered', *CJ* 74: 229–35.
—— (1986), *Unity and Design in Horace's* Odes (Chapel Hill and London).
SCHANZ, M., and HOSIUS, C. (1927), *Geschichte der römischen Literatur* (Munich).
SCHULZ, F. (1951), *Classical Roman Law* (Oxford).
SCULLARD, H. H. (1970), *From the Gracchi to Nero*, 3rd edn. (London).
SHACKLETON BAILEY, D. R. (1949), 'Propertiana', *CQ* 43: 22–9.
—— (1956), *Propertiana* (Cambridge).
—— (1984), *Q. Horati Flacci Opera* (Stuttgart).
SIKES, E. E. (1931), *The Greek View of Poetry* (London).
SILK, M. S. (1974), *Interaction in Poetic Imagery* (Cambridge).
SITTL, C. (1890), *Die Gebärden der Griechen und Römer* (Leipzig).
SKOIE, M. (2002), *Reading Sulpicia: Commentaries 1475–1990* (Oxford).
SKULSKY, S. (1985), '"Inuitus, regina...": Aeneas and the Love of Rome', *AJP* 106: 447–55.
SKUTSCH, F. (1901), *Aus Vergils Frühzeit* (Leipzig).
—— (1906), *Gallus und Vergil* (Leipzig).
SKUTSCH, O. (1969), 'Symmetry and Sense in the *Eclogues*', *HSCP* 73: 153–69.
—— (1975), 'The Second Book of Propertius', *HSCP* 79: 229–33.
—— (1985), *The* Annals *of Q. Ennius* (Oxford).
SMITH, K. F. (1913), *The Elegies of Albius Tibullus* (Baltimore).
SMYTH, W. R. (1970), *Thesaurus Criticus ad S. Propertii textum* (Leiden).
SOLMSEN, F. (1961), 'Propertius in his Literary Relations with Tibullus and Vergil', *Philologus* 105: 273–89.
—— (1962), 'Three Elegies of Propertius' First Book', *CP* 57: 73–88.
SPURGEON, C. F. E. (1935), *Shakespeare's Imagery and What it Tells Us* (Cambridge).
STAHL, H.-P. (1985), *Propertius: 'Love' and 'War'* (Berkeley).

References

STANFORD, W. B. (1961), *Homer:* Odyssey Books *I–XII* (London).
STAVELY, E. S. (1963), 'The fasces and *imperium maius*', *Historia* 12: 458–84.
STEINBY, E. M. (ed.) (1993–9), *Lexicon Topographicum Urbis Romae.* 6 vols. (Rome).
STEVENSON, J. (2005), *Women Latin Poets* (Oxford).
STROH, W. (1971), *Die römische Liebeselegie als werbende Dichtung* (Amsterdam).
SUDHAUS, S. (1907), 'Die *Ciris* und das römische Epyllion', *Hermes* 42: 469–505.
SULLIVAN, J. P. (1962), *Critical Essays on Roman Literature* (London).
—— (1976), *Propertius: A Critical Introduction* (Cambridge).
SYME, R. (1933), 'Some Notes on the Legions under Augustus', *JRS* 23: 14–33.
—— (1939), *The Roman Revolution* (Oxford).
—— (1978), *History in Ovid* (Oxford).
—— (1986), *The Augustan Aristocracy* (Oxford).
SYNDIKUS, H. P. (1984–90), *Catullus.* 3 vols. (Darmstadt).
—— (2001), *Die Lyrik des Horaz.* 2 vols. (Darmstadt).
TAPLIN, O. (1977), *The Stagecraft of Aeschylus* (Oxford).
TATUM, J. (1984), 'Allusion and Interpretation in *Aeneid* 6.440–76', *AJP* 105: 434–52.
TESCARI, O. (1936), *Quinto Orazio Flacco, I* Carmi *e gli* Epodi (Turin).
THOMAS, R. F. (1978), 'An Alternative to Ceremonial Negligence (Catullus 68.73–78)', *HSCP* 82: 175–8.
—— (1988), *Virgil:* Georgics. 2 vols. (Cambridge).
THOMSON, D. F. S. (1997), *Catullus* (Toronto).
THORNTON, A. (1962), 'A Catullan quotation in Virgil's *Aeneid* Book VI', *Journal of the Australasian Universities Language and Literature Association* 17: 77–9.
TRAINA, A. (1986), *Poeti latini (e neolatini). Note e saggi filologici* (Bologna).
TRÄNKLE, H. (1960), *Die Sprachkunst des Properz und die Tradition der lateinischen Dichtersprache* (Wiesbaden).
—— (1967) 'Neoterische Kleinigkeiten', *MH* 24: 87–103.
—— (1990), *Appendix Tibulliana* (Berlin and New York).
TREGGIARI, S. (1975), 'Jobs in the Household of Livia', *PRBS* 43: 48–77.
—— (1991), *Roman Marriage* (Oxford).
TUPLIN, C. J. (1981), 'Catullus 68', *CQ* 31: 113–39.
VAHLEN, J. (1914), *Beiträge zu Aristoteles' Poetik*, ed. H. Schöne (Leipzig).
VAN SICKLE, J. (1980), 'Catullus 68.73–78 in Context (vv. 67–80)', *HSCP* 84: 91–5.
VESSEY, D. W. T. C. (1971), 'The Reputation of Antimachus of Colophon', *Hermes* 99: 1–10.
VOIGT, E.-M. (1971), *Sappho et Alcaeus: Fragmenta* (Amsterdam).
VOSS, J. H. (1810), *Albius Tibullus und Lygdamus* (Tübingen).
VOX, O. (1993), 'Alc. 395 V. e Hor. Epod. 13.13–4', *RhM* 136: 190–1.
WATSON, L. C. (2003), *A Commentary on Horace's* Epodes (Oxford).
WEBSTER, T. B. L. (1964), *Hellenistic Poetry and Art* (London).
—— (1967), *The Tragedies of Euripides* (London).
WEINSTOCK, S. (1971), *Divus Iulius* (Oxford).
WELLS, S., and TAYLOR, G. (eds.) (1986), *William Shakespeare: The Complete Works* (Oxford).

WEST, M. L. (1966), *Hesiod*: Theogony (Oxford).
—— (1974), *Studies in Greek Elegy and Iambus* (Berlin).
—— (1982), *Greek Metre* (Oxford).
—— (1989), *Iambi et Elegi Graeci i.*, 2nd edn. (Oxford).
—— (2003), *Homeric Hymns* (Cambridge, Mass., and London).
WETMORE, M. N. (1911), *Index Verborum Vergilianus* (New Haven).
WHEELER, A. L. (1934), *Catullus and the Traditions of Ancient Poetry* (California).
WHITBY, M., et al. (eds.) (1987), *Homo Viator: Classical Essays for John Bramble* (Bristol, 1987).
WHITE, P. (1993), *Promised Verse. Poets in the Society of Augustan Rome* (Cambridge, Mass.).
WHITEHEAD, D. (1986), *The Demes of Attica* (Princeton).
WIGODSKY, M. (1972), *Vergil and Early Latin Poetry* (Wiesbaden).
WILAMOWITZ, U. VON (1924), *Hellenistiche Dichtung* (Berlin).
WILKINSON, L. P. (1969), *The Georgics of Virgil* (Cambridge).
—— (1970), '*Domina* in Catullus 68', *CR* 20: 290.
WILLIAMS, G. (1968), *Tradition and Originality in Roman Poetry* (Oxford).
—— (1980), *Figures of Thought in Roman Poetry* (London).
WILLIAMS, R. D. (1967), 'The Purpose of the *Aeneid*', *Antichthon* 1: 29–41. Repr. in Harrison (1990), 21–36.
—— (1979), *Virgil, The Eclogues and Georgics* (Basingstoke).
WILKINSON, L. P. (1963), *Golden Latin Artistry* (Cambridge).
WIMMEL, W. (1960), *Kallimachos in Rom* (Wiesbaden).
—— (1976), *Tibull und Delia. Erster Teil. Tibulls Elegie 1.1* (Wiesbaden).
WIMSATT, W. K. (1970), *The Verbal Icon* (London).
WIRSZUBSKI, Ch. (1950), Libertas *as a Political Idea at Rome during the Late Republic and Early Principate* (Cambridge).
WISEMAN, T. P. (1969), *Catullan Questions* (Leicester).
—— (1974), *Cinna the Poet and Other Roman Essays* (Leicester).
—— (1985), *Catullus and his World* (Cambridge).
WISSOWA, G. (1912), *Religion und Kultus der Römer* (Munich).
WOODMAN, T. (2002), '*Biformis Vates*: The Odes, Catullus and Greek Lyric', in Woodman and Feeney (2002), 53–64.
—— and WEST, D. (eds.) (1984), *Poetry and Politics in the Age of Augustus* (Cambridge).
—— and POWELL, J. (eds.) (1992), *Author and audience in Latin literature* (Cambridge).
—— and FEENEY, D. (eds.) (2002), *Traditions and Contexts in the Poetry of Horace* (Cambridge).
WRIGHT, G. M., and JONES, P. V. (eds.) (1997), *Homer: German Scholarship in Translation* (Oxford).
WYKE, M. (1987), 'Written Women: Propertius' *scripta puella*', *JRS* 77: 47–61.
ZANKER, P. (1987), *Augustus und die Macht der Bilder* (Munich).
—— (1988), *The Power of Images in the Age of Augustus* (Ann Arbor).
ZETZEL, J. E. G. (1982), 'The Poetics of Patronage in the Late First Century B.C.', in Gold (1982), 87–102.

Index Locorum

In the references, a line-number often indicates, not that line alone, but a passage beginning with that line.

ACCIUS
Fragmenta (ed. Ribbeck)
156: 128 n. 26
Ad Herennium
4.67: 139 n. 10
AELIUS ARISTIDES
On Behalf of the Four (ed. Jebb)
228: 215
AESCHYLUS
Agamemnon
374: 11
668: 302
Persae
301: 302
Prometheus Vinctus
356–74: 46
Supplices
23: 302
ALCAEUS
Testimonia (ed. Campbell)
1: 295
10: 295 n. 15
11: 294 n. 6
Fragmenta (ed. Voigt)
fr. 5: 297
fr. 34: 295 n. 14, 297
fr. 34a: 295 n. 14
fr. 38a: 295 n. 14, 317, 319, 320, 324
fr. 50: 300
fr. 67: 297
fr. 68: 295 n. 11, 297
fr. 69: 295 n. 11, 297
fr. 71: 294 n. 6
fr. 75: 294 n. 6
fr. 208: 312
fr. 286: 312
fr. 305b: 312
fr. 306c: 312
fr. 307a: 299
fr. 307c: 305
fr. 308: 297 n. 26, 299
fr. 332: 312
fr. 335: 319
fr. 338: 301, 305, 317, 319
fr. 340–8: 300
fr. 342: 303, 306
fr. 343: 299
fr. 346: 317, 319
fr. 347: 317, 319
fr. 349b: 300
fr. 352: 317, 319
fr. 362: 319
fr. 367: 317, 319
fr. 395: 326 n. 45
fr. 447: 300
fr. 453: 295–6
fr. 455: 298 n. 28
Anthologia Palatina
5. 22: 89
5. 85: 223, 225, 264
5. 100: 86–7
5. 123: 18
5. 212. 5–6: 200
5. 230: 87
5. 275: 1
5. 275. 2: 6 n. 14
5. 302. 15–16: 88
7. 19: 78 n. 50
7. 31. 3–4: 332 n. 68
7. 735. 5–6: 260 n. 31
11. 44. 1–6: 285–6
12. 48. 1: 194

Anthologia Palatina (cont.)
12. 50: 324
12. 101: 194, 202
12. 157: 27 n. 9
12. 169: 88–9
Anthologia Planudis
207. 1: 351
APOLLODORUS
Epit. 3. 29: 213 n. 9
Epit. 3. 30: 215
APOLLONIUS RHODIUS
1. 79: 346
1. 790–1: 139
3. 297–8: 142
APULEIUS
Metamorphoses
10. 17: 19 n. 64
ARCHILOCHUS (ed. West)
fr. 13: 338 n. 97
frr. 188–92: 298
fr. 193: 330
fr. 195: 298, 329
fr. 196a: 329
fr. 199: 330
fr. 215: 316 n. 7
fr. 318: 298 n. 29
ARISTOTLE
Historia Animalium
5. 21: 112
6. 18: 111
6. 21: 111
Nicomachean Ethics
1157^{a}7: 88
Poetics
1449^b: 65 n. 15
Rhetoric
1408^b: 333 n. 71
ATHENAEUS
562c–d: 199
589b: 87–8
AUGUSTUS
Res Gestae
1. 2: 51
4: 116

6: 307 n. 72
13: 116
21: 134
26: 307
26–33: 116

BACCHYLIDES
3. 7: 323
5. 168: 277 n. 84
27. 34–45: 320–2

CAESAR
De Bello Gallico
2. 14: 115
De Bello Civili
3. 19. 1: 198
CALLIMACHUS
Fragmenta (ed. Pfeiffer)
fr. 1: 65 n. 16, 77 n. 45,
   152–3
fr. 1. 3: 152
fr. 1. 11–12: 157
fr. 1. 18: 154
fr. 1. 26: 239
fr. 1. 32: 239
fr. 2: 234, 236–7
fr. 2. 1–2: 236, 249
fr. 2a. 20: 249
fr. 7: 349
fr. 7. 22: 240
frr. 67–75: 77
fr. 75. 77: 240
fr. 112. 5–6: 236, 249
fr. 112. 9: 244, 333 n. 71
fr. 178. 2: 302
frr. 226–9: 336
fr. 398: 64 n. 12, 77
fr. 546: 302
Iambi
1: 336
1. 3: 335 n. 81
1–13: 336–8
13: 336, 338
14: 338

14–17: 336–8
Hymn to Apollo
17: 27 n. 7
47–54: 86
Hymn to Delos
234: 8
Epigrams (ed. Pfeiffer)
6: 153
27: 153, 237
CALVUS
Fragments (ed. Morel)
1–3: 66
4–5: 70
9–14: 67
15–16: 74
17–19: 66
Carmina Epigraphica
1325: 211 n. 3
CASSIUS DIO
40. 46. 2: 254
40. 56. 1: 242
53. 1. 3: 256
53. 13. 4: 252 n. 5
53. 23. 5: 255
53. 29. 3–8: 255
CATO
De Agri Cultura
1. 2: 39 n. 5
CATULLUS
1. 6–7: 349
3. 12: 324
5: 224–5, 242, 264, 290
7: 224–5, 264, 265
7. 3–8: 290
7. 7: 291 n. 31
7. 9–11: 290
8. 18: 273 n. 62
10: 283–4
10. 5–9: 284
10. 12–13: 283–4
10. 29–30: 63–4, 66
12. 6: 285
14: 63, 64
16. 3–4: 66

16. 4: 204 n. 56
22: 349
22. 14: 270 n. 56
25. 1: 204 n. 56
28: 66, 283–4
28. 6–7: 284
28. 9–10: 284
29: 66
30: 284–7
30. 3–5: 285–6
30. 6: 287
30. 10: 285
30. 11: 285
32. 1–3: 290–1
34. 17–24: 287–8
35. 1: 63
35. 14: 70
36: 64, 349
38: 64
38. 6–8: 66
42: 349
43. 3: 276 n. 82, 278 n. 87
45. 11: 12
48: 290
50: 63, 64
51. 11: 197 n. 32
53: 63
56: 64
61: 69–70, 76, 79
61. 1–2: 351
61. 5–9: 291
61. 17–20: 290
61. 31–2: 288
61. 109–12: 290–1
61. 185–8: 142
61. 199–203: 290
61. 203–4: 290
62. 23: 190
62: 69–70, 76, 79
63: 70, 76, 77 n. 47, 79
63. 66: 16
63. 75: 197 n. 32
63. 91: 70
64: 76, 79

CATULLUS (cont.)
64. 1: 62
64. 15: 69
64. 28: 62
64. 61: 287
64. 71–2: 62
64. 77: 69
64. 115: 69
64. 132–5: 172–3
64. 155–6: 173
64. 141: 173
64. 148: 286
64. 228: 62
64. 306: 325–6
64. 319: 69
64. 325: 62
64. 357–61: 325–6
64. 359: 326 n. 45
64. 362: 326
64. 383: 323
65. 2: 246
65: 65, 66, 76, 81, 333
65. 12–14: 27 n. 7
65. 19–24: 16, 138
66: 333
66. 39–40: 167–74
66. 47: 171
66. 56: 172
66. 59–61: 173
66. 59–62: 172
66. 62: 171
66. 64: 168
66: 65, 76, 80–1, 83
67: 76
68: 76, 80–1, 83
68. 49: 76
68. 68: 90 n. 17, 288
68. 70–86: 216–17, 289
68. 73: 80, 221
68. 73–4: 288–90
68. 74: 220, 223
68. 75–84: 221
68. 79–81: 220
68. 84: 218, 221
68. 85–6: 220, 221
68. 89: 292
68. 105: 80
68. 105–7: 221
68. 105–14: 217–18
68. 106–7: 219
68. 107: 221
68. 119–24: 218, 221
68. 125–30: 218, 221
68. 131–2: 218
68. 135: 219
68. 136: 89
68. 145: 16 n. 54
68. 156: 289
68. 159–60: 219
68. 160: 289
72: 225
76. 9: 7 n. 19
77. 5: 287
77. 6: 287
87: 225
95: 63, 64
95. 3: 66
95. 6: 68
95b: 64 n. 12
96: 63, 74, 365
96. 4: 74
102: 365
105: 235
109: 225
109. 5–6: 265
113. 1: 64
116: 65
CICERO
Ad Atticum
4. 6. 1–2: 94, 96, 192
5. 4. 1: 344
7. 2. 1: 60–3, 68, 71, 79, 80
10. 10. 5: 187 n. 9
11. 1. 1: 348
15. 11. 1: 19
15. 29. 3: 348

Index Locorum

Ad Familiares
4. 3. 4: 344
4. 4. 5: 344
4. 6. 1: 344
4. 14. 1: 192
5. 7. 3: 188
11. 28. 3: 94–5, 97
13. 37. 4: 344
Ad M. Brutum
6: 133 n. 33
Ad Quintum fratrem
3. 5. 4: 94
Brutus
247: 66
De Amicitia
44: 193
59: 193
De Divinatione
1. 97–8: 45 n. 24
1. 98: 48
2. 132: 69
De Haruspicum Responsis
27: 190
De Lege Agraria
1. 11: 5
De Natura Deorum
2. 6: 17 n. 57
2. 14: 43 n. 20
De Officiis
1. 35: 115, 120
1. 55: 292
1. 62: 115
1. 62–3: 117
De Oratore
2. 25: 270 n. 55
3. 44: 270 n. 55
De Re Publica
2. 55: 252 n. 5
In Catilinam
3. 2: 200 n. 39
3. 18: 45
In Verrem (*actio secunda*)
1. 104: 187 n. 9
1. 135–40: 187 n. 9
3. 98: 245 n. 67
4. 8: 252
5. 38: 187 n. 9
5. 39: 252
5. 28: 190
Orator
81: 39 n. 9
139: 139 n. 10
161: 60
Paradoxa Stoicorum
praef. 3–4: 93 n. 27
36: 93 n. 26
Philippics
2. 20: 187 n. 9
6. 7: 286
7. 19: 286
9. 12: 344
11. 24: 94
13. 40: 35 n. 17
Pro Caelio
28: 187 n. 9, 290
39: 290
42: 187 n. 9, 200, 290
73: 186 n. 7, 190, 283 n. 2
Pro Flacco
16: 192
Pro Murena
83: 117 n. 7
Pro Rabirio Perduellionis Reo
22: 189 n. 18
Pro Roscio Amerino
75: 270 n. 54
Pro Sestio
97: 189 n. 16, 200
99: 189 n. 17
139: 189 n. 16
Pro Sulla
88: 35 n. 17
Tusculans
2. 5: 231
3. 45: 60, 81

Tusculans (cont.)
4. 11–21: 118 n. 10
4. 16: 119 n. 14
4. 43–9: 117–18
4. 44: 118 n. 10
4. 56: 119 n. 14
CINNA
Fragmenta (ed. Morel)
1–5: 83–4
6–7: 67
9–14: 66
14: 68
CLAUDIAN
De Raptu Prosperpinae
1. 19: 12
CORNIFICIUS
Fragmenta (ed. Morel)
1: 66
Corpus Inscriptionum Latinarum
4. 4371: 346
6. 3996: 345–6
6. 11252: 211 n. 3

DEMOSTHENES
57. 45: 88
DICAEARCHUS OF MESSANA (in Müller *GGM*)
i. 103: 278 n. 88
DIONYSIUS OF HALICARNASSUS
Antiquitates Romanae
5. 19. 3: 252 n. 5
DOMITIUS MARSUS (in Courtney *FLP*)
fr. 7: 204
DONATUS
On the Aeneid
12. 65: 144
DRACONTIUS
Romulus
10. 275: 12

ENNIUS
Annales
208–9 Sk.: 234–5
210 Sk.: 235

352 V (= 361 Sk.): 139 n. 7
558 V (= 572 Sk.): 19 n. 63
Varia
18V: 243
EPICURUS
Kuriai Doxai
1: 177 n. 28
EUBULUS (ed. Hunter)
fr. 41: 199
EURIPIDES
Alcestis
348–53: 226
357–62: 212
Hippolytus
1281: 33
Iphigenia in Aulis
1062–75: 320
Fragmenta (ed. Nauck, 2nd ed., and Snell, *Supplementum* to Nauck)
646a: 214
655: 213 n. 10, 214, 226

FESTUS (ed. Marx)
216: 292

GELLIUS
6. 3. 52: 115
19. 9. 7: 67

HEPHAESTION
12. 3: 77 n. 46
HERMESIANAX (ed. Powell in *CA*)
fr. 7. 1–14: 212
fr. 7. 35–6: 204 n. 55
HERODOTUS
6. 61. 5: 321 n. 26
HESIOD
Theogony
5–7: 236, 249–50
7: 235
22: 246
22–34: 234
22–35: 250

Index Locorum 389

23: 249
243–62: 302
Fragmenta (ed. Merkelbach–West)
283–5: 322 n. 28
HIPPONAX (ed. West)
fr. 115: 316
HOMER
Iliad
1. 45–6: 197
1. 196: 277 n. 83
1. 315: 221 n. 30
1. 361: 321 n. 26
2. 538: 346
2. 698–702: 212, 219
2. 701–2: 213 n. 8
2. 702: 221
3. 284: 277 n. 83
3. 380–2: 352
4. 141–2: 140
4. 146: 140 n. 14
4. 222: 120 n. 15
5. 470: 120 n. 15
6. 208: 120 n. 15
7. 449–50: 220
9. 610: 323 n. 35
11. 783: 120 n. 15
12. 3–9: 220
13. 71–2: 278 n. 89
16. 492–501: 123 n. 19
16. 791: 125 n. 23
16. 795: 140 n. 14
17. 36: 212 n. 7
17. 204–6: 125
18. 38–51: 302
18. 91–3: 120 n. 15
19. 199–214: 120 n. 15
19. 284–5: 272 n. 61
19. 365–6: 126 n. 24
21. 219: 326 n. 45
21. 268: 326 n. 45
21. 361: 325 n. 41
22. 82–9: 137
22. 388: 323 n. 35
23. 99–101: 225
23. 100–1: 176

23. 282: 302
Odyssey
4. 197–8: 263 n. 39
5. 70: 302
5. 181: 321 n. 26
5. 306: 168, 170
6. 107–8: 277 n. 84
11. 489: 158
14. 83–4: 186
23. 192: 212
Homeric Hymns
5. 299: 304–5
19. 3: 300 n. 41
19. 19: 300 n. 41
21: 300
HORACE
Ars Poetica
80: 204
Carmen Saeculare
47–8: 288
Epistles
1. 1. 77–8: 206
1. 4: 206
1. 13. 2: 349
1. 14: 258
1. 18. 40: 346
1. 19. 23–5: 316
1. 19. 32–3: 294
Epodes
1. 2–4: 339
1. 16: 335
1. 19: 323
2: 316
2. 67: 328
6: 340
6. 13–14: 316
10: 316
11: 91–2, 329, 340
11. 1: 329
11. 1–2: 339 n. 103
11. 2: 330
11. 5: 339 n. 103
11. 6: 329
11. 10: 329
11. 14: 329

Epodes (cont.)
11. 15–16: 91
11. 20: 91, 329 n. 58
11. 23: 339 n. 103
11. 23–7: 91
11. 24: 329
11. 25: 339 n. 103
12: 298, 329
13: 314–30, 338–9
13. 1–3: 322
13. 1–10: 324
13. 3: 314, 338
13. 4: 323–4
13. 6: 319–20, 327, 338
13. 7: 327
13. 7–8: 324
13. 8: 330
13. 8–9: 320
13. 8–10: 325
13. 9: 323–4, 327–8
13. 9–10: 327
13. 10: 330
13. 11: 323
13. 11–12: 327
13. 12: 324
13. 13: 326
13. 13–14: 325
13. 14: 330
13. 14–15: 325
13. 15–16: 324
13. 17: 327
13. 17–18: 325
13. 18: 327, 330
14: 330–8, 339
14. 1–4: 332
14. 3: 334
14. 5: 334, 339
14. 7: 324, 335–6
14. 7–8: 332
14. 8: 334
14. 9: 332
14. 11: 332 n. 68
14. 13–14: 331
16. 66: 324

Odes
1. 1. 32–4: 293–4
1. 1. 34–5: 297
1. 1. 35: 298
1. 2: 304, 307
1. 2. 13: 314
1. 2. 41: 134
1. 2. 43–4: 304
1. 2. 45–8: 291
1. 2. 52: 304
1. 3: 297
1. 4: 293, 298, 307, 319
1. 4. 17: 314 n. 4
1. 4. 18: 317
1. 5: 297, 309
1. 6: 297
1. 6. 1–5: 240
1. 7: 298, 307, 319
1. 8: 297
1. 9: 294, 299, 300–6, 312, 319
1. 9. 7: 320
1. 9. 7–8: 302
1. 9. 9–11: 305
1. 9. 13: 305
1. 9. 14: 305
1. 10: 300–5, 312
1. 10. 13: 304
1. 10. 17–18: 304
1. 10. 17–20: 305
1. 11: 264, 284–5, 300–6, 312, 319
1. 11. 1: 305
1. 11. 2: 305
1. 11. 4–5: 305
1. 11. 8: 305
1. 12: 301, 307
1. 16: 311
1. 17: 311
1. 18: 285, 303, 306, 312
1. 18. 1: 303
1. 19: 306
1. 20. 1–2: 302
1. 24: 307
1. 26. 11: 294

1. 27: 311
1. 28: 306–7
1. 28. 21: 307
1. 29: 307, 309
1. 29. 16: 307
1. 30: 307, 309
1. 30. 6: 309
1. 31: 307–9
1. 31. 1–2: 308
1. 31. 3–17: 308
1. 31. 17–20: 308
1. 32: 294, 301
1. 33. 14–16: 92 n. 22
1. 34: 311
1. 35: 311
1. 36: 319
2. 3: 319
2. 7. 13: 304
2. 7. 25: 317 n. 15
2. 9. 1: 322
2. 12. 13–14: 314 n. 5
2. 13. 13: 296
2. 16. 17: 314 n. 5
2. 17. 29–30: 304
2. 20. 1: 350
3. 3. 1: 119 n. 12
3. 4: 118
3. 4. 65–7: 118
3. 6. 23–5: 190
3. 12: 313
3. 12. 1: 290
3. 15. 12: 290
3. 18. 1–4: 291
3. 19: 319
3. 21: 320
3. 21. 1: 327 n. 49
3. 21. 6: 320
3. 28: 319
3. 30. 12: 231
4. 1. 65: 306
4. 5. 1–2: 288
4. 8: 287
4. 10: 285
4. 11: 25 n. 2, 319

4. 12: 319
4. 13. 19: 11
4. 15. 4–5: 116
4. 15. 49–56: 116
Satires
1. 1. 120–1: 310 n. 84
1. 2: 90–1
1. 2. 81: 345
1. 4. 73–4: 207 n. 61
1. 8. 8–10: 292
1. 8. 14: 292
1. 10. 1–2: 204
1. 10. 19: 68 n. 25
2. 3: 310
2. 6: 208, 258
2. 6. 4–5: 304
2. 7: 87 n. 12, 93 n. 28
Hyginus
Fabulae
103–4: 213, 214 n. 12, 226

Jerome
Adversus Iouianum
1. 46: 344

Laevius (ed. Courtney *FLP*)
fr. 13–19: 216
Livy
1. 59. 1: 190
3. 15. 7: 174
5. 11. 16: 5
5. 34. 6–7: 47
6. 27. 1: 188
8. 23. 9: 174
9. 3. 5: 245 n. 67
21. 30. 6–8: 47
23. 23. 6: 123 n. 19
29. 17. 20: 45
33. 12. 7: 115
37. 40. 12: 202 n. 48
41. 15: 47
Lucian
Dialogues of the Dead
28: 215

Menippus
1: 232

LUCRETIUS
1. 33: 174
1. 88: 197 n. 32
2. 162: 19 n. 61
2. 600–60: 70
3. 128–9: 176
3. 214–15: 176
3. 257: 13 n. 40
3. 400–1: 176
3. 455–6: 176
3. 912–15: 324
3. 1034: 314 n. 5
4. 1–25: 340
4: 1073: 187 n. 9
4. 1075: 187 n. 9
4. 1083: 187 n. 9
4. 1117: 187 n. 9
4. 1121: 90
4. 1122: 187 n. 9
4. 1123–30: 200
4. 1124: 187 n. 9
4. 1274–7: 290
5. 259: 292
5. 1127–30: 174
4. 1177: 33 n. 8
5. 392: 11
6. 47: 232 n. 19
6. 50–1: 232 n. 19

MACROBIUS
Saturnalia
5. 19. 2: 177
6. 5. 13: 68

MARTIAL
1. 96. 1: 205
4. 89. 1–2: 334 n. 73
7. 26. 1: 205
10. 35: 343
10. 38: 343

MENANDER
Misumenus
fr. 2: 87–8

Fragmenta (ed. Sandbach)
568: 87

MOSCHUS
Europa
117–19: 278 n. 90

NICANDER
Theriaca
11–13: 250

NONIUS MARCELLINUS
(ed. Marx)
142: 317 n. 15

NONNUS
Dionysiaca
7. 275: 351
48. 107: 351

OVID
Amores
1. 1. 4: 204
1. 1. 30: 204
1. 2: 350
1. 2. 11: 4
1. 2. 24: 351
1. 2. 32: 351
1. 6: 98 n. 37
1. 7. 13: 8 n. 22
1. 10. 15: 351
1. 11. 1–2: 16 n. 55
1. 15. 29–30: 281–2
2. 11. 10: 161
2. 17. 19–22: 205
2. 18. 38: 226
3. 1. 8: 204
3. 1. 10: 204
3. 7. 74: 5
3. 11. 17: 14
3. 15. 8: 350

Ars Amatoria
1. 8: 350
1. 23: 14
1. 623: 190
2. 24: 161
2. 185–96: 195 n. 29

3. 17: 226
Epistulae ex Ponto
1. 5. 57–8: 207 n. 61
3. 1. 109–10: 226
3. 3. 80: 14
5. 14. 5: 350
Fasti
2. 139: 190
4. 91–103: 33
6. 408: 12
Heroides
13. 80: 226
13. 105–10: 226
13. 151–8: 226
13. 163–4: 226
Metamorphoses
1. 4: 151
1. 497–505: 159
1. 568: 67
1. 656: 17 n. 57
2. 709: 276 n. 79
2. 798: 44
3. 339–510: 148
3. 395: 148
3. 502: 148
6. 241–7: 150
6. 252–3: 149
6. 258–60: 149
6. 310–12: 27 n. 7
7. 87: 14
8. 20: 56
8. 462: 149
9. 795: 19 n. 63
10. 254: 5
10. 298–502: 147
10. 402: 17 n. 57
11. 421: 146
11. 566–7: 146
11. 573–6: 146
11. 663: 146
11. 676–707: 146
11. 719: 146
11. 725: 146
12. 293–5: 149

12. 325–6: 149
13. 898: 68
15. 376: 350
15. 378: 350
15. 379: 350
Remedia Amoris
378: 12 n. 39
723–4: 226
Tristia
1. 6. 20: 226
2. 427: 72
2. 431–2: 66
2. 432: 74
2. 433–4: 66
2. 435: 66
2. 436: 66
2. 437–8: 74 n. 36
2. 441–2: 66
3. 1. 11: 204
3. 1. 11–12: 205
3. 7: 343
3. 7. 51–2: 350
4. 10. 7–8: 207
4. 10. 33: 207

Pausanias
2. 4: 213, 219–20
9. 29. 5: 249
Persius
Prol. 13: 344
Philostratus
Heroicus
2. 130: 215
Pindar
Olympians
1. 17: 333
2: 301
Isthmians
7: 301
Nemeans
10: 301
Pythians
4. 109: 302
9. 39–65: 320

PLATO
Laws
639d–641: 317–18
712b: 291
Phaedo
89b: 321 n. 26
Phaedrus
238e: 87 n. 12
Republic
387b: 158
Symposium
179b–d: 212
183e: 88
184b–c: 88
213e: 318
219e: 88
PLAUTUS
Asinaria
656: 267 n. 47
Bacchides
92: 92
Persa
24: 267 n. 47
Pseudolus
14: 92
PLINY THE ELDER
Natural History
7. 19: 301
PLINY THE YOUNGER
Epistles
5. 3. 5: 66
PLUTARCH
Moralia
620a–622b: 317–18
655a: 291 n. 31
PORPHYRIO
On Horace, Odes
1. 10 pr.:
   296 n. 19
1. 10. 9: 296 n. 19
1. 12. 46: 296 n. 18
1. 15: 296 n. 19
1. 22. 10: 296 n. 18
1. 27: 296 n. 18

1. 32. 11: 296 n. 19
3. 30. 13–14: 296 n. 19
On Horace, Satires
1. 2. 81: 345
PROPERTIUS
1. 1: 184–210, 350
1. 1. 1: 280
1. 1. 1–3: 95
1. 1. 1–4: 37
1. 1. 2: 202
1. 1. 3: 202
1. 1. 4: 188
1. 1. 5: 189–91
1. 1. 6: 185, 188, 200
1. 1. 7: 185, 189
1. 1. 9–16: 195
1. 1. 17–18: 195, 199
1. 1. 25–8: 91 n. 18, 193
1. 1. 27–8: 34, 96, 99–100, 185, 186,
   191–3
1. 2: 185–6
1. 2. 1: 185
1. 2. 8: 351
1. 2. 27: 343
1. 2. 27–8: 274
1. 2. 27–30: 246
1. 3: 1–22
1. 3. 1–8: 2, 12
1. 3. 1–10: 8–13
1. 3. 2: 9, 21
1. 3. 3: 9
1. 3. 4: 9
1. 3. 5: 21
1. 3. 6: 9
1. 3. 7: 13, 22
1. 3. 8: 12
1. 3. 9–12: 12
1. 3. 9: 4
1. 3. 11–12: 13
1. 3. 11–16: 2
1. 3. 11–20: 13–15
1. 3. 12: 22 and n. 83
1. 3. 13–16: 18
1. 3. 14: 13

Index Locorum

1. 3. 15: 22
1. 3. 15–16: 5–6
1. 3. 17–18: 13
1. 3. 17–20: 2
1. 3. 19: 22
1. 3. 19–20: 14
1. 3. 21–30: 15–18
1. 3. 23: 16, 21
1. 3. 27–30: 16–18
1. 3. 24–6: 6–7
1. 3. 27: 6, 21
1. 3. 31–3: 2 n. 2, 18–19
1. 3. 34: 22 and n. 81, n. 83
1. 3. 35: 4, 20
1. 3. 35–6: 186
1. 3. 36: 20
1. 3. 38: 20, 21
1. 3. 39–40: 20–1
1. 3. 40: 22
1. 3. 41: 4, 21, 22 n. 77
1. 3. 42: 21
1. 3. 43: 21
1. 3. 44: 23
1. 3. 45: 7–8
1. 3. 46: 16
1. 4: 185
1. 4. 1–4: 33
1. 4. 4: 95
1. 4. 22: 33 n. 8
1. 5: 32–7, 185, 241
1. 5. 11: 32
1. 5. 11–18: 36, 37
1. 5. 11–22: 32
1. 5. 12: 32–3
1. 5. 13: 33–4, 36
1. 5. 14–15: 34
1. 5. 16: 35, 99
1. 5. 18: 35
1. 5. 19: 37, 95
1. 5. 20: 36
1. 5. 21: 36
1. 5. 21–2: 35–6
1. 5. 23–6: 36–7
1. 5. 25–6: 32

1. 5. 27: 37
1. 6: 186, 206, 207, 252, 257
1. 6. 5–6: 259
1. 6. 14: 252, 254
1. 6. 16: 263 n. 39
1. 6. 19–20: 252, 254
1. 6. 25–8: 260, 164
1. 6. 29–30: 267
1. 7. 5: 205
1. 7. 11: 246
1. 7. 19: 204
1. 7. 22: 350
1. 9. 1–4: 96
1. 10: 241
1. 10. 21–4: 96
1. 11. 7–8: 352
1. 11. 29: 191
1. 12. 15–16: 271
1. 12. 18: 95
1. 12. 18–20: 92 n. 21
1. 12. 20: 265
1. 14: 207, 257, 267–8
1. 14. 8: 267
1. 14. 14: 260, 265, 268
1. 14. 15: 268
1. 14. 23–4: 267–8
1. 16. 7: 16
1. 17: 261–2, 274
1. 17. 4: 7 n. 19
1. 17. 5: 262
1. 17. 5–6: 27, 261
1. 17. 5–12: 261–2
1. 17. 9: 27, 261, 262
1. 17. 11: 273
1. 17. 15–18: 261
1. 17. 19: 273
1. 17. 19–24: 262
1. 17. 23: 273
1. 18. 3: 34 n. 13, 96
1. 18. 8: 35, 99
1. 18. 25–6: 96
1. 19: 3 n. 3, 222–6, 260, 274
1. 19. 1–4: 260–1
1. 19. 5–12: 223

PROPERTIUS (cont.)
1. 19. 6: 223
1. 19. 9–10: 225, 226
1. 19. 10: 223
1. 19. 11: 225
1. 19. 12: 222
1. 19. 18: 223
1. 19. 19: 223
1. 19. 21–4: 261
1. 19. 22: 223
1. 19. 25: 242
1. 19. 25–6: 224, 264, 265
1. 19. 26: 265
1. 22: 207
2. 1: 201, 208, 228, 233, 241, 245, 247–8, 275, 281, 306
2. 1. 1–2: 203, 204, 208, 209, 275
2. 1. 3–4: 240, 246
2. 1. 5: 203
2. 1. 7–8: 203
2. 1. 9–10: 203
2. 1. 11: 203
2. 1. 17: 208
2. 1. 23: 33
2. 1. 25: 247
2. 1. 28: 247
2. 1. 39: 247
2. 1. 43–5: 239
2. 1. 47: 247
2. 1. 73: 208
2. 1. 75–6: 247
2. 1. 77–8: 247
2. 1. 78: 208
2. 2: 237–8, 241, 245, 276, 279, 280
2. 2. 1: 203
2. 2. 1–8: 276
2. 2. 6: 203
2. 2. 13–14: 276
2. 3: 237–8, 241, 245, 276
2. 3. 1–4: 279
2. 3. 3: 256
2. 3. 4: 203, 227, 228, 245
2. 3. 9: 203
2. 3. 9–26: 279–80

2. 3. 10–12: 142
2. 3. 19–22: 246
2. 3. 20: 246
2. 3. 21–2: 343
2. 3. 23–32: 239
2. 3. 25: 238, 245
2. 3. 25–9: 281
2. 3. 29–32: 247
2. 3. 29–38: 281
2. 3. 39–40: 281
2. 3. 41: 253
2. 3. 41–4: 281
2. 3. 44: 241
2. 4: 241
2. 5. 18: 33
2. 5. 21–8: 269, 271
2. 5. 28: 270
2. 6. 28: 191
2. 7: 256
2. 8: 242
2. 8. 1–16: 239
2. 8. 14: 201
2. 8. 17–28: 239
2. 8. 33: 35 n. 16
2. 8. 38: 231
2. 9: 242
2. 9. 15: 239
2. 9. 25–8: 243
2. 9. 45–6: 242
2. 10: 227–48
2. 10. 1: 230
2. 10. 1–4: 232
2. 10. 2: 230–1
2. 10. 4: 245
2. 10. 5: 233
2. 10. 6: 247
2. 10. 7–8: 232, 247
2. 10. 10: 240
2. 10. 11: 231, 233, 234, 243
2. 10. 13: 231, 243
2. 10. 13–18: 233, 240, 245
2. 10. 15: 255
2. 10. 15–16: 231
2. 10. 20–6: 232

Index Locorum 397

2. 10. 21–2: 232, 234
2. 10. 23: 231–2, 233, 247
2. 10. 24: 232
2. 10. 25: 232, 236, 249
2. 10. 25–6: 234, 237
2. 10. 26: 236
2. 11: 237–48
2. 11. 1: 239, 245
2. 11. 3: 245
2. 11. 3–4: 238
2. 11. 3–6: 247
2. 11. 5–6: 248
2. 11. 6: 246
2. 12: 196–210, 228, 240, 242
2. 12. 1–12: 197, 198
2. 12. 2: 209
2. 12. 3–4: 200
2. 12. 5–6: 199
2. 12. 6: 197
2. 12. 7–8: 199
2. 12. 10: 197
2. 12. 13: 197, 198
2. 12. 13–16: 198, 200
2. 12. 15: 197
2. 12. 17: 209
2. 12. 18: 198
2. 12. 19: 201–2
2. 12. 21–4: 202–3
2. 13: 240, 242, 271
2. 13. 11: 248
2. 13. 19: 273
2. 13. 25–6: 227, 228
2. 13. 25–38: 271–2
2. 13. 29: 273
2. 13. 32: 273
2. 13. 33: 273
2. 13. 35–6: 98 n. 36, 273
2. 14: 242
2. 14. 1–10: 242
2. 14. 10: 242
2. 14. 11–20: 242
2. 14. 16: 242
2. 14. 23: 242
2. 14. 23–4: 210

2. 15: 242
2. 15. 7: 19 n. 62
2. 15. 11–30: 239
2. 15. 12: 242
2. 15. 23–4: 242
2. 15. 41: 210
2. 15. 49: 242
2. 15. 49–54: 239
2. 16. 12: 7
2. 16. 37: 210
2. 18. 13: 232 n. 19
2. 20. 18: 137
2. 20. 26: 33
2. 22A: 3
2. 23: 243
2. 23. 17–18: 201
2. 24. 1–10: 243
2. 24B. 22: 206
2. 24B. 35–8: 206
2. 24B. 49: 206
2. 25. 4: 75
2. 27. 1–12: 230
2. 28: 243
2. 29. 5: 5
2. 29A: 2 n. 2
2. 29A. 22: 4
2. 29B: 2 n. 2, 4
2. 29B. 1–2: 4
2. 29B. 31–8: 186
2. 30. 19–22: 210
2. 30B. 33: 246
2. 30B. 38: 246
2. 31: 210, 256
2. 34: 210
2. 34. 1–24: 241
2. 34. 25–94: 241
2. 34. 55–6: 206
2. 34. 59–62: 239–40
2. 34. 81–94: 72–5
2. 34. 89: 74 and n. 36
2. 34. 91–2: 255
2. 34. 93: 240
3. 1. 1: 204, 208
3. 1. 6: 204

Propertius (cont.)
3. 1. 13: 208
3. 1. 15: 208
3. 1. 15–18: 240
3. 1. 19: 208
3. 1. 31–2: 208
3. 2: 209, 246
3. 2. 1–2: 205
3. 3: 209
3. 4: 209
3. 5: 209
3. 6. 19–34: 186
3. 9: 208, 209
3. 9. 21–4: 273
3. 10: 24–31, 354
3. 10. 1–4: 26
3. 10. 4: 27
3. 10. 5–6: 26, 27
3. 10. 5–7: 28
3. 10. 7: 27
3. 10. 7–10: 26
3. 10. 8–10: 27
3. 10. 10: 27
3. 10. 11–12: 28–9
3. 10. 11–18: 29–30
3. 10. 12–15: 28
3. 10. 15–16: 25–6, 29
3. 10. 17–18: 29–30
3. 10. 19–20: 30
3. 10. 21: 30–1
3. 10. 22: 30
3. 10. 23: 30
3. 10. 24: 30
3. 10. 25: 30
3. 10. 27: 31
3. 10. 28: 31
3. 10. 29–30: 31
3. 11. 4: 33
3. 11. 40: 35
3. 12. 15: 190
3. 12. 37: 190
3. 15. 10: 33
3. 16. 21: 273
3. 21. 14: 227

3. 23. 1–11: 349–50
4. 1. 1: 209
4. 1. 12: 270 n. 56
4. 1. 39: 209
4. 1. 55: 209
4. 1. 59: 273
4. 1. 62: 209
4. 1. 67: 209
4. 1. 129–30: 206
4. 1. 134: 206
4. 3. 50: 4
4. 4. 67: 10 n. 28
4. 5. 61–2: 30
4. 6: 340
4. 7. 13–94: 186
4. 8. 73–80: 186
4. 11. 1: 263 n. 38

Pseudo-Acro
On Horace, Satires
1. 8. 10: 292

Pseudo-Lucian
Erotes
39–40: 29

Pseudo-Vergil
Ciris
20: 204
180: 139
291: 36

Publilius Syrus
C29: 190

Quintilian
Institutio Oratoria
2. 4. 26: 198
8. 3. 83: 139 n. 10

Rhianus
Fragmenta (ed. Powell in *CA*)
10: 86

Sallust
Bellum Catilinae
12. 4: 115–16

SENECA THE ELDER
Controversiae
2. 2. 12: 160
4 *praef.* 2: 207 n. 61
6. 27: 334 n. 73
SENECA THE YOUNGER
De Clementia
1. 21. 1–2: 133 n. 33
2. 3. 1: 116 n. 3
2. 6. 4: 119 n. 14
De Constantia Sapientis
7. 4. 7: 66
De Ira
2. 32. 1: 133 n. 33
De Matrimonio (ed. Bickel)
fr. 28: 344
Epistulae Morales
86. 15: 109
Medea
69: 12
SERVIUS
On the Aeneid
3. 46: 177
4. 345: 83
10. 50: 83
On the Eclogues
6. 72: 82–3
10. 46: 195 n. 29
SERVIUS AUCTUS
On the Aeneid
12. 66: 144
STATIUS
Silvae
5. 3. 273: 226
STRABO
1. 2. 3: 154, 158
9. 2. 19: 249
10. 1. 3: 346
SUETONIUS
Augustus
34. 2: 256 n. 14
Caligula
27. 3: 35 n. 17

De Grammaticis et Rhetoribus
11: 75 n. 39
18: 75 n. 39
Divus Julius
73: 66
TACITUS
Dialogus
18: 333 n. 71
Agricola
39: 16 n. 56
TERENCE
Eunuchus
57–8: 187 n. 11
84: 34 n. 10
1026–7: 89
THEOCRITUS
Idylls
1: 108
3. 21: 16
3. 40: 101
4. 1–4: 101
5: 105
7. 43: 78, 107–8
11: 106–7
13: 78
14. 70: 323 n. 35
18: 78
Epigrams
21: 298 n. 30
THEOGNIS
891: 346
THUCYDIDES
5. 47. 8: 221 n. 30
TIBULLUS
1. 1: 207, 266
1. 1. 1–6: 257, 267
1. 1. 5: 258
1. 1. 5–6: 206
1. 1. 7: 258
1. 1. 8: 270
1. 1. 19–20: 206, 258
1. 1. 41: 257, 267
1. 1. 41–2: 206

TIBULLUS (cont.)
1. 1. 41–4: 267
1. 1. 43: 206, 267
1. 1. 46: 258
1. 1. 49: 259
1. 1. 49–52: 267
1. 1. 49–58: 257
1. 1. 55–6: 258–9
1. 1. 55–60: 262
1. 1. 57–60: 260
1. 1. 59–60: 264, 265
1. 1. 61–8: 262–3, 271
1. 1. 62: 273
1. 1. 68: 263 n. 39, 272
1. 1. 71–4: 265
1. 1. 73: 269
1. 1. 73–5: 270
1. 1. 75–8: 266
1. 2. 71–6: 259
1. 2. 99–100: 98 n. 38
1. 3: 207
1. 3. 14: 138
1. 3. 55–6: 273
1. 3. 83: 4 n. 10
1. 4. 77–8: 34
1. 5: 258
1. 5. 5–6: 99
1. 5. 20: 259
1. 5. 21–34: 259, 274
1. 5. 43–4: 275, 277 n. 83, 180
1. 5. 43–6: 276
1. 5. 45–6: 275
1. 5. 62: 14
1. 5. 66: 278
1. 6. 57: 281
1. 6. 73–4: 270
1. 6. 85–6: 266
1. 7: 207, 354
1. 7. 3–8: 254
1. 7. 63–4: 291, 351
1. 8. 33–4: 269 n. 50
1. 9. 19–22: 99
1. 10. 51–65: 268–9
1. 10. 61–5: 270
1. 10. 63–4: 271

2. 1. 71: 14
2. 2: 346, 354
2. 3: 346, 354
2. 3. 11–32: 98 n. 36
2. 4. 1–2: 98 n. 36
2. 4. 14: 6
2. 5. 5: 273
2. 5. 46: 352
2. 5. 71: 49
2. 5. 111–12: 204
3. 1–6: 341
3. 4. 30–4: 142
3. 6. 15: 33
3. 7: 341, 342
3. 8–12: 341
3. 8–18: 342
3. 9. 1: 346
3. 11: 25 n. 2, 354
3. 12: 25 n. 2, 354
3. 13: 348–54
3. 13–18: 341, 342–3, 348–67
3. 13. 1–2: 351–2
3. 13. 3: 354
3. 13. 3–4: 352
3. 13. 5–6: 352–3
3. 13. 6: 347
3. 13. 7–8: 346, 353
3. 13. 9–10: 353–4
3. 14: 354–7
3. 14. 1: 354
3. 14. 3: 355
3. 14. 4: 344, 355
3. 14. 5: 344
3. 14. 5–6: 355–6
3. 14. 7: 356
3. 14. 8: 356–7
3. 15: 357–9
3. 15. 1: 357–8
3. 15. 2: 358
3. 15. 3–4: 358–9
3. 16: 347, 359–62
3. 16. 1: 347
3. 16. 1–2: 359–60
3. 16. 3–4: 360–1
3. 16. 4: 344, 346, 347

3. 16. 5–6: 361–2
3. 16. 6: 346
3. 17: 347, 362–4
3. 17. 1: 347, 362–3
3. 17. 2: 363
3. 17. 3: 363
3. 17. 3–4: 364
3. 17. 4: 364
3. 17. 5: 347, 364
3. 17. 6: 347, 364
3. 18: 347, 364–7
3. 18. 1: 366
3. 18. 3: 348, 366–7
3. 18. 4: 367
3. 18. 5: 367
3. 18. 6: 367
3. 19: 341, 342
3. 20: 341, 342

VALERIUS MAXIMUS
1. 6. Ext. 1: 200 n. 39
VARRO
De Lingua Latina
5. 25: 292
Menippean Satires
144: 12
Res Rusticae
2 *praef.*: 39 n. 5
2 *praef.* 3: 55 n. 55
2. 1. 6: 39 n. 5
2. 1. 18: 111
2. 5. 12: 111
3. 1. 4: 39 n. 5
VERGIL
Aeneid
1. 46–7: 277 n. 85
1. 94–6: 168–70
1. 54–5: 57
1. 101: 121
1. 148–52: 118–19
1. 289–90: 123 n. 19
1. 291–6: 118
1. 405: 278
1. 482: 14

2. 184: 47
2. 288: 17 n. 57
2. 296–7: 54
2. 314: 119
2. 314–15: 286
2. 428: 51
3. 43: 49 n. 40
3. 175: 49 n. 40
3. 578–82: 45
4. 1–2: 141
4. 34: 177 n. 28
4. 67: 141
4. 69: 141
4. 143: 181
4. 305–6: 172
4. 307: 137
4. 314: 137
4. 316: 172
4. 324: 137
4. 333: 170
4. 345: 83
4. 357: 170, 173
4. 379–80: 177 n. 28
4. 384: 141, 177
4. 393–6: 119
4. 412: 189
4. 455: 45
4. 492–3: 171
4. 688: 202
4. 689: 141
4. 690: 19 n. 64
4. 693–700: 171
4. 702–4: 171
4. 704–5: 176–7
5. 90: 17
5. 509: 202 n. 48
6. 447: 226
6. 458–60: 167–74
6. 685: 197 n. 32
6. 842–3: 314 n. 5
6. 846: 175
6. 851–3: 120, 174–5, 307 n. 72
6. 853: 131

Aeneid (cont.)
7. 53: 137, 138
7. 55: 138
7. 352: 178
7. 417: 45
7. 525–6: 43 n. 18
8. 29: 120 n. 17
8. 293: 68
8. 394: 174
8. 514–19: 122
8. 537–40: 120–1
8. 665–6: 190
9. 72: 46
9. 373–4: 125
9. 384: 125
9. 692–3: 46
10. 449–50: 123
10. 495–505: 122–3
10. 811–32: 122
10. 819–20: 177
11. 108–19: 121
11. 177–80: 132
11. 507: 14
11. 785–8: 301
12. 4–5: 141
12. 19: 137, 138
12. 55–6: 137
12. 57–8: 137
12. 64–70: 136–45
12. 67–9: 178
12. 101–2: 126
12. 107–8: 126
12. 108: 128
12. 109: 126
12. 176: 126, 129
12. 189: 129–30
12. 189–91: 126–7
12. 229–30: 127
12. 234–7: 127
12. 238: 127
12. 277–9: 130
12. 313–14: 127
12. 324: 128
12. 387: 128

12. 398: 128
12. 405: 128
12. 435–6: 128 n. 26
12. 466–7: 128
12. 494–9: 128–9
12. 554: 129
12. 565–73: 129
12. 570: 130
12. 579–82: 130
12. 620: 130
12. 643: 130
12. 653: 130
12. 669: 130
12. 694–5: 130
12. 697: 130
12. 794–5: 173
12. 864: 45
12. 876: 45
12. 896: 140
12. 930–8: 130–1
12. 938–41: 131
12. 941–50: 131–2
12. 952: 177
Eclogues
1: 107
1. 1–5: 103
1. 18: 104
1. 19–25: 104
1. 20: 103
1. 26: 104
1. 27: 104
1. 45: 104
2: 106, 108, 111
2. 46: 302
2. 58: 287
3: 106
3. 1: 102
3. 40: 102
3. 100: 287
5: 106, 340
5. 64: 331 n. 63
6: 108, 285
6. 3–9: 331
6. 6–8: 239

6. 64: 108
6. 64–5: 249
6. 64–73: 82–3, 108, 234–6
6. 70: 236–7
7: 106
8: 106
8. 16: 103
8. 37–42: 102
8. 49: 189
8. 58–60: 102–3
8. 72: 352
8. 109: 352
9: 105–6, 107
9. 26–9: 285
9. 27–9: 105–6
9. 35: 75 n. 38
10: 108–9
10. 46: 108, 195 n. 29
10. 50: 82
Georgics
1. 1–2: 55
1. 4: 48
1. 14: 52
1. 17–18: 291
1. 19: 53
1. 25: 54
1. 43: 53
1. 45: 53
1. 48: 110
1. 55: 39
1. 60–1: 40, 110
1. 64: 52
1. 65: 55
1. 67: 39
1. 69: 39
1. 80: 52
1. 87: 52
1. 94: 53
1. 98: 53, 55
1. 100: 49
1. 105: 52
1. 106: 48
1. 111: 39
1. 115: 48

1. 119: 55
1. 121: 39, 40, 55 n. 52, 110
1. 121–4: 40
1. 125–8: 40
1. 128: 40
1. 130: 49, 55 n. 52
1. 139–40: 40
1. 145: 39
1. 147: 55
1. 155: 53
1. 157: 55
1. 160: 53, 110
1. 162: 53
1. 164: 53
1. 167–8: 53
1. 168: 270 n. 54
1. 169–75: 53
1. 192: 52
1. 213: 53
1. 260: 49
1. 261: 53
1. 263: 48
1. 265: 57
1. 269: 48
1. 278–9: 40
1. 311–34: 42–3
1. 318–19: 52
1. 319: 39
1. 326–7: 48
1. 328: 39, 49
1. 332: 314 n. 5
1. 338: 110
1. 340: 49
1. 341: 52
1. 348: 55
1. 352: 39, 110
1. 355: 48
1. 357: 42
1. 393: 49
1. 424–6: 50
1. 426: 49
1. 439: 45
1. 441: 42
1. 444: 48

Georgics (cont.)
1. 453–6: 42
1. 461: 49
1. 461–3: 42
1. 463: 44, 45
1. 463–514: 38–59
1. 464–5: 42–4
1. 464–8: 43
1. 465: 51
1. 466–8: 43
1. 464: 44, 54
1. 466: 50
1. 467–8: 47
1. 468: 51, 55
1. 469: 50
1. 469–88: 44
1. 470: 45
1. 471: 46–7
1. 471–3: 45
1. 472: 48
1. 474: 47
1. 476–8: 47
1. 478: 47
1. 479: 47, 48, 49–50
1. 480: 48
1. 481: 50
1. 482–3: 48
1. 483: 49, 50
1. 483–4: 47
1. 485–6: 49
1. 487–8: 49
1. 488: 51
1. 489: 50, 52
1. 489–92: 50
1. 491: 51, 56
1. 491–2: 52
1. 493–7: 52–3
1. 494–5: 55
1. 498: 54
1. 500: 54–5
1. 501: 56

1. 502: 44, 56
1. 503: 50
1. 504: 54
1. 505: 55
1. 506–8: 55
1. 507: 52
1. 509: 47, 56
1. 510: 56
1. 510–11: 57
1. 511: 56
2. 5: 46
2. 136–76: 111
2. 458: 40 n. 11
2. 458–542: 111
2. 461–71: 285
2. 513: 53
2. 515: 48
2. 538: 40 n. 11
2. 541: 230
2. 541–2: 243
2. 542: 231
3. 8–9: 243
3. 22: 243
3. 209: 111, 141
3. 310: 49 n. 40
3. 339–82: 114
3. 404–6: 286
3. 407: 49
3. 471–2: 286
3. 486: 111
3. 537: 49
3. 551–2: 111
3. 566: 202 n. 48
4. 116–48: 112
4. 197: 112
4. 201: 112
4. 206: 112
4. 210: 112
4. 334–44: 302
4. 435: 49

General Index

Greek words have been alphabetized as they would be transliterated.

accent and ictus 347
Achilles 122, 130, 132, 274, 281, 320–1, 323, 325–8
Actium 51, 113, 309 n. 76, 322 n. 31
actualizing indicative 281 n. 100
addressees/addresses, in Catullus 284–5; in Horace 285, 338–9; in Propertius 184, 185, 186, 208
Aeneas xiv, xv, 119, 136, 168–74, Ch. 8 *passim*
Aeschylus 179
aestheticism 154–5, 162; Callimachean 101, 154, 158; Ovidian (*Metamorphoses*) 149, 150, 161; Propertian 271; Vergilian (*Georgics*) 114
aetiology, in Callimachus 158
Aetna 45, 46, 56
affective fallacy 178 n. 33
aims and methods, in imperialism and war 115, 116, 118, 123, 126, 127, 128, 129, 130, 132, 133, 134
Ajax 128
Alcaeus xvii, Ch. 17 *passim*
Alcestis 177, 212, 214–16, 222, 226
Alcyone 146–7
allegory: in *Eclogues* 103–6; in *Georgics* 112, 113, 114
Allen, Woody xvii
alliteration 62, 69, 315
allusion xvi, 4, 167–9, 170, 174 n. 20, 180; in *Aeneid* 140, 141; metrical 285, 306, 312
Althaea 149–50
Amata 136–8
ambiguity 42; Propertian 202, 210; transient 12 n. 37, 37 n. 25, 202;
Vergilian 42, 105, 106, 107, 114, 139, 140, 141, 143
ambivalence, in *Georgics* 58
amici 253; in Propertius 193; *see also cohors*
Amor: Cynthia equated with 37; naked 351; winged 197–200
Anacreon, and Horace 332–3
anaphora 150
Anchises 120, 131, 137 n. 3, 174, 175
Andromeda 9, 10
anger 122, 124, 127, 134; of Aeneas 123, 126, 132–3; Stoics on 117
Anglo-Saxon empiricism 167 n. 2, 170, 182
Angst, Propertian 26, 29, 31, 257, 263, 264, 268, 271, 274
annales 66
Antimachus 75 n. 39, 77 and n. 46
antonomasia 60, 62
Antonius, M. 187 n. 9; 309 n. 76; as slave of Cleopatra 100
anxiety, Propertian *see Angst*
aoros (ἄωρος) 122 and n. 18
Apollo 159, 274, 275; Citharoedus 308 and n. 75; in Alcaeus and Horace 299–301, 303, 305, 309; Medicus 308–9 n. 76; temple of 256, 307, 308
Apollonius Rhodius 77 n. 46
apostrophe 67, 239
Appendix Vergiliana 342
apples, as gift to beloved 7, 16
Arabia, Roman expedition to 231, 255, 307
Aratus 153
Archilochus 297, 298; model for Horace 316 and Ch. 18 *passim*

Argus, guardian of Io 14–15, 17
Ariadne 9, 10, 11; in Catullus 172–3
Aristaeus, in *Georgics* 112
Aristarchus 61; edition of
    Alcaeus 294–5, 297 n. 25, 301, 310–13
Aristophanes of Byzantium: edition of
    Alcaeus 294–5
Aristotle, *Poetics* 146 and n. 1, 147
    nn. 2–4, 151 n. 13, 153, 154 and n. 23,
    158 and n. 38, 220
arma 5 and n. 11; of farmer's tools 39
    and n. 7, 53, 56
Arruns 301
art (τέχνη) 152, 154 and n. 26; Art over
    Life 162; *Georgics* on 113
'art for art's sake' *see l'art pour l'art*
Artemis, in Callimachus 158, 161
ascent: epic as 243; of Helicon 233–4;
    metaphor of 232
assonance 69
asynarteta 329 and n. 57
at: in apodosis 285; anaphoric 285
Atalanta 195
Attis 70, 77
audience limitation, fallacy of 178–80
Augustus / Octavian xiii, xvi, 50, 51, 54,
    55, 56, 57, 103–4, 123, 240, 255 n. 12,
    304, 309 n. 76; avenger of Julius
    Caesar 134; in *Georgics* 112, 113;
    patron of the arts 209; policy of
    mercy 116; and Propertius 245, 247
axes *see secures*

Bacchante 10
Bacchylides 320–2, 323, 325
Barbey d'Aurevilly 155
Barthes, Roland 183
Bassus, in Propertius 185 and n. 4, 188
Bathyllus, in Anacreon 332–3
Bathyllus, beloved of Maecenas 331 and
    n. 62, 338
Baudelaire 155, 163–5
Berenice 168, 169 n. 8, 171–3
biographical approach to elegy 2

birthday: in elegists 25–6, 27, 29, 254,
    354; in Sulpicia 358, 359; poem
    (*genethliakon*) 342, 354
blush 138–9 and n. 7
Boileau 151 n. 13
bonds, of love 33
book division: of Alcaeus 294; *see also*
    Propertius, 'Book 2'
books, length of: of Augustan
    poetry 341; of Callimachus 337; of
    Propertius 227, 242–3; of Sappho and
    Alcaeus 311 n. 89
books, physical form of xvii, xix, 348–9;
books, of poetry 334
bravery 118, 120; Stoics on 117
Brutus 50
bucolic 78, 331, Ch. 7 *passim*

Cacus 126 n. 24
cado 'be ruined' 360
Caecilius 63–4, 69, 74, 75, 79
Caelius 187 n. 9, 191 n. 23, 290
Caesar, Julius 43–5, 47, 50, 51, 54,
    56, 66, 73; assassination and
    deification 106
Callimacheanism 77, 78–80, 82, 84, 108,
    114; in *Eclogues* 102
Callimachus 64–5, 66 n. 15, 76, 86, 101,
    153, 233–5; *Coma Berenices* 168,
    169 n. 7; *Iambi* and Horace xvii,
    336–8; on Permessus 249; Ch. 10
    passim; and *Metamorphoses* 152; and
    Propertius 273
Calliope 275
calque 197, 303, 314, 325 n. 41
Calvus 14 n. 46, 63–5, 67, 69, 71 n. 30,
    72, 74, 75, 79, 83, 84
Camenae 26, 352
career, Roman *see cursus honorum*
carmen perpetuum
    (ἓν ἄεισμα διηνεκές) 151–2, 158, 160
carmina: of Horace 296; Horace's *Iambi*
    as *carmen* 324
Cassagne 158

General Index

Cassius 50
castae puellae 189–90, 191 and n. 24
castus 190; *see also* chastity
catalogue 159, 160
Cato the Elder, on love 187 and nn. 9–10
Cato, Valerius *see* Valerius Cato
Catullus xi, xiii, xiv, xvii, 205 n. 56, 211, 257, 264, 265, 326, Chs 5 and 16 *passim*; order of poems in 81 and n. 64; on *otium* 85; model for Sulpicia 365, 366–7; on Protesilaus and Laodamia 216–25; source text for Vergil 168–74
Cerinthus 345–6, 352, 357, 358, 359, 360, 362
Ceyx 146
character and psychology, in *Aeneid* 136, 137, 139 n. 7
chastity, wifely 190
cheek-tearing 272 and n. 61
Chelidon (prostitute) 187 n. 9
Chiron 315, 320–1, 323–8
Choerilus 231, 232 n. 20
choral lyric 320
Cicero, on chastity 190–1; on Clodia 191 and n. 123; on female speech 347 and n. 16; on freedom of speech 94–7, 192; on friends 193; on *improbi* and *optimates* 189; on love 187 and n. 9, 200, 265, 266; on *ludus* 290; on neoteric poets 60–3, 65, 68, 71, 79–82; on *otium* 85; on Roman war 115, 120 and n. 16; on slavery of lover 93, 98; on Servius Sulpicius Rufus 344
Cinna 63–5, 66, 67, 68, 71 n. 30, 74, 75, 79, 83, 84
Cinyras 147
civil war 38, 39, 42, 44, 45, 47, 49, 50, 51, 52, 56, 57, 58, 97, 109, 110, 111, 112, 113, 124, 131, 208
clementia 116 n. 3, 124, 127, 131, 134
Cleopatra 307
cletic hymn *see* hymn, cletic
Clodia 191 and n. 23

closure (and false closure): 228; in *Georgics* 243; Horatian 306, 307 and n. 70, 316, 324, 328–30, 334–5, 336–7, 339, *see also* penultimacy; Propertian 241–8, 255, 281, 310 n. 83; Sulpician 343; Tibullan 258 n. 28, 273 n. 67, 274 n. 69, 276 n. 78
cohors 283; *see also amici*
colloquialism (everyday language): 5, 12, 92, 93, 97; Greek 89; in Horace 334; in Sulpicia 347, 352, 359, 360, 361, 365
colonus 38–9, 55
colour (φάρμακον) 136
comedy 89; Greek 199; Roman 187
commentators, ancient: on Alcaeus 294 n. 6; on Archilochus 335 n. 79; on Horace 296 and n. 19
comparative constructions, in Sulpicia 364
compassion *see* mercy
complexion, female 279 n. 93
compound adjective (Ennian) 285
confiscations *see* land confiscations
Conon, astronomer 102
consciousness, literary 180, 181
consilium 188–90, 200
contamination (*contaminatio*) 126, 130
contingo, contactum 202 and n. 48
Cornficia, poetess 343
Cornificius 64, 66, 68, 74, 75
Cornutus, M. Caecilius 345 n. 10, 346
country: in Theocritus 102; in Tibullus 258; *see also rusticus*
Cupid 198–203
Cupidines 4, 26
cursus honorum 192, 206, 283 n. 2
Cybele 70, 77, 78
Cyclopes 46
Cynthia 72–3, 343, Chs 1–3, 6, 12, 14–15; choice of name 274; as *docta* 246, 248; *domus* of 191 n. 24; as Muse 246, 275; as 'wife' 4, 20
Cytheris 187 n. 9, 235; *see also* Lycoris

Daphne 159
daughters xviii
death *see* mortality
decimal structures, in poetry books 306, 307, 310 and n. 82, 311, 340
deconstruction xii
deduco 160
deification of beloved 33 and n. 3, 275–6, 277–8 n. 85, 278
Delia 138, 191 n. 23, Ch. 15 *passim*; choice of name 274, 346
dialectic *see* dialogue
dialogue: of *Aeneid* with itself 177; between texts xvii; Horatian with elegists 92 and n. 22; Propertian with Catullus 222–5; Propertian with Gallus 282; Propertian with Greek poetry 198–9; Tibullan with *Georgics* 258 and n. 25; two-way between Propertius and Tibullus 251 n. 1, 252, 255 n. 10, 257, 261 n. 34, 264 n. 42, 265–6, 269–72, 279–80 and Ch. 15 *passim*; Vergilian with Lucretius 174, 175
diction, in *Aeneid* 140–1; of Callimachus 153
didactic epic 77; Callimachus and 157
Dido xiv, xv, xviii, 119, 120, 137–8, 141, 145, 168, 169 n. 8, 170–4, 176–7, 277 n. 83
diminutives 329 n. 58
discontinuous narrative 157
disengagement *see* dissociation
displacement of poems, Horatian 307 n. 70; *see also* penultimacy
dissociation from public world, Propertian 188, 194, 196, 200, 210
distancing 150
disturbing: *Aeneid* as 133, 137, 173; (and non-disturbing) elements in *Metamorphoses* 147, 148
diuina puella see deification of beloved
diuitiae see wealth

doctus/doctrina 67, 246
dolor, in love elegy 27
domina 13; in Catullus 90 n. 17, 288–9 and n. 21; in Propertius 95
domus 36 and n. 21, 288–9
door *see paraklausithyron*
door-breaking: in Tibullus 266, 268–70

ebrius 12
echo 167
Echo and Narcissus 148
Eco, Umberto 247, 248
'effects' 155; in Baudelaire 163–4, 165; in Callimachus 158, 161, 163; in *Metamorphoses* 150, 151 and n. 13, 161
eheu 287
elegiacs, Callimachean 101
elegy Ch. 6 *passim*, 2, 63, 236; narrative 152; parity with epic 274 n. 68
elevation 9, 18; myth as elevating 279
Eliot, T. S. 183
elision 347
emotions: reader's (not) engaged in *Metamorphoses* 147, *see also* reader, insulation of; passions
emphasis (ἔμφασις) *see significatio*
engagé: poetry as 156, 158; Alcaeus as 306; *see also* political commitment
Ennius 60, 73, 234–5, 243, 250, 352; *see also* compound adjective
epic 61, 62, 64, 67, 73, 76, 77, 101, 152, 331; cyclic 153 and n. 18; heroes 52, 53; historical 65 n. 13, 152, *see also annales*; Homeric 152; laudatory 108; mythological 73; post-Homeric 153
epicedion 74–5, 83
Epicureanism 174, 177 n. 28, 187 n. 9; and Horace 308–9
epigram 209; Alexandrian 86–8, 89, 91; Callimachean 101; Greek 31; Roman 65, 71, 76, 89
epigrammatic style, in *Metamorphoses* 149

epitaphs 273; Propertius' 247–8, 273
epithalamia 69–70, 78, 79, 142
Epodes, not title of Horace's book 316
epyllion 63, 67, 68–9, 77, 78, 79, 82, 83, 101, 108
equites 186 and n. 7, 190, 192, 206–7, 273, 283 n. 2
erotic: lyric 332; poems 66, 67, 295 n. 14, 306
Erysichthon 161
etymologizing: in Hellenistic poets 221 and n. 31; in Homer 213 n. 8; Varro 292
Eubulus 199
Eudoxus, astronomer 102
Euphorion 60, 68–9, 75 n. 39, 79 n. 55, 82, 83
Euripides xviii, 321; *Protesilaus* 213–16; *Alcestis* 226
Euryalus 125
Eurydice 212 n. 4, 215
Evander 122, 123, 132, 133, 137 n. 3
everyday language *see* colloquialism
exchanges *see* dialogue
exclusus amator 20, 32, 33–34 and n. 8, 35, 36, 91, 92 and n. 22, 255 n. 10, 259 n. 30
exempla 161

fable 319
face, of beloved 276, 281, 282
fair hair *see flauus* and *fuluus*
fallacy of audience limitation *see* audience limitation, fallacy of
fantasy: Catullan 289; Tibullan 258, 259
farce 260
Farmer, metaphor of 38, 39, 49, 52, 109–11
fasces 252–3 n. 5
fatum sequi 117
female speech 346–7; *see also* Sulpicia: syntactical idiosyncrasy; feminine logic
feminine logic 20
feminism 347; *see also* gender
fiction 155; in *Eclogues* 105, 106

figo 14, 19
fire imagery of love 367; in *Aeneid* 139–41
flauus 171 and n. 12, 277 and n. 83; calques Ξάνθος 314
flower imagery 29–30, 142
focalization, embedded xi
form and content (style and content) 149, 150, 151 and n. 12, 163, 164; congruence of style and content 150, 161, 163, 164–5 and nn. 59, 62
form for form's sake 154, 155, 160–1
fraus 44
freedom of speech 94, 99–100, 185 and n. 3, 186, 191, 192, 193, 194
friends *see amici*
fuluus 277 and n. 83
funerals, in Propertius and Tibullus 260–1 and n. 34, 271
funerary ritual 262
Furius 'Alpinus' 65 n. 13
Furius Bibaculus 65 n. 13
furor xiv, 122, 126, 132, 189 and n. 17, 190, 195 n. 28; in *Aeneid* 118, 123, 128, 133, 134
furta, as subject of neoteric poetry 71, 74
further voices *see* voices
future tense (publishing futures) 350

gait: Cynthia's 203, 278; female 278 n. 88
Gallus, poet xiii, 73, 79 n. 55, 82–3, 84, 195 and nn. 28–9, 234–7, 240, 250, 257, 260 nn. 32–3, 274, 280 n. 99, 281–2; death of 255; on *seruitium amoris* 90; in *Eclogues* 108–9
Gallus, character in Propertius 32, 37, 96, 185, 188
garlands, given to beloved 16
Gautier 155, 156 and n. 32
gender xii, xviii, xix, 346; in Catullus 219 and n. 27; in Propertius 185
genre: and Alcaeus 295

generic games xiii
Germany 45, 47
Giants 45, 46, 48
gloria 117
Golden Age, in *Georgics* 39, 48, 52, 109–10
grandeur, epic 152, 156
gratum est quod 359, 365
great men, (not) addressed by poets 184, 188, 207, 209, 210, 247–8, 320 and n. 22, 354
Grecisms 281–2, 285
Grecizing 60, 62, 76, 79, 84
Greek names 9; in *Eclogues* 103
grotesque: in Callimachus 158; in *Metamorphoses* 150, 151
Grynean grove 82–3, 234–5, 237
guilt, Roman 44, 51, 54, 55, 56, 57

Habans, J. 165 n. 62
hair: arranging hair of beloved 16; beloved arranging her hair 28–9; Cynthia's 203; as funerary offering 262, 263 and n. 39, 273 and n. 63; severed lock 168–74
hamartia (ἁμαρτία) 220
happy ending 147
Hector 125, 130
height, of beautiful heroines 277 and n. 84
Helen 281
Helicon 233–6, 249–50
Hercules 217 n. 22
Hermes, in Alcaeus 299–303
hero: epic 67, 79, 119; Homeric 119; and kings 152, 159
Hesiod 82, 153, 235–7, 249–50; Χείρωνος Ὑποθῆκαι 321, 322 n. 28; Vergil as Roman Hesiod 109
heterometria (ἑτερομετρία) 294 n. 8, 205 n. 11
heu 287
high-mindedness, in *Aeneid* 122, 123, 129, 134, 135, 137; *see also* idealization
Hippocrene 234, 236, 249

Hipponax 297; model for Horace 316 and Ch. 18 *passim*
Homer x, 73, 153, 156, 158, 177, on Protesilaus 212, 219–22; source text for Lucretius 176; source text for Vergil 167, 168, 169, 172
Homeric Hymns 77
homoiocatarcton 150
homoiometria (ὁμοιομετρία) 294 n. 8, 205 n. 11
homoioteleuton 150
honour and dishonour, in *Aeneid* 120, 123, 124, 131–2
Horace xiii, xvi, xvii, 191, 207 and n. 61, 240, 284–5, 287, 292, Ch. 18 *passim*; on Augustus and war 118; dialogue with elegists *see* dialogue, Horatian with elegists; disconcertingly unAugustan views in 307; humour in 307 and n. 71, 309; 'Italianization' of Alcaeus 303 and n. 56; on love 265, 266; 'Parade Odes' 296 and n. 20, 301, 303, 306, 309; as poet laureate 116, 134; public and personal in 307–8; as Roman Alcaeus 299, 301, 306; on *seruitium amoris* 90–1
horse, image for epic 231, 233
Hortensius 66, 67, 71 n. 30
Hugo, Victor 165
humour 65, *see also* puns; Callimachean 154; Catullan 284; in *Ciris* xii; Horatian 92 and n. 22, 332, 333, 334, 337; Lyne's own xii, xv; Ovidian (*Metamorphoses*) 159; Propertian xiii, 2, 3, 4, 206, 208, 209, 236–7, 240, 242, 257, 270, 273; Propertian and Tibullan 251 n. 1; Sulpician 351, 354, 355, 356; Theocritean 102, 107; Tibullan 257, 260, 263, 264 nn. 40, 42, 265, 266, 267 and n. 47, 268; Vergilian (*Eclogues*) 108–9
hunting 346

hybris, in *Metamorphoses* 151
hymn, cletic 291, 351
hymnic parody 320
hymns, Callimachean 101; of Alcaeus 295
hyperbaton 361, 364, 365
hyperbole 149, 253
'hyperintertextualists' 178–80

iambi 316, 324; Callimachus' *Iambi* 335; *Iambi* as title of Horace's *Epodes* 316, 335 and n. 77; metrical iambics versus *iambi* in generic sense 316 n. 7, 332, 333 n. 70, 336–7
iambic poets/poetry 185
ianitor 259 and n. 30; *see also* door; *exclusus amator*
ictus *see* accent and ictus
idealism, in *Metamorphoses* 147, 148, 150, 162; in *Georgics* 112–13
idealization 3, 7, 8, 10, 11, 12, 13, 15, 16, 17, 18, 21, 22, 29; of war 116–18, 119; *see also* high-minded principles
ideology 175
illness, of *puella* of elegy 362
imperialism xiv, Ch. 8 *passim*
improbus 189 and nn. 15–16, 190
inceptive poems (inceptive sequence) 184 n. 2, 227, 228, 241, 242, 245, 246, 251 n. 2; *see also* introductory poems; in Horace 301, 306; in Propertius 271, 273, 275 n. 72, 276 n. 78, 280; in Tibullus 258 n. 28, 270, 274 n. 69
incongruity, in Theocritus 102, 107
independence of poets xiii, 207; Horace's 307
India, submission of to Rome 231, 255
individual/individuality 112, 113
instruction/moralizing (paraenesis): in Horace 317, 323, 324
intentional fallacy 178, 181–2

intentionalism/intentions of author 167–70, 180, 181; *see also* intentional fallacy
interaction, in poetic imagery 323 and n. 36
intertexts, work like similes or contrast similes 172–3, 175
intertextuality x, xiii, xvi, Ch. 11 *passim*
introductory poems, in Propertius Ch. 12 *passim*, esp. 186, 191, 196, 201, 203, 208–9, 251 n. 2; in Sulpicia 343, 348, 350; in Tibullus 257
ira see anger
irony x–xi, xv, 19, 36, 21, 22, 147; in *Aeneid* 173–4, 175; Propertian 246–7
Italy, idea of 38 n. 3

Junia Aurunculeia 288, 290
Juno 118, 278
Jupiter 39, 40, 42, 45, 48, 59, 281; in *Aeneid* 118; Feretrius 123; in *Georgics* 110, 111
Juturna 127, 128, 129

Kreuzung (generic crossing) 306, 307, 316, 317, 319, 338
Kristeva, Julia 167 n. 2, 183

labor, in *Georgics* 40
Laevius 66, 67, 71 n. 30; *Protesilaodamia* 216
land confiscations 206; in *Eclogues* 103–5
Laodamia xvii, 288, 289 and n. 25, Ch. 13 *passim*; partial identification with Catullus 219 and n. 28
Laomedon 44, 51, 56
Lapiths and Centaurs 149, 151 n. 12
Larkin, Philip 178 n. 33
l'art pour l'art 154 and n. 26, 155, 160, 161, 162, 164
Lausus 122, 128
Lavinia Ch. 9 *passim*

leisure, life of *see otium*
lena 259 n. 30
leptaleos, leptos
  (λεπταλέος, λεπτός) 152–3
Lesbia xii, 71–3, 216–19
Lesbous, in Horace 294, 297
Leuconoe, in Horace 302, 304
Levallois, Jules 165
libertas 41, 91, 94, 96; and *lex* (in Nature) 41; *loquendi see* freedom of speech; in love 34 and n. 12, *see also seruitium amoris*
liberty: of speech *see* freedom of speech; political 94
Liebestod 221, 242, 247–8; *see also* love
life imitating art 72
life of love 86, 100, 242, 257–60
limen 33–4
Linus 234
literary apologetics 333 and n. 72
literary polemic 64; Callimachean 156
literary theory xiv
literature versus life 2
love: in Callimachus 158; and death xvii; conquers death 242, 260 and n. 33, 264, 310 n. 83, Ch. 13 *passim*; until death (in Tibullus) 260, 262–3; Greek view of 194, 198–200; in Horace (*Epodes*) 332; love-in-death 272; Lucretius on 90, 187 n. 9, 200; reciprocal 146; Roman view of 187, 188 n. 12; as sickness 187 and n. 9, 188; in Vergil (*Eclogues*) 107, (*Georgics*) 111, 113, (*Aeneid*) 119; whole love 211
love-poetry xiii, xvi
Lucretius 174–6, 70; in *Georgics* 111; Vergilian dialogue with *see* dialogue, Vergilian with Lucretius
ludus 290–1; love as 187 n. 9
Lutatius Catulus 66
Lycidas 106
Lycoris 73, 274, 282; *see also* Cytheris
Lygdamus 341

Maecenas xvi, 205, 207–10, 247–8, 273 n. 63, 320 n. 22, 330–1 and n. 61, 333 n. 72, 339
magic 275
magnanimity, Roman 115, 116, 120, 121, 127, 128
manumission: of Tityrus 104–5
Marathus 274 n. 69
Mark Antony *see* Antonius, M.
marriage 4, 20, 36 n. 21
marriage law 256 and n. 14
Mars 56, 57
martial epic xiv; *see also* historical epic
medical terminology, in Sulpicia 363
Meditrinalia 308 and n. 76
Meineke's Law 287
mele (μέλη), of Alcaeus 295–6
Meleager 71, 194, 196, 200 n. 38, 202
melodrama 148
Memmius 66, 67, 71 n. 30, 253, 283 nn. 2–3, 283–4
Menalcas 105–6
Menander, on slavery of love 87, 88
Menelaus 140–1
Menippean *saturae* 70
Mercury: in Horace 302–4, 309; *see also* Hermes
mercy 115, 116, 118, 119, 120, 121, 122, 123, 129, 133 and n. 33; *see also clementia*
Messalla 66 n. 18, 207, 254 and n. 9, 258 n. 26, 273, 274 n. 69, 320, 341–2, 354–7; uncle of Sulpicia 344, 345, 347
Messapus 127, 128, 129
metaliterary/metapoetic 203, 205, 210, 258 n. 28, 301; 307 n. 70; in Horace 334, 337
metamorphosis 146, 147, 148, 150, 159, 161
metaphor 38–40, 42
metre: alcaic stanza 297 n. 25, 301; anacreontean 333 n. 70; Archilochean metres in Horace *Epodes* 316; Archilochus' works cited by 335;

aristophanean 298; asclepiad stanzas 297; blazon metre *see* metrical blazon; *breuis in longo* 329; choliambics 316 and n. 10; choliambics 333 n. 71, 335 n. 81; choriambic tetrameters anaclastic 333 n. 70; dactylic hexameter 330; epodic metres 298, 329; first Archilochean 298, 307, 329; galliambics 70, 77 and n. 46, 78; glyconics and pherecratean 69; greater Archilochean 298 n. 30; greater asclepiad 284–5, 300 and n. 38, 301, 303, 306; greater sapphic 297; hemiepes 329, 330; hiatus 329; iambic dimeter 329, 330, 333 n. 70; iambic metres in Anacreon 333 n. 70; iambic metron 333; iambic trimeter 298 n. 30, 326; neglect of Hermann's Bridge in Catullus 76; pentameters ending in short vowel in Sulpicia 347; sapphic eleven-syllable line 297 n. 26; Sapphic sixteen-syllable 300 n. 38; sapphic stanza 301; Sappho's books arranged by 295; *scazon* 205; second Archilochean 329–30; shift in metrical pattern in Horace *Epodes* 329; *spondeiazon see spondeiazon*; stichic asclepiads 297; stichic iambics 329; Sulpicia's use of hexameter 347; third Archilochean 298 and n. 30, 329; two monosyllables ending hexameter 364

metrical: allusion *see* allusion, metrical; blazon 297, 299, 300, 316; dexterity, Horatian 296–7, 340, *see also* ἑτερομετρία; puns 204–5

Milanion 158, 194–5; in Gallus 195 and n. 29

military metaphor: of Farmer 110: in *Georgics* 39, 40, 52, 53

militia 253, 257 and n. 22, 258, 259, 267; *amoris* 5, 242, 267, 268, 274

military imagery 5
mimesis 147, 148, 150, 151 and n. 13, 154 and n. 23, 155, 162, 163
Mimnermus 77 n. 46, 156–7
minae, in Propertius 27
Minos 158
misericordia see mercy
mollis 204 and n. 56
monstrous, the 126 and n. 24; *see also* Giants
moral values, Vergilian 38, 105, 109–10, 112, 141–2; *see also* Vergil, personal views
morality (immorality/amorality): in *Aeneid* 124–5; in *Metamorphoses* 147, 148, 150, 151, 153, 161; of poetry 154, 155, 156, 158, *see also engagé*; Propertian 25–6, 30, 31
Moschus 68
munera (gifts to beloved) 7, 16, 237–8, 245
Murra 147, 149
Muses 234–5
Mutina 208
myth, mythology xiii, 8, 11, 14, 77, 79, 155; in Propertius 276–7, 279; in Theocritean bucolic 101; in Tibullus 275, 279
mythical exemplum 319, 320, 323

narro 'gossip about' 353
naturalism: in bucolic poetry 101–2
nature, in *Georgics* 110
ne... si... 365
nec... sed... 286
negotium see otium
neoteric poets xi, xii; Ch. 5 *passim*
neoteroi (νεώτεροι) 60–2, 65
nightingale 27
Niobe and Niobids, in *Metamorphoses* 27, 149, 150, 151, 166
non sibi sed patriae natus see patriotism; subordination of self
nota 99
nox 31

numbers of poems in poetry book: in Alcaeus (book 1) 310; in Callimachus (*Iambi*) 311, 336–8, (*Aetia* book 4) 311–12; in Horace (*Odes* 1) 306, 310, (*Odes* 2–4) 311, (*Epistles* 1) 311, (*Epodes*) 311, 336–8, (*Satires* 1) 310; in Propertius (book 1) 310 and n. 83; in Tibullus (book 1) 310
nymphs: in Alcaeus and Horace 299, 301–3, 309 and n. 79

occasional poetry 66, 70, 71
Odysseus, Aeneas as 168, 172
old age, amorous conduct in 265, 266
optimates 189
optimism 52, 53, 57, *see also* pessimism; in Georgics 111
order, in *Georgics* 40
Orpheus: love triumphs over death 211–12 and n. 4, 222
oscillation, in *Eclogues* 105, 106, 107
otium (leisure) 85, 257–8
Ovid 207, 342, 347, Ch. 10 *passim*

pacificism xiii
painting, and Propertius 198
Pallas 122–5, 131–2, 137 n. 3
Panegyricus Messallae 342
para prosdokian (παρὰ προσδοκίαν) 14, 18, 149
parablepsy 232, 358
paradox: in Propertius 95; in Theocritus
paraklausithyron 81, 91, 255 n. 10
Parcae 325–6
parody xvii, 260, 266
Parthenius 74, 75 n. 37, 78, 79 n. 55, 82, 83, 84
Parthians 231
passions 118 and n. 10, 119, 127–8, 133–4, 187 n. 9, *see also furor*; in *Aeneid* 137, 138, 141, 143
pathos 9, 10, 16, 21, 23, 122 and n. 18, 146; in *Metamorphoses* 148, 151; in Theocritus 102

patriotism, in *Georgics* 112
Patroclus 176
patronage, and Propertius 205 and n. 58, 207–10; *see also* great men
Paulus Silentarius 1 n. 2, 87
peace 39, 49, 53, 54, 309; in *Aeneid* 115, 116, 118, 120, 121, 123, 124, 127, 129, 130, 133, 134
Penelope 4
penultimacy, exploited by Horace 307 and n. 70
Perilla 343
Permessus 234–6, 249
Perseus 9, 10
personal experience 1, 2; of Catullus 80–1; of Vergil 107
personal poetry x; *see also* public poetry
personality, of author x, xiii
perturbatio 119, 121
Perugia 208
pes ('foot' and 'verse-foot') 204, 333
pessimism xiv; in *Eclogues* 105; in *Georgics* 111
Pharsalus 50
Philippi 50, 51, 52, 58, 206, 208, 322 n. 31
Philitas 77 n. 46
Pindar 157; in Horace 301, 303; number of poems in books 311
pity *see* mercy
Plato: on Homer 158; on slavery of love 88
pleasure: from *mimesis* 151 n. 13; from poetry 153–4
plough 53, 55–6
poetic initiation 234
poetry: edifying / educational 153 and n. 20, 154, 156; pleasurable *see* pleasure
political commitment: of Vergil in *Eclogues* 107–8; *see also engagé*; public and political life
political values xvii
Pollio and *recitatio* 207 and n. 61

polyeideia (πολυείδεια) 338
polymetrics 65, 70–1, 75
Pompey 66, 254
Ponticus, character in Propertius 96, 185 n. 4, 204, 246
Porcius Licinus 66
Porphyrio 296 nn. 18–19
portents *see prognostica*
poverty, relative 206, 267
praxis 146, 151
preconceptions, critics' 169
Priam 281
proem in the middle 241, 340
prognostica 39, 42–50, 52
programme, poetic (programmatic poem) 62, 65, 69, 71, 76, 80–4, 95 and n. 31, 98, 99 n. 41. 188, 194, 204, 228, 245, 246, 270, 274 n. 69, 275, 306, 335 n. 81, 340
promissory deferral 244; *see also recusatio*
propaganda 94
propempticon 83, 84
Propertius xii–xiii, xvii, Chs 1–2, 6, 15 *passim*; 'Book 2' 184 n. 2, 191 n. 24, 201 n. 43, 251 and n. 2, 255, Ch. 14 *passim*; equestrian 190, 192, 206; on love-poets 72–5; temperament of 208, 210; *see also* Angst, Propertian
prophecy, in *Eclogue* 4 106
prosaism: in Sulpicia 347, 361; *see also* colloquialism; medical technical terminology
Protesilaus Ch. 13 *passim*
pseudonyms, poetic 274, 346
public and political life, in Propertius 186–7, 188, 189, 191, 196, 200–1, 206, 207; *see also* dissociation; political commitment
public poetry x, xiv, xvi, xvii; *see also* personal poetry; political values
publication 334, 346; dates of (Propertius book 1) 252–4, (Propertius 'Book 2') 254–7, 255 and n. 12, (Tibullus book 1) 254; of *Odes* 1–3 293; poetic influence prior to 255 n. 10, 256; *see also* future tense (publishing futures)
publishing poem 342, 343, 348, 350
puns: in Callimachus 221 n. 31; in Propertius 203–4, 205

quamuis with indicative 357
quasillus 361
Quintilia 74
quod noun-clause 365
quotation, of source text 168, 175

rationality 118, 120, 121
raw material (non-significant source text) 167, 169; *see also* significant source text
reader: emotional involvement of 150, 151, 155, 162; insulation of (in *Metamorphoses*) 148, 149, (in Baudelaire) 164, *see also* emotions: reader's emotions (not) engaged; responses of complicated 149
realism: in *Eclogues* 103, 107; *see also* naturalism; unreality
reality (vs idealization) 3, 15, 20, 29, 37–8, 41, 55, 57; in *Aeneid* 128, 134, 135
reality and fiction, in *Metamorphoses* 147, 148
reason *see* rationality
reception 183
recitation 207, 255 n. 10, 256
recusatio 108, 306, 330 n. 61; parodied 331–2 and n. 64; in Propertius 208, 239; Prop. 2.10 not a *recusatio* 232–3, 240, 244
regere imperio 174–5
revenge, in *Aeneid* 123–4, 130, 134
rhetoric 198; in *Metamorphoses* 149, 151
rhyme, internal 69

rhythm: in Catullus 76; of Euphorion's hexameter 69; of neoteric hexameter 60, 62; *see also* metre
ring-composition 228 n. 10; in Horace 305; in Propertius 247, 248; in Tibullus 259; metrical, in Horace 330
romantic: Catullus as 291; Propertius as 265–8
romanticism (romantic vision) xiii, 2, 4, 7, 9, 10, 11, 12, 18, 92 n. 22, 213, 221, 222; *see also* idealization
'running on' in the myth 323, 324, 326; *see also* trespass
rustic life *see* country
rusticus 269–70

's', elided 60
sacrifice: human 122; neglected 219–20
Sainte-Beuve 165
Sallustus 115–16
Sappho 78, 294 and n. 5, 295, 297, 312, 352
sapping xvi; *see also* subversion
saviour: in *Eclogues* 106; in *Georgics* 112–13
Scamander 34, 315 n. 5, 325 and n. 40, 326 and n. 45
Schadenfreude 34
scholia 294 n. 6
scortum 360–1
scribo, self-referentially used in Propertius 245 and n. 66, 247
seafaring, love as 261
sealing motif 348, 350
secures 252–3 n. 5
Seneca, on Ovid 160
sequence of poems: in Horace 301, 302, 304, 305, 306, 309, 311, 312; in Sulpicia 342–3
seruare modum, in *Aeneid* 122, 125
seruitium amoris xii–xiii, 16, 31, 33, 34, 35, 36, 37, 186, 191, Ch. 6 *passim*; *see also domina*

servility 192
Servius Sulpicius Rufus 344–5 and n. 11
Servius: on *Eclogues* 104
sexism 346
Shakespeare 162–3, 179 and n. 39, 183
sibilance 60
sickle 55–6
significant source text, significant allusion 167–9; *see also* raw material
significatio 139 and n. 10
simile 323; in *Aeneid* 136, 140, 178, 189 n. 17; of *auriga* 57–8; in Catullus (poem 68) 217; contrast simile 172 and n. 15, 173, 175; Homeric 140, 323 n. 34; in Propertius 232; relation between simile and narrative 118, *see also* 'running on' in the myth; trespass
Simois 325
Simonides 66
sin, Roman *see* guilt
sinus 7
smugness, Tibullan 257, 263, 268, 271, 274; *see also* Angst, Propertian
social class, in Rome 191, 192, 193, 200, 205; of poets 207; *see also equites*
sodales 207
Sophocles xviii
Soracte 301, 305
source text 167
spinning 4, 360
spoils: in *Aeneid* 122–5, 131–2, 137 n. 3; in Homer 123 n. 19, 125 and n. 23; *spolia opima* 123 and n. 19
spondeiazon (σπονδειάζων) 60, 76
Stasiotica, of Alcaeus 295 and n. 14, 296
Stoicism, in *Aeneid* 127
Stoics, on war ('Stoic imperialism') 115, 117–18, 119, 120, 123, 127, 128, 133, 134
stola, metonymy for high-class women 360
storm image: of love 27; at sea (Alcaeus and Archilochus) 322; in Vergil

(*Georgics*) 42–3, 52, (*Aeneid*) 118; of woman 261
structure x, xi, 340
style: and content *see* form and content; Callimachean 153, 156; Catullan 285, 286; of *Metamorphoses* 149; neoteric 79, 80
subjective style, of Vergil 141, 142
subordination of self 117 and n. 7, 118 n. 11, 119
subversion x, xi, xii, xiii, xiv, xvi, xvii, xviii–xix; *see also* sapping; in *Aeneid* 174, 175, 177 and n. 28; *see also* undermining irony
Suffenus 349
Sulpicia xviii, Ch. 19 *passim*; life 343–5; metre in 365; syntactical idiosyncrasy 346, 364–5
sun 43–4, 47; Julius Caesar as 43, 50
supplication, Turnus' 131
sweetness, of poetry 153
'swords into ploughshares' 39, 110
syllepsis 5
sympathy *see* mercy; the reader's 147, 148, *see also* emotions, reader's (not) engaged
symposiarch (συμποσίαρχος) 317–19, 323
symposium 324, 325, 338
sympotic poems 295 n. 14, 301, 306, 316, 317, 318, 319

tableaux, poetic 157; in *Metamorphoses* 159
tears, as funerary offering 273 and n. 63
teasing: Horace as 297, 298, 303, 339; Propertius as 256; Sulpicia as 346; Tibullus as 258 n. 25
temptare 5
terra/Terra 40, 45, 46, 48
textual criticism: of Catullus 216 and n. 20, 217 n. 21, Ch. 16 *passim*; of Horace 314, 338–9; of Propertius 5, 32, 36, 197–8, 230–2, 276 nn. 79–80, 279 n. 93, 280 and n. 94; of Sulpicia Ch. 19 *passim*, exx. 351, 353, 356–7,

358–9, 361, 362, 364; of Tibullus 259 n. 29, 266 n. 4
Theocritus 78, 101–8, 297
Theseus 158
Tibullus xiii, xvii, 33, 35, 85, 86, 91, 98–9, 204, 207, 341, Ch. 15 *passim*; as equestrian 206; *see also* smugness, Tibullan
Tibur 303 and n. 56
Ticida xii
Titans 40, 46
Tityrus 103–5
toga, worn by prostitutes 360–1
toilette, of beloved 28–9; *see also* hair
Tolumnius 127
tombstones, Roman 211, 222
tone, change of, in Propertius 184
torch imagery 331
torches 4
Torquatus, Manlius 288–91
tragedies, read 179
tragedy, tragic 27, 51, 58, 81, 212, 213, 214, 215, 220, 221; in *Aeneid* 125, 169 and n. 7, 172, 174; in *Metamorphoses* 146, 147, 148, 161
transitions, in *Metamorphoses* 159, 160
trespass ('intrusion' by a tenor term into the vehicle of a simile) 140–1 n. 14, 141 n. 16, 232 and n. 22; *see also* 'running on' in the myth
Trojan war 281, 325
Tullus, in Propertius 186, 187–8, 191, 194–5, 196, 207, 252–3, 267
Tullus, L. Volcacius (*cos.* 33 BC) 186 and n. 7, 252–4
Turnus 121–5, 126, 128–32, 136–7, 141, 143
Typhoeus 40 and n. 12, 45, 46

uates, Horace as 308 n. 74, 324
uersiculi 329 and n. 58, 332; *see also* versicles
umbilici 334

undermining irony x, 175; in Propertius 209
unity, of poetry 157; in *Metamorphoses* 159
unreality, of Vergilian bucolic world 103

Valerius Aedituus 66
Valerius Cato 64, 66, 68, 74, 75 and n. 39, 79, 84 n. 72
Varro, M. Terentius (of Reate) 38, 39 n. 5, 70, 109, 111
Varro, P. (of Atax) 73
Varus, P. Alfenus 285, 303 and n. 57
vengeance, in *Metamorphoses* 151
Venus 4, 278, 352; in *Aeneid* 172–3
Vergil x, xiv–xvi, 61, 297, Chs 4, 7, 11 *passim*; Caesarianism 58; contrasted with Horace 134; homosexual? 107; intervenes in narrative 122, 124–5; personal views of 106, 110, 117, 124–5, 126, 134–5, 141–2; Propertius on 73
Verres 187 n. 9
versicles 65–6, 70–1, 75; *see also uersiculi*

violence 149; in Propertius 5; in Tibullus 269–70, 271 and n. 57, 74; in Vergil (*Georgics*) 40, 46, 47, 49, 50, 53, 110, (*Aeneid*) 49 n. 41, 128, 134, 135, 143
voices (further voices) xiv, xvi
Volusius 63–4, 67, 349 and n. 19

war xiii–xiv, xv; Roman Ch. 8 *passim*
wealth 267
weather, imagery of 322
weather-signs *see prognostica*
Wilde, Oscar 155, 161–2
wine 319–20, 325, 327; metapoetic 301–2
wit *see* humour
women poets in Rome 343–4
word-patterning 76
wound, imagery of in *Aeneid* 140–1
writing, self-referentially used in Propertius *see scribo*

Xanthus *see* Scamander

Zeus 46 *see also* Jupiter; in Callimachus 158